Justification and

Justification and Variegated Nomism

Volume I

The Complexities of
Second Temple Judaism

edited by

D. A. Carson, Peter T. O'Brien,
and Mark A. Seifrid

Mohr Siebeck · Tübingen
Baker Academic · Grand Rapids

Distributors

For the United States and Canada
Baker Academic
P.O. Box 6287
Grand Rapids, Michigan 49516-6287
USA

for Europe
Mohr Siebeck
Wilhelmstrasse 18, Postfach 2040
72010 Tübingen
Germany

Printed in the United States of America

Die Deutsche Bibliothek – CIP-Einheitsaufnahme

Justification and variegated nomism / ed.: D. A. Carson; Peter T. O'Brien;
Mark A. Seifrid. – Tübingen: Mohr Siebeck
Vol. 1. The complexities of second temple Judaism. – 2001
  (Wissenschaftliche Untersuchungen zum Neuen Testament: Reihe 2; 140)
  ISBN 3-16-146994-1

*Library of Congress Cataloging-in-Publication Data is on file at the Library of
Congress, Washington, D.C.*
ISBN 0-8010-2272-X

© 2001 by J.C.B. Mohr (Paul Siebeck)

ISSN 0340-9570

Preface

This is the first of a two-volume set. The subtitle of the second will be *The Paradoxes of Paul*. The idea was conceived when Peter O'Brien spent a sabbatical year at Trinity Evangelical Divinity School. He and I enjoyed many hours talking over recent publications variously connected with the "new perspective" on Paul. In due course Mark Seifrid joined the discussions. Despite the fact that we were approaching the subject from various angles, we soon reached agreement that what was needed was a fresh exploration of the literature of Second Temple Judaism, followed by a fresh treatment of Paul that took into account the findings of the first exploration. In our view, the theses of E. P. Sanders regarding covenantal nomism, articulated in his seminal work on *Paul and Palestinian Judaism* (1977) and in subsequent publications, though they obviously provided valuable correctives, needed further examination. It was not as if nothing had been done. Hundreds of reviews and articles, and not a few monographs, have been published on the views of Sanders and on the constellation of fairly diverse reconstructions that make up the "new perspective," but nothing had been published of which we were aware that looked afresh at virtually all the literature of Second Temple Judaism, aiming simultaneously for comprehensiveness and depth, before turning again to Paul.

These goals meant that we soon abandoned the hope of achieving our purpose in one fat volume. Hence this two-volume set. At one point we briefly toyed with the idea of attempting a straight-line chronological study; indeed, one or two distinguished scholars urged us to take this route. But eventually we settled on the outline reflected here. A straight-line chronological study is very difficult in any case, owing to protracted debates about the dates of many of the sources. More importantly, however, we were concerned not to lose the interpretive gains that depended on being sensitive to distinguishable literary genres. One of the criticisms raised against the category "covenantal nomism" is that it is suspect precisely because it paints with such a broad brush, or (to change the metaphor) because it is such a powerful vortex that it sucks in diverse literary genres without much historical and literary sensitivity.

The result was that we divided up the literature of Second Temple Judaism and invited distinguished specialists to look at it afresh, asking fundamental questions about the pattern of the relationships between God and human beings, about righteousness and salvation and eschatology and grace and works and faith and law. We tried to make the categories broad enough that each scholar could "tweak" the approach – the questions asked and the categories for the results – according to the literature. Several of the contributors decided to follow a roughly chronological schema within the corpus of literature being studied.

Inevitably, this approach led to a bit of overlap: both Philip R. Davies and Donald E. Gowan, for instance, treat 4 Maccabees; despite some specific assignment of sources, there is a little overlap between the treatment of apocalyptic (Richard Bauckham) and of the Dead Sea Scrolls (Markus Bockmuehl). In our view, however, this has proved beneficial: we did not attempt to impose an artificial uniformity on the findings, and the small degree of diversity that resulted has probably enhanced the project's credibility. On two fronts, we decided to commission essays of a topical nature (which of course ensured a bit more overlap with the other essays): Mark A. Seifrid wrote an essay on the "righteousness" words of the Hebrew Bible and of Second Temple Judaism, while Roland Deines embarked on a major study of Pharisaism. The most serious lacuna in the present volume is the absence of a separate treatment of the LXX. We intend to include something on that subject in the second volume, in an essay dealing with Greek "righteousness" words.

As the first draft of each essay was received, it was circulated to the other contributors to the first volume, who were invited to offer their suggestions and criticisms. About half of them did so. Essays were then revised and edited. I must make special mention of the written responses of Markus Bockmuehl, who (apart from the editors, of course) offered the most detailed and penetrating comments. Though they are now unseen by those who read these pages, his critical suggestions have probably made almost as great a contribution to this volume as his own essay.

Within the limits of reasonable uniformity of presentation, I have tried in final editing to allow some diversity of stylistic preferences. For instance, individual authors could choose for themselves between B.C.E./C.E. and B.C./A.D.

I want to record my thanks to those who have contributed to this project, some of them very substantially. First of all, I am grateful to the writers, whose erudition has been matched by consistent courtesy and efficiency as suggestions have been followed up, proofs read, questions answered. Prof. Martin Hengel and Georg Siebeck have been unflagging in their support of this project, even when there were some painful delays occasioned by the ordinary but always unexpected vicissitudes of life. Several scholars contributed to the translation of the essay by Roland Deines: their names are in the first footnote of that piece. The co-editors have been wonderfully rapid and insightful in their suggestions. My graduate assistant, Sigurd Grindheim, prepared the indexes with his customary attention to detail; my indefatigable secretary, Judy Tetour, prepared the camera-ready copy. Trinity Evangelical Divinity School has an enviable track record of encouraging scholarship, and in this instance provided funds to offset various expenses. To all of them I owe a great deal, and extend my heartfelt thanks.

Soli Deo gloria.

Trinity Evangelical Divinity School, April 2001

D. A. Carson

Table of Contents

Contributors

ALEXANDER, Philip S., Professor of Post-Biblical Jewish Literature, University of Manchester

BAUCKHAM, Richard, Professor of New Testament Studies and Bishop Wardlaw Professor, St. Mary's College, University of St. Andrews

BOCKMUEHL, Markus, Fellow and Tutor, University Lecturer in Divinity, Fitzwilliam College, University of Cambridge

CARSON, D. A., Research Professor of New Testament, Trinity Evangelical Divinity School

DAVIES, Philip R., Professor of Biblical Studies, University of Sheffield

DEINES, Roland, Completing his Habilitationsschrift, University of Tübingen; Research Scholar, Corpus Judaeo-Hellenisticum Project in Jena

ENNS, Peter, Associate Professor of Old Testament, Westminster Theological Seminary

EVANS, Craig A., Director of the Graduate Program in Biblical Studies, Trinity Western University

FALK, Daniel, Assistant Professor of Ancient Judaism and Biblical Studies, Department of Religious Studies, University of Oregon

GOWAN, Donald E., Emeritus Robert C. Holland Professor of Old Testament, Pittsburgh Theological Seminary

HAY, David M., Joseph E. McCabe Professor of Religion, Department of Philosophy and Religion, Coe College

KUGLER, Robert A., Associate Professor of Religious Studies, Gonzaga University

MCNAMARA, Martin, Missionaries of the Sacred Heart

O'BRIEN, Peter T., Senior Research Fellow in New Testament and Vice-Principal, Moore Theological College

SEIFRID, Mark A., Professor of New Testament, Southern Baptist Theological Seminary

SPILSBURY, Paul, Associate Professor of New Testament, Canadian Bible College

Abbreviations

With only rare exceptions (such as in the use of roman font for Targums), these essays have followed the abbreviations set out in Patrick H. Alexander et al., ed., *The SBL Handbook of Style* (Peabody: Hendrickson, 1999). In addition, the following abbreviations, not found in the *Handbook*, have been used:

CSCT	Columbia Studies in the Classical Tradition
DSSSE	*Dead Sea Scrolls: Study Edition* (ed. F. García Martínez)
EnAC	Entretiens sur l'antiquité classique
EOS	Eos. Commentarii Societatis Philologae Polonarum
GAP	Guides to Apocrypha and Pseudepigrapha
JSJSup	Journal for the Study of Judaism Supplement
JudChr	Judaica et Christiana
NBL	*Neues Bibel-Lexikon*
NEB.EAT	Neue Echter Bibel. Ergänzungsband zum Alten Testament
SFSHJ	South Florida Studies in the History of Judaism
SSAW.PH	Sitzungsberichte der sächsischen Akademie der Wissenschaft zu Leipzig: Philologisch-historisch Klasse
T&T	Texts and Translations
WdF	Wege der Forschung

1. Introduction

by

D. A. CARSON

The "new perspective" on Paul is in some respects not new, and in any case cannot be reduced to a single perspective. Rather, it is a bundle of interpretive approaches to Paul, some of which are mere differences in emphasis, and others of which compete rather antagonistically. Taken together, however, they belong to the "new perspective" in that they share certain things in common, not least a more-or-less common reading of the documents of Second Temple Judaism, and a conviction that earlier readings of Paul, not least from the Protestant camp, and especially from the German Lutheran camp, with lines going back to the Reformation, are at least partly mistaken, and perhaps profoundly mistaken. The sometimes mutually reinforcing, sometimes mutually competing, interpretive grids share enough in common that together they have generated a reigning paradigm that to some extent controls contemporary discussion on Paul, the genesis of early Christianity, justification, grace, the identity and boundaries of the people of God, Torah, and a host of related themes. This new perspective (for so we shall continue to call it) is now so strong, especially in the world of English-language biblical scholarship, that only the rare major work on Paul does not interact with it, whether primarily by agreement, qualification, or disagreement.

Perhaps it is true that the origins of this new perspective, at least insofar as this new perspective became a reigning paradigm, lie with the 1977 volume by E. P. Sanders.[1] Arguably, however, some of the elements in the debate stretch back centuries. Within the twentieth century, some of Sanders's views on Second Temple Judaism were anticipated by C. Montefiore,[2] G. F. Moore,[3] and K. Stendahl,[4] among others.[5] In 1963, the last-named scholar wrote a

---

[1] *Paul and Palestinian Judaism: A Comparison of Patterns of Religion* (Philadelphia: Fortress, 1977).

[2] *Judaism and St. Paul* (London: Goschen, 1914).

[3] "Christian Writers on Judaism," *HTR* 14 (1921): 197–254; ibid., *Judaism*, 3 vols. (Cambridge: Harvard, 1927–30).

[4] *Paul Among Jews and Gentiles* (Philadelphia: Fortress, 1976).

[5] For a useful overview of Jewish thought regarding Paul, see D. A. Hagner, "Paul in Modern Jewish Thought," in *Pauline Studies* (ed. D. A. Hagner and M. J. Harris; Grand Rapids: Eerdmans, 1980), 143–65.

seminal essay of extraordinary influence,[6] in which he argued that Luther's position on justification reflected rather more his own internal struggles than the teaching of the Pauline letters. In Stendahl's view, Luther's influence was continuing to make difficult an historically accurate reading of Paul. Several years before his 1977 volume, E. P. Sanders anticipated his own book in one of his articles.[7] The title of the article and the subtitle of the book are significant: Sanders was looking for "patterns of religion," essentially an approach that borrows from the sociology of religion rather more than from theology. Over against a focus on "reduced essences" (e.g. faith vs. works, liberty vs. law, and the like) or of "individual motifs" (e.g. one starts with Pauline motifs and looks for their origin in Judaism), Sanders deploys a "holistic comparison of patterns of religion," in which the function and context of individual motifs are traced within the "whole," within a "more or less homogeneous entity."[8] "A pattern of religion, defined positively, is the description of how a religion is perceived by its adherents to *function* – how getting in and staying in are understood."[9]

Despite the title of his book, Sanders's focus was on some of the literature of Second Temple Judaism, not on Paul. Almost four hundred pages were devoted to the former, a mere ninety-two to the latter. That scarcely mattered, for it was his treatment of Palestinian Judaism that proved broadly convincing to many. In the forms of Judaism that he treated, Sanders found a common pattern that he labelled "covenantal nomism." This pattern Sanders summarized as follows:

> The "pattern" or "structure" of covenantal nomism is this (1) God has chosen Israel and (2) given the law. The law implies both (3) God's promise to maintain the election and (4) the requirement to obey. (5) God rewards obedience and punishes transgression. (6) The law provides for means of atonement, and atonement results in (7) maintenance or re-establishment of the covenantal relationship. (8) All those who are maintained in the covenant by obedience, atonement and God's mercy belong to the group which will be saved. An important interpretation of the first and last points is that election and ultimately salvation are considered to be by God's mercy rather than human achievement.[10]

More simply put, the "pattern of religion" in Second Temple Judaism, according to Sanders, is that "getting" in is by God's mercy, while "staying in" is a function of obedience. Despite the many branches or emphases in first-century Judaism, this "covenantal nomism" is the common pattern. Sanders

---

[6] Krister Stendahl, "The Apostle Paul and the Introspective Conscience of the West," *HTR* 56 (1963): 199–215.

[7] E. P Sanders, "Patterns of Religion in Paul and Rabbinic Judaism," *HTR* 66 (1973): 455–78.

[8] Sanders, *Paul and Palestinian Judaism*, 16.

[9] Sanders, ibid., 17 (emphasis his).

[10] Ibid., 422.

acknowledges, of course, that some documents are notably "defective" (Sanders thinks in particular of 1 Enoch),[11] but the pattern, he insists, is pervasive.

To determine just how pervasive this pattern is, is one of the purposes of this volume. Whatever the results, the implications of this reading of Second Temple Judaism are certainly pervasive. For a start, it means that the theory that apocalypticism and legalism constitute substantially different religious streams within Second Temple Judaism of the period is profoundly misguided. More importantly for our purposes, the Protestant (and especially Lutheran) reading of Paul, which pits Paul's theology of grace against an ostensible Judaism of legalism, cannot (on this view) withstand close scrutiny of the primary texts. The Protestant reading of Paul is grounded not only on a terribly anachronistic reading of late texts – after all, apart from other evidence a fifth-century talmudic source is as relevant to Paul as mid-twentieth-century existentialism is for the evaluation of Shakespeare – but also on a chronic failure to discern the *pattern* of religion that Sanders believes he has uncovered. Paul's primary problem with the Judaism of his day, according to Sanders, has little to do with merit theology. His primary complaint is that it is not Christianity. Otherwise put, the most significant dividing line between Paul and his Jewish opponents was not merit theology but Christ. Of course, once Paul had come to accept that Jesus was the Messiah, he had to work out the theology of that position, and sometimes that drove him to theological constructions that emphasized differences between himself and unconverted Jews – sometimes even caricaturizing his opponents, rather than dealing with them fairly. Moreover, one must distinguish (Sanders says) between the way that Paul arrived at his conclusion, and the theological construction he later developed to support it. Thus, the relationship between Romans 1:18–3:20 and Romans 3:21–6 may be that of plight and solution, but that is surely after the fact: as Paul actually experienced things, he came to accept Jesus as the Messiah, and then worked out the theology: he moved from solution to plight.

Even now, almost two and a half decades later, reading the initial reviews of Sanders's work is a profitable exercise,[12] not only for their intrinsic value

---

[11] Ibid., 423.

[12] These include: C. Scobie, *SR* 4 (1978): 461–3; J. Murphy-O'Connor, *RB* 85 (1978): 122–6; G. B. Caird, *JTS* 29 (1978): 538–43; J. Neusner, *HR* 18 (1978): 177–91; Bruce J. Malina, *BTB* 8 (1978): 190–91; C. Bernas, *TS* 39 (1978): 340–41; J. C. Beker, *ThTo* 35 (1978): 108–111; J. Drury, *Theology* 81 (1978): 235–6; J. T. Pawlikowski, *ChrCent* 95 (May 10, 1978): 511–12; D. E. Aune, *ChrToday* 22 (Apr. 21, 1978): 34; S. S. Smalley, *Chm* 92 (1978): 71–2; R. Smith, *CurTM* 6 (1979): 33–4; M. McNamara, *JSNT* 5 (1979): 67–73; G. Brooke, *JJS* 30 (1979): 247–50; A. J. Saldarini, *JBL* 98 (1979): 299–303; W. Baird, *PSTJ* 32 (1979): 39–40; G. Nickelsburg, *CBQ* 41 (1979): 171–5; D. J. Lull, *QR* 1 (1980): 81–7; N. King, *Bib* 61 (1980): 141–4; B. R. Gaventa, *BTB* 10 (1980): 37–44; E. Best, *SJT* 33 (1980): 191–2; J. F. Collange,

but also to discover how prescient (or otherwise!) they were. At the risk of generalization, most of them thought that Sanders's views on Paul needed a good deal more work, while his portrait of post-biblical Judaism received generally favorable notice. A. J. Saldarini (in *JBL*) was one of several exceptions: he protested that the pattern of "covenantal nomism" could not be sustained in pre-70 Judaism. Although many reviewers predicted that the book would prove important, few signalled that they thought it would bear the influence it has in fact enjoyed.

What has happened is that, for a sizable proportion of the New Testament guild, "covenantal nomism" has become the shibboleth for understanding Second Temple Judaism, and the necessary background for understanding Paul. So influential has this proportion become that few serious students of Paul say much about his writings without interacting with the "new perspective," whether as supporters or as detractors (or some mix of both).[13]

To track these developments here would be inappropriate, not least because the lead essay in the second volume of this two-volume set attempts just such an exercise. But it would surely not be inappropriate to mention the work of two scholars in particular. In 1983, James D. G. Dunn gave a highly positive assessment of the work of Sanders,[14] and this was eventually followed up by major commentaries on Romans[15] and Galatians[16], not to mention a bevy of articles and books aimed at re-constructing parts of first-century Christianity, especially in Pauline circles. Dunn and his students have repeatedly insisted that the "works of the law" that draw the focus of interest in our literature have little to do with merit theology, and much influence as "boundary markers": Sabbath observance, the importance of kosher food, and circumcision have to do with preserving Jewish identity. Paul's insistence on breaking down these barriers has less to do with his opposition to some sort of ostensible legalism, than with his opposition to cultural elitism. Meanwhile, the growing corpus of N. T. Wright argues, among other things, that for Paul justification does not so much mark the entrance point into the Christian way, as that justification is God's righteous declaration that someone actually belongs to the covenant. Inevitably, Sanders, Dunn, and Wright all disagree with one another in various ways, even though they are among the leading lights of the new perspective. What all sides would agree upon, I think, is that Sanders's "covenantal nomism" has been a shaping feature of the new

---

RHPR 61 (1981): 196–7; N. Hyldahl, *DTT* 46 (1983): 223–4.

[13] The exceptions stand out: e.g. Joseph A. Fitmyer's commentary on *Romans* (AB 33; New York: Doubleday, 1993), for the most part, simply ignores the new perspective on Paul, which tends to make his commentary on Romans simultaneously refreshing and obsolete.

[14] "The New Perspective on Paul," *BJRL* 65 (1983): 95–122.

[15] *Romans* (WBC; Dallas: Word, 1986).

[16] *Galatians* (BNTC; Peabody: Hendrickson, 1993).

perspective on Paul, even though there are other elements of Second Temple Judaism that some parties within this trajectory judge to be no less significant (e.g. Wright's insistence that for most first-century Jews the exile was viewed as still not over).

This means that the place to begin is with the literature of Second Temple Judaism, and the questions to be asked have to do with whether or not "covenantal nomism" serves us well as a label for an overarching pattern of religion. The scholars who have contributed the chapters of this book are not in perfect agreement on this point. The disagreement may spring in part from legitimate scholarly independence, but it springs even more (as the following chapters show) from the variations within the literature: the literature of Second Temple Judaism reflects patterns of belief and religion too diverse to subsume under one label. The results are messy. But if they are allowed to stand, they may in turn prepare us for a more flexible approach to Paul. It is not that the new perspective has not taught us anything helpful or enduring. Rather, the straitjacket imposed on the apostle Paul by appealing to a highly unified vision of what the first-century "pattern of religion" was really like will begin to find itself unbuckled.

The bearing of these matters on Paul must await the second volume. For the moment, it is enough to attempt a fresh evaluation of the literature of Second Temple Judaism.

2. Psalms and Prayers

by

DANIEL FALK

1. Introduction

As expressions of the heart poured out before God, prayers and religious poetry potentially offer richer insights into the affective theology of a group than theoretical speculation or admonition. This is especially the case with topics such as salvation and atonement for sin which are regular concerns in Jewish prayer. The large corpus of Jewish prayers and psalms from the Second Temple period,[1] however, brings its own problems. Only part of this diverse literature is found in collections; much is scattered throughout all kinds of genres as embedded texts, and consequently the corpus has so far received remarkably little systematic treatment. Furthermore, because of the generic nature of the language of prayer it is notoriously difficult to determine the date, provenance, and *Sitz im Leben*, let alone whether we are dealing with "real" prayer or a literary construct for some other purpose.[2] It must also be acknowledged that the language of prayer is to a great extent conventional. Because of this constraint, a straightforward reading of a prayer text cannot always be assumed to represent accurately the pray-er's theology.

A comprehensive study of the entire corpus is not feasible here.[3] Instead, I will examine a few select examples of psalms and prayers. First, I will survey briefly various penitential prayers, all definitely pre-Christian, with separate treatments of *Words of the Luminaries, Communal Confession,*

---

[1] See J. H. Charlesworth, "Jewish Hymns, Odes, and Prayers (ca. 167 B.C.E.–135 C.E.)," *Early Judaism and Its Modern Interpreters* (The Bible and its Modern Interpreters; ed. R. A. Kraft and G. W. E. Nickelsburg; Philadelphia: Fortress Press, 1986), 411–36.

[2] E. Schuller, "Prayer, Hymnic and Liturgical Texts from Qumran," *The Community of the Renewed Covenant: The Notre Dame Symposium on the Dead Sea Scrolls* (Notre Dame: University of Notre Dame Press, 1994), 153–71.

[3] For surveys, see: R. S. Sarason, "On the Use of Method in the Modern Study of Jewish Liturgy," *Approaches to Ancient Judaism 1: Theory and Practice* (BJS 1; ed. W. S. Green; Missoula: Scholars, 1978), 97–172; R. S. Sarason, "Recent Developments in the Study of Jewish Liturgy," *The Study of Ancient Judaism 1: Mishnah, Midrash, Siddur* (ed. J. Neusner; New York: KTAV, 1981), 180–87; J. H. Charlesworth, "A Prolegomenon to a New Study of the Jewish Background of the Hymns and Prayers in the New Testament," *JJS* 33 (1982): 265–85; J. H. Charlesworth, "Jewish Hymns, Odes, and Prayers (ca. 167 B.C.E.–135 C.E.)"; D. Flusser, "Psalms,

Psalm 154, Psalm 155, Plea for Deliverance, and *Prayer of Manasseh*. Such prayers flourished during the Second Temple period and provide an important background for understanding motifs that were becoming stereotyped in prayer. This is followed by a discussion of various series of petitions that appear in the late Second Temple period and seem to have been drawn upon by the formulators of the statutory synagogue prayer known as the *Amidah* (Eighteen Benedictions). Two of the later texts to be considered – book 7 of the *Apostolic Constitutions* and pap. Egerton 5 – supply information of Jewish prayers in a Diaspora context. I will then consider at greater length three large collections. The *Hodayot* from Qumran (second century B.C.) and the *Psalms of Solomon* (first century B.C.) have featured prominently in studies of early Jewish soteriology because of their preponderance of relevant terminology and motifs. They are thus worthy of special attention here, even though the *Hodayot* are treated comparatively in M. Bockmuehl's chapter on the *Rule of the Community* from Qumran. The *Odes of Solomon* is also considered as an extended collection of prayers from a different context, that of Jewish-Christianity probably around the end of the first century A.D.

2. Penitential Supplications

Penitential prayers became prominent in the reconstruction piety of the Second Temple period, prompted especially by reflection on the covenantal warnings such as Lev 26:40–45: "but if they confess their iniquity and the iniquity of their ancestors . . . if then their uncircumcised heart is humbled and they make amends for their iniquity, then I will remember my covenant . . ." (cf. Deut 30:1–10; 1 Kgs 8:22–53; Jer 3:12–13; 14:20–21; Ezek 30:10–20).[4] These prayers are predominantly characterized by four elements, in slightly varying orders: (1) confession of sins, usually in the form of a historical recollection; (2) confession that God's judgment is just; (3) recital of God's mercies in the past; (4) petition for mercy.[5] The focal point of the

---

Hymns and Prayers," *Jewish Writings of the Second Temple Period. Apocrypha, Pseudepigrapha, Qumran Sectarian Writings, Philo, Josephus* (CRINT 2.2; ed. M. E. Stone; Assen: Van Gorcum, 1984), 551–77; M. Harding, "The Lord's Prayer and Other Prayer Texts of the Greco-Roman Era: A Bibliography," *The Lord's Prayer and Other Prayer Texts from the Greco-Roman Era* (ed. J. H. Charlesworth; Valley Forge, PA: Trinity Press, 1994), 103–274; M. Kiley et al., ed., *Prayer from Alexander to Constantine: A Critical Anthology* (London: Routledge, 1997).

[4] R. A. Werline, *Penitential Prayer in Second Temple Judaism: The Development of a Religious Institution* (SBL Early Judaism and its Literature 13; Atlanta: Scholars, 1998). Biblical citations will be according to the NRSV unless otherwise indicated.

[5] E.g., Neh 9:6–37; Ezra 9:6–15; Dan 9:4–19; Pr Azar 1:3–22; Bar 1:15–3:8; *Words of the Luminaries* 4Q504 1–2 v–vii (prayer for Friday); *Communal Confession* 4Q393. See further the

prayer is the petition for mercy (sometimes implied rather than verbalized), even if the content is dominated by the confession of sin and God's justice.[6] The latter elements, along with the recital of God's past mercies, are conventional and support an appeal for God's mercy in the present.

So, for example, in the prayer in Neh 9:6–37 there is no explicit petition for mercy, but the prayer drives unmistakably toward its unstated object, ending "and we are in great distress" (Neh 9:36–37). The most conventional of the elements is the confession that God's judgments are just, for example: "You have been just in all that has come upon us, for you have dealt faithfully and we have acted wickedly" (Neh 9:33); "O Lord, God of Israel, you are just . . . here we are before you in our guilt, though no one can face you because of this" (Ezra 9:15); "righteousness is on your side, O Lord, but open shame, as at this day, falls on us, the people of Judah, the inhabitants of Jerusalem, and all Israel . . . because of the treachery that they have committed against you. Open shame, O Lord, falls on us, our kings, our officials, and our ancestors, because we have sinned against you" (Dan 9:7–8; very similarly Bar 1:15; 2:6); "for you are just in all you have done; all your works are true and your ways right, and all your judgments are true. You have executed true judgments in all you have brought upon us . . . by a true judgment you have brought all this upon us because of our sins . . . and now we cannot open our mouths" (Pr Azar 1:4–10).

Accompanying the declaration that God is righteous in his judgment are also expressions to the effect that the petitioners can speak nothing in their defense ("shame is on us," etc.), which along with the confessions of sin are not uncommonly in apparent tension with expressions of piety/righteousness: in Prayer of Azariah, the petitioners who confess their sins and cannot open their mouths are also those "with a contrite heart and a humble spirit," who "trust" in God, "follow" God with all their heart, "fear" God and "seek" his presence (1:16–19); in Bar 1:15–3:8, those who confess their sins are also those who fear God, call on his name, and have "put away from our hearts all the iniquity of our ancestors who sinned against you" (3:7). The tension is only apparent, however. The pious suffer because of the sins of the nation/ ancestors, and suffering is regarded as atoning for sin. In Pr Azar 1:15–19, it is requested that God in his mercy will accept penitence as atonement in the place of sacrifice. In Baruch and *Words of the Luminaries*, there can be no basis for appeal to merit, because the desire to repent itself is a gift of God (Bar 3:7; for *Words of the Luminaries*, see below).

---

references cited in D. K. Falk, "4Q393: A Communal Confession," *JJS* 45 (1994): 199–207.

[6] The one exception is 1QS 1:18–2:4, where the prayer form is significantly modified. See D. K. Falk, *Daily, Sabbath, and Festival Prayers in the Dead Sea Scrolls* (Leiden: Brill, 1998), 71, 222.

The conventional nature of much of the language is easily apparent; that is, this is how one petitions when the situation of distress is perceived to be a result of sin, even the sins of ancestors. One humbly accepts God's judgment and appeals on the basis of election, the covenant and God's mercy,[7] even if one's own congregation is pious. An explanation is not hard to find: this body of penitential prayers seems to be a product of taking the covenantal warnings (Lev 26:40–45, etc.) as a prescription for restoration.

The language of much subsequent Jewish prayer is marked with a strong imprint from such penitential supplications. To ignore this is to risk misinterpreting stereotyped motifs such as God's righteousness. This becomes particularly important in considering the *Psalms of Solomon* below, since the degree to which they are steeped in the language of the penitential prayer tradition has not often been appreciated.[8] In order to give due weight to this body of penitential prayers and the range of soteriological perspectives within it, then, I will consider a few specific examples.

2.1. Words of the Luminaries

A collection of prayers for each day of the week found in Qumran Cave 4 (4Q504, 4Q506),[9] entitled דברי המארות (*Words of the Luminaries*), is the earliest known example of penitential supplications used in a daily liturgy. The two fragmentary copies date around the middle of the second century B.C. and the middle of the first century A.D. Although they were likely used at Qumran, they were composed prior to the sectarian settlement at Qumran and probably outside the *Yahad* community.[10] They appear to be the product of professional literary composition, but for liturgical purposes.[11]

---

[7] E.g., Dan 9:18, "we do not present our supplication before you on the ground of our righteousness, but on the ground of your great mercies"; Pr Azar 1:11–13, 19–20; Bar 2:19, 27; 3:2. Appeal is also made to God's reputation and his deeds in the past.

[8] But see Werline, *Penitential Prayer in Second Temple Judaism: The Development of a Religious Institution*, 188.

[9] Edition: M. Baillet, "Paroles des Luminaires," *Qumrân grotte 4, III (4Q482–4Q520)* (DJD 7; Oxford: Clarendon, 1982), 137–75; reconstruction and commentary: E. G. Chazon, "A Liturgical Document from Qumran and Its Implications: 'Words of the Luminaries' (4QDibHam)"[Hebrew], Ph.D. dissertation, Hebrew University, 1991); translation: E. G. Chazon, "Prayers from Qumran: Issues and Methods," *SBL 1993 Seminar Papers* (ed. E. H. Lovering; Atlanta: Scholars, 1993), 758–72; F. García Martínez and E. J. C. Tigchelaar, ed., *The Dead Sea Scrolls Study Edition* (2 vols.; Leiden: Brill, 1997–1998), 2.1008–10; discussion: Falk, *Daily, Sabbath, and Festival Prayers*, 59–94. Translations used here are my own.

[10] E. G. Chazon, "Is *Divrei Ha-Me'orot* a Sectarian Prayer?" *The Dead Sea Scrolls: Forty Years of Research. Papers Read at a Symposium Sponsored by Yad Izhak Ben-Zvi at the University of Haifa and at Tel Aviv University March 20–24, 1988* (ed. D. Dimant and U. Rappaport; Leiden: Brill, 1992), 3–17.

[11] E. G. Chazon, "4QDibHam: Liturgy or Literature?" *RevQ* 15 (1992): 447–55.

The supplications for each week day[12] evince a profound sense of sinfulness. Current situations of distress are understood as God's chastening discipline for their sin. There is no basis for appeal to one's own behavior. They are without excuse for their sin because Adam was created with "understanding and knowledge," and God "established for him not to stray" (4Q504 8 recto 5–8). Likewise, Israel was created and chosen to be distinct from the nations, and given knowledge so that they would not sin. But they rebelled anyway, and it can be said to be because of Israel's election that God disciplined them. God's justice is thus his punishment of their sin. Moreover, God called them in their sin, gave them his holy spirit so that they might repent and turn to God, and implanted Torah in their heart that they might not stray from his commands. Thus, even when they repent, atone for their sin (רצינו את עווננו), and obey (4Q504 1–2.vi.2–9), this cannot be claimed as merit, but comes by God's grace.

> You were gracious toward your people Israel in all [the] lands to which you banished them, to cause them to turn their heart(s) to return to you and to obey your voice [according] to all you commanded by the hand of Moses your servant. [Fo]r you poured out your holy spirit on us [to br]ing your blessings to us, so that (we) might seek you in our distress [and so that (we) might mu]rmur (prayers) in the distress of your correction. (4Q504 1–2.v.11–17)

They can appeal only to God's mercy and love, God's election and covenant with Israel, and God's reputation (4Q504 1–2.ii.7–11; 1–2.v.6–9). Not only does the community pray for deliverance, but also for forgiveness and spiritual help to obey:

> But you, ransom us and forgive, [*please*], our sin and [our] of[fence. . . . the law which [you] com[manded] by the hand of Mos[es] . . . Circumcise the foreskin [of our heart . . .] Strengthen our heart to do [. . . to] walk in your ways [. . . Blessed] be the Lord, who has made [us] to kn[ow . . .] (4Q504 4:7–14).

The praying community identifies itself with Israel, as is evident from the close interchange of Israel and "us" with regard to events such as the Exodus, the Mosaic covenant, and the exile. It is unlikely that there is a sense here of a limited Israel, although there are possible hints that may be obscured by the fragmentary nature of the remains. For example, immediately after pleading that God restore dispersed Israel, there occurs the phrase "everyone who is written in the book of life [. . .]" (1–2.vi.14). It is not clear how this phrase relates to the context, or whether the "book of life" terminology here has to do with inclusion versus exclusion as in Ps 69:29. Toward the end of the prayer for Sunday, the community asks that God "not re]ckon to us the sins of the former ones in all their wick[ed] dealings . . . but you, ransom us and forgive, [please], our iniquity and [our] s[in]" (4:6–7). It is possible that the

---

[12] Sabbath has instead a hymn of praise.

community here distances itself from the fathers who sinned, and that forgiveness should be extended to the community *in contrast to* the previous sinners. In the light of the identification with the sins of Israel elsewhere, however, this is unlikely.

The language of such a classic presentation of penitential supplication corresponds very well to the covenantal nomism pattern described by E. P. Sanders,[13] since a sense of corporate solidarity as the covenant people is at the forefront. God punishes sin and assists with repentance and keeping Torah because these are his chosen people. Keeping of Torah is not the means of repairing relationship with God, but rather the goal. Sin is atoned by submitting to God's discipline and by means of the penitential prayer itself (4Q504 1–2.v.4–8) which is provided for in Torah (cf. Lev 26:40–45; Deut 4:29–31; 30:1–10).

It is not the case, however, that even in such a stereotyped genre the language will be consistently used. Two further examples illustrate wide differences in the perception of the nature of human sinfulness and the need for divine grace.

2.2. Communal Confession (4Q393)

A fragmentary manuscript found in Qumran Cave 4 contains a communal prayer of confession probably dated no later than about the latter half of the first century B.C.[14] There is no compelling reason to conclude that this prayer is a product of the *Yaḥad*.

In literary terms, the prayer is an expansion of Moses' prayer in Deut 9:26–29 along the lines of *Jub* 1:4–25, generously adapting language from Ps 51 and Neh 9. God's just judgment is contrasted with the people's guilt: "and what is evil [in your eyes] I have [done,] so that you are just in your sentence, you are pu[re . . . when] you [jud]ge. Behold, in our sins w[e] were founded, [we] were [br]ought forth [   ] in imp[urity of . . .] and in st]iffness of neck." (4Q393 1–2.ii.2–4). Supplication is made to God for forgiveness and help in obedience, appealing to God's compassion ("your people have fainted on account of [your gr]eat ang[er]. Continually they [have relied] upon [your] forg[iveness]," 1–2.ii.8), God's reputation ("Nations and kingdoms will sa[y]," 1–2.ii.9), and the election and covenant ("do not abandon your people

---

[13] E. P. Sanders, *Paul and Palestinian Judaism: A Comparison of Patterns of Religion* (Philadelphia: Fortress, 1977), 422-3.

[14] Falk, "4Q393"; D. K. Falk, "Biblical Adaptation in 4Q392 *Works of God* and 4Q393 *Communal Confession*," *The Provo International Conference on the Dead Sea Scrolls: Technological Innovations, New Texts, and Reformulated Issues* (STDJ 30; ed. D. W. Parry and E. Ulrich; Leiden: Brill, 1999), 126–46; D. K. Falk, "4Q Communal Confession," *Poetical and Liturgical Texts, Part 2* (DJD 29; ed. M. Broshi et al.; Oxford: Clarendon, 1999), 45-61. Translations are my own.

[and] your [in]heritance," 3:3; "You are the YHWH who chose our fathers from ancient times. May you confirm us as a remnant for them to give to us (that which) you established with Abraham (and) Israel," 3:6–7).

Although the profound sense of sinfulness and guilt is adapted from Psa 51:7, it is particularly striking here because the context of communal confession lends the language an implication of universal guilt. Even more striking is the modification of Psa 51:11–15, whereby the community apparently speaks of itself as the sinners and transgressors who need to be returned to God and taught his ways (4Q393 1–2.ii.4–8).

2.3. Prayer of Manasseh

Prayer of Manasseh is a penitential prayer of an individual. It was composed as a narrative production by a Jew probably between the second century B.C. and the first century A.D., self-consciously attempting to supply the penitential prayer of Manasseh mentioned in 2 Chronicles 33:12–13, 18–19 by echoing phrases from the narrative. Still, it reflects to a certain degree actual patterns of Jewish penitential prayers, and at least by the third century it was used liturgically by Christians.[15] Scholars are divided as to the original language (Greek or semitic) and provenance.

Prayer of Manasseh begins with (1) an invocation (vv. 1–5) which praises God as the God of the patriarchs, creator of all, and fearsome. The complaint is hinted at: God is the God of the righteous and none can endure God's wrath against sinners. (2) The individual then expresses confidence in God's mercy (vv. 6–8), appealing to his character in terms particularly reminiscent of the biblical lists of God's attributes but especially Joel 2:12–13 (LXX; see also

---

[15] See J. H. Charlesworth, "Prayer of Manasseh," *OTP*, 2.627-8. The earliest manuscripts are in Syriac (*Didascalia*, third century A.D.) and in Greek (*Apostolic Constitutions*, fourth century A.D.; from the fifth century codex Alexandrinus included among the Odes attached to the Psalter). Greek edition: A. Rahlfs, ed., "Προσευχὴ Μανασση," *Septuaginta: Id Est Vetus Testamentum Graece Iuxta LXX Interpretes* (Duo volumina in uno; Stuttgart: Deutsche Bibelgesellschaft, 1979), 180–81; Syriac: W. Baars and H. Schneider, "Prayer of Manasseh," *The Old Testament in Syriac According to the Peshitta Version* (Leiden: Brill, 1972), i–vii, 1–9. Translations and notes: H. E. Ryle, "The Prayer of Manasses," *The Apocrypha and Pseudepigrapha of the Old Testament in English* (2 vols.; ed. R. H. Charles; Oxford: Clarendon, 1913), 1.612–24; E. Osswald, *Das Gebet Manasses* (Jüdische Schriften aus Hellenistisch-Römischer Zeit 4,1; Gütersloh: Gerd Mohn, 1974), 1–27; J. H. Charlesworth, "Prayer of Manasseh." Introductions: J. B. Frey, "Apocryphes de l'A.T., 13. La Prière de Manassé," *Dictionnaire de la Bible, Supplément* 1 (1928), 442–5; A.-M. Denis, "La Prière de Manassé," *Introduction aux Pseudépigraphes grecs d'Ancient Testament* (Studia in Veteris Testamenti Pseudepigrapha 1; Leiden: Brill, 1970), 177–81; E. Schürer, *The History of the Jewish People in the Age of Jesus Christ. A New English Edition* (3 vols. in 4 parts; revised and edited by G. Vermes, F. Millar, M. Black and M. Goodman; Edinburgh: T & T Clark, 1973–1987), 3.2:730–3; J. H. Charlesworth, *The Pseudepigrapha and Modern Research with a Supplement* (Septuagint and Cognate Studies 7s; Chico, CA: Scholars, 1981) 156–9, 296.

Exod 34:6; Ps 103:8): God has great compassion, is long-suffering, and abundant in mercy, and "repents concerning the evils of men." The latter phrase probably means that God has pity on the people suffering as punishment for sin and is willing to relent.[16] God's mercy is part of his promise, which assures forgiveness for those who repent of their sins. Thus, God appointed repentance to sinners for their salvation.[17] Here the psalmist anticipates the answer to his problem: God is the God of the righteous, such as the patriarchs who did not sin and for whom God did not appoint repentance ("grace" in the Syriac), but his concern for sinners is evident in appointing repentance for them. (3) Next, the individual confesses his sin, the justice of the suffering he is experiencing,[18] and his unworthiness to see heaven (vv. 9–10). (4) Now the petitioner pours out a moving plea for forgiveness (vv. 11–13). The depiction of repentance is graphic – "and now I bend the knees of my heart before you, beseeching your kindness" – and the tone urgent – "I have sinned, O Lord, I have sinned . . . forgive me, O Lord, forgive me." He ends the petition with an expression of hope: "for you, Lord, are the God of those who repent." Thus, God is not only the God of the righteous who do not sin, but he is also the God of sinners who repent. (5) This leads to a confession of confidence that God will forgive and deliver (v. 14): "and in me you will show your goodness, for although I am unworthy you will save me according to the abundance of your mercy." The prayer concludes with (6) a vow (v. 15a) to praise God continually, and (7) a doxology (v. 15b).

In contrast to the universality of guilt assumed in *Communal Confession*, *Prayer of Manasseh* raises the prospect of sinlessness.[19] The patriarchs did not sin, and their true offspring are the righteous. These apparently do not need repentance, or as in the Syriac, God's grace (v. 8). In contrast to the righteous are the sinners. These are not hopelessly lost, because God out of his mercy promised repentance for sinners as the means to forgiveness and salvation. Both the righteous – those who do not sin – and the sinners who repent enjoy God's covenant. It is implied that those excluded from the covenant are sinners who refuse to repent.

The overarching presupposition of the prayer is God's covenant with the patriarchs and his unlimited grace and unmerited mercy. To this extent,

---

[16] Ryle, "Prayer of Manasses," 621.

[17] Verse 7b is found in the Syriac and Latin manuscripts, and – somewhat differently – in only some Greek manuscripts. It is likely original, however, as argued by Ryle, "Prayer of Manasses," 621.

[18] The verse "and now, O Lord, I am justly afflicted, and as I deserve I am harrassed; for already I am ensnared" (Charlesworth, "Prayer of Manasseh," 636, verse 9b) is absent from the Greek. It is likely original, however, as argued by Ryle, "Prayer of Manasses," 622.

[19] For a few other texts that seem to countenance the possibility of sinlessness see the references in Charlesworth, "Prayer of Manasseh," 629, n. 52.

Sanders's model of "covenantal nomism" might be seen to apply in general terms. But the language is suggestive of a double track to enjoyment of God's covenant. Those who do not sin and never need repentance are the true offspring of the patriarchs, and repentance may be read as a concession for those who fail. If the repentant sinner considers himself undeserving of God's goodness due to his sins (vv. 10, 14), does this imply that the righteous person is deserving of God's goodness because of righteous conduct? It must be kept in mind that the perspective of the prayer is limited: it is specifically the sin of idolatry that is in view,[20] and this is to be the prayer of a notorious sinner. Perhaps this should be read merely as the humble response of the sinner: at first reluctant to compare himself with the heroes of the faith or even consider himself among the righteous because of his many sins, he nonetheless comes to recognize that God is his God because God provides repentance for sinners. The brevity of the prayer and the limited viewpoint do not allow for a clear answer. Nevertheless, the language does set this prayer apart as making a distinction within the covenant.

2.4. The Qumran Covenant Ceremony

The penitential prayer form we have been considering was modified in a distinctive way in the exclusivistic covenant ceremony in the sectarian texts from Qumran (*Rule of the Community* 1QS 1:18–2:18; *Damascus Document* CD B 2:27–30).[21] In the ceremony, the people (1) ascribe praise to God, (2) recount God's merciful acts, and (3) confess the sins of the fathers and their own sin, and confess that God's judgments are just. So far, this corresponds to the typical pattern of communal penitential prayers. However, there is no petition for mercy. Instead, (4) the priests and Levites pronounce blessings on the community, and curses on the men of Belial's lot and apostates. The meaning of confession of sin is thus significantly modified by the eschatological and sectarian setting: it functions as an affirmation of one's position in the covenant, since God's elect are those who confess sins (cf. CD B 2:27–30). The scope of the covenant, moreover, is limited to the community.[22] Repentance no longer serves merely to repair and maintain relationship with God in the covenant with Israel, but serves as a formulaic part of an exclusivistic rite of passage into the sectarian community.

---

[20] Ryle, "Prayer of Manasses," 615.

[21] On the *Rule of the Community* generally, see the chapter by M. Bockmuehl in this volume. On the adaptation of the penitential prayer form in the covenant ceremony, see further Falk, *Daily, Sabbath, and Festival Prayers*, 219–36.

[22] On the modification of soteriological categories in apocalyptic Judaism, see M. A. Seifrid, *Justification by Faith: The Origin and Development of a Central Pauline Theme* (NovTSup 68; Leiden: Brill, 1992), 78–99.

2.5. Summary

The genre of penitential petitions grew out of reflection on classic covenantal texts to understand and remedy the travails of the exile.[23] It should come as no surprise that many of these prayers – and numerous other texts influenced by them – exhibit motifs that find resonance in the pattern of covenantal nomism described by Sanders. This is not to say, however, that all such texts fully correspond to the notion of covenantal nomism. The language is constrained by convention, but is used with very different meanings in different contexts, particularly with regard to how inclusive or exclusive the covenant is conceived and the means of attaining God's mercy. It cannot be ruled out that in some instances the penitential prayer itself may become a pious activity that merits God's favor. This of course is virtually impossible to track, but certainly in the sectarian covenant ceremony the penitential prayer is transformed into a formulaic part of a ritual to reinforce the boundaries between those under God's favor and those excluded in the last days.

God's righteousness is an important motif in the penitential prayers. Predominantly in these prayers it has to do with declaring God just in his judgments in contrast to the people's guilt. When the prayers speak of God's forgiveness in the face of the people's guilt, the language is usually of his mercy. It has been argued that God's righteousness in the penitential prayers is also God's help and forgiveness to which the supplicant appeals.[24] This is demonstrable in some instances (e.g., Psa 51:16; *Plea for Deliverance* 11QPs[a] 19:4b–5a, 11), but it can be overestimated. For example, one of the cases where God's righteousness most clearly seems to be his forgiveness in the face of the people's guilt is in the *Words of the Luminaries*: "you [remov]ed fr[o]m us all ou[r] transgressions, and you [p]urified us from our sin for you sake. To you, yes, you, O Lord, (belongs) righteousness! For you have done all these things" (4Q504 1–2.vi.2–3, prayer for Friday). However, one needs to ask what is meant by removing transgressions and purifying from sin. It is not simple forgiveness despite sinfulness. Rather, there are two circles of action involved in the context. On God's part, he has sent severe distress as correction on the people ("tests and blows," 4Q504 1–2.vi.7), and poured out his holy spirit on them so that they might pray to him "in the distress of your correction" (4Q504 1–2.v.15–17). On the people's part, they have submitted to God's discipline and humbled their hearts, and in so doing "we have atoned for our iniquity and the iniquity of our fathers" (4Q504 1–2.vi.4–9). That is, God is declared righteousness for accepting the people's

---

[23] Werline, *Penitential Prayer*, 191–2.

[24] P. Stuhlmacher, "The New Righteousness in the Proclamation of Jesus," *Reconciliation, Law, and Righteousness. Essays in Biblical Theology* (Philadelphia: Fortress, 1986), 34.

repentance and submission to his purifying discipline. In this, the emphasis is probably on God's response as just or consistent rather than specifically lenient. The opposite would be God acting out of caprice. When leniency is in view, the language is almost always of God's grace and mercy (4Q504 4:5 cf. 4Q506 131+132:11; 4Q504 1–2.v.11). It is possible that even in Daniel 9:16 – "O Lord, in view of all your righteous acts, let your anger and wrath, we pray, turn away" – the righteous acts spoken of are especially his discipline for which God was declared "just" in 9:14 (but cf. Dan 9:18). In many of the prominent examples of this genre (e.g., Ezra 9:6–15; Neh 9:9–37; Bar 1:15–3:8; Pr Azar) God's righteousness is consistently his justice or right action. Key to this usage in the penitential prayers is the idea that the people have experienced God's discipline and repented. God is then seen as acting in accordance to his promise in Lev 26:40–45.

3. The Amidah and Series of Petitions

One of the two central liturgical elements of the synagogue service is a prayer known as the *Amidah*, also called the Eighteen Benedictions because it comprises a series of short benedictions (now nineteen). Although it is impossible to speak of a particular authoritative text of the *Amidah* prior to the geonic period (8th–11th c. A.D.), it is important to consider for the present study because the prayer was apparently constructed out of ancient series of petitions with traditional thematic structures and forms dating back to the Second Temple period.[25]

For our purposes, then, it will be useful first merely to summarize the essential substance of the benedictions as known on the basis of some of the earliest explicit evidence for the *Amidah*.[26] Secondly, we will examine several examples of the earliest series of petitions that bear an apparent relationship

---

[25] J. Heinemann, *Prayer in the Talmud: Forms and Patterns* (SJ 9; Berlin: Walter de Gruyter, 1977), 37, 219–29; L. A. Hoffman, *The Canonization of the Synagogue Service* (University of Notre Dame Center for the Study of Judaism and Christianity in Antiquity; Notre Dame: University of Notre Dame, 1979), 1–9.

[26] I base the following discussion primarily on the Palestinian version of the *Amidah* in a medieval manuscript from the Cairo Genizah that preserves the original number of eighteen benedictions (text reprinted in J. J. Petuchowski, ed., *Contributions to the Scientific Study of Jewish Liturgy* [New York: KTAV, 1970], 373–8, 379–448, especially 375–8 and 405–10; translation in J. Heinemann and J. J. Petuchowski, *Literature of the Synagogue* [Library of Jewish Studies; New York: Behrman House, 1975], 33–6). Also taken into account are the earliest known prayer-book (Babylonian, 9th c.), by R. Amram Gaon (D. Hedegård, *Seder R. Amram Gaon. Part I. Hebrew Text with Critical Apparatus, Translation with Notes and Introduction* [Lund: A.-B. Ph. Lindstedts Universitets-Bokhandel, 1951], 83–98), and the two versions of an abbreviated form of the middle petitions (known as *Habinenu*) cited in the Palestinian and Babylonian talmuds (*y. Ber.* 4:3,8*a* and *b. Ber.* 29*a*).

to what became the *Amidah* and consider what meaning the petitions had in those contexts.

The *Amidah* begins with three ascriptions of praise to God:[27]

1. as God and protector of the patriarchs
2. as the God of power
3. as unique and holy

Then follows a series of petitions:

4. for knowledge of Torah
5. for perfecting/acceptance of repentance[28]
6. for forgiveness
7. for redemption/deliverance
8. for healing
9. for fruitfulness of the land
10. for the gathering of the dispersed
11. for judgment of the wicked[29]/restoration of judges
12. for the destruction of the wicked
13. for blessing of the righteous
14. for restoration of Jerusalem, the temple, and Davidic monarchy[30]
15. for the acceptance of prayer

The *Amidah* concludes with three prayers that originally were probably related to the temple service:[31]

16. petition for the acceptance/restoration of the temple service
17. thanksgiving for God's mercies
18. petition for peace

The middle petitions may be regarded as addressing spiritual concerns (4–6), material concerns (7–9), and national concerns (10–15), giving the whole a very structured progression, but this does not necessarily reflect on the genesis of the petitions or their original meaning. On the basis of formal

---

[27] I follow here the numbering of the text from the Cairo Geniza, which preserves the original number of eighteen benedictions.

[28] Assistance with keeping Torah seems to have been the original emphasis of this petition. Cf. "circumcise our hearts to fear you" in the *Habinenu* (*b. Ber.* 29a) and "bring us back in perfect repentance" in *Seder R. Amram*; also some of the prayers to be discussed below: the Prayer of Levi (verses 6–7, 10; M. E. Stone and J. C. Greenfield, "The Prayer of Levi," *JBL* 112 [1993]: 259); *Words of the Luminaries* (4Q504 4:11); 2 Macc 1:3–4; *Plea for Deliverance* (11QPs^a 19:14–16); *Psalm 155* (11QPs^a 24:12–13).

[29] See Heinemann, *Prayer in the Talmud*, 223.

[30] In the prayer books the petition concerning David is a separate benediction (#15, so that the total is 19), but most scholars agree that this was originally a single benediction as in the Cairo Geniza manuscript.

[31] E. Bickerman, "The Civic Prayer for Jerusalem," *HTR* 55 (1962): 167–8.

features, E. Bickerman isolated different clusters of benedictions that he believed at one point were independent units of prayer, and argued that the *Amidah* formed around the nucleus of a "civic prayer for Jerusalem": invocation of God of the Fathers (*Amidah* #1), prayer for health (*Amidah* #8), prosperous harvest (*Amidah* #9), peace for Jerusalem (*Amidah* #14), and concluding with an appeal for God to heed the prayer (*Amidah* #15).[32] Another cluster consists of the prayers for knowledge, repentance, and forgiveness (*Amidah* #4–6), concluding with petition for mercy/deliverance (*Amidah* #7).

Although specific developmental models are difficult to prove, many early petitionary prayers fall into two broad patterns corresponding in a general way to these two prayer clusters. On the one hand are prayers whose focus is appeal for physical and community needs on the basis of God's character and special relationship with his people.

The prayer in Sirach 36:1–17 (first quarter of the second century B.C., Palestine)[33] falls into three parts. Verses 1–9 – the greatest part – petitions God to save "us" and to destroy foreign oppressors (evidently Seleucid rulers). It is an extended and nationalistic expression of petition *Amidah* #12.[34] Verses 10–15 ask for God's blessings on Israel, closely corresponding to the themes of four of the *Amidah* petitions: "gather all the tribes of Jacob" (cf. *Amidah* #12), compassion on Israel (cf. *Amidah* #7), compassion on and God's glory in Jerusalem and the temple (cf. *Amidah* #14), and reward to those who hope in God (cf. *Amidah* #13). Verses 16–17 express confidence that God will hear the prayer (cf. *Amidah* #15). The nationalistic tone is unmistakable. There is no confession of sin or petition for repentance or forgiveness, but nor is there appeal to righteous behavior. Rather, God is asked to deliver and bless the nation for the sake of his reputation and character, especially his holiness and power (cf. *Amidah* #3 and *Amidah* #2), to fulfill prophecies, and on the basis of his special relationship with his people: "called by your name," "your city," "your temple," "those who hope in you," "according to your favor[35] toward your people." Although the term is not used, the covenant is the assumed basis of God's gracious dealings with Israel.[36]

---

[32] Bickerman, "The Civic Prayer for Jerusalem," 173–4. Bickerman found support in parallel petitions for health, prosperity, and peace in Greek prayers for the *polis*.

[33] The Hebrew text of the prayer is extant in the fragments from the Cairo Geniza. See I. Lévi, *The Hebrew Text of the Book of Ecclesiasticus* (Semitic Study Series. 3; reprint; Leiden: Brill, 1951); M. H. Segal, *Sēper Ben-Sîrāʿ Ha-Šālôm* (Jerusalem: Bialik, 1972); P. W. Skehan and A. A. Di Lella, *The Wisdom of Ben Sira* (AB; New York: Doubleday, 1987).

[34] Compare "shake your hand against the foreigners" (Sir 36:2) with the twelfth petition in the *Habinenu* "shake your hand against the wicked" (*b. Ber.* 29a).

[35] Following the Hebrew כרצונך, supported by the Syriac.

[36] The psalm following Sir 51:12 in the Hebrew text from the Cairo Geniza also bears strong

The prayer in 2 Maccabees 1:24–29 may well belong to a fictitious letter, but "the author gives the words of the prayer because he wishes the Jews of Egypt to use them in observing the Feast of Purification."[37] Thus, this prayer attests an attempt by a Palestinian author near the end of the second century or beginning of the first century B.C. to establish a custom of public prayer for Hanukkah, and probably reflects a prayer custom associated with the celebration of Booths which serves as the model (cf. 2 Macc 10:6–7). Although the prayer is strongly dependent on biblical language, the prayer juxtaposes in a way unprecedented in the Hebrew Bible themes and phrases corresponding to benedictions of the *Amidah*. The style and the prayer themes – although not the order – are remarkably similar to the prayer in Sirach 36:1–17. These two prayers, then, assume the existence of a tradition of series of petitions with customary themes similar to the *Amidah*.[38] The prayer in 2 Macc 1:24–29 begins with an invocation to God as creator, awesome and strong (cf. *Amidah* #1), just and merciful king (cf. *Amidah* #11), provider (cf. *Amidah* #9), just and almighty and eternal (cf. *Amidah* #2), who rescues Israel from every evil (cf. *Amidah* #7), and who chose and consecrated the patriarchs (cf. *Amidah* #1 but especially the Sanctification of the Day in the *Amidah* for festivals).[39] The prayer then petitions God to "accept this sacrifice on behalf of all your people Israel and preserve and make holy your portion" (cf. *Amidah* #16), "gather together our dispersed and set free those enslaved among the gentiles" (cf. *Amidah* #10), "look upon the rejected and despised" (cf. *Amidah* #8), "make known to the gentiles that you are our God" (cf. *Amidah* #3), "afflict the oppressors and arrogant" (cf. *Amidah* #12), and "plant your people in your holy place, as Moses said" (cf. *Amidah* #14). Once again, the prayer is nationalistic, there is no confession of sin or petition for forgiveness, nor appeal to righteous behavior. Appeal is made to God's character but above all to the relationship between God and the nation: "all your people Israel." The essence of the prayer is the plea that God accept the sacrifice and fulfill promises of the covenant, which is assumed. Although Israel is God's people, the language of election is not appropriated for the contemporary nation, but rather for the patriarchs alone. It is acknowledged that God chose and sanctified the patriarchs, but the prayer asks that God sanctify Israel. Goldstein is probably correct that the prayer envisages the nation currently in the Age of Wrath prior to fulfillment of prophecies that God will again choose and sanctify his people (e.g., Isa 14:1; Ezek 37).[40]

---

similarities to the *Amidah* benedictions (*Amidah* #2?, 7, 10, 14, 15, 1, 17, 11?).

[37] J. A. Goldstein, *II Maccabees* (AB; Garden City: Doubleday, 1983), 177.

[38] See Falk, *Daily, Sabbath, and Festival Prayers*, 199–201 and the literature cited there.

[39] The Sanctification of the Day in the festival *Amidah* reads in the prayer-book "you have chosen us . . . and been pleased with us . . . and sanctified us by your commandments."

[40] See Goldstein, *II Maccabees*, 179.

On the other hand are prayers where spiritual needs are in the foreground. The festal letter attached to the beginning of 2 Maccabees – probably genuinely from Jewish leaders in Jerusalem to Jews in Egypt to urge observance of Hanukkah – includes a short prayer for the well-being of the recipients (2 Macc 1:2–6). After invoking God's covenant with the patriarchs, it asks that God strengthen them to worship him and do his will, open their heart to his law and commandments, hear their prayers and forgive them, and not forsake them in time of evil. This is effectively an abbreviated form of a cluster of petitions corresponding to the *Amidah* benedictions concerning knowledge, repentance/perfecting,[41] and forgiveness, concluding with a plea for deliverance, and prefaced with an invocation of God of the patriarchs. The order is only slightly different – *Amidah* #1, 5, 4, 6, 7 – and highlights the key matter: proper worship. In the context of the festal letter, the prayer implies that the Egyptian community has sinned by maintaining a schismatic temple at Leontopolis and is in need of repentance, which should involve demonstrating their commitment to the Jerusalem temple by observing the feast of Dedication (Hanukkah).[42] Thus, this is not an abstract prayer for spiritual assistance, but is pointed toward concrete sin. Nevertheless, the addressees are regarded as kindred Jews (τοῖς ἀδελφοῖς τοῖς κατ' Αἴγυπτον Ἰουδαίοις) belonging to the covenant made with the patriarchs.

Such prayers for spiritual needs were not confined to cases of concrete sin. As Weinfeld noted, prayers for knowledge, repentance, and forgiveness (hence corresponding to the themes of *Amidah* #4, 5, 6) became a stereotyped cluster in the Second Temple period, as attested by numerous examples including especially two non-canonical psalms,[43] several Qumran hymns,[44] a narrative prayer attributed to Levi,[45] and a collection of daily prayers found at Qumran.[46] Almost always these petitions were combined with explicit or implicit petition for deliverance (cf. *Amidah* #7.)[47] In the regularizing of such

---

[41] The petition "may he give you all a heart to worship him and to do his will with a strong heart and a willing spirit" (NRSV) thematically corresponds to the petition for repentance of the *Amidah* (#5), for which the abbreviated form in the Babylonian talmud (*b. Ber.* 29a) reads "circumcise our hearts to fear you." See n. 28 above.

[42] Goldstein, *II Maccabees*, 138–9.

[43] *Psalm 155* (11QPsᵃ 24:3–17 and Syriac Psalm 3); *Plea for Deliverance* (11QPsᵃ 19:1–18).

[44] *Hodayot*, especially 1QHᵃ 8(=16):8–20.

[45] *4QAramaic Leviᵇ* (4Q213a) 1 i–ii; see Stone and Greenfield, "The Prayer of Levi." The preceding examples, as well as an early Christian catechetical prayer (*Apostolic Constitutions* 8.6.5–7) were noticed and discussed by M. Weinfeld, "The Prayers for Knowledge, Repentance and Forgiveness in the 'Eighteen Benedictions' – Qumran Parallels, Biblical Antecedents, and Basic Characteristics (Hebrew)," *Tarbiz* 48 (1979): 186–200.

[46] *Words of the Luminaries*, especially the prayers for Sunday (4Q504:4 4–14) and Thursday (4Q504 1–2.ii.7–17). Chazon, "Liturgical Document," 13 (English abstract), 104–5.

[47] Falk, *Daily, Sabbath, and Festival Prayers*, 69–71, 77–8. Cf. Bickerman, "The Civic Prayer for Jerusalem," 172.

prayer, repentance comes to the fore not only as reparation but also for maintaining relationship with God. But repentance is not presented as a purely human action by which one gains God's favor. Rather, knowledge of Torah is a prerequisite for repentance and is sought as God's gift.[48] The petitioner also acknowledges the need for divine assistance with repentance and with keeping God's Torah.[49] Forgiveness is sought on the basis of God's mercy and his special relationship with the people, specifically the covenant, although there is relatively less emphasis on any national distinction than with the previous pattern.[50] Two examples will serve here.[51]

Plea for Deliverance (11QPs[a] 19:1–18) is an individual lament that petitions God for deliverance from some threat. The nature of the danger is unknown since both the beginning and end are lost, but it is apparently perceived as life-threatening (probably illness, see 11QPs[a] 19:15). The psalmist considers himself among the pious (חסידים) who love God's name and to whom God shows mercy (11QPs[a] 19:5–7), but he does not appeal to any righteous behavior or qualities of his own. Rather, he acknowledges his sinfulness but argues that even "those whose feet stumble" are of more value than the dead because they can praise God when shown God's mercy and righteousness (11QPs[a] 19:1–3). He throws himself on God's mercy (11QPs[a] 19:4–5), recalling that previously his life had been in jeopardy because of his sins and God had saved him (11QPs[a] 19:9–11). This remembrance gives him confidence in his present danger (11QPs[a] 19:11–13). He pleads for God to forgive his sin and also to give him spiritual assistance to avoid sin in the future: a faithful spirit, knowledge, and protection from the rule of Satan or the evil inclination (11QPs[a] 19:13–16).

The thought and language are biblical.[52] Forgiveness of sins and God's saving action are grounded solely in God's character: his goodness, mercy, righteousness, faithfulness, lovingkindness, and grace. Here, God's righteousness is interchangeable with his mercy (11QPs[a] 19:4b–5a, 11). Neither the covenant nor Israel are mentioned; although the petitioner is part of a community, the focus is predominantly individual.

---

[48] Cf. the Palestinian *Amidah* from the Cairo Geniza: "Graciously favor us, our Father, with understanding from thee. . . ."

[49] See n. 41 above.

[50] E.g., *Words of the Luminaries* 4Q504 1–2.ii.7–9 (prayer for Thursday) and *Plea for Deliverance* 11QPs[a] 19:4–6.

[51] See also the discussion of *Words of the Luminaries* above, pp. 10–12.

[52] J. A. Sanders, "Non-Masoretic Psalms (4Q88=4QPs[f], 11Q5=11QPs[a], 11Q6=11QPs[b])" (with J. H. Charlesworth and H. W. L. Rietz), *The Dead Sea Scrolls. Hebrew, Aramaic, and Greek Texts with English Translations 4A: Pseudepigraphic and Non-Masoretic Psalms and Prayers* (The Princeton Theological Seminary Dead Sea Scrolls Project; ed. J. H. Charlesworth and H. W. L. Rietz; with P. W. Flint et al.; Tübingen: Mohr [Siebeck], 1997), 193.

Psalm 155 (11QPs[a] 24:3–17 = Syriac Psalm III) is an individual thanks-giving song thanking God for delivering the psalmist from wicked accusers. The core of the psalm (Syriac 3–14; 11QPs[a] 24:4b–13a) is the lament.[53] Thoroughly biblical language and tone pervade the psalm, and there is no hint of an exclusivistic perspective. The assumed scenario seems to be similar to that in Job: the psalmist has been struck with illness[54] which his accusers interpret as divine judgment for his sins. In his despair, the psalmist cries out for God not to abandon him before the wicked, and as the true judge to deliver him from his illness ("recompense of evil," "the evil scourge"; Syriac 7, 13; 11QPs[a] 24:6, 12) that appears as a divine judgment. He does not claim to be sinless, but appeals for God not to judge him according to his sins, "for no one living is righteous before you" (Syriac 8; 11QPs[a] 24:7). He petitions God for spiritual assistance: for instruction in Torah, for safeguarding from what is too difficult, for the forgiveness of his sins. The psalmist offers no personal qualifications to elicit God's help, but appeals only to God's reputation, his simple trust, and God's election of Israel/Jacob (Syriac 10, 17, 21; 11QPs[a] 24:9, 15).

In all of the prayers reviewed in this section, God is able and willing to answer the prayers of his people, who appeal to him on the basis of his mercy and usually also his covenant. On the surface at least, both those prayers which focus on physical and/or community needs and those which focus on spiritual needs correspond in a general way to the "covenantal nomism" described by Sanders. Nevertheless, to apply a broad theological banner over all these prayers would obscure somewhat the significantly different emphases with regard to how the people are related to God. In the first group of prayers the preoccupation is national, so that evil is centered in the "other." The trouble from which Israel needs deliverance is external, especially foreign oppressors. Harm comes because one belongs to Israel: either as punishment for sins of the nation or persecution. Israel also is the realm of God's saving action. In the second group of prayers, we are still dealing with Israel as the covenant people, but the real trouble from which they need deliverance is not external to the people but internal, individual and spiritual: community and personal sin, and in some cases, demonic threat.[55] The keeping of Torah is a spiritual problem for which divine assistance is necessary, particularly when demonic attack is in view as in *Plea for Deliverance* and the Prayer of Levi. Sinfulness is endemic and so the concern

---

[53] M. Noth, "Die fünf syrisch überlieferten apokryphen Psalmen," *ZAW* 7 (1930): 15.

[54] Noth, "Psalmen," 15.

[55] On the petitions for protection from demons, see D. Flusser, "Qumrân and Jewish 'Apotropaic' Prayers," *IEJ* 16 (1966): 194–205 and Stone and Greenfield, "The Prayer of Levi," 262–3.

of harm has to do with one's humanness. The realm of saving activity is more that of the individual than of the nation.

Furthermore, it must be acknowledged that these have become conventional patterns of prayer with stereotyped language, and for the most part we can know little of their significance to petitioners in a life setting. For example, in apotropaic prayers – of which *Plea for Deliverance* and Prayer of Levi are examples – the language may be formalized as incantation.[56] In drawing conclusions about soteriology from traditional prayers, then, one must distinguish between the language of the prayer and the practical appropriation of the prayer which often remains unclear.

For comparison it will be useful to consider two later expressions of the *Amidah* in the Diaspora, still well before a standardized text. Book Seven of the *Apostolic Constitutions* (33–38) contains an extended Christian adaptation of the Jewish Seven Benedictions of the *Amidah* for Sabbaths that probably originated in Jewish Greek synagogues in Syria sometime between 150–300 A.D.[57] The Seven Benedictions for the Sabbath correspond to the first and last three benedictions of the *Amidah* with a special sanctification of the Sabbath in between. Apart from the lack of the final benediction, the Greek Syrian version[58] behind the *Apos. Con.* 7.33–38 corresponds very closely in themes, phrasing, and order. God is powerful (*Apos. Con.* 7.34, cf. *Amidah* #2) and holy (*Apos. Con.* 7.35, cf. *Amidah* #3) and the people are inadequate to give God due praise (*Apos. Con.* 7.38, cf. *Amidah* #18). Yet the prayer begins with the base of approach to God: his special relationship to the people (God of our fathers) and his mercy. Both of these motifs are sounded repeatedly throughout the prayer. Israel is the assembly chosen out of the nations on earth to worship God in conjunction with the angels (*Apos. Con.* 7.35, cf. *Amidah* #3). They are the special people that God redeemed and to whom God gave the Torah and the Sabbath (*Apos. Con.* 7.36, cf. Sanctification of the Sabbath). The sole petition of the prayer is for God to fulfill promises of the prophets for national restoration: Zion, Jerusalem and the Davidic kingdom. This prayer reflects the first pattern described above: its focus is primarily national and there is no petition concerning repentance or forgiveness.

An ancient Jewish Greek version of the *Amidah* from Egypt has been recognized in a papyrus (pap. Egerton 5) dated to the end of the fourth or the

---

[56] Compare the use of the Aaronic blessing as an amulet. It is possible that the purification ritual preceding the Prayer of Levi belongs to the context of the prayer. See Stone and Greenfield, "The Prayer of Levi," 249–50.

[57] D. A. Fiensy, *Prayers Alleged to Be Jewish: An Examination of the Constitutiones Apostolorum* (BJS 65; Chico: Scholars, 1985); see pp. 215–28 for his discussion of provenance.

[58] For a reconstruction of the Jewish prayer minus the Christian redaction, see Fiensy, *Prayers Alleged to Be Jewish*, 198–201. Reference is to Fiensy's translation of his proposed reconstruction.

beginning of the fifth century A.D.[59] What is extant of the prayer contains reflections of at least a dozen of the *Amidah* benedictions,[60] mixing spiritual, physical, and communal needs. Spiritual needs, however, are at the root. In addition to petitions for knowledge (line 4), perfecting (line 5),[61] and forgiveness (lines 14–19a), the request for healing is spiritualized: "of our sick soul you are the only doctor." Wickedness is "a product of our thoughts" (lines 25–26). As typical, appeal is made to both God's special relationship with the people whom he has redeemed and chosen (lines 5b–12a), and to his mercy (lines 33b–35). Although the covenant people are thus assumed, there are no explicit national elements: no reference to the patriarchs, Israel, Jerusalem, or David/Messiah.[62] Thus, this prayer aligns with the second pattern described above.

It certainly cannot be assumed that the two patterns of prayer explored here represent mutually exclusive soteriologies. Nevertheless, the different orientations are significant. The individualism of the second pattern and its focus on the problem of human sinfulness may lead more naturally – although not necessarily – to a strict bifurcation between righteous and sinners within Israel, since within the covenant individuals struggle against evil/Satan. In a heightened apocalyptic and sectarian context such as in the *Yaḥad* the primary distinction becomes the sons of Belial versus the sons of Light. This latter perspective comes to expression in the *Hodayot* from Qumran.

4. Hodayot

The basic features of the soteriology of the Qumran *Hodayot* (frequently called *Thanksgiving Hymns*) have been touched on in Markus Bockmuehl's chapter on the *Rule of the Community* from Qumran. Because of their importance to the debate and much new information to be gathered from recent scholarship,[63] it is appropriate to give separate treatment to the message of the *Hodayot* hymns on their own terms and in relationship to their function.

The *Hodayot* are a collection of songs named for a stereotypical formula frequently found in them: "I give you thanks, O Lord," or "I praise you, O

---

[59] P. W. van der Horst, "Neglected Greek Evidence for Early Jewish Liturgical Prayer," *JSJ* 29 (1998): 278–96. As van der Horst notes, it may in fact be parts of two separate prayers (p. 279). Quotations are from his translation (pp. 283–94).

[60] Fiensy, *Prayers Alleged to Be Jewish*, 289.

[61] It does not seem previously to have been recognized that "make perfect" (line 5) corresponds to the theme of the "repentance" benediction of the *Amidah*. See n. 41 above.

[62] van der Horst, "Neglected Greek Evidence for Early Jewish Liturgical Prayer," 292–3.

[63] E.g., Sanders's treatment of the *Hodayot* was based on the hymns in the faulty order in which they were known prior to the publication of Puech's reconstruction. Sanders, *Paul and*

Lord." The collection is not homogeneous, and since the 1960s there has been a virtual consensus that the songs are of two main types distinguished by form, style, vocabulary, and theology, although more recent research has shown that these are not strictly exclusive.[64] On the one hand are individual songs of thanksgiving in which a very distinct personality – usually identified with the Teacher of Righteousness, and hence these songs are often called Hymns of the Teacher – speaks of his distress and divine deliverance from persecution and betrayal.[65] On the other hand are hymnic songs of confession in which the "I" that speaks generically represents the collective community (sometimes as the Maskil or "Instructor") – hence these are commonly called Hymns of the Community. These latter are characterized by confession of God's acts of salvation in juxtaposition with reflection on the desperate human condition.

Different settings are probable for the two types of songs. The Hymns of the Community are more liturgical in tone and point to a cultic context in connection with the annual covenant ceremony, where confession of sin and God's faithfulness were stereotyped elements (cp. 1QS 1:18–2:4).[66] The rhetoric of these songs, then, is to express commitment to the covenant of the community in the form of humble praise to God. The Hymns of the Teacher are so specifically individualized that they carry a didactic quality when included in a collection of songs. Newsom has convincingly suggested that the rhetorical function of these songs in the collection is to discourage

---

Palestinian Judaism, 239–323; E. Puech, "Quelques aspects de la restauration du Rouleau des Hymnes (1QH)," *JJS* 39 (1988): 38–55; E. Puech, "Un hymne essénien en partie retrouvé et les Béatitudes, 1QH V 12–VI 18 (=col. XIII–XIV 7) et 4QBéat," *RevQ* 13 (1988): 59–88.

[64] S. Holm-Nielsen, *Hodayot, Psalms from Qumran* (Acta Theologica Danica 2; Aarhus: Universitetsforlaget i Aarhus, 1960), 316–48; G. Morawe, *Aufbau und Abgrenzung der Loblieder von Qumrân. Studien zur gattungsgeschichtlichen Einordnung der Hodajôth* (Theologische Arbeiten 16; Berlin: Evangelische Verlagsanstalt, 1961), 107; more precisely G. Jeremias, *Der Lehrer der Gerechtigkeit* (SUNT 2; Göttingen: Vandenhoeck & Ruprecht, 1963), 171; J. Becker, *Das Heil Gottes* (SUNT 3; Göttingen: Vandenhoeck & Ruprecht, 1964), 50–6. For a summary see J. Murphy-O'Connor, "The Judean Desert," *Early Judaism and Its Modern Interpreters* (ed. R. A. Kraft and G. W. E. Nickelsburg; Philadelphia: Fortress Press, 1986), 130–32. On "hybrid" songs, see E. Schuller, "A Thanksgiving Hymn from 4QHodayot^b (4Q428 7)," *RevQ* 16 (1995): 538–9.

[65] The debate about whether these hymns were actually composed by the Teacher is important, but not of critical concern here, since in the collection they functioned as the spiritual expression of an authoritative leader of the community. For convenience, I will speak of the Teacher as the author.

[66] More general use of these hymns (as suggested by some of the introductions restored by E. Puech (see n. 63), still would recall the solemn ceremony of entering the covenant. See H.-W. Kuhn, *Enderwartung und gegenwärtiges Heil: Untersuchungen zu den Gemeindeliedern von Qumran* (SUNT 4; Göttingen: Vandenhoeck und Ruprecht, 1966), 29–33; Falk, *Daily, Sabbath, and Festival Prayers*, 100–103.

disaffection from the community by framing it as betrayal of the now deceased Teacher.[67]

There is some evidence that the two types of songs originated at different times and circulated in different collections.[68] Paleographic dates for the eight surviving manuscripts (two from Qumran Cave 1–1QH^a, 1QH^b – and six from Cave 4 – 4QH^{a-f}) extend throughout most of the first century B.C.[69] Only the latest – 1QH^a – is extensive. At least the core of the Hymns of the Teacher apparently go back to his lifetime around the middle of the second century B.C., whereas some of the Hymns of the Community could be even earlier. As a collection, they bear the imprint of the Qumran community in terms of theological outlook, institutions, and history.

These data need to be taken into consideration when discussing the theology of the *Hodayot*. As with other of the Qumran texts, one needs to take into account heterogeneity within a text in relation to different functions and the probability of different stages of theological development.[70] Furthermore, we should not expect in hymns such as these a theology systematically or comprehensively worked out.

4.1. God and Humans

The dominant tone in the *Hodayot* is praise of God as creator of all, and gratitude for his undeserved mercy. In contrast to God, depictions of the human condition appear remarkably pessimistic. God alone is righteous and humans are utterly frail in their dust and water mortality. Morally frail as well and without spiritual insight, all humans are sinful and incapable of comprehending God or their condition.[71] The universality of human

---

[67] C. A. Newsom, "Kenneth Burke Meets the Teacher of Righteousness: Rhetorical Strategies in the Hodayot and the Serek Ha-Yahad," *Of Scribes and Scrolls: Studies on the Hebrew Bible, Intertestamental Judaism, and Christian Origins Presented to John Strugnell on the Occasion of His Sixtieth Birthday* (College Theology Society Resources in Religion 5; ed. H. W. Attridge, J. J. Collins and T. H. Tobin; Lanham, MD: University Press of America, 1990), 121–31.

[68] E. Schuller, "The Cave Four Hodayot Manuscripts: A Preliminary Description," *JQR* 85 (1994): 141, 144, 148–9. 1QH^a (the latest and most complete manuscript) contains the Hymns of the Teacher (roughly columns 10–17 [=2–9]) in a block surrounded by Hymns of the Community. 4QH^c (late Hasmonean-early Herodian) may have contained only the Hymns of the Teacher. 4QH^a (late Hasmonean-early Herodian) may have contained only Hymns of the Community.

[69] Starcky, "Quatre étapes," 483 n. 8, refers to Strugnell's judgment that the oldest manuscript (4QH^b) dates around 80 B.C.; Starcky himself dates it around 100 B.C.

[70] See the appropriate cautions in S. Holm-Nielsen, *Hodayot*, 273–4.

[71] 1QH^a 7(=15):15–16, 24; 9(=1):21–23, 25–27; 22(=fragment 1):4, 8. J. P. Hyatt, "The View of Man in the Qumran 'Hodayot'," *NTS* 2 (1956): 276–84; S. Holm-Nielsen, *Hodayot*, 274–7; E. H. Merrill, *Qumran and Predestination. A Theological Study of the Thanksgiving Hymns* (STDJ 8; Leiden: Brill, 1975), 25–9; H. Lichtenberger, *Studien zum Menschenbild in Texten der Qumrangemeinde* (Göttingen: Vandenhoeck & Ruprecht, 1980), 76–87, 92–3. Unless otherwise

sinfulness is all the more accented by the self-analysis of the speaker in the hymns of the Teacher.

> What is flesh compared to this? What is a creature of clay to do great wonders? He is in iniquity from the womb, and until old age in guilt of unfaithfulness. But I know that to man does not belong righteousness nor to a son of Adam perfection of way. (1QH[a] 12(=4):29–31; cf. 1QS 11:9–10)

This inclines in the direction of a doctrine of original sin, but in the *Hodayot* there is no speculation about the origin of the human sinful nature.[72] Rather, the point of such statements in hymnic contexts is to stress human nothingness before God.

Nevertheless, the *Hodayot* mark a fundamental bifurcation of humanity, between those whose ultimate destiny is salvation and those who will be destroyed in God's judgment.[73] Various expressions designate the opposing groups in this soteriological dualism, for example the good and the evil (1QH[a] 6[=14]:11–12); the righteous (and the perfect of way, 1QH[a] 9[=1]:36) and the wicked (1QH[a] 12[=4]:38; 15[=7]:12); sons of truth and sons of wickedness/guilt (1QH[a] 14[=6]:29–30); those in communion with the congregation of the sons of heaven (1QH[a] 11[=3]:22) and the congregation of Belial (1QH[a] 10[=2]:22); those who have knowledge and walk in God's ways and those who do not (1QH[a] 7[=15]:18, 21; 12[=4]:17–18, 21, 24); the elect of God and those excluded from God's covenant (1QH[a] 6[=14]:15, 21–22; cf. 7[=15]:26–8).[74]

4.2. Salvation

Salvation in these hymns means deliverance from the wicked, release from the guilt of sin and the weakness of humanity, and participation in the heavenly community (1QH[a] 7[=15]:19–20; 10[=2]:31–36; 11[=3]:19–23; 19[=11]:9–14). In comparison with those destined for destruction there is room for a certain confidence – even if it is always expressed in terms of God's gracious election – because of a strong emphasis on the present realization of salvation, especially in terms of forgiveness, purification from sin, spiritual strengthening, knowledge of divine mysteries, and communion with the angelic community.[75] There is still a future expectation to salvation,

---

noted, translations will be mine and references from the *Hodayot* will be that of García Martínez and Tigchelaar, *DSSSE*. The column number of the Sukenik edition (E. L. Sukenik, ed., *The Dead Sea Scrolls of the Hebrew University* [Jerusalem: Magnes, 1955]) will be provided in square brackets. Line numbers often differ, and will be different again in the official edition yet to be published (DJD).

[72] J. Licht, "The Doctrine of the Thanksgiving Scroll," *IEJ* 6 (1956): 11.

[73] 1QH[a] 7(=15):17–20; 12(=4):24–27; 14(=6):29–33.

[74] See S. Holm-Nielsen, *Hodayot*, 290–93 for a more complete discussion of terms.

[75] See the references above. The hymn recovered in 4QH[a] (4Q427) 7 i–ii speaks in the

however: only in the eschaton will the wicked be destroyed, a remnant be restored and purified, and the elect ultimately freed from human frailty.[76]

On the surface, salvation has to do with traditional categories: belonging to the covenant and the people God has graciously chosen. But the distinctive features of the theology of the *Hodayot* become apparent when one asks who specifically is elect. The division of humanity is not Israel versus the nations. In fact, "Israel" is not once mentioned and the nation as such never comes into view, except perhaps implicitly as a remnant in the future.[77] Rather, in *Hodayot* the contrast is with non-sectarian Jews – and apostates[78] – who are excluded from the covenant.

4.3. Covenant and Law

Any notion of covenant membership by birth is displaced by a fundamental individualism. One enters the covenant only by individual choice, and apparently can choose to abandon the covenant. Expressions of human free will are prominent. Accordingly the dualism is largely expressed in terms of ethical behavior (e.g., good, righteous, perfect of way) and passages speak of judgment on the basis of actions (1QH^a 9[=1]:9; cf. 7[=15]:20–23; 12[=4]:18–22; 14[=6]:8–9).[79] In comparison with other humans, one can acknowledge different levels of innocence and knowledge (17[=9]:15–16; 18[=10]:27–28). In consideration of human standing before God, however, the individual can take no credit and there can be no room for merit. On the contrary, the individual confesses utter dependence on God's mercy (1QH^a 7[=15]:16–26; 9[=1]:28–33; 11[=3+frg. 25]:19–22; 12[=4]:29–31, 36–7; 15[=7]:28–31; 17[=9]:14–16, 33–34; 19[=11]:8–14). Thus, as expected for hymnic material (cf. also 1QS 10–11) the stress is on God's activity, and hence predestination.[80] Here again, however, it is predestination of the

---

strongest manner of exaltation to the ranks of the angels and the abolition of sickness and sin, but it is uncertain whether this is intended as rejoicing in the proleptic experience of eschatological blessings or as a prophetic hymn by an eschatological figure. E. Schuller, "A Hymn from a Cave Four *Hodayot* Manuscript: 4Q427 7i+ii," *JBL* 112 (1993): 605–28; J. J. Collins, "A Thrice-Told Hymn: A Response to Eileen Schuller," *JQR* 85 (1994): 151–5.

[76] 1QH^a 6(=14):15–16; 7(=15):17–20; 14(=6):7–8, 29–30; on these passages, see the discussion by Sanders, *Paul and Palestinian Judaism*, 250, 280–81.

[77] See the interpretation of 1QH^a 14(=6):7–8 by Sanders, *Paul and Palestinian Judaism*, 250. It is far from clear whether this passage refers to the eschatological remnant of Israel or the establishment of the Teacher's community.

[78] On the problem of whether the *Hodayot* truly address apostasy, see Sanders, *Paul and Palestinian Judaism*, 256–7.

[79] On ethical dualism in the scrolls, see J. H. Charlesworth, "Qumran, John and the Odes of Solomon," *Critical Reflections on the Odes of Solomon. Volume 1: Literary Setting, Textual Studies, Gnosticism, the Dead Sea Scrolls and the Gospel of John* (JSPSup 22; Sheffield: Sheffield Academic Press, 1998), 201–2.

[80] Merrill, *Qumran and Predestination*; P. Garnet, *Salvation and Atonement in the Qumran*

individual. Humans are distinguished according to their "spirits,"[81] either good or evil (1QH^a 6[=14]:11–12) and their ultimate destiny has been determined since creation (1QH^a 7[=15]:15–22; 9[=1]:7–8, 19–20, 23–24; 11[=3]:22–23; 12[=4]:38). The dual motifs of predestination and free will co-exist throughout Qumran literature in unresolved but seemingly untroubled tension (e.g., 1QH^a 7[=15]:20–21; 14[=6]:5–10). Holm-Nielsen is probably correct that we are concerned with theoretical speculation on the one hand versus practical observation on the other.[82]

The severely restricted nature of the election is apparent above all in the observation that God's covenant comes effectively to be equated with those who follow the Teacher of Righteousness and belong to his community ("those who walk on the path of your heart have listened to me," 1QH^a 12[=4]:24; cf. 6[=14]:21–22; 13[=5]:8–9, 23; 15[=7]:12, 19–23). To belong to God's covenant is effectively to join the *Yaḥad*. Those excluded from God's covenant are the enemies of the Teacher and the community (1QH^a 12[=4]:7–20; 15[=7]:12). Bockmuehl cautions in the light of the larger Qumran corpus that this sort of language is not likely an ultimate rejection of the nation as replaced by the sectarian community, but rather has to do with how the community understood its representative role in the restoration of the last days.[83] Nevertheless, the critical point is that salvation is conceived as available only in connection with the Teacher and his community. Hope for the eschatological restoration of Israel[84] is not envisaged in any way other than submission to the "new covenant" of the Teacher's community (see e.g., 1QH^a 15[=7]:12).

Salvation in the *Hodayot* involves a transfer from outside the sectarian community to inside.[85] As is natural for hymns of praise, the process of this transfer is described most prominently in terms of God's actions:

> for you have instructed them in the secret of your truth and enlightened them in your wonderful mysteries. For the sake of your glory you have purified man from sin, so that he can sanctify himself for you from all impure abominations and guilt of unfaithfulness, so that he can be united wi[th] the sons of your truth and in the lot with your holy ones . . . and so that he can take his stand in the assembly before you with the eternal host and the spirits . . . (1QH^a 19[=11]:9–13; cf. 11[=3]:21–22; 15[=7]:29–31).

That is, God grants knowledge, God purifies from sin, God unites the individual with the holy community (earthly and heavenly, i.e., "to make them stand in your presence, forever and ever," 1QH^a 15[=7]:31). But the

---

Scrolls (WUNT 2:3; Tübingen: Mohr [Siebeck], 1977), 59; Sanders, *Paul and Palestinian Judaism*, 266–7, 292.

[81] See Licht, "The Doctrine of the Thanksgiving Scroll," 91.

[82] S. Holm-Nielsen, *Hodayot*, 279–84.

[83] Pp. 389–90.

[84] Sanders, *Paul and Palestinian Judaism*, 250.

[85] Sanders, *Paul and Palestinian Judaism*, 283.

human element is also essential. Individuals must repent, and dedicate themselves to observe the law according to sectarian interpretation:[86] "there is hope for those who repent of offence and abandon sin . . . to walk on the path of your heart, without injustice" (1QH[a] 14[=6]:6; cf. 6[=14]:23–24; 10[=2]:9–10).

Life in the covenant requires continued commitment to observe the law, to resist sin by God's help, and to atone for sins committed (e.g., 1QH[a] 4[=12]:21–24; 6[=14]:9, 17–18; 8[=16]:18–19, 23). However, Sanders overstates the significance of such passages when he argues that what distinguishes the two categories of humanity is not that the elect are saved from being "in sin" – that is, a transfer out of the sphere of human frailty – but rather that God pardons the elect from acts of sin – that is, transgressions of the covenant – and does not pardon the non-elect.[87] He is correct that there is not a totally realized eschatology and that those who are saved continue to confess their human nothingness,[88] but a number of passages in the *Hodayot* make clear that the community already experiences a significant release from the problem of human frailty through the impartation of divine knowledge to enjoy communion with the heavenly congregation (1QH[a] 19[=11]:10–14; 9[=1]:31–33; 11[=3]:19–22; 14[=6]:7–8; 15[=8]:19–20). "For the sake of your glory you have purified man (אנוש) from sin . . ." (1QH[a] 11[=3]:10–14) does not merely mean the pardoning of particular acts of sin but cleansing of impurity associated with being human (cf. 1QS 11:14–15). It is not possible to dismiss all such passages as concerning eschatological redemption,[89] because these are often in the context of asserting the union with the heavenly congregation that is an important part of the community's present experience.[90]

Furthermore, we may inquire as to the basis on which God pardons some and not others. From one perspective, membership in the covenant is purely by God's grace, since all human action requires God's prior action and empowering. Thus, even repentance is possible only because God enlightens the individual (4QH[b] 7:1–10; 1QH[a] 18[=10]:27; cf. 6[=14]:8–16, 25).[91] Although the wicked are judged for their sinful works, the elect are judged not according to their deeds but according to God's mercy (13[=5]:5–6; cf.

---

[86] "Volunteers"(המתנדבים, הנדבים) is a stereotypical designator of the sectarians in the *Rule of the Community* especially. The term appears certainly only once in the *Hodayot* (frg. 47 2), but the idea of individual choice to live by the (sectarian) covenant is well attested.

[87] Sanders, *Paul and Palestinian Judaism*, 272–84.

[88] Sanders, *Paul and Palestinian Judaism*, 280–81.

[89] Sanders, *Paul and Palestinian Judaism*, 279–80.

[90] See also Newsom's comments on the function of the *Songs of the Sabbath Sacrifice*. C. Newsom, *Songs of the Sabbath Sacrifice, a Critical Edition* (HSS 27; Atlanta: Scholars, 1985), 71–72.

[91] Merrill, *Qumran and Predestination*, 58.

5[=13]:22–23; 12[=4]:35–36; 15[=7]:29–31).[92] On the other hand, however – and often in the same context – are statements that God will purify individuals of sin because of their obedience, and in relation to special divine knowledge granted to them. For example,

> You will purify them to cleanse them from guilt for all their deeds are in your truth, and in your mercies you will judge them with a wealth of compassion and abundant forgiveness, and according to your mouth you teach them . . . (1QH[a] 14[=6]:8–9)

> Those who are in harmony with you, will stand in your presence always; those who walk on the path of your heart will be established permanently. (1QH[a] 12[=4]:21–22; trans. García Martínez and Tigchelaar; *DSSSE*, 1.161)

> In your goodness is abundance of forgiveness and your mercies for all the sons of your favor, for you have made them know the counsel of your truth and you have enlightened them in your wonderful mysteries. (1QH[a] 19[=11]:9–10)

Such statements do not imply the thought that one "earns" salvation by obedience.[93] Nevertheless, it is not completely true that obedience to law is merely "the *consequence* of being in the covenant and the *requirement for remaining* in the covenant" as Sanders argues.[94] This overemphasizes a disjunction between repentance, entry into the community, and obedience to law. Practically speaking, repentance involves commitment to the law of the community (1QH[a] 12[=4]:24; 6[=14]:21–22).[95] The prior enlightening is special knowledge, effectively the secret teaching of the community (e.g., 1QH[a] 19[=11]:8–10). Human righteousness – impossible without God – is, as Sanders pointed out, perfection in Torah observance, but this is specifically adherence to the precepts of the *Yaḥad*. No one is admitted to the community apart from evidence that one is elect (1QH[a] 6[=14]:21–22), and this can only be adherence to sectarian law (1QH[a] 12[=4]:24–5). Thus, although one can agree with Sanders that observance of the law cannot be said to be the means of election in a theological sense, it is the sign that one is elect. Practically speaking, observance of law (according to sectarian interpretation) is not just the consequence of election as Sanders maintains ("once in the covenant, members took upon themselves to obey its regulations").[96] Instead, taking upon themselves to obey the covenant regulations was an essential element in the process of entering the covenant; it was the requisite evidence for admittance to the community apart from which there

---

[92] See Sanders, *Paul and Palestinian Judaism*, 293.

[93] Sanders, *Paul and Palestinian Judaism*, 293, 295–6.

[94] Sanders, *Paul and Palestinian Judaism*, 320, cf. 296.

[95] According to the *Rule of the Community* and the *Damascus Document*, the sins which one rejects at entry include transgression of the "hidden things," that is, sectarian interpretation of Torah.

[96] Sanders, *Paul and Palestinian Judaism*, 320.

is no salvation or atonement.[97] This point is clearest in texts of an admonitory nature like 1QS 1–4 and CD 1–8, but even on the basis of the *Hodayot* alone it is not possible to imagine the declaration of God's grace to an individual not living according to the community's laws (e.g., 1QH[a] 6[=14]:8–22).

4.4. Function of the Hodayot

Along with these observations we must consider the nature of the *Hodayot*. Although confession of human sinfulness is prominent, and repentance from sin is a central topic, these hymns include no actual direct petitions for the forgiveness of sin. The closest we find are descriptions of penitence (1QH[a] 6[=14]:24; 8[=16]:14–15, 18–20) and petitions to protect from sin (1QH[a] 8[=16]:23). Nitzan has highlighted this point starkly in contrast to the overall prominence of penitence and petition for forgiveness in prayers of the Second Temple period, including numerous other prayers found at Qumran.[98] Her explanation that the *Hodayot* are theoretical reflections of the individual in contrast to the public prayers of the sect is no longer satisfactory, however. Several introductory formulas restored by Puech for the Hymns of the Community suggest a liturgical as well as didactic function,[99] and the hymn in 1QH[a] 26 largely recovered by Schuller with the help of fragments from Cave 4 seems to assume the context of public worship.[100] Furthermore, the public prayers from Qumran that Nitzan had in mind are for the most part generally considered to be of non-sectarian origin.[101] That is, of the considerable corpus of prayers now known from Qumran, direct petitions for forgiveness are common in those prayers not likely – or at least without evidence – of origin in the *Yaḥad*, although many of these were undoubtedly used by the sect.[102] Those clearly of sectarian origin commonly contain confession of sins and the justice of God's judgment, and malediction against sinners, but generally lack direct petition for forgiveness.[103] This is most

---

[97] Cf. Sanders, *Paul and Palestinian Judaism*, 275.

[98] B. Nitzan, *Qumran Prayer and Religious Poetry* (STDJ 12; trans. J. Chipman; Leiden: Brill, 1994), 333–43.

[99] See n. 66 above.

[100] Schuller, "A Hymn from a Cave Four *Hodayot* Manuscript." Alternating with descriptions of communion with angels, eschatological blessings, and God's grace to frail humans are plural imperatives to praise with liturgical directions ("proclaim and say," "they are to say").

[101] See e.g., C. A. Newsom, "'Sectually Explicit' Literature from Qumran," *The Hebrew Bible and Its Interpreters* (ed. W. Propp, B. Halpern and D. N. Freedman; Winona Lake, IN: Eisenbrauns, 1990), 167–87; E. G. Chazon, "Sectarian Prayer."

[102] E.g., *Words of the Luminaries* 4Q504 4:7; 1–2.ii.11; *Communal Confession* 4Q393 1–2.ii.4–5; *Plea for Deliverance* 11QPs[a] 19:13–16.

[103] Note that even in the purification liturgies (4Q414; 4Q512), purification is linked with atonement from sins and the individual blesses God for forgiving and purifying sin, but there is no direct petition for forgiveness.

strikingly seen in the liturgy for the covenant ceremony described above,[104] which passes from confession of sin to blessing and cursing of the covenant members and outsiders/apostates respectively – without a petition for forgiveness and mercy. I have argued that this phenomenon is to be explained by the unique self-understanding of the sect: they are those who have repented and are thus God's elect and under God's blessing.[105] Confession of sin and submission to God's judgment have atoning value.[106] The liturgy itself functions primarily to confirm one's place in the covenant and to reinforce the boundaries between insider and outsider. It is a fundamentally sectarian liturgy.

These considerations are relevant for the present study because the sect's covenant ceremony appears to have influenced their liturgical life very broadly, and it is likely that the *Hodayot* were used in connection with the covenant ceremony and/or served to bolster commitment to the covenant. It is consistent with this that despite the emphasis on human nothingness and sinfulness in contrast with God these hymns are thanksgiving for mercy received and not direct petitions for mercy. Overall these hymns maintain a predominantly confident tone as the speaker glories in God's gracious actions toward them as the elect. They serve primarily not the need for penitence, but the need to express and reinforce one's standing in the covenant, marking the boundaries of the community as those who repent (שבי פשע, 1QH[a] 6[=14]:24; 10[=2]:9; 14[=6]:6).

4.5. Summary

It is important to recognize both that the *Hodayot* serve sectarian purposes, and that they do not give an accurate picture of the overall piety of the sect. Whether repentance was really open to anyone as Sanders maintains is a purely theoretical question.[107] What defines the distinctive quality of the practice of religion glimpsed in the *Hodayot* is its sectarian context, above all that one is a member of the covenant only by individual transfer into the community of the Teacher and by submission to its authority and laws. It is meaningless in this context to make a theoretical separation between adherence to sectarian law and entrance to the community. Even if many motifs are held in common, the category of covenantal nomism is not satisfactory for the *Hodayot* to take into account the fundamental individual-ism of these hymns and their focus on the problem of sin endemic to human nature more than deliverance of Israel as such.

---

[104] See p. 28.
[105] Falk, *Daily, Sabbath, and Festival Prayers*, 222–5.
[106] E.g., 1QS 8:1–10; 9:4–5.
[107] Sanders, *Paul and Palestinian Judaism*, 267.

5. Psalms of Solomon

The *Psalms of Solomon* comprise a collection of 18 non-canonical psalms currently extant in Greek and Syriac,[108] but probably originally composed in Hebrew.[109] They are the product of a Jewish community – not likely a single author – in Palestine, and probably Jerusalem because of the preponderance of focus on the city.[110] There is no evidence of Christian redaction.[111]

Two interrelated concerns dominate the content.[112] On the one hand national peril from foreign invasion is blamed on the sins of Jewish leaders, and there is longing for national restoration under a Davidic messiah. Historical allusions in psalms 2, 8, and 17 are generally agreed to refer to Pompey's invasion of Jerusalem in 63 B.C., and psalm 2:26–27 refers to Pompey's death in Egypt in 48 B.C. Consequently, these psalms – together with the lack of any likely allusion to Herod – suggest a dating around the

---

[108] Greek text: A. Rahlfs, ed., *Septuaginta* (two volumes in one; Stuttgart: Deutsche Bibelgesellschaft, 1979), 2: 471–89 (convenient presentation of von Gephardt's classic critical edition). Syriac text: W. Baars, *The Old Testament in Syriac According to the Peshitta Version 4, fasc. 6: Psalms of Solomon* (1972). Translations and notes: H. E. Ryle and M. R. James, *Ψαλμοὶ Σολομῶντος: Psalms of the Pharisees, Commonly Called the Psalms of Solomon. The Text Newly Revised from All the MSS, Edited, with Introduction, English Translation, Notes, Appendix, and Indices* (Cambridge: University Press, 1891); G. B. Gray, "The Psalms of Solomon," *The Apocrypha and Pseudepigrapha of the Old Testament in English* (2 vols.; ed. R. H. Charles; Oxford: Clarendon, 1913), 2.625–52; R. B. Wright, "Psalms of Solomon," *The Old Testament Pseudepigrapha* (2 vols.; ed. J. H. Charlesworth; Garden City: Doubleday, 1985), 2.639–70; J. Viteau and F. Martin, *Les Psaumes de Salomon: Introduction, texte Grec et traduction. Avec les principales variantes de la version Syriaque* (Documents pour l'étude de la Bible; Paris: Letouzey et Ané, 1911); S. Holm-Nielsen, *Die Psalmen Salomos* (Jüdische Schriften aus Hellenistisch-Römischer Zeit 4,2; Gütersloh: Gerd Mohn, 1977), 51–112; J. L. Trafton, *The Syriac Version of the Psalms of Solomon: A Critical Evaluation* (SBLSDS 11; Atlanta: Scholars, 1985). See the bibliography in J. H. Charlesworth, "Psalms of Solomon," *The Pseudepigrapha and Modern Research with a Supplement* (Septuagint and Cognate Studies 7; Chico: Scholars, 1981), 195–7, 303–4 and J. L. Trafton, "The *Psalms of Solomon* in Recent Research," *JSP* 12 (1994): 3–19.

[109] Most scholars agree that the Greek was translated from an original Hebrew (e.g., Viteau and Martin, *Les Psaumes de Salomon: Introduction, texte Grec et traduction. Avec les principales variantes de la version Syriaque*, 105–25), but although many believe that the Syriac was translated from the Greek, an argument that the Syriac derives primarily from the Hebrew has recently been reasserted (J. L. Trafton, *The Syriac Version of the Psalms of Solomon: A Critical Evaluation*). In any case, Trafton has shown that the Syriac preserves important readings.

[110] Viteau and Martin, *Les Psaumes de Salomon*, 92–94; Wright, "Psalms of Solomon," 641.

[111] Schürer, *History of the Jewish People*, 3.1:195.

[112] These do not distinguish genres or types of psalms as attempted by G. W. E. Nickelsburg, *Jewish Literature Between the Bible and the Mishnah* (Philadelphia: Fortress, 1981), 204, 209–10. See S. Holm-Nielsen, "Erwägungen zu dem Verhältnis zwischen den Hodajot und den Psalmen Salamos," *Bibel und Qumran: Beiträge zur Erforschung der Beziehungen zwischen Bibel- und Qumranwissenschaft (Festschrift H. Bardtke; ed. S. Wagner; Berlin: Evangelische Haupt-Bibelgesellschaft, 1968), 128, and Seifrid, *Justification*, 115.

middle of the first century B.C., and a setting of harsh opposition to the Hasmonean dynasty. The other dominant concern of the psalms is with matters of personal piety, particularly conflict and contrast between "sinners" and "righteous" within Israel. It is unlikely that all of the content belongs to the same circumstances as the allusions to Pompey's invasion.[113] The collection as a whole must have been completed after 48 B.C., and Wellhausen's range of 80–40 B.C. for the psalms is useful as a general estimate.[114]

In comparison with the genres of biblical psalms the *Psalms of Solomon* evidence mixed forms, including community and individual lament, hymn, song of thanksgiving, and didactic poems.[115] The psalms contain eschatological motifs, especially concerning messianic redemption.[116] Although it is often repeated that the *Psalms of Solomon* were composed for liturgical use in the synagogue,[117] there is slender concrete support for this.[118] The psalms lack the web of indicators of liturgical use that mark numerous prayers and psalms found at Qumran,[119] and historical references are more specific than is typical of liturgy.[120] References to the "synagogues of the pious" (*Pss. Sol.* 17:16) and "the synagogues of Israel" (*Pss. Sol.* 10:7) are not evidence for the use of these psalms because there is as yet no certain evidence that there was a regular and substantial prayer liturgy in synagogues by this time. In any case, the strong anti-Hasmonean polemic signals that these psalms cannot have been for any general and public use, but must rather have functioned in the context of a specific and private group(s). Regardless of the specific format of their use, the frequently observed didactic and edifying character of these psalms[121] as well as their polemical content leave little doubt that an

---

[113] See S. Holm-Nielsen, "Erwägungen zu dem Verhältnis zwischen den Hodajot und den Psalmen Salamos," 119, and J. Schüpphaus, *Die Psalmen Salomos. Ein Zeugnis Jerusalemer Theologie und Frömmigkeit in der Mitte des vorchristlichen Jahrhunderts* (ALGHJ 7; Leiden: Brill, 1977), 76–8.

[114] J. Wellhausen, *Die Pharisäer und die Sadducäer* (Greisswald: L. Bamberg, 1874), 112; cf. Viteau and Martin, *Les Psaumes de Salomon*, 38–45; Wright, "Psalms of Solomon," 641.

[115] O. Eissfeldt, *The Old Testament: An Introduction* (trans. P. R. Ackroyd; Oxford: Blackwells, 1965), 611.

[116] M. Winninge, *Sinners and the Righteous. A Comparative Study of the Psalms of Solomon and Paul's Letters* (ConBNT 26; Stockholm: Almquist & Wiksell, 1995), 17–8.

[117] Holm-Nielsen, *Die Psalmen Salomos*, 59–60; Schüpphaus, *Psalmen Salomos*, 155–6; Seifrid, *Justification*, 113, 117; Winninge, *Sinners*, 18–19.

[118] Flusser, "Psalms, Hymns and Prayers," 573; Wright, "Psalms of Solomon," 646.

[119] Falk, *Daily, Sabbath, and Festival Prayers*, 16–17. The occurrence of διάψαλμα in *Pss. Sol.* 17:29 and 18:9 may owe only to biblical literary convention.

[120] Wright, "Psalms of Solomon," 646.

[121] H. L. Jansen, *Die spätjüdische Psalmendichtung, ihr Enstehungskreis und ihr "Sitz im Leben": Eine literaturgeschichtlich-soziologische Untersuchung* (Oslo: Dybwad, 1937), 100–119; Flusser, "Psalms, Hymns and Prayers," 573.

intended function was to encourage and admonish a particular community that felt threatened within Israel.[122]

In treating these psalms, then, we must distinguish between the surface level of the language of prayer and piety directed toward God and the rhetorical function directed toward the community. The extended denouncements of enemies (e.g., *Pss. Sol.* 4), threats of punishment (e.g., *Pss. Sol.* 3:9–12; 15:6–13), and frequent parading of correct conduct (e.g., *Pss. Sol.* 3:3–8; 5:5–7) are self-consciously meant to be overheard, not by those denounced, but by the community.[123] The concern is not to persuade the "sinners" but to reinforce group boundaries and to prevent disaffection in the context of external pressure.[124]

Interpretations of the soteriology assumed in the *Psalms of Solomon* are surprisingly polarized. On the one hand some scholars find in the *Psalms of Solomon* a clear example of righteousness attained by works. Wellhausen argues that God's mercy is viewed as a reward for obedience to law.[125] Braun notes that mercy is a key term in the *Psalms of Solomon*, but argues that it is not received merely as an unmerited free gift from God. Rather, the righteous are entitled to God's mercy because of their righteousness, attained through their conduct.[126] Seifrid has recently presented a more nuanced view.[127] Because of the apocalyptic eschatology of the *Psalms of Solomon*, the motifs of God's righteousness and mercy, Israel and covenant are redefined in terms of the opposing categories pious/sinners rather than Israel/Gentiles. Consequently, individual choice and behavior are determinative for one's destiny.

On the other hand are scholars who find in the *Psalms of Solomon* a sincere piety that depends solely on God's unmerited mercy, refuting any thought of righteousness attained by works. Büchler argues that the confidence of the pious rested not in their righteous deeds, but solely in God's mercy, which was not regarded in any way as a reward.[128] Schüpphaus emphasizes the wisdom overtones of the dichotomy pious/sinner, and that in the *Psalms of Solomon* the opposition has to do with one's basic relationship

---

[122] Seifrid, *Justification*, 61–2, 113–14.

[123] *Pss. Sol.* 4:1 addresses the "profaner" who is "sitting in the council of the devout," but this is rhetorical, as indicated by the immediate switch to the third person.

[124] See similarly with regard to the *Hodayot* Newsom, "Kenneth Burke Meets the Teacher of Righteousness."

[125] J. Wellhausen, *Die Pharisäer und die Sadducäer*, 118–9.

[126] H. Braun, "Vom Erbarmen Gottes über den Gerechten: Zur Theologie der Psalmen Salomos," *ZNW* (1950–1951): 1–54.

[127] Seifrid, *Justification*, 109–33.

[128] A. Büchler, *Types of Jewish Palestinian Piety from 70 B.C.E. to 70 C.E.* (New York: Ktav, 1922), 130.

to God rather than specific qualities.[129] Sanders maintains that *Psalms of Solomon* is a classic representation of the "covenantal nomism" pattern of religion that he expounds throughout his book *Paul and Palestinian Judaism*.[130] God's judgment and mercy to the sinners and righteous flow out of God's election and covenant with Israel. Winninge follows Sanders in understanding Israel in an inclusive rather than severely limited sense.[131]

On both sides, there is a tendency to reduce the message of *Psalms of Solomon* to a single voice. Braun, for example, finds a contrast between God's mercy to Israel as grace freely bestowed to the covenant nation on the basis of God's election, and mercy to the pious as earned, bestowed on those who display the prerequisite works of righteousness.[132] In the end, he finds the authentic voice in an emphasis on righteousness achieved by one's conduct; the apparently opposing perspective is illusory.

Sanders on the other hand also recognizes the two perspectives, high-lighted in the contrast between statements that the pious live by the law (*Pss. Sol.* 14:1–3) and by God's mercy (*Pss. Sol.* 15:12–13). He argues, however, that these statements are not truly in conflict. The opposite of God showing mercy to the righteous would be God rewarding "the righteous *for their merits*."[133]

> The 'free grace' passages (God's mercy to Israel) have to do with the *election and preservation of Israel*. They show . . . that all Israel is elect and as such is 'saved'. The passages dealing with *God's mercy to the righteous* have to do with their *relative protection from temporal harm*. The wicked are considered to be those who have transgressed the covenant so severely that they are treated as Gentiles; that is, they have forfeited their place in the free, unmerited grace bestowed by God in electing and preserving Israel, and consequently are destroyed.[134]

In the end, he finds essentially the same pattern of religion he has found elsewhere: mercy is to all Israel on the basis of the covenant, and the emphasis on mercy to the righteous is a rejection of the idea of merit.[135]

The problem, then, is to determine what language – that about God's mercy or about religious conduct – to take more seriously. Sanders is certainly correct to find a partial answer to these two types of statements in their different contexts as pious language. Concerning God's treatment of humans, one wants to avoid any implication of caprice, and therefore one emphasizes that mercy and judgment are according to conduct. When the focus is why some receive God's mercy, "*particularly in the form of prayer*

---

[129] Schüpphaus, *Psalmen Salomos*, 95.
[130] Sanders, *Paul and Palestinian Judaism*, 387–409.
[131] Winninge, *Sinners*, 181–212.
[132] Braun, "Erbarmen," 35.
[133] Sanders, *Paul and Palestinian Judaism*, 395 (italics his).
[134] Sanders, *Paul and Palestinian Judaism*, 396 (italics his).
[135] Sanders, *Paul and Palestinian Judaism*, 389, 395.

to God, one would hesitate to attribute good treatment by God to one's own merit."[136] On the other hand, Seifrid is correct to point to the polemical tone of the *Psalms of Solomon* as indication of intense conflict with other Jews over the relationship of Torah obedience and mercy to election and belonging to the covenant people.

To put it another way, modern scholars seem to divide in their interpretations of the *Psalms of Solomon* as to whether they focus on the intent of the language as prayer and expressions of piety, or whether they focus on reading the polemic between the lines. In order to move the discussion forward, it will be helpful to be more explicit about the two levels at which *Psalms of Solomon* operates: the surface level of the language of prayer and piety, and the level of the rhetorical function of the prayers to exhort and maintain boundaries. In this way, we can better take account of the genuine insights from both ends of the debate and at the same time clarify some of the misrepresentations. We will consider four constellations of language in the *Psalms of Solomon,* the first two of which predominate: God's justice and mercy, sinners and righteous, sin and atonement, covenant and law. To anticipate the ensuing discussion, and to use just two representatives of the current debate, we can say in response to Seifrid that whatever the rhetorical function of the psalms, the language itself belongs to prayer forms, and must be understood first on that level. Thus, we should be cautious about using the specific language itself against the psalmist, as it were, since much of it is conventional. In response to Sanders we can say that regardless of the language of prayer, these psalms have a group-specific rhetorical function that cannot be ignored.

5.1. God's Justice and Mercy

It is widely recognized that the language of God's righteousness in the *Psalms of Solomon* is not concerned with his saving activity, but almost exclusively associated with his judgment.[137] That is, God's judgments are "just" or "right" (δίκαιος), and thus in his judgment he displays his "righteousness" (δικαιοσύνη).[138] The verb of the δικ- root (translating the Hebrew צדק root) is used only of the community declaring God's judgments just. For example, "I shall declare you just (δικαιώσω), O God, in upright-

---

[136] Sanders, *Paul and Palestinian Judaism,* 395 (italics his).

[137] Braun, "Erbarmen," 25–6; Sanders, *Paul and Palestinian Judaism,* 407; Seifrid, *Justification,* 119.

[138] *Pss. Sol.* 2:10, 18, 32; 4:24; 5:1; 9:5; 10:5; 17:29; 18:7; cf. 8:32, 34. References to the *Psalms of Solomon* will be given according to the verse numbers of Wright's translation. Unless otherwise noted, I will cite his translation.

ness of heart; for in your judgments is your righteousness (τοῖς κρίμασίν σου ἡ δικαιοσύνη σου), O God."[139]

There is, however, a tension in the statements about God's justice. Although it is "impartial" (*Pss. Sol.* 2:18) and meted out "according to the individual and the household" (*Pss. Sol.* 9:5), there is a fundamental group distinction. Towards "sinners," God is proved right when he judges on the basis of behavior (*Pss. Sol.* 2:16; 17:8–10) leading to expulsion from the "righteous" and ultimate destruction.[140] Toward the "righteous," however, God is proved right when he responds to their sins instead with corrective discipline, leading to restoration.[141] Furthermore, God's mercy applies only to the righteous who are disciplined, and stands in stark contrast to the destruction of sinners in judgment.[142] In fact, God's discipline of the righteous is an act of his mercy, since it rescues them from the fate of the sinners (*Pss. Sol.* 16:3, 6). Statements about the discipline of Israel (*Pss. Sol.* 9:2) and God's mercy toward Israel (*Pss. Sol.* 11:1, 7–9; 17:45; 18:1–5) are found where Israel represents the covenant nation generally or the purified nation of the Messianic age.

As noted above, how scholars deal with this apparent conflict largely determines their interpretation of the soteriology in the *Psalms of Solomon*. It is critical, then, to determine the proper relative position of the motifs of God's justice and his mercy, and to understand the use of the language in the context of prayer forms. In this regard, it is important to recognize that the *Psalms of Solomon* show influence from the type of penitential supplications that came to flourish in the Second Temple period. Key examples of these were considered above (section 2). It is sufficient to note here that these prayers are at their root petitions for divine mercy and help, but under the strong influence of covenantal warnings – especially Lev 26:40–45 and Deut 30:1–5 – they dedicate a large portion of the content to confession of sin and the acceptance of God's judgment as "right." It certainly cannot be said that the *Psalms of Solomon* is a collection of this type of penitential prayers, but the influence of the language of these prayers on the *Psalms of Solomon* – whether deliberate or unconscious – is unmistakable. The same thematic network pervades the *Psalms of Solomon*, often with very similar language. Especially significant for our purposes is the language about God's justice. Despite the high frequency of this language, the *Psalms of Solomon* are not primarily concerned with a theological exposition of God's righteousness. It frequently functions as a conventional prayer motif. Rather, there is more

---

[139] *Pss. Sol.* 2:15; my translation; also 3:3, 5; 4:8; 8:7, 23, 26; 9:2.

[140] *Pss. Sol.* 2:15; 4:8, 24; 8:7–8; concerning Gentiles, 8:23; 17:29.

[141] *Pss. Sol.* 3:5; 10:5; 18:7.

[142] Discipline: *Pss. Sol.* 9:6–8; 10:2–4, 6–7; 16:15; cf. 7:5, 8; 8:27–28; 13:12; 14:1, 9; 16:3, 6, 15; destruction: 13:7–11; 14:9; 15:13; 17:3.

immediate concern with God's mercy in various situations of crisis, either national (war) or personal (disaster).[143] Whether or not the *Psalms of Solomon* had a particular liturgical application, they functioned to encourage a community in the midst of such crisis: ultimately things will turn out well for the pious who maintain their relationship with God. In each case, the ultimate cause of distress is perceived to be sin, either hidden sins of national leaders or unintentional sins of the righteous. Influence from penitential petitions should not be surprising. The main difference is the heightened note of confidence in the *Psalms of Solomon*, which may reflect the sapiential application of the prayer motifs.[144]

Against the backdrop of the penitential petitions, a very important and often misunderstood psalm also gains new clarity. *Psalms of Solomon* 9 is frequently looked to as the clearest example of God's mercy earned by conduct, and Sanders on the other hand specifically expounds this psalm as exemplifying the "covenantal nomism" pattern of religion.

> For none that do unrighteous deeds shall be concealed from your knowledge, and the righteousness of your pious ones is before you, Lord. Where will one hide from your knowledge, O God? [4] Our works are in the choosing and power of our souls, to do right and wrong in the works of our hands, and in your righteousness you oversee human beings. [5] The one who does what is right saves up life for himself with the Lord, and the one who does what is wrong causes his own life to be destroyed; for the Lord's righteous judgments are according to the individual and the household. (*Pss. Sol.* 9:3–5; translation mine)

At first glance, verse 3 could imply that one's "righteousness" – which in the context is Torah observance – is what determines one's standing before God, and verses 4–5 could seem like an explicit statement that God's favor is earned by one's conduct. Ryle and James read verses 4–5 as a statement that "every man makes his own fate": life for those who do righteousness and death for those who sin. Verses 6–7 would then be a concession: the sinner may be able to attain pardon if he repents, although the righteous does not need to repent.[145] Seifrid finds in these verses clear evidence that "the destiny of the individual can be said to be contingent upon behavior."[146]

Leaving aside for the moment the question as to whether or not such confidence in one's behavior may be read between the lines, it is necessary first to render to the author of this psalm the same courtesy Seifrid pleads for Paul – one must seek to understand the aims of the author in his use of language before passing judgment.[147] On the basis of formal considerations

---

[143] Some scholars have expressed a similar point by noting that the *Psalms of Solomon* are about theodicy; e.g., Schüpphaus, *Psalmen Salomos*, 30.

[144] I.e., they are not penitential prayers themselves.

[145] Ryle and James, *Psalms of Solomon*, 89.

[146] Seifrid, *Justification*, 120.

[147] *Ibid.*, 3.

I argue that the interpretations cited above run completely counter to the psalmist's intent in his use of language. The psalm reflects the formal pattern of the penitential supplications discussed earlier: confession of sin (vv. 1–2a); the justice of God's judgment (vv. 2b–7); recollection of God's mercies (vv. 9–10); petition for mercy (vv. 8, 11). Thus, in this psalm, the community as Israel appeals for mercy from God in the face of threat from Gentiles. It begins by recounting the causes for the exile: the people neglected the Lord who had redeemed them, and God was just in his judgment. Next, the community confesses that the sin was inexcusable and that the people bear full responsibility, for "our works (are) in the choosing and power of our souls." Nevertheless, coming to God repentant as a sinner is only to be in a position able to receive God's mercy: "whose sins will he forgive except those who have sinned? . . . your goodness is upon those that sin, when they repent." Finally, the community appeals for help on the basis of God's kindness, mercy, loving choice of Israel, and his covenant with Abraham.

Verse 3 is not, then, about the mechanics of God's evaluation of persons, but the universal fact that no one can hide from God: God sees the evil deeds done in secret as well as the righteous deeds of the pious. Verses 4–5 reflect familiar motifs (e.g., Deuteronomy 30:11–20): the law is do-able and a source of life, and God punishes sin. In the context, these verses express the idea of culpability – the people are without excuse before God. That this is the point is made clear in verse 6c, "so that for all these things the shame is on us." This language of shame is merely that common in the penitential supplications.[148] These verses, therefore, are not a statement of confidence in one's righteous deeds. The one who finds God's favor is the one who confesses his sin (v. 6b). This presupposes that all have sinned, including the righteous: "and whose sins will he forgive except those who have sinned? You bless the righteous, and do not accuse them for what they sinned. And your goodness is upon those that sin, when they repent" (v. 7). One cannot appeal to one's own righteousness, but only to God's kindness, mercy, loving choice of Israel, and his covenant with Abraham (vv. 8–11). The righteous are not those who by their effort have avoided sin, but those who confess their sins and seek God's mercy.

Another psalm further illustrates the point. *Pss. Sol.* 3 contrasts the way of life of the righteous and the sinner, and their different destinies. As Schüpphaus noted, the psalm is best understood primarily as instruction intended to encourage a religious community (the diction alternates between the singular – the individual representing the community – and the plural) wearied by trouble: to see the trouble as God's discipline, to adopt a proper

---

[148] E.g., "righteousness is on your side, O Lord, but open shame, as at this day, falls on us . . . because we have sinned against you" (Dan 9:7–8); cf. Ezra 9:6, 15; Pr Azar 1:10.

response, and to praise anew God's righteousness.[149] The righteous and the sinner are distinguished by their differing response to God's judgment. "The righteous does not lightly esteem discipline from the Lord" (v. 4). When the righteous experiences misfortune,[150] understood as God's discipline for his sins, he declares God's judgments right (v. 5). What defines the sinner is that he does not recognize such misfortune as God's discipline, but curses his life (v. 9). The pious behavior described of the righteous – he is vigilant to remove unintentional sins from his household and to atone for sins of ignorance (v. 7–8) – is not raised as a basis for the mercy he receives from God. Rather, in the context of the psalm it is an expression of his proper response to God's discipline, in contrast to the sinner who continues to sin (v. 10). That is, the psalmist does not mention pious behavior to indicate that the righteous has earned God's favor. The confidence of the righteous is not in their piety, but comes "from God their savior" (v. 6).

In the light of the preceding, to cite language from the *Psalms of Solomon* about pious behavior as expressions of meriting God's mercy is to misunderstand the context and contradict the psalmist's use of his language. At this level, then, Sanders does more justice to the psalms than many of his critics. On the other hand, for Sanders to claim that these psalms are perfect examples of "covenantal nomism" is to ignore the rhetorical function of these psalms to reinforce sharp group boundaries. In this regard, Seifrid and others are correct to perceive that behind the language are sharp group distinctions. We will take up this matter in the following section on sinners and righteous, but for now a brief consideration of a further psalm can illustrate the situation well.

In *Pss. Sol.* 16, the psalmist expresses his gratitude to God for drawing him back from dangerous sin (seemingly sexual) by means of discipline. Were it not for this, he would have perished along with the sinners. The psalm undercuts any notion that the righteous can appeal to qualities of their own to commend them as the "righteous" in contrast to the "sinners." The psalmist portrays himself as helpless in the grips of sin ("when my soul slumbered . . . I sank into sleep, far from God," v. 1), rescued only by God ("thus my soul was drawn away from the Lord God of Israel, unless the Lord had come to my aid with his everlasting mercy," v. 3). Indeed, he was "near the gates of Hades with the sinner" (v. 2) and had no ability to perceive or resist his sin on his own (vv. 3–4). Nevertheless, although the psalm excludes the possibility of appealing to anything other than God's mercy, Seifrid is correct to note that God acted graciously toward the psalmist because he

---

[149] Schüpphaus, *Psalmen Salomos*, 31.

[150] "Stumble" (προσέκοψεν) in 3:5 and 3:9 cannot mean moral failure, but the sense is similar to Prov 24:16–18. Ryle and James, *Psalms of Solomon*, 33; Schüpphaus, *Psalmen Salomos*, 32; Winninge, *Sinners*, 39.

belonged to the righteous (and not the sinners): God "did not count me with the sinners for (my) destruction" (v. 5).[151] We need to inquire as to the basis of this group distinction. Is Sanders correct to equate the righteous in *Psalms of Solomon* with Israel of the covenant and the sinners as those who through flagrant transgression have exempted themselves from the covenant?

5.2. Sinners and Righteous

Throughout the *Psalms of Solomon*, God's treatment of humans falls strictly along a fundamental distinction between the "sinners" and the "righteous." God separates between the righteous and the sinner (*Pss. Sol.* 2:34), sending retribution on the sinners for their oppression of the righteous and bestowing mercy on the righteous (*Pss. Sol.* 2:34–35). God's judgment on the sinners is for their destruction, but on the righteous it is discipline for their restoration.[152] This opposition between the "sinners" and the "righteous" dominates the content of the psalms. Does it reflect a soteriology based on behavior, that is, a salvation earned by righteous deeds? The identification of the sinners and righteous, and more importantly on what basis they are distinguished, is therefore critical to our task.

Throughout the *Psalms of Solomon* there are three main groups in view. The psalmist and the community represented by him identify themselves with (1) the "righteous" and the "pious" in Israel. Israel is threatened by (2) foreign oppressors, who are called "sinners" (ἁμαρτωλοί) and "enemies."[153] These are "arrogant," hate Israel without cause, and ruthlessly attack Jerusalem, trampling and defiling the sanctuary.[154] An underlying theme throughout the *Psalms of Solomon* is the concern to encourage the community in the midst of this suffering, which is blamed on (3) Jewish "sinners" (ἁμαρτωλοί).[155] These must be sinning in secret, and exceeding the Gentiles in their sins: like them, they are "arrogant," "sinners," and have defiled the sanctuary.[156] Thus, the gentile attackers are God's instrument of judgment on Israel for her sins, but although this will mean destruction for the Jewish sinners, it will be purifying discipline for the righteous.

It is seldom disputed that the gentile attackers predominantly in view are the Romans led by Pompey.[157] This provides a general context in which to

---

[151] Seifrid, *Justification*, 131 n. 249.

[152] See p. 40 above.

[153] "Lawless nation" (*Pss. Sol.* 17:24); the gentile leader is called "one alien to our race," (17:7); "heart alien to God," (17:13); sinners: 1:1; 2:1; 17:23 (the latter passage may also include Jewish sinners); enemies: 17:13, 45.

[154] *Pss. Sol.* 1:1; 2:1–2, 19, 22–30; 4:24; 7:1–2; 17:13, 22.

[155] *Pss. Sol.* 1:1-8; 2:3-21; 4:1-25; 17:5-9, 15.

[156] *Pss. Sol.* 1:5–8; 2:3, 9, 12; 4:5; 8:9, 12–13, 22; 17:6, 15.

[157] E.g., Ryle and James, *Psalms of Solomon*, xl–xliv.

understand the conflict between the "righteous" and Jewish "sinners." Since Wellhausen, this has commonly been understood as the conflict between Pharisees and Sadducees,[158] especially since allusion to Hyrcanus and Aristobulus can be found in *Pss. Sol.* 8. On the other hand, the specific evidence for identifying the *Psalms of Solomon* with the Pharisees is equivocal,[159] and comparable arguments can be made in favor of other Jewish groups.[160] Furthermore, there is no evidence to indicate that the opponents are specifically Sadducees. The polemic against the Jewish "sinners" is stereotypical, and where the language becomes more specific, opposition is to the Hasmonean rulers rather than the Sadducees.[161] Especially telling is that disdain is expressed equally for Hyrcanus and Aristobulus. There is no evidence, then, that the distinction between righteous and sinners is along clear lines of religious parties, and in the end this is unlikely.[162] According to *Pss. Sol.* 4, separation between the righteous and the sinners is not yet effected but is hoped for.[163] It is not certain that the "council of the devout" in this psalm is the Jerusalem Sanhedrin, but the important observation for our purposes is that like the tares among the wheat, the two groups may not readily be distinguished from the outside.

Nevertheless, there is still a strong group distinction. This becomes apparent when one considers that there are other Jews lurking in the shadows apart from the righteous and the sinners. A distinction is made between the "sinners" who are the primary object of scorn and a generic class of "sinners" who are victims of the hypocritical severity of the former (*Pss. Sol.* 4:1–3, 8). Similarly, although the righteous are part of ideal Israel, the blurring is seldom complete. In the present, the righteous seem to stand apart as a group. Only in the Messianic age do the two merge so that Israel and the righteous are coterminous.[164] The question of the identity of Israel is important and will

---

[158] Wellhausen, *Pharisäer*, 112.

[159] J. O'Dell, "The Religious Background of the Psalms of Solomon," *RevQ* 3 (1961): 241–57; R. B. Wright, "The Psalms of Solomon, the Pharisees and the Essenes," *1972 Proceedings: International Organization for Septuagint and Cognate Studies and the Society of Biblical Literature Pseudepigrapha Seminar* (SBLSCS 2; ed. R. A. Kraft; Missoula: Society of Biblical Literature, 1972), 136–54.

[160] Qumran, or Essenes in general: A. Dupont-Sommer, *The Essene Writings from Qumran* (trans. G. Vermes; Oxford: Blackwell, 1961), 296, 337; Eissfeldt, *The Old Testament: An Introduction*, 613; R. R. Hann, "The Community of the Pious: The Social Setting of the Psalms of Solomon," *Studies in Religion/Sciences religieuses* 17 (1988): 169–89. *Hasidim* (broadly defined): O'Dell, "The Religious Background of the Psalms of Solomon"; Wright, "The Psalms of Solomon, the Pharisees and the Essenes"; Wright, "Psalms of Solomon," 642. Impossible to define to one specific group: J. H. Charlesworth, *Pseudepigrapha and Modern Research*, 195.

[161] J. L. Trafton, "Solomon, Psalms of," *ABD* 6.116.

[162] Sanders, *Paul and Palestinian Judaism*, 403–14.

[163] Schüpphaus, *Psalmen Salomos*, 33.

[164] See pp. 50–51 below.

be taken up below, but it is crucial to recognize that this ambivalence in the use of terms is because of the rhetorical function of these psalms: they serve a religious community that regarded itself as the righteous – oppressed and thus the "poor" – and they demonize opponents as a group as "sinners." In the face of opposition they encourage strict adherence to Torah and reinforce group boundaries. There is little concern to identify the place of other Jews.

On what basis do the psalms themselves distinguish between the two groups? The distinction is primarily drawn on the basis of contrasting stance toward God. "The righteous" (οἱ δίκαιοι, probably = הצדיקים) and "the pious" (οἱ ὅσιοι, probably = החסידים)[165] are "those who fear God" and "those who love God."[166] They praise and give thanks to God readily[167] and are humble (*Pss. Sol.* 5:12). When in need they remember God, call upon him, and hope in him.[168] The Jewish sinners, on the other hand, are "godless" (ἀσεβής, *Pss. Sol.* 13:5), they do not fear God, listen to him, or remember him (*Pss. Sol.* 2:8; 4:21; 14:7), but they anger God (*Pss. Sol.* 4:21) and are arrogant (*Pss. Sol.* 1:5–6; 17:6).

It is not the absence of sinning that defines the righteous. The psalmist readily confesses that they sin, using some of the same terminology as for the sinners.[169] Nevertheless, the language applied to the righteous is only that of failure and lapse (ἁμαρτίαι παραπώμα). They are never called "sinners" (ἁμαρτωλοί) or accused of being unrighteous or lawless.[170] Rather, their sins are unintentional and out of ignorance, and when they sin they willingly submit to God's discipline, atone for their sins, and are vigilant to root out sins from their household.[171] They know and confess that God's judgments

---

[165] "Righteous": *Pss. Sol.* 2:34, 35; 3:3, 4, 5, 6, 7, 11; 4:8; 9:7; 10:3; 13:6, 7, 8, 9, 11; 14:9; 15:3, 6, 7; 16:15; 17:32. "Pious": *Pss. Sol.* 2:36; 3:8; 4:1, 8; 8:34; 9:3; 10:6; 12:4, 6; 13:10, 12; 14:3, 10; 15:3, 7; 17:16.

[166] Fear: *Pss. Sol.* 2:33; 3:12; 4:23; 5:18; 6:5; 12:4; 13:12; 15:13; love: Sol. 4:25; 6:6; 10:3; 14:1.

[167] *Pss. Sol.* 5:1; 6:4; 10:6; 15:2; 16:5.

[168] *Pss. Sol.* 2:36; 3:3; 5:5, 8; 6:1, 6; 7:7; 8:31; 9:10; 15:2; 17:3.

[169] *Pss. Sol.* 3:5; 9:7; 16:11. Of the righteous: ἁμαρτίαι (9:7; 10:1; 16:7; 17:5), παραπτώματα (13:10). Of the sinners: ἁμαρτίαι (1:7; 2:7; 4:3; 8:8, 13; 14:6; 15:11; 16:7, 8; 17:20), παραπτώματα (13:5).

[170] For "sinners" see n. 155 above. Also: the "unrighteous" (ἄδικοι 15:4), the "lawless" (παράνομοι 4:19; 12:1, 3, 4; 14:6; cf. 16:8; ἄνομοι 17:18), the "wicked" (πονηρός, 12:1, 2; 16:7), "slanderers" (ψιθύποι, 12:4), the "profaner" (βέβηλε, 4:1), the "godless" (ἀσεβής, 13:5[the common emendation to x is unsupported in the manuscripts, unnecessary, and unlikely; see Wright, "Psalms of Solomon" 663, n. 13c]). Only the sinners are accused of ἀδικία (2:12, 4:24; 9:4, 5), ἀνομίαι (1:8; 2:3, 12; 15:8, 10), παρανομία (4:1, 12; 8:9; 17:20).

[171] *Pss. Sol.* 3:4, 6–8; 6:5; 7:3, 9; 10:2; 13:7; 14:1; 16:15; 18:4. With regard to 3:6–8, Wright notes that "the devout eliminate all possible sins: repeated sins (vs. 6), accidental sins (vs. 7), and unknown sins (vs. 8)." Wright, "Psalms of Solomon," 655.

are just.[172] The "sinners" sin habitually (*Pss. Sol.* 14:6) and do not recognize God's discipline but curse and sin all the more (*Pss. Sol.* 3:9–10).

It is undeniable that there is a behavior component to the contrast between the two groups. The designations "righteous" and "pious" imply behavior – doing what is right – and this is made explicit in several passages. "The one who does righteousness stores up life for himself with the Lord" and is contrasted with "the one who does unrighteousness" (*Pss. Sol.* 9:5; translation mine). The pious are "those who walk in the righteousness of his commands, in the law, which he commanded us for our life; the devout live in it forever" (*Pss. Sol.* 14:2–3; translation mine). Do these passages indicate that the standing of righteous is gained by one's behavior? With regard to *Pss. Sol.* 9:3–7,[173] I have already argued that such a reading runs counter to the psalmist's intent in using such language in the context of a prayer form. Similarly, with regard to *Pss. Sol.* 14:2–3, δικαιοσύνη προσταγμάτων is not "the state of holiness produced by the observance of the commandments."[174] Rather, "in the righteousness of his commandments" (ἐν δικαιοσύνη προσταγμάτων) is parallel "in the law, which he commanded us for our life" (ἐν νόμῳ ᾧ ἐνετείλατο ἡμῖν εἰς ζωὴν ἡ-μῶν). Thus, the phrase seems to be functionally equivalent to living according to God's righteous command-ments. That is, "righteousness" pertains to the commandments, rather than being a qualification attained by the individual on the basis of Torah observance. We could paraphrase that the devout are those "who walk in the righteousness – that is the law – that he has commanded as the way of life for us." The passage as a whole is a loose paraphrase of Ps 1:2–3: those who base their lives on God's law will flourish and be secure (image of tree), as opposed to sinners who will perish.

Furthermore, throughout the *Psalms of Solomon* the righteous display confidence in the face of their sin and God's discipline, but it is not expressed as confidence in their behavior. Rather, the righteous appeal to God's mercy on the basis of the election of Israel and God's covenant with their forefathers (*Pss. Sol.* 9:8–11; 10:4). Although sinners are said to be rewarded/judged according to their deeds/sins,[175] there is no comparable statement concerning the righteous. God's treatment of the righteous according to his mercy stands in contrast to God repaying the sinners according to their works. For example,

> the Lord's mercy is upon those who fear him with judgment, to separate between the righteous and the sinner, to pay back sinners forever *according to their works* and to

---

[172] *Pss. Sol.* 5:1; see also the references in n. 138.

[173] See pp. 41–43.

[174] Viteau and Martin, *Les Psaumes de Salomon*, 325; similarly Ryle and James, *Psalms of Solomon*, 111.

[175] *Pss. Sol.* 2:15–18, 34–36; 17:8–10.

show mercy to the righteous . . . for the Lord is good to those who steadfastly call upon him, to do to his devout *according to his mercy* (*Pss. Sol.* 2:33–36; translation and emphasis mine).

It must also be recalled that according to *Pss. Sol.* 16, God showed mercy to the devout person when he was helpless in sin and when his behavior was leading him to the fate of the sinners.[176] The psalmist confesses his inability to add anything to his case before God.

For you are good and merciful, the shelter of the poor. When I cry out to you, do not ignore me. For no one takes plunder away from a strong man, so who is going to take (anything) from all that you have done, unless you give (it)? For an individual and his fate (are) on the scales before you; he cannot add any increase contrary to your judgment, O God. (*Pss. Sol.* 5:2–4)

In fact, the *Psalms of Solomon* show the unreliability of religious conduct as grounds for righteousness in parodies on their opponents. Indeed, the sinners "sit in the council of the pious" (κάθησαι ἐν συνεδρίῳ ὁσίων, *Pss. Sol.* 4:1),[177] they quote the law and do works – which in the context are presumably works of Torah – in order to impress people, and the psalmist gives the impression that they are generally successful (*Pss. Sol.* 4:7–8). Yet God is not impressed by appearances (*Pss. Sol.* 2:18) and the psalmist pronounces the judgment that they are hypocrites and that their works are all deceit.

While this polemic should caution us against finding expressions of confidence in works of Torah in the surface language of the psalms, it does betray an anxiety on the part of the psalmist to distinguish his community from their opponents. A sense of frustration emerges in several psalms that the sinners seem to share the same public image and authority as the righteous. This is particularly apparent in the wish that God "expose" the sinners and separate them from the righteous (*Pss. Sol.* 2:17–18; 4:6–8). Although the former might appear righteous (*Pss. Sol.* 1:2–3; 8:6) the psalmist insists that they must be sinning "secretly" (*Pss. Sol.* 1:7; 4:5; 8:9) and accuses them of a stereotypical list of generic sins.[178] That is, the distinction between the two groups apparently is not on the basis of observable flagrant transgression of Torah. How could it be said with Sanders, then, that the righteous are essentially coterminous with Israel, and that they include – besides the especially scrupulous – all who fear and love

---

[176] See pp. 43–44 above.

[177] It is a group in view throughout this psalm; the individual "profaner," etc., functions as a representative of the group. Schüpphaus, *Psalmen Salomos*, 33.

[178] The three cardinal sins of which they are accused are sexual sins (*Pss. Sol.* 2:11, 13; 4:5; 8:9–10), defilement of the sanctuary (1:8; 2:3; 8:12, 22), and illegal wealth (8:11; cf. 1:6; 4:9–13, 20, 22); cf. the three "nets of Belial" in CD 4:14ff. Other traditional sins include: arrogance (1:5–6; 17:6), intemperance (4:3), lust (4:4), lying (4:4; 12:1), deceit (4:8, 10, 11; 12:1), covetousness (4:9).

God, excluding only those who exclude themselves by "insolently and heinously" transgressing God's will?[179]

The investigation so far suggests that there is no convincing evidence that the *Psalms of Solomon* intend to communicate confidence in one's righteous deeds before God, or that the various actions of the righteous towards God are "pious qualities which provide the presupposition for the bestowal of God's mercy."[180] The matter is played out at the deeper level of the rhetorical function of the psalms to reinforce community boundaries. The distinction between righteous and sinners must be considered further below under the heading law and covenant, after a brief consideration of sin and atonement.

5.3. Sin and Atonement

The sins of the righteous are described as unintentional (e.g., 3:8); intentional sins are associated with the sinners who are judged. Even the potentially mortal sins of the righteous in *Pss. Sol.* 16 are possibly to be regarded as unintentional – the righteous man needs to be wakened. Do the *Psalms of Solomon* envisage that only unintentional sins can be forgiven, then? This may be the case, but caution is in order. The psalms serve to encourage a pious community in trouble blamed on sinners. A complete catalogue of sin would not be appropriate.[181]

Given the emphasis on righteousness and the righteous versus sin and sinners throughout the *Psalms of Solomon*, it might at first seem surprising that forgiveness of sins is explicitly mentioned only once, "and whose sins will he forgive except those who have sinned?" (*Pss. Sol.* 9:7). It is also alluded to in 9:6, "He will cleanse from sins the soul in confessing, in restoring," and 13:10, "he will wipe away their mistakes with discipline." On the whole, however, forgiveness of sin in the *Psalms of Solomon* is subsumed under the exercise of God's righteousness: God disciplines the righteous when they sin. The righteous atone for their sins by submitting to God's discipline (*Pss. Sol.* 7:9; 10:1; 13:10) and repenting ("fasting and humbling his soul," *Pss. Sol.* 3:8; "confessing," 9:6). The lack of reference to sacrifice as atoning is curious in light of the psalmist's high regard for the temple and concern for the purity of its cult, but it probably is due to the function of the psalms rather than to a rejection of sacrifice as atonement.[182] On the one hand, the Jewish "sinners" also made sacrifices (since they are accused of defiling them, *Pss. Sol.* 1:8; 2:3–5; 8:12); what distinguished the "righteous" was their humble submission to God. More importantly, on the other hand,

---

[179] Sanders, *Paul and Palestinian Judaism*, 389, 405.

[180] W. L. Lane, "Paul's Legacy from Pharisaism: Light from the Psalms of Solomon," *Concordia Journal* 8 (1982): 133.

[181] Seifrid, *Justification*, 123.

[182] Sanders, *Paul and Palestinian Judaism*, 398. Cf. Büchler, *Piety*, 170–74.

it probably highlights the influence of penitential prayer based on covenantal warnings. For example, Lev 26:40–45 and Deut 30:1–5, which seem to have served as important theological bases for the penitential prayers that flourished during the Second Temple period, prescribe the route to restoration after punishment for breaking the covenant: sacrifice is not mentioned, but rather repentance and humbling oneself. The community represented by *Psalms of Solomon* interpreted the woes of Israel in light of the covenantal warnings and believed that they as a community were responding to the covenant prescription for restoration.

5.4. Covenant and Law

Now we can return to consideration of the self-perception of the righteous in *Psalms of Solomon*. Although covenant is rarely explicitly mentioned,[183] God's covenant with Israel is unmistakably an underlying presupposition of this community's self-perception. The theodicy of *Psalms of Solomon* assumes a covenant theology: the hardship experienced by the people at the hands of foreigners is from God as in the covenantal warnings of the Bible (Lev 26; Deut 28) and it is intended to turn the people back to God. The righteous are those who, when they become conscious of sin, diligently follow the prescription in Lev 26:40–45 and Deut 30:1–5 for restoring the covenant: they humble themselves under God's discipline and repent. Sinners on the other hand are those who spurn God's covenant discipline and arrogantly neglect repentance. That is, God responds to human behavior on the basis of the covenant.

However, it is not covenant Israel but the psalmist's community that is of primary concern, in keeping with the rhetorical function of the psalms. Furthermore, Israel is not coterminous with the devout in *Psalms of Solomon*. The devout are in Israel, but Israel also contains sinners who will be judged by the standards of the covenant and excluded from the eschatological blessings. In psalm 8, for example, although the psalmist blames Pompey's attack on Jews who were deliberately sinning in secret, and distinguishes from these "the devout of God," the main contrast is between Israel and the Gentiles. Only in the messianic future envisioned in *Pss. Sol.* 17–18 is Israel simply coterminous with the pious. The wish "may God cleanse Israel for the day of mercy in blessing, for the appointed day when his Messiah will reign" (*Pss. Sol.* 18:5) implies that up to the messianic age Israel includes sinners who must be purged (cf. *Pss. Sol.* 17:15–18). In the end, then, the language is not used consistently. From one perspective, their Jewish enemies may be regarded as non-Israel, but from another perspective, they are still Israel in

---

[183] *Pss. Sol.* 9:8–11; 10:4; 17:15; cf. 11:7; 17:4–5, 23; Nickelsburg, *Jewish Literature Between the Bible and the Mishnah*, 210.

contrast to the Gentiles, to be purged in the messianic age. The community focus is particularly apparent when the psalmist distinguishes between the "assemblies of the devout" and the sinning "children of the covenant" who persecute them (*Pss. Sol.* 17:16–17). Thus, for the purposes of the psalms, what is important is that the community is (among) the righteous and continues the covenant promises; all their opponents (Jews and Gentiles alike) are sinners.

Finally, what is the role of law in the *Psalms of Solomon*? As has been noted already, keeping the law is never portrayed as the means of gaining the status of righteousness. But then, appeal to one's law observance would hardly be appropriate in the context of prayer language where humble confession is a stereotyped norm. Law is everywhere assumed, however, in the group distinctiveness that pervades these psalms: "we" are a law-keeping group and "they" are a law-breaking group. Of the two paths that diverge between these two groups, this may make all the difference.

5.5. Summary

In conclusion, we may return to ask how suitable is Sanders's concept of "covenantal nomism" to the *Psalms of Solomon*. The answer is somewhat equivocal. If we have in mind a formulation that the psalmist(s) would recognize and agree with, there is little doubt in my mind that they would find Sanders's "covenantal nomism" more congenial than the judgments of his critics. To them, their enemies had self-evidently excluded themselves by flaunting the demands of the covenant. They would almost certainly be indignant at any implication that they do Torah to earn God's favor. With such charges they cast aspersions on their opponents. This, however, does not do justice to the rhetorical function of the *Psalms of Solomon*. A major preoccupation of these psalms is to reinforce community boundaries and one cannot escape that religious conduct is central to their group distinction. Opponents as a group are excluded as sinners, charged with stereotyped sins. This does not at all necessarily add up to a system of entitlement to God's mercy based upon one's actions, but to designate this restricted group-centered soteriology "covenantal nomism" is ultimately not very helpful. Very similar to the ethos of *Psalms of Solomon* is Psalm 154.

6. Odes of Solomon

The forty-two *Odes of Solomon* comprise a hymnbook of a Jewish Christian community, probably from Syria (Antioch and Edessa are commonly proposed) and dating probably from the early second century A.D. or possibly the end of the first century. Syriac is more probable than Greek as the original language. Despite earlier claims, it is misleading to call them gnostic, and it is unlikely that the Jewish nature that pervades them points to a Jewish original. Rather, it points to the milieu of Jewish Christianity, and probably a single author. The *Odes of Solomon* display impressive affinities with the Gospel of John and the Qumran *Hodayot*, but a direct relationship with either is unlikely. Although most of these conclusions continue to be contested, they reflect the closest to a consensus that exists and will serve the purposes of the present study.[184]

The description of the *Odes* as an early Christian hymnbook is intentional and important to the interpretation of them. These are not private mystical poems, but were intended for public use in the context of communal worship, as suggested especially by the "hallelujah" response at the end of each ode and numerous plural imperatives.[185] Despite the use of some initiation/ baptismal imagery, this is not a collection of "hymns of the baptized" as Bernard argued.[186] Rather, on the basis of the Odist's prominent claim to divine inspiration, the repeated blurring of the Odist's voice with that of Christ, and the emphasis on present experience of eschatological salvation, Aune is likely correct that the *Odes* should be regarded as prophetic or charismatic hymns of praise such as described in Pauline churches. According to this view, these spiritual hymns served as a vehicle for the leader and congregation in their communal worship to realize eschatological salvation as restoration to the primal rest of Paradise, mediated by the Spirit.[187]

It must be kept in mind that as hymns, the *Odes of Solomon* do not enunciate a comprehensive doctrine of atonement.[188] This at least partly

---

[184] Recent summaries of the *status quaestionis* and extensive bibliographies on the Odes of Solomon make it unnecessary to replicate references here. See J. H. Charlesworth, *Pseudepigrapha and Modern Research*, 189–94, 301–3; M. Franzmann, *The Odes of Solomon: An Analysis of the Poetical Structure and Form* (NTOA 20; Göttingen: Vandenhoeck & Ruprecht, 1991), 1–7; J. H. Charlesworth, *Critical Reflections on the Odes of Solomon. Volume 1: Literary Setting, Textual Studies, Gnosticism, the Dead Sea Scrolls and the Gospel of John* (JSPSup 22; 2 vols.; Sheffield: Sheffield Academic Press, 1998), 21–6, 261–85. Texts and translations of the *Odes of Solomon*: J. H. Bernard, *The Odes of Solomon* (Cambridge: University Press, 1912); J. R. Harris and A. Mingana, *The Odes and Psalms of Solomon. Re-edited for the Governors of the John Rylands Library* (2 vols.; Manchester: Manchester University Press, 1916–1920); J. H. Charlesworth, *The Odes of Solomon* (SBLTT; corrected reprint; Missoula: Scholars, 1977); J. A. Emerton, "The Odes of Solomon," *The Apocryphal Old Testament* (ed. H. F. D. Sparks; Oxford: Clarendon, 1984), 683–731; J. H. Charlesworth, "Odes of Solomon," *OTP*, 2.725–71.

[185] D. E. Aune, *The Cultic Setting of Realized Eschatology in Early Christianity* (NovTSup 28; Leiden: Brill, 1972), 174–5.

[186] Bernard, *Odes of Solomon*, 16–25, 32–9; see the detailed refutation in Harris and Mingana, *Odes and Psalms of Solomon*, 2:187–97.

[187] Aune, *Cultic Setting*, 174–84.

[188] H. Chadwick, "Some Reflections on the Character and Theology of the Odes of Solomon," *Kyriakon. Festschrift Johannes Quasten* (2 vols.; ed. P. Granfield and J. A. Jungmann; Münster:

accounts for three distinctive features of the soteriology of the *Odes*.[189] First, there is no direct reference to sin, repentance, and forgiveness. There are a couple implicit allusions to the idea of sin: the Odist "did not err in anything" because he obeyed Truth (personified, *Odes Sol.* 38:4–5); Christ "pitied" the Odist and granted him to receive of his "sacrifice" (*Odes Sol.* 7:10, cf. Ps 51:1).[190] In place of forgiveness of sin, the Odist speaks especially of the banishment of ignorance (also error, falsehood) at the coming of the knowledge (also truth, wisdom) of the Lord (e.g., *Odes Sol.* 7:21). Second, the Odist does not dwell on either the sacrificial nature of Christ's death or his resurrection. There is only brief allusion to these: "he was gracious to me in his abundant grace, and allowed me to seek from him and to benefit from his sacrifice" (*Odes Sol.* 7:10);[191] "then I [Christ] arose and am with them" (*Odes Sol.* 42:6). Instead, the Odist focuses on Christ's incarnation, suffering (including death), and descent into Hades as the primary redemptive acts. Third, although it is not absent (e.g., *Odes Sol.* 3:7) the future aspect of salvation is muted in favor of a prominent focus on eternal life experienced as a present actuality ("realizing eschatology").[192]

The *Odes* assume a dualism of two worlds: the world "above" and the world "below" which is a mere shadow of the former (*Odes Sol.* 34:4–5). Christ descended to the world "below" bringing knowledge and light, dispelling ignorance and darkness (*Odes Sol.* 7:3–6; 22:1; 41:11–15). In his death he descended to the underworld, conquering the "abyss" and the "dragon" and releasing prisoners (*Odes Sol.* 17:7–11; 22:1, 5; 31:1–2; 42:11–20). His descent was a mission of restoring primal paradise:[193] the experience of salvation for the believer is described as receiving a living crown (related to the tree of paradise, see *Odes Sol.* 20:7–8; cf. 1:1–5; 17:1–2), bearing fruit, being released from illness, being reclothed and becoming a new person, receiving knowledge and light, and enjoying eternal rest (see especially *Odes Sol.* 10, 11, 15, 17, 21, 25). This is described both as a present experience and as ascent (*Odes Sol.* 21:6; 36:1). Hence, in the world humans are divided between those who live the life of above or "eternal life" and those who live the "below" life of darkness. The predominant metaphor for the division is knowledge/truth (*Odes Sol.* 11:3; 23:4) versus ignorance/error (*Odes Sol.* 15:6; 18:14).

Aschendorff, 1970), 1.270.

[189] For the following three points, see Harris and Mingana, *Odes and Psalms of Solomon*, 2:84.

[190] See Bernard, *Odes of Solomon*, 60–62. Unless otherwise indicated, citations from the *Odes of Solomon* will use the translation by J. H. Charlesworth, "Odes of Solomon."

[191] Bernard, *Odes of Solomon*, 61–2.

[192] Charlesworth, "Qumran, John and the Odes of Solomon," 210 (originally published in J. H. Charlesworth, *John and Qumran* (1972), 107–36.

[193] Aune, *Cultic Setting*, 194.

Humanity is divided on the basis of response to Christ, and Charlesworth is correct to note that this "soteriological dualism" is dominant in the *Odes*.[194] The emphasis rests on the divine initiative. For example in *Odes Sol.* 11, salvation is described purely in terms of divine actions; the Odist merely receives.

> My heart was pruned and its flower appeared, then grace sprang up in it, and it produced fruits for the Lord. For the Most High circumcised me by his Holy Spirit, then he uncovered my inward being toward him, and filled me with his love. And his circumcising became my salvation, and I ran in the Way in his peace, in the Way of truth. From the beginning until the end I received his knowledge. (*Odes Sol.* 11:1–4)

In the imagery that follows, God gave him living water with which he became intoxicated, gave up vanity and turned toward God and received God's favors; God gave him new clothes; God's light shone on him, giving him immortal rest and enlightening him.

The *Odes* thus speak prominently about salvation by God's grace (e.g., *Odes Sol.* 11:1; 31:6–7; 33:10; 34:6; 41:3), and the divine initiative is based on God's faithfulness to his covenant with Israel.

> And I bore their bitterness because of humility; that I might save my nation and instruct it. And that I might not nullify the promises to the patriarchs, to whom I was promised for the salvation of their offspring. (*Odes Sol.* 31:12–13)

Christ's redemption, then, was fulfillment of God's covenant promise with Israel, and the Christians belong to the "true covenant of the Lord" (*Odes Sol.* 9:11; cf. 3:6). The inclusion of Gentiles in the covenant seems still to have been a sensitive enough issue that a special point is made about it.

> And the gentiles who had been scattered were gathered together, but *I was not defiled by my love* (for them), because they had praised me in high places. And the traces of light were set upon their heart, and they walked according to my life and were saved, and *they became my people* for ever and ever (*Odes Sol.* 10:5–6, italics mine).

Those who are saved are the elect, but the *Odes of Solomon* are far from espousing predestination. Election is foreknowledge, not predetermination.

> And he who created me when yet I was not knew what I would do when I came into being. On account of this he was gracious to me in his abundant grace, and allowed me to seek from him and to benefit from his sacrifice. (*Odes Sol.* 7:9–10)

The elect are those who seek God, and thus respond to Christ's call and grasp the mystery of divine knowledge (*Odes Sol.* 8:8–11). As Charlesworth has noted, there is therefore an implicit universalism in the *Odes*:[195] in the metaphor of a stream, the gospel flowed over the whole earth so that "all the thirsty upon the earth drank" (*Odes Sol.* 6:10–11). Two cosmic spirits appear

---

[194] Charlesworth, "Qumran, John and the Odes of Solomon," 211–12.

[195] Charlesworth, "Qumran, John and the Odes of Solomon," 212.

in the *Odes* – good and evil – but rather than controlling humans, they preach to humans to win their allegiance (*Odes Sol.* 33). The role of human preachers ("ministers of that drink, who have been entrusted with his water," *Odes Sol.* 7:13) is prominent, for they are able to rescue people from Death (*Odes Sol.* 7:15).

Appeal to ethical life is important in the *Odes*, and personal choice is assumed.[196] The Odist urges "offer your inward being faultlessly," and lists several injunctions of what this means (*Odes Sol.* 20:5–9). But the ethical life is not prerequisite for salvation, but living out the life of salvation. When the Odist declares "I abandoned the way of error, and went toward him and received salvation from him generously" (*Odes Sol.* 15:6), this is only as a response to God's prior grace. God first gave him new eyes, ears, and knowledge (*Odes Sol.* 15:3–5), so that the Odist confesses "I have put on incorruption through his name, and stripped off corruption by his grace" (*Odes Sol.* 15:8). The believer is united with Christ in his suffering (*Odes Sol.* 42:1–8) and his life (*Odes Sol.* 3:1–7).

There is no real role for law in the *Odes* to provide for atonement or to maintain the covenant relationship. Salvation is already achieved. What is eschatological in Judaism is present in the *Odes*. The life of obedience is not maintenance of covenant obligation but part of being united with Christ, a benefit of eschatological salvation that has invaded the present: "and there was not danger for me because I constantly walked with him; and I did not err in anything because I obeyed him" (*Odes Sol.* 38:5). Furthermore, covenant is no longer all Israel except those who flagrantly exempt themselves, but all those who know God through the mystery of Christ's incarnation comprise the true covenant. Thus, the *Odes* are distinguished by features deriving from its Christian outlook, especially its altered eschatology and universalism.

7. Conclusion

Songs and prayers do not provide systematic statements of theology, but they do allow potential insights into practiced piety. Many pious Jews of the Second Temple period associated the troubles of their people with consequences of national and individual sin and hence were deeply concerned about the problem of sin and the reparation of the covenant, and yearned for God's salvation. Following the covenantal admonitions of the Bible, they made penitential prayers an important part of their piety and these left their mark on much of Jewish prayer and psalmic literature. The language of prayer means of course that emphasis will be on God's grace and words of

---

[196] Charlesworth, "Qumran, John and the Odes of Solomon," 212.

confession will be stereotyped. It is only to be expected that the motifs associated by Sanders with the pattern "covenantal nomism" recur frequently throughout these prayers. No doubt, from the perspective of those who prayed them, all of the prayers reviewed here would be seen to reflect something very like such a traditional covenantal perspective. If the aim was to define a sort of "lowest common denominator" soteriology that would be recognized by most of the divergent expressions of Judaisms, Sanders's covenantal nomism would serve fairly well, given his generous allowances of flexibility. To do so, however, would be akin to grouping apples, oranges, and bananas together as "fruit." For comparative purposes, such a harmonizing approach is of limited value. It masks very different conceptions of the problem of sin, the balance of focus on nationalism and individualism, and most significantly the boundaries of the covenant.

In classic penitential prayers such as in *Words of the Luminaries* one finds perhaps the best correspondence to covenantal nomism. The framework is the covenant people. Trouble is interpreted as God's punishment on the people because of collective guilt and deliverance is sought in corporate terms on the basis of God's mercy and the covenant relationship. When the primary need from which salvation is sought is spiritual and universal, there is a greater focus on individualism. In the context of a heightened eschatological perspective the categories of Israel and the nations become less important than distinctions of righteous and sinner. When prayers and psalms function substantially to maintain these boundaries, as in *Psalms of Solomon* and even more so in the *Hodayot* and the sectarian covenant ritual, one is a long way from the truly corporate concern for Israel assumed in the concept of covenantal nomism, even if the language is little changed. With realized eschatology, whether partial as in the *Hodayot* or more fully as in the Christian *Odes of Solomon*, the category of Israel slides increasingly into practical irrelevance to the degree that experienced salvation gains importance.

3. Scripture-Based Stories in the Pseudepigrapha

by

CRAIG A. EVANS

Among the writings broadly defined as pseudepigrapha are several narratives which are more or less based on biblical characters and biblical narratives. Exegetical questions and theological interests of various sorts are what usually prompt their production.[1] These fictitious works provide us with no authentic historical traditions pertaining to the worthies whose stories are being retold, but they often do tell us much about the way Scripture was understood and applied in the intertestamental and New Testament periods. Moreover, they sometimes provide us with important indications of the development of the various doctrines that would eventually become part of the theologies of Judaism and Christianity. It is with this latter feature that the present essay is principally concerned.

In what follows four Scripture-based pseudepigrapha will be examined: *Martyrdom and Ascension of Isaiah, Joseph and Aseneth*, the *Life of Adam and Eve*, and the *Lives of the Prophets*. All of these works were composed in the first century C.E. or earlier, although most of them betray evidence of later redaction, often at the hands of Christian scribes. We are particularly interested in what these texts say about humanity's relationship to God, viz., who are the elect and why, what constitutes sin, how one may be forgiven and reconciled to God, and what role grace and good works play in bringing about forgiveness and reconciliation. We shall find among these writings a remarkable degree of consistency in the answers to these questions.

1. Martyrdom and Ascension of Isaiah[2]

The *Martyrdom and Ascension of Isaiah* is made up of Jewish and Christian elements, with 1:1–3:12 + 5:1–16 comprising the *Martyrdom of Isaiah*, 3:13–

---

[1] For a representative sampling, see J. H. Charlesworth and C. A. Evans, eds. *The Pseudepigrapha and Early Biblical Interpretation* (JSPSup 14; SSEJC 2; Sheffield: JSOT Press, 1993).

[2] Principal texts, translations, and studies of the *Martyrdom and Ascension of Isaiah* include R. H. Charles, *The Ascension of Isaiah* (London: Black, 1900); idem, "The Martyrdom of

4:22 comprising the *Testament of Hezekiah*, and chs. 6–11 comprising the *Vision of Isaiah*. Originally the *Martyrdom* was probably Hebrew and Jewish (though it contains Christian interpolations) and could date as early as the Maccabean period, while the *Testament* and the *Vision* originally were probably Greek and certainly Christian.[3] These Christian additions probably date to the late first century of the Common Era. Only the Jewish components are of interest for the present study (i.e. 1:1–2a; 1:6b–3:12; 5:1b–14).[4]

Isaiah," in *The Apocrypha and Pseudepigrapha of the Old Testament* (ed. R. H. Charles; 2 vols.; Oxford: Clarendon, 1913), 2.155–62; V. Burch, "The Literary Unity of the Ascensio Isaiae," *JTS* 20 (1919): 17–23; idem, "Material for the Interpretation of the Ascensio Isaiae," *JTS* 21 (1920): 249–65; D. Flusser, "The Apocryphal Book of *Ascensio Isaiae* and the Dead Sea Sect," *IEJ* 3 (1953): 34–47; J. Flemming and H. Duensing, "The Ascension of Isaiah," in *New Testament Apocrypha* (ed. E. Hennecke and W. Schneemelcher; 2 vols.; Philadelphia: Westminster, 1963–65), 2.642–63; M. Philonenko, "Le *Martyre d'Ésaïe* et l'histoire de la secte de Qoumrân," in *Pseudépigraphes de l'Ancien Testament et manuscrits de la Mer Morte* (ed. M. Philonenko; Cahiers de la RHPR 41; Paris: Presses universitaires de France, 1967), 1–10; A.-M. Denis, "Les fragments grecs du Martyre d'Isaïe," in *Introduction aux pseudépigraphes grecs d'Ancien Testament* (ed. A.-M. Denis; SVTP 1; Leiden: Brill, 1970), 170–76; idem, *Concordance grecque des pseudépigraphes d'Ancien Testament* (Leuven: Peeters; Leiden: Brill, 1987), 904; A. K. Helmbold, "Gnostic Elements in the 'Ascension of Isaiah'," *NTS* 18 (1972): 222–7; A. Caquot, "Bref commentaire du 'Martyre d'Ésaïe'," *Sem* 23 (1973): 65–93; E. Hammershaimb, "Das Martyrium Jesajas," in *Jüdische Schriften aus hellenistisch-römischer Zeit*, vol. 2 (ed. W. G. Kümmel et al.; Gütersloh: Mohn, 1973), 15–34; J. M. T. Barton, "The Ascension of Isaiah," in *The Apocryphal Old Testament* (ed. H. F. D. Sparks; Oxford: Clarendon, 1984), 775–812; G. W. E. Nickelsburg, "Stories of Biblical and Early Post-Biblical Times," in *Jewish Writings of the Second Temple Period* (ed. M. E. Stone; CRINT 2.2; Assen: Van Gorcum; Philadelphia: Fortress, 1984), 33–88, esp. 52–56; M. A. Knibb, "Martyrdom and Ascension of Isaiah," in *The Old Testament Pseudepigrapha* (ed. J. H. Charlesworth; 2 vols.; ABRL 13–14; New York: Doubleday, 1983–85), 2.143–76; idem, "Isaianic Traditions in the Apocrypha and Pseudepigrapha," in *Writing and Reading the Scroll of Isaiah: Studies of an Interpretive Tradition* (ed. C. C. Broyles and C. A. Evans; 2 vols.; VTSup 70.1–2; FIOTL 1.1–2; Leiden: Brill, 1997), 2.633–50; C. D. G. Müller, "The Ascension of Isaiah," in *New Testament Apocrypha* (ed. W. Schneemelcher; 2 vols.; Cambridge: James Clarke; Louisville: Westminster John Knox Press, 1991–92), 2.603–20; J. L. Trafton, "Isaiah, Martyrdom and Ascension of," in *ABD* 3.507–509; J. Knight, *Disciples of the Beloved One: The Christology, Setting and Theological Context of the Ascension of Isaiah* (JSPSup 18; Sheffield: Sheffield Academic Press, 1996); idem, *The Ascension of Isaiah* (Guides to the Apocrypha and Pseudepigrapha 2; Sheffield: Sheffield Academic Press, 1995).

[3] Some scholars think the *Vision* betrays gnosticizing tendencies and so may in fact be a fragment of an early gnostic work. In my judgment the evidence is too slim to draw this conclusion.

[4] Some scholars have suggested that the entire work is Christian. But many portions of this document resist this simple explanation. Most scholars rightly remain convinced that a Jewish core underlies the *Martyrdom*. The entire work is extant in Ethiopic. There also exist Greek and Latin fragments, as well as Coptic and Slavonic recensions. The original Jewish work was probably composed in Hebrew.

On the significance of the Christian additions to some of the Jewish apocryphal and pseudepigraphal works, see J. H. Charlesworth, "Christian and Jewish Self-Definition in Light

The *Martyrdom and Ascension of Isaiah* begins with Hezekiah king of Judah commanding his son Manasseh to serve the Lord (the object of these commands is implied, not stated explicitly). These commands are uttered in Isaiah's presence, but the prophet tells Hezekiah that his words will have no effect upon the prince (1:1–2, 6–7). Isaiah predicts his (Isaiah's) martyrdom at the hands of Manasseh and further predicts that Satan will guide the new king. Hezekiah weeps, but nothing can be done: "Sammael's plan against Manasseh is complete" (1:11). Hezekiah contemplates putting his son to death, but Isaiah tells him that such a plan will not come to pass.

True to Isaiah's prophecy Manasseh forgets his father's commands, Sammael dwells within him, and the new king begins to commit terrible evil (2:1). Manasseh abandons the Lord and begins to serve Satan and his angels (2:2). This results in apostasy, sorcery, adultery, persecution of the righteous, and all manner of iniquity in Jerusalem (2:3–6). Isaiah and other prophets withdraw from the city and dwell in a spartan fashion in neighboring mountains. A false prophet from Samaria named Belkira arises and begins to persecute the true prophets. Learning of his whereabouts the Samaritan accuses Isaiah to Manasseh, who then seizes him (3:1, 11–12).

Isaiah is condemned by Belkira for speaking of Jerusalem's coming judgment (3:6) and for calling Jerusalem "Sodom" and the princes of Judah the "people of Gomorrah" (3:10; cf. Isa 1:8–10). Manasseh and the princes of Judah seize Isaiah and cut him in two with a wood saw (5:1, 12). While Isaiah is being sawn Belkira attempts unsuccessfully to persuade the prophet to recant. Isaiah instead utters an imprecation against the false prophet (or perhaps against Satan who dwells within him) and his house (5:9). Before dying he tells his disciples to go to Tyre and Sidon, reassuring them that his cup of suffering is meant only for him (5:13). The original Jewish composition ends by noting that Isaiah did not cry out or weep (5:14).

Our pseudepigraphal story of Isaiah is based loosely on Old Testament materials (2 Kgs 18:13–20:19; Isa 36–39; cf. Sir 48:17–25).[5] Casting Manasseh in the role of executioner of the great prophet may have been suggested by 2 Kgs 21:16 ("Manasseh shed very much innocent blood"). Knowledge of the tradition of Isaiah being sawn in two is attested in first-century compositions such as Hebrews (11:37) and *Lives of the Prophets* (1:1) and elaborated on in later literature (e.g. *y. Sanh.* 10:2; *b. Yebam.* 49*b*).[6]

---

of the Christian Additions to the Apocryphal Writings," in *Jewish and Christian Self-Definition.* Volume Two: *Aspects of Judaism in the Greco-Roman Period* (ed. E. P. Sanders, A. I. Baumgarten, and A. Mendelson; London: SCM Press; Philadelphia: Fortress, 1981), 27–55, 310–15, esp. 41–46.

[5] Although, as is noted by Knibb ("Martyrdom and Ascension of Isaiah," 150), there is "no trace of the more sympathetic picture of Manasseh which is given in 2 Chronicles 33 and is presupposed in the Prayer of Manasseh."

[6] According to the rabbinic tradition Isaiah hides in a cedar tree, which is then sawed in two

Isaiah's command that his disciples go to Tyre and Sidon and his assurance that "for [him] alone the Lord has mixed this cup" (5:13) approximate Jesus' promise to go before his disciples to Galilee and his willingness to drink the "cup" of suffering and death (cf. Mark 14:28, 36).

The author's understanding of good and evil is sharply dualistic. The piety of Hezekiah is exaggerated – he was willing to put his son to death to avert evil. The evil of Manasseh is exaggerated, especially that of his advisors (i.e. the "false" prophets). The author's pronounced dualism also encompasses the supernatural world. Manasseh is said to be indwelt by Satan,[7] and even Belkira the principal false prophet may be understood as Satan himself. Thus, Manasseh's evil acts are explained in part as the result of satanic influence.[8] This feature also parallels the tradition of Judas the betrayer, at least according to Luke and John, who say that Satan entered the disciple's heart (cf. Luke 22.3, John 13:2, 27). The influence of Satan in the life and activities of Manasseh stands in sharp contrast to the pious Isaiah who in death "did not cry out, or weep, but his mouth spoke with the Holy Spirit" (*Mart. Ascen. Isa.* 5:14; cf. again the vague parallel with the passion of Jesus).

The prominence of Isaiah in the New Testament and especially the fourth evangelist's citation of Isa 6:10 and 53:1 in reference to Jesus may very well account for the Christianization of the *Martyrdom and Ascension of Isaiah*. Indeed, the very basis for accusing Isaiah of heresy lay in his claim of having seen God, something that the great lawgiver Moses was never privileged to experience (*Mart. Ascen. Isa.* 3:7–9; cf. Isa 6:1; Exod 33:20; John 12:37–41).[9] Sirach's assertion that knowledge of what was to occur at the end of time was granted to Isaiah (Sir 48:24–25) no doubt encouraged early Christians to append to this pseudepigraphal book visions in which the

---

with him still in it. Although there is in *Martyrdom and Ascension of Isaiah* no mention of a tree, the reference to the wood saw suggests that this tradition is probably in view.

[7] "Beliar" will dwell in him (1:9) and "Sammael Malkira will serve Manasseh" (1:8) and will dwell in him (2:1; cf. 3:11; 5:1). Reference to Beliar is found in 2 Cor 6:15. The Belial/Beliar epithet, which is used in reference to Satan, is ubiquitous in Qumranic (CD 4:13, 15; 16:5; 1QS 1:18; 1QM 13:11; 14:19; 17:5–6) and pseudepigraphal (*Jub.* 1:20; *T. Sim.* 5:3; *T. Levi* 3:3; 18:12; *T. Ash.* 3:1–2) literature. In *Mart. Ascen. Isa.* Satan, Beliar, Malkira, and Sammael are synonymous.

[8] The dualism of this work, as well as putative parallels between the details of the story and events in late antiquity, have led some scholars to identify the *Martyrdom and Ascension of Isaiah* as a work emanating from Qumran. See the succinct summary of this discussion provided by Knibb, "Martyrdom and Ascension of Isaiah," 152–3.

[9] In fact, elsewhere in the Pentateuch Moses is said to have *spoken* with God "face to face" (e.g. Exod 33:11) or to have *known* God "face to face" (e.g. Deut 34:10). Biblical interpreters in the New Testament era apparently saw no contradiction, evidently assuming that what Moses requested in Exod 33:18 ("show me your glory"), which God refused in v. 20 ("you cannot see my face; for no one shall see me and live"), involved something beyond what is described in the descriptive and perhaps metaphorical phrase "face to face."

coming of Christ and the church was foretold (*Mart. Ascen. Isa.* 3:13–4:22; 9:6–18; 11:1–33).

The principal theological contributions that the *Martyrdom and Ascension of Isaiah* makes to the literature and thought of late antiquity concern demonology, particularly with respect to the idea of direct influence over human beings, as well as strongly defined dualism, with respect to morals and to the cosmic struggle between the forces of evil and the forces of good. But perhaps of more interest is the observation that the original Jewish form of this work entertained ideas of moral election. Manasseh's reign of evil was certain, and there was nothing Hezekiah (or Isaiah) could do to ameliorate it. Hezekiah's words would have no effect (1:7); even his plan to kill Manasseh was prevented (1:12–13). Even if Manasseh's wickedness was foretold, he remains morally culpable for his deeds. Finally, there is no indication that Isaiah's death was understood by the original Jewish author of the *Martyrdom and Ascension of Isaiah* as having atoning value (as, say, in the case of the martyrs in 2 Macc 6–7).

2. Joseph and Aseneth[10]

This pseudepigraphal work, composed in Greek and extant in various other languages, is now widely regarded as Jewish and as deriving from the turn of

---

[10] Principal texts, translations, and studies of *Joseph and Aseneth* include V. Aptowitzer, "Asenath, the Wife of Joseph: A Haggadic Literary-Historical Study," *HUCA* 1 (1924): 239–306; M. Delcor, "Un roman d'amour d'origine thérapeute: Le Livre de Joseph et Asénath," *BLE* 63 (1962): 3–27; C. Burchard, *Untersuchungen zu Joseph und Aseneth: Überlieferung-Ortsbestimmung* (WUNT 8; Tübingen: Mohr [Siebeck], 1965); idem, "Zum Text von 'Joseph und Aseneth'," *JSJ* 1 (1970): 3–34; idem, "Joseph und Aseneth Neugriechisch," *NTS* 24 (1977): 68–84; idem, "Joseph and Aseneth," in *OTP*, 2.177–247; idem, "Ein vorläufiger griechischer Text von Joseph und Aseneth," *Dielheimer Blätter zum Alten Testament* 14 (1979): 2–53; idem, "The Importance of Joseph and Aseneth for the Study of the NT," *NTS* 32 (1986): 102–34; idem, "The Present State of Research on Joseph and Aseneth," in *Religion, Literature, and Society in Ancient Israel: Formative Christianity and Judaism*, vol. 2 (ed. J. Neusner *et al.*; Lanham: University Press of America, 1987), 31–52; idem, *Gesammelte Studien zu Joseph und Aseneth* (SVTP 13; Leiden: Brill, 1996); T. Holtz, "Christliche Interpolationen in 'Joseph und Aseneth'," *NTS* 14 (1968): 482–97; M. Philonenko, *Joseph et Aséneth: Introduction, texte critique, traduction et notes* (SPB 13; Leiden: Brill, 1968); A., "Le livre de la Prière d'Asénath," in *Introduction aux pseudépigraphes grecs d'Ancien Testament*, 40–48; idem, *Concordance grecque des pseudépigraphes d'Ancien Testament*, 851–9; S. West, "Joseph and Asenath: A Neglected Greek Romance," *CQ* 24 (1974): 70–81; H. C. Kee, "The Socio-Religious Setting and Aims of 'Joseph and Asenath'," in *Society of Biblical Literature 1976 Seminar Papers* (ed. G. W. MacRae; Missoula: Scholars Press, 1976), 183–92; idem, "The Socio-Cultural Setting of Joseph and Aseneth," *NTS* 29 (1983): 394–413; R. I. Pervo, "Joseph and Aseneth and the Greek Novel," in *Society of Biblical Literature 1976 Seminar Papers*,

the era, perhaps as early as 30 BCE.[11] Although a few Christian interpolations have been proposed here and there,[12] there is nothing distinctively Christian about the work; it reflects a strongly hellenized Judaism and was probably composed in Egypt.

Joseph and Aseneth tells a delightful tale of romance, conversion to Judaism, and political intrigue. According to the story, the son of Pharaoh loves but is rebuffed by the beautiful Aseneth, daughter of Pentephres the priest of Heliopolis. When she meets the handsome Joseph she falls in love, but he will have nothing to do with her because of her conceit and idolatry. After a week of repentance and fasting she is visited by an angel. Fully converted to the Jewish faith, she marries Joseph. Eight years later the son of Pharaoh conspires to murder his father and Joseph and take Aseneth as his wife. He tries to enlist Simeon and Levi, but they refuse. However, he succeeds in persuading Dan and Gad to undertake this wild adventure. Several of Jacob's sons intervene and foil the plot. Pharaoh's son is wounded and shortly thereafter dies. His grief-stricken father also dies. Joseph then reigns over Egypt forty-eight years.

A major factor that drives this tale is theological concern over Joseph marrying the daughter of a pagan priest (cf. Gen 41:45). The biblical account does not say so, but *Joseph and Aseneth* reassures Jewish readers of, and perhaps intends to impress upon pagan readers, the complete and even supernaturally assisted conversion of the young woman to Judaism, before her marriage (cf. 10:2–17:10). She is not just any Egyptian woman, she is the daughter of a priest. Her conversion, therefore, is all the more impressive.

Biblical language and style permeate this account, especially with regard

---

171–81; Nickelsburg, "Stories of Biblical and Early Post-Biblical Times," 65–71; D. Cook, "Joseph and Aseneth," in *The Apocryphal Old Testament*, 465–503; G. Delling, "Die Kunst des Gestaltens in 'Joseph und Aseneth'," *NovT* 26 (1984): 1–40; D. Sänger, *Antikes Judentum und die Mysterien: Religionsgeschichtliche Untersuchungen zu Joseph und Aseneth* (WUNT 2.5; Tübingen: Mohr [Siebeck], 1985); R. D. Chesnutt, "The Social Setting and Purpose of Joseph and Aseneth," *JSP* 2 (1988): 21–48; idem, "Joseph and Aseneth," in *ABD* 3.969–71; idem, *From Death to Life: Conversion in Joseph and Aseneth* (JSPSup 16; Sheffield: Sheffield Academic Press, 1995); A. Standhartinger, *Das Frauenbild im Judentum der hellenistischen Zeit: Ein Beitrag anhand von Joseph und Aseneth* (AGJU 26; Leiden: Brill, 1995); G. Bohak, *Joseph and Aseneth and the Jewish Temple in Heliopolis* (SBLEJL 6; Atlanta: Scholars Press, 1996); E. M. Humphrey, *The Ladies and the Cities: Transformation and Apocalyptic Identity in Joseph and Aseneth, 4 Ezra, the Apocalypse and The Shepherd of Hermas* (JSPSup 17; Sheffield: Sheffield Academic Press, 1996); R. Kraemer, *When Aseneth Met Joseph: A Late Antique Tale of the Biblical Patriarch and His Egyptian Wife Reconsidered* (Oxford: Oxford University Press, 1998).

[11] See Burchard, "Joseph and Aseneth," 181–8.

[12] Holtz ("Christliche Interpolationen," 482–97) believes that a Christian redactor reworked a Jewish text. The majority opinion is still that *Joseph and Aseneth* is a Jewish work with perhaps a few later Christian interpolations.

to Aseneth's soliloquies in chs. 11–13. The young woman's conversion may also have been intended as an example for pagans to follow (perhaps modeled after the example of Ruth). This is not to say, however, that the author of *Joseph and Aseneth* was overly ecumenical in outlook.[13] But an evangelistic and apologetic thrust does seem to be intended. The conversion of Aseneth, the virtues of Joseph, and the gallantry of Joseph's brothers in defense of the Egyptian king are surely meant to garner admiring sympathy, to deflect criticisms aroused by the Jewish presence in Egypt, and to attract proselytes.

The author of *Joseph and Aseneth* clearly presupposes the choice and election of Israel, as over against the nations. One might say that according to *Joseph and Aseneth* salvation is for the Jew to lose, for the pagan to gain. Hopes of Aseneth's conversion are perhaps anticipated when in ch. 1 she is said to possess the grace and beauty of Israel's matriarchs Sarah, Rebecca, and Rachel (cf. vv. 4–6).[14] Aseneth's virtue, though marred by her conceit and idolatry, is also underscored when it is noted that no man approached her, and no male ever sat on her bed (2:7–9). Thus the young woman possessed beauty and purity, the prerequisites for marriage to a Jewish patriarch.

The repentance of Aseneth begins with her admission that she was rash in repudiating her father's suggestion that she marry Joseph. When Joseph enters her house she recognizes him as "a son of God" (6:3, 5), who possesses and exudes great light (6:4, 6). She prays: "And now be gracious to me [ἵλεώς μοι], God of Joseph" (6:7).[15] For the first time in her life she petitions the true God, not one of her idols. Later Joseph himself prays for her, saying, "Lord, bless this virgin, and renew [ἀνακαίνισον] her by your spirit, and form her anew by your hidden hand, and make her alive again [ἀναζωοποίησον] by your life, and let her eat your bread of life, and drink your cup of blessing" (8:9). The language of renewal is found in Hebrews (6:6), which speaks of being renewed to repentance [ἀνακαινίζειν εἰς μετάνοιαν], while the idea of being made alive again is also found in the New Testament, though using the word ἀναζάω (cf. Luke 15:24; Rom 7:9).[16] Even the use of ἀναπλάσσω ("form her anew [ἀνάπλασον] by your hidden hand") may allude to the

---

[13] Burchard ("Joseph and Aseneth," 195) says that "Proselytes are welcomed, not sought."

[14] Haggadic traditions extoll the beauty and wisdom of these women.

[15] Her words may contain an echo of Joseph's reassurance to his frightened brothers (Gen 43:23).

[16] ζωοποιέω is found some ten or eleven times in the New Testament. See especially 1 Pet 3:18 (ζωοποιηθεὶς δὲ πνεύματι). Because the language of *Joseph and Aseneth* approximates that of the New Testament, some scholars have suspected the presence of Christian interpolations in Joseph's prayer for Aseneth. But ἀναζωοποιέω appears in the *Testament of Abraham*, thus showing that its usage was not necessarily a Christian innovation: καὶ ἀπέστειλεν ὁ θεὸς πνεῦμα ζωῆς ἐπὶ τοὺς τελευτήσαντας, καὶ ἀνεζωοποιήθησαν (18:11). Furthermore, the absence of elements that are distinctively Christian caution against the view that Joseph's prayer has been edited by Christians.

formation of the first human being (Gen 2:7, 8, 15, 19; cf. 1 Tim 2:13), perhaps suggesting that Joseph has asked God to recreate Aseneth. If so, then this too parallels the New Testament idea of believers being recreated upon their conversion (2 Cor 5:17; Gal 6:15).

Following Joseph's prayer Aseneth weeps and repents of her devotion to idols (ch. 9). Her repentance continues for a week, complete with ashes and sackcloth and the destruction of her idols (10:2–17; cf. 13:2). Aseneth gives eloquent expression to her repentance in two soliloquies. In the first, Aseneth says that she has heard that "the God of the Hebrews is a true God, and a living God, and a merciful God, and compassionate and long-suffering and pitiful and gentle, and does not taken into account the sin of a humble person [μή λογίζόμενος ἁμαρτίαν ἀνθρώπου ταπεινοῦ]" (11:10). Therefore she too "will take courage and will turn to him, and take refuge with him, and confess all (her) sins to him [ἐξομολογήσομαι αὐτῷ πάσας τὰς ἁμαρτίας]" (11:11; cf. 12:3). This language parallels expressions in the New Testament. In Rom 4:8 Paul quotes Ps 31:2, which may have been alluded to in Aseneth's soliloquy: μακάριος ἁνὴρ οὗ οὐ μὴ λογίσηται κύριος ἁμαρτίαν ("Blessed is the man whose sin the Lord does not take into account"). Similar expressions are found elsewhere in Jewish sources (cf. *1 Enoch* 99:2; *Pss. Sol.* 16:5). Aseneth's confession of her sins is also reminiscent of the Jews who went to John the Baptist ἐξομολογούμενοι τὰς ἁμαρτίας αὐτῶν (Mark 1:5; cf. Jas 5:16; 1 John 1:9). Again, there is nothing distinctively Christian here (cf. Sir 4:26; *T. Gad* 2:1). Her statement that God does not "take into account the sin of the humble" echoes a common theme in the Old Testament.[17]

In her second soliloquy Aseneth regards herself as wretched, as an orphan, and as desolate. If the Lord strikes her for her sins, she is confident that he will heal her; though he be furious at her, "he will again be reconciled with (her) and forgive (her) every sin [διαλλαγήσεταί μοι καὶ ἀφήσει μοι πᾶσαν ἁμαρτίαν]" (11:16–18). Paul also speaks of humanity's reconciliation to God (using καταλλάσσω in Rom 5:10; 2 Cor 5:19–20; ἀποκαταλλάσσω in letters many regard as deutero-Pauline; cf. Eph 2:16; Col 1:20, 22; διαλλάσσομαι is found in Matt 5:24).

Following her soliloquies, Aseneth lifts her eyes to heaven and prays. She proclaims God as Creator of all. She again confesses her sins (ἥμαρτον; cf. Luke 15:18, 21) and asks that God spare her (12:3–5). Her prayer ends with a petition that God protect Joseph (13:15). An angel appears and tells Aseneth that her prayer has been heard. She is told to replace her sackcloth with fresh apparel. The angel then tells Aseneth that her humiliation has been

---

[17] See for example Isa 66:2 . . . καὶ ἐπὶ τίνα ἐπιβλέψω ἀλλ ἢ ἐπὶ τὸν ταπεινὸν καὶ ἡσύχιον καὶ τρέμοντα τοὺς λόγους μου; Ps 24:18 ἰδὲ τὴν ταπείνωσίν μου καὶ τὸν κόπον μου καὶ ἄφες πάσας τὰς ἁμαρτίας μου (cf. Zeph 2:3).

observed. Indeed, her tears and the ashes have formed "plenty of mud" (15:3). Her name is now "written in the book of the living in heaven" and "will never be erased" because it was written by the finger of the angel (15:4; cf. v. 12).[18] To have one's name written in the book of life by a celestial being is a signal honor and may be intended as an echo of Deut 9:10 where it is said that the commandments of Sinai were written by the finger of God himself. But it may also recall Exod 32:32–33, where Israel, having committed idolatry, is in danger of being blotted out of the book that God has written. These deliberate allusions are probably meant to indicate that although Aseneth had been an idolator, because of her repentance she is securely placed in the covenant.

Her repentance, Aseneth is told, has made her a "City of Refuge" behind whose walls many others may attach themselves to God (15:7; cf. 11:3; 12:3, 6, 13; Ps 142:5). The angel adds: "For Repentance is in the heavens, an exceedingly beautiful and good daughter of the Most High. And she herself entreats the Most High God for you at all times and for all who repent in the name of the Most High God, because he is the father of Repentance." Personification of μετάνοια is found elsewhere in Jewish literature of this period (cf. *1 Enoch* 40:9; *T. Gad* 5:7–8).

Aseneth's soliloquies and prayer of repentance are reminiscent of various expressions of contrition and repentance found in the Old Testament and elsewhere *(Prayer of Manasseh*; cf. 2 Chr 33:12–13). Her confession of God's compassion and mercy (11:10) recalls the language of Scripture (cf. Exod 34:6; Ps 86:15); so also her confidence that God "does not count sin" (11:10; cf. Ps 32:2). Her admission that she has "sinned much . . . and committed lawlessness and irreverence, and said wicked and unspeakable things" (12:4) is reminiscent of Israel's confession (cf. 1 Kgs 8:47; Ps 106:6). The angel's pronouncement of forgiveness, complete with a new name (15:7), recalls God's naming of Abraham and Sarah (Gen 17:5, 15), as well as the renaming of God's redeemed people (cf. Isa 62:4; Hos 1:10; 2:23). Indeed, the name assigned Aseneth – "City of Refuge" – may allude to passages in the LXX (cf. Zech 2:15; Isa 54:15; Jer 27[50]:5).

Although God's grace is extolled in *Joseph and Aseneth*, the author believes that salvation comes through obedience to the Torah. According to Burchard: "Divine life . . . is obtained through the right use of food, ointment, and by the avoidance of the pagan way of partaking of them."[19] This assessment appears to be correct. Israel's food laws are summed up several times in these words: ". . . eat blessed bread[20] of life and drink a blessed cup

---

[18] Being written in a book of life is found in Jewish and Judeo-Christian works (Exod 32:32–33; Ps 87:6; *Jub.* 30:22; 1QM 12:1–2; Luke 10:20; Rev 20:12, 15). The threat to be blotted out of the book of life is found in the revised twelfth benediction of the *Amidah*.

[19] Burchard, "Joseph and Aseneth," 191.

[20] This "blessed bread . . . of incorruption" (ἄρτος εὐλογημένος . . . ἀφθαρσίας) may refer

of immortality and anoint himself with blessed ointment of incorruptibility"
(8:5; cf. 8:9). These elements play the principal role in the conversion of
Aseneth.

An angel descends from heaven and informs Aseneth that her confession,
prayer, fasting, and self-abasement have been observed (15:2–3). She may
now "eat blessed bread of life, and drink a blessed cup of immortality, and
anoint [herself] with blessed ointment of incorruptibility" (15:5). After
dressing, Aseneth is given to eat of a honey comb generated by the "bees of
paradise" (16:14). In eating the comb, she has received the promised bread
of life, etc. (16:16; cf. 19:5; 21:21). Eating the bread of life has the happy
effect of nullifying her idolatrous past, in which she had eaten from bread
sacrificed to idols (21:13–14). From these statements one is left with the
impression that the change of lifestyle, not least the change of diet, plays a
vital role in the redemption of Aseneth. God's grace is the presupposition, to
be sure, but apart from wholesale adoption of Jewish food and purity laws,
the conversion of Aseneth could not have taken place.[21]

3. Life of Adam and Eve[22]

The presence of Hebraisms suggests that the *Life of Adam and Eve*, in both
its Latin and Greek recensions, was originally composed in Hebrew, though
no trace of the Hebrew text has survived. The language and themes of this

---

to manna (Burchard, "Joseph and Aseneth," 191), while the words "of life, and drink a blessed
cup of immortality and anoint oneself with a blessed anointing" (ζωῆς καὶ πίνει ποτήριον
εὐλογημένον ἀθανασίας καὶ χρίεται χρίσματι εὐλογημένῳ) may be a Christian interpolation;
cf. Holtz, "Christliche Interpolationen." Eating bread of life and drinking a cup of immortality
may reflect Johannine tradition.

[21] This feature of Joseph and Aseneth appears to stand in tension with aspects of
"covenantal nomism," as E. P. Sanders (*Judaism: Practice and Belief 63 BCE – 66 CE* [London:
SCM Press/ Philadelphia: Trinity Press International, 1992], 277) has defined it: "[P]re-
Christian and non-Christian Jewish theologians held that God's grace underlay all of life, that
God chose and redeemed Israel from bondage before requiring obedience to the law, and that
God would remain true to his promises *despite* disobedience. They understood obeying the law
as the Jews' appropriate response to the prior grace of God."

[22] Principal texts, translations, and studies of the *Life of Adam and Eve* include L. S. A.
Wells, "The Books of Adam and Eve," in *The Apocrypha and Pseudepigrapha of the Old
Testament*, 2.123–54; J. M. Evans, *Paradise Lost and the Genesis Traditions* (Oxford:
Clarendon, 1968); A.-M. Denis, "Le Vie de Adam et Eve," in *Introduction aux
pseudépigraphes grecs d'Ancien Testament*, 3–7; idem, *Concordance grecque des
pseudépigraphes d'Ancien Testament*, 815–18; A. B. Kolenkow, "Trips to the Other World in
Antiquity and the Story of Seth in the Life of Adam and Eve," in *Society of Biblical Literature
1977 Seminar Papers* (ed. P. J. Achtemeier; SBLSP 16; Missoula: Scholars Press, 1977), 1–11;
G. W. E. Nickelsburg, "Some Related Traditions in the Apocalypse of Adam, the Books of
Adam and Eve, and 1 Enoch," in *The Rediscovery of Gnosticism* (ed. B. Layton; Studies in the

work, in relation to other works of late antiquity, point to a date of composition probably toward the end of the first century C.E.[23] The few Christian interpolations (in *Vita* 29:14; 42:2–5; 51:9) support the early date.[24] The Greek recension, called the *Apocalypse of Moses* (because of a late, misleading preface),[25] and the Latin recension, called *Vita Adae et Evae*, contain overlapping traditions, as well as materials not paralleled in one another. Whereas the Greek recension appears to be directly dependent on the Hebrew, the Latin recension gives evidence of being dependent partly on Greek and partly on Hebrew materials.[26]

The *Life of Adam and Eve* recounts the story of how Satan deceived Eve (no fewer than twice according to *Vita*) and how the first-formed humans fell into sin, were driven from earthly paradise, repented, and qualified for entry into the paradise of heaven. This pseudepigraphon is especially interested in the negative effects of sin and the elaborate penance performed by Adam and Eve. The story represents an imaginative and greatly expanded embellishment of Genesis 3–4. At many points these midrashic elements parallel early rabbinic traditions and other earlier Jewish interpretive traditions (e.g. *Vita* 50 and Josephus, *Ant.* 1.2.3 §70–71).

In many ways the theology of the *Life of Adam and Eve* is consistent with that of early Christianity and emerging rabbinic Judaism. Adam is formed from earth (or clay) and God's breath (*Vita* 27:2). He therefore posseses the image of God, which though damaged is not erased by the fall (*Apocalypse* 10:3; 12:1; *Vita* 13:3; 14:1–3). While in Paradise Adam and Eve ate "the food of angels" (*Vita* 4:2, alluding to Ps 78:25), but now they will toil for their

---

History of Religions 41; Leiden: Brill, 1981) 515–39; idem, "The Bible Rewritten and Expanded," in *Jewish Writings of the Second Temple Period*, 110–18; M. D. Johnson, "Life of Adam and Eve," in *The Old Testament Pseudepigrapha*, 2.249–95; D. A. Bertrand, *La Vie grecque d'Adam et Eve* (Recherches Intertestamentaires 1; Paris: A. Maisonneuve, 1987); J. R. Levison, "The Exoneration of Eve in the Apocalypse of Moses," *JSJ* 20 (1989): 135–50; idem, "Adam and Eve, Life of," *ABD*, 1.64–66; M. de Jonge and J. Tromp, *The Life of Adam and Eve and Related Literature* (Guides to the Apocrypha and Pseudepigrapha 4; Sheffield: Sheffield Academic Press, 1997).

[23] See Johnson, "The Life of Adam and Eve," 252.

[24] Johnson ("The Life of Adam and Eve," 254) comments: "The absence of any and all messianism is most striking and completely unexplainable on the assumption of a Christian origin of the material."

[25] The preface reads: "The narrative and life of Adam and Eve the first-formed, revealed by God to Moses his servant when he received the tablets of the Law of the covenant from his hand, after he had been taught by the archangel Michael. May the Lord bless." The preface is misleading, as Johnson ("The Life of Adam and Eve," 259) notes, for Moses plays no role in the *Life of Adam and Eve*. But the preface no doubt attempts to answer the question of how Moses, understood to be the author of Genesis, could have known of the story of the creation and subsequent fall of Adam and Eve.

[26] See the convenient summary of evidence, as well as additional bibliography, in Johnson, "The Life of Adam and Eve," 251.

food. At one time clothed with righteousness and glory (*Apocalypse* 20–21) Adam now has an evil heart (*Apocalypse* 13:5) and is subject to hard labor, pain, illness, and death (*Apocalypse* 24–25). At death his body is buried in the ground (*Apocalypse* 40), but his soul ascends to the third heaven (*Apocalypse* 37; cf. 2 Cor 12:2–4).

The *Life of Adam and Eve* understands sin as lust (ἐπιθυμία; *Apocalypse* 19:3: "lust is the head of all sin") and desire to be equal to God (*Vita* 15:3: "I will set my throne above the stars of heaven and will be like the Most High"; *Apocalypse* 21:3: "You shall be as God"). Both recensions insist that sin entered humanity through Eve (*Apocalypse* 9:2; 11; 14:2; 21:2, 6: "O evil woman! Why have you wrought destruction among us? You have estranged me from the glory of God"; *Vita* 18:1; 26:2; 35:2; cf. 1 Tim 2:13–14).

Eve wonders what penance is required (*Vita* 5:1–2). The Lord orders the angels to continue driving the man and woman out of Paradise, but he does have this to say to Adam: "If you guard yourself from all evil, preferring death to it, at the time of the resurrection I will raise you again, and then there shall be given to you from the tree of life, and you shall be immortal forever" (*Apocalypse* 28:4; cf. 41:3).

The extravagance of Adam's and Eve's penance is especially interesting. Adam is first to repent, speaking to the angels that are driving them out of Paradise: "Let me be a little while so that I may beseech God that he might have compassion and pity me, for I alone have sinned" (*Apocalypse* 27:2). It is noteworthy that whereas the author blames Eve for sin entering the world, Adam is portrayed rather nobly as assuming the responsibility. Adam again begs of the angels: "Let me take fragrances from Paradise, so that after I have gone out, I might bring an offering to God so that God will hear me" (*Apocalypse* 29:3). There is no recounting, however, of Adam offering up an offering.

According to the Latin recension Adam and Eve "mourned for seven days, weeping in great sorrow" (*Vita* 1:1). Eve admits her culpability, saying to Adam: "O that I would die! Then perhaps the Lord God will bring you again into Paradise" (*Vita* 3:1; 5:2). Adam fasts for forty days (*Vita* 6:1). They immerse themselves in the Tigris (*Vita* 6:1–2: Eve) and Jordan Rivers (*Vita* 6:3: Adam), with the hope: "Perhaps the Lord God will pity us."

According to the Greek recension, Adam enjoins Eve to "pray to God until I shall give back my spirit into the hands of the one who has given it. For we know not how we shall meet our maker, whether he shall be angry with us or turn to have mercy on us" (*Apocalypse* 31:4). As Adam dies, Eve confesses: "I have sinned, O God; I have sinned, O Father of all; I have sinned against you . . . I have sinned much" (*Apocalypse* 32:2). Even the angels intercede for Adam, saying, "Forgive him, O Father of all, for he is your image [εἰκών]" (*Apocalypse* 35:2; cf. 33:5).

The penance and prayerful petitions prove to be efficacious. A heavenly trumpet sounds and an angel shouts: "Blessed be the glory of the Lord over his works; he has had mercy on Adam, the work of his hands" (*Apocalypse* 37:2). Adam is then carried up to heaven, where he is washed in the presence of God. Adam is consigned to the third heaven and "the angels sang an angelic hymn marveling at the pardoning [συγχωρήσει] of Adam" (*Apocalypse* 37:6). God then tells Adam that Satan's joy will be turned into sorrow and that Adam's dominion will be established and he will sit on the throne of his seducer (*Apocalypse* 39:1–3).

According to the *Life of Adam and Eve* the first-formed humans fell into sin through their disobedience but were able to reclaim all that might have been theirs through their repentance: the Tree of Life (*Apocalypse* 28:4), the healing oil (*Apocalypse* 13; *Vita* 42), a godly heart (*Apocalypse* 13), the throne on which Satan had sat (*Apocalypse* 39; *Vita* 47), and Paradise (*Apocalypse* 37). However, the pardoning of Adam and Eve was not entirely the result of God's grace; it was in response to their vigorous penance. To be resurrected and to gain access to the "Tree of Life," Adam must "guard [himself] from all evil" (*Apocalypse* 28:4).[27] Adam hopes to gain a hearing from God by offering up "fragrances from Paradise" (*Apocalypse* 29:3). After repeated immersions, Adam and Eve hope that the Lord will take pity on them (*Vita* 6:1–4), but there is little indication that such pity may be assumed. At the end of their mortal lives, Adam and Eve have no assurance of reconciliation with God: "we know not how we shall meet our maker, whether he shall be angry with us or turn to have mercy on us" (*Apocalypse* 31:4). At this point the perspective of the author of the *Life of Adam and Eve* stands in tension with that of the author of the *Prayer of Manasseh* (esp. vv. 7–14), who believes that God will forgive the most wretched sinner, if only he repent.

4. Lives of the Prophets[28]

Although C. C. Torrey years ago argued that the *Lives of the Prophets* was originally composed in Hebrew,[29] the evidence suggests that this pseudepi-

---

[27] The concern expressed in *Life of Adam and Eve* with regard to assurance of resurrection may not square with Sanders's discussion of the topic (cf. *Judaism: Practice and Belief,* 298–303).

[28] Principal texts, translations, and studies of the *Lives of the Prophets* include T. Schermann, *Prophetarum vitae fabulosae indices apostolorum discipulorumque Domini Dorotheo, Epiphanio, Hippolyto aliisque vindicate* (Leipzig: Teubner, 1907); idem, *Propheten- und Apostellegenden nebst Jüngerkatalogen des Dorotheus und verwandter Texte* (TU 31.3; Leipzig: Hinrichs, 1907); C. C. Torrey, *The Lives of the Prophets: Greek Text and Translation* (JBLMS 1; Philadelphia: Society of Biblical Literature, 1946); M. de Jonge, "Christelijke

graphon was composed in Greek. D. R. A. Hare dates the original work to the first quarter of the first century C.E., when there was great interest in the building of monuments to the prophets (cf. Matt 23:29 = Luke 11:47; Josephus, *Ant.* 16.7.1 §182) and some years before Herod Agrippa (41–44 C.E.) erected the new south wall of the city of Jerusalem (assuming that reference to the place of Isaiah's burial is properly understood; cf. *Lives* 1:1, 8–9).[30] However, there are several scribal glosses and later Christian interpolations. Most are easily identifiable, but some are disputed.

The Greek Codex Marchalianus summarizes the *Lives of the Prophets* as providing "the names of the prophets, and where they are from, and where they died and how, and where they live." The summary is apt, for that is precisely what this pseudepigraphon does. *Lives* includes Isaiah, Jeremiah, Ezekiel, Daniel, the Twelve, and seven non-writing prophets who are mentioned in Scripture.[31] Hare comments that the "author's interest in the prophets relates not to their importance as ethical teachers but, rather, to their numinous quality as workers of miracles, intercessors, and foretellers of future events."[32] Much of the material represents summarizing recapitulations of the biblical narratives themselves. Sometimes explanatory glosses and embellishments are added.

The theme of the prophets as intercessors is mentioned in a few cases. Isaiah plays a post-mortem intercessory role in providing water at the pool of Siloam (1:8). Concerning poisonous asps Jeremiah's prayers were of benefit to the Egyptians (2:3) and to people long after the prophet's death (2:4–6). During the Babylonian captivity Ezekiel defended the Jewish people against aggression and on occasion provided food (3:5–10). Through Elisha's intercession the water of Jericho was made pure and remains so to this day (22:6).

A major theme of the *Lives of the Prophets* is the martyrdom of the prophets. Isaiah was martyred by Manasseh by being sawn in two (1:1; cf. *Mart. Ascen. Isa.* 5:1–15). Jeremiah was stoned and buried in the vicinity of

---

Elementen in de Vitae Prophetarum," *NedTT* 16 (1961–62) 161–78; M. Philonenko, "Prophetenleben," in *Biblisch-historisches Handwörterbuch* (ed. B. Reicke and L. Rost; 3 vols.; Göttingen: Vandenhoeck & Ruprecht, 1962–66), 3.1512–13; M. E. Stone, "Prophets, Lives of the," *EncJud* 13.1149–50; A.-M. Denis, "Les Vies des Prophètes," in *Introduction aux pseudépigraphes grecs d'Ancien Testament*, 85–90; idem, *Concordance grecque des pseudépigraphes d'Ancien Testament*, 868–71; D. R. A. Hare, "The Lives of the Prophets," in *The Old Testament Pseudepigrapha*, 2.379–99; idem, "Prophets, Lives of," *ABD*, 5.502–503.

[29] Torrey, *The Lives of the Prophets*, 7.

[30] Hare, "The Lives of the Prophets," 380–81.

[31] These include Nathan (2 Sam 7:2), Ahijah (1 Kgs 11:29), Joad (1 Kgs 13:1–32, where no name is given, but see Josephus, *Ant.* 8.8.5 §231), Azariah (2 Chr 15:1–15), Elijah (1 Kgs 17:1), Elisha (1 Kgs 19:16), and Zechariah son of Jehoiada (2 Chr 24:20–22).

[32] Hare, "The Lives of the Prophets," 382.

Pharaoh's palace (2:1–2). Ezekiel's exilic ministry largely consisted of rebuking the faithless (3:14) and pronouncing judgment upon those who "were committing sacrilege against the Lord by persecuting those who were keeping the Law" (3:16). The prophet was killed in Chaldea by the ruler of the Jewish people (3:1–2). Micah was killed by Joram son of Ahab, "because he rebuked him for the impieties of his fathers" (6:2). Amos was tortured to death by Amaziah (7:2). It is interesting that *Lives* does not develop either the theme of Israel's persistent rejection and persecution of the prophets (cf. 2 Chr 24:19; 36:14–16; Neh 9:26; *Jub.* 1:12; Matt 23:37 = Luke 13:34) or the theme of the atoning efficacy of the prophets' martyrdoms.

Two of the retellings of the lives and ministries of the prophets potentially bear on the concerns of the present essay more directly. We are told that the prophet Nathan taught King David the Law of the Lord and foresaw his sin with Bathsheba (17:1–2). However, before he could reach David to avert this catastrophe "Beliar hindered him." This hindrance took the form of a naked dead man lying by the road, which made it necessary for Nathan to remain that day (17:3).[33] This retelling may mitigate David's culpability somewhat in suggesting that Satan was in some way involved. A timely prophetic warning would have brought David to his senses and would have prevented his serious transgression.

The second interesting narrative is that concerning Daniel, who is described as chaste (4:2), who is said to have fasted (4:3) and to have prayed for Nebuchadnezzar (4:4). Much of this narrative retells the story of the Babylonian king's pride, insanity, and eventual restoration (cf. Dan 4). What is of interest is the heightened depiction of the king's repentance. The author of *Lives* says that Nebuchadnezzar "prostrated himself to the Lord and confessed his impiety, and after the forgiveness of his wickedness he restored to him the kingdom" (4:13). Going well beyond the biblical story, the author of *Lives* adds that the Babylonian king "neither ate bread or meat nor drank wine as he made his confession, for Daniel had ordered him to appease the Lord with (a diet of) soaked pulse and greens" (4:14; cf. Dan 1:12). The king's repentance is sufficient for forgiveness, but it is interesting to observe the distinctively Jewish direction that it takes.

The *Lives of the Prophets* tells us little directly about justification, election, salvation, or judgment. In the case of Nebuchadnezzar, like the story of Adam and Eve, the efficacy of repentance is emphasized. This emphasis is consistent with the later rabbinic refrain: "Great is the power of repentance!"

---

[33] Despite the obvious parallel to Luke 10:30, there is no reason to suspect the presence of Christian redaction.

5. Conclusion

Heartfelt repentance and confession make reconciliation between a human being and God possible. Repentance may entail dramatic outward signs, such as sackcloth, ashes, bathing; and it may require careful observation of basic Mosaic laws, such as observing the Sabbath, observing *kashrut*, and renouncing idolatry. What was especially interesting was the observation that forgiveness and reconciliation were possible without sacrifice (as in *Life of Adam and Eve* and *Joseph and Aseneth*). Of course, our more obvious examples – Adam and Eve and the Babylonian king Nebuchadnezzar – were not Jewish and had no access to the Jerusalem temple. Perhaps this reality influences theology.

Nevertheless, as these Scripture-based stories stand, their understanding of election, sin, and redemption is largely consistent with what we find in early Christianity and in some strands of emerging rabbinic Judaism. The obvious difference, of course, is that these pseudepigrapha have no counterpart to Christianity's idea of atonement wrought through the death of Jesus. But even Christianity's understanding of atonement, in that all that is required is repentance, confession of sin, and faith in God's provision in Christ, is in some important ways anticipated in these writings. However, elements are present in some of the writings reviewed above that still reflect a works-righteousness understanding of justification, with which the Apostle Paul sharply disagreed (as seen especially in his letters to the churches in Galatia and Rome). Obedience to the Law appears to be the requirement for Aseneth to become a member of the people of God, while repentance and self-effacing acts on the part of Adam and Eve carry a measure of hope, but no assurance of God's acceptance.

This is not to say that the authors of these writings did not view God as gracious and forgiving; they did. There is no indication, however, that they believed that people could gain God's acceptance apart from obedience to the Law.[34]

---

[34] This is not the place to engage E. P. Sanders and the applicability of his formulation of "covenantal nomism" to Paul; the second volume will do that. However, the Jewish literature of late antiquity that has been reviewed in this chapter, as well as the literature treated in other chapters of the present volume, supports the conclusion reached by R. H. Gundry, in his critical assessment of Sanders's comparison of the theologies of Palestinian Judaism and Paul: "Despite some formal similarities, then, Paul and Palestinian Judaism look materially different at the point of grace and works" ("Grace, Works, and Staying Saved in Paul," *Bib* 66 [1985]: 1–38, quotation from p. 37).

4. Expansions of Scripture

by

PETER ENNS

"Expansions of Scripture" is a collective term given to a number of Second Temple texts[1] that add to a biblical book or well-known biblical story. The nature of these expansions is certainly varied, so much so that no one rubric can do full justice to the contents of the individual works so designated. For example, even in the relatively few works treated in this essay, there is much variety. 1 Esdras, a retelling of the substance of 2 Chron 35:1–36:23, Ezra, and Neh 7:38–8:12, adheres quite closely to the biblical books (the most significant exception is the story of the three bodyguards in chaps. 3–4). Other apocryphal material – Song of the Three, Susanna, Bel and the Dragon, and Additions to Esther – are deliberately presented as additions to existing biblical books, and so they add substantive information not treated in their canonical precursors. Finally, the pseudepigraphal books *Jubilees* and Ps.-Philo's *Biblical Antiquities*, are expansions of another sort. They are retellings that have as their framework large portions of canonical material, but change the biblical accounts significantly, either by altering the biblical stories themselves or simply introducing new material altogether. The result is essentially a new "version" of the biblical story.

The purpose of this essay, however, is not to discuss the nature of these expansion of Scripture per se, but to glean from these texts any information they might contain on the nature of "justification" in Second Temple Judaism.[2] These texts are, to be sure, nothing approaching a systematic handling of this topic, so caution must be exercised in reading too much into

---

[1] This essay evaluates 1 Esdras, Song of the Three, Susanna, Bel and the Dragon, Additions to Esther, *Jannes and Jambres, Biblical Antiquities, Jubilees.*

[2] Of course, even using the word "justification" could be considered reading into Judaism categories better known in connection with Paul and, perhaps more importantly, the understanding of Paul throughout the history of Christianity. I use the word here without any conscious prejudice as to how precisely it should be understood, since that is the collective purpose of the essays of this two-volume work, but merely as a short-hand description of what it meant for someone to be considered among the "people of God," i.e., Sanders's notion of "getting in and staying in" (*Paul and Palestinian Judaism: A Comparison of Patterns of Religion* [London: SCM, 1977], 17; hereafter *PPJ*).

them.[3] Nevertheless, this is not to say that they are silent on the subject. They are documents written with some religious purpose in mind, and so they do discuss on some level how being a Jew was understood during this period, at least by the writers themselves and, presumably, the communities those writers represented. The intention of this essay, therefore, is to attempt to see what these particular texts have to say about what being Jewish meant during the Second Temple period, specifically, whether Sanders's notion of "covenantal nomism" adequately describes the religious stance of any, some, or all of these texts. To be sure, what we will see in these texts are general directions and tendencies that give us glimpses rather than full-blown discussions such as we find in the Pauline corpus.

Of the texts to be discussed in this essay, only *Jubilees* was given special attention by E. P. Sanders in *Paul and Palestinian Judaism*.[4] This is likely the case because *Jubilees* is both relatively early (first half of the 2nd century B.C.)[5] and has much more to say on the topic than the other works (although I would argue that *Biblical Antiquities*, although later, should not be overlooked). Our discussion of *Jubilees* will be left to the end. The other works are of varied relevance to the discussion, and will be treated one at a time. The apocryphal material will be treated first followed by the pseud-epigraphal material.

1. 1 Esdras

1 Esdras, known as Esdras A in the LXX and 3 Esdras in the Vulgate, is a fairly close retelling of the biblical accounts[6] beginning with Josiah's

---

[3] It has been a criticism of Sanders that he has imposed questions, especially on the apocryphal and pseudepigraphal material, "that seem distinctly peripheral to the authors' interests" (N. King, review of *Paul and Palestinian Judaism*, in *Bib* 61 [1980]: 143).

[4] *PPJ*, 362–87.

[5] J. VanderKam has argued this position at length (*Textual and Historical Studies in the Book of Jubilees* [HSM 14; Missoula: Scholars, 1977]). He dates the book between 160 and 150 B.C.

[6] The vexing question of the precise relationship between 1 Esdras and the canonical books (e.g., whether it is an independent translation from the Hebrew, whether it is based on a Greek version different from the LXX version of the canonical material, whether 1 Esdras is at all based on the canonical books or is itself a piece of the Chronicler's own work) is not germane here, since the focus of this essay is the religious ideas purported in 1 Esdras. As for the consensus view that 1 Esdras is a translation from Hebrew (despite the story of the three young bodyguards in chaps. 3–4 for which there is no extant Hebrew source), see Z. Talshir, "The Milieu of 1 Esdras in the Light of Its Vocabulary," *De Septuaginta: Studies in Honour of John William Wevers on His Sixty-Fifth Birthday* (ed. A. Pietersma and C. Cox; Mississauga, Ontario: BENBEN, 1984), 129–47; R. Hanhart, *Text und Textgeschichte des 1. Esrabuches* (Göttingen: Vandenhoeck & Ruprecht, 1974), 11–18. For general discussions of the relationship

celebration of the Passover and ending somewhat abruptly with Ezra's reforms as described in Neh 8:12, a historical period of nearly 200 years. Because it is such a close retelling, we find in 1 Esdras a number of themes represented in the canonical books, e.g., the people's disobedience to the law, the importance of the temple, feasts, offerings, and sacrifice.[7] Nevertheless, although it is heavily dependent on the canonical literature, it is not merely a translation,[8] and thus deserves to be read as a work in its own right. The content of this book is fairly focused. It is the story of the last years of Judah's existence as an independent nation, the deportation to Babylon, the return under Ezra, and the reconstruction of the temple. It is the well-known story of rebellion, punishment, and restoration. But why bother retelling this particular story? Why was 1 Esdras composed at all? For one thing, the omission of references to Nehemiah in a number of places (e.g., compare 1 Esd 9:49 to Neh 8:9) suggests the writer's desire to bring to the foreground Ezra's role in the reforms. Moreover, he mentions Zerubbabel much more frequently than do the canonical books.[9] These facts may imply some sort of a political agenda on the part of the writer, and therefore serve as another reminder that the types of questions we are asking of the text may not be those the text is fully prepared to give. Hence, we proceed with some caution.

Having said this, however, it seems to be the case that 1 Esdras generally supports Sanders's understanding of Second Temple Judaism, albeit indirectly. It tells the story of an elect people, a people who are "in" but who have transgressed the law, and the steps taken in response to this transgression. In the words of 1 Esd 1:47–51 (LXX vv. 45–49), Zedekiah "did what was evil in the sight of the Lord" (ἐποίησεν τὸ πονηρὸν ἐνώπιον κυρίου).

---

between Ezra and both canonical and extra-canonical traditions of Ezra, see R. Kraft, "'Ezra' Materials in Judaism and Christianity," *Principat 19.1* (*ANRW* II; Berlin: de Gruyter, 1979), 116–36. For other helpful treatments of introductory matters, see R. J. Coggins and M. A. Knibb, *The First and Second Books of Esdras* (Cambridge: Cambridge University Press, 1979), 1–7; J. M. Myers, *I and II Esdras* (AB 42; Garden City: Doubleday, 1974), 1–19; B. Metzger, *Introduction to the Apocrypha* (New York: Oxford University Press, 1957), 11–19; A. E. Gardner, "The Purpose and Date of I Esdras," *JJS* 37 (1986): 18–27; H. W. Attridge, "Historiography," *Jewish Writings of the Second Temple Period* (CRINT 2/2; ed. M. Stone; Philadelphia: Fortress, 1984), 157–60; T. C. Eskenazi, "The Chronicler and the Composition of 1 Esdras," *CBQ* 48 (1986): 39–61.

[7] To be specific, Eskenazi argues that the theological distinctives of 1 Esdras parallel closely those of the Chronicler over against those of Ezra-Nehemiah ("The Chronicler and the Composition of 1 Esdras").

[8] See M. Carrez, "Esdras Septante," *RHPR* 74 (1994): 13–42. R. J. Coggins has suggested that the purpose of the book was "to set out a less confused account of the traditions relating to Ezra," but the actual reasons are certainly more involved than that (Coggins and Knibb, *The First and Second Books of Esdras*, 5).

[9] S. Japhet, "Sheshbazzar and Zerubbabel against the Background of the Historical and Religious Tendencies of Ezra-Nehemiah," *ZAW* 95 (1983): 218–29.

He stiffened his neck and hardened his heart and transgressed the laws of the Lord God of Israel" (σκληρύνας αὐτοῦ τὸν τράχηλον καὶ τὴν καρδίαν αὐτοῦ παρέβη τὰ νόμιμα κυρίου θεοῦ Ισραηλ). Likewise, the "leaders of the people and of the priests committed many acts of sacrilege and lawlessness beyond all the unclean deeds of all the nations" (οἱ ἡγούμενοι δὲ τοῦ λαοῦ καὶ τῶν ἱερέων πολλὰ ἠσέβησαν καὶ ἠνόμησαν ὑπὲρ πάσας τὰς ἀκαθαρσίας πάντων τῶν ἐθνῶν). "They mocked his messengers and . . . scoffed at his prophets" (αὐτοὶ δὲ ἐξεμυκτήρισαν ἐν τοῖς ἀγγέλοις αὐτοῦ . . . ἐκπαίζοντες τοὺς προφήτας αὐτοῦ.[10] The point of 1 Esdras is how the evil deeds of Judah's leadership, as opposed to the godliness of Josiah (1:23), set the people of God on a path toward exile as a form of punishment.

But as the exile is at God's command, so too is the return under Cyrus (2:3–4). Upon their return, the Judahites vowed to rebuild the temple (5:44) and sacrifice "in accordance with the directions in the book of Moses the man of God" (5:49; LXX v. 48, ἀκολούθως τοῖς ἐν τῇ Μωυσέως βίβλῳ τοῦ ἀνθρώπου τοῦ θεοῦ διηγορευμένοις; see also 7:6–15). The returnees were in fact quite scrupulous in keeping the law in great detail. Ezra is described as possessing "great knowledge, so that he omitted nothing from the law of the Lord or the commandments, but taught all Israel all the ordinances and judgments" (8:7; πολλὴν ἐπιστήμην περιεῖχεν εἰς τὸ μηδὲν παραλιπεῖν τῶν ἐκ τοῦ νόμου κυρίου καὶ ἐκ τῶν ἐντολῶν διδάξαι τὸν πάντα Ισραηλ πάντα τὰ δικαιώματα καὶ τὰ κρίματα). This sentiment should probably be contrasted to Ezra 7:10, where Ezra is said merely to "devote himself to seek after and observe the law" (LXX: ἔδωκεν ἐν καρδίᾳ αὐτοῦ ζητῆσαι τὸν νόμον καὶ ποιεῖν). In any event, such scrupulousness must be maintained "so that wrath may not come upon the kingdom of the king and his sons" (8:21; ἕνεκα τοῦ μὴ γενέσθαι ὀργὴν εἰς τὴν βασιλείαν τοῦ βασιλέως καὶ τῶν υἱῶν).

It seems, however, that these warnings to maintain legal precision must be understood within a covenantal framework. The heart of that framework may be found in 8:74–80 (LXX vv. 71–77).

> O Lord, I am ashamed and confounded before your face. For our sins have risen higher than our heads, and our mistakes have mounted up to heaven from the times of our fathers, and we are in great sin to this day. And because of the sins of our fathers we with our kindred and our kings and our priests were given over to the kings of the earth, to the sword and exile and plundering, in shame until this day. And now in some measure mercy has come to us from you (καὶ νῦν κατὰ πόσον τι ἐγενήθη ἡμῖν ἔλεος παρὰ σοῦ), O Lord, to leave us a root and a name in your holy place, and to uncover a light for us in the house of the Lord our God, and to give us food in the time of our servitude. Even in our bondage we were not forsaken by our Lord (καὶ ἐν τῷ δουλεύειν ἡμᾶς οὐκ ἐγκατελείφθμεν ὑπὸ κυρίου ἡμῶν). . . .

---

[10] All translations of apocryphal material are taken from the NRSV.

The pattern is well-known from the Hebrew Bible itself: sin leads to captivity/punishment, but mercy is to follow. The transgression that followed God's mercy, intermarriage (8:82–90), is therefore a cause for great shame which prompted "confession, weeping and lying on the ground before the temple" (8:91). It also prompted Ezra to lead the people in an oath to put away foreign wives (8:93) and "to offer rams in expiation of their error" (εἰς ἐξιλασμὸν κριοὺς ὑπὲρ τῆς ἀγνοίας αὐτῶν; 9:20). We have, in other words, transgression by the people of God, but for which there is a means of rectifying their position before God. Despite the disobedience of their fathers, God has mercy and leaves a "root." Continued transgression is dealt with by means of contrite confession, an oath to follow the law scrupulously, and sacrifice for the "expiation of their error."

The general picture presented in 1 Esdras, as it speaks to the topic at hand, is not in any way surprising. It is the pattern demonstrated time and again in the pages of the Hebrew Scriptures. God has chosen a people for himself. If they sin, he will punish but not forsake them. They are his by election and they, or at least a "root" or remnant, will remain so. Their own efforts, whether they are confession, oaths, or sacrifice, pertain to those who are already in, not the outsiders seeking entrance.

The temptation, however, to understand this pattern on essentially a personal level, i.e., how individual Jews had their own sins expiated, should be guarded against. One of the central themes of the book is the restoration of the temple, which reaffirms the relationship between an elect people and a saving God in their own land.[11] This is likely at least one reason why there is no mention of Nehemiah's efforts in rebuilding the city walls, a fact that also helps explain Nehemiah's relative unimportance in the book mentioned above. This is also where the story of the three bodyguards takes us. Darius seeks to know "what is strongest." It is Zerubbabel's answer to the question that prompts Darius to release the people: "Great is truth, and strongest of all" (4:41). This is no mere contest of wits. For 1 Esdras, Zerubbabel's answer is the means by which the Israelites are permitted to return and rebuild the temple. This is the focus of this curious story, and it is a significant indication as to the covenantal purpose of the book as a whole.

2. Additions to Daniel: Song of the Three, Susanna, Bel and the Dragon

These three texts are brief additions to the canonical book of Daniel. One general theme they share is the behavior of the faithful in Babylon, which is

---

[11] Gardner, "Purpose and Date," 21.

a theme that, at least in the abstract, may hold some promise for the purpose of the present volume. It is perhaps in the context of a non-covenantal setting that the covenantal relationship between Yahweh and his people can be emphasized. Nevertheless, there is little of great importance that will advance the discussion, although some salient points surface here and there.

The Song of the Three recounts the prayer uttered by Azariah (Abednego) and the song sung by the three men (Shadrach, Meshach, and Abednego) as they walked about in the fire (Pr Azar 1:1). The biblical trigger for this story is the fiery furnace of Dan 3:22–30, and the contents of this book would have occurred between their falling into the furnace in Dan 3:23 and Nebuchad-nezzar's order for them to come out in 3:26.

Azariah's prayer (1:1–22) is quite surprising in the context. It is no prayer for help or protection as one might expect, nor is it praise to God for not being harmed. It is rather praise for God's just judgments: he has brought Israel into exile on account of their sin and lawlessness (1:6). But, as we have seen in 1 Esdras, the covenant God is asked to act justly yet one more time, not to judge further but to save. Azariah appeals to the covenant with the patriarchs (1:12–13) as the basis for Israel's eventual deliverance from Babylon.

> For your name's sake (διὰ τὸ ὄνομά σου) do not give us up forever, and do not annul your covenant. And do not withdraw your mercy from us, for the sake of Abraham your beloved (δι' Αβρααμ τὸν ἠγαπημένον) and for the sake of your servant Isaac and Israel your holy one (1:11–12).[12]

At this point Azariah laments that the proper means by which God's mercy may be dispensed are missing. There are no princes, prophets, or leaders outside of native soil, nor are there burnt offerings, sacrifices, oblations, or incense (v. 15) apart from the temple. What they do have, however, is a contrite heart which may be accepted as an ersatz sacrifice. Yet with a contrite heart and a humble spirit may they be accepted, *as though it were* with burnt offerings of rams and bulls, and with tens of thousands of fat lambs (v. 16).

It is not the case that the writer expresses here the unimportance of these typical means of re-establishing a proper relationship with God. His purpose is not to subvert Jewish identity.[13] What he is saying is that even in the absence of these vital means, God is still "connected" to his people by virtue of the covenant (v. 11), which will not change. They will, therefore, *as a people* not be abandoned because of what individuals have done. Their election remains sure, i.e., they (the people) will not be given up utterly (v.

---

[12] A similar plea may be found in *T. Mos.* 4.

[13] I do not think, for example, that the writer means to communicate to the reader the "spiritualization" of sacrifice as an advance over mere literalism, as Metzger suggests (*Introduction*, 104).

11). But it is incumbent upon these covenant people to make a humble and contrite move toward God, not to "get in" but precisely because they already are in.

Moreover, as with 1 Esdras, we should not understand such an admonition on a purely personal level. Although it is true that humility and a contrite heart are expressed by individuals, the focus of this prayer is certainly national, i.e., the return from Babylon. This is one significant difference between the apocryphal book and the story of the fiery furnace in Daniel 3. In the latter, the preservation of the three men results in the vindication of God and the promotion of the three (Dan 3:28–30). But here, it is the return to the land that will manifest plainly God's continued maintenance of his covenant faithfulness. In this respect, it is hard to miss the symbolism of the fire. The release of Azariah and his two companions from the fire represents Israel's release from Babylon. This is why the prayer from the very start focuses the reader's attention on Israel's collective deliverance from Babylon rather than on the individual deliverance of the three men, which one might expect. Azariah, after all, really has nothing to be contrite about.[14] He is not in the fire because of his lawlessness. If anything, the exact opposite is the case. He finds himself in his present circumstance because of his unwavering commitment to worship the true God rather than an image of gold (see Dan 3:1–18). Azariah's prayer, therefore, should be understood not on the level of the personal deliverance of the three, but on the covenantal/nationalistic level. This is what the author means in v. 20 (LXX 343): "Deliver *us* [both the three and Israel as a whole] in accordance with your marvelous works and bring glory to your name, O Lord" (καὶ ἐξελοῦ ἡμᾶς κατὰ τὰ θαυμάσιά σου καὶ δὸς δόξας τῷ ὀνόματί σου, κύριε).

There is more at work in this prayer than "God helps those who pray," as might seem to be the case on the surface. God gives glory to his name by maintaining his covenantal promises to the patriarchs on behalf of his people as a whole. The point is made once again at the end of the song, in v. 66.

---

[14] G. W. E. Nickelsburg correctly observes that "the contents of the prayer hardly fit the young man's present predicament" (*Jewish Literature between the Bible and the Mishnah* [Philadelphia: Fortress, 1981], 28). He concludes that the prayer is a "previously existent composition," thus implying that it was simply inserted in its present context, perhaps not very wisely. This is a dubious assumption. Moreover, irrespective of its (hypothetical) point of origin, the purpose of the prayer in the present context cannot be dismissed as a by-product of poor editing. Certainly C. Moore's confident pronouncement that the prayer and the song "were independently circulating works, originally having no relationship whatsoever to their present context" seems to hinge on his own notions of how the parts of the book ought to fit together (*Daniel, Esther and Jeremiah: The Additions* [AB 44; Garden City: Doubleday, 1977] 7; see also 26, 40, 63–65). In Moore's view, the present form of the text would be the result of, not surprisingly, a somewhat inept editor.

Bless the Lord, Hananiah, Azariah, and Mishael; sing praise to him and highly exalt him forever. For he has rescued us from Hades (ἡμᾶς ἐξ ᾅδου) and saved us from the power of death (χειρὸς θανάτου), and delivered us from the midst of the burning fiery furnace (καμίνου καιομένης φλογός); from the midst of the fire he has delivered us.

Hades is not simply a figurative description of the fiery furnace, but also a reference to Babylon, the place of death. God has delivered us – the three and the Israelites – from two types of Hades: Babylon and the furnace. The ambiguity is intentional, as it forces the reader to see this story as a metaphor of national deliverance, an act which is founded upon God's unchanging covenantal character as seen in his promise to the patriarchs.

Susanna[15] is essentially the story of a holy woman who maintains her trust in God's justice against the false accusations of two corrupt Israelite elders. As with the other additions to Daniel, the setting is Babylon. As the Prayer of Azariah and Bel and the Dragon (see below) concern the opposition of the Babylonians against God's people, Susanna speaks of another situation, that of corruption on the part of the people of God themselves while on foreign soil. Despite the Israelite identity of the adversaries, the similarities with the other Daniel additions is obvious. Susanna is an Israelite who "feared the Lord" (v. 2; φοβουμένη τὸν κύριον) to the point where she would rather resist sin, thus falling into the hands of the ungodly, than sin against God by giving in to their heinous plan. To be sure, the story comes to a resolution in the wise and compassionate intervention of Daniel, who foils the plot of the elders (vv. 44–59), and this climax of the story should give us a clue as to at least part of the story's focus. We can safely presume that Daniel's just behavior was intended to capture the reader's imagination.[16]

There is little in the way of specifics to be gleaned from Susanna that advances significantly our understanding of Second Temple Judaism other than a general observation or two, similar to what we have seen above with the Prayer of Azariah. Even on enemy soil, Israel is expected to obey God. His people are to resist sin, even to the point of death (as does Susanna), and punish offenders according to the law of Moses (a process instigated by Daniel; see vv. 60–62 and the citation of Exod 23:7 in v. 53). Even in Babylon God's people are to behave as though they were in the land, in

---

[15] On the complex relationship between the OG and TH for this text, see M. J. Steussy, *Gardens in Babylon: Narrative and Faith in the Greek Legends of Daniel* (SBLDS 141; Atlanta: Scholars, 1993) 101–43; H. Engel, *Die Susanna-Erzählung: Einleitung, Übersetzung und Kommentar zum Septuaginta-Text und zur Theodotion-Bearbeitung* (Göttingen: Vandenhoeck & Ruprecht, 1985).

[16] I agree with Moore that Susanna is likely the central focus of the book, although I would not want to dismiss Daniel's role as merely peripheral, as Moore seems to do (*Daniel, Esther and Jeremiah*, 90–91). Verse 64 is especially clear on this point: "And from that day onward Daniel had a great reputation among the people" (Δανιηλ ἐγένετο μέγας ἐνώπιον τοῦ λαοῦ ἀπὸ τῆς ἡμέρας ἐκείνας καὶ ἐπέκεινα).

accordance with God's law. Without wishing to read too much into this short story, the theme of moral rectitude in accordance with the law of Moses suggests an assumed covenantal perspective from which to view the behavior of both Susanna and Daniel. Thus, the story is more than simply an abstract call to "do the right thing." Neither is it intended to highlight sexual purity for its own sake, and it is most certainly not a story of a "strong woman."

It is a story of *Israel* in captivity, a people faced with constant temptation to follow the ignoble path of spiritual impurity, perhaps on pains of physical harm. Do not the words of vv. 22–23 remind us of the words of the three men in Dan 3:16–18, who were likewise innocent of wrongdoing, when faced with the option of sure death in the fire, or of innocent Daniel's (Dan 6:22) quiet resolve to disobey Darius's order, even though it meant certain death in the lion's den?

> I am completely trapped. For if I do this, it will mean death for me; if I do not, I cannot escape your hands. I choose not to do it; I will fall into your hands, rather than sin in the sight of the Lord. (Οἶδα ὅτι ἐὰν πράξω τοῦτο, θάνατός μοί ἐστι, καὶ ἐὰν μὴ πράξω, οὐκ ἐκφεύξομαι τὰς χεῖρας ὑμῶν· κάλλιον δέ με μὴ πράξασαν ἐμπεσεῖν εἰς τὰς χεῖρας ὑμῶν ἢ ἁμαρτεῖν ἐνώπιον κυρίου.)

Without wanting to paint these stories with the same broad brushstrokes, there is certainly a theme that unites the additions to Daniel. God is with *his people* even in Babylon. He is always with them, not because an occasional hero proves himself or herself worthy, but because Israel belongs to him. The examples of Susanna, Daniel, and the others serve to provide models of proper behavior for God's people living in a pagan (Hellenistic?) environment, but not simply to be good people individually, but to behave in such a way as is worthy of the covenant with which they as a people have been entrusted. Again, this is a long way from saying that Susanna proves or disproves Sanders's thesis. We can say, however, that it is in general consistent with such a thesis.

The third addition to Daniel, Bel and the Dragon, is actually two stories in one.[17] The first deals with the Daniel's proof that the idol of Bel, the chief god of the Babylonian pantheon, did not eat the food left for him each evening, but that it as eaten secretively by the priests and their families. The second has Daniel exposing not an idol, but a live "god," a snake (dragon, δράκων). He kills the snake, is threatened with death, and receives a

---

[17] How these two stories came to be included in one book is not known. It is, however, simply an assumption to insist that they were "originally" separate stories brought together for some unknown purpose. Moreover, it is further doubtful that the story of the dragon itself consists of three shorter stories (killing of the dragon, lion's den, Habakkuk's meal) that were "originally separate tales" (Moore, *Daniel, Esther and Jeremiah*, 121–22). Any such explanation would have to make some attempt to account for why the stories were brought together in the first place.

miraculous provision of food from the hands of none other than the prophet Habakkuk. Like Susanna, one of the themes of the book is certainly to highlight Daniel's sagacity[18] in exposing the utter absurdity of the notion that the gods of Babylon are in any way real; the idol Bel does not eat, and the dragon-god can be killed with boiled cakes of pitch, fat, and hair. Moreover, like the other additions to Daniel as well as the biblical Daniel, these are stories of the vindication of God's people amid hostile situations. Hence, the conclusions drawn above can be generally applied to this book as well.

In the story of Bel, Daniel steadfastly worships the true God even though King Cyrus worships the idol. Daniel is a companion of Cyrus and had earned the respect of, presumably, important members of the king's court (vv. 1–2). Daniel's acceptance by the Babylonians, as is the case with the canonical book of Daniel, provides a tension: will Daniel live like a Babylonian or like a Jew? The answer the book provides is that being a Jew means living like one everywhere and in any circumstance, not just in persecution (Susanna, Song of the Three), but when things are going well. David challenges the power structure of which he himself is a part, which supports his own privileged status, and chooses rather to follow God, whom he reveres (v. 5).

Daniel's exposé of the Bel idol results in the just punishment of the priests and their families and the destruction of the idol and the temple (vv. 21–22). But Daniel's steadfastness extends to times when the outcome is not so favorable. Perhaps exposing an idol is one thing, but killing a snake worshiped as a god was apparently not taken so lightly. Daniel's boldness in this regard results in a second stint in the lion's den (see Dan 6). Here, too, Daniel is to live as a Jew no less than at any other time. The puzzling element in this story of Habakkuk's meal (vv. 33–39) cannot be fully unraveled here, but it seems to serve at least one purpose. The chronological problem of having Habakkuk, the late 7th century prophet, present a meal to Daniel toward the end of the latter's life (the Persian Cyrus ended Babylon rule in 539) has been noted by most commentators as a gross anachronism. This is certainly true, but I wonder how much is gained by simply dismissing it as such, as if the ancient author would not have known this or be unconcerned by it.

There is more here than dischronology. For example, M. Steussy correctly remarks on the thematic and lexical overlap between Habakkuk and Bel and the Dragon, thus providing a rationale for the reference to Habakkuk. Specifically, it is "Habakkuk's polemic against idolatry [that] suits the Daniel story theme of unmasking false gods."[19] I agree with Steussy's observation, but this does not answer fully the matter of chronology. My suggestion is that this overt appeal to the past, which any ancient reader would certainly have

---

[18] A number of commentators refer to the Bel episode as a "detective story."

[19] M. Steussy, *Gardens in Babylon*, 160 (see also 156–63 for a more detailed discussion of the lexical connections).

recognized as posing a chronological problem, is not so much a miraculous story in the abstract, but an object lesson on behalf of Diaspora Jews of the Second Temple period. As I have suggested with the other additions to Daniel, the protagonist of the story is to be understood at least on one level as representing the people as a whole.[20] In this sense, the lesson of the story of the dragon is that help in *present* circumstances comes from appealing to the *past*, a principle that is concretely demonstrated in introducing Habakkuk, of all people, to the story. Rather than being a "later interpolation" and having "no vital connection with the rest of the narrative,"[21] the reference to Habakkuk forces the reader to ponder why such a chronological tension would have been created in the first place. The reason as I see it is to demonstrate that the same God of the past is present in the Diaspora. This would have served as another reminder to the people of God that they are vitally connected now to the God who acted in the past. In other words, there is at least implicit in the appeal to Habakkuk a covenantal understanding of Israel's Diaspora setting, and as such supports generally the notion that being a Jew during the Diaspora would have been viewed in terms of a conscious connection to the past.

At the very least, the perspective on Bel and the Dragon, and on the additions to Daniel as a whole, suggested here is worth introducing to the general discussion of "getting in and staying in" raised by Sanders. Being a Jew on enemy turf meant being a faithful Torah-keeper, which in the case of these stories can be boiled down to this: worship the true God whatever the circumstances. Remain true to him and he will deliver you, certainly a common theme in Hellenistic Judaism (e.g., *Testament of Moses, Testament of Job*, 2 Macc 6:7–7:42). In striving toward this end, these stories also remind the people of God that obedient faith in God is not only required by him, but is engendered by him as well. Such faith also serves the purpose of connecting the Jews of the Second Temple period to the Israelites of biblical times. The implicit message is that *God's* faithfulness to his people remains intact, and that provides the proper perspective from which to view the *people's* faith which God demands of them.

---

[20] To take this one step further, I agree with others that the reference to Bel and the dragon are "judaized" versions of the battle between Marduk and Tiamat as told in the *Enuma Elish* (Moore, *Daniel, Esther and Jeremiah*, 123–25; F. Zimmermann, "Bel and the Dragon," *VT* 8 [1958]: 438–40.) Hence, not only would Daniel represent the people, but the subtle appeal to the primordial creation struggle between Bel and the dragon would represent the Babylonian religious system as a whole.

[21] W. Davies, *Bel and the Dragon, APOT* 1.663, cited approvingly by Moore (*Daniel, Esther and Jeremiah*, 145).

3. Additions to Esther

As Metzger and others have observed, the purpose of the six additions to Esther (labeled A through F) was likely to add an overt religious element to the canonical Esther, in which God is not mentioned.[22] The fact that the additions and the canonical book do not coincide in a number of details, which contributes to their doubtful historical value, raises some question as to why the problem of God's absence was handled so sloppily. Added to this is the very difficult subject of the relationship between the three extant Greek versions of Esther (LXX, the so-called "alpha-text," and Josephus' version) and their Hebrew *Vorlagen*.[23] These otherwise interesting topics will not enter into the discussion here, as our concern is the religious themes contained in these additions.

With the book of Esther and its additions, we find ourselves once again in a situation characterized by fierce opposition to Judaism by an oppressive rule, in this case Persia. This is a theme we have seen in the additions to Daniel. It is precisely because the additions to Esther are geared toward adding overt religious content to the canonical book that we can catch a glimpse of the religious mind set that engendered these additions.[24] This is not to say that we will find here a systematic or well-rounded picture of the types of things called for in this essay, but the prospects look promising at the outset. The additions attempt to draw out (create) the religious dimension of the book of Esther, and so give us some insight into how those responsible

---

[22] B. Metzger, *Introduction*, 61–62. See also Nickelsburg, *Jewish Literature*, 173; Nickelsburg, "The Bible Rewritten and Expanded," *The Writings of the Second Temple Period* (CRINT 2/2; ed. M. Stone; Philadelphia: Fortress, 1984), 137; H. Bardtke, *Zusätze zu Esther* (*JSHRZ* 1/1: Historisch und legendarische Erzählungen; Gütersloh: Gerd Mohn, 1973), 20–21; Moore, *Daniel, Esther and Jeremiah*, 153. Of course, this does not address the question of why Esther itself has such little "traditional" biblical content about God. On this question, see the essay by R. Gordis, which discusses the issue in general and posits an interesting solution: Esther was written by a Jewish author as a chronicle of the Persian (Gentile) court ("Religion, Wisdom and History in the Book of Esther – A New Solution to an Ancient Crux," *JBL* 100 [1981]: 359–88).

[23] See the recent study, K. Jobes, *The Alpha-Text of Esther: Its Character and Relationship to the Massoretic Text* (SBLDS 153; Atlanta: Scholars, 1996). See also C. V. Dorothy, *The Books of Esther: Structure, Genre and Textual Integrity* (JSOTSup 187; Sheffield: Sheffield Academic Press, 1997) and M. V. Fox, *The Redaction of the Books of Esther: On Reading Composite Texts* (SBLMS 40; Atlanta: Scholars, 1991). On the possible interpretive and ideological bases for the differences between the alpha-text and the LXX, see Fox, *Redaction*, 71–89.

[24] As with all of the apocryphal material treated in this essay, the additions to Esther are difficult to date precisely. Add Esth 11:1 mentions a certain Lysimachus, resident of Jerusalem, who translated the book of Esther in 114–113 B.C.E. It is speculated by a number of commentators that he is a likely source for at least some of the additions.

for the additions understood the relationship between God and his people while in duress.

A number of the elements of these additions are worth highlighting for our purposes. The first addition (A, 11:2–12:6) was inserted into Esther before Esth 1:1. It contains Mordecai's dream (explained in Add Esth 10:4–13), which revealed to him the impending crisis of Haman's charge against the Jews and "what God had determined to do" (Add Esth 11:12; τί ὁ θεὸς βεβούλευται ποιῆσαι). Mordecai was apparently a man of some importance, since he was "serving in the court of the king" (Add Esth 11:3; θεραπεύων ἐν τῇ τοῦ αὐλῇ τοῦ βασιλέως), and this insertion no doubt intended to explain how Mordecai could be sitting at the king's gate (Esth 2:19) to overhear the guards discussing their plans to assassinate Xerxes (Esth 2:21–23).[25] The point of the dream is that God is with his people and he is very involved to ensure that they will not be annihilated. Despite their exile, which they deserve (Add Esth 14:6–7), they remain his "inheritance" (Add Esth 13:17; κλῆρος).

A notion clearly consistent with covenantal nomism comes across in additions C and D (13:8–14:19 and 15:1–16). Israel is God's "portion" redeemed by him from Egypt (13:16; μερίς). This is part of Mordecai's prayer to God, in which he calls people to remember "all the works of the Lord" (13:8; πάντα τὰ ἔργα κυρίου). The appeal to the past for a proper perspective on Israel's present situation is something we have seen above in Bel and the Dragon. After recounting to God Haman's intentions, Mordecai puts his trust in the "God of Abraham" to prevent Haman from destroying "the inheritance that has been yours from the beginning" (13:15; τὴν ἐξ ἀρχῆς κληρονομίαν σου). This beginning is the Exodus, referred to in v. 16, the concrete event that forms the basis for the confidence in Mordecai's prayer. Israel simply *is* God's people. Mordecai's prayer is that God act accordingly.

So, too, is Esther's prayer (14:1–19). Like her older cousin Mordecai, she appeals to God's past actions.

> Ever since I was born I have heard in the tribe of my family that you, O Lord, took Israel out of all the nations, and our ancestors from among all their forebears, for an everlasting inheritance, and that you did for them all that you promised (v. 5). (ἐγὼ ἤκουον ἐκ γενετῆς μου ἐν φυλῇ πατριᾶς μου ὅτι σύ, κύριε, ἔλαβες τὸν Ισραηλ ἐκ πάντων τῶν ἐθνῶν καὶ τοὺς πατέρας ἡμῶν ἐκ πάντων τῶν προγόνων αὐτῶν εἰς κληρονομίαν αἰώνιον καὶ ἐποίησας αὐτοῖς ὅσα ἐλάλησας.)

It is this that forms the proper backdrop for her confession of national sin in vv. 6–7 mentioned above. But despite what they deserve, Esther appeals essentially to God's honor as the basis for deliverance. She pleads that God

---

[25] See C. Moore, "Esther Revisited: An Examination of Esther Studies over the Past Decade," *Biblical and Related Studies Presented to Sam Iwry* (ed. A. Kort and S. Morschauser; Winona Lake: Eisenbrauns, 1985), 164.

not surrender his scepter or allow the people to be mocked, which would be mockery against God (v. 11). He is to make *himself* known as "King of the gods and Master of all dominion" (v. 12; βασιλεῦ τῶν θεῶν καὶ πάσης ἀρχῆς ἐπικρατῶν). In other words, Esther's prayer is based on her confidence that the annihilation of Israel is an affront to God. Esther understands that it is contrary to *God's character* to let anything happen to his people.

The appeal in vv. 15–19 shifts from national deliverance to that of Esther's personal empowerment to face the king with eloquence and courage in an effort to get him to reverse his decree to destroy the Jews. And here the basis of Esther's appeal shifts as well. She emphasizes her own piety, her own zeal in living a consistently godly life: she abhors the fineries of the wicked and the bed of the uncircumcised; she remains humble despite her high position; she has refrained from cavorting with the enemy or honoring the king's pagan feasts. This list of virtues, however, has little to do with our topic, let alone do they constitute an argument against covenantal nomism. The question here is neither one of "getting in" nor "staying in" but of Esther's fitness to be the instrument of God to confront the king. She is asking God to honor her piety in order to perform this specific task. And this is precisely what happens. Despite being "frozen with fear" (15:5; ἀπεστενωμένη ἀπὸ τοῦ φόβου), she is able to confront Artaxerxes successfully.

Add Esth 16:1–24 (addition E) is the second letter (the first letter is addition B, 13:1–7) included in the additions. Whereas the first letter indicates the degree of hostility to which the Jews were subjected, the second letter is in effect the acknowledgment by Artaxerxes that God "rules over all things" (ὁ πάντα δυναστεύων θεός) and has delivered the Jews (16:21).[26] After a lengthy denunciation of Haman (16:1–14), Artaxerxes affirms a number of things.

> But we find that the Jews, who were consigned to annihilation by this thrice-accursed man, are not evildoers, but are governed by the most righteous laws and are children of the living God, most high, the most mighty, who has directed the kingdom both for us and for our ancestors in the most excellent order (16:15–16). (ἡμεῖς δὲ τοὺς τοῦ τρισαλιτηρίου παραδεδομένους εἰς ἀφανισμὸν Ἰουδαίους εὑρίσκομεν οὐ κακούργους ὄντας, δικαιοτάτοις δὲ πολιτευομένους νόμοις, ὄντας δὲ υἱοὺς τοῦ ὑψίστου μεγίστου ζῶντος θεοῦ τοῦ κατευθύνοντος ἡμῖν τε καὶ τοῖς προγόνοις ἡμῶν τὴν βασιλείαν ἐν τῇ καλλίστῃ διαθέσει [LXX vv. 14–15].)

This confession is more than an acknowledgment of Israel's "right to exist." It is rather a demonstration to the readers of these additions of the final outcome of God's plan. Their covenant God is not merely interested in

---

[26] I do not think that such a Jewish confession put into the mouth of a Persian king is an indication of the author "unintentionally" showing his hand, nor is it "secondary" (Moore, *Daniel, Esther and Jeremiah*, 237). The confession was certainly put into the mouth of the Persian king, but it was quite intentional for the author's purpose, as discussed below.

Israel's own well-being, but in having the nations as a whole know the true God, a theme enunciated clearly as early, for example, as Moses' confrontation with Pharaoh (e.g., Exod 6:7; 7:5, 17, etc.). Israel will be used by God to bring glory to himself throughout the world.[27] In keeping with my comments above on the Daniel additions, Esther's behavior symbolizes the behavior that the people as a whole ought to have among the nations. They are to be a holy and pure people in order to proclaim to the world the true God. There is more at stake, therefore, in "staying in" than simply maintaining a people of God. Rather, these people will play a role in a broader campaign. The discussion of the importance of being and remaining a Jew, in other words, cannot be considered simply on the personal level, although I am not suggesting that should be ignored. But from the point of view of the overarching plan of God to be acknowledged by the nations, the continued existence of Israel is of central importance. That "the people of God" will remain does not come seriously into question. In other words, God's election of a people (getting in) must succeed for the sake of God's honor, which will be ultimately vindicated when the world at large, like Artaxerxes, acknowledges him.

4. Jannes and Jambres

We move now for the remainder of this essay to the pseudepigraphal texts.[28] The help that *Jannes and Jambres* will give us in our discussion is at best minimal. This is for two reasons. First, the text is so fragmentary that little of confidence can be said.[29] Second, the date of origin for both the tradition and the written text are extremely difficult to ascertain. Few deny the Jewish roots of either, but it seems that the present form of the text is, at least to a certain extent, a product of Christian reflection.[30] If this is true, it has little if any relevance for the topic before us.

---

[27] The broader implications of what God is about to do for the Jews is already hinted at in the "cosmic" overtones (dragons, cosmic upheaval) of Mordecai's dream (addition A). See Moore, *Daniel, Esther and Jeremiah*, 181.

[28] All English references to the Pseudepigrapha will be taken from the translations in J. Charlesworth, *Old Testament Pseudepigrapha* (vol. 2; Garden City: Doubleday, 1985).

[29] For the details of the textual history, see S. Gero, "Parerga to 'The Book of Jannes and Jambres'," *JSP* 9 (1991): 67–85; A. Pietersma, "The Apocryphon of Jannes and Jambres," *Congress Volume: Leuvan 1989* (ed. J. A. Emerton; Leiden: E. J. Brill, 1991), 383–95; A. Pietersma, "Jannes and Jambres," *ABD* 3.638–40; A. Pietersma and R. T. Lutz, "Jannes and Jambres," *OTP* 2.427–36.

[30] The Latin text dates to the 11th century A.D. The Greek fragments are 3rd to 4th century A.D. (see *OTP* 2.431–32). The earliest Hebrew reference seems to be in CD 5:17–19 (but see Pietersma, "Apocryphon," 384–5). The earliest Greek reference is 2 Tim 3:8. The earliest

Any conclusions that could be drawn from this text would have to be so qualified and tentative as to be of very little benefit. Even assuming (1) the Jewish origin of the tradition, and (2) that the Greek and Latin texts are not "tainted" with Christian influence, it is still the case that the text is quite fragmentary. As Pietersma and Lutz put it, "The fragmentary nature of our text makes it hazardous, if not impossible, to arrive at any definitive conclusions. . . . We may have no more than a general condemnation of idolatry, necromancy included, which is well attested in early literature of both religions [Jewish and Christian]."[31] We really have very little idea who wrote it or for what purpose, nor do we even have a clear impression of the details of the story, since it is preserved only in fragmentary form (although *OTP* 2.430–31 does provide a helpful story line). In view of these many variables, it seems the wisest course of action not to press this text into service for interacting with Sanders's thesis regarding covenantal nomism.

5. *Ps.-Philo's* Book of Biblical Antiquities

This pseudepigraphal text is worthy of closer attention. As mentioned above, Sanders does not engage this text, but this is likely due to considerations of space and the date of *Biblical Antiquities*.[32] Despite the fact that this document was likely composed after the rise of Christianity, it is nevertheless a thoroughly Jewish work[33] that provides some helpful insights into how Judaism was understood by this writer.

I would like to begin this discussion by providing several quotations from *L.A.B.* These are not presented as an exhaustive or even systematic collection

---

reference to a book "Jannes and Jambres" is in Origen's Matthew commentary (3rd century A.D.). On the possibility of the 2nd century A.D. pagan author Numenius knowing *Jannes and Jambres* see *OTP* 2.428. On the possibility of the Jewish historian Artapanus (100 B.C.) being responsible for the story, see *OTP* 2.427–8; 433–4. On the possibility of the book being of the genre of a Christian confession, see *OTP* 2.433; 435.

[31] *OTP* 2.434.

[32] The date of composition of *L.A.B.* is usually judged to be the second half of the 1st century A.D., perhaps before the destruction of Jerusalem (D. J. Harrington, "Pseudo-Philo," *OTP* 2.299; see also F. Murphy, *Pseudo-Philo: Rewriting the Bible* [New York: Oxford University Press, 1993], 6; C. Perrot and P. M. Bogaert, *Pseudo-Philon: Les Antiquités Bibliques* [vol. 2; Paris: Éditions du Cerf, 1976], 66–74). H. Jacobson, however, rehearses the arguments for a pre-A.D. 70 date and finds them wanting. He prefers a date somewhere between A.D. 70 and the middle of the second century (*A Commentary on Pseudo-Philo's* Liber Antiquitatum Biblicarum, *With Latin Text and English Translation* [AGJU 31; Leiden: E. J. Brill, 1996], 1.199–210).

[33] Harrington has argued the consensus position that the Latin manuscripts (11th–15th centuries) are translations from Greek, which are themselves dependent on a Hebrew *Vorlage* ("The Original Language of Pseudo-Philo's *Liber Antiquitatum Biblicarum*," *HTR* 63 (1970): 503–14; see also *OTP* 2.298–9; *ABD*, 5.344–5).

of passages around a central theme, nor are they intended as proof texts to support a particular point of view. They serve, rather, to form an impression of the types of things the author of *L.A.B.* considers descriptive of the relation between God and his people. They are a way of entering into the discussion rather than settling matters.[34]

9:4 Amram's trust in God over against Pharaoh's edict that the Israelites not have children
For God will not abide in his anger, nor will he forget his people forever, nor will he cast forth the race of Israel in vain upon the earth; nor did he establish a covenant with our fathers in vain. . . .

9:7–8 God's response to Amram's faith
Because Amram's plan is pleasing to me, and he has not put aside the covenant established between me and his fathers, so behold now he who will be born from him will serve me forever, and I will do marvelous things in the house of Jacob through him. . . . I will show him my covenant that no one has seen. And I will reveal to him my Law and statutes and judgments. . . .

11:1 The law is a light for Israel
I will give a light to the world and illumine their dwelling places and establish my covenant with the sons of men and glorify my people above all nations. For them I will bring out the eternal statutes that are for those in the light but for the ungodly a punishment.

13:10 A command regarding "the salvation of the souls of the people"
If they will walk in my ways, I will not abandon them but will have mercy on them always and bless their seed; and the earth will quickly yield its fruit, and there will be rains for their advantage, and it will not be barren. But I know for sure that they will make their ways corrupt and I will abandon them, and they will forget the covenants that I have established with their fathers; but nevertheless I will not forget them.

19:9 Moses' farewell speech
And you gave them the Law and statutes in which they might live and enter as sons of men. For who is the man who has not sinned against you? And unless your patience abides, how would your heritage be established, if you were not merciful to them? Or who will yet be born without sin? Now you will correct them for a time, but not in anger.

30:7 Deborah's speech
And behold now the LORD will take pity on you today, not because of you but because of his covenant that he established with your fathers and the oath that he has sworn not to abandon you forever. Know, however, that after my departure you will start sinning again until the end of your days. On account of this the LORD will work wonders among you and hand over your enemies into your hands. For our fathers are dead, but the God who established the covenant with them is life.

35:3 The angel explaining to Gideon the reason for Israel's oppression by the Midianites
. . . you have not been mindful of the commandments of God that those who were before you commanded you, so that you have come into the displeasure of your God. But he will have mercy, as no one else has mercy, on the race of Israel, though not on account of you but on account of those who have fallen asleep.

---

[34] All English quotations are from Harrington's translation ("Pseudo-Philo," *OTP* 2.304-77).

39:6 Jephthah's speech
You know that, while our leaders were still alive, they warned us to follow our Law. And Ammon and his sons turned the people from their way in which they walked, and they served foreign gods who would destroy them. Now therefore set your hearts on the Law of the LORD your God, and let us beg him together, and so we will fight against our enemies, trusting and hoping in the LORD that he will not deliver us up forever. Even if our sins be overabundant, still his mercy will fill the earth.

Again, my purpose here is not to isolate these passages from their contexts and construct an argument around them. The point still remains, however, that any attempt to explain the conception of Judaism in *L.A.B.* will have to account for passages such as those cited here. The umbrella under which these and other statements in *L.A.B.* are typically subsumed is the idea of the covenant. In my view this is entirely correct. Commentators routinely note how central the abiding, eternal, covenant is to the writer of *L.A.B.*, and these passages are among many that bear this out quite clearly. L. Cohn, whose seminal essay in 1898 brought *L.A.B.* to the attention of the scholarly world, sums up the matter nicely.

In all the speeches the same idea recurs again and again: God has chosen the people of Israel and has made his covenant with them for ever; if the children of Israel depart from God's ways and forget his covenant, he delivers them for a time into the hands of their enemies; but God is ever mindful of his covenant with the patriarchs; he always delivers the Israelites through leaders of his choice, and he will never entirely abandon them.[35]

The fact that Ps.-Philo puts such stress on the covenant certainly suggests that he felt the need to press the matter with his audience. As Levison argues, it seems that they were specifically in danger of abandoning the covenant for idols and false gods.[36] The text that both he and Murphy[37] adduce to show the writer's preoccupation with idols and false gods is *L.A.B.* 2:9. Ps.-Philo changes Gen 4:22, "Tubal-Cain made all kinds of bronze and iron tools [כָּל-חֹרֵשׁ נְחֹשֶׁת וּבַרְזֶל]" to refer to the beginning of idolatry: "And those inhabiting the earth began to make statues and to adore them."

The citations offered above not only highlight the covenant, but the importance of the law as well, which raises a logical question: What is the relationship between law and covenant in *L.A.B.*? Levison's excellent essay

---

[35] L. Cohn, "An Apocryphal Work Ascribed to Philo of Alexandria," *JQR* 10 (1898): 322. Cohn's view has found a firm foothold in the scholarly world, as can be seen by the frequency with which his position is cited. See Murphy, *Pseudo-Philo*, 244; J. R. Levison, "Torah and Covenant in Pseudo Philo's *Liber Antiquitatum Biblicarum*," *Bund und Tora: Zur theologischen Begriffsgeschichte in altertestamentlicher, frühjüdischer und urchristlicher Tradition* (ed. F. Avemarie and H. Lichtenberger; WUNT 92; Tübingen: Mohr [Siebeck], 1996), 116.

[36] J. R. Levison, *The Spirit in First Century Judaism* (AGJU 29; Leiden: E. J. Brill, 1997), 266–7; Levison, "Torah and Covenant," 120; 122.

[37] Murphy, *Pseudo-Philo*, 252.

is focused specifically on this question. He concludes, however, that law and covenant are essentially interchangeable, to the extent that "*entrance* into the covenant requires adherence to the Law."[38] But Ps.-Philo is certainly writing to Jews, so one might question whether "entrance" into the covenant is ever really the writer's concern. The example Levison adduces to support his position, 16:5, is not convincing. When Korah asks his seven sons to join in his plot against Moses, they respond as follows:

> Just as a painter does not produce a work of art unless he has been instructed beforehand, so we have received the Law of the Most Powerful that teaches us his way; and *we will not enter them except to walk in them*. Our father has not begotten us, but the Most Powerful has formed us. And now if we walk in his ways, we will be his sons. But if you are unbelieving, go your own way [emphasis mine].

The conversation here is among Israelites, those who are members of the covenant, not outsiders considering entrance requirements. The phrase "we will not enter them except to walk in them" is not about non-Israelites considering the question of "getting in" to the covenant, but Israelites who are already in and considering the responsibilities of that status. To rephrase the clause: "Being part of the covenant implies that we walk in its ways." In my view, Levison himself puts the matter much more accurately several pages later: "*adherents to the covenant* are required to abide by the Law."[39] With such a statement there can be no quarrel. Moreover, while it is true that *L.A.B.* refers occasionally to the relationship between the law and non-Israelites, very little if anything can be clearly gleaned as to the precise nature of that relationship.[40] At the very least, it must be admitted that *L.A.B.* is not prepared to give an answer to this question. And in any event, answering the question of the nations does not help us in understanding the relationship of the Israelites, God's covenant people, to the law.

Nickelsburg is much closer to the mark when he says that "election and covenantal status are fundamental to Pseudo-Philo's exposition," and that in *L.A.B.* we find the "affirmation of Israel's covenantal status."[41] The specific perspective Nickelsburg brings to this discussion further highlights the importance of covenant, and therefore the proper understanding of law, in *L.A.B.* Ps.-Philo seems to spend an inordinate amount of attention on the

---

[38] "Torah and Covenant," 122 (my emphasis).

[39] Ibid., 124; my emphasis.

[40] The information Ps.-Philo provides on this is ambiguous (Murphy, *Pseudo-Philo*, 229). T. L. Donaldson argues that whatever reference *L.A.B.* makes to the possibility of Gentile conversion is hypothetical, posed "simply as a justification for the condemnation of the wicked, displaying no interest at all in moving beyond the hypothetical" (*Paul and the Gentiles: Remapping the Apostle's Convictional World* [Minneapolis: Fortress, 1997], 59).

[41] G. W. E. Nickelsburg, "God and Bad Leaders in Pseudo-Philo's *Liber Antiquitatum Biblicarum*," in *Ideal Figures in Ancient Judaism: Profiles and Paradigms* (ed. G. W. E. Nickelsburg and J. J. Collins; SBLSCS 12; Chico: Scholars, 1980), 59.

period of the Judges. Significant portions of the OT have either been deleted or greatly abbreviated from his retelling. Apart from Judg 1:1–3:6, however, the book of Judges remains essentially intact (albeit with some revisions, variations, or replacement of some biblical stories with others).[42] Nickelsburg argues that the reason for this attention to the Judges is that the pattern of rebellion, punishment, repentance, and deliverance in these stories, particularly the role of the judges themselves, provided examples of covenant fidelity or infidelity to Ps.-Philo's readers.[43] In other words, examples from Israel's past were meant to inspire the present elect, covenant people, to covenant fidelity. This is why so much of *L.A.B.*, especially chaps. 22–65, recount how Israel "has not lived up to its side of the bargain."[44] It also helps explain why the book ends as abruptly as it does, with Saul's death in ch. 65. The message is, "Don't let this happen to you." This is not a book for outsiders, but insiders to the faith who are beset with challenges to their covenantal status, and who are warned not to turn away. But despite the trauma, precisely because they are God's covenant people, the *L.A.B.* strives to show that God will never completely abandon them. Ps.-Philo never ceases to remind his readers of the obligations God makes on them, but these obligations are nothing less than the special privilege of those who already enjoy covenant status. Covenant precedes law.

6. Jubilees

As mentioned above, *Jubilees* is the one work treated in this essay that Sanders has systematically incorporated into his own discussion on the nature of Second Temple Judaism.[45] This section of the essay will offer a summary and critique of Sanders's argument.

Sanders begins his argument by providing a large number of references in *Jubilees* that indicate the foundational importance of the concept of election/covenant for the author. It is this concept (Sanders argues) that forms the basis for discussing the theology of the book as a whole. Election is not the possession of a privileged few, but the gift of the covenant God to

---

[42] Ibid., 49. On the relevance of Judges as a narrative base as it relates to the author's notion of covenant and the land in *L.A.B.*, see B. Halpern-Amaru, *Rewriting the Bible: Land and Covenant in Postbiblical Jewish Literature* (Valley Forge: Trinity, 1994), 66–94.

[43] Ibid., 60–62; Murphy, *Pseudo-Philo*, 233–41.

[44] Murphy, *Pseudo-Philo*, 16.

[45] *PPJ*, 362–85. For a brief summary of the basic argument, see E. P. Sanders, "The Covenant as a Soteriological Category and the Nature of Salvation in Palestinian and Hellenistic Judaism," in *Jews, Greeks and Christians: Religious Cultures in Late Antiquity* (Fs. W. D. Davies; ed. R. Hamerton-Kelly and R. Scroggs; SJLA 21; Leiden: E. J. Brill, 1976), 15–17.

his people, the Israelites.[46] The importance of election may be seen in that it forms a frame for the book as a whole.

> Set your mind on everything which I shall tell you on this mountain, and write it in a book so that their descendants might see *that I have not abandoned them on account of all the evil which they have done to instigate transgression*[47] *of the covenant* which I am establishing between me and you today on Mt. Sinai for their descendants. And thus it will be, when all of these things happen to them, that they will know that I have been more righteous than they in all their judgments and deeds. And they will know that I have truly been with them (1:5).

> And Jubilees will pass *until Israel is purified* from all the sin of fornication, and defilement, and uncleanness, and sin and error. And they will *dwell in confidence* in all the land. And then it will not have any Satan or any evil (one). *And the land*[48] *will be purified from that time and forever* (50:5).

There are a number of other passages to which Sanders refers in an effort to buttress his view of the centrality of election/covenant for the author of *Jubilees* including: 1:17ff., 25, 28; 16:18, 26; 19:18; 21:24; 22:11ff., 27; 24:29; 25:3; 33:20; 36:6.[49]

But election is not all there is to *Jubilees*. "Israel's role in the covenant relation is to keep the commandments."[50] The emphasis of the author of *Jubilees* is on commands between God and the people, rather than on social law. This includes even sexual sins, since the point of keeping the commands, as Sanders argues, is to set Israel apart as a people vis-à-vis the Gentiles. This is why the Israelites are to avoid any practice that might make them indistinguishable from the Gentiles, thus obliterating their chosen, covenantal status before God. Sanders lists the following as commandments in *Jubilees* that serve to set Israel apart: keep the Sabbath (2:18), cover their nakedness (3:31), observe period of uncleanness after childbirth (3:8–11), don't eat meat with blood in it (6:10), observe the Feast of Weeks (6:17) and Tabernacles

---

[46] Sanders argues against the thesis of M. Testuz (*Les Idées religieuses du Livre des Jubilées* [Geneva and Paris: Droz, 1960]) that the phrase "elect of Israel" indicates a sect within the larger group. Testuz equates the *Jubilees* community with the Essenes. Sanders reads the genitive appositionally: the elect, Israel.

[47] VanderKam reads the verb in question as "in straying from" rather than as a causative (*The Book of Jubilees* [CSCO 511; Louvain: Peeters, 1989], 2).

[48] B. Halpern-Amaru argues that the reference to land here is eschatological, not historical. It concerns the "restoration of the primeval human condition and total fruition of the covenantal relationship ordained at Creation, not . . . return to the Land" (*Rewriting the Bible*, 54).

[49] Sanders's view is in no way controversial. See the recent study by E. J. Christiansen, who discusses the centrality of Israel's covenant consciousness as it serves to set up boundary markers vis-à-vis Gentiles (*The Covenant in Judaism and Paul: A Study of Ritual Boundaries as Identity Markers* [AGJU 27; Leiden: E. J. Brill, 1995], 77–87; the full discussion on *Jubilees* is found on pp. 67–103).

[50] *PPJ*, 364.

(16:29), tithe (13:34), do not commit incest (33:10), and several others.[51] In other words, being an elect people, it is now Israel's responsibility to act accordingly.

That election and covenant are central not only to *Jubilees* but to biblical Israelite faith is a matter that is beyond dispute. The question, however, is how a system of commandments fits into this broader scheme. Specifically, what are the consequences for disobedience of these commands? It is here that we come to the heart of Sanders's understanding of covenantal nomism in *Jubilees*. The data of the book itself create a tension and ambiguity concerning the role of obedience in election. This tension, and Sanders's apparent struggle to maintain that tension, is evident already at the outset of Sanders's discussion of the basis of Israel's salvation (pp. 367–74). Citing *Jub*. 15:26–28, Sanders remarks, "It is repeatedly emphasized that the *basis* of salvation is *membership* in the covenant *and loyalty* to it."[52] Are *both* membership (i.e., election, covenant, "getting in") *and* loyalty (i.e., obedi- ence) the *basis* of salvation? Not only does this seem to contradict the notion of covenantal nomism, it also seems to contradict statements Sanders will make later on in his argument. We will return to this below.

In any event, according to 1:5 and 18, God has chosen Israel and he will not forsake them. Nevertheless, having been chosen they are now bound to keep the commandments, lest they "forsake the covenant." Election, as Sanders repeatedly emphasizes, is the basis for salvation, but the elect people are still required to act in a certain way. But not all transgressions are equal. Some may be repented of, but others are breaches of "eternal commands." These are commands

> transgression of which is a "sin unto death" for which there is *no atonement*. Rejection of any one of these commandments, like transgression of the commandment to circumcise, was regarded by the author as forsaking the covenant and thus *forfeiting one's status as a member of Israel* and one destined for eternal salvation.[53]

Sanders goes on to list these eternal commands on pp. 368–9, which include Sabbath keeping, eating of blood, intermarriage, incest, and others. That a "sin unto death" is one for which there is no atonement can be seen in 33:13–14. Regarding incest we read,

> And there is no forgiveness in order to atone for a man who has done this, forever, but only to execute him and kill him and stone him and to uproot him from the midst of the people of our God. For any man who does this in Israel should not have life for a single day upon the earth because he is despicable and polluted.

---

[51] *PPJ*, 364–5.

[52] *PPJ*, 367 (my emphasis).

[53] *PPJ*, 368 (my emphasis).

Other sins may be atoned for but "eternal commands" that are broken can only result in that individual's destruction.

This raises a rather obvious question that Sanders spends some time discussing. How is it that Israel is God's eternal, elect, covenantal people, whom he will never forsake, while at the same time there are sins for which there is no possibility of atonement, and this results in the loss of that person's elect status? The tension is obvious in a number of junctures in Sanders's argument.

> Thus we see that *all Israel* will be saved. *Excluded from Israel* are those who transgress a commandment which is, in the author's view, tantamount to denying the covenant . . . or those who blatantly commit heinous transgression which is, by inference, a denial of the God who gave the commandment. . . . [54]

> We conclude, then, that the soteriology of the book of Jubilees is that which we have found to be so widespread in Palestinian Judaism: salvation is given graciously by God to his establishing the covenant with the fathers, a covenant which he will not forsake (1.18); individuals may, however, be excluded from Israel if they sin in such a way as to spurn the covenant itself.[55]

To put it most succinctly, according to Sanders, "salvation is not earned by obedience, although it may be forfeited by disobedience." "Obedience . . . is the *condition* of salvation . . . , but not its cause." "Obedience *preserves* salvation."[56] Again, it is not clear how these statements square with that given above at n. 52. It seems that the whole thrust of Sanders's argument is that the "basis of salvation" is *only* "membership in the covenant" (i.e., election) and not "loyalty to it," which is obedience. I will not venture to suggest that Sanders is contradicting himself. He is, after all, attempting to bring clarity to a difficult issue by means of a somewhat unaccommodating text. Nevertheless, his choice of words at this point serves to augment that lack of clarity.

How then does *Jubilees* square with Sanders's theory of covenantal nomism? For one thing, he is quite correct in saying that Israel's salvation is based in its elect status, which is purely an act of God's good pleasure. This can be seen in contrast to the status of the Gentiles for whom there will be "no portion in the future world" and who will be judged by Israel.[57] Gentiles will receive thorough condemnation, which is why Israel is repeatedly warned not to mingle with them. The message to Jews is that if they deny the covenant, they in effect become Gentiles. How does one become Jewish?

---

[54] *PPJ*, 369–70.

[55] *PPJ*, 370–71.

[56] *PPJ*, 371 (his emphasis).

[57] *PPJ*, 374. J. C. Endres also speaks of an "anti-Gentile mood" pervading the book (*Biblical Interpretation in the Book of Jubilees* [CBQMS 18; Washington, D. C.: Catholic Biblical Association of America, 1987], 236). See also the comments by T. L. Donaldson, *Paul and the Gentiles*, 52–53.

Election. How does one lose that status? By disobeying the eternal commands. This means mingling with the Gentiles, acting like them – to "become" Gentile. Since there is essentially no hope whatsoever in *Jubilees* for the salvation of the Gentiles, Sanders's notion that election is the basis of salvation certainly seems in order.

But what of mercy and grace for those who are "in" but have sinned? Sins not unto death are presumably dealt with in the conventional manner, through biblical methods of atonement. But these types of transgressions are not the author's focus. He has much more to say about heinous sins unto death, sins that obliterate the Jewish/Gentile distinction. For these there is no atonement. But it is precisely here that even the author of *Jubilees* is not entirely consistent. In one instance in Israel's history, we read that mercy even extends to Reuben who broke the "eternal command" of incest. Yet he is forgiven. How can this be? Because "the ordinance and judgment and law had not been revealed till then (as) completed for everyone" (33:16). He was excused because he didn't know, but the readers of Jubilees are not afforded such leniency. Elsewhere Judah is forgiven his incest because "he made great supplication and because he mourned and did not do it again" (41:24). But how can Judah be forgiven for breaking an eternal command? Why would the author allow this contradiction to stand? Because, as Sanders puts it, "he was faced with the fact that Judah had not been burned and his descendants not immediately destroyed."[58] In other words, he had to account for the very fact of Israel's existence despite the fact that Israel's father, Judah, committed a sin unto death. Hence, there simply *had* to be a reason why the rules of the game did not apply to him. Such forgiveness, however, although granted in the past and promised for the future, will not be extended to the present day, where "the crisis of the author's time is so acute that certain transgressions permit no atonement."[59]

Nevertheless, the tension remains between election and obedience, and Sanders is quite up front in recognizing it.

> It thus appears that the author's view that there is no atonement for forsaking the covenant, when it conflicts with the *historical reality of the continuation of Israel* and with his *conviction that Israel is elect and will ultimately be cleansed and saved*, yields. It must be confessed that we cannot achieve complete clarity on this matter.[60]

Yet one wonders whether Sanders is being too skeptical here. At least the example of Judah is quite consistent with the primacy of the covenant as the basis for salvation. Since it is Judah from whose line will come the covenant people, it is by God's special mercy that he accepts Judah's – and only

---

[58] *PPJ*, 377.
[59] *PPJ*, 378.
[60] *PPJ*, 378 (his emphasis).

Judah's – sincere repentance (Reuben is not said to repent). The covenant people must come about, and this is by grace, and that principle of grace is illustrated in no better way than by doing what is in the mind of the author of *Jubilees* unthinkable – by forgiving the patriarch Judah of breaking an "eternal command." This is why this past disobedience is forgiven; the *individual* transgression has *national* consequences.[61] It is also why future transgressions of the covenant, predicted in 1:5, will also be ultimately forgiven. The people of God must go on, and as a result, they will learn that God is righteous and truly with his people.

The point is that the author of *Jubilees*, from first to last, is concerned to emphasize God's promise never to forsake his *people. Israel as a people* will always remain because God is faithful. Transgression of eternal commands, however, will result in individual punishment and forfeiture of one's individual covenant status. The fact of Israel's election, however, remains sure. In fact, it is precisely the fact that God destroys individuals while maintaining the whole that demonstrates to the people that he is *faithful to the covenant*: the actions of individuals cannot affect God's purpose and plan – Israel's existence is his doing. Although *Jubilees* does not provide us with an unequivocal, systematic soteriology, Sanders's basic assessment of the situation in *Jubilees* seems to be sound. As he himself concludes his discussion,

> Despite a strict legalism of one sort, the author's view is not the kind of legalism which is summed up in the phrase "works righteousness," for salvation depends on the grace of God.[62]

7. Conclusions and Further Questions

Having said all this, however, there are still a number of problems that persist, perhaps not so much with Sanders's basic thesis but with the almost nagging imprecision of the nature of soteriology in *Jubilees*. Despite Sanders's arguments, it is still not entirely clear how "salvation" can be by grace but "staying saved" is a matter of strict obedience. If salvation can be lost by disobedience – i.e., if obedience is necessary to "preserve" salvation – in what sense can we say with Sanders that "salvation *depends* on the grace of God"? How can there be sins unto death when *election* is the basis of salvation? More basically, what meaning does "election" have when it can so easily be

---

[61] Endres also argues for the centrality of Jacob in understanding the author's conception of the covenantal relationship between God and Israel (*Biblical Interpretation*, 228–31). See also Christiansen, *The Covenant in Judaism and Paul*, 88–9.

[62] PPJ, 383.

undone by the actions of frail people whose very existence as a covenant people depends on grace/election to begin with?

Not only is there imprecision in *Jubilees*, but one must also leave open the possibility of – quite simply put – exaggeration on the part of the author, which, if true, would place the entire discussion on a wholly different plane. Does the writer of *Jubilees* really mean that any individual who breaks any of these commandments under any circumstances is irrevocably lost? Might such harsh black and white categories simply be part of the rhetoric of warning in a time of perceived crisis? In this respect, might the examples of forgiveness for Reuben and Judah be a veiled reminder of how God will *actually* deal with his people despite the unforgiving tone evinced elsewhere in the book? I have not explored this line of reasoning fully, although I cannot help but have some suspicions. Still, I am more than willing to allow the author of *Jubilees* and other Second Temple authors to speak for themselves without presuming to guess their psychological motives.

I wonder, too, whether we should equate salvation with election, as Sanders seems to do. Is salvation the best word to describe one's *initiation* into the covenant wholly apart from the final outcome? Despite the fact that covenant is the "basis" of salvation, as Sanders argues, the fact remains that the texts discussed in this essay, and *Jubilees* especially, certainly emphasize the importance of obedience in maintaining that covenantal status, in staying saved. It might be less confusing to say that *election* is by grace but *salvation* is by obedience. In fact, getting in and staying in may not be categories that do justice to the evidence provided by the Second Temple sources. Since election is the beginning point, and this is solely Israel's property according to *Jubilees*, perhaps we should speak of "being in" rather than getting in, since the latter is never really in view. This is more than merely a semantic distinction. "Being in" is by birth; it is nationalistic. Staying in, however, is a matter of individual effort. Now, to be sure, that individual effort must be seen within the context of the individual's self-understanding and confidence as a Jew, a confidence that rests on God's faithfulness in calling a particular people to himself, and that he is predisposed to forgive transgression, an obvious fact seen in the biblical institution of a system of atonement. The point still remains, however, that the final outcome is based on more than initial inclusion in the covenant.

5. Didactic Stories

by

PHILIP R. DAVIES

1. Introduction

1.1 What Is a Didactic Story?

What is a *didactic* story? The stories that have been preserved for us in the Jewish and Christian scriptural canons or among the so-called "Pseudepigrapha" clearly function as *didactic* in some way: whether or not that is why they were written, that is how they have been read and transmitted as vehicles of religious instruction.

Didactic means "instructional," "teaching"; usually it is employed in biblical scholarship as a "wisdom" adjective. How do stories *teach*, as distinct from proverbs, or sermons, or laws? Narrative texts construct a world: and however much that world represents itself as the real one of the reader's experience, the story world is not the world of experience, for it is ordered into an author's narrative. The world created in a story is an artificial world, however much it aims to portray the "real," since shape and meaning are given to selected events by devices such as plot, character and point of view.

Moreover, the order of a narrative world is fabricated with moral, ethical or aesthetic dimensions. Indeed, such dimensions are usually an important ingredient of a story. Is the world of a story a tragic world or a comic one? Is it orderly or disorderly? Is it just? And by what values does the reader interpret characters in a story as "good" or "bad," as heroes or villains? The clearest example of a didactic story is the parable, but really most stories aim to convey both ethical and aesthetic values, from the fables of Aesop to Gibbon's *Rise and Fall of the Roman Empire*, from the biblical tale of Eden in Gen 2–3 to the *Hitchhiker's Guide to the Galaxy*.

It is equally true and obvious that stories also have to entertain. Stories function by engaging the interest of the reader in the plot, the characters or the point of view: devices such as suspense, irony, humor and pathos address the emotions and the intellect of the reader. To try and distill from stories a didactic "message" can sometimes be mistaken, because dramatic effect can override or even blur the contours of any "teaching" as well as enhance it.

Indeed, stories are a perfect vehicle for conveying ambiguity, tension, and even different points of view. While the ethical/aesthetic and the dramatic aspects of a story often collude, sometimes they can be in tension, or at least not in harmony.

These points need to be borne in mind in considering how ancient Jewish "didactic stories" present their characters in relation to the Deity, and how they understand and communicate the way in which humans *justify* their lives, to themselves, their neighbors and, above all, to the higher powers (in this case, the Jewish God), both as individuals, and as members of various groups and societies.

1.2 Genre

Are there any characteristics of the stories under review (Jewish didactic stories of the Greco-Roman period) that mark them out for generalization? We can start by considering generic features. In stories, as with other forms of literature, the expectations of the reader (and thus the potentialities of the author) are conditioned by the perception of genre, by a sometimes unconscious recognition of the "way" a story is to be taken because of its formal markers.

The texts under review are Tobit, Judith, the Letter of Aristeas, 3 Maccabees and 4 Maccabees: all extant in Greek. But Tobit was composed, it seems, in Aramaic or Hebrew,[1] and the language of Judith also suggests a Semitic original. The other texts were composed in Greek. The choice of language, in works emanating from the Greco-Roman period, is not insignificant, of course: such a decision implies a certain kind of original audience (the distinction between Hebrew and Aramaic is equally important, but cannot be exploited here). It is not necessarily merely a Palestinian versus a diaspora audience, but of the literary and aesthetic conventions that each language (and its culture) imports. Questions of social identity, class and even politics can also be entailed in the choice of language. For content, as well as form, can define a genre, and the values extolled in the wisdom literature of the ancient Near Eastern world can also be taken as characteristic features. Thus, our Jewish didactic stories might feature certain kinds of setting, hero, villain, virtue and vice – such as the royal court and the jealous courtier, or the threatened destruction of the Jews – that we could well call "generic." Since there is no *single* genre of "Jewish didactic story," and therefore no single genealogy of the Jewish didactic story, it is valuable to consider briefly the generic backgrounds of the various types of story, or story elements, to be considered here.

---

[1] Fragments of four Aramaic and one Hebrew manuscripts have now been identified from Qumran Cave 4 (4Q196–200).

1.2.1 Scribal Didactics

The most important, and the most ancient, generic influence on the Jewish didactic story is the court tale, and all the stories being considered here are influenced in some way (however slightly) by it. There are, of course, examples of this tale in the Jewish Scriptures, too (Joseph, Esther, Daniel). A brief consideration of this important genre will therefore enable us also to sketch the cultural and scriptural background to the Jewish didactic story of the Greco-Roman period.

Instruction and storytelling belong in many levels and occasions in ancient society, including the home, the village square, the school, the banquet and the royal court. But the didactic story is essentially a product of the scribal class, those professionally educated administrators who, virtually alone possessing the gift of literacy, served the governing class.[2] Scribes served administrative, economic and diplomatic functions, recording gifts to temple and king, property transactions, legal decision, decrees, annals, letters and treaties. They also served as librarians and archivists, responsible for the preservation and arrangement of material knowledge about the world. This knowledge came to include what we would now call science and philosophy. Among the earliest kinds of written texts are rituals, omen lists and lists of names of objects (gods, trees, sacrifices), astronomical observations, myths – and ethical instruction. For the cultivation of correct behavior was as much a part of their concern as correct records and knowledge of the natural world.

Ethical instruction, then, is intimately bound up with the other genres produced by the ancient scribes. Scribal ethical instruction addresses the behavior of the *individual*, and needs to be distinguished from genres such as lawcodes, historiography or certain kinds of prophetic oracles, which typically address the behavior of a *society*. The ethical instruction of the scribe perhaps had its origin, and certainly its counterpart, in the instruction of the child by the parent: it was the convention of scribal "Instructions" to address the reader as "my son" (as found in the early chapters of the book of Proverbs). While the ethical instruction of women was probably also carried out, there were, to our knowledge, no female scribes in the ancient civilizations of Egypt and Mesopotamia, nor in ancient Israel and Judah.

The name given in Hebrew to an understanding of *both* the external world *and* how to live properly in it, is חכמה, "wisdom." These two aspects of wisdom are connected in two ways, which can be illustrated from the Jewish Scriptures. The first is that both are derived experientially. While the divine revelation of laws or oracles was a necessary part of the ideology of justice,

---

[2] For a fuller description of the origin and function this class, see Philip R. Davies, *Scribes and Schools: The Canonization of the Hebrew Scriptures* (Louisville: Westminster John Knox, 1998).

kingship and intermediation, rules for how to live well *as an individual* come from the accumulated wisdom of ancestors or predecessors. This is the essence of the Instruction genre in ancient Near Eastern as well as biblical texts, where the reputation of the author as a wise king or administrator recommends the wisdom contained. Thus, in the Jewish Scriptures, Solomon is credited with proverbs and (as a transparent fiction) with Ecclesiastes. (Ben Sira is an apparent exception: his own reputation may have been sufficient to recommend his book – we do not know.) Personal experience, then, is the basis of knowledge of both the natural and the moral world, though the virtues conveyed are generally traditional: prudence above all; piety; restraint; justice; truthfulness. All these comprise *wisdom* and come from *understanding*.

The second connection between knowledge of the world and correct behavior in it is at the theological level. In some ancient civilizations ethical behavior falls under the aegis of a divinity (such as the Egyptian Maat). In Greece the gods tended to punish *hubris*. There were divine sanctions against what transgressed natural and moral law. In the wisdom of the Jewish Scriptures, two important presuppositions must be appreciated: one is monotheism, the other the finality of death (except, of course, for the last chapter of the book of Daniel). The scribal theology of Judah did not seek to explain the symptoms of moral disorder by appealing to a plurality of gods. Rather, there was one God responsible for the state of the world, and, effectively, this God was the only one to whom piety was to be addressed. The existence of one God made possible the creation of a distinctive moral philosophy. The finality of death also confined all theological-philosophical speculation to the observable, and preempted speculations about an after-life as a solution to the problems that lived experience highlighted (again, the ending of the book of Daniel breached this confine). These two presuppositions together, monotheism and the finality of death, permitted a rational moral theology.

That theology is expressed most clearly in Prov 8:22–23:

> Yahweh created me at the beginning of his activities, the very first of his primordial acts. I was set up long ago, from the very beginning, before the world itself.

The natural world, then, it was claimed, was created *according to a moral order*, and wisdom consists of discerning not only the workings of that world, but the moral order that underlies it. The correct way to live is according to "natural law."

The experiential principle of the "wisdom" tradition (for which the term "philosophy" would be quite appropriate) in the ancient Near East remained primary, and the continual questioning that it provoked led to profound disagreements. The simple rational, retributional system of Proverbs (good deeds earn good rewards in this world) was challenged by the authors of Job and Ecclesiastes, then Daniel. Job affirmed the ability of humans to understand the natural world but not the moral order – this was known only to its divine Creator. Ecclesiastes, expressing less wonder than the book of Job at the natural world, also affirms human inability to discern a moral order, and recommends indifference to it. He does this, however, on the basis of personal experience and observation, turning the tradition against itself and advocating (surely under the influence of Greek thought) independent observation and critical judgment. The book of Daniel finally addresses itself to the fate of the righteous martyr, and in that turn away from rationality towards manticism that is sometimes called "apocalyptic" abandons understudying to divine mystery that can only be revealed, not discovered, and delivers a (literal) *deus ex machina* in the form of a resurrection.

There are three important features, possibly later developments, of this wisdom tradition that can be detected in our didactic stories. One is the mingling of the personal with the national, and can already be seen in the book of Daniel, where the fate of this wise man is a microcosm of the fate of all of righteous Israel, and his loyalty, persecution and deliverance symbolize that of the nation. As we shall see, Tobit, Judith and 4 Maccabees all mingle personal and national in different ways. This may be due to the influence of another scriptural tradition, national historiography, and to the recognition in the Greco-Roman period that the survival of Judean culture was threatened on both the national and the personal level. Both individual Jews and also Judaism itself needed vigorous preservation.

A second development of the late Second Temple period is the tendency to equate acquired wisdom with revealed *torah*. Already in Sir *torah* (not necessarily in this case to be simply equated with the Mosaic law, though the Mosaic law was an authoritative expression of it) wisdom is *revealed* and the wise person *obeys* rather than *questions*. The equation of piety and wisdom is also celebrated in Ps 1 and at greater length in Ps 119: the wise person receives instruction not from his natural parent or his teacher, but from the Parent and Teacher in heaven. Thus, while Job and Ecclesiastes suggest the unknowability of the ultimate sense of things by rational reflection, revealed law emerges to fill the vacuum, as the starting point for the constructing of a personal ethic. Simultaneously, however, the culture of the Greeks offered to the Jewish scribes a new challenge to address the question of ethics *intellectually*; the result of these conflicting influences was that sometimes "law" and "reason" were opposed, and sometimes they were equated.

A third development, clearly related to the other two, is the presence of the national God as an agent of rescue. In the older wisdom tales of Sinuhe, Wen-Amon, and Ahiqar, it was the individual's virtue, resourcefulness or cunning that won the day. In the (Hebrew version of) the story of Esther this is still observable, as it is, largely, in the Joseph story, too. But in the Greek forms of Esther, and in Daniel, divine action is made more prominent.

Finally, we need to note the amalgamation of another genre (alluded to earlier) into the scribal wisdom tradition: historiography. If the genre of scribal instruction occupies itself with the identity and values of the *individual*, the tracts of historiography in the Jewish Scriptures (Joshua-Kings, Chronicles, Ezra, Nehemiah) are concerned with the identity and values of the group "Israel." This nation is guided as a whole, not by the intellectual reflection of its ruling caste but by the revealed law of God, and, as in the scribal instructional literature reviewed earlier, there is a strong retributional basis: obedience to its constitution (the laws of the God who chose it – its patron deity in other words) guarantees Israel's safety and survival. As already mentioned, this law more and more became identified with "wisdom" and *as an Israelite/Jew* the wise person was constituted by obedience to that law. For if "wisdom" could be universalized, the law gave Israel its unique identity. In Jewish didactic stories, being a good *person* is not the issue, but being a good *Jew*. And in an age when there was no agreed meaning as to what that meant, "Judaism" had to be defined. [3]

Nevertheless, in stories about heroes who rescued Israel, we find. as in the wisdom-derived stories, an occasional tension between divine action and human initiative. The book of Judges tells of heroes who were "raised up," but often they acted on their own cunning. Thus we find no miraculous intervention in the tale of Judith. It is not the case, in any Jewish didactic story, that the hand of God is banished. But the storyteller may wish to recommend different human responses: patient suffering, obedience, or, sometimes, acting on one's own conscience. But it is certainly not possible to generalize about the way in which the heroes of these tales relate directly to the Jewish God, or the means by which their own or Israel's survival is accomplished.

The literatures of Judean wisdom and historiography, therefore, are the main sources for the Jewish didactic story. More specifically, each has generated its own kind of narratives. Among the relevant historiographical narrative genres is the miraculous deliverance of Israel through the intervention of a woman, while among the wisdom narrative genres the tale of the wise courtier is paramount. This genre, reflected, as mentioned earlier, in the stories of Joseph, Esther and Daniel, goes back to the ancient tales of Sinuhe, Wen-Amon and to the popular Persian-period story of Ahiqar. Here the wise man, despite the devices of other men and the vicissitudes of fortune, remains

---

[3] Significantly, it is in 2 Maccabees that the word Ἰουδαϊσμός first appears (several times). On the significance of this, see D. Schwartz, *Studies in the Jewish Background of Christianity* (Tübingen: Mohr [Siebeck], 1992), 11. See also M. Hengel, *Judaism and Hellenism* (2 vols.; London: SCM, 1974), 95ff.

true to his principles and is finally vindicated. These narratives will be considered in more detail when discussing the individual didactic tales that they have influenced. Here it is necessary only to point out that the hero of the Jewish didactic tale is generally about danger averted. That danger may be to an individual or to the nation, or both; the hero may be male or female, and the role of the Deity may be unseen or highly prominent. In approaching our examples of Jewish didactic stories, we should be aware of the different possibilities for understanding the nature of the human-divine relationship that the genres entail, including the ethical system that guarantees a person divine favor and, indeed, what it is that earns one "salvation."

1.3 The Audiences of Jewish Didactic Stories

In this section we shall consider briefly the historical and cultural context in which the generic features just discussed were deployed. This also provides the opportunity to introduce some generic influences on the Jewish didactic story that do not emanate from the scribal tradition but from the Hellenistic world.

The authors of most of the scriptural literature, both instructional and historiographical, were members of a scribal class. They wrote for their own class and for the ruling class that they served. Their world was privileged, their values circumscribed by their own interests, their instincts and training rational and their monopoly of high literacy (the writing down of literary works) virtually complete. They also wrote in Hebrew. But one of the most important developments of the late Persian and early Hellenistic periods in Palestine was the expansion of a lay class whose wealth was based on commerce, whose lifestyle was cosmopolitan, and who wrested from the scribal class their virtual monopoly of literacy. Ben Sira taught such people, and for these, too, no doubt, the words of the scribal author of Ecclesiastes were written. If wisdom (as represented in the surviving literature) had been until this time a scribal tradition, reserved for those engaging in the life of government, it was now becoming accessible to a wider public, for whom the Greek language, Greek forms of political life, Greek ways of thinking, and, above all, the Greek emphasis on education were the keys to responsible citizenship of the city and the world. Libraries were no longer confined to palaces and temples, but collected by individuals and even instituted in cities. We can speak, to a limited extent, of a "democratization of learning" as a corollary of the more frequently cited term "Hellenization." With the permeation of Greek notions of citizenship, the greater extent of contact between persons of different cultures through trade and travel, we also find a corresponding emphasis in Jewish literature on the *identity and the responsibilities of individuals towards their own ethnic group and others.* For the stories of Esther, Daniel (and Joseph) the traditional generic setting of life in a foreign court, a traditional setting, is utilized as a vehicle for considering the fate of Jews in a non-Jewish world. But Jonah, on the other hand, has the hero (or anti-hero) mixing with sailors and going on a business trip to a huge foreign metropolis. Travel, of course, had long been the prerogative of the scribe engaged in diplomatic duties (as reflected in the stories of Wen-Amon and Sinuhe, below): but now merchants regularly roamed the civilized world, while pilgrims and relatives visited sites and family in other lands. Ruth, by contrast, is a foreigner brought to live in Judah. Here is a tale about what makes a non-Jew into a Jew, as well as about how women can create history.

This "democratization of learning" is a factor also needing to be taken into account in considering the Jewish didactic tale, for it points us to a readership whose Judaism is not deniable, but nevertheless negotiable. The question *"Who* is a Jew?", *"What* is a Jew?", *"What sort of Jew* am I?" and *"What sort of Deity* do Jews worship?" are questions that not only fell from the lips of foreigners but echoed in the minds of Jews themselves.

It is this literate, substantially hellenized, Jewish reader to whom the stories we are considering are, in fact, largely addressed. And while the theology of scribal piety is nowhere displaced, some interesting modifications can be observed, in the influence of Greek literary forms (the romance, the pathetic historiography, the martyr legend, the philosophical treatise), in the identities of the heroes, and in the introduction of women as major characters. A detailed discussion of Greek literary influences on Jewish didactic stories is unfortunately too large and complex a topic for the present essay.

This brief account of the background of the Jewish didactic story illustrates their likely readership (and thus, perhaps their likely *purpose*). A familiarity with the Jewish Scriptures is usually evident, and sometimes taken for granted. Such a fact is not surprising, given the role of these writings in constituting a Jewish identity through its continuity with an historical "Israel." The appeal to the past and to classical examples in constructing the didactic stories (some of which were themselves to be scripturally canonized by some Christian communities) is thus entirely understandable. Yet the implication of a widespread familiarity among literate Jews, inside and outside Palestine, with these Scriptures is itself a remarkable enough phenomenon. That one such as ben Sira should commend this to the scribe is not striking; but that it should become more widely known suggests an extent of private and probably also institutional education among Jews of the kind that flourished in the Greek cities of the Hellenistic world. Here, the bequest of the Scriptures had to be negotiated side by side with the political and religious requirements of a non-Jewish world that could be challenging, attractive and also threatening. It is these issues that give rise to the Jewish didactic story, with its varying styles, settings – and solutions.

1.4 An Introduction to the Stories

The variety of styles, ideas, and solutions just mentioned can be illustrated by a brief review of the stories to be considered. In the story of Tobit we find a story whose genealogy lies in the court tale. Yet its focus is not on the court, but on the family. In Judith, we find a different genre of didactic tale, whose origin does not lie in the scribal tradition of ethical philosophy, but rather seems to rely on a curious and interesting archetype: the female warrior, as represented not only by the divine figures of Ishtar or Athena or Astarte, but also by human figures like Deborah and Jael, or even the Greek Bacchae.[4] Like Ruth and Esther, Judith is concerned with the preservation of the Jewish people, but she acts independently of any man, slightly more independently than Ruth (and Naomi), and much more so than Esther. The wisdom of the Hebrew Bible does not concern itself with the role of women, except marginally as good wives. Women are not bound to Torah, nor do they professionally practice "wisdom." Here, however, her gender possibly underscores the lesson that strength can be defeated by virtuous "weakness," and one ancestor of this story is clearly the tale of David and Goliath.

The books of Aristeas, and 3 and 4 Maccabees, composed in Greek, reflect Greek rather than Semitic genres. They deal explicitly with the conflict of Jewish and foreign culture, and their didactic is addressed to the question of Jewish identity and survival in a world whose general character is different, and in which Judaism will stand out as something very distinctive, and for that reason always under threat, whether of discrimination or assimilation. Despite the identity of purpose, however, the three books deliver their didactic message in different ways. One unifying feature is the confrontation between the foreign king and the pious Jew(s): in Aristeas this is a friendly exchange; in 3 Maccabees the king is finally won over; in 4 Maccabees he is destroyed (the same three options can be seen in Daniel 6, 2 and 5 respectively). Each resolution implies a different perception of the way in which Jews might address their non-Jewish environment, but also of how they perceive divine activity in history. Only in the case of 4 Maccabees is the problem of theodicy presented in individualistic terms (what is the nature of true virtue?). But, as will be argued, even Tobit, the most apparently individualistic of the five stories under consideration, the didactic message concerns Judaism and the Jewish people rather than the individual Jew. Explicit obedience to, and conformity with, a "Jewish" norm is perhaps what emerges as the major unifying characteristic of all these stories, which in different ways represent

---

[4] For the interesting suggestion that Judith is modeled on Moses, see J. W. van Henten, "Judith as Alternative Leader," in *A Feminist Companion to Esther, Judith and Susanna* (ed. A. Brenner; Sheffield: Sheffield Academic, 1995), 224–52. Van Henten also suggests (232 n. 1) the story of Abigail as an influence.

how Judaism in the Hellenistic period dealt, in narrative form, with its corporate essence and survival.

Following a rather extended general introduction, the stories will now be considered individually. In each case, as appropriate, the treatment will follow the same pattern: first a rehearsal of the course of the narrative, then an indication of relevant literary (including generic) features and scriptural influence, and finally suggestions as to what the story may say about Jews and their relationship with their God.

2. Tobit

2.1 The Story

The story takes place in the realm of Assyria in the time of one of its great kings. Tobit has been exiled from the court of the Assyrian king Shalmaneser. He had always been pious (like Job), and was rewarded by the king by becoming his purchasing agent. But he defies a royal decree not to bury the bodies of those executed by the king. (Here one is reminded of Sophocles' *Antigone*, which need not be ruled out as a possible influence, though such a duty was widely extolled in Jewish as well as Greco-Roman society.) Tobit's property is confiscated, but the king is later murdered and through the intervention of his nephew Ahiqar, Tobit is reinstated. So far the plot is extremely conventional.

Tobit then buries another Jewish corpse, and although he has made himself ritually clean, remains outside the city where sparrow droppings make him blind; he is looked after by Ahiqar, then by his own wife. Accused by him of theft, she rebukes him by asking what his own righteousness has earned him. He repents and (like Jonah) asks God that he may die. Coincidentally, a young Jewish woman in the city of Ecbatana, Sarah, is also praying for death because seven bridegrooms to whom she was successively betrothed died on the wedding night through the agency of a demon Asmodeus (here one thinks of the fate of Tamar, Gen 38). God sends the angel Raphael to assist both. Tobit sends his son Tobiah from Nineveh to Media to seek money left by Tobit there, and Raphael, in disguise as a human with the name of Azariah, offers himself as a guide. Tobit pronounces, unwittingly, that a good angel will accompany Tobiah. On the way Tobiah hooks a fish which will later heal his father's blindness. On arrival in Ecbatana, Raphael suggests that Tobiah marry Sarah, who is a relative and to whom Tobiah will be performing his Jewish duty as next of kin. He is assured that his fate will not be that of his predecessors. In the bridal chamber, Tobiah burns the fish's entrails and repels the demon as far as Egypt, where Raphael binds him. After much celebration, the married couple return to Nineveh and Tobiah heals his father's blindness with the fish gall.

On being offered half of all that Tobiah brought back, Raphael discloses his identity, explains his mission and bids Tobiah and Tobit write down the story for the instruction of others. Tobit composes a hymn of thanksgiving, in which the return to Jerusalem and rebuilding of the temple are anticipated. Later, on his deathbed, Tobit remembers the prophecies against Nineveh and tells his son to take his family elsewhere. He alludes to the fortunes of Ahiqar and his reward for his piety, and dies. Tobiah leaves for Ecbatana, and finally dies wealthy, witnessing the destruction of Nineveh and the bringing of Assyrian prisoners to Ecbatana.

2.2 Literary Features

Recent scholarship on Tobit[5] exhibits no unanimity on whether it is a unity, and to what genre(s) it ought best be assigned. Though there seems little reason to quibble that this tale is strongly didactic, its genealogy is nevertheless quite complex, drawing on a number of genres and works. Among the many genres deployed in Tobit are the romance (the book is essentially a successful quest), prayer and wisdom instruction. Here we shall simply indicate some of the book's probable and possible ancestry.

2.2.1 The Courtier Tale

Tobit clearly stands within the tradition of the courtier tale,[6] examples of which are Sinuhe, Wen-Amon and (especially) Ahiqar. This genre, with distinctive Jewish adaptations, is represented in the story of Joseph and the books of Esther and Daniel, and features the vicissitudes of the royal servant falling in and out of favor with the king.[7] The genre perhaps originated as a means of conveying in an entertaining way the virtues required, and the perils to be faced, of one in the service of a ruler and subject to the intrigues of rivals as well as the vagaries of royal favor.[8] Here, human virtue, with some element of coincidence and fortune, secures a happy ending.

---

[5] For a review, see conveniently Moore, *Tobit*, 15–21 (and the bibliography in that volume). For bibliographical information regarding Tobit and the other primary literature treated here, see the "Select Bibliography" at the end of this essay.

[6] For a convenient discussion of the "courtier" tale, see Lawrence M. Wills, *The Jew in the Court of the Foreign King* (Minneapolis: Fortress, 1990), 39–74. On Ahiqar, see J. M. Lindenburger, *The Aramaic Proverbs of Ahiqar* (Baltimore/London: Johns Hopkins University, 1983).

[7] See Lawrence M. Wills, *The Jew in the Court of the Foreign King*, 39–74. For the texts, see W. W. Hallo and K. L. Younger, eds., *The Context of Scripture* (vol. 1; Leiden: Brill, 1997), 77–82 (Sinuhe), 89–93 (Wen-Amon).

[8] The story of Sinuhe (from the end of the third millennium B.C.E.) tells of a courtier who flees his native Egypt for fear of a civil war, and lives with foreigners, achieving fame as a wise,

Sometimes such stories (as in the case of Tobit in ch. 4) were actually combined with "Instructions," lists of wise sayings, making their didactic intent even clearer.[9] The earliest example of this combination is the story of Ahiqar.[10] Such a mixture of narrative and instruction is present in the book of Job (though the instruction takes the form of a series of monologues between conversants), and also in the Egyptian *Instruction of Onkhsheshonq*, from roughly the same (Persian-Hellenistic) period.[11] Here the hero is thrown into prison as a result of intrigue, and is rescued when a conspiracy against the Pharaoh is uncovered. Parallels between these writings and the stories of Joseph, Daniel and Esther are not hard to construct; they have a royal court setting, tell of the vicissitudes of court life, including the envy of others, and show the hero(ine)'s cunning. But the court is a foreign one, the hero is (or represents) a Judean, and human cunning is subservient to divine guidance – except perhaps in the Hebrew version of Esther.

2.2.2 The Folk-tale

Three folk-tales in particular, all from Egypt, have often been cited as influences upon the book of Tobit.[12] *The Grateful Dead*[13] tells of a man who went to great trouble to bury the corpse of a physician and is finally rewarded by the dead man's spirit, by being rescued from drowning and acquiring a bride. *The Bride of the Monster* is more or less self-explanatory, while the

---

brave and prosperous man, before being welcomed home, reinstated and honored. Accounts of the travels of Wen-Amun belong to about a thousand years later. Both of these scribal compositions probably became classics in scribal schools, being intended for the instruction, but not without entertainment, of the pupils.

[9] Wills has suggested, however, that the story form lends itself readily to irony and ambiguity, and believes that where a set of instructions was attached, in some cases the stories actually undermine the teaching, showing how "wisdom" is not necessarily of paramount value in everyday life. Such a view makes problematic the suggestion that such stories were intended to be educative, though it does not dispose of it. For the scribe being trained for a career in court life had to be aware of the limits of his own rational philosophy in the face of the irrationality of rulers as well as the envy of rivals.

[10] Found among the documents from Elephantine, a Jewish military colony (end of 5th century B.C.E.). The story, which circulated widely in the Levant, tells of a wise courtier (a royal scribe) of the Assyrian kings Esarhaddon and Sennacherib, who is tricked by his heir, escapes execution and finally returns to royal favor and serves the king by his wisdom, turning the tables on his betrayer.

[11] Wills notes (*The Jew in the Court*, 43) that there are narrative sections attached to earlier Egyptian works of instruction, but not fully developed.

[12] See Moore, *Tobit*, 11–14.

[13] For a discussion of the possible relationship of this text with Tobit, see E. Schürer, *The History of the Jewish People in the Age of Jesus Christ* (ed. G. Vermes, F. Millar, M. Goodman and M. Black; Edinburgh: T & T Clark, 1973–87), 3/1.226.

Tractate of Khons relates how a princess, possessed by a demon, was exorcized by the god of Thebes through Khons.

The problem with positing folk-tale influences is that their motifs tend to circulate widely and originate independently in similar forms. There are undoubtedly such sources in the book of Tobit, and a strong indication of an Egyptian background. But the presence of such motifs tells us little about direct influence.

2.3 Dependence on the Jewish Scriptures

The author is clearly aware of the contents of the Scriptures, since Amos (2:6) and Nahum (14:4) are mentioned. It is also possible that the "dangerous bride" motif was inspired by the case of Tamar (Gen 38) rather than any other, and that Tobit's prayer for death might just recall that of the less pious Jonah. But while the story has its setting within the history of Israel (as presented in the Jewish Scriptures) the story makes little or no explicit reference to biblical texts or motifs. Interestingly, Tobit, like Judith, is set among the "lost" tribes of the kingdom of Israel deported to Assyria. It would be interesting to speculate on whether this device carries any significance for the self-identity of some of the readers: whether these tribes were taken to symbolize diaspora Jews in a particular way.

2.4 "Justification" and "Salvation" in Tobit

As explained earlier, the traditional problem of "wisdom" writings was not the fate of the non-pious, but of the exceptionally pious: Job and Daniel, like Tobit and Judith, display high, even exaggerated piety. Because of the monotheistic premises of the classic wisdom theodicy, innocent suffering is both a metaphysical and an ethical problem. It denies order in the universe, denies the goodness of God, and challenges the individual's commitment to being pious. The suffering of the innocent (Hebrew צדיק can be translated as both "righteous" and "innocent") is the fundamental problem of a monotheistic theodicy.

The piety of Tobit is stressed (as is Job's) almost to the point of absurdity.[14] His affliction is not caused by human agency, either. The explanation given by Raphael of Tobit's affliction does not even say that his affliction was a test; rather Raphael's own mission *included* a test (12:14). Sarah's misfortunes are caused by a demon; and yet no account is given of the

---

[14] The episode in 2:11–14 is not necessarily an exception. The blind Tobit suspects that he is about to eat a stolen kid goat, and does not believe his wife when she says it is a gift. There is hyper-morality here, a concern not to do anything wrong, but this leads to the sin of false accusation towards his wife. His remorse, however, demonstrates his basic goodness.

origin of demons, nor of the basis of their power. But Raphael can bind
Asmodeus, just as God bound Azazel (see *1 Enoch* 6–11).

In stressing (a) concern for the poor and (b) the vindication of the
righteous in prosperity and in a peaceful death after a long life, the book of
Tobit reinforces the traditional philosophy of the wise as reflected in the book
of Proverbs. However two important features deserve comment. One is the
role of obedience to the Jewish Law, and the other is the corporate fate of the
exiled Jewish people (underlined by Tobit being a member of one of the "lost"
tribes). The Torah has become part of the law of the natural world, as in
Sirach (and as we shall also see, as also understood in Jewish didactic stories
written in Greek). Such an amalgamation introduces, of course, a notion of
revelation into an otherwise rational-empirical system. But so does the notion
of the special status of Israel. And the *Jewishness* of Tobit is paramount. His
son must marry an Israelite wife; he must bury the dead according to the
dictates of Jewish Law. That Law is expressed here in terms of those
practices that express the solidarity of Jews in another country: support of the
poor, fasting, prayer to their God, marriage with other Jews only, reverence
for the dead. Of these, the giving to the poor seems to be more emphasized
than the others, for above all it reinforces the mutual ties of Jews.

Finally, however, it can be suggested that Tobit is a symbolic figure. The
restoration for which he prays, and the theme with which the book ends, is the
restoration of Israel to its land and the rebuilding of its temple. *Individual
fulfillment of the life of a Diaspora Jew entails national restoration.* As in
the book of Daniel, it may also be that the fortunes of the hero are a model
for those of his people. If so, Tobit's blindness, perhaps, is the blindness of
Israel, and certainly his exile is that of Israel. The restoration of the fortunes
of the righteous individual are, then, understood as a guarantee of the
restoration of Tobit's people. Perhaps that is why the origin of Tobit's
blindness is not dwelt upon, as if the author shares with the poet of Isaiah
40–55 the notion that the fate of the Israelite/Jewish nation is not simply a
matter of punishment but rather a mysterious affliction on a chosen people.
And is the joyous marriage of Tobiah and the riches that he brings back to his
father a symbol of the joyful remarriage of the people of Israel and Jerusalem,
when they return (as they did from Egypt and from Babylon) with gifts?

It may be an overstatement that the story of Tobit is *purely* symbolic; but
the intertwining of personal and ethnic identities is so strong that one cannot
avoid concluding that the problem of this book is less one of theodicy in the
abstract or even as applied to the individual, than of the problem of the fate
of the chosen people, Israel. It is as a member of the covenant people that
divine grace is extended to Tobit. All humans suffer, but only Israel (so Jews
believed) has a God who can exert a righteous will. Righteousness consists
not only in obedience to the Law, but in all acts that guarantee the preservation of Israel.

2.5 Conclusion

How are Tobit and Tobiah reconciled to God? One can see two dimensions to this. The personal, the traditional concern of the "wise" is shown in the healing of Tobit, the marriage of Tobiah and the long life of each. They are blessed through the large family, social respect, wealth and long life. However, it is not the natural order of things that brings this about, but a divine act: an agent is sent to correct the wrongs, and these wrongs are partly caused by the workings of demons. A purely natural and mechanical theology of retribution has been abandoned in favor of a folkloristic perception that the world is full of vicissitudes to which no-one is immune and for which remedy is uncertain.

More significant, however, is the corporate aspect. It is as an Israelite, as a Jew that the heroes behave righteously and it is the survival and restoration of the Jewish people that ultimately matters. The problem of the individual righteous sufferer masks, as it does in Daniel, the fate of the chosen people. Ultimately their survival, that of their home and their cult, are the goals of individual piety, just as they are ultimately the parameters by which individuals are related to God and through which they become blessed.

3. Judith

3.1 The Story

Despite the title of the book, Judith herself does not appear until about halfway through (ch. 8). The story opens with the great king Nebuchadnezzar (wrongly set over the Assyrians)[15] who aspired to rulership of the entire world. However, all those living West of the Euphrates (more or less) refused to assist him in his campaign of conquest against king Arphaxad to the East, because "they did not fear him, but regarded him as an ordinary man." After his success, Nebuchadnezzar orders his general Holofernes to conduct a campaign of revenge, which is successfully conducted as the general moves towards the Judean highlands.

The reaction of the Judeans (who had, again anachronistically, shortly before returned from exile!) is to fortify the country and occupy the mountain passes. Then, on the instructions of the high priest and council, they pray and fast at the temple.

Meanwhile, Holofernes consults the Moabites and Ammonites concerning the Israelites and is told by Achior the Ammonite leader about their history,

---

[15] There is much debate about whether such "errors" are accidental or deliberate. Among those who claim the latter are Toni Craven, *Artistry and Faith in the Book of Judith* (SBLDS 70; Chico: Scholars, 1983) and J. W. van Henten, "Judith as Alternative Leader."

from their beginnings in Chaldea, from which they were driven out because they worshiped their own God, not the gods of Chaldea. They settled in their land, where they suffered defeats when they sinned against their God: "for theirs is a God who hates sin" (5:17). The nub of Achior's advice is: "If they are sinning against their God, and we discover this, we should go and fight them. But if they are not guilty, my lord should pass them by, since *their* Lord and God will protect them" (5:20–21).

Holofernes rates the power of Nebuchadnezzar superior to that of the Israelite God, and Achior is punished for this advice by being handed over to the Israelites, tied up at the foot of the hill where stood the city of Bethulia. But the Israelites of the town take him, question him and welcome him into their midst. The siege of Bethulia then begins, and rather than being subjected to a direct assault, the city is surrounded and the well guarded so as to starve the inhabitants. At this, the people of Bethulia turn on their leader, Uzziah, who asks for five more days, in the belief that God will not abandon them. The stage is thus set for the entry of Judith.

Judith is presented as a rich and beautiful widow, but also exceptionally pious, fasting every day (cf. Tobit). She advises her fellow-townspeople not to put God to the test, but to allow him to protect as he wishes. Rather, God is putting *them* to the test, and they should praise him. Having said this, however, she indicates that she already has a plan of action herself. But first she utters a prayer at the time of the evening offering in the temple (as did Dan 9), citing the case of Simeon and Levi's revenge for Dinah, pointing to the arrogance of the Assyrians and asking that they be destroyed by the hand of a woman, so as to show that human strength does not matter. "Show to every nation and tribe that you are God, the God of all power and might, and that there is no-one else who protects the people of Israel" (9:14). If not actually putting God to the test, she is at least challenging him!

Judith transforms herself from sedate widow to siren, and, taking her maid, leaves the city and is taken into custody by the Assyrians. She asks to be taken to Holofernes, whom she claims she can help to overcome the city. She tells him to wait, since the townspeople will soon break the divine law by eating food forbidden to them. Thus they will sin and lose God's favor. She asks to leave the camp every evening to pray and learn from God when these offenses have been committed; then the city can be overcome.

Judith thus becomes a guest of Holofernes, but maintains her purity by bathing every evening outside the camp, where she prays for deliverance for Israel. On the fourth day she is invited to a party by Holofernes, who wishes to seduce her. Left alone in the tent with the drunken general, she beheads him and smuggles his head back to Bethulia, where she celebrates the power of God who enabled her to carry out her plan and to remain pure and sinless throughout. Achior believes in the Israelite God and is accepted into the congregation of Israel. Holofernes's head is hung on the city wall, the townspeople rush out armed, the Assyrians look to Holofernes, and his corpse is discovered. In their ensuing flight, the enemy are cut down by the Bethulians and all the Israelites in the area. The victory is finally celebrated by a hymn, led by Judith. This hymn has three parts: the first is very militaristic, praising the God who crushed his enemies; the second part narrates Judith's exploits; and the third part praises God as Creator, and warns that all nations who rise against Israel will be crushed by him "on the day of judgment."

The celebrations continue with sacrifices and dedications, and a brief final note explains how Judith lived to an old age, when she freed her maid and distributed her wealth. The Israelites were unthreatened during her life and for a long time afterwards.

3.2 Literary Features

The genre of this story has been much debated,[16] as has its composition and indeed its unity (many scholars find it hard to see any intrinsic connection between chs. 1–7 and 8–16). But the clue to both its structure and its theology lies in the book of Judges (which is also an explicit model for the book of 1 Maccabees). The story may reflect Jewish fear of being overrun, militarily and/or culturally, not by individual neighbors, but by an empire, or by a collection of nations.

That there is a level of irony in the book is generally agreed, though how deep this runs is debated. The victory of a woman over a general is itself mildly ironic; but perhaps the irony runs deeper, almost to the level of parody, as scenes, genealogies and historical details are deliberately confused; in particular "Israel" and "Judah," and the monarchic and post-monarchic eras, are entirely jumbled.[17] On the other hand, Judith's final slide into obscure conformity may be seen as another touch of irony, or as a final victory for patriarchal values.[18]

If Judith addresses a specific contemporary situation, for which nation, if any, might the Assyrians stand? Antiochus IV and the Seleucid kingdom have been suggested, as has the Roman Empire and even the Parthian. It may be, nevertheless, that no particular military threat lurks here: possibly Hellenism itself (despite the fact that Judaism absorbed a good deal of it) was seen, in quasi-military guise, as a threat to the bulwark of Jewish identity. At all events, the book betrays a nervousness, an insecurity against a threat that is presented in terms of physical annihilation, in much the same way as the book

---

[16] See Moore, *Judith*, 71–6 for discussion.
[17] So van Henten, "Judith as Alternative Leader."
[18] So A.-J. Levine, "Sacrifice and Salvation," in *Esther, Judith and Susanna*, 208–33.

of Esther. How far this situation itself might be seen as ironic is a good question. Van Henten suggests that within a predominantly male story there are female voices. It remains a possibility, however, that this is substantially a woman's story, in which case modern readers are in danger of misrepresenting the target of a possible parody as the message of the book itself! It is also worth pointing to the instance of the "good Gentile" in Achior, alluding, perhaps (like Ruth) to the circumstances of absorption *into* the Jewish ethnos. His role is a useful reminder than in many Jewish stories from and about the diaspora, attitudes to Gentiles are often nuanced: and those who defend the Jews are equally subject to the protection of the Jewish God. In this connection, the inclusion of the people west of the Euphrates, and not just Israelites/Judeans, in the original resistance to Nebuchadnezzar, is suggestive.[19])

3.3 Dependence on the Jewish Scriptures

The author has drawn very richly upon other scriptural antecedents. These references may be impossible to demonstrate in every individual case, but the cumulative evidence of even likely allusions is overwhelming enough. From the book of Judges itself, we can discern the figure of Ehud who assassinates a foreign king in his private chamber and escapes to his own camp. Much more obvious, of course, is the story of Deborah, which is surely the dominant scriptural model – but the story, rather than the figure of Deborah herself, since it is Jael on whom Judith is more closely modeled; Jael it is who kills the general in her tent, and Jael whose wifeliness is foregrounded more than Deborah's. The concluding song in Judith also recapitulates scriptural songs by two women: the "song of Deborah" in Judg 5, mostly in its second part, and the song of Miriam (/Moses), in its first part (the victory song).

The most detailed treatment of scriptural parallels in Judith is that of van Henten, who finds Judith presented as an alternative to Moses, though in the service of a Hasmonean ideology. Other scriptural influences include Balaam, who may be seen behind the figure of Achior when Achior rehearses the history of Israel to Holofernes and advises him against attack, and Daniel, in which two themes are especially shared: the confrontation between the arrogant human king and the Jewish God, and the individual piety of the hero. The resemblance between Holofernes's attempted seduction of Judith and Haman's of Esther is also inescapable; whether one can suggest influence either way is another matter. Finally, we ought to mention the story of 2 Chr

---

[19] As is Ezra's mission to bring the Jewish Law to the satrapy of Beyond the River (Ezra 7:25), behind which may lie some claim to a Jewish territory equivalent not only to the satrapy but the extent of the land over which David is said to have ruled.

20, in which an invading army is averted by the king and people fasting at the temple, and the victory celebrated by a psalm of praise.

In addition to unacknowledged models such as those mentioned, there are explicit recollections of individuals: Abraham, Isaac and Jacob are mentioned, and the revenge of Simeon and Levi in Gen 34 involved as a precedent. But detailed allusions to scriptural events are rare, for the history of Israel is surveyed in a rather vague way. Moses is not mentioned, nor the lawgiving on Sinai, and no kings are mentioned. This lack of specificity, and the absence of explicit allusion to antecedents such as Deborah is in fact rather curious.

Indeed, the relationship between the story of Judith and the Jewish Scriptures is perplexing. On the one hand, the models just suggested, and the outline of Israel's past, together with numerous names of humans and places that occur in the Scriptures, indicates that the author knew the Scriptures, and probably expected the readers to have some familiarity. But the story of Judith appears to exploit a range of scriptural sources rather freely, and the lack of concern for scriptural chronological and geography, whether deliberate or otherwise, compounds the problem.

3.4 "Justification" and "Salvation" in Judith

Judith is an individual who delivers her people from a foreign oppressor, after which she lives a long time, and Israel is free from further aggression. In this basic outline, the theology of Judith is basically Deuteronomistic: if Israel keeps the divine law it is inviolate; only if it sins can it be overcome by foreign nations. The secret of national survival is rigid adherence to the divine laws, and particularly the cultic laws.

Judith herself is made to portray her achievement as an act of God. But her own bravery and cunning are paramount to the interest of the narrative. Unlike biblical heroes who consult oracles or respond to divine commissions, Judith is in practice self-reliant, as are Mordecai and Esther, for whom, indeed, at least in the Hebrew edition of the book, there is little or no allusion to divine activity.[20] The story thus engages directly an issue that Jews from the Seleucid to the Roman periods were obliged to address: is deliverance from foreign rule (or even foreign influence) to be left to God, or is the initiative to be taken by individuals? As in the case of 1 Maccabees, the answer is clearly that human ingenuity and activity are necessary tools for divine deliverance. (As with 4 Maccabees, the prominence of a woman *might* disguise a critique of contemporary male passivity.)

Justification of the individual is hardly an issue in Judith, except to the extent that the individual owes to his or her nation a total obedience to the

---

[20] As is well known, the absence of clear reference to divine assistance is remedied in the Greek text(s) of Esther.

Law given to them. And in this story, while there are murmurings of discontent at one point from the townspeople of Bethulia (ch. 7), Israel is not in fact overrun, merely threatened. This is because it has *not* sinned. Hence we are dealing with a case of the suffering of the innocent. Here Israel plays the innocent sufferer. This could mean that while in Tobit we have a story about Israel disguised as a story about individuals, in Judith we arguably have a story about individuals disguised as a story about the nation. One of the classic explanations of innocent suffering is divine testing, and Judith offers this in the key speech of ch. 8, where, indeed, the examples she gives are all individuals. Indeed, the argument is pushed further: "the Lord harms those who come near to him in order to admonish them" (8:27). *Individual* as well as corporate suffering is thus a sign, not of divine *dis*approval, but the opposite. Trust is ultimately rewarded, in this case by copious booty plundered from the enemy (16:11).

Adherence to the law, as Judith herself shows, is in the end an individual matter, too. She herself must be exemplary in order to win divine favor. There is also perhaps a stronger hint of the individual dimension of this tale, a feature, indeed, that makes the story truly "didactic," in Judith's final hymn (16:16):

> For a sacrifice with its pleasant smell is a minor thing
> And fat of a burnt offering insignificant to you
> Whoever fears the Lord is always great

What is also particularly intriguing is the following verse:

> Woe to the nations that rise against my people
> The all-powerful Lord will take vengeance on them at the day of judgment
> He will consign their bodies to fire and to worms
> And they will remain in pain forever

While this may be interpreted to point to the belief in a final destruction of invading foreign nations, in the manner of Ezek 38–39, the references to punishment of the dead, rather than just destruction, hint, as in Dan 12, at a theodicy that demands postmortem resolution. There is, to be sure, no statement of a resurrection of righteous dead; the righteous, as Judith herself exemplifies, are rewarded for their piety by long life, respect, honor, wealth. But the wicked must be punished beyond the grave. To this extent, the logic of postmortem reward for the righteous sufferer, even if not spelled out, seems to be congenial.

But the logic only. As in the case of Daniel, the idea of postmortem retribution ("in pain forever") appears at the close, and is far from theologically developed. Both books, then, perhaps reflect the beginnings of a considered theological approach to the question of a full divine recompense after death. The most a commentator on Judith can say in this regard is that like Daniel, Judith earned her own earthly reward. The hint of anything more as reward for the righteous individual remains faint.

3.5 Conclusion

The book of Judith stresses the need for both individual initiative and self-reliance and also for piety and strict obedience to the law. The problem of the suffering of the righteous is treated at a corporate rather than individual manner, though there are hints that beneath the corporate issue lies, ultimately, the individual one. God can be trusted to protect his chosen people so long as they do not sin, though he will test them for their trust. It is that trust which ultimately proves the identity of Israel and secures divine deliverance. However, such trust must not be considered as a merely passive attitude of mind. It must express itself not only in the appropriate responses of fasting, prayer and expressions of hope, but also through direct physical action. Judith's confidence in divine protection during high risk delivers a message about individual justification as much as the story as a whole about the justification of Israel. Moreover, those who trust in God, even of non-Israelite birth, can become Israelites, and the enemies of Israel may suffer eternal torment at the hands of its avenging God.

4. Aristeas

4.1 The Story

The keeper of the library of King Ptolemy II (284–47 B.C.E.), Demetrius, is commissioned to collect as many books in the world as possible, and has heard about the lawbooks of the Jews; but these need translating from their strange language and script. The king orders that the Jewish high priest be sent a letter. The narrator (Aristeas, who is apparently not a Jew himself) bargains with the king for the release from slavery and military service of Jews deported on previous occasions to Egypt. This is granted (the text of this and other decrees is, as is conventional, provided).

Demetrius reports that existing translations of the Jewish Law are defective and that competent translators must come from Judea – Demetrius specifies six from each tribe. The king has the letter sent, together with gifts, and receives a favorable reply. The names of the translators are given and their tribes (but these are numbered, not named). A digression describes the gifts for the Jerusalem temple sent by the Egyptian king, then the temple itself, and some of its rituals; this is followed by a description of the country.[21]

---

[21] The suggestion by Jellicoe (developing a comment by Momigliano) ("The Occasion and

During the deputation to the High Priest Eleazar, the Egyptian party (including Aristeas) asks him about the distinction between clean and unclean foods and animals, prompting a long speech on the subject that takes in monotheism and separation from other peoples. (The explanations for such distinctions in diet, ultimately, are rational: clean beasts are inherently nicer than unclean ones.) On their arrival in Egypt with a law book in Hebrew, the Jewish delegates are very warmly greeted by the king. During a banquet he asks them in turn various questions about statecraft, and receives answers all of which, as the king gratefully acknowledges, make God the basis. The procedure is repeated the next six days, with more questions that spread to cover general ethics and wisdom.

The narrative resumes as the translators are taken to an island and prepare to work. They finish in seventy-two days; and the translation is highly commended for its accuracy. It is asked why other authors had not quoted from this ancient work, and two instances are given of non-Jewish authors who had wished to quote misleadingly and were smitten by God. The king sends the translators away, with more gifts, offering to welcome them back any time because he enjoys the company of men of culture.

4.2 Literary Features

The narrative epistle is a well-known Hellenistic genre (cf. 2 Maccabees in particular). The purpose is not, as the letter frequently claims, to give an accurate account of particular events, but to offer a purportedly non-Jewish (Aristeas never refers to Jews as "us") account of the Law. It is indeed possible that the letter is an apology for a Greek translation of the Jewish Torah, but it covers rather more than merely the process of translation.[22] It is, rather, an apology for Judaism directed at non-Jews, seeking to explain the rationality of the law, the wisdom of the Jews, the high culture of its leaders, the nobility and opulence of its customs, and, not least, the favor in which it was regarded by the king. This last is most important if, as seems likely, the work reflects some antagonism towards Jews by Greek-Egyptians. The story of the translation is thus a pretext for the endorsement of Judaism as a sound philosophy. The reference to Hecataeus (31), the Greek-Egyptian writer who may have written a treatise on the Jews, and almost certainly wrote in an informed and neutral manner about the expulsion of Jews from Egypt in the

---

Purpose") that the *Letter* was written to express solidarity with the Jerusalem temple, rather than with the temple in Leontopolis, remains a possibility; certainly solidarity with Jerusalem is expressed, though how popular the Leontopolis temple really was with all Egyptian Jews we do not know.

[22] The weight given to this text as evidence for the dating and origin of the Greek translation of the Pentateuch is rather surprising, given the general recognition of its highly legendary features.

distant past, is not accidental. Thus the episode of the freeing of Jews taken to Egypt, the request to bring Jews to the Egyptian court, their wisdom in matters asked by the king, their warm welcome and manner of departure, all gloss the scriptural story, as well as other stories about Jews in Egypt that would have been circulating.

4.3 Dependence on the Jewish Scriptures

Although the Jewish Scriptures from part of the subject matter of this narrative, there is no use made of them in composing the narrative itself. For this an obvious reason can be offered: the narrator, Aristeas, is presented as a non-Jew, so that such a usage would be unexpected. Such a device was not uncommon at the time, and several Jewish writers in Greek (such as Pseudo-Hecataeus) may have disguised their ethnic identity so as to give added credence to their praise of Judaism. Nevertheless, it is possible to consider the story as to some extent a reversal of the Exodus. The "exodus" story was clearly known, in some form, to Egyptians, as both Hecataeus and Manetho relate it. Here, instead of an enslaving Egyptian king, we are presented with one who liberates Jewish captives: the law, given to Moses after the exit from Egypt, is triumphantly returned and its glory acknowledged. Enmity between Egypt and Judah is replaced by amity. The presence of the translators in twelve tribes may hint at the growth of these tribes in Egyptian captivity. In this regard, it is instructive to compare the Wisdom of Solomon, where a much different attitude towards the Exodus and the Egyptians is maintained.

It is also worth noting a similarity with 1 Esd 3–4, the story of the three bodyguards, in which the (Jewish) Zerubbabel triumphs in a debate about the greatest virtue. But here is almost certainly a case of a common (Greek?) genre rather than of direct influence either way.

4.4 "Justification" in Aristeas

The narrative of itself gives little insight into the manner in which Jews were seen to be justified by God. However, the extensive descriptions of the temple and land, and the seven days of conversation between king and delegates, seem to bear the brunt of the argument, which is a rational account of Judaism. The Law is both perfect and revealed, and in accord with the best of Greek philosophy. God is the sovereign of all, and guides the hearts even of non-Jews, and especially of foreign rulers.

Because the writing proposes to minimize as much as possible the differences between Judaism and Greek philosophy, there is little emphasis on any peculiarly Jewish justification as distinct from that of non-Jews. One is justified, whether Jew or Gentile, by obedience to the Law, but also by obedience to reason, which is the same thing. God is the model for all human rulers to obey, and his will in found, as well as in reason, in rational thought. For God works in the hearts of all humans. To one of the questions (195): "What is the supreme blessing in life?" the answer is: "to know that God is lord over everything and that we do not ourselves control our plans in the best actions, but God brings about all human affairs and guides humans by his sovereign power." In another answer, it is acknowledged that all people have been created by God as equal.

Here in fact we find a hellenized version of the ancient wisdom philosophy, which held that, regardless of ethnic affiliation, if one acts according to wisdom one will be blessed, for there is one god, one law of nature and thus one ethic. "Wisdom" in this case means life and thought according to the will of God, to whom prayer should be addressed for guidance. God is essentially to be equated with providence. He directs every human thought when it is aimed at good goals. One's lot in life is a gift from God and ordained as such (206). The explicit virtues of the law and of proper social behavior are identical: honor to parents and friends, justice and piety. Thus, while obedience to Torah brings joy, so does clear conscience – if that is not, according to the writer, the same thing (260–61). Boccaccini's argument that this story develops a "true theology of grace" perhaps overstates what is an attempt to make God the source of all things.[23]

4.5 Conclusion

Of all the stories considered here, Aristeas is the most open and positive towards Greek philosophy. Jewish writings belong with the best of the world's philosophy, and Jewish Law expresses perfectly the truths to which reason, according to Greek philosophy, also aspires. Revelation and reason, Jew and Greek are subject to the one Deity; and the goal of the good life – "justification" – is virtue in itself.

5. 3 Maccabees

5.1 The Story

The opening of the story, in which an unknown ex-Jew rescues the king from a plot, employs a familiar element of the courtier-tale (Sinuhe, Esther). The king is Ptolemy IV (Philopator), and, though he begins as a sympathetic figure, distributing gifts and accepting an invitation to visit Jerusalem, he wishes to enter the sanctuary. Following a prayer from the high priest,

---

[23] G. Boccaccini, *Middle Judaism: Jewish Thought 300 B.C.E. to 200 B.C.E.* (Minneapolis: Fortress, 1991), 171.

Ptolemy is stricken before he enters (we may compare the case of Heliodorus in 2 Maccabees 3). Returning to Egypt he seeks revenge on the Jews by depriving them of their rights, and having them branded with the sign of Dionysus, but also bribing them with the gift of citizenship[24] to participate in that cult. Most resist, upon which they are commanded to be brought to Alexandria and executed. They are so numerous that numbering them takes forty days. The king orders that they should be trampled to death by elephants, but the attempt is postponed because the king falls into a deep sleep. Another miraculous intervention entails another postponement. Finally, after another prayer from an aged Jew called Eleazar, the elephants are turned back by two angels against the royal troops, whereupon the king reverses his attitude and commands a festival to be celebrated, ever after commemorated by the Jews. The Jews also slay their own apostates, hold another festival, and return to their homes.

5.2 Literary Features

This work conforms to the Greek romance, namely a fictitious story about a historical character, with much drama, a religious theme, and elements of the miraculous.[25] It shows no signs of having been composed in any language other than Greek. Its "Maccabean" title, whatever the origin, indicates its resemblance to the second book of Maccabees (see next section). It does contain a stock martyrdom scene, though unlike that popular genre (especially in Christian circles) the martyrdom is not accomplished: instead there is a happy ending. The theme of the conversion, rather than destruction, of the king recalls the stories of Dan 1–4 and 6, where miraculous acts of divine deliverance persuade the ruler of his folly. The celebration of a feast to mark the occasion is another fairly stock item (as in Esther, but also in both 1 and 2 Maccabees, where they relate the origin of the "feast of lights" at the rededication of the altar). The text of a royal letter is another feature of such stories (as in Ezra, Esther, 1 Maccabees) granting certain rights to Jews in perpetuity. Finally, one feature of the self-purging of the Jewish community of apostates is interesting: the Jews request this of the king on the grounds that those who do not obey the Jewish Law are unfit subjects of the king as well.

5.3 Dependence on the Jewish Scriptures

Precise dependence upon any scriptural writing is hard to pin down, but the

---

[24] Citizenship status was a case of ongoing contention in Alexandria, where the Jewish community continually strove for it, to be on a par with the Greeks and above the majority of Egyptians.

[25] M. Hadas, *The Third and Fourth Books of Maccabees* (New York: Harper, 1953), 13–16.

book of Esther provides a number of parallels: the foiled plot against the king;
the destruction of enemies (here apostates) by Jews, the commemorated feast.
Like 2 Maccabees, where the largest number of parallels can be detected, it
includes an attempt by a foreigner to enter the Jerusalem sanctuary, but unlike
it, does not really glorify individual martyrdom or dwell on postmortem
retribution. The trampling by elephants recalls 1 Macc 6, where the hero, as
here, is also named Eleazar (but he also appears as a martyr in 2 Macc 6). The
massacre of apostates recalls the episodes of Phinehas (Num 25) and the
levites (Exod 32). The former episode is also recalled by Mattathias in his
speech in 1 Macc 2 (v. 54), and may possibly also have underlain the adoption
of the name "zealot" (Greek translation of the Hebrew קנא used of Phinehas)
by some of those rebelling against Roman rule in the first Jewish revolt.

5.4 "Justification" and "Salvation" in 3 Maccabees

The absence of themes that one might expect here – martyrdom and afterlife
– is noticeable, at least in a work presumably emanating from Alexandria
during the Greco-Roman period.[26] The issue, as with Esther, is the preservation of the Jewish people, and, like Daniel, idolatry provides the point of
conflict, as a foreign king seeks to persuade them to abandon their religion.
The danger to Jews comes from within as well as without; very probably this
reflects the concerns of Alexandrian Jews in particular, where, despite
political discrimination and occasional riots, the pressure was felt rather in
terms of steady assimilation. For that reason, H. Anderson[27] is probably right
to doubt that any specific persecution prompted this story. If apostasy is an
issue, as the slaughter of apostates in ch. 7 implies, then what of the report
that it is an *apostate* Jew, Dositheus, who rescues the king in ch. 1? Must this
be read in a disapproving way? (3 Macc 1:3 states that Dositheus "arranged
that a certain insignificant man should sleep in the tent; and so it turned out
that this man incurred the vengeance meant for the other one.") Perhaps,
however, the intended vengeance was not divine. The reader might wonder
whether this Dositheus survived the end of the story, however. If there is
salvation for a king, there is apparently none for an apostate, even when an
apostate rescued a king.

The issue of the political loyalty of Jews is not directly raised, as it is in
both Esther and Daniel, but by alluding to the unfitness of apostates to be
subjects of the king, and by bringing harmony to relations between Jews and
king, the story clearly proposes that there is salvation for Jews on earth where
God intervenes. Indeed, as the Jews end by praising the king, the story affirms

---

[26] The exact date of 3 Maccabees is hard to fix. Most scholars suppose the first century B.C.E.
as the most likely.

[27] "3 Maccabees," in *OTP*, 2.511–12.

the desirability of harmonious relations as much as it depicts the folly of the king in resisting the Jews and their God, whom he himself finally proclaims as the "Deliverer of Israel" (7:23).

What is it, then, that defines Jews? We are not really told: the issue is "apostasy" and this means adopting the city's religious rites. But it is profanation of the temple that instigates the conflict. No doubt here we have a reflection of Maccabean times. But here, no more than in Aristeas, do we see what role the temple plays in defining the relationship between Jews and their God. No doubt the sanctity of that place and of its cult were essential in the construction of a stable world. But how were Jews saved, and how were they "justified"? The story does not seem much concerned to tell us.

5.5 Conclusion

The narrative interestingly combines features of the individual courtier story with those of a national persecution, but without the adhesive of individual martyrdom. There is little interest on what Judaism *means* to a Jew, while the persecution is based, it seems, on the king's desire to rid himself of this religion. There are some curious features: the wicked king is finally honored as he does honor; but the apostate Jews, like the one who first rescued the king, are executed by their own people. One cannot find much literary or theological value in this poor narrative, which manages to be both contrived and derivative at the same time.

6. 4 Maccabees

6.1 The Story

Like Aristeas, this narrative is in the service of an essentially philosophical agenda, as the beginning of the work makes clear: "whether pious reason is in absolute control of the passions." The martyrdom of Eleazar and the seven brothers, narrated in 2 Maccabees, is taken as the author's illustration that this thesis is correct.

The author, then, first defines wisdom as knowledge, acquired from the Law, the highest virtue that we learn being prudence (φρόνησις). Those who conduct themselves according to the Law overcome their natural tendency and perform justly, wisely, temperately; it subdues all vices. Biblical examples are given of such control (Moses, Levi, David).

The narrative commences (ch. 4) when Simon, an opponent of the virtuous high priest Onias, incites Apollonius, governor of Syria, to plunder the temple. On his approach, with priests, women and children at the temple praying to God for deliverance, Apollonius is rebuffed by angels on horseback. Appealing to the high priest to pray for him, Apollonius is spared and reports to king Seleucus.

Seleucus's successor, Antiochus, however, deposes Onias in favor of Jason, and after Jason's Hellenizing measures, proscribes Judaism, ordering every Jew to eat pork and food sacrificed to other gods. The first of these to be featured is Eleazar, a priest and expert in the Law, as well as known for his philosophy. In response to threats of torture, Eleazar again retorts that the Law is not contrary to reason (as, he says, the king thinks) and he will not break it. A description of the tortures follows, during which Eleazar refuses even to pretend to eat unclean food, lest he make a poor example to others. At the point of death Eleazar prays that his sufferings may be a δίκη for his people, and his life an ἀντίψυχον for them (for the meaning of the terms, see below). For the author, Eleazar's death furnishes another instance of the power of reason/Law over pain as well as over pleasure.

The account of Eleazar's death is followed by that of seven brothers and their mother. Faced with torture, the young men respond in the same defiant way to Antiochus, claiming that their suffering will win them "the prize of virtue" and that through it they will be "with God" (9:8). "As though being transformed into incorruption by the fire" the eldest exhorts his brothers to fortitude before he dies. The remaining brothers follow, each making his own speech.

The author finally dwells on the piety of the mother, whose maternal instinct is totally governed by her piety. She throws herself into the fire, thus showing that she too has the reason that conquers passion, and the narrative concludes with further reflections on the meaning of the martyrdoms.

6.2 Literary Features

Although the author uses an embellishment of the narrative of Eleazar and the seven youths in 2 Maccabees, this work is essentially a philosophical treatise. Just as it attempts to equate the Jewish Torah with the reason of Greek philosophy, rather in the manner of Aristeas, so it also elaborates the theme of Jewish martyrdom in the face of a Hellenizing monarch; and to this end it deploys a range of Greek subgenres: the trial scene, the pathetic history, the rhetorical speech.

As with 3 Maccabees, it is doubtful whether such a work requires a context of actual persecution for its composition. The martyrdom accounts are taken from another source and embellished with a philosophical argument; it seems more likely that the purpose of the work is to demonstrate the supremacy of reason/Law over passion, while neither the rewards of martyrdom nor the fate of the tyrannical king are given prominence. Thus, the purpose of the work is to illustrate a philosophical-religious principle, and not to inspire those currently under persecution to withstand it.

6.3 Dependence on the Jewish Scriptures

Exemplary figures from the Jewish Scriptures are given extensive mention. The final address of the mother (18:6–19) is a recollection of how her husband had acquainted his sons with the "law and the prophets," with specific mention of Abel, Isaac, Joseph, Phinehas, the three youths of Dan 3 and Daniel himself. Abraham, Isaac, Jacob, David, Moses, and the heroes of the book of Daniel are mentioned elsewhere too, while the mother is likened (15:31) to Noah's ark.

The closing chapter also cites a number of scriptural prooftexts: Isa 43:2; Ps 34:19; Prov 3:18, Ezek 37:3 and Deut 32:39. Apart from this device, which is unusual for a work of this kind (and may be part of a secondary addition), the function of allusions to Scripture elsewhere is to provide historic examples of the supremacy of Law and reason over passions, just as the martyrs understand themselves as exemplars to their fellows and to future generations.

6.4 "Justification" and "Salvation" in 4 Maccabees

More than in any other of the didactic narratives discussed here, 4 Maccabees concerns itself with the significance of martyrdom for the fate of the individual and the people as a whole. It also presents such an act in terms of "justification." But the theology of martyrdom presented here does not function as a means of personal vindication, as it does, to a large extent, in 2 Maccabees. The value of the martyr is in the example, and also in the demonstration itself of the supremacy of reason. Martyrdom in and of itself is the demonstration of truth as well as virtue. Herein lies the ultimate demonstration of "righteousness"; the mastery of passion and supremacy of reason displayed in a human life. This inevitably implies obedience to the Law, one of the prevailing definitions of צדיק in the Jewish Scriptures. To a much lesser degree, if at all, does it convey "innocence," a forensic sense clearly present in both wisdom and prophetic books of the Hebrew Bible. There, as with late Second Temple Judaism, and with Paul, it is "innocence *before God*" that is supremely conveyed. Had this sense been present in 4 Maccabees, the personal salvation of the martyr would surely have been more emphasized. My impression is that "righteousness" in 4 Maccabees is closer to the Stoic ideals of αὐτάρκεια and ἀπαθεία.

And so, somewhat surprisingly for a work modeled in 2 Maccabees, the individual fate of the martyr, as of the oppressor, is not accorded any prominence, though both are alluded to. Thus, Antiochus will be punished in death as well as life (12:18), and eternal torment awaits the souls of those who break the commandments of God (13:15). The seven youths are also described "as if running on the road to immortality." And they did, after all, receive "pure and deathless souls from God" (18:23).

One might indeed expect such concentration on the frailty of the body to be accompanied by rather more emphasis on the immortality of the soul, especially in the youths' speeches. But this theme is very muted, as if the author, who clearly has a philosophical bent, wished to avoid some of the implications of stressing a soul-body dichotomy as he also wished to avoid any suggestion that martyrs suffered for the sake of a reward (for that, too, could be seen as a matter of passion, not reason). Immortality and heavenly glory are not the chief prizes of martyrdom, though they are acknowledged as an outcome.

Martyrdom is not, then, according to 4 Maccabees, a matter of achieving glory in the eternal world. It is exemplary and followed for the sake of nobility. This reflects a good deal of Greek philosophy, both Stoic and Platonic. However, there is a distinctive and important Jewish element. Though it is not part of the author's main argument, it acquires significance because of the implications it carries for the theology of martyrdom in early Christian writing, and especially for certain forms of Christology. This is the notion that the martyr's death achieves a benefit for others – the martyr, in other words, as a vehicle for the justification and salvation of others as well.

The idea is presented in two places. One is in 6:27–29:

Σὺ οἶσθα, θεέ, παρόν μοι σῴζεσθαι βασάνοις καυστικαῖς ἀποθνῄσκω διὰ τὸν νόμον. ἵλεως γενοῦ τῷ ἔθνει σου ἀρκεσθεὶς τῇ ἡμετέρᾳ ὑπὲρ αὐτῶν δίκῃ. καθάρσιον αὐτῶν ποίησον τὸ ἐμὸν αἷμα καὶ ἀντίψυχον αὐτῶν λαβὲ τὴν ἐμὴν ψυχήν.

You know, O God, that while it is open to me to be preserved, I am dying for the law, in fiery torments. Be merciful to your people, our sentence being satisfaction on their behalf. Make my blood a means of their purification and take my life as their ransom.

The other passage is 17:19–22, which is an eulogy on Eleazar and the seven youths:

καὶ γάρ φησιν ὁ Μωυσῆς Καὶ πάντες οἱ ἡγιασμένοι ὑπὸ τὰς χεῖράς σου. καὶ οὗτοι οὖν ἁγιασθέντες διὰ θεὸν τετίμηνται, οὐ μόνον ταύτῃ τῇ τιμῇ, ἀλλὰ καὶ τῷ δι᾽ αὐτοὺς τὸ ἔθνος ἡμῶν τοὺς πολεμίους μὴ ἐπικρατῆσαι. καὶ τὸν τύραννον τιμωρηθῆναι καὶ τὴν πατρίδα καθαρισθῆναι, ὥσπερ ἀντίψυχον γεγονότας τῆς τοῦ ἔθνους ἁμαρτίας. καὶ διὰ τοῦ αἵματος τῶν εὐσεβῶν ἐκείνων καὶ τοῦ ἱλαστηρίου τοῦ θανάτου αὐτῶν ἡ θεία πρόνοια τὸν Ισραηλ προκακωθέντα διέσωσεν.

For Moses says, "All the holy ones are in your hands." These, therefore, having been sanctified by God are esteemed, not only by this honor, but also in that through them enemies did not overcome our nation, and the tyrant punished and the land purified, since they became a ransom for the sin of the nation. Through the blood of these righteous persons and through the propitiation [effected by] their death, divine providence saved an afflicted Israel.

The death of the martyr can thus atone for the sins of others. Nor should it be overlooked that in this connection Isaac is mentioned (7:14). The antiquity of the notion of vicarious atonement in Judaism is a vexed question. The value of an animal's sacrificial death for atonement is certainly an ancient and widespread notion. That human sacrifice can appease the gods is attested throughout the ancient Near East and in classical culture too; it is indeed an almost universal phenomenon. However, the scriptural view is overwhelmingly that animal, not human, sacrifice secures atonement. It is possible, though certainly much disputed, that the germ of this idea is present in the "Servant Songs" of Isaiah. The role of martyrdom in post-Second Temple Judaism is probably to be seen in the context of theological reaction to the disappearance of the temple cult as the ordained means of removing sin. Thus, according to both the Qumran Community Rule (1QS) and the rabbis, good deeds could atone, so the ultimate "good deed" of martyrdom could seen as especially efficacious. Certainly the figure of Isaac was developed in this direction, though here the line between bravery under threat and an atoning effect must be carefully distinguished (as is not always done in scholarship on this subject). In 7:14 it is Isaac's "reason" (like Aaron's in 7:11) that is appealed to, not necessarily any atoning value resident in his (near-) sacrifice. Again, in 16:20, while Isaac's bravery is commended, we have no suggestion that his fortitude was efficacious for Israel as a whole. In Pseudo-Philo (late first century or early second C.E.), Jephthah's daughter suggests that her death may be of atoning value (ch. 40).

Fourth Maccabees' acceptance of some atoning value for martyrdom in its paying the price (ransom, ἀντίψυχον) for the sins of Israel raises an interesting question about whether the temple and the cult were still standing at the time of writing; but this is not a question that can be answered firmly. However, the atoning value of the exploits of Eleazar and the youths is not actually given great prominence. More important seems to be their *exemplary* role. We may go further and suggest that this exemplary role does not necessarily apply to Jews threatened by death. Many of the examples cited from Scripture did not die under such circumstances. Rather, they showed the supremacy of reason over passion in other ways. It follows that the value of martyrdom, according to the purpose of this author, is as an extreme illustration of the control of passion by reason. In the end, the law is something to live by, not because it offers a reward of eternal blessedness, nor because it achieves recompense for the sins of Israel (both of which are acknowledged), but because it is intrinsically good and proper to do so. Ultimately, this idea, to which belongs the theme of the "noble death,"[28] owes more to the Greek world than to the Judean.

---

[28] On this well-known *topos* of Greco-Roman culture, see e.g. D. Seely, *The Noble Death: Graeco-Roman Martyrology and Paul's Concept of Salvation* (JSNTS 28; Sheffield: JSOT, 1990).

The notion of the atoning value of an exemplary death is also present. The role this idea plays has perhaps been overemphasized by many commentators because of its theological connection with the New Testament. That vicarious atonement is present anywhere in the Hebrew Bible is a contentious issue: the Servant of Isaiah 40-55 is often held as an example, but such an interpretation has been disputed. The idea that human sacrifice (whether by death or perfection of way) can replace animal offerings is found in the Qumran Community Rule (8:1-10), where suffering (death is not mentioned) is said to be "atonement for the land." But the atoning value of martyrdom is at best hinted at in Daniel and 2 Maccabees, and seems to have taken root after the destruction of the Second Temple, notably in the rabbinic notion of the "merits of the fathers" and the doctrine of the Aqedah, which emerged as a haggadah about the Tamid sacrifice (which was also "tied," Heb. עקד), and later influenced by Christian ideas. In 4 Maccabees, the notion that a righteous martyr's death can serve the function of a sacrifice appears in the speech of Eleazar (6:28-29) and in 17:22 where the narrator regards death as a "propitiation" (ἱλαστήριον) by means of which God saved (διέσωσεν) Israel. But while there are other references to divine pity on Israel (e.g. 9:24; 12:18) the notion of martyrdom as atonement is not expressed here – and indeed, it cannot be said, on the basis of such scanty reference, to form a main element in the theology of the book. To speak of 4 Maccabees presenting a doctrine of atonement through martyrdom is not incorrect, but is somewhat exaggerated. For the author, martyrdom is efficacious mainly in other ways. Whether the word ἱλαστήριον is used here in a precise, technical sense, as indicating an acknowledged instrument of propitiation, or somewhat more poetically (especially in 6:28-29) to suggest that divine pity on Israel might be provoked by the sight of innocent suffering, is difficult to know. The view taken here inclines to the latter alternative.

Martyrdom, then, is presented here in a guise that Greeks would find familiar. But the Greek character of the "righteousness" that the book extols, and the central identification of reason with Law, are both put to the service of an anti-Hellenistic message, in which Hellenism is presented as the vehicle of religious apostasy. The phrase "children of Abraham" (e.g. 6:23 and also 18:7 and 23) is often repeated; the persistence of *Israel* itself counterbalances the *philosophical* value of martyrdom.

6.5 Conclusion

In 4 Maccabees, as in the other stories discussed, the individual and Israel are entwined. In this particular case, the individual value seems to rest to a great extent on the demonstration of a Stoic virtue itself (self-control, αὐτάρκεια, of passion by reason). The "salvation" that achieves for the individual may be understood in terms of an immortality, but much more emphasis is laid on the effect for Israel as a whole of such martyrdom: it is exemplary, a demonstration of the superiority of Jewish virtue; and it can also accomplish a recompense for others.

To what end, then, is it necessary, in the view of 4 Maccabees, to secure the future of Judaism? We are not told: the answer, we can suppose, is self-evident to the sympathetic reader. Yet, as with 3 Maccabees, we may ask whether Hellenism itself did threaten Judaism by such violent means as are ascribed to Antiochus (or Ptolemy), rather than by the more subtle means of persuasion and attractiveness. For in the end this particular story engages a philosophical argument and, it must be admitted, sets out (with 2 Maccabees) also to satisfy the reader's delight at reading of gruesome tortures (we need not deny this fairly universal human trait). Whether it engaged with real persecution or even discrimination must remain in doubt.

7. General Conclusion

We have seen that all the stories in different ways link the justification of the individual with the justification of the Jewish people. Tobit shows what the essential virtues of Jewish life are, but also draws in quite clearly the question of the fate of the whole Jewish people, of whom Tobit is a representative, not merely an instance. In Judith strong individual initiative and piety can achieve salvation for the people, with divine providence well in the background – and provided that the people are free from sin. In Aristeas, indeed, there is little about the individual dimension at all. Third Maccabees makes much of the dangers, and the fate, of apostasy and the availability of divine intervention when the Jews are persecuted for what is never clearly explained. But like Aristeas, it seems concerned essentially with the question of accommodating foreign culture to Jewish life and vice versa. Finally, 4 Maccabees shows that martyrdom has both personal and communal meaning.

With the exception of Aristeas, none of these stories, however, gives a very clear hint as to what it is about Judaism and the Jewish people that makes it important for them to be preserved. Such a question, perhaps, was not worth asking and the answer taken as self-evident. But certainly all of these narratives make it clear that it was as a member of the Jewish people that each individual had to relate to God, and that equally the fate of that people depended on the allegiance, resourcefulness, reliability and honor of every single member. In these stories, no Jew is an island, and in the fate of every Jew lies, potentially, the fate of the Jewish people.

Select Bibliography

General

Barclay, J. M. G. *Jews in the Mediterranean Diaspora: From Alexander to Trajan.* Edinburgh: T&T Clark, 1996.

Charles, R. H., ed. *Apocrypha and Pseudepigrapha of the Old Testament in English.* 2 vols. Oxford: Clarendon Press, 1913.

Charlesworth, J. H., ed. *The Old Testament Pseudepigrapha.* 2 vols. New York: Doubleday, 1983, 1985.

Cohen, S. J. D. *From the Maccabees to the Mishnah.* Library of Ancient Christianity 7. Philadelphia: Westminster, 1987.

Collins, J. J. Between *Athens and Jerusalem: Jewish Identity in the Hellenistic Diaspora.* New York: Crossroads, 1983.

Collins, J. J. *Jewish Wisdom in the Hellenistic Age.* Louisville: Westminster John Knox, 1997.

Kraft, R. A. and Nickelsburg, G. W. E., eds. *Early Judaism and its Modern Interpreters.* Philadelphia: Fortress/Atlanta: Scholars, 1986.

Martínez, F. García. *The Dead Sea Scrolls Translated. The Qumran Texts in English.* 2d ed. Leiden: Brill/Grand Rapids: Eerdmans, 1996.

Nickelsburg, G. W. E. *Jewish Literature Between the Bible and the Mishna.* Philadelphia: Fortress, 1981.

Nickelsburg, G. W. E. and Stone, M. E. *Faith and Piety in Early Judaism: Texts and Documents.* Philadelphia: Fortress, 1983.

Stone, M. E., ed. *Jewish Writings of the Second Temple Period: Apocrypha, Pseudepigrapha, Qumran Sectarian Writings, Philo, Josephus.* CRINT, section 2. Philadelphia: Westminster Press, 1984.

Wills, L. M. *The Jew in the Court of the Foreign King.* HDR 26. Minneapolis: Fortress, 1990.

Tobit

Deselaers, P. *Das Buch Tobit: Studien zu seiner Entstehung, Komposition und Theologie.* OBO 43. Freiburg: Universitätsverlag/Göttingen: Vandenhoeck & Ruprecht, 1982.

McCracken, D. "Narration and Comedy in the Book of Tobit." *JBL* 114 (1995): 410–18.

Moore, Carey A. *Tobit.* AB 40A. New York: Doubleday, 1996.

Nickelsburg, G. W. E. "Tobit." Pp. 40-46 in Stone, ed., *Jewish Writings.*

Rabenau, M. *Studien zum Buch Tobit.* BZAW 220. Berlin: De Gruyter, 1994.

Simpson, D. C. "The Book of Tobit," in *APOT,* 1.174–241.

Judith

Craven, T. *Artistry and Faith in the Book of Judith.* SBLDS, 70. Chico: Scholars, 1983.

Doran, R. "Narrative Literature," in Kraft and Nickelsburg, *Early Judaism*, 287–310.

Enslin, M. S. and Zeitlin, S. Z. *The Book of Judith.* Leiden: Brill, 1972.

Levine, A. J., "Sacrifice and Salvation: Otherness and Domestication in the Book of Judith." Pages 208-33. *A Feminist Companion to Esther, Judith and Susanna.* Edited by A. Brenner. Sheffield: Sheffield Academic, 1995.

van Henten, J. W. "Judith a Alternative Leader," in Brenner, *Feminist Companion*, 234–52.

Letter of Aristeas

Andrews, H. T. "The Letter of Aristeas," in *APOT*, 2.3–122.

Boccaccini, G. *Middle Judaism: Jewish Thought 300 B.C.E. to 200 C.E.* Minneapolis: Fortress, 1991. 161–85.

Hadas, M. *Aristeas to Philocrates.* New York: Harper, 1951.

Howard, G. E. "The Letter of Aristeas and Diaspora Judaism," *JTS* 22 (1971): 337–48.

Shutt, R. J. H. "Letter of Aristeas," in *OTP*, 2.7–34.

Tcherikover, V. "The Ideology of the Letter of Aristeas," *HTR* 51 (1958): 59–85.

3 Maccabees

Anderson, H. "3 Maccabees," in *OTP*, 2.509–29.

Emmet, C. W. "The Third Book of Maccabees," in Charles, *APOT*, 1.156–73.

Hadas, M. *The Third and Fourth Books of Maccabees.* New York: Harper, 1953.

4 Maccabees

Anderson, H. "4 Maccabees," in *OTP*, 2.531–64.

Breitenstein, U. *Beobachtungem zu Sprache, Stil und Gedankengut des Vierten Makkabäerbuches.* Basel and Stuttgart: Schwabe, 1978.

Emmet, C. W. *The Fourth Book of Maccabees.* London: SPCK 1918.

Hadas, M. *The Third and Fourth Books of Maccabees.* New York: Harper, 1953.

Townshend, R. B. "The Fourth Book of Maccabees," in *APOT*, 2.653–85.

6. Apocalypses

by

RICHARD BAUCKHAM

The apocalypses are a literature of revelation in which seers receive, by heavenly agency, revelations of the mysteries of creation and the cosmos, history and eschatology. Within the common literary genre and this rather broad definition of the kind of content the genre can be used to convey, the Jewish apocalypses of this period are fairly diverse, and on the subjects of covenant, law, and salvation present a spectrum of approaches such as also characterizes other Jewish literature of the same period. Apocalyptic is not an ideology but a genre, and we must abjure the habit of considering that the apocalypses propound a certain kind of Judaism different from that expressed in other forms of Jewish literature. Those who read and valued apocalypses also read and valued hymns and halakah and retellings of Israel's history and wisdom literature. Even those who wrote apocalypses may well have written other forms of religious literature too. Not the ideology but the kind of content determined genre. Certainly there were traditions of thought continued in a succession of apocalypses, especially the Enoch literature, but there are also groups of apocalypses characterized by their varied responses to similar issues, as in the case of *4 Ezra*, *2 Baruch* and *3 Baruch*. Some apocalypses have more in common with certain other works of different genre than they do with other apocalypses. However we characterize the variety of ideologies in early Judaism – which can easily be either smoothed over or exaggerated – we should not confuse it with the variety of literary genres.

The apocalypses included are those which are non-canonical, indubitably or probably non-Christian Jewish, and which date from before 200 C.E. Two which fulfill these conditions (the *Apocalypse of Abraham* and the *Ladder of Jacob*) have been omitted for reasons explained in section 3.1 below.

1. The Enoch Tradition

1.1 Introduction

The work we know as *1 Enoch* consists of several distinct compositions, all or most of which probably existed as independent works before being incorporated in this compilation of Enochic works: (1) the Book of Watchers (chs. 1–36); (2) the Parables (or Similitudes) of Enoch (chs. 37–71); (3) the Astronomical Book (chs. 72–82); (4) the Book of Dreams (chs. 83–90); (5) the Epistle of Enoch (chs. 91–105); (6) the Noah Appendix (chs. 106–107); (7) another Writing of Enoch (ch. 108). The complete text of this corpus of Enochic writings survives only in the Ethiopic version, but Greek versions of sections (1), (4), (5) and (6) are partially extant. Whether these are from a compilation of Enochic works in Greek corresponding to the scope of the Ethiopic *1 Enoch* we cannot be sure. All of the four sections partially extant in Greek are also evidenced among the fragments of Enoch writings in Aramaic from Qumran. These fragments are from several manuscripts,[1] some of which show that at Qumran there was a compilation of Enochic writings somewhat different from that which we know as *1 Enoch*. It comprised: (1) the Book of Watchers; (2) the Book of Giants; (3) the Book of Dreams; (4) the Epistle of Enoch; (5) the Noah Appendix. As well as manuscripts which probably contained all these five components, there are manuscripts which probably contained only the Book of Watchers, which probably contained only the Book of Giants, and which perhaps contained only the Epistle of Enoch, suggesting that these were also known as independent works. In addition, there are fragments of manuscripts of the Astronomical Book, in a considerably longer form than that preserved in the Ethiopic version, too long to be incorporated with other Enochic works in a single manuscript. Thus the Qumran fragments preserve, in fragmentary form, the original Aramaic of all sections of Ethiopic *1 Enoch*, except for the Parables, which, so far as the evidence goes, was not known at Qumran, and chapter 108. (The Parables probably was first written in Aramaic, but we still know only the Ethiopic version. Chapter 108 may have been added to the Enochic collection in Greek, but is still only extant in Ethiopic.) It also appears likely that the particular collection of Enochic works we know as *1 Enoch* has been formed on the basis of the collection known at Qumran,[2] with the Parables of Enoch substituted for the Book of Giants, and an abridged version of the Astronomical Book integrated into the collection. This second compilation of writings

---

[1] On the scope of the manuscripts, see J. T. Milik, ed., *The Books of Enoch: Aramaic Fragments from Qumrân Cave 4* (Oxford: Clarendon, 1976); F. García Martínez, *Qumran and Apocalyptic: Studies on the Aramaic Texts from Qumran* (SJDJ 9; Leiden: Brill, 1992), 46–47; L. T. Stuckenbruck, *The Book of Giants from Qumran* (TSAJ 63: Tübingen: Mohr [Siebeck], 1997).

[2] It is possible that *1 Enoch* is a compilation of Enochic works known to the compiler only as independent works. But (1) it shares with the Qumran collection the order: Book of Watchers, Book of Dreams, Epistle of Enoch; and (2) it has the Noah Appendix (chs. 106–107) which most probably owes its place in both Enoch collections not to a pre-existing connection with the Epistle of Enoch in particular, but to its having been added to the Qumran collection as an appendix to the whole collection. See García Martínez, *Qumran and Apocalyptic*, 95–96.

of Enoch is almost certainly also a Jewish compilation from the Second Temple period, but very probably made at a considerably later date than the compilation known at Qumran.

It is probable that all the Enoch writings known at Qumran date from before the middle of the second century B.C.E. The Book of Watchers and the Book of Giants[3] (the latter written with knowledge of the former) date from the third century, as does the Astronomical Book, which many regard as the oldest of the Enochic works. The Epistle of Enoch, though it has often been dated to the first century C.E., is probably pre-Maccabean,[4] while the Book of Dreams was certainly written during the Maccabean revolt. Thus the Enochic writings known and valued at Qumran all date from before the foundation of the Qumran community (which may also be true of most of the pseudepigraphal works known but not written at Qumran). The absence of the Parables of Enoch shows only that it was written outside Qumran at a later date. Since it probably presupposes the Book of Watchers, but also seems to incorporate traditions both similar to and differing from those in the Book of Watchers,[5] it is evidence that the Enoch writings were read and traditions about Enoch transmitted in circles outside Qumran. On internal evidence, the Parables are most plausibly dated to the first century C.E. before 70. The New Testament letter of Jude, which alludes to material in the Book of Watchers, chapter 80 of *1 Enoch* (whether or not this is an original part of the Astronomical Book), and the Book of Dreams,[6] is also evidence that the major Enochic writings were known and valued outside Qumran, as is the popularity of Enochic writings in post-apostolic Christianity.[7] Thus, although

---

[3] On the date of the Book of Giants, see Stuckenbruck, *The Book of Giants*, 28–31.

[4] I agree with García Martínez, *Qumran and Apocalyptic*, 79–94, who argues, contrary to much previous scholarship, that there are no convincing arguments for treating the Apocalypse of Weeks (*1 En.* 93:3–10; 91:11–17) as an independent work which pre-existed the rest of the Epistle of Enoch. He also argues correctly that the Apocalypse of Weeks must have been written before the Maccabean Revolt, and so that the whole Epistle of Enoch, of which the Apocalypse of Weeks is an originally integral part, must also be pre-Maccabean.

[5] D. W. Suter, *Tradition and Composition in the Parables of Enoch* (SBLDS 47; Missoula: Scholars, 1979), esp. ch. 4.

[6] R. Bauckham, *Jude, 2 Peter* (WBC 50; Waco: Word Books, 1983), 7, 37–40, 50–53, 87–91, 94–99; idem, *Jude and the Relatives of Jesus in the Early Church* (Edinburgh: T. & T. Clark, 1990), 137–41, 188–201, 211–16. In *Jude and the Relatives,* ch. 7, I also argued that the Lukan genealogy of Jesus derives from the same early Christian circle as the letter of Jude and depends on the scheme of history found in the Book of Watchers and the Apocalypse of Weeks in the Epistle of Enoch.

[7] R. Bauckham, "The Fall of the Angels as the Source of Philosophy in Hermias and Clement of Alexandria," *VC* 39 (1985): 313–30; J. C. VanderKam, "*1 Enoch*, Enochic Motifs, and Enoch in Early Christian Literature," in *The Jewish Apocalyptic Heritage in Early Christianity* (ed. J. C. VanderKam and W. Adler; CRINT 3/4; Assen: Van Gorcum/ Minneapolis: Fortress, 1996), 33–101.

the major Enochic writings may derive from a community or tradition that the Qumran community regarded as its predecessor,[8] it would be a mistake to associate them too closely with Qumran. The Enochic tradition was continued also apart from Qumran.

This is clear also from the last Enochic work[9] that concerns us: *2 Enoch*, which is unfortunately preserved only in an Old Slavonic version and in differing recensions that make it very difficult to distinguish earlier and later forms of the text. It is a single work (though some think the final chapters, 69–73, a secondary addition), probably presupposing at least some of the earlier Enochic writings and representing itself as Enoch's last testament to his descendants, recounting the last revelations made to him before his final translation to heaven. Since, unlike the other Enochic works, *2 Enoch* uses the scheme of seven heavens, through which Enoch ascends, viewing the contents of each and the throne of God in the highest, it is unlikely to date from before the first century C.E., when other evidence suggests that that particular form of visionary ascent was first employed in apocalypses.[10] If its references to the temple are to the Jerusalem temple, it would date from before 70, but they may not be. If *3 Baruch* stands in a polemical relationship to it,[11] then the early second century is the latest plausible date.

It is clear that the various Enoch writings form a distinctive tradition of thought and writing. This does not necessarily imply that they derive from a single, historically continuous socio-religious group, though this may be plausible for some or all of the Enochic writings known at Qumran. It does mean that later writers in the tradition knew and depended on earlier Enochic writings, and that certain central themes and concerns run through the literature, in spite of some ideological variations between some of the Enochic works. It is likely that the Book of Watchers was known to the authors of all the other Enochic works, apart from the Astronomical Book, which may have been written before the Book of Watchers. It was certainly the most influential of the Enochic writings and it set the agenda of themes and concerns which run through the others to a greater or less extent. For this reason we shall begin our survey with the Book of Watchers and discuss it at greatest length. The survey will not include the Book of Giants, whose

---

[8] See now G. Boccaccini, *Beyond the Essene Hypothesis: The Parting of the Ways between Qumran and Enochic Judaism* (Grand Rapids: Eerdmans, 1998).

[9] Other Jewish and Christian Enochic works, including so-called *3 Enoch* and the *Seventh Vision of Enoch*, date from too late a period to be relevant to our present purpose.

[10] R. Bauckham, *The Fate of the Dead: Studies on the Jewish and Christian Apocalypses* (NovTSup 93; Leiden: Brill, 1998), 84–85.

[11] Bauckham, *The Fate of the Dead,* 67.

surviving fragments are too small to provide material for our present purpose, or the Astronomical Book, whose relevance to our concerns is very limited.[12]

1.2 Book of Watchers (1 Enoch 1–36)

From the Qumran manuscripts which begin with the first five chapters of *1 Enoch* and seem to have included only the Book of Watchers, we know that these first five chapters formed the introduction to the Book of Watchers when it was an independent book and were not written as an introduction to the whole collection of Enochic works, admirably as they also fulfill this latter function. Very probably the Book of Watchers incorporates earlier sources, but we cannot easily tell how far they were rewritten in the book as we have it, and, since it was this book that was influential on the rest of the Enoch tradition and much more widely also, we are justified in considering the Book of Watchers as a unity.

The book has three main themes, corresponding to successive parts of it. The first is Enoch's prophecy of the universal judgment to come, addressed to the elect who will live at the time of this judgment, seventy generations after Enoch's own lifetime (chs. 1–3). The second is the story of the Watchers (chs. 6–16), disobedient angels who, in the time of Enoch's father Jared, descended from heaven to satisfy their lust for women. The offspring of these unions were the giants, who tyrannized the earth with their violence in the period before the flood. The Watchers also corrupted humanity by revealing forbidden and dangerous heavenly knowledge. The story is a myth of the origin of evil (cf. esp. 10:8). Although the Watchers were chained in the underworld, the giants were exterminated by their own violence, and the earth was cleansed of its corruption by the flood, their evil has continued to influence humanity, since the ghosts of the giants survived as the evil spirits who are abroad in the world until the last judgment and are responsible for idolatrous religion. The story is linked to Enoch because he is commissioned by God to announce to the Watchers their irrevocable judgment. The third element in the Book of Watchers is the cosmological tours on which Enoch is taken by the angels, revealing the mysteries of the cosmos to him (chs. 17–36).

Clearly the Book of Watchers is concerned with the origin and nature of evil, and provides, probably for the first time in extant Jewish literature, a fully-fledged account of evil as due to supernatural beings who corrupt almost all humanity and the earth itself. But it is even more concerned with the judgment of evil.[13] The relevance of the antediluvian world to Enoch's implied

---

[12] Relevant material is in chs. 80–82, which readers may easily compare with our studies of the other Enochic works.

[13] For the eschatological judgment as the focal point of the whole of *1 Enoch*, see G. W. E. Nickelsburg, "The Apocalyptic Construction of Reality in *1 Enoch*," in *Mysteries and*

readers in the last generation of history before the last judgment is that it was a thoroughly corrupt world whose evil was comprehensively judged by God. Only the family of Noah was saved to make a fresh start after the flood. The world in Enoch's time functions as a type of the implied readers' world and the judgments on the Watchers and humanity at the time of the flood are a type of the coming last judgment, through which the righteous will be saved from angelic and human evil. Whereas in the first judgment in Enoch's time evil was provisionally defeated, but survived to corrupt the world again, in the second and last judgment God will remove the threat of evil altogether. The same concern for judgment also appears in Enoch's journeys, where, alongside other cosmological secrets, he sees both the places where the dead and the Watchers are presently awaiting the last judgment, and also the places where the Watchers and the unrighteous will be punished and the righteous will enjoy the blessings of paradise after the judgment. The introductory chapters also exploit the typological parallel in that Enoch's condemnation of the wicked (chs. 2–5) parallels his announcements of judgment to the Watchers (13:1–3; 16:2–4).[14] These chapters, with their vivid evocation of the coming theophany of the divine Judge (ch. 1), and their prophecy of salvation for the elect but irrevocable doom for the ungodly, are programmatic in that they define the book's subject as the eschatological judgment and direct the implied readers to read the rest of the book with this in mind.[15]

The antediluvian story perhaps inevitably gives the immediate impression that the book is not concerned with the specifically Israelite themes of Abrahamic or Sinai covenant and Mosaic law, but only with universal evil affecting the world as a whole.[16] Sacchi argues that, in the Book of Watchers, the "problem of evil is not connected in any way to the Law, nor does salvation come in any through the Covenant."[17] This enables him to interpret the Enochic tradition as distinct from and opposed to the "official" or "nomistic" tradition of Jerusalem in early Second Temple Judaism, which

---

Revelations: Apocalyptic Studies since the Uppsala Colloquium (ed. J. J. Collins and J. H. Charlesworth; JSPSS 9; Sheffield: Sheffield Academic, 1991), 52–53. He concludes that "there is scarcely a page of *1 Enoch* that is not in some sense related to the expectation of an impending divine judgment" (53).

[14] In both cases there is reference to hardness of heart (5:4; 16:3), and in both cases there can be neither mercy nor peace for the offenders (5:4–5; 13:1–2; 16:4).

[15] On chs. 1–5 as introduction to the Book of Watchers, see especially L. Hartman, *Asking for a Meaning: A Study of 1 Enoch 1–5* (ConBNT 12; Lund: Gleerup, 1979), 138–145.

[16] But note that on his travels Enoch sees the land of Israel and the environs of Mount Zion and Jerusalem (unnamed and, of course, in Enoch's time, before there was a city or temple there) (chs. 26–27), and is told about the temple in Jerusalem in the eschatological age (25:5–6).

[17] P. Sacchi, *Jewish Apocalyptic and its History* (tr. W. J. Short; JSPSS 20; Sheffield: Sheffield Academic, n.d.), 22.

relied on Moses and the law.[18] In neglecting both Moses and the prophets, the Book of Watchers "gives the impression of a conscious break with the tradition."[19] However, we should note that Sacchi is able to maintain this position only by ignoring chs. 1–5, which, as we have seen, must be included if we are to characterize the theology of the Book of Watchers in the only form we know it, rather than excavating sources behind it.

However, before considering this question in relation to chs. 1–5, we should first reject the possibility that Enoch and his teaching are presented in the Enochic tradition, or the Book of Watchers in particular, as an alternative to Moses and the Law. The real contrast is between Enoch and the Watchers, both presented in terms of the ancient idea of culture-heroes who were responsible for introducing the arts and knowledge of civilization revealed to them by the gods.[20] The Watchers are negative culture-heroes, who descended from heaven with secrets that led humanity astray and proved to be only "a worthless mystery" (16:3).[21] In this sense the story is doubtless a polemic and warning against pagan culture and learning. But in contrast to the misleading and harmful secrets revealed by the descending and disobedient angels there is the genuine revelation of heavenly secrets given to Enoch when he ascends to heaven and keeps company with the holy angels. In this aspect, therefore, the stories of Enoch and the Watchers function to draw a sharp distinction between pagan culture and the wisdom cultivated in the Jewish circles from which the early Enochic literature comes. For this purpose, in view of the importance attached to antiquity in such contexts, the antediluvian Enoch, as ancient as any of the culture-heroes to whom pagans traced their culture, was more useful than Abraham or Moses, who were also portrayed as culture-heroes in some Jewish literature. But the secrets revealed and communicated by Enoch in the Book of Watchers (chs. 17–36), as also in the Astronomical Book and in the Parables, in no way compete with the Torah. Their subject-matter is different and complementary.

There is certainly a genuine element of universalism in the Book of Watchers, which persists through much of the rest of the Enochic tradition. The coming judgment is emphatically represented as a universal one (1:7–9), while, when the earth has been cleansed of evil, "all the children of men are to become righteous and all nations shall serve and bless me [God], and all

---

[18] Sacchi, *Jewish Apocalyptic,* 18–19, 106–107. A rather similar view is taken by M. Barker, *The Older Testament* (London: SPCK, 1987).

[19] Sacchi, *Jewish Apocalyptic,* 58.

[20] Bauckham, "The Fall of the Angels," 314–319.

[21] This translation follows the Ethiopic rather than the Greek, with M. A. Knibb, *The Ethiopic Book of Enoch,* vol. 2 (Oxford: Clarendon Press, 1978), 102–103, against M. Black, *The Book of Enoch or 1 Enoch* (SVTP 7; Leiden, Brill, 1985), 35, 155, who prefers an emended form of the Greek text at this point. Elsewhere my quotations of *1 Enoch* are from Black's translation unless otherwise noted.

shall worship me" (10:21). On the other hand, Hartman has argued at length and convincingly that chs. 1–5 evoke God's covenant with Israel as their "referential background."[22] We may note especially that 1:1, 3–4, 9 allude unmistakably to Deut 33:1–2 (along with other passages in the Hebrew Bible), implying that the author, like some other Jewish writers, read Deut 33–34, the last words of Moses in the Torah, as prophecy of the future history of Israel, and 33:2 as referring to the eschatological theophany of God as judge.[23] The reference to Sinai as the location of the theophany (*1 En.* 1:4) is borrowed from Deut 33:1, but did not have to be had the author not wished to evoke the giving of the Law by which God will judge the world.[24] Hartman also shows the affinity of chs. 2–5 with the covenantal denunciation speeches of the Hebrew Bible and early Jewish literature, in which those addressed and denounced are those who had violated the covenant.[25] It looks as though, while speaking of universal judgment, these chapters focus on those who are faithful to God's covenant with Israel and those who have committed apostasy from it.

The two categories of people are designated in these chapters, on the one hand, "the righteous" (Aramaic קשיטין: 1:1, 8, 5:6) and "the elect" (בחירין: 1:1, 3, 8; 5:7, 8), and, on the other hand, "the sinners" (חטאין: 1:9; 5:6, 7) and "the wicked" (רשיעין: 1:1, 9; 5:6, 7). Of these terms, the most interesting is "the elect," which also occurs once more in the Book of Watchers (25:5), occurs just twice in the Epistle of Enoch (93:2, 10),[26] and is frequent in the

---

[22] Hartman, *Asking for a Meaning*. The reason for which J. J. Collins, *The Apocalyptic Imagination* (New York: Crossroad, 1984), 38, rejects Hartman's argument is not cogent. He claims that chs. 2–5 refer to the law of nature rather than the law of Moses. But the example of the works of creation which never deviate from obeying God's commandments to them cannot supply humans with the content of what God requires of them. The meaning is that, by contrast with nature's obedience to God's commands *to them*, the apostates are disobedient to God's commands *to them* (in the Torah).

[23] Cf. D. J. Harrington, "Interpreting Israel's History: The *Testament of Moses* as a Rewriting of Deut. 31–34," in *Studies on the Testament of Moses* (ed. G. W. E. Nickelsburg; SBLSCS 4; Cambridge, MA: Scholars, 1973), 59–68. *T. Mos.* 10:1–7 describes the eschatological theophany in similar terms to *1 En.* 1:3–9, because both passages allude to the same OT sources.

[24] In Deut 33:2 YHWH comes "from Sinai," whereas in *1 En.* 1:4 he will "tread upon the earth upon Mount Sinai" (a mixed allusion to Mic 1:3 and Deut 33:2). The difference does not indicate that "Sinai has a place in Enoch's revelation, but it is not the ultimate source," as Collins, *The Apocalyptic Imagination,* 37, suggests. Rather *1 Enoch* corrects the text of Deuteronomy because it understands God to dwell in heaven, not on Mount Sinai.

[25] Hartman, *Asking for a Meaning*, 49–95.

[26] Sacchi, *Jewish Apocalyptic*, 115, claims that "for the first time the righteous are called 'elect'" in 93:2, while conceding in a footnote (5), "The word 'elect' appears also in the first chapter of *Enoch*, where it constitutes a problem by reason of its isolated character." He missed the occurrences not only in 5:7, 8, but also in 25:5. He correctly refers to Trito-Isaiah, but is

Parables of Enoch (38:2, 3, 4; 39:6, 7; 40:5; 41:2; 45:3, 5; 48:1, 9; 50:1; 51:5; 56:6, 8; 58:1, 2, 3; 60:1; 61:4, 13; 62:7, 8, 11, 12, 13, 15; 70:3), often used alongside "the righteous" to refer to the same people as "the righteous and elect." The prominent use of the term in *1 En*. 1–5 is very significant. The plural of the noun בחיר ("chosen ones," "elect") is rare in the Hebrew Bible. On just four occasions, in closely related texts, it refers to Israel as "his" or "your [YHWH's] chosen ones" (Pss 105:6, 43; 106:5; 1 Chron 16:13). But also three times in Isa 65 "my [YHWH's] chosen ones" (vv. 9, 15, 22), parallel with "my servants" (vv. 8–9, 13–15) and "my people" (v. 22), refers to the righteous remnant of faithful Israelites contrasted with the apostates of Israel whom God will destroy (vv. 1–8, 11–15). That this chapter of Isaiah is the actual source of the usage of "the elect" in *1 En*. 1–5 must be virtually certain since *1 En*. 5:6 clearly alludes to Isa 65:15, one of the three verses in which "my chosen ones" appears in that chapter. There are other echoes of this and neighboring chapters of Isaiah in the Book of Watchers: 10:17–19 (cf. 5:9) alludes to Isa 65:20–23; the repeated theme that the righteous will have peace (1:8; 5:6–7, 9; 10:17) but the sinners will not have peace (5:4–5; 12:5–6; 13:1; 16:4) derives from Isa 57:19, 21 (cf. 48:22; 60:17); and the idea of "the plant of righteousness" (10:16, cf. v. 3) probably echoes Isa 60:21b (cf. 61:3), while the first half of the same Isaianic verse seems to have influenced *1 En*. 5:6–8 (cf. 10:21).

Barker argues that the people whose prophet speaks in Trito-Isaiah, Israelites opposed to the innovative Deuteronomic temple establishment of the restoration period, actually were the people who preserved the Enoch traditions.[27] It is less speculative to assume that the third-century author of the Book of Watchers, like many others in the Second Temple period, read the later chapters of Isaiah as the key eschatological prophecies depicting the coming judgment and restoration of Israel. He saw the widespread apostasy of his own time, as he viewed it, predicted in Isa 65, and the faithful Israelites of his time, with whom he identified, as the elect of YHWH to whom the same chapter refers. These chosen ones were such because they constituted the true Israel, the elect nation, YHWH's true covenant partners, while other Israelites had excluded themselves from Israel by their apostasy.

The apostasy is described only in general terms (5:4), while it is left entirely unstated what is entailed by being righteous. The righteous are evidently not sinless, since they are promised that they will be sinless after the judgment, as a result of God's gift of wisdom to them (5:8–9).[28] What is at

---

mistaken in thinking that the term there refers to "the Jews." He also fails to notice the significant influence which *1 En*. 1–5 has exercised on the Epistle of Enoch.

[27] Barker, *The Older Testament*, chs. 1, 7, 8.

[28] This is clear in the Ethiopic, translated by Knibb, *The Ethiopic Book*, 66–67, but the matter is more obscure in the additional material found in the Greek at this point.

stake seems to be a fundamental attitude and practice of loyalty to God and his law, contrasted with a fundamental refusal of obedience. The lack of reference to specific commandments of the Law does not mean that they are unimportant.[29] In part, this is a matter of genre.[30] It is possible that behind the accusation of apostasy lie disputes about the correct interpretation of the Law, but halakhic discussion does not belong to the genre of apocalypse and would not be appropriate on the lips of Enoch. Our text presupposes its readers know what is involved in keeping the Law properly and focuses on the fundamental distinction between those who live by it and those who reject it. This is also why there is an absolute and apparently exclusive division of people into the righteous and the wicked, a characteristic that continues in the rest of the Enochic tradition and in other apocalypses too. (But it may be noted that in this respect chs. 1–5 seem not entirely consistent with what Enoch sees, according to ch. 22, in the place where the dead are kept awaiting the judgment. Here there are two classes of the wicked: sinners who escaped justice in their lifetime and will be assigned to punishment at the last judgment, and those "who were not wholly lawless" but "collaborated" with the lawless. The latter will experience neither punishment nor resurrection at the day of judgment. This passage is not only the earliest Jewish depiction of the intermediate state of the dead. It is also unique: no other Second Temple period Jewish text classifies the dead into more than the two categories of righteous and wicked.)

In chs. 1–5 there is no exhortation to the wicked to repent or to the righteous to continue in obedience. There is simply announcement of judgment on the apostates and mercy and peace for the righteous. Presumably, there is no possibility of forgiveness for the wicked, any more than there is for the paradigm apostates, the Watchers (12:4–14:7). As for the righteous, the text simply presupposes that they are living obediently and need primarily the reassurance that justice is going to be done. Similarly, there is no indication of the way the two attributes "righteous" and "elect" relate to each other: it is simply assumed that the elect are those who are loyal and obedient to God. This is generally true of the rest of the Enochic literature also, though exhortations to the righteous not to be deflected from the path of righteousness sometimes occur (e.g. 91:3–4, 19).

---

[29] On previous discussion of this issue in the apocalypses generally, see J. C. H. Lebram, "The Piety of the Jewish Apocalyptists," in *Apocalypticism in the Mediterranean World and the Near East* (ed. D. Hellholm; 2d ed.; Tübingen: Mohr [Siebeck], 1989), 177–8.

[30] The Qumran community provides clear evidence that one and the same religious community could read and value apocalypses, halakah and wisdom paraenesis. These are different genres of literature with different and complementary functions in the life of a Jewish group. There are no necessary lines of ideological difference between the genres.

1.3 The Epistle of Enoch (1 Enoch *91–105*)

The Epistle of Enoch comprises, in the first place, introductory material, including an account of Enoch's writing of the letter for his children and for later generations, and exhortations addressed to his children (91:1–10, 18–19; 92:1–5). Secondly, there is the Apocalypse of Weeks, a summary and interpretation of world history from creation to new creation (93:1–10; 91:11–17). Thirdly, there are several chapters of admonitions addressed to the righteous and woes addressed to the sinners in the last days (94–105).

The Apocalypse of Weeks helps to set the context of the work as the writer himself envisages it. The first event after the destruction of the first temple is that "a perverse generation shall arise, and many shall be its misdeeds and all its doings shall be apostate" (93:9). Then "the elect shall be chosen, as witnesses to righteousness, from the eternal plant of righteousness" (93:10). There can be no doubt that these elect are the group with whom the real author identifies and whom he regards as the righteous remnant of Israel in his own time. The description of them recalls 91:2: "the children of righteousness and the eternal elect sprung from the plant of righteousness and uprightness" – evidently the same people. It also recalls the description of Abraham at an earlier point in the Apocalypse of Weeks: "a man shall be chosen as a plant of righteous judgment; and his posterity shall come forth as a plant of eternal righteousness" (93:5). The plant (cf. also 10:3, 16; 62:8; 84:6) is an image, drawn from Isa 60:21, of the chosen ones, stressing God's gracious act of election. The picture appears to be that from the descendants of Abraham God chose those who now constitute the elect ones in a time of widespread apostasy when the rest of Israel no longer qualify for that description. Again the existence of this group is attributed to God's act of choice. But in all cases, as in *1 En.* 1–5, this language of election and the plant is closely associated with language of righteousness (93:2, 5, 10). The elect ones are also "the children of righteousness" (93:2; cf. 105:2), "witnesses to righteousness" (93:10) and simply "all the righteous" (91:12). In this case, we may say a little more about the relationship of God's grace and human activity in righteousness than was possible for the Book of Watchers. Here the righteous are exhorted "to seek and choose for yourselves righteousness, and a life of goodness" (94:4): thus election is not envisaged as contradicting human freedom to choose the good.[31] But it is also noteworthy that, in the resurrection, when for the first time people will be

---

[31] Some scholars, including Sacchi, *Jewish Apocalyptic,* 114, cite 98:4 as evidence that the Epistle of Enoch stresses human responsibility for sin to the extent of denying that evil was brought into the world by the Watchers or Satan. But the text of 98:4 is very uncertain: see Black, *The Book of Enoch,* 301. The myth of the fall of the Watchers is so integral to the rest of the Enochic literature that we should need better evidence to conclude that the Epistle of Enoch rejects it.

able to be wholly righteous forever, this is the result of God's grace and power (92:3–5; cf. 91:17): God "will be gracious to the righteous and give him eternal uprightness" (92:4).

After the Apocalypse of Weeks, the righteous are not called "the elect" again, no doubt because the admonitions and woes concern the contrast between the ways of life of the two categories of people. Besides "the righteous," they are occasionally called "holy" (100:5), "pious" (100:5; 103:9; 104:12) and "wise" (98:1, 9, 99:10; 100:6; 104:12). The last is an indication of the influence of wisdom tradition, with its contrasts of wise and foolish, righteous and sinners. In line with this, we also find the image of the two ways: "the paths of righteousness" and "the paths of wrong-doing" (91:18–19; cf. 93:14; 94:1–4; 99:10; 104:13). All this accords with the absolute and exclusive distinction between the two groups which, as in *1 En.* 1–5, runs through the whole of chs. 94–105. It also accords with the assumption that what is at stake is a matter of fundamental loyalty and life-orientation. The only warning to the righteous is, in effect, to keep to the way of righteousness and not to apostatize (94:3; 99:10; 104:5), while of "the truly righteous"[32] it is said that "no unrighteousness has been found in them till they die" (102:10). We hear nothing of repentance or forgiveness, though a single verse addressed to the wicked exhorts them not to do evil (104:9).

The contrast between righteous and sinners is also given quite concrete social definition. The sinners are powerful, rich, arrogant, unscrupulous, and oppress the poor, such that "the paths of wrong-doing" can also be called "the paths of oppression" (91:19). They are not Gentiles,[33] but Jewish apostates, some of whom cause others to apostatize (99:1): these "alter the words of truth, and pervert the everlasting law, and count themselves to be without sin" (99:2; cf. 98:15). The righteous, who by comparison with the wicked are few (103:9, 15), are objects of their contempt, persecution and oppression (94:11; 95:7; 96:8). This situation explains why it is that, whereas the sins of the oppressors are amply characterized, almost nothing is said about what the way of righteousness entails. It is assumed that they are pursuing that path, and what they primarily need is hope and courage, not to be intimidated by the oppressors, not to be discouraged by their apparent impunity (95:3; 96:1, 3; 97:1; 104:2, 4, 6). The message of the certain doom of the wicked provides for this need.

The wicked, who might suppose that their evils go unnoticed, are assured that "all your iniquities are written down day by day until the day of judgment" (98:8; cf. 104:7). The well-known formula that they will be judged

---

[32] On the translation, see Black, *The Book of Enoch,* 113.

[33] But the rulers, who ignore the complaints of the righteous against the oppressors (103:14–15), could be Gentiles. Pagans appear in 91:9, and perhaps in 99:7–10 (though here the meaning may be that Jewish apostates practice pagan idolatry).

according to their deeds is also used (95:5; 100:7).[34] Neither of these motifs should be understood in the sense of a nice calculation of the guilt of individual deeds. Both are consistent with the holistic sense of judgment on a whole way of life, and the main rhetorical function is to stress that the wicked will not escape justice.

1.4 The Book of Dreams (1 Enoch 83–90)

We need pause only briefly over this Enochic work, which contains little of direct relevance to our theme, though it continues the dominant interest of the Enoch tradition on the origin and nature of evil and especially on its coming eradication through eschatological judgment and renewal. Most of the work consists of the Animal Apocalypse, an allegory of history from creation to new creation. Up to the flood it follows the Book of Watchers. The account of the history of Israel differs in emphasis from the Apocalypse of Weeks, in that it stresses not only the repeated apostasy of the people but also the hostility of the Gentile nations, whom God permits to punish Israel. (The relative dates of the two works, before and during the persecution of Antiochus and the Maccabean revolt, may well account for this difference.) The theme of angelic evil affecting human history is also extended from the antediluvian period, the subject of the Book of Watchers, to the period of Israel's history from the exile onwards, in which Israel's sufferings are attributed to angelic shepherds who abuse their God-given position over their flock. Finally, the Animal Apocalypse illustrates again the universal element in the Enoch tradition: although the Gentile nations feature in most of the history as enemies and oppressors of Israel, in the eschatological age all the nations will worship God in the temple, and the very distinction between Israel and the nations will disappear (90:33–38). The point is strikingly made by the symbolism. During the history of Israel, the pagan enemies of Israel are represented by unclean animals, following the notion found in Leviticus that the food laws serve to represent the distinction between the holy people of God and the other nations as profane. (Thus the Mosaic law, never explicitly mentioned in the Animal Apocalypse, is not absent from its conceptuality.) But in the eschatological age all the species, representing the various nations, are transformed into white bulls (90:38), as Adam had been (85:3).

1.5 E. P. Sanders on 1 Enoch

Since Sanders excludes the Parables of Enoch from his discussion, this is the appropriate point at which to pause to compare our findings with those of

---

[34] On this motif in OT and OT Pseudepigrapha, see K. L. Yinger, *Paul, Judaism, and Judgment According to Deeds* (SNTSMS 105; Cambridge: Cambridge University, 1999), chs. 1–2; and for early Christian literature, see Bauckham, *The Fate of the Dead,* 195–8.

Sanders's investigation of *1 Enoch*,[35] which is one of the two apocalyptic works he discusses. Sanders's work depends on an earlier stage of scholarly study of *1 Enoch*, still dominated by the work of R. H. Charles and unaffected by the Qumran evidence, but this is not decisive for his assessment of the ideological stance of the major Enochic writings. Broadly, our findings coincide with Sanders's. It is true that, in the perspective of the texts, the righteous are the true Israel, sharply distinguished from the sinners, who are Jewish apostates or Gentile oppressors. It is true that the classifications are holistic, concerned with fundamental and permanent loyalties rather than with individual transgressions or good works. Obedience to the Law is a matter of "staying in" rather than "getting in." It is usually taken for granted that the true Israel will inherit the promises God in his grace has made to his elect people. Indeed, the general picture of the coming judgment is not that the righteous will come well out of the same judgment according to works in which the sinners are condemned, but that only the sinners are judged.[36]

Sanders recognizes that the texts tend to presuppose a rather narrow definition of the righteous or the true Israel, compared with the broader definition he finds in the rabbinic literature, but that the texts offer few clues to the criteria which distinguish the faithful from the apostates. (In passing, we may note that this enabled these writings to be popular among groups, such as the early Christians, who would have used different criteria from those used by the circles in which the texts originated.) The reason is that the implied readers are in no doubt that they belong to the category of the righteous, and understand the boundaries of this category from other genres of literature. (Sanders does not here make this latter point, but it would be congenial to his general approach to Second Temple Judaism.)

However, it is less clear that Sanders does justice to these texts by claiming that they exhibit "much the same pattern of religion" as he finds in the Rabbis.[37] This claim results from isolating the particular question he is pursuing from its wider context of thought, as well as from playing down the material difference between larger and narrower definitions of the true Israel in favor of a purely formal understanding of the issue. It must be recognized that the Enoch literature deals with issues of righteousness and salvation in the context of a vision of a world presently dominated by evil. Evil on a cosmic and universal scale is the inescapable problem to which the solution is eschatological judgment. The righteous are those who are already part of God's solution to the cosmic problem of evil. Their election and perseverance

---

[35] E. P. Sanders, *Paul and Palestinian Religion* (London: SCM, 1977), 346–62.

[36] But it is debatable whether Yinger, *Paul*, is right to cite 60:6 as evidence of this point: I am inclined to think the reference (in a disordered textual context) is to the flood and to the Noahic covenant.

[37] Sanders, *Paul*, 361.

(getting in and staying in) take place in a context in which apostasy (getting out) is widespread and domination by the pagan enemies of God and his people an all too familiar fact, while behind these earthly realities the seductive and oppressive power of supernatural evil is vividly perceived. Addressed to the righteous in such a context, the texts modulate between, on the one hand, assuring them of their election, of God's mercy to the elect and of the certainty of his promises to them, and, on the other hand, encouraging them to remain loyal to God and his law in very adverse situations. Less often remarked is the striking combination of the focus on the righteous remnant of Israel and of the universal and cosmic vision of these writings. Contrary to some caricatures of apocalyptic literature, the Enochic tradition retains the prophetic hope for the time when all the nations will acknowledge and worship the God of Israel. Not merely the vindication of the righteous, important as that is in this literature, but universal righteousness is the outcome of the contest against evil in which the righteous are currently engaged.

1.6 The Parables of Enoch (1 Enoch 37–71)

Read as part of the collection of Enochic writings, the Parables of Enoch seems in many respects a less coherent version of the Book of Watchers. Most of the key themes of the latter recur, though without the narrative framework of the Book of Watchers and with more movement between the events of Enoch's time and tableaux of the coming last judgment. As in *1 En.* 1–5 and the Epistle of Enoch the main focus is the respective destinies of the righteous and the sinners, and as in the Epistle of Enoch the righteous are an oppressed group while the sinners are the powerful oppressors. The most innovative and most studied feature of the Parables is the figure of the Son of Man, a heavenly being who, as the Righteous One and the Elect One, is a kind of heavenly counterpart of the righteous and elect, and who will be God's agent in the judgment, enacting the vengeance of the righteous on their enemies. He functions as a kind of guarantee of the destiny of the righteous, who will live with him in blessedness for ever.

Of the various terms for the righteous, "righteous" is the most common (40 occurrences), followed by "elect" (30) and "holy" (8, used more commonly of the angels). Other key descriptions are "the righteous and elect whose works depend on the Lord of spirits" (38:2), "the elect who depend on the Lord of spirits" (40:5), "the faithful who depend on the Name of the Lord of spirits" (46:8), those "who believe on the Name of the Lord of spirits for ever and ever" (43:4), those "who have made supplication to my glorious Name" (45:3), "those who hold fast to righteousness" (61:4). These descriptions are distinctive of the Parables, not found in the other Enochic writings, and, along with the frequent use of "elect" (paralleled only in *1 En.* 1–5), serve to emphasize the grace of God and the corresponding belief, faith and reliance on God on the part of the elect. In view of what we have already said about *1 En.* 1–5 and the Epistle of Enoch, it will not be surprising that nothing is said about the righteous deeds of the righteous (other than that they "hold fast to righteousness") or their obedience to the Law, presumably not because these things are denied, but because they are taken entirely for granted. They do not need exhortation to be righteous, but assurance that God and the Son of man are on their side, that they will be vindicated against the wicked, and that they have a secure destiny of blessing and righteousness. It is important that righteousness is represented as a quality (alongside mercy in 39:5 and wisdom in 48:1) which characterizes not only the coming judgment but also the life of the righteous with the Son of man for eternity (71:16–17). There is also a notion that righteousness in human and divine affairs corresponds to the order of the creation as Enoch perceives it in his cosmological journeys.

The wicked are called not only sinners, but, more revealingly, "those who have denied the Name of the Lord of spirits" (38:2; 45:2), those who "deny the name of the Lord of spirits" (41:2; 45:1), those who "have denied the Lord of spirits and his Anointed One" (48:10), those who "have denied the Lord of spirits" (67:8, cf. 10) and "do not extol the Name of the Lord of spirits" (46:6). These expressions might suggest Jewish apostates, as in *1 En.* 1–5 and the Epistle of Enoch, but 46:7 characterizes them as idol-worshipers and therefore presumably pagans. There and in most places the sinners are the kings, the mighty, the powerful, those who occupy or possess the earth (or the land). The judgment is to be a reversal of status, such that from then onwards "those who possess the earth will be neither powerful nor exalted" (38:4). But there are some passages which seem to acknowledge a general class of sinners other than the powerful and the rulers (53; cf. 42). Jewish sinners seem never to be mentioned, and so the usual view that, as in other Enochic works, the righteous (called "the congregation of the righteous" [38:1] and "the congregations of the godly" [41:2]) are a group within the nation who considered themselves the true remnant of Israel is hard to verify.

The powerful and the rulers are to be judged according to their works (45:3; 63:9; cf. 41:1), with a justice they themselves acknowledge (63:8–9). This justice requires that mercy is refused them even when at the time of judgment they ask for it (62–63; 38:5–6). But although this refusal of mercy applies to the arrogant oppressors, for Gentiles in general the Parables offers much more hope, in line with the ultimately universal emphasis of the Enochic tradition. When the Gentiles[38] witness the victory of the elect over their oppressors, then they may repent and renounce their idols, and God will have

---

[38] This depends on Black's interpretation of "others" (50:2) as Gentiles: see Black, *The Book of Enoch*, 213. But it is in accord with the Isaianic expectation to which the description of the Son of man as "the light of the Gentiles" (58:4) clearly also alludes.

compassion on them. His compassion grants salvation to those who repent, while his righteousness requires that those who do not repent must perish (50:2–5).

1.7 2 Enoch[39]

Second Enoch has much in common with other Enochic works, and probably presupposes specifically at least the Book of Watchers (some such background would be necessary, for example, to understand the appearance of the Watchers themselves in chapter 7). Enoch's cosmic tour, accompanied by angels who show him cosmological and eschatological secrets, does not here take him to the edges of the world, as in the Book of Watchers, but upwards through the seven heavens to the throne of God. But this merely corresponds to a shift of cosmological picture in late Second Temple Judaism. As in the Book of Watchers and the Parables, revelations to Enoch are about the workings of the cosmos as well as eschatological matters, and the topics are probably connected by a sense that God's judgment is part and parcel of God's ordering of the cosmos. As in the Book of Watchers, Enoch in *2 Enoch* sees the places of eschatological judgment, reward and punishment, already prepared as an integral part of creation. As in all the Enoch literature, eschatological judgment is a very dominant theme. Similarly, *2 Enoch* seems to rely on the implicit typology of its setting before the flood: the sinfulness of humanity before the flood parallels that of the end-time, the readers' own time, and the flood itself prefigures the eschatological judgment. More novel in the Enoch tradition is the considerable attention *2 Enoch* gives to questions of cosmological origins: the processes of God's creation of the world and of Adam.

An important difference from the other Enoch literature is that *2 Enoch* does not seem to address a situation in which the readers, a righteous minority, are troubled by widespread apostasy or by oppression. The function of eschatological promise and judgment as encouragement and consolation for the faithful is largely missing.[40] Instead, there are considerable portions of ethical paraenesis, in which, exceptionally among the Enoch literature, the content of righteous living is expounded in some detail, and ethical exhortation is both accompanied by eschatological sanctions of punishment and reward and also frequently grounded in creation. But it is hardly correct to characterize the content of the exhortation as only "a simple ethical code,"[41] since there are also cultic requirements, including animal sacrifice (2:2;

---

[39] For a survey of scholarship on *2 Enoch*, see C. Böttrich, "Recent Studies in the *Slavonic Book of Enoch*," *JSP* 9 (1991): 35–42.

[40] Chapter 50 is a partial exception, but even here the form is ethical exhortation.

[41] F. I. Andersen, "2 (Slavonic Apocalypse of) Enoch," in *OTP* 1.96.

45:1–3; 59:1–5; 62:1; 66:2)[42] and thrice-daily attendance at "the Lord's temple" (51:4).[43] (These references are decisive in demonstrating the Jewish origin of *2 Enoch*, which, if the references are to the Jerusalem temple cult, must date from before 70 C.E. But the Jewish temple at Leontopolis in Egypt might be in view, if, as many have argued, *2 Enoch* was written in Egypt.) Set as it is in the time of Enoch, Enoch has no reference to the covenants with Israel, the Torah or the history of Israel, except in a very indirect sense in the predictive reference to the preservation of Enoch's books until the last generation of his descendants, when they will be revealed (35:2–3). This rather obscure statement may refer to *2 Enoch*'s implied readers as "the faithful men." The ethical teaching is not obviously based on the Torah, but, as wisdom instruction, need not be seen as competitive with the Torah,[44] just as Ben Sira's wisdom was not meant to be an alternative to the Law. Like the Law, Enoch's teaching is referred to as a yoke (48:8–9), no doubt because it embodies God's commandments, also described as a yoke (34:1). It was not uncommon for Jews to see the essence of the Torah, without its specifically Jewish features, as known to people from the time of Adam. The strong insistence on monotheistic belief and worship throughout *2 Enoch* is very typical of late Second Temple Jewish literature, and, since *2 Enoch* is not plausibly a work of propaganda aimed at pagan readers, the implied readership can hardly be other than Jews and those Gentiles who attached themselves to synagogues and worshiped the God of Israel as the only god.

The universalistic, not specifically Jewish, tenor of the book is therefore to be understood as a requirement for a work set in the antediluvian period and attributed to Enoch. The question is whether *2 Enoch* takes for granted the specifically Jewish teaching known to its readers in the Hebrew scriptures or whether it defines a form of religion for which Enoch's writings would take the place of the Torah of Moses. The former is more likely. But the consequence of this feature of *2 Enoch* is that there are no covenantal features in *2 Enoch*, no election or covenantal promises, only God's commandments and rewards and punishments for observance or neglect of them.

The major concerns of *2 Enoch*'s many references to the last judgment are that nothing in a person's life, inward or outward, will escape scrutiny, and that strict justice will be done, such that retribution or reward will correspond to merit. Several conventional motifs convey this. One is the light from which

---

[42] The book also depicts the practice of animal sacrifice by the righteous in the antediluvian period (68:5–7; 69:9–18; 70:2, 19–21), though no temple is mentioned.

[43] Quotations of *2 Enoch* are from the translation of Andersen, "2 (Slavonic Apocalypse of) Enoch."

[44] *Second Enoch* 47:2J seems to claim superiority for Enoch's books over all other books ever to be written, but the relevant words are found only in recension J, and may not be original.

no one can hide, so that "there will be true judgment, without favoritism, for true and untrue alike" (46:3J). Another is the book in which all the deeds of every person are recorded, so that they can be made known at the judgment (50:1; 52:15; 53:2–3; cf. *1 En.* 98:8; 104:7; *2 Bar.* 24:1; *Apoc. Zeph.* 7). According to 19:5(J) angels keep this exhaustive record of each life, but elsewhere Enoch himself is the scribe (50:1; 53:2–3).[45] In either case, the scribe has the benefit of God's total knowledge of a person, their inward thoughts as well as their outward deeds (53:3; cf. 66:3, 5), so that, once again, nothing can be hidden and noone can escape God's judgment (50:1; 66:3, 5). *Second Enoch*'s strong emphasis on the heart (in the biblical sense of the seat of thought and motivation) as the interior source of behaviour and on the need for purity of heart (e.g. 2:3; 45:3; 46:2; 61:1; 63:2) requires an emphasis on the full exposure of the heart to the divine scrutiny. Another aspect of judgment which emphasizes its absolute justice is the eschatological *lex talionis,*[46] in which the punishment is described in a way that fits the crime or the reward in terms that parallel the righteous act. For example, "He who expresses anger to any person without provocation will reap anger in the great judgment" (45:3J), while someone who willingly suffers financial loss for the sake of a brother can expect to receive "a full treasury" in the age to come (50:5J; for other examples, positive and negative, see 2:2; 44:3bJ; 45:1–2; 50:6A; 60:3).

Finally, there is the image of weighing people or their deeds in the scales of justice (44:5; 49:2; 52:15).[47] This motif is found also elsewhere in the Jewish apocalypses with reference to eschatological judgment (*1 En.* 41:1; 61:8; *Apoc. Zeph.* 8:5). Tempting as it is to trace this motif to Egyptian origins,[48] it is in fact no more common in Jewish and Christian literature of Egyptian origin than elsewhere,[49] and its immediate source is certainly biblical:

If you say, "Look, we did not know this" –
does not he who weighs the heart perceive it?
Does not he who keeps watch over your soul know it?
And will he not repay all according to their deeds (Prov 24:12 NRSV; cf. also Prov 16:2; 21:2; Job 31:6; Dan 5:27).

---

[45] For this role of Enoch, cf. *Jub.* 4:23–24; *T.Ab.* B10–11, and Coptic Christian literature discussed in B. A. Pearson, "The Pierpont Morgan Fragments of an Enoch Apocryphon," in *Studies on the Testament of Abraham* (ed. G. W. E. Nickelsburg; SBLSCS 6; Missoula: Scholars, 1972), 244–9.

[46] On this see Bauckham, *The Fate of the Dead,* 123–4, 210–15.

[47] In 52:15 both scales and books are mentioned together at the judgment; the two images are also combined in *T.Ab.* A12–13.

[48] S. G. F. Brandon, *The Judgment of the Dead* (London: Weidenfeld & Nicolson, 1967), 37–48, 120–126.

[49] Pearson, "The Pierpont Morgan Fragments," 249.

The significance of this text is that it couples the image of weighing with the formula about requiting each according to his or her deeds (also in Ps 62:12; Job 34:11; Jer 17:10), which became a standard way of describing the justice of the eschatological judgment in early Jewish literature.[50] Though *2 Enoch* does not use the formula, the image of weighing deeds is clearly intended in the same sense. Particularly interesting is the extended image in 44:5, which shows how it refers to the use of instruments for measuring by weight and quantity in the marketplace:

> Because on the day of the great judgment every weight and every measure and every set of scales will be just[,] as they are in the market. That is to say, each [person] will be weighed in the balance, and each will stand in the market, and each will find out his own measurement and in accordance with that measurement each will receive his reward (44:5J).

Evidently the just weights and measures are the divine standard of justice, and the correct price (reward) will be paid for each person's weight or measurement on those scales.[51] Peculiar to *2 Enoch* seems to be the notion that a scale for weighing each person is already prepared for that person, along with a place for their judgment, before the person existed (49:2–3; cf. 23:4). This is the extreme case of the notion, important in *2 Enoch*, that judgment is an integral part of the cosmos as God has created and ordered it, as is expressed more generally in Enoch's viewing of paradise and hell, already awaiting the inhabitants to be assigned to them at the last judgment (8–10; cf. 61:2–3).

It is not explained how the assessment of recorded deeds or the weighing of people's lives operates such as to produce two distinct categories of people, the righteous and the wicked. Even if there are also gradations of reward or punishment within each category (cf. 43:3J), the overall division into two categories, one destined for paradise, the other for hell, is everywhere taken for granted in *2 Enoch*, as in other apocalypses and most early Jewish literature. In the *Testament of Abraham* (A12–14; B9) it is clear that people are assigned according to whether their sins outnumber their righteous deeds. But this crudely arithmetical notion can hardly be intended literally. We should probably think of a process of just judgment on the overall quality of a person's whole life. In other apocalypses, we can detect the idea that the division into two categories at the judgment rests on the fundamental choice and loyalties of people, who direct their lives either in accordance with God's commandments or in rejection of them, and that the deeds done and the lives lived are the outworking of this basic orientation of life in one or the other

---

[50] Yinger, *Paul*, chs. 1–2; Bauckham, *The Fate of the Dead*, 195–8.

[51] Cf. the "measure for measure" idea and terminology in Jewish and Christian literature: Bauckham, *The Fate of the Dead*, 212.

direction. One way in which this is expressed is the well-known picture of the two ways, one of which everyone must choose to take. This image is used of Adam in *2 Enoch* 30:15J:

> And I [God] gave him [Adam] his free will; and I pointed out to him two ways — light and darkness. And I said to him, "This is good for you, but that is bad"; so that I might come to know whether he has love toward me or abhorrence, and so that it might become plain who among his race loves me.

It is clear that for *2 Enoch* all of Adam's descendants have the same free choice as Adam had. It may also be that *2 Enoch*'s considerable emphasis on monotheistic faith and worship as opposed to polytheism and idolatry implies that other acts follow from a fundamental choice between faith in or rejection of the one true God.[52] Something like this is suggested by the images of the two yokes and the sowing of two kinds of seed:

> I [God] know the wickedness of mankind, how they have rejected my commandments and they will not carry the yoke which I have placed on them. But they will cast off my yoke, and they will accept a different yoke. And they will sow worthless seed, not fearing God and not worshipping me, but they began to worship vain gods, and they renounced my uniqueness. And all the world will be reduced to confusion by iniquities and wickednesses . . . (34:1–2J: the reference is to the period before the flood).

Carrying the yoke is doubtless undertaking to obey the commandments of the one true God, and the seed are the deeds that follow from such an undertaking. Using the same image of the yoke for the commandments of God as conveyed in his own writings, Enoch says that those "who are discerning so that they may fear God" delight in them, but "those who are undiscerning and who do not understand the Lord" renounce them and find the yoke a burden weighing them down (48:7–8).

At first sight, *2 Enoch* 41:2 suggests total perfectionism: someone who avoids being sent to hell is one who "has not sinned before the face of the Lord." This appears to justify Andersen's note that *2 Enoch* "does not admit the possibility of any remedy for sin through repentance and reparation from the human side, let alone compassion and forgiveness from the divine side."[53] But such statements are not usually intended in as absolute a sense as they seem. That *2 Enoch* allows for repentance and forgiveness in the case of some sins we should probably conclude from the fact that for certain sins there is explicitly said to be no possibility of repentance or forgiveness: murder and other forms of serious harm against another person, and failure to fulfill a vow made to God (60–62). It is likely that for more minor sins, repentance (and sacrifice?) obtain forgiveness if repentance takes place in this life. What is truly remarkable is that *2 Enoch* (a work of 72 chapters) has no reference

---

[52] 10:4J could well imply this.
[53] Andersen, "2 (Slavonic Apocalypse of) Enoch," 167.

whatever to the mercy of God. As Andersen justifiably puts it: "A blessed afterlife is strictly a reward for right ethical conduct."[54]

E. P. Sanders judged *4 Ezra* as, among the early Jewish works he studied, a unique exception to the general pattern of covenantal nomism as he defined it, especially because it lacks the notion that "the basically righteous but not always obedient members of Israel" require God's mercy in order to be saved.[55] As we shall see, *4 Ezra* does not in fact exclude God's mercy entirely (10:24; 12:34; 14:34), though it so marginalizes it that all the emphasis is on the merit of good works. Had he taken account of *2 Enoch*, Sanders would have found it even more worthy of the description: "the closest approach to legalistic works-righteousness which can be found in the Jewish literature of the period."[56] Andersen gives the verdict for him: "harsh legalism,"[57] "rigorous legalism."[58] Yet we should remember that according to *2 Enoch*, for those "who are discerning," Enoch's writings, containing the commandments of God and their eschatological sanctions, "will be more enjoyable than any delightful food on earth" (48:7J). Only for the undiscerning do they seem a burden (48:8). And there is just one hint that *2 Enoch*'s religion of the heart is not devoid of grace. After his parting summary of his ethical instruction to his children in chapter 2, Enoch prays: "may God make your hearts true in reverence for him" (2:3J).

2. Apocalypse of Zephaniah[59]

Although the *Apocalypse of Zephaniah* has not yet acquired a generally recognized place among the Jewish apocalypses of the Second Temple period, there is a reasonable probability that it belongs there. But a Christian origin cannot be ruled out,[60] and so, until more thorough studies are made, its evidence must be treated cautiously. It may well be the earliest extant

---

[54] Andersen, "2 (Slavonic Apocalypse of) Enoch," 96.

[55] Sanders, *Paul*, 422.

[56] Sanders, *Paul*, 418.

[57] Andersen, "2 (Slavonic Apocalypse of) Enoch," 167.

[58] Andersen, "2 (Slavonic Apocalypse of) Enoch," 188

[59] It is generally thought that the long fragment of an apocalypse in Akhmimic, first called an "Anonymous Apocalypse" by Steindorff, belongs to the same work as the smaller fragment in Sahidic, in which the speaker is Zephaniah. I threw some doubt on this in Bauckham, "The Apocalypses in the New Pseudepigrapha," in *New Testament Backgrounds: A Sheffield Reader* (ed. C. A. Evans and Stanley E. Porter; Biblical Seminar 43; Sheffield: Sheffield Academic, 1997), 71–74 (this article was first published in 1986), but for convenience I use the title *Apocalypse of Zephaniah* which has become standard scholarly usage.

[60] *Ap. Zeph.* 10:9 almost certainly betrays a Christian editor, if not origin, and 2:2–4 (cf. Matt 24:40–41; Luke 17:34–35) needs careful assessment in relation to this issue.

example of a specific type of apocalypse, in which the seer is taken on a tour of the places of the dead and sees the dead in their various conditions. Whereas in Enoch's cosmic tours, in the Book of Watchers and *2 Enoch*, Enoch sees the places prepared for the dead but also many other contents of the hidden parts of the cosmos, Zephaniah's travels in the other world are confined to the places of the dead and to sights of the living on earth in relation to their fate after death.[61] Abraham's cosmic journey in the *Testament of Abraham* provides the closest parallel in extant literature of the Second Temple period. The *Apocalypse of Zephaniah* reflects that view of the intermediate state, gaining ground towards the end of the Second Temple period, according to which the dead already enjoy or suffer, in a provisional way, the fates to which they will be finally assigned at the day of judgment.[62] As far as can be gathered from the fragmentary and probably abbreviated Coptic texts, Zephaniah follows the path of a dead person through Hades to paradise. The fragmentary beginning of the Akhmimic text (1:1–2) may describe his body appearing to be dead. Evidently Zephaniah has gone into a cataleptic trance in which his soul could leave his body and be taken by an angel through the world of the dead. His angelic guide protects him from the angels of punishment who seize the souls of the wicked when they die (4:1–10). Entering Hades, he encounters the angel Remiel (cf. *1 En.* 20:7), who is in charge of the souls in Hades, and another terrifying angel, who is Satan in his traditional, biblical role of judicial accuser (8:5; cf. Zech 3:1). He reads out all Zephaniah's sins from a scroll; Zephaniah prays to God for mercy and is told that he has triumphed over the accuser; another angel reads out the record of his righteous deeds (though this part of the text is lost). He travels from Hades to paradise, where the patriarchs are (7–9). From here it is possible to look back to Hades and down into its pit, where the wicked dead are being punished.

This is a text whose primary concerns are with the postmortem judgment of the dead on the basis of their deeds done in this life and also with the possibilities for God's mercy after death. The recording angels whom we have met in *2 Enoch* appear here observing people during their lifetimes from the gates of heaven. Some record "all the good deeds of the righteous," and the records are taken to God who then records the names of these people in the book of the living (3:5–7).[63] Others, the angels of Satan, record sins, so that Satan can accuse people when they die (3:9). As we can see in the case of

---

[61] For such apocalypses, see Bauckham, *The Fate of the Dead,* 80, 85–86, 91–94; M. Himmelfarb, *Tours of Hell: An Apocalyptic Form in Jewish and Christian Literature* (Philadelphia: University of Pennsylvania, 1983).

[62] Bauckham, *The Fate of the Dead,* 86–90.

[63] Quotations from the *Apocalypse of Zephaniah* are from the translation by O. S. Wintermute, "Apocalypse of Zephaniah," in *OTP* 1.497–515.

Zephaniah himself, certainly a righteous man (4:9), two books, one of sins and of righteous deeds, are read out in relation to each soul when it comes into Hades (7). The picture is similar to that in the *Testament of Abraham* (A12–13), though Satan does not appear there. As in *2 Enoch* and the *Testament of Abraham*, the image of the two books of deeds is associated with the alternative image of the scales (8:5).

We would expect that, as in the *Testament of Abraham*, the assessment of each soul would be a matter of whether sins outnumber righteous acts or vice versa. Unfortunately, the section of the text describing the reading of the scroll of Zephaniah's righteous deeds (7:10–11) and what happens then is missing. But it is notable that after hearing the painfully accurate record of his sins, Zephaniah prays for God's mercy: "may you wipe out my manuscript [i.e. the record of his sins] because your mercy has come to be in every place and has filled every place" (7:8). Then, even before his righteous deeds have been read out, the angel tells Zephaniah that he has "prevailed" and "triumphed over the accuser" and has "come up from Hades and the abyss" (7:9). This places the text firmly in the tradition that holds that even the righteous can be saved only by the mercy of God in forgiving their sins.

Another feature of the two books is remarkable. It is on the basis of the record of the good deeds of the righteous that God writes their names in "the book of the living" (3:7; for this term, also in 9:2, rather than "book of life," see *1 En.* 47:3; *Jos. Asen.* 15:4). The biblical source of this term is Ps 69:28:

> Let them be blotted out of the book of the living;
> let them not be enrolled among the righteous.

The idea is found quite often in the context of eschatological judgment, distinguished from the books recording the deeds of people,[64] and functioning rather as a register of the elect who are to be saved (Dan 12:1; *1 En.* 47:3; 108:3; Rev 20:15). Therefore, as in Ps 69:28, the usual image is not of names being added to the book, but of the names of sinners being blotted out of it (Exod 32:33; *Jub.* 30:22; *1 En.* 108:3; Rev 3:5; *Jos. Asen.* 15:4), even though the second line of Ps 69:28 could be read (and may well have been read by the author of the *Apocalypse of Zephaniah*) as indicating a process of adding names, additional to the process of subtracting names to which the first line of the verse refers. The usual use of the image of the book of life therefore coheres with the covenantal view that Israelites belong to the elect people of God and will receive the eschatological promises of life *unless* they apostatize and are blotted out of the book of life. By contrast, the *Apocalypse of Zephaniah* suggests that the righteous qualify by their righteousness to be included in the people of God who will receive eschatological salvation.[65]

---

[64] Our text is helpful in making the distinction clear, since scholars sometimes confuse these books: e.g. Black, *The Book of Enoch,* 209.

[65] I know only one other example of the idea that people who live righteous lives get to have

Zephaniah's view of the wicked undergoing punishment in the abyss leads him to ask God to be merciful to them (2:8–9).[66] He also learns that at a certain hour of every day, Abraham, Isaac and Jacob prays for God's mercy on these sinners, and are joined in their prayer by all the righteous in paradise (11:1–6). We do not learn God's response to the prayers, but Zephaniah's angelic guide does tell him that repentance by sinners in hell after death is possible up to the last judgment (10:10–11). This is a very unusual view in the context of Second Temple Judaism (or early Christianity). *Fourth Ezra*, for example, says, specifically of sinners after death and before the last judgment, that "they cannot make a good repentance so that they may live" (7:82). But in limiting the possibility of repentance to the time before the last judgment, the *Apocalypse of Zephaniah* conforms to the usual view, in the Jewish apocalypses, that the possibility of repentance and mercy for the wicked comes to an end at the last judgment (*1 En.* 60:5–6; *4 Ezra* 7:33–34; *2 Bar.* 85:12–13) and that God will not listen to prayers for mercy by the damned after the judgment (*1 En.* 62:9–10). These works also, rather emphatically, deny that intercession by the especially righteous for the wicked will be possible or efficacious at the last judgment (*4 Ezra* 7:102–115; *1 En.* 38:6; *2 En.* 53:1; *2 Bar.* 85:12–13). This is a denial of the argument that, just as such people as Moses and the prophets had successfully interceded for the sinners of Israel in this world (*T. Mos.* 11:17; 12:6; *4 Ezra* 7:106–111; *2 Bar.* 85:1–2), surely they might do the same in the next?[67] The *Apocalypse of Zephaniah* seems to have taken advantage of the possibility of recognizing the finality of the last judgment but allowing for intercession, repentance and forgiveness between death and the last judgment.

That the principal intercessors in the *Apocalypse of Zephaniah* are the three patriarchs is surely significant. Despite this apocalypse's unusual use of the image of the book of life, the appearance of the patriarchs suggests that they are pleading for the sinners among their descendants on the basis of the covenant God made with them. Though it is a much later text, it is worth comparing the medieval Hebrew *Story of Daniel* according to which, at the end of history, the three patriarchs will stand at the three entrances to Gehenna and ask God to remember his covenants with them. In response God will be merciful to all Israelite sinners and none of them will be sent to Gehenna.[68] While it is not likely that the *Apocalypse of Zephaniah* goes as far as this in its notion of the intercession of the patriarchs and the extent of

---

their names put into the book of life: *T. Jac.* 7:27, a clearly Christian passage.

[66] This theme is common in later Christian apocalypses which doubtless derived it originally from Jewish sources: see Bauckham, *The Fate of the Dead,* 137.

[67] On this whole subject, see Bauckham, *The Fate of the Dead,* 136–48.

[68] G. W. Buchanan, *Revelation and Redemption* (Dillsboro, NC: Western North Carolina, 1978), 476.

God's mercy, it evidently expresses a generous view of God's willingness to be merciful to members of his covenant people. (There is no evidence for the author's view of Gentiles.)

3. Responses to the Fall of Jerusalem

3.1 Introduction

It is well known that the destruction of Jerusalem and the temple by the Romans in 70 C.E. was a traumatic event which eventually provoked major changes in Jewish religion and thought, though many of these may have been less obvious after 70 than they were after the failure of the second Jewish revolt in 135. Some of these changes were practical accommodations to a radically changed situation, but, as the apocalypses written between the two revolts or perhaps after the second show, the catastrophe also raised profound theological and existential questions. The perplexing issues, which actually threatened faith in the God of Israel unless they could be adequately met, concerned the covenant and theodicy. That the catastrophe was divine punishment for Israel's sin was the most obvious interpretation available, but how could punishment to such a degree and involving the triumph of Israel's pagan oppressors, God's enemies over God's people, be understood in the light of God's covenant with Israel? Was the covenant invalidated? How were the justice, the mercy and the faithfulness of YHWH to be understood in this unexpected new event in his history with Israel? Such questions challenged not so much those who already presupposed a very restrictive definition of the true Israel who would inherit the promises (though they may well have had problems of their own unrepresented in our literature), but rather those who understood the promises to belong to the whole of ethnic Israel (excepting only those who actually renounced Jewish identity).

It was natural that people accustomed to understanding God and his purposes for his people from the biblical narratives should explore these perplexing issues by putting themselves imaginatively within the story of the closest analogy in Israel's history: the fall of Jerusalem to the armies of Nebuchadrezzar. Hence the three apocalypses attributed to Baruch and Ezra and set at the time of the fall of Jerusalem or the exile that followed. Another appropriate literary vehicle was an apocalypse attributed to one of the patriarchs to whom God gave the covenant promises that he would never forsake their descendants. Two other apocalypses probably written in the period after 70 fall into this category: the *Apocalypse of Abraham* and the

Ladder of Jacob.[69] Unfortunately, the state of the extant texts (both in old Slavonic) of these two works is such that their treatment of the topics of interest to our present concerns is obscure in the extreme, and so they have had to be omitted from the present study.

3.2 4 Ezra

Fourth Ezra[70] is a sustained theological reflection on the justice and mercy of God in his dealings with Israel in particular and humanity in general. The special problematic, as well as the agonized character, which this issue has in *4 Ezra* derives from its context following the destruction of Jerusalem and the temple by the Romans in 70. The fictional setting, according to which Ezra, in Babylon in the thirtieth year of the Babylonian exile, is in severe distress and theological bewilderment over the fall of Jerusalem to the Babylonians in the late sixth century B.C.E., is plainly meant to be read as typological of the situation of the real author and his readers at the end of the first century C.E. The starting-point for the theological journey Ezra undertakes in the book is the apparent fact that, if the destruction of Jerusalem is understood as God's judgment on Israel's sin, as much of the Hebrew Bible would suggest, then God must be understood to treat even his own covenant people with merciless justice. How can this be consistent with the merciful character of the God of Israel portrayed in Israel's scriptures and with the covenant he made with Abraham and his descendants?

Fourth Ezra is carefully structured in seven episodes (I: 3:1–5:20; II: 5:21–6:34; III: 6:35–9:26; IV: 9:27–10:59; V: 11:1–12:51; VI: 13:1–58; VII: 14:1–48).[71] The first three are dialogues (each initiated by Ezra's prayer to God) between Ezra and the angel Uriel, who speaks for God, sometimes directly in God's name. At first sight it might seem that throughout these

---

[69] There are close resemblances between the *Ladder of Jacob* and the *Apocalypse of Abraham* which probably indicate that the former is to be dated in the same period as the latter. It is remarkable that the *Ladder of Jacob*, misleadingly included in volume 2 of Charlesworth's Old Testament Pseudepigrapha, has not been recognized as an apocalypse. There can be no question that generically it is.

[70] Among other studies of *4 Ezra* I am especially indebted to B. W. Longenecker, *Eschatology and the Covenant: A Comparison of 4 Ezra and Romans 1–11* (JSNTSS 57; Sheffield: Sheffield Academic, 1991) and *2 Esdras* (GAP; Sheffield: Sheffield Academic, 1995), though I differ from his views in significant ways. The fine commentary of M. E. Stone, *Fourth Ezra* (Hermeneia; Minneapolis: Fortress, 1990) is now indispensable for all study of *4 Ezra*, though it is not especially alert to the issues that are of particular concern in the present context. There are useful reviews of scholarship in Longenecker, *2 Esdras*, ch. 2, and Stone, *Fourth Ezra*, 9–21.

[71] Chapters 1–2 and 15–16 of the work known, in English editions of the Apocrypha, as 2 Esdras, do not belong to the original Jewish apocalypse (*4 Ezra*) but are later Christian additions (often known respectively as *5 Ezra* and *6 Ezra*).

dialogues Ezra doggedly maintains his own perspective on the matter, resisting the alternative theological approach recommended by Uriel, but closer attention shows that in fact Ezra step by step accepts elements of Uriel's case, so that by the fourth and central episode he appears to have wholly accepted Uriel's view.[72] This episode and the two which follow consist of visions which are then interpreted by Uriel. At the beginning of the fourth episode, Ezra, although he has accepted Uriel's account of God's justice, is no less distressed than he has been all along. The three visions of God's eschatological judgment and salvation have the effect of consoling him, so that at the end of the sixth episode he is full of praise for God's sovereignty (13:57–58). In the last, distinctive episode, Ezra is inspired to rewrite both the twenty-four books of the Hebrew scriptures, which had been lost, and seventy other secret books.

The whole book is evidently composed as a progressive argument, which must be understood as a whole for the message of the book to be appreciated. It may well be that, as Longenecker argues, the process of Ezra's dispute with Uriel, conversion to Uriel's position, and the fuller understanding which follows reflect the real author's own dialogue with himself and the way his own thinking changed and developed.[73] Stone may also be correct in arguing that the psychological process of what could be termed the author's religious conversion is reflected especially in the fourth episode.[74] But it is unlikely that the purpose of the work is autobiographical. Ezra's intellectual and spiritual progress is more likely a rhetorical strategy designed to carry readers who start where Ezra does at the opening of the book through a process of enlightenment, conversion and consolation similar to that which Ezra undergoes. From chapters 12 and 14 it is clear that these implied readers are not the generality of Jews, but "the wise among your people"[75] (12:38; 14:46). Plausibly they are the Jewish theological elite, such as the sages who assembled at Yavneh in the period between the two Jewish revolts. But they are not envisaged as an insider group who already perceive themselves as the few who are to be saved. They are expected to be sympathetic with Ezra's starting-point rather than his concluding position; they need to follow Ezra on his theological journey. In that sense, although, as we shall see, the understanding of salvation which *4 Ezra* read as a whole propounds is not dissimilar to that in the Enoch tradition, *4 Ezra* differs from the works comprising *1 Enoch* in not presupposing the narrow definition of the true

---

[72] For the progressive character of the dialogues, see Stone, *Fourth Ezra*, 24–28, and his commentary on the passages.

[73] Longenecker, *2 Esdras*, 96–98.

[74] Stone, *Fourth Ezra*, 32–33; also M. E. Stone, "On Reading an Apocalypse," in *Mysteries and Revelations*, 65–78.

[75] Quotations from *4 Ezra* are from the NRSV version of 2 Esdras.

Israel which the Enoch literature could evidently expect its readers to take for granted. Otherwise put, *4 Ezra* does not address a sectarian audience, but rather those, such as the rabbis at Yavneh, who understood themselves as religious leaders of all Israel. The choice of Ezra, the man who taught all Israel the whole Torah (1 Esd 8:7), as the work's pseudonymous author, is in this, as in several other respects, appropriate.

Ezra's position in the dialogues is based on an understanding of God's purpose in creation and world history as centered on his covenant people Israel. These are the descendants of Abraham, with whom God made an eternal covenant, promising that he would never forsake them (3:15). Even after Uriel has told Ezra that he should see himself as one of the very few righteous, not one of the many sinners (Jewish and Gentile), he continues to identify himself with the whole of Israel (9:29–37; contrast the significant alternation of first and second person plurals in 14:29–35). Throughout the first three episodes it is the failure of God's mercy that Ezra cannot understand. He accepts that Israel has sinned, but not that this explains God's abandonment of his people to their enemies. Although God gave Israel his law, how could he have expected them to obey it, since he did not remove the evil inclination[76] which all people have inherited from Adam and hardly any succeed in resisting (3:20–23; cf. 7:48)? In any case, Israel has certainly kept the commandments much better than Babylon or the other nations, who prosper while Israel suffers (3:28–36). Having deliberately selected the one people Israel from all the nations, why has God now handed his people over to the nations who oppose God (5:23–30)? God intended Israel to rule the world, but instead the nations rule over Israel (6:55–57). These arguments imply that God has broken his covenant with Israel in that he has not exercised mercy to his people in order to fulfill his covenant promises to them.

The point is reinforced by Ezra's eloquent appeal to God's character as merciful, revealed in the revelation to Moses which played a foundational role in the Jewish understanding of God (7:132–140; cf. Exod 34:6–7). But by this stage Ezra's argument has developed, under pressure from Uriel's responses, to a consideration of the whole of humanity as sinful and bound to perish unless God were merciful. This is in considerable tension with his earlier appeal to God's declared estimation of the Gentile nations as nothing (6:56–57) and Ezra's real concern remains Israel (cf. 8:15–16). The shift to considering sin and its punishment as universal is significant not as indicating a more sympathetic attitude to the Gentiles, but as indicating the difficulty Ezra is having, through the long dialogue that forms the third episode, in maintaining his view of ethnic Israel as having a special claim on God's

---

[76] On the evil inclination in *4 Ezra*, see Stone, *Fourth Ezra*, 63–67.

mercy. Though he cannot yet accept it, he is being prepared for the view that God is as little concerned for Israelite sinners as he is for Gentile sinners (cf. Uriel in 7:59–61). The high point of the unconverted Ezra's argument is his prayer for God to be merciful (8:20–36). He pleads with God to consider not the sinners, but the righteous in Israel, sparing the whole people for the sake of the latter (8:26–30). He ends by claiming that God will be seen to be merciful, righteous and good, not by rewarding the righteous, if there are such, who have stored up good works, but by being merciful to those who have no such store of good works (8:32–35).

It is important to appreciate in what an eloquent and appealing form Ezra voices an inclusive covenantal view of God's gracious and forgiving relationship with Israel. It is a view that takes human and Jewish sinfulness very seriously, such that God's covenantal promises to his people can be fulfilled only if he is gracious to those who deserve nothing. It founds this hope on the Torah's own revelation of God's character. This view is certainly not caricatured. It is presented so sympathetically, even persuasively, that it must be part of the book's rhetorical strategy to allow this view its full weight. Not that the book is in the least equivocal about which view it finally endorses. But the unconverted Ezra's position must be given its full due, which is considerable, if the need for it to be superseded is to be presented convincingly to those whose response to the fall of Jerusalem Ezra voices. In the overall context of the book, Ezra's position in the first three episodes fails in that it cannot provide what he is seeking. It cannot account for God's actual abandonment of his people to his and their enemies in late first-century history.

Uriel's position in the dialogues is very different from Ezra's. Ezra's anguished desire to understand how the destruction of Jerusalem can be consistent with the covenant promises of God to Abraham and his descendants is initially met by Uriel's insistence that Ezra, a mortal creature of God, should not expect to understand God's ways. Uriel does not, it should be noted, deny the covenant promises, only that Ezra can understand how God will fulfill them (5:40). All the same, the initial impression that Ezra is going to be left, like Job, in chastened agnosticism about the problem of theodicy he confronts is not entirely confirmed by the rest of the book, in which Ezra in fact learns a good deal about the outworking of God's justice and mercy, both from Uriel and from the visions he is given.[77]

The key elements in Uriel's account of the matter are a stark eschatological dualism and a corresponding distinction between the way God treats the

---

[77] According to Stone, *Fourth Ezra*, 373, what cannot be revealed are "cosmological and uranological speculation, mystical ascent and theosophical speculations" (all to be found in other apocalypses, such as those in the Enoch tradition), whereas "eschatological secrets" are seen in *4 Ezra* as "a proper subject of revelation" (cf. 3:14; 14:5).

many, who are sinners, and the way he treats the few righteous: "The Most High made this world [or age[78]] for the sake of many, but the world [or age] to come for the sake of only a few" (8:1). This age is dominated by sin, which has frustrated God's good intentions for humanity and for which sinners themselves, not God, are to be held responsible (8:59–61). In this age the righteous are bound to suffer while sinners prosper. Only with the advent of the age to come will God intervene on behalf of the righteous. Only then will God act in judgment on sinners and act with mercy to the righteous, and only then will the evil inclination be removed from human nature (6:26–28).

Uriel agrees with Ezra that, given the difficulty of keeping the Law in this age, only a few succeed in doing so, such that they can be considered righteous. But whereas Ezra found it intolerable that therefore only these few could be saved, Uriel strongly affirms that this is indeed the case. Difficult though it may be to keep the commandments, those who do not are unequivocally to blame and deserve no mercy. God rejoices over the few who will be saved, but wastes no grief on the many who will perish (7:59–61). So Ezra should not be concerned for them either, nor should he count himself among them. As Sanders fairly puts it, with allusion to 7:20, "It is better for transgressors to perish than for the glory of the law to be besmirched by having mercy on them."[79]

We shall return shortly to the precise terms in which the righteousness of the righteous is understood and their salvation brought about. First, it is important to notice what the visions add to what Ezra has already learned from Uriel in the dialogues. One point which the three visions consistently make is that eschatological salvation will be brought about by God alone (10:53–54) or through the sole agency of his Messiah, who achieves victory without the use of military means (12:31–34; 13:8–11, 37–38). This is a forceful rejection of the kind of militaristic messianic activism which had issued in the Jewish revolt and led to the destruction of Jerusalem by the Romans. It also distinguishes *4 Ezra* from the Enoch tradition as represented in *1 Enoch* (though not in *2 Enoch*), where the righteous are expected to take an active part in God's judgment on the wicked (*1 En.* 1:1; 38:5; 90:19; 91:12; 95:3). For *4 Ezra* the role of the righteous is to keep God's law; judgment and salvation should be left to God alone. In the post-70 context it is clear how this functions to direct faithful Jews away from the political and military activism that had proved futile and instead into renewed effort to keep God's law faithfully. The latter remained possible even in the circumstances of suffering and oppression which *4 Ezra* does not expect to be lifted other than by the sheer initiative of God himself at the eschatological moment which he has already determined and which Ezra reveals to his readers at the

---

[78] See the "Excursus on the Term 'Age'" in Stone, *Fourth Ezra,* 218– 19.

[79] Sanders, *Paul,* 416.

end of the first century to be soon. In the wake of the tragedy of 70 C.E., *4 Ezra* does not shift emphasis from eschatological hope to keeping the commandments, as the rabbinic movement in general would eventually do, but does define rather carefully the relationship between the eschatological hope and the observance of Torah.

Apart from the exclusion of human participation in God's eschatological victory, the visions depict the eschatological events in ways that are scriptural and traditional, drawing, like most Jewish eschatology, especially on Isaiah and Daniel. By no means alien to this tradition, but probably not a feature of the hopes that had accompanied the revolt of 66–70 for most of its Jewish participants, and certainly a feature of special significance in *4 Ezra*, is the fact that not the whole of ethnic Israel, but only a righteous remnant will be the beneficiaries of eschatological salvation (12:34; 13:48–49). (It seems to have escaped the attention of most scholars writing on *4 Ezra* that the Ezra of the biblical book of Ezra also expresses a remnant theology: Ezra 9:13–15; cf. also 1 Esdras 8:78, 86–90. The implied readers of *4 Ezra* could understand this theology to have been learned by Ezra through the experiences recounted in *4 Ezra*, set chronologically earlier than the story of Ezra recounted in biblical Ezra.) This idea of the remnant is, of course, coherent with Uriel's insistence on the fact that only the righteous few within Israel will be saved. Uriel had used "remnant" language in this sense already in the dialogues (6:25; 7:28; 9:7–8).[80] Thus the visions do not simply reaffirm the traditional hope for Israel; they reaffirm it in a form different from the inclusive covenantalism expressed by the Ezra of the first three episodes and expressive rather of Uriel's distinctive position against Ezra in those dialogues.[81]

This does not mean that we should downplay the traditional material which comprises most of the visions and much even of Uriel's interpretations of the visions. The traditional hopes of God's fulfillment of his covenant promises to his people Israel, as expressed in the prophets, are not being denied in favor of a thoroughly individualistic understanding of salvation. Rather the visions and their interpretations affirm that God will indeed fulfill his covenant promises while at the same time explaining that fulfillment as salvation only for the righteous remnant of Israel. (It is important that the remnant is emphatically the remnant *of Israel:* see 12:34; 13:48.) Both aspects are important to the overall message of *4 Ezra*. That God, in the eschatological hope expressed in these visions, is fulfilling his covenant with Abraham and his descendants becomes especially clear in a special feature of the last vision (ch. 13). Here not only the remnant of Israel in the land participate in the

---

[80] On the terminology – "those who remain" or "the survivors" – see M. E. Stone, *Features of the Eschatology of IV Ezra* (HSS 35; Atlanta: Scholars, 1989), 103–4.

[81] Demonstrating this is a major contribution of Longenecker's work on *4 Ezra*; cf. already, very briefly, Collins, *The Apocalyptic Imagination*, 167.

messianic salvation, but also the nine and a half (or ten) exiled tribes of northern Israel, who return to the land of Israel as a "peaceable multitude" (13:12, 39). Probably the author and his readers knew a tradition in which the ten tribes were expected to return to join in the messianic war against Israel's oppressors.[82] This role for the northern tribes he not unexpectedly repudiates: they are peaceable and arrive only after the Messiah has already defeated the innumerable multitude of hostile Gentile nations (13:8–13). Their function in this vision is quite different. They are a kind of eschatological surprise revealing to Ezra that the righteous remnant is not as tiny as he had been inclined to think, rather as Elijah, thinking himself the only faithful Israelite left, learned that the remnant actually numbered seven thousand (1 Kgs 19:14–18). But the point is not simply to encourage Ezra. It shows that God will in fact fulfill his promise to Abraham that he would be the ancestor of *a multitude* (Gen 17:4) with whom God would maintain his covenant for ever.[83] This is the covenant to which Ezra referred in his first prayer to God (3:15) and to which he felt the destruction of Jerusalem to be in inexplicable contradiction. This is the covenant promise which seemingly could not be fulfilled if only a very few were to be saved, as Ezra feared and Uriel insisted. Not until the third of his visions, which adds to the message of the second vision precisely the fact that, through the return of the ten tribes, the remnant who are finally saved will be a multitude, does Ezra discover that, after all, God will be faithful to his covenant with Abraham. This is why it is only after this vision that Ezra, finally consoled, glorifies God for the wonders of his sovereign governance of history (13:57–58). Uriel's contrast between the few saved and the many who will perish is not contradicted by the vision, but is put in a different light: the ten tribes are a multitude (13:12, 39, 47), but the Gentile nations whom the Messiah destroys are an *innumerable* multitude (13:5, 11, 34; cf. 3:7).[84] Thus *4 Ezra*'s remnant theology finally maintains the distinction between Israel and Gentile sinners as more significant than that

---

[82] R. Bauckham, *The Climax of Prophecy: Studies on the Book of Revelation* (Edinburgh: T. & T. Clark, 1993), 219–20.

[83] *Fourth Ezra* is not alone in seeking the fulfillment of the promise of very numerous descendants of Abraham in the exiled ten tribes: Josephus also does so (*Ant.* 11.133: "countless myriads whose number cannot be ascertained"), alluding to the promise of *innumerable* descendants to Abraham (Gen 15:5). However, it is significant that, by contrast, *4 Ezra* does not call the ten tribes an *innumerable* multitude: see below. Like *4 Ezra* and also with allusion to the covenant with Abraham, Rev 7 juxtaposes the innumerable company from all nations with the determined number (144,000) of Israelites; cf. Bauckham, *The Climax*, 223–5.

[84] Once the importance of the term "multitude" as part of the covenant with Abraham is recognized, its occurrence elsewhere in *4 Ezra* acquires more significance: 7:140; 8:55; 9:22; 10:10–11. Note that in Uriel's definitive statement in 8:1–3, the contrast is between the "many" *created* and the "few" saved (not between many and few Israelites), as is also the case in 9:19–22.

between righteous and sinners within Israel. The *concerns* of Ezra's opening prayer (ch. 3) turn out to be fully met in the end, though he has only been able to come to appreciate this by adopting Uriel's apparently quite contradictory theology. Incidentally, these concerns also exclude from *4 Ezra*'s vision of the future any such hope for the Gentile nations as is found in the Enoch tradition.

The function the ten tribes fulfill in this vision is only possible by virtue of a novel element *4 Ezra* introduces into their story. Not only have they repented of the sins for which they were exiled; they also decided to leave the land of their exile, among Gentiles, and migrate to an uninhabited region,[85] "so that there at least they might keep their statutes that they had not kept in their own land" (13:40). This is how it comes about that, whereas of Israel in the land only a few manage to keep the commandments adequately, all of the exiles of the ten tribes apparently succeed in doing so. They are a model of what the Israel to which *4 Ezra*'s implied readers concretely belonged could have been. *Fourth Ezra*'s "individualism" – in which righteous individuals in Israel manage to keep the Law while most of their neighbors do not – is thus not represented as inevitable, though it seemed so to Ezra in his ignorance of the history of the ten tribes before his third vision. All Israel could have kept the Law and have been saved. But this would have only been possible through national effort and determination equivalent to the ten tribes' journey of a year and a half to a land distant from any other nation. This determined self-isolation (assisted by divine action: 13:44) represents the kind of isolation Israel could have achieved in the land had they rigorously kept themselves apart from Gentile contamination as the Torah commanded.[86] Thus the account of the ten tribes, while diverging from Ezra's original view that observing the Law was near impossible because of the evil inclination, coheres

---

[85] The name Arzareth, given to this land in *4 Ezra* 13:45, probably derives from אֶרֶץ אַחֶרֶת in Deut 29:28, which according to *m. Sanh.* 10:3 R. Aqiva and R. Eliezer ben Hyrcanus, contemporaries of *4 Ezra*, applied to the ten tribes, debating whether it implied that they would or would not return. For *4 Ezra*, the true meaning of Deut 29:28 is one of the "secret things" to which Deut 29:30 refers (cf. *4 Ezra* 14:6), i.e. secrets not revealed by Moses to the people in the Torah but revealed by God to Ezra and thereby to the wise among the people only (14:46).

[86] Longenecker, *Eschatology*, 128, sees the significance of the ten tribes' distant habitation rather in showing that "keeping the law does *not* depend on the existence of the temple, the priesthood or any sacrificial offering." But (1) the usual Jewish view was that the key elements of the temple cult – such as daily burnt-offerings and the day of atonement ritual – were efficacious for Israelites wherever they lived and without their attending the temple in person. As long as the temple stood, the ten tribes in exile were not without its benefits. (2) *Fourth Ezra* nowhere shows any awareness that the absence of the temple cult could be a problem for observing the Law. In the fictional historical setting, the temple had been in ruins for thirty years, but this is never a point of attention. (3) In any case, the explicit emphasis in the narrative about the ten tribes is on their remoteness from all other nations, not on their lack of access to the temple.

with Uriel's view that it is not impossible but does demand very considerable determination and effort.

Much study of *4 Ezra* has found the question of the coherence between the dialogues and the visions highly problematic. The older source-critical approaches tended to solve the problem by dissolving the unity of the work; the more recent work which rightly sees *4 Ezra* as a deliberately and carefully constructed unity tends to argue, in varying ways, that the problems Ezra raises in the dialogues, silenced rather than met by Uriel in the dialogues, are overcome by the visions, but in a psychologically or existentially rather than rationally satisfying way.[87] What has been missed is the crucial role of the ten tribes in relation to God's faithfulness to his covenant with Israel. It is this that provides Ezra at last with a rationally coherent way of understanding how God can fulfill his covenant promises without relaxing the strict demand for observance of the Torah that Uriel, along with the fall of Jerusalem itself, had persuaded Ezra God must maintain however small the number of the saved may in consequence be. The multitude of Abraham's descendants whom God had promised never to forsake will be found after all in the form of the ten tribes who have, in their hidden remoteness, remained faithful to the Torah as very few of the Israelites in the land or in the later Diaspora have been.

We must now consider in more detail the question of the relation between the covenant, keeping the Law and salvation in *4 Ezra*. Bruce Longenecker usefully characterizes the options that have been taken by various scholars thus:

(1) *Fourth Ezra* ultimately supports a kind of covenantal framework in which God's gracious faithfulness to ethnic Israel is assured in the end, even if it looks suspect in the present; (2) *4 Ezra* redefines traditional covenantalism, narrowing the scope of divine grace and thereby limiting covenant membership to include only a remnant, a much smaller group than the whole of ethnic Israel; (3) *4 Ezra* breaks out of traditional covenantal confidence in God's faithfulness to corporate Israel and postulates another concept of the ways of God, in which salvation is a matter of the efforts of each individual in order to overcome sin and to amass works of righteousness in one's favor before God. Perhaps these approaches can be entitled "covenantal confirmation," "covenantal redefinition," and "covenantal abrogation" respectively.[88]

In his earlier full study of *4 Ezra*, Longenecker himself had taken the third view, arguing that *4 Ezra* replaces the "ethnocentric covenantalism," which Ezra expresses in the early chapters and which could not cope theologically with the destruction of Jerusalem, with a "legalistic individualism," in which God's grace, the primary quality of God in his covenant with Israel, is given up and salvation, restricted to those who fulfill the Law perfectly without sin,

---

[87] Collins, *The Apocalyptic Imagination*, 168–9, is quite typical.

[88] *2 Esdras*, 31–32.

is made to depend entirely on their good works.[89] In his later work, Longenecker opts rather for the second of the three views, arguing that the third
view depends on too one-sided an emphasis on certain elements in *4 Ezra*.
Thus *4 Ezra* is "animated by a covenant theology," but one defined by an
ethical rigorism, such that the benefits of the covenant are available only to
exceptionally righteous people. While "confidence in God's justice and
faithfulness" characterize *4 Ezra*'s covenant theology, God's graciousness,
so important to the general Jewish view of the covenant, has practically
disappeared: "traditional notions such as atonement and divine mercy are
practically vacuous."[90] Thus the redefinition of the covenant is not merely a
matter of numbers – not all Israel but only the righteous within Israel – but
a matter of the very basis on which people are saved.

We have seen that *4 Ezra* certainly does not regard the covenant as
abrogated, though only in the third vision does it finally become clear how
this can be so. We have also seen how the inclusive covenantalism with which
Ezra begins his theological journey, which depends on expecting God to be
merciful to those who not observe the Law faithfully, is replaced by a
restriction of the benefits of the covenant to those who succeed in the very
demanding task of fulfilling the Law in the adverse circumstances of the
human condition in this age. The covenantalism with which *4 Ezra* evidently
expects its readers to begin, as Ezra himself does, is redefined in the course
of the book. But it is not clear that the conception of the covenant that
emerges from *4 Ezra* is novel in itself. The understanding we have observed
in the Enoch tradition similarly divides Israel into the righteous and the
sinners and restricts the eschatological benefits of the covenant to the former.
In Sanders's terms, the righteous "stay in" by observing God's commandments, while the sinners, by in effect repudiating the covenant, opt out. Is this
not also the case in *4 Ezra*? This is what Uriel says of sinners in general,
Israelite as well as Gentile:

> they were not obedient [to God's commands] and spoke against him;
> they devised for themselves vain thoughts,
> and proposed to themselves wicked frauds;
> they even declared that the Most High does not exist,
> and they ignored his ways.
> They scorned his law,
> and denied his covenants;
> they have been unfaithful to his statutes,
> and have not performed his works (7.22–24, cf. 37, 79; 8:55–56; 9:9–11).

Just as Gentile sinners have repudiated God by abandoning the commandments he gave them, so Jewish sinners have themselves repudiated the

---

[89] See the summary of his findings in Longenecker, *Eschatology*, 149–57.
[90] Longenecker, *2 Esdras*, 99–100.

covenant by not keeping the Torah faithfully. Significantly, Uriel's only explicit quotation of Scripture[91] – taken strategically from the closing words of 'Moses' address to Israel in Deuteronomy[92] – reminds Ezra that Moses "spoke to the people, saying, 'Choose life for yourself, so that you may live!'" (7:129, quoting Deut 30:19;[93] and cf. *4 Ezra* 8:56: "when they had opportunity to choose, they despised the Most High"). The difference between the righteous and the sinners seems to consist in a fundamental choice to observe the Law faithfully or not to take it seriously. The latter option is described in terms of fundamental apostasy from God and his ways. Of course, it is also true, as Sanders stresses,[94] that the righteous who "choose life" must maintain their choice by continuous effort to be faithful to the Law: loyalty must be fulfilled in obedience. But the foundational importance of the basic choice between God and apostasy means that for the sinners who have made the wrong choice there remains, while this life lasts, the possibility of repentance, i.e. of changing the whole direction of their lives in order to align it with the Law they have previously neglected (7:82; 9:11). This, after all, is what the exiles of the ten tribes did (13:42).

Significant ways in which Ezra and Uriel describe the righteous are as follows:[95] They are those who keep God's commandments (Ezra: 3:35–36; 7:45, cf. 72; Uriel: 13:42) or his ways (Uriel: 7:79, 88)[96] or the Law (Uriel: 7:94; Ezra: 9:32) or God's covenants (Ezra: 8:27). In this way they have stored up "good works" or "works of righteousness" with God (Uriel: 7:77; Ezra: 8:32–33, 36). They will be rewarded for their deeds (Ezra: 8:33; Uriel: 7:35, cf. 83, 98; 8:39) at the last judgment, when all deeds, righteous and unrighteous, will be made manifest (Uriel: 7:35; 14:35) and "all shall bear their own righteousness and unrighteousness" (7:105). As well as the language of "works," the language of "faith" (*fides*) is also common. The heavenly store of works can also be called "treasures of faith" (6:5), where "faith" seems to mean fidelity or faithfulness in keeping the Law (as probably in 5:1; 6:28;

---

[91] The rarity of Uriel's explicit allusions to Scripture is not an indication that the author of *4 Ezra* sees his position as radically novel in relation to the Hebrew Bible. Uriel is an angel who comes from God and speaks on God's behalf; he does not need to bolster his own authority by citing Scripture.

[92] This, together with the allusion to Deut 29:28 in *4 Ezra* 13:45 and the allusion to Deut 29:29 in *4 Ezra* 14:6, shows that *4 Ezra* found special eschatological significance in the final chapters of Deuteronomy, just as we have observed is the case in *1 En.* 1:3–9 in relation to Deut 33:2.

[93] The description of the Torah as "the law of life" in *4 Ezra* 14:30 is probably also based on Deut 30:19–20.

[94] Sanders, *Paul*, 416.

[95] These citations show that there is no significant difference in the ways Uriel and Ezra describe the righteous.

[96] For this sense of God's "ways" as his commandments, cf. 7:23–24; 8:56; 9:9; 14:31.

7:34, cf. 114). The remnant are described as those "who have works and faith towards the Almighty" (Uriel: 13:23; cf. Ezra: 8:30), or as those who "escape on account of their works, or on account of the faith by which they have believed" (Uriel: 9:7). In these cases, "faith" seems to be trust or belief in God, and the point may be that the righteous live by the faith that God will save and reward them in the eschatological future, just as this is probably the sense of the description of them as those "who believed the covenants of the Most High" (Uriel: 7:83; cf. Ezra: 3:32; 5:29). In any case, it seems clear that faith and works are not alternatives but necessary complements in the righteousness of the righteous. We should also note the ways in which Uriel speaks of the fulfillment of the Law by the righteous as very laborious: "they have striven with great effort to overcome the evil thought that was formed in them, so that it might not lead them astray from life into death" (7:92); and the righteous have to "pass through the difficult and futile experiences" in this age in order to receive their inheritance in the next (7:12–14). Finally, we should notice two passages which especially lend credence to the description of *4 Ezra*'s soteriology as "legalistic perfectionism":[97] the righteous kept the Law "throughout their life" (7:94; cf. 6:32) and they are those who "laboriously served the Most High, and withstood danger every hour so that they might keep the law of the Lawgiver perfectly" (7:89).

Does this mean that they never transgress? It is hard to be sure, since *4 Ezra*'s dualistic division of humanity into the two categories of sinners and righteous is typically expressed in extreme terms: apostates who repudiate God and his commandments, and the righteous who keep the Law perfectly. It is never a case of weighing the righteous and unrighteous deeds of an individual to see which outweighs the other. As we have noticed, in *4 Ezra* as in the Enoch tradition, being righteous or wicked is primarily a matter of a fundamental choice to orientate one's life in accordance with or in repudiation of God's law. The former choice must be faithfully maintained in order to lead to salvation, but we should not too readily conclude that keeping the Law "perfectly" excludes the commission of sins which are regretted and forgiven while the overall adherence of the person to God and his law is maintained.[98] Since salvation is not represented as the result of weighing an individual's righteous deeds against his or her sins, the storing up of good deeds is not a matter of calculating merit on an abstract scale, but of rewarding the kind of life the righteous person has led in faithfulness to God and the Torah. This is why, as we have seen, repentance is a possibility.

---

[97] Sanders, *Paul*, 409, cf. 416.

[98] Sanders, *Paul*, 422, takes the view that for *4 Ezra* any disobedience to the Law (rather than, as in other Jewish literature, only certain extreme violations) constitutes denial of God and the covenant, but Collins, *The Apocalyptic Imagination*, 169, objects that we "do not know what level of legalistic performance was regarded as necessary."

We have considered the contribution of the righteous to their salvation. What of God's grace? It is not true that God's mercy is entirely excluded from *4 Ezra*'s vision of God's dealings with humanity. While sinners at the judgment receive merciless justice (7:33–34), it is in mercy to the righteous that God saves them in the end (12:34; 14:34; cf. 10:24). This could mean that, while the righteous have not lived completely sinless lives and would not in strictest justice merit salvation, God overlooks their comparatively minor failings in order to reward their general faithfulness. More likely, mercy is here God's favor to the covenant people to whom he promised salvation. It was in God's free grace that he chose Israel and made his covenant with this people. The terms of the covenant – understood in *4 Ezra* as God's promise to give the eschatological reward to those who themselves keep the covenant by observing the Law – make salvation for the righteous both a matter of reward, within the terms God has given, but also a matter of God's grace, in that he freely chose to make such a covenant with Israel. To suppose that for *4 Ezra* God gives the righteous eschatological salvation not because they are members of his elect people but because, regardless of their corporate affiliation, they have individually merited salvation,[99] is to pose a false alternative. God gives salvation to those members of his elect people who have kept the terms of the covenant and so merit the salvation promised in the covenant. The remnant, as we have seen, is the remnant of God's elect people Israel. What God does not do, according to *4 Ezra*, is exercise mercy to Israelite sinners by withholding judgment from them. Ezra had wanted God to do this because it seemed to him the only way in which God could be faithful to the covenant himself, but by the end of the third vision Ezra had learned how God will fulfill his covenant promises by rewarding only those who keep his law.

Undoubtedly the result is a strong emphasis on the need to merit eschatological reward by difficult obedience to the Law. (That divine assistance accompanies human effort is very rarely mentioned: 9:21–22; 13:44.) This does not make it, as Sanders thought, a unique exception to the "covenantal nomism" he described: "the closest approach to legalistic works-righteousness which can be found in the Jewish literature of the period."[100] The idea that God will fulfill his covenant promises in the end only for the faithful remnant and not for the unfaithful mass of ethnic Israel is not new in *4 Ezra*, though

---

[99] This contrast plays a key role in the argument of Longenecker, *Eschatology*.

[100] Sanders, *Paul*, 418. Sanders's view is to some extent dependent on his sympathy with the older source-critical views of *4 Ezra*, which enable him to assign at least chs. 13–14 to a later redactor who was not in agreement with the author of the original apocalypse. Recent work has demonstrated more than adequately the literary unity of *4 Ezra*, indeed that *4 Ezra* is a very carefully constructed whole. In his *Eschatology*, Longenecker, broadly speaking, finds Sanders's view of *4 Ezra*'s relation to covenantal nomism valid while rejecting Sanders's source-critical views.

it is presented here as a view to which the work seeks to lead readers who are expected to begin with a more inclusive covenantalism. But *4 Ezra* does rather importantly illustrate how the basic and very flexible pattern of covenantal nomism could take forms in which the emphasis is overwhelmingly on meriting salvation by works of obedience to the Law, with the result that human achievement takes center-stage and God's grace, while presupposed, is effectively marginalized. In the case of *4 Ezra*, this emphasis was a reaction to the failure of the Jewish revolt and the fall of Jerusalem, which for the author made it clear that God does not deal leniently with his erring people but punishes them in strict justice. As Collins rightly comments: "The pessimism of the book springs not so much from its lofty standards as from historical experience."[101]

The seventh and last episode (ch. 14) presents the two sides of the solution Ezra has reached to the distressing dilemma that preoccupied him at the beginning of the book. They are represented by the two categories of books: the twenty-four books of the Hebrew scriptures, which may be read by "the worthy and the unworthy," and the seventy secret books which are reserved for the wise (14:45–47).[102] The former, containing the Law, make salvation possible: they are given to the people "so that people may be able to find the path, and that those who want to live in the last days may do so" (14:22). The path to salvation is what it has always been and what Israel has always known it to be: fulfilling God's commandments. Accordingly, in his last speech to the people, Ezra tells them that their present sufferings are God's judgment on them for not keeping the Law (14:29–33). Therefore what they must now do is put renewed effort into the demanding task of observing the Law ("rule over your minds and discipline your hearts") in order to obtain mercy from God after death (14:34). Thus the way to salvation is genuinely open to any of God's people who manage to follow it. In this sense, *4 Ezra* remains, at the end, non-sectarian[103] literature for those, like Ezra himself, who are teachers of the Law to all Israel. The distinction between them, the wise, and the rest of Israel is not a soteriological distinction between the saved and the wicked.[104] The secret books which can be entrusted only to the wise do not reveal the way to attain salvation, which is made known to all in the Torah.

---

[101] Collins, *The Apocalyptic Imagination*, 169.

[102] The two categories derive from Deut 29:29, to which *4 Ezra* 14:6 alludes. On the significance of the number seventy as indicating "secret," see Longenecker, *Eschatology*, 143–4.

[103] Cf. Collins, *The Apocalyptic Imagination*, 169: "There is no reason to regard 4 Ezra as sectarian in any sense."

[104] The phrase "the worthy and the unworthy" (*digni et indigni*) in 14:45 does not mean "worthy and unworthy of salvation," but, as 12:36–38 shows, capable and incapable of understanding the eschatological secrets revealed to Ezra.

Rather they reveal to the wise what Ezra has learned[105] about the way in which God will fulfill his covenant promises in spite of the fact that the people as a whole deserve the judgment God has inflicted on them by handing them over to their Gentile oppressors.

3.3 2 Baruch[106]

Second Baruch has so many resemblances to *4 Ezra*, from broad structural and thematic similarities down to precise verbal correspondences, that all scholars agree that a close literary relationship must be postulated. Most likely the author of one work was very familiar with the other work, but the direction of dependence is debated. Without being able to argue the case here, I will state my preference for the view that *2 Baruch* is indebted to *4 Ezra* rather than vice versa. The typological situation in *2 Baruch* is similar to that of *4 Ezra* in that it focuses on the fall of Jerusalem to the Babylonians: in this case the setting is Jerusalem shortly before and shortly after the destruction of the city and the temple. Like *4 Ezra*, *2 Baruch* divides into seven sections (I: 1–9; II: 10–12; III: 13–20; IV: 21–34; V: 35–47; VI: 48–77; VII: 78–86),[107] which contain prayers of Baruch, dialogues between Baruch and God, symbolic visions (in sections V and VI), and addresses of Baruch to the people. Broadly, there is a movement from problems to solutions, and from Baruch's great distress over the destruction of Zion to consolation for himself and the people. As in *4 Ezra*, much of the dynamic of the earlier sections is due to the religious problem which the fall of Jerusalem is for Baruch.

However, along with these broad similarities, there are equally broad differences. One of great importance is that, whereas the revelations to Ezra

---

[105] That the seventy books include Ezra's own work seems clear from the parallelism between 12:36–38 and 14:45–46.

[106] Among recent studies of *2 Baruch*, the most relevant to our present concerns are G. B. Saylor, *Have the Promises Failed? A Literary Analysis of 2 Baruch* (SBLDS 72; Chico: Scholars, 1984); and F. J. Murphy, *The Structure and Meaning of Second Baruch* (SBLDS 78; Atlanta; Scholars, 1985); cf. also M. Desjardins, "Law in 2 Baruch and 4 Ezra," *SR* 14 (1985): 25–37. Surveys of scholarship on *2 Baruch* can be found in Murphy, *The Structure*, 1–9; A. F. J. Klijn, "Recent Developments in the Study of the Syriac Apocalypse of Baruch," *JSP* 4 (1989): 3–17. E. P. Sanders, *Paul*, does not discuss *2 Baruch* except in passing in a comparison with *4 Ezra* (427), but devotes more attention to *2 Baruch* in his article, "The Covenant as a Soteriological Category and the Nature of Salvation in Palestinian and Hellenistic Judaism," in *Jews, Greeks and Christians* (ed. R. Hamerton-Kelly and R. Scroggs; SJLA 21; Leiden: Brill, 1976), 17–20.

[107] This understanding of the structure is that of Collins, *The Apocalyptic Imagination*, 170. It has the strong advantage of depending on clear structural markers in the text, such as ancient readers required to discern major divisions of a work. Other proposals accept many of the same divisions between sections but differ at some points: see the summary of proposed structures in Murphy, *The Structure*, 12.

are eschatological secrets to be communicated only to the wise, making *4 Ezra* as a whole intended for a select circle of readers, while only 14:27–36 exemplifies the message these teachers may give the people on the basis of the Torah, in *2 Baruch* the revelations to him[108] lead directly to addresses to the people. By the end of the fourth section of the book Baruch is already sufficiently instructed and consoled himself to be able to instruct the people. He addresses them at the end of the fourth, fifth and sixth sections,[109] while the whole of the seventh section is a letter addressed by Baruch to the exiles of the northern tribes, in effect digesting the message of the whole book into paraenesis of general application. The implied readership must be a general Jewish audience. The content and the message of the book are appropriate to this. While Baruch's distress over the fall of Jerusalem parallels Ezra's in its concern with the respective fortunes of God's people and the Gentile nations (5, 11, 14), and while Baruch like Ezra implores God to show mercy to the people and is told that justice cannot be compromised (48), the peculiar intensity with which Ezra explores the problem of sin and salvation is lacking in *2 Baruch*. Ezra's convictions about the ineradicable root of sin and the near impossibility of keeping the Law, his anguish about the fact that only few will be saved[110] and his persistence in sceptical questioning of God's justice, are all missing from *2 Baruch*. In *2 Baruch* the problem and the solution are both simpler, and Baruch is accordingly more easily satisfied and more quickly enlightened. Furthermore, the solution is not simply understanding of God's ways, but strongly paraenetic: the book's overall message is that, since God has not abandoned his covenant with Israel, it is imperative that Israel keep the Law in order to benefit from the covenant promises.

One could imagine that a Jewish leader, deeply impressed by and very familiar with *4 Ezra*, the work of a colleague, wished to write a comparable work for the people in general, containing not esoteric revelations for the wise, but what needed to be said in response to the general distress over the

---

[108] According to 54:4–5, God's revelations of eschatological secrets are made to those who fear him and obey the Law.

[109] The speech at the end of the fifth section (44–46) is directly addressed to the leaders of the people, but with a view to their instruction of the people generally.

[110] *2 Baruch* 18:1 suggests that only "few" kept the Law, but the reference is to Moses' own generation (cf. 19:1). Saylor, *Have the Promises*, 62, translates 48:19 as "behold the few who have submitted to you," but R. H. Charles translates: "Behold the little ones that are subject to Thee," P.-M. Bogaert: "Regarde les humble qui te servent," and A. F. J. Klijn: "Look at the small ones who submit to you." Saylor's argument for a literary connection between 18:1 and 48:19 fails because the Syriac words "few" and "little ones" are different. According to 21:11, "while many have sinned once, many others have proved themselves to be righteous." "Many" in 44:15 ("the habitation of the many others will be in the fire") is textually uncertain, but if it is read it need not mean that the saved are few. *Second Baruch* simply does not seem to be exercised with the numerical problem as *4 Ezra* is. Probably in consequence it also retains a relatively generous hope for the Gentile nations (72:4–5), as *4 Ezra* does not.

fall of Jerusalem. *Second Baruch* enters into the questioning that any Jew might have felt after 70, offers such insight into God's ways and visions of the eschatological future as the people in general could understand, and thus provides them with the eschatological urgency and hope needed to sustain their obedience to the Law. It is a full-scale apocalypse elaborating and reinforcing the message of Ezra's concise discourse to the people in *4 Ezra* 14:27–36. Accordingly, its presentation of the problem is milder, its theological approach more familiar and less demanding, its message more encouraging and more practical. This is certainly not to deny that there are some real theological differences between *4 Ezra* and *2 Baruch*, or that the author of the latter may have felt he had more satisfactory explanations of some problems than the former. But since it is hard to read the relationship between the two works as actually polemical, this view of their relationship can explain how they may both have belonged to the rather diverse circle of Jewish sages and teachers in the period between the two revolts, both conscious of their role as teachers of the Torah to the whole people, one concerned in his work to address the problems of this theological elite themselves lest their own belief in the God of the covenant fail, the other writing to fulfill directly his calling as a teacher of the Law to Israel.

In *2 Baruch*'s theological response to the fall of Jerusalem there are two main elements. One is that salvation is to be found not in this transient world, but in the eternal age to come. The other is an understanding of Israel's punishment as chastisement with Israel's repentance in view. Both themes are announced in the first section of the book (1:5; 4), developed throughout the book and strongly affirmed in the final section, the letter. The first theme is shared with *4 Ezra*,[111] but is developed in a characteristic way as a dominant feature of *2 Baruch*. Again and again the point is made that the present world is transient and soon to pass away (e.g. 83:9–20; 85:10), so that any good to be had in this world is worthless by comparison with the transcendent good of the age to come: "For that which is now is nothing. But that which is in the future will be very great" (44:8).[112] Suffering in this world is well worth bearing if it leads to eternal reward in the next (15:8). The restoration of Israel is to be understood in terms of this contrast between the two ages:

> . . . if we direct and dispose our hearts, we shall receive everything which we lost again by many times. For that which we lost was subjected to corruption, and that which we receive will not be corruptible (85:4–5).

Particularly is this true of Zion, the temple and the city (cf. 31:2–32:6), whose destruction is the fundamental problem the book resolves. The city which God promised never to forget or forsake (Isa 49:16, quoted in 4:2), the city whose

---

[111] On this point I think Murphy, *The Structure*, 140–42, probably misrepresents *4 Ezra*.

[112] Quotations from *2 Baruch* are from the translation by A. F. J. Klijn in *OTP* 1.615–52.

glorious restoration the prophets predicted, is not the earthly Jerusalem at all, but the heavenly Zion, prepared before the creation of humanity, preserved in heaven for the faithful to enter in the age to come (4:1–6). The eternal dwelling of God with his people was never intended to be the temple that, forsaken by God, has fallen to their enemies, but rather the heavenly temple.

The second theme is that Israel's punishment by God is not intended to result in her destruction, but to produce repentance to which God will respond with mercy and restoration. Like *4 Ezra*, *2 Baruch* understands the Mosaic covenant especially in the terms given by the final section of Moses' address to the people in Deuteronomy (both 19:1 and 84:2 quote Deut 30:19, which is also quoted in *4 Ezra* 7:129), but *2 Baruch*'s understanding of Deut 28–30 differs significantly from *4 Ezra*'s. There is the same emphasis on the decisive choice between obedience and apostasy, life and death (Deut 30:19–20, to which *2 Bar.* 46:3; 76:5 allude), but from these chapters as a whole, especially 28:58–68; 30:1–10, *2 Baruch* derives the following pattern of God's dealings with his errant covenant people: (1) Israel's disobedience to the Law; (2) God's punishment of Israel by destruction and exile; (3) Israel's repentance; (4) God's mercy in restoring Israel; (5) the punishment of Israel's enemies. This pattern is found, wholly or partially, in all of Baruch's addresses to the people as well as the letter to the ten tribes.[113] The pattern functions both to console the people with the prospect of future salvation and future punishment of their enemies, and also to require them to rededicate themselves to the fulfillment of the Law, so that, point (4) being the case, point (5) may follow. Hence the paraenetic sections of the book contain many conditional propositions, such as: "For when you endure and persevere in his fear and do not forget his Law, the time again will take a turn for the better for you" (44:7; cf. 32:1; 46:5–6; 75:7–8; 77:6, 16; 78:6–7; 84:6; 85:4).[114] Such propositions are instances of the general principle which is *2 Baruch*'s own summing up of the Mosaic covenant as taught by Moses to Israel in Deuteronomy: "If you trespass [*sic*] the law, you will be dispersed. And if you shall keep it, you shall be planted" (84:2). Therefore Baruch can tell the tribes in exile that, assuming they are repentant, they "have suffered now for your good so that you may not be condemned at the end and tormented" (78:6). Israel is chastised in this age in order to be saved in the next, whereas judgment is withheld from her enemies in this age so that they may be punished finally (13:3–11).

Baruch generally addresses and speaks about the people as a whole. (In the narrative context of most of the work this means those who survived in

---

[113] See the detail in Murphy, *The Structure,* 117–20, with the chart on p. 119, following the work of O. H. Steck.

[114] Murphy, *The Structure,* 126–30, relates these to the similar conditional forms in Deuteronomy.

Jerusalem after the Babylonian capture of the city, but the same message is also conveyed by letter to both the exiles of the southern tribes and those of the northern tribes: 77:11–26.) But this does not mean that all of ethnic Israel will be saved. With regard to humanity in general Baruch makes a clear distinction between righteous and sinners, of whom only the former will be saved (21:11; 24:1–2; 51:1–5; 54:21). As for the Israel who inherit the eschatological promises, Baruch himself asks God: "For whom and for how many will these things be?," raising the question because he sees "many of your people who separated themselves from your statutes and who have cast away from them the yoke of the Law" (41:1, 3). Such apostates and their exclusion from Israel's salvation are, after all, clearly envisaged in the key chapters of Deuteronomy on which *2 Baruch*'s covenantalism is especially based (Deut 28:18–21). As well as these apostates who have rejected God's law, Baruch also notes that there are proselytes who have taken on the yoke of the Law. Since both categories have obeyed the Law, but only for a part of their lives, he wonders how they can be justly rewarded: "Their time will surely not be weighed exactly, and they will certainly not be judged as the scale indicates?" (41:6). Though the reply in ch. 42 is at some points very obscure,[115] the essential answer seems clear: the obedience of the apostates before their apostasy is not counted in their favor, while the disobedience of the proselytes before their conversion is not counted against them in the judgment. The passage is important, not only because it shows that the author is concerned about issues of equitable correspondence between obedience to the Law and salvation, but also because it shows that, for *2 Baruch*, the Israel who will be saved is constituted by those who either remain within the covenant by remaining faithful to the Law or opt into the covenant by subjecting themselves to the Law. *Second Baruch* almost completely lacks (cf. 40:2) the remnant language which is so important in *4 Ezra*, and therefore probably does not regard faithful Israel as no more than a minority of ethnic Israel. This is certainly a more inclusive covenantalism than *4 Ezra*'s, much more like the position with which Ezra begins than the one he learns in the course of that book, and we must shortly consider the reasons for this difference. But it should be noted that, in principle, *2 Baruch*'s position is no less "individualistic" than the remnant theology of *4 Ezra*: if it is possible to be excluded from Israel's salvation through apostasy, then every individual's participation in that salvation is dependent on his or her continued faithfulness to the covenant through subjection to the Law.

Sinners in general are "those who have not subjected themselves to [God's] power" (54:14), "those who do not love your Law" (54:14), those

---

[115] See the discussion in P.-M. Bogaert, *Apocalypse de Baruch*, vol. 2 (SC 144; Paris: Editions du Cerf, 1969), 76–78.

who "have once rejected the understanding[116] of the Most High" (54:17), those who "did not know [God's] Law because of their pride" (48:40), and those who "despised [God's] Law and stopped their ears lest they hear wisdom and receive intelligence" (51:4).[117] Jewish apostates are "those who have withdrawn" (42:4), those who "withdraw from the way of the Law" or "from the commandments of the Mighty One" (44:3). As we have seen in earlier sections to be typical of our literature, the distinction between righteous and sinners comes down to a fundamental acceptance or rejection of the Law. With regard to sinners, *2 Baruch* is notably concerned to make clear that they are those who consciously and deliberately act wrongly (48:29, 40).

That being righteous is a matter of fundamental alignment of life with the Law appears in descriptions of them as "those who subjected themselves to [God] and [God's] law in faith" (54:5, where "faith" probably means faithfulness, as in 54:21; for righteousness as subjection to God, cf. also 66:1; 75:7) and as those who "always feared [God] and did not leave [God's] ways" (14:5; cf. 54:4; 38:4). Like *4 Ezra*, *2 Baruch* can speak of them both in terms of good works (14:11; 24:1) and as "those who have believed" (42:2; 54:16; 59:2; cf. 83:8), where the object of belief may be primarily the eschatological reward prepared for those who obey the Law (cf. 57:2).[118] Like *4 Ezra*, *2 Baruch* speaks of the good works that the righteous have stored up for themselves in heaven and because of which they can be confident of salvation (14:11; 24:1; 44:14). Similarly, they are "those who are saved because of their works and for whom the Law is now a hope, and intelligence, expectation and wisdom a trust" (51:7), where the last phrase refers, in a way characteristic of *2 Baruch*, to the understanding to be found in the Torah (cf. the similar passage in 51:3; also 38:1; 44:14). It is clear that salvation is perceived as reward for adherence to the Law (cf. also 54:16; 59:2).

At the same time, the righteous (or at least most of them) are not sinless (85:15) and their salvation is attributed to God's mercy (77:6–7; 78:7; 84:10). In its frequent reference to God's mercy (not only in Baruch's prayer for the people [48] but also in authoritative statements), *2 Baruch* resembles the Ezra of the early dialogues in *4 Ezra* more than the position which *4 Ezra* as a whole endorses. Without God's mercy, none, except perhaps a very exceptional few, could be saved (75:5–6; 84:11): the implication here, unlike the similar assertion in *4 Ezra*, is that many are indeed saved by God's mercy. Significantly, the righteous are those who "have not withdrawn from mercy"

---

[116] Understanding is here knowledge of the right way to live which the Law gives.

[117] Like *4 Ezra*, *2 Baruch* evidently considers that Gentile nations have had the opportunity to be subject to God's law (though perhaps not in its Sinaitic form) but have rejected it; cf. 15:3.

[118] On the meaning of "belief" in *2 Baruch*, see Murphy, *The Structure*, 64–66; Yinger, *Paul*, 84–85.

(44:14), as apostates have. God's mercy deals with the sins of those who subject themselves to his Law, but those who reject the Law have cut themselves off from mercy. Therefore the book's concluding summary of the fate of people at the judgment reads:

> Then he will make alive those whom he has found,
> and he will purge them from their sins,
> and at the same time he will destroy those who are polluted with sins (85:15).

As in *1 En.* 5:8–9, sinlessness is eschatological gift for those who have proved sufficiently righteous in this life.

While this view of God's mercy contributes to *2 Baruch*'s more inclusive covenantalism, as compared with *4 Ezra*, and makes *2 Baruch* resemble the Ezra of the dialogues more than the position which *4 Ezra* as a whole endorses, *2 Baruch*'s view of God's mercy still stops far short of that advanced by Ezra in his plea to God for mercy (*4 Ezra* 8:20–36). For the unconverted Ezra, the exceptional people who are truly righteous secure their reward by their deeds, while God's mercy must be mercy for sinners who have no store of good works (8:31–36). This is not *2 Baruch*'s view of God's mercy. For *2 Baruch*, as for the Enoch tradition, mercy is for the righteous, who live in accordance with the Law and have a store of good works, but are not perfect (as well as passages already cited, cf. 61:9). For *2 Baruch*'s more inclusive covenantalism depends not only on emphasizing God's mercy for the righteous, as *4 Ezra* does not, but also on taking a more optimistic view than *4 Ezra* of the possibilities of keeping the Law faithfully. *Second Baruch* does not mention the problem of the evil heart, and while at one point the book appears to share *4 Ezra*'s view of the legacy of Adam (48:42–43) it later clarifies the point, making clear that Adam merely set an example which his descendants are free to copy or not (54:15–19).[119] *Second Baruch* does not refer to the difficulty of keeping the Law.

Because the Law can be kept adequately, if not perfectly, because God will be merciful to those who keep the Law adequately, though not perfectly, and because the fall of Jerusalem is his chastisement of his people for their own good, not his destruction of irredeemable apostates, *2 Baruch* does not face the most acute problems in Ezra's theological journey nor require the unusual solutions he is given.

E. P. Sanders contrasts the two works in order to contrast the "legalistic perfectionism" unique, in the literature of early Judaism, to *4 Ezra*, and the view of *2 Baruch*, which he sees as representative of the covenantal nomism characteristic of the rest of early Jewish literature.[120] He gives "the usual

---

[119] On the differences between *4 Ezra* and *2 Baruch* in this respect, see P.-M. Bogaert, *Apocalypse de Baruch*, vol. 1 (SC 144; Paris: Editions du Cerf, 1969), 402–5.

[120] Sanders, *Paul*, 427; "The Covenant," 17–22.

formulation" of the latter as: "God punishes the wicked *for their deeds,* while bestowing *mercy on the righteous.*"[121] Yet this contrast between *4 Ezra* and *2 Baruch* is probably overdrawn. As we have seen, *4 Ezra* does not altogether exclude God's mercy for the righteous, while it is difficult to tell what standard of law observance qualifies as keeping the Law perfectly. With reference to *2 Baruch*, it would be more accurate to say not simply that God bestows mercy on the righteous, but that God has mercy on the righteous *because of their good works.* As Carson puts it, mercy "is a kind response to merit."[122] As *2 Baruch*'s discussion of apostates and proselytes (41–42) shows, the notion of salvation as the reward for the good works of the righteous does not imply a nice calculation of merit and reward, but it does make salvation dependent on adherence to God and his Law. As we have seen in discussion of *4 Ezra*, the idea of salvation as reward for righteousness need not be alternative to the idea of salvation as God's covenantal grace. It is in his grace that God makes the covenantal promises and lays down the requirement of obedience to the Law as the condition for receiving them. Within this general framework it is possible to emphasize the need for human achievement to the point of marginalizing grace, as *4 Ezra* does, and it is possible to stress the need for human achievement at the same time as assuring people who adhere to the Law that God will be merciful to them, as *2 Baruch* does. While *4 Ezra*'s pessimism about the prospects of salvation for Israel in the land in his time would make it thoroughly discouraging for a general audience and suitable only for a learned elite who can appreciate its novel way of maintaining God's covenant faithfulness, *2 Baruch* is addressed to Israel as a whole, encouraging that renewed adherence to the Law which, along with God's mercy, would ensure salvation.

3.4 3 Baruch

This apocalypse is extant in Greek and Slavonic versions, which frequently differ in textual detail and both of which have been subject to Christian influence, though the original work was undoubtedly non-Christian Jewish.[123] The differences between the versions are one factor which make interpretation difficult, but this work has proved curiously resistant to coherent interpretation for other reasons too. The fact that the interpretations offered in the most significant recent studies – by Picard,[124] Nickelsburg[125] and Harlow[126] – differ

---

[121] Sanders, *Paul*, 421: italics original.

[122] D. A. Carson, *Divine Sovereignty and Human Responsibility* (London: Marshall, Morgan & Scott, 1981), 69.

[123] This has been adequately demonstrated by D. C. Harlow, *The Greek Apocalypse of Baruch (3 Baruch) in Hellenistic Judaism and Early Christianity* (SVTP 12; Leiden: Brill, 1996), ch. 3.

[124] J.-C. Picard's essays on *3 Baruch* are now collected in *Le Continent Apocryphe: Essai*

very widely suggests that we must be very cautious about any conclusions drawn from this work. However, certain points may be made. Since the indubitably Christian additions to the text are in every case found only in one of the two recensions, never in both, we should also be very cautious about accepting the originality of other material present in only one of the recensions. This applies to references to the fate of righteous and sinners after death which occur only in the Greek version (4:3, 4–5, 15; 10:5) as well as to 16:4–8 in the Slavonic version.[127] It is likely that the original work referred to existence after death only in the special case of its depiction of the planners and builders of the tower of Babel in the second and third heavens (3–4). Scribes who expected an apocalypse to deal with this subject supplied the lack, differently in the two versions. Therefore I cannot accept Harlow's argument that *3 Baruch* substitutes personal eschatology for a national, collective eschatology such as would involve the restoration of Jerusalem.[128] Surprisingly, there is no explicit eschatology at all in *3 Baruch*. Another important point at which I differ from Harlow also concerns the differences between the versions. In chs. 11–16, evidently the climactic part of the revelation given to Baruch, the Slavonic version refers consistently to what the angels bring as prayers (11:4, 9; 14:2; 15:2–3), while the Greek, after first referring to prayers (11:4), subsequently refers to virtues and good works (11:9; 12:5; 14:2; 15:2).[129] It is surely probable that the Slavonic is more original in this. Most other parallels to the general notion concern prayers (Tob 12:12, 15; *1 En.* 47:1–2; 99:3; *T. Adam* 2:7; Rev 8:3–4), but the *Apocalypse of Paul* speaks of deeds. The clumsy mixture of the two in the Greek version of *3 Baruch* may well reflect the influence of the *Apocalypse of Paul* on it. Therefore I must dissent also from Harlow's interpretation of the significance of chs. 11–16 for the meaning of the whole apocalypse: "A present and universal system of rewards and punishments replaces any hope for an eschatological restoration of Jerusalem that would involve the

---

sur les Littératures Apocryphes Juives et Chrétiennes (Instrumenta Patristica 36; Turnhout: Brepols, 1999), 55–161.

[125] G. W. E. Nickelsburg, *Jewish Literature between the Bible and the Mishnah* (London: SCM, 1981), 299–303.

[126] Harlow, *The Greek* Apocalypse.

[127] In Bauckham, *The Fate of the Dead*, 67–69, I argued that these verses in the Slavonic summarize the original ending of *3 Baruch*. I no longer think this, mainly because I am impressed by the inclusio which 16:1–3 forms with 1:2 (see below). I now think that 16:4–8 in the Slavonic must have been added by a scribe who knew other cosmic tour apocalypses which follow this pattern.

[128] Harlow, *The Greek* Apocalypse, argues this at various points; see the summary on p. 208. Nickelsburg, *Jewish Literature*, 300–305, also takes this view.

[129] Harlow, *The Greek* Apocalypse, 148, notes these differences but proceeds as though the originality of the Greek version can be taken for granted.

collective salvation of the Jewish people."[130] Thus I cannot agree with his overall understanding of the way *3 Baruch* aims to deflect concern from the restoration of Jerusalem by attention instead to individual eschatology and to good works as the only means of access to God.[131] If this were the case it would be of considerable interest for our present concerns, but the evidence is against it.

Third Baruch, surely in dependence on *2 Baruch*, opens with a scene in which Baruch laments and questions God about the fall of Jerusalem, posing the problem in much the same way as the opening chapters of *2 Baruch* do, with evident reference to the way the event seems to contradict the special status of Israel as the covenant people by contrast with the nations. But then an angel, announcing that Baruch's prayer has been heard, promises to reveal mysteries to him and does so by conducting him through the various heavens up to the fifth. This follows the model of other heavenly tours through the heavens, except that others proceed to the presence of God in the seventh heaven. The climax in *3 Baruch* is different: he sees how the prayers of people on earth are received and rewarded in the heavenly temple, where the angelic high priest Michael officiates before God. The significance, for the overall meaning of the book, of what Baruch sees in the lower heavens is obscure, and we should probably not expect too much coherence in this kind of apocalypse, which typically discloses miscellaneous contents of the various heavens. We shall focus here on the way the events that transpire in the fifth heaven and the book's conclusion might relate to the opening problem.

Nickelsburg has provided a major key by showing how Baruch's opening question (1:2) and Michael's closing words (16:1-3) form an inclusio by both alluding to Deut 32.[132] Admittedly, the most important part of Michael's words for this observation (16:2) occurs only in the Greek, but here it may be permissible to rely on the Greek because we have already seen how the closing chapters of Deuteronomy were a regular resource of Jewish eschatology, including those apocalypses which wrestled with the problem of understanding God's purpose for Israel in the light of the catastrophe of 70 C.E. Deut 32 depicts the punishment of Israel by God for faithlessness and idolatry. God's instrument is a pagan nation which foolishly takes the credit for itself, not recognizing that its victory was possible only because God handed over his people to it. This is exactly the issue in *3 Bar.* 1:2, and

---

[130] Harlow, *The Greek* Apocalypse, 156.

[131] These are two of the four themes Harlow, *The Greek* Apocalypse, 148, specifies; cf. 208–209.

[132] Nickelsburg, *Jewish Literature*, 302–3; Harlow, *The Greek* Apocalypse, 155–6, reports and even develops the argument a little, before rejecting it on the grounds that 16:2 is only in the Greek text and that the interpretation is inconsistent with the rest of Harlow's argument about the meaning and purpose of *3 Baruch*.

16:2–3, by alluding to Deut 32:21–27, explains how this was an appropriate form of punishment for God to give his faithless people.[133] It was a response to the evil of those of his people who did not invoke him (their guardian angels are those in ch. 13 who have no human prayers to bring, and who beg not to have to accompany such evil people). Since they did not pray for mercy, God punished their evils justly. But those angels who do bring prayers to God receive mercies in response – to a degree corresponding to their prayers (15:1–3 Slavonic). Deut 32 goes on to declare that, following his punishment of his people by means of their enemies, God will have mercy on them and vindicate them (Deut 32:36) by taking vengeance himself on their enemies. The implicit message must be that, just as God has punished his people in response to their evil, so he will have mercy in response to their prayers. Thus, despite the arguments of other scholars precisely to the contrary, it seems that *3 Baruch* is solely concerned with the corporate destiny of the covenant people, not at all with the destiny of individuals after death.

In a way which is parallel to but also different from *2 Baruch*, *3 Baruch* understands the punishment of Israel as just, and also as consistent with the covenant promises of God because God's mercy will in the future supervene. Instead of directing attention to observance of the Law, as *2 Baruch* does, *3 Baruch*'s implied message is that prayer for God's mercy is the appropriate action to take.

4. The Sibylline Tradition

The Jewish *Sibylline Oracles* are a form of prophetic oracle, not apocalypses, but they share with the apocalypses the character of literature of revelation, and so may be conveniently included here. Since two of the major oracles (4 and 5) were written in the wake and under the impact of the fall of Jerusalem in 70 C.E., this is also a reason for considering the oracles at this point in our chapter. There were pagan Sibylline oracles, attributed to prophetesses known as Sibyls, and the Jewish oracles continue this literary tradition, making the Sibyl into a daughter-in-law of Noah, who was inspired to prophesy by the one true God. The original intention must have been to gain a hearing for their message from Gentile readers who would take them seriously as ancient prophecy. Though it is debatable whether Jewish literature that has the appearance of apologetic for Gentile readers was really intended for outsiders, some at least of the Sibyllines are very likely propaganda, promoting an

---

[133] The repetition of "provoke" in both Deut 32:21 and in the virtual quotation of it in *3 Bar.* 16:2 indicates a *lex talionis* judgment, i.e. one which is just by virtue of the correspondence between the crime and the punishment.

ethical code that condemned the practices Jews found objectionable in pagan life (especially sexual misconduct and infanticide) and urging worship of the one God the Creator in place of idolatry. The role of the Jewish people in this one God's purpose is also a significant topic. Typically the Sibyllines contain many oracles of destruction on nations, places, cities and empires, condemned for their various misdeeds, and reviews of world history culminating in an imminent climax of judgment leading to a golden age on earth, in which God will be universally honored and his people Israel central. With the exception of the conclusion to book 4 (179–192) and a probably Jewish part of book 8 (401–423) there is no reference to resurrection or judgment of the dead,[134] one of the features which limits the significance of these works for our theme. The ultimate salvation of individuals is no more a concern here than in most of the Old Testament prophets.

In view of their genre and implied audience, it is not surprising that the Sibyllines are a literature of the Diaspora. Oracles 3, 5 and 11 were written in Egypt, with the bulk of the earliest (book 3) coming from the mid-second century B.C.E., and the fifth book written between 70 C.E. and the Egyptian Jewish revolt of 115. The Jewish parts of books 1–2 were written in Asia Minor, probably in the first century C.E. Book 4 may come from the vicinity of Palestine and was written after 70 C.E. The Jewish parts of book 8 date from the end of the second century C.E.

The third book refers to the Mosaic law as given by God to "the people of the twelve tribes," such that whoever disobeys it is punished by humans or by God (256–259).[135] Israel's life in obedience to the Law (245: "fulfilling the word of the great God, the hymn of the law") is eulogized (218–247, 594–600) in terms which refer to none of the specifically Jewish features of the Law but only those which are commended also to Gentiles. But as well as the ethical requirements of the Law, the cultic worship of the one God, centered on Jerusalem, is also prominent (574–594, cf. 273–294). Both are commended to Gentiles, since the Jews are to be "guides of life for all mortals" (195). The Sibyllines in general, as well as most of the apocalypses we have studied, take for granted that the basic ethical commandments of the

---

[134] Book 2 contains a long eschatological section (154–338) in which resurrection and the judgment and destinies of the dead are prominent subjects. But most of this section (178–338) is a paraphrase of the Christian *Apocalypse of Peter*, supplemented by passages taken from *Sib. Or.* 8. All the material on resurrection and judgment of the dead is from the *Apocalypse of Peter*. This dependence on the *Apocalypse of Peter* was already demonstrated conclusively by M. R. James, "A New Text of the Apocalypse of Peter," *JTS* 12 (1911) 39–44, 51–52, but his work is not known to J. J. Collins, who therefore underestimates the extent of the Christian material in book 2: "Sibylline Oracles," in *OTP* 1.330–4; and *The Apocalyptic Imagination*, 192. Thus the only eschatological material from the original Jewish book 1–2 is in 2:154–177.

[135] Quotations from the *Sibylline Oracles* are from the translation in Collins, "Sibylline Oracles," 317–472.

Torah are also God's commandments to all people, and that the requirement to worship not idols, but the God who has made himself known to Israel and dwells in Jerusalem is also incumbent on all people. Therefore Gentiles are judged for "transgressing the holy law of the immortal God" (599–600) and "because they knew not the law nor the judgment of the great God" (686–687), this ignorance understood as culpable. In the eschatological age, seeing the blessed state of Israel in the holy land the Gentiles will wish to worship Israel's God and to "ponder the Law of the Most High" (719). When, finally, God puts "in effect a common law for men throughout the whole earth" (757–758), the Stoic language refers to the essence of the Torah. In all this the covenant with Israel appears only in the favored status of Israel as those given the Law and the understanding it brings (585–586) and as those destined to share this knowledge with others. Jews and Gentiles alike are punished for disobeying God's commandments and enjoy this-worldly well-being as a result of keeping them.

The assumption that God's law is for Gentiles as well as Jews – with no attempt to define the difference between its universal and specifically Jewish features – appears particularly strikingly in a passage in book 8, in which the notion of the two ways in the form in which it is presented by Moses to Israel at the end of Deut 30 expresses God's address to all his human creatures: "I myself proposed two ways, of life and death, and proposed too the judgment to choose good life. But they turned eagerly to death and eternal fire" (399–401). *Fourth Ezra* too, quoting this very text (Deut 30:19), assumes that, though spoken by Moses to Israel, it is also the choice that confronts every human being (*4 Ezra* 7:127–129). The expectation that in the future the Gentile nations will also worship God and obey his law is also found in the fifth Sibylline book: "they will have a mind in their breasts that conforms to your [Jerusalem's] laws" (265, cf. 357). The Egyptian book 5 includes an impressive prophecy of judgment on Egypt's idolatry and her conversion to the true God (484–511). Book 4 issues a call to repentance and conversion to all humanity, threatening the eschatological destruction of the world as punishment for continued disobedience to God (162–178).

Books 4 and 5 both respond to the fall of Jerusalem in 70 C.E., in very different ways but both much more simply than the three apocalypses we have considered. Neither seems concerned about the question of the validity of the covenant that so distressed the apocalyptists. Book 5 responds entirely with denunciation of Rome and prophecies of her doom. Book 4, perhaps a product of one of the Jewish baptist sects, treats all human-made temples and animal sacrifices as inappropriate to the true God (6–30), in such a way that the Jerusalem temple can hardly be an exception. This, of course, reduces the impact of the fall of Jerusalem to a minimum, and the latter is unproblematically treated as punishment for Israel's folly and sin (115–118).

7. Testaments

by

ROBERT A. KUGLER

E. P. Sanders first formulated his notion of "covenantal nomism" in 1977 with the publication of *Paul and Palestinian Judaism*.[1] According to Sanders this pattern of religion was "based on election and atonement for transgressions, it being understood that God gave commandments in connection with the election and that obedience to them, or atonement and repentance for transgression, was expected as the condition for remaining in the covenant community."[2] Sanders's claim that the pattern was pervasive in early Jewish literature has serious implications for understanding the beginnings of Judaism and Christianity. Thus it is worth checking its consistency in Jewish works from the turn of the era. Our interest in this essay is in testamentary compositions.[3] The outcome is not entirely favorable for Sanders's thesis.

---

[1] E. P. Sanders, *Paul and Palestinian Judaism* (Minneapolis: Fortress, 1977).

[2] Ibid., 236.

[3] Among ancient texts given the title "testament" only the *Testaments of the Twelve Patriarchs*, the *Testament of Moses*, and the *Testament of Job* exhibit the fundamental characteristics of the genre. Testaments are defined chiefly by a *narrative framework* that includes an introduction in which the testator gathers family or friends to give his near-death speech and a conclusion that narrates the speaker's death (see John J. Collins, "Testaments," in *Jewish Writings of the Second Temple Period: Apocrypha, Pseudepigrapha, Qumran Sectarian Writings, Philo, Josephus* [CRINT II.2; ed. Michael Stone; Assen/Philadelphia: Van Gorcum/Fortress, 1984], 325). While it is not possible to define the genre by content alone, it is true that testaments usually include something about the testator's life, moral exhortation, and/or predictions of the future (cf. Collins, "Testaments," 325–6, for caution against relying on content to define the genre testament). Some works from the turn of the era that are called "testaments" but lack these basic genre characteristics include the *Testament of Abraham* and the *Testament of Solomon*. *Testament of Abraham* is in no way a deathbed speech, though it is certainly concerned with Abraham's demise (see E. P. Sanders, "Testament of Abraham," in *OTP* 1.871–902). For the critical edition of the *Testament of Abraham*, see M. E. Stone, *The Testament of Abraham: The Greek Recensions* (T&T 2; Pseudepigrapha Series 2; Missoula: Scholars, 1972). The *Testament of Solomon* is a compendium of demonological lore with only the faintest trace of testamentary character in its claim that Solomon composed the work before his death (*T. Sol.* 15:14; see D. C. Duling, "Testament of Solomon," in *OTP*, 1.935–88). For the critical edition of the *Testament of Solomon*, see C. C. McCown, *The Testament of Solomon* (Leipzig: J. C. Hinrichs, 1922). See also K. Preisendanz, "Ein Wiener Papyrusfragment zum

Although the *Testaments of the Twelve Patriarchs* do evince Sanders's covenantal nomism, the *Testament of Moses* embraces the concept of election but rejects the idea that "obedience [to the laws] . . . or atonement and repentance for transgression" are ultimately necessary "for remaining in the covenant community." And while the *Testament of Job* admits a God-fearer into the community of the elect, it only requires of him trust in God to maintain that relationship.

1. Method

Our approach to discerning the theology of these works requires some explanation. In this essay theology is understood as *proposals regarding God's character in relationship to humanity.* So we ask how these texts understand the relationship between God and humanity to have been generated. In what ways do people come into relationship with God? How is that relationship sustained by God or by the human being? What can terminate the relationship? Furthermore, we understand these proposals always and everywhere to have been created in response to real human experiences. Thus it is incumbent upon the critic to ascertain as much as possible the historical context in which a text was composed. Finally, we assert that the contents of the proposals never derived purely from the imagination of the author, but consistently took up and argued with existing theological arguments known from the Hebrew Bible. Given these presuppositions our investigation will be focused on the ways in which the testaments reshaped the Hebrew Bible, on the historical situations to which they responded, and on how they made those responses using biblical and nonbiblical resources.

2. Testament of Moses[4]

The work begins with Moses summoning Joshua to give him final instructions and it concludes by beginning to narrate Moses' death.[5] While the scene

---

Testtamentum Salomonis," *EOS* 48 (1956): 161–7, for an important fragment that may extend our knowledge of the work, but that also adds support to the view that it was not a testament.

[4] The book exists in a single Latin sixth-century palimpsest discovered in Milan by A. M. Ceriani in 1861; for the text see R. H. Charles, *The Assumption of Moses* (London: Blackwell, 1897) and Johannes Tromp, *The Assumption of Moses: A Critical Edition with Commentary* (SVTP 10; Leiden: Brill, 1993). The work's original language is widely agreed to have been Hebrew (see D. H. Wallace, "The Semitic Origin of the Assumption of Moses," *TZ* 11 [1955]: 321–8), although the Latin manuscript is almost certainly a translation of an intermediate Greek version (see the evidence cited by Tromp, *A Critical Edition*, 78–85). Ceriani thought the manuscript reflected the *Assumption of Moses* because of the correspondence between 1:14 and

recalls Deut 31:7, 14, the introductory chapter introduces some unique elements. First, Moses reassures Joshua that all will be well for Israel beyond his death because God created the world for the people of Israel (1:12). He also tells Joshua that he himself was created from the beginning of time as the mediator of God's covenant (1:14). In 2:1–3:14 Moses predicts the future from the conquest to the exile and blames the eventual expulsion from the land on the last four kings of Judah, all of whom violate the "covenant and oath" (2:7). But once in exile the people will implore God to recall the covenant with Abraham, Isaac, and Jacob (3:9), and according to 4:1–4 a mediator (Daniel?) will appeal to God's pride by noting the awful conditions the people experience in captivity, implying that a chosen people should not suffer so. Then, says Moses, following this intercession God will raise up a king from a foreign nation to deliver some of the tribes from their exile

a quotation from an *Assumption of Moses* by Gelasius (Eusebius, *Hist. eccl.* 2:17.17); but the further reference made to the work by Gelasius includes a debate between the devil and Michael (*Hist. eccl.* 2:21.7) and the absence of such a dialogue in Ceriani's manuscript raises doubts regarding the identification. Moreover, Collins points out that Nicephorus's reference in the *Stichometry* to a *Testament of Moses* just after the *Assumption* suggests that the Latin text is the *Testament* and that the *Assumption* existed independently (Collins, "Testaments," 344). For Greek citations indicating the existence of a *Testament of Moses,* see M. Black and A.-M. Denis, ed., *Apocalypsis Henochi graece Fragmenta pseudepigraphorum quae supersunt Graeca una cum historicorum et auctorum judaeorum hellenistarum fragmentis collegit ed ordinavit Albert-Marie Denis* (PVTG 3; Leiden: Brill, 1970), 63–67. For presentations of the text with varying degrees of commentary, see R. H. Charles, *APOT* 2.407–24; C. Clement, "Die Himmelfahrt Moses," in *Die Apokryphen und Pseudepigraphen des Alten Testaments* (ed. E. Kautzsch; Tübingen: Mohr [Siebeck] 1099), 2.311–31; E. M. Laperrousaz, "Le Testament de Moïse (généralement appelé 'Assomption de Moïse'): Traduction avec introduction et notes," *Semitica* 19 (1970); idem., "Testament de Moïse," in *La Bible. Ecrits Intertestamentaires* (ed. A. Dupont-Sommer and M. Philonenko; Paris: Bibliothèque de la Pléiade, 1987), 993–1016; J. Priest, "The Testament of Moses," in *OTP,* 1.919–34; and J. Tromp, *A Critical Edition.* In addition to the aforementioned, some of the basic studies on the *Testament* are the following: D. C. Carlson, "Vengeance and Angelic Mediation in *Testament of Moses* 9 and 10," *JBL* 101 (1982): 85–95; Adela Yarbro Collins, "Composition and Redaction of the Testament of Moses 10," *HTR* 69 (1976): 179–86; H. Cousin, "Le Testament de Moïse," *Foi et Vie* 89 (1990): 39–48; Robert Doran, "*T. Mos.* 4:8 and the Second Temple," *JBL* 106 (1987): 491–2; K. Haacker, "Assumptio Mosis – eine samaritanische Schrift?" *TZ* 25 (1969): 385–405; J. Licht, "Taxo, or the Apocalyptic Doctrine of Vengeance," *JJS* 12 (1961): 95–103; C. Lattey, "The Messianic Expectation in 'The Assumption of Moses'," *CBQ* 4 (1942): 9–21; S. Mowinckel, "The Hebrew Equivalent of Taxo in As. Mos. ix," *VTSup* 4 (1953): 88–96; G. Theissen, "*Pax Romana et Pax Christi:* Le Christianisme primitif et l'idée de paix," *RTP* 124 (1992): 61–84, esp. 66–70; and S. Zeitlin, "The Assumption of Moses and the Bar Kochba Revolt," *JQR* 38 (1947/48): 1–45. See also the essays assembled in G. W. E. Nickelsburg, ed., *Studies on The Testament of Moses* (SBLSCS 4; Cambridge: Society of Biblical Literature, 1973).

[5] The conclusion is lost from the manuscript so one cannot be certain that it actually completed the narration of Moses' death. It is possible that the death is recounted in *Assumption of Moses;* see D. Flusser, "*Palaea Historia.* An Unknown Source of Biblical Legends," in *Scripta Hierosolymitana* 22, 72–4.

(4:6–7), though two tribes will not join in the restored sacrificial cult, and ten will spread among the nations during the period of captivity (4:8–9).

A new prediction passage in 5:1–6 recalls the Hasmoneans as apostates whose sins against God and people are punished first by the traumas imposed by Herod (6:1–7) and then by the campaign of Varus in 4 B.C.E. (6:8–9). *T. Mos.* 7:1–8:5 recites another cycle of apostasy and its consequences, this time focusing on a catalogue of priestly sins which defy assignment to any particular period of Israelite or Jewish history (7:1–10); these sins are punished by a cornucopia of sufferings which also cannot be ascribed to a particular period in Jewish history (8:1–5). Then, just as 4:1–4 introduced an intercessor who seemed to provoke God into action on behalf of the people, 9:1–7 introduces a parallel figure, Taxo, who promises that, if necessary, he and his sons will die as martyrs to prompt the advent of God's kingdom. *T. Mos.* 10:1–10 describes the future kingdom and states that it will be established by God alone. Having concluded his predictions, in 10:11–15 Moses admonishes Joshua to lead well, but in 11:1–19 Joshua voices his fear that without the mediation of Moses the people will not survive the predicted future, filled as it is with "tears and sobbings" (11:4). The work concludes with Moses answering Joshua by repeating his assertion that God made the world from before time for Israel (12:3–5; cf. 1:12–13). Although God did appoint Moses from the beginning of time as a mediator and intercessor (12:6–7; cf. 1:14), it is God who controls all things in Israel's favor, not Moses' prayers or the people's righteous deeds (12:8–9). So while God determines that in the present time and world the righteous enjoy goodness and the wicked suffer (12:10–11), in the end God will vindicate all Israel and remain true to God's covenant and oath (12:12–13).

Narration of events from the Hasmonean period in *T. Mos.* 5:1–6 has prompted some to date *Testament of Moses* in the late second century B.C.E.;[6] but the allusions to Herod (6:2–6), to his sons – who by the time of writing had not yet reigned longer than their father (6:7) – and to Varus, the Roman commander who put down a revolt around 4 B.C.E. (6:9) prove that the present form of the testament was composed some time between 4 B.C.E. and 30 C.E.[7] Given the familiarity with the campaign of Varus and the interest in

---

[6] See especially George W. E. Nickelsburg, "An Antiochan Date for the Testament of Moses," in *Studies on the Testament of Moses* (ed. G. W. E. Nickelsburg; SBLSCS 4; Missoula: Scholars, 1973), 33–7.

[7] See, for example, John Collins, "The Date and Provenance of the Testament of Moses," in *Studies,* 15–32; but note Tromp, *A Critical Edition,* 116–7, who thinks the allusion to Varus is not so certain and so prefers a slightly broader period that would extend to the middle of the first century C.E.; see also the (widely discredited) view of Haacker, "Assumptio Mosis," *passim,* that it is a second century C.E. Samaritan work. And see E. Stauffer, "Probleme der Priestertradition," *TLZ* 81 (1956): col. 141, who suggests that the different references indicate the work was a collection of statements from different epochs.

the priesthood, a Palestinian provenance seems likely.[8] As for assigning the work to a particular Jewish group of that period and locale, nothing can be said with confidence.[9]

Attempts to determine the theology of *Testament of Moses* range widely in their results. J. Priest simply calls its theology "deuteronomic."[10] Meanwhile, John Collins considers the work to be a good example of "covenantal nomism," inasmuch as the testament seems to indicate that the people of Israel are elected to their status, but are required to keep the law to retain their place in relationship to God and God's choosing.[11] Other commentators suggest the testament argues that God works unilaterally on behalf of Israel, and is unconditionally merciful to a sinful, punished, and only nominally repentant Israel.[12] We turn now to ask whether a look at the material that the *Testament* borrows from the Hebrew Bible, the manner in which it adapts that material, and its likely historical context support one or another of these views.

At least in part the *Testament of Moses* takes from the Hebrew Bible its testamentary form. Relying heavily on Deut 31–32, the *Testament* exhibits the standard narrative framework that includes at the beginning announcement of the speaker's impending death and his intention to pass on words of wisdom to his successor(s) and concludes with an account of the speaker's death.[13] And like Deut 31–32 it mixes exhortation and future prediction.[14]

The *Testament of Moses* also borrows a narrative strategy typical of apocalyptic texts and reminiscent especially of Daniel. In *T. Mos.* 2–9 Moses repeatedly characterizes Israel's future as a pattern of sin followed by punishment, intercession and deliverance (see 2–3, followed by 4; 5–6 and 7–8, followed by 9).[15] While a great deal of effort has been devoted to identifying each of these predictions with specific events in Israelite, Judean,

---

[8] See J. Tromp, *A Critical Edition,* 117; but see the contrasting possibility hinted at by Daniel Schwartz, "The Tribes of *As. Mos.* 4:7–9," *JBL* 99 (1980): 217–23. For a fuller treatment of the sociohistoric context, see David Rhoads, "The Assumption of Moses and Jewish History: 4 B.C.–A.D. 48," in *Studies,* 53–58.

[9] See Laperoussaz, "Le Testament," 88–95, for a summary of the various views on the topic; but see especially the thesis of Haacker, "Assumptio Mosis," *passim,* noted above.

[10] J. Priest, "Some Reflections on the Assumption of Moses," *PRSt* 4 (1977): 92–111; see also J. Tromp, *A Commentary,* 123, who seems to take roughly the same view.

[11] Collins, "Testaments," 347.

[12] Daniel Harrington, "Interpreting Israel's History: The Testament of Moses as a Rewriting of Deut 31–34," in *Studies,* 59–68; and Betsy Halpern-Amaru, *Rewriting the Bible: Land and Covenant in Postbiblical Jewish Literature* (Valley Forge: Trinity Press International, 1994), 55–68.

[13] See n. 3 above.

[14] For other biblical testaments with such a mixture, see Gen 49; Josh 23–24; 1 Sam 12; 1 Kgs 2:1–9.

[15] For this structure in *Testament of Moses,* see Halpern-Amaru, *Rewriting,* 157 n. 44.

and Jewish history,[16] a look at the whole document suggests that it actually engages in the narrative approach known from apocalyptic texts, wherein the same general future is repeatedly narrated from a variety of different perspectives.[17] This pattern is well known from Daniel, *1 Enoch*, and perhaps some of the *Sibylline Oracles*.[18]

In terms of content, the text leans heavily on Deut 31–32. Chapter 1 aligns nicely with Deut 31:1–8, 14–15, 23–26; chs. 2–9 correspond to 31:16–21; and ch. 10 recalls 32:1–43.[19] As for chs. 11–12, which narrate the transfer of leadership, and would seem to move beyond Deut 31–32, Halpern-Amaru comments, " . . . but the transfer of leadership [of chs. 31–34] is the point of departure for the dialogue which sets forth the theological perspective of the work."[20] Perhaps it is more accurate to say that chs. 11–12 complete (apart from any precise biblical precedent) the agenda begun in chs. 1–10. In that way the *Testament* extends beyond the limits of Deut 31–32.

The language in the *Testament of Moses* evokes still other Pentateuchal traditions. According to Halpern-Amaru especially the phrase "covenant and oath" in 1:9; 2:7[21]; 3:9; 11:17; and 12:13 would have called to mind Exod 32:13 and Gen 22:16–18. She denies that the phrase directs the reader to Deut 29:9–14, even though it is there, in close proximity to the passage being echoed by the work as a whole, that the terms appear together. Instead, she suggests that when the content of the covenant and oath is spelled out in *T. Mos.* 3:8–9 attention is directed to Exod 32:13 by the explicit reference to God swearing an oath "upon himself," which in turn recalls Gen 22:16–18, the only other occasion in the Hebrew Bible where God swears out a

---

[16] See the discussions of date and historical referents cited in nn. 8–9 above.

[17] For this insight regarding apocalyptic narrative strategies, see John J. Collins, *The Apocalyptic Imagination* (New York: Crossroad, 1984), 85–86.

[18] Collins, *Apocalyptic Imagination*, 85, also cites as examples *4 Ezra, 2 Baruch*, and Similitudes of Enoch, all of which might be too late for the earliest readers of *Testament of Moses* to have known them. But Daniel was certainly well known to them, and it is from that work that the strategy seems to have developed.

[19] Halpern-Amaru, *Rewriting*, 152 n. 1. Like many others, Harrington, "Interpreting," 66–68, suggests that in general the antecedent text is Deut 31–34. Yet his treatment of the *Testament* shows that the substantive parallels only extend as far as Deut 31–32. Notably, Deut 31–32 records Israel's history as a repeated pattern of election, apostasy, punishment, and vindication by God; for more on this, see below (Halpern-Amaru, *Rewriting*, 61; contrast Nickelsburg, "The Antiochan Date," 33 n. 2, who suggests that Taxo's death provides the equivalent of repentance; yet it is not clear from the text that Taxo actually does die, and his threat to die of starvation seems designed more to bully God into action than an act of contrition intended to earn God's mercy for others).

[20] Halpern-Amaru, *Rewriting*, 55.

[21] For the emendation that provides both *testamentum* and *jusjurandum* in 2:7, see Charles, *The Assumption of Moses Translated from the Latin Sixth Century MS, the Unemended Text of Which is Published Herewith, Together with the Texts in its Restored and Critically Emended Form* (London: Blackwell, 1897), *ad loc.*

covenant "upon himself."[22] Halpern-Amaru is correct in seeing the connection to Exod 32:12–13 and Gen 22:16–18 at 3:8–9, yet there is good reason to think that where the phrase appears before that (1:9; 2:7) the referent would more likely have been taken to reflect Deut 29:9–14.[23] Moreover, the reference in 3:8–9 would not only call Exodus 32:12–13 and Gen 22:16–18 to mind, but Gen 15 as well. *T. Mos.* 3:8–9 refers only to descendants becoming so numerous as the stars in the sky, while Gen 22:17 also uses the metaphor of the sand on the seashore; but in Gen 15:6, like *T. Mos.* 3:8–9, God compares descendants only to the stars of the heavens. Furthermore, although Gen 15 makes no explicit reference to God swearing an oath upon himself, there God *acts* out the swearing of an oath upon himself by passing between the pieces. Thus while the first two occurrences of the phrase "covenant and oath" echo Deut 29 and its bilateral covenant, its third occurrence directs the audience to Exod 32:12–13; Gen 22:16–18; and Gen 15, all passages which give expression to a unilateral covenant.

The *Testament of Moses* also takes up some *topoi* typical of apocalyptic works. It is highly deterministic in outlook[24] and it has something of apocalyptic's more severe division of Judaism between those who are righteous and those who are wicked by their lack of concern for the law.

What are the theological consequences of the mixture of these biblical genre patterns, narrative strategies, and content in the *Testament of Moses*? First, the testamentary genre leads one to expect narration of future realities and moral exhortation on the basis of those realities. The references in 1:9; 2:7 to a covenant and oath that echoed Deut 29:9–14 would also support the view that God would reward or terminally punish Israel for its success or failure in the covenant relationship (cf. Deut 29:18–28). But already in *T. Mos.* 1:6, 9 the fulfillment of such genre and content-based expectations is put into question by the echoes of Deut 31:7, 14, the opening salvos in an unusual testamentary passage that predicts the people's corporate failure and God's remedial action *in place* of repentant and rectifying human activity. *T. Mos.* 1:13 underscores this tilt toward the outlook of Deut 31–32 by announcing God's prehistoric determination that creation would be for the people of Israel. But 1:14 introduces a third possible understanding of the relationship between God and people, stating that Moses himself was determined from the beginning of the world to be God's covenant mediator, and implying that

---

[22] Ibid., 57.

[23] This is no small matter in that the text leads its readers toward the fulfillment of one set of expectations by harkening to Deut 29:9–14, which, taken with the rest of ch. 29 makes clear the bilateral character of God's covenant, only to upend the reader in mid-stream, forcing a reconsideration that shapes one's reading of the rest of the work.

[24] Note, however, Collins' reserve regarding the deterministic character of *Testament of Moses* stemming from his view that Taxo's action could change the course of history ("Testaments," 347).

Moses' mediation and intercession are necessary for the people's prosperity in relationship to God (and that his impending death and the end of his mediation would cut them off from God's will).

The tension among these possible ways of conceiving the relationship between God and humanity is maintained by the content, genre clues, and narratives strategies that follow. Predictions of future wickedness and punishment, followed by successful intercession on the part of the unnamed figure in ch. 4 and Taxo in ch. 9, uphold the possibility that it is only through intercession that the people can survive. Meanwhile, the parallels with Deut 31–32 bolster the prospect of God deciding in the people's favor no matter how they behaved. Likewise, the consistent adherence to the basic elements of the testamentary genre preserves the chance that God rewards those who respond to exhortation and leaves to their fate those who do not. And the narrative strategy of rehearsing the same future from different perspectives recalls apocalyptic literature and its deterministic theological nature. And so it goes throughout chs. 2:1–9:7. Rehearsing the future in a way that echoes known events (e.g., the Antiochan persecution, the reign of Herod and the campaign of Varus) and clearly establishing the pattern of the future as one of apostasy, punishment and intercession, the text maintains a vexing neutrality on the question of just who God is and what God intends in relationship to the people of Israel.

Although the clarification of the content of the covenant and oath in 3:8–9 had already revealed something of the outlook of the *Testament*, the resolution of the tension among the three options begins to emerge most fully in ch. 10 with Moses' eschatological hymn. Like the hymn in Deut 32, it announces that the people, sinful and weighed down by the burden of their punishment, will be delivered by God who will not be denied the chance to make of God's people what God wants.[25] Yet Joshua's speech in ch. 11 immediately renews the tension. He expresses his assent to the intercessory approach and his fear that it meets its demise with the death of Moses (11:9–19). Then in ch. 12 Moses resolves the tension. He acknowledges that the people cannot do for themselves what God would do (12:8); he says that although he was chosen from the beginning of time and his intercession has been effective it has been so only by God's will (12:6–7); and he affirms that though people will suffer the natural consequences of good and bad action in this life (12:10–11), from the beginning God, who is in control of all things (12:4b–5, 9), made creation for Israel and will not let Israel be vanquished completely at the end, but will be faithful to his covenant and oath to sustain

---

[25] See, however, Collins, "Composition and Redaction of the Testament of Moses," *HTR* 69 (1976): 179–86, whose suggestion regarding the eagle of 10:8 would counter this view; but see also the reading of J. Tromp, *A Critical Edition*, 236.

the people (12:4a, 12–13). Thus in the contest of various perspectives, Moses' closing speech affirms the position established in Gen 15; 22; Exod 32; and Deut 31–32.

What would have been the wider impact of this work on an audience living in first-century Palestine? Varus' campaign proves that Herod's death in 4 B.C.E. encouraged in some Jews a renewed yearning for freedom from oppressive rule. But Varus' quick and brutal success, and the renewed control exerted by Rome over the region, would have put an end to all such hopes, at least for a time. It might also have served as a warning to those with further nationalistic hopes. Where such hopes survived, they may have worried more cautious Jews that they could lead to further difficulties for the people. It is in this context that the *Testament of Moses* emerges with its argument regarding the sovereignty of God over creation and the fate of Israel, and its claim that, while Israel may suffer at the hands of its enemies, God will vindicate her in the end of time. Coming in the wake of frustrated nationalistic aspirations and in opposition to theological and political notions of retributive justice, the *Testament of Moses* offered a critique of those perspectives and evoked the alternative theological horizon already evident in Gen 15; 22; Exod 32 and Deut 31–32. As such it is easy to imagine that *Testament of Moses* opened up a horizon of theological thought for Palestinian Jews of the first century C.E. that was latent in the biblical text. Thus the *Testament of Moses* meets Sanders's notion of covenantal nomism at least half-way: the *Testament* does understand Israel to have been elected by God, but it seems to preclude the possibility that Israel could "unelect" itself by a failure to keep the law.[26]

3. Testament of Job[27]

Although modeled on the Book of Job,[28] the *Testament of Job* differs vastly in theological outlook from the biblical work. In true testamentary fashion,

---

[26] It is important to note, however, that Sanders says with respect to *Testament of Moses* that it embodies the "common theology, covenantal nomism. God has chosen Israel and will redeem his nation by his own initiative. People should obey his law. He punishes sinners severely and chastises the righteous for their transgressions" (*Judaism: Practice and Belief, 63 B.C.E.–55 C.E.* [London: SCM, 1992], 457). In these words Sanders himself seems to hint that covenantal nomism embraces the idea that God's election cannot be undone.

[27] For the text of the *Testament of Job*, see R. A. Kraft, *The Testament of Job* (T&T 5; Pseudepigrapha Series 5; Missoula: Scholars, 1974); and S. P. Brock and J.-C. Picard, *Testamentum Iobi/Apocalypsis Baruchi Graece* (Leiden: Brill, 1967), 3–59. It is preserved in four major Greek manuscripts and three Slavonic manuscripts. For a convenient presentation of the text in translation with introduction and notes, see R. P. Spittler, "Testament of Job," in *OTP* 1.829–68. Significant studies on the *Testament of Job* include, among others, the following

it begins with Job[29] summoning his children in advance of his own death to recall for them the events of his life (ch. 1). He explains to them that his suffering was caused by his destruction of the temple of Satan. An angel of God had confirmed his suspicion that a local temple was actually Satan's and advised him that he could tear down the temple, but that Satan would destroy his wealth and cause him great suffering as a consequence; but if he endured all of that while trusting in God his prosperity and happiness would be restored twofold and he would know resurrection, for in δίκαιος καὶ ἀληθινὸς καὶ ἰσχυρὸς ἐνισχύων τοὺς ἐκλεκτοὺς αὐτοῦ ("the Lord is just, true and strong, giving strength to his elect ones") (4:11; chs. 3–5). Job destroyed the temple and retreated home to weather the coming storm.

Satan then comes to Job's home disguised as a beggar. The doormaid does not recognize Satan, but Job, wise to his ploys, instructs her to send the beggar away (ch. 6).[30] Satan returns to plead again for bread and again the doormaid is ignorant of the beggar's identity and reports to her master the stranger's request. Aware that it is yet Satan at his door, Job tells the maidservant to give the beggar a charred and worthless loaf. Loath to shame her master, she gives instead a good loaf; Satan scorns her ignorance and charges her to give the burnt loaf. Satan announces that Job's life will soon

---

works: C. T. Begg, "Comparing Characters: The Book of Job and the Testament of Job," in *The Book of Job* (ed. W. Beuken; Leuven: Peeters, 1994), 435–45; Randall Chesnutt, "Revelatory Experiences Attributed to Biblical Women in Early Jewish Literature," in *"Women Like This:" New Perspectives on Jewish Women in the Greco-Roman World* (ed. Amy-Jill Levine; SBLEJL 1; Atlanta: Scholars, 1991), 107–25; John J. Collins, "Structure and Meaning in the Testament of Job," *1974 SBL Seminar Papers* (ed. G. W. MacRae; Missoula: Scholars, 1974), 35–52; Susan Garrett, "The 'Weaker Sex' in the *Testament of Job*," *JBL* 112 (1993): 55–70; H. C. Kee, "Satan, Magic, and Salvation in the *Testament of Job*," *1974 SBL Seminar Papers* (ed. G. W. MacRae; Missoula: Scholars, 1974), 53–76; D. Rahnenführer, "Das Testament des Hiob und das Neue Testament," *ZNW* 62 (1971): 68–93; B. Schaller, "Das Testament Hiobs und die Septuaginta-Übersetzung des Buches Hiob," *Bib* 61 (1980): 377–406; H. M. Wahl, "Elihu, Frevler oder Frommer? Die Auslegung des Hiobbuches (Hi 32–37) durch ein Pseudepigraphen (TestHi 41–43)," *JSJ* 25 (1994): 1–17.

[28] B. Schaller, "Das Testament Hiobs und die Septuaginta-Übersetzung des Buches Hiob," *Bib* 61 (1980) 377–406, proves that the author relied in particular on LXX Job.

[29] *T. Job* 1:1 begins, Βίβλιος λόγων Ιωβ τοῦ καλουμένου Ιωβαβ ("The book of the words of Job, the one called Jobab," apparently in reliance on LXX Job 42:17d. *T. Job* 2:1 indicates it is the Lord who changes Job's name (cf. Gen 17:5; 32:29).

[30] The theme of unenlightened women in the *Testament of Job* has been dealt with at length by Pieter van der Horst, "Images of Women in the Testament of Job," in *Studies in the Testament of Job* (ed. Michael Knibb and Pieter van der Horst; SNTSMS 66; Cambridge: Cambridge University, 1989), 273–89; and Susan Garrett, "The 'Weaker Sex' in the *Testament of Job*," *JBL* 112 (1993): 55–70; see also Collins, "Testaments," 353; and Randall Chesnutt, "Revelatory Experiences Attributed to Biblical Women in Early Jewish Literature," in *"Women Like This:" New Perspectives on Jewish Women in the Greco-Roman World* (ed. Amy-Jill Levine; SBLEJL 1; Atlanta: Scholars, 1991), 107–25.

be as the loaf, a scorched and worthless thing. Job challenges Satan to do his best (ch. 7). With that Satan asks and receives God's permission to afflict Job (ch. 8).

Next Job's wealth and generosity to the poor are described (chs. 9–15) and his losses to Satan are circumscribed (chs. 16–26).[31] Much of this account relates to Job's wife Sitidos (chs. 21–26).[32] Job sees his wife carrying water as a servant for the wealthy to obtain bread for Job and herself (ch. 21). The nobles reduce her portions so that she can no longer feed herself and Job, and Satan, disguised as a breadseller, offers bread in exchange for the hair of her head. She permits Satan to shave her head in the open marketplace, after which she goes to Job, with Satan secretly following, to explain her predicament and to ask Job to curse God and die so as to end their suffering (chs. 22–24). Following is a lament for Sitidos that describes her former wealth (ch. 25; cf. chs. 9–15 and Job's wealth).[33] Job responds to Sitidos' invitation to curse God with a rebuke and his claim that to do so would alienate him from his great wealth, his inheritance in heaven (26:3). Job exhorts Sitidos to the same endurance he exhibits. Since God gave goodness it is not too much to endure some evil, and he tells her that Satan is the driving force in her attempt to lead Job astray (26:4–6). Then Satan comes forward and admits that even though he is the stronger of the two combatants in their wrestling match, Job is the more persistent of the two and has wearied Satan into withdrawal and defeat (ch. 27).

Next Job's fellow kings, Eliphaz, Baldad, and Sophar arrive and remain silent for the first seven days because they are astonished at Job's great fall from wealth and fitness to poverty and sickness (chs. 28–30). Then Eliphaz establishes that this is really Job (ch. 31) and laments Job's loss of wealth and position, repeating the refrain ποῦ οὖν τυγχάνει ἡ δόξα τοῦ θρόνου σου ("Where is the glory of your throne?") (ch. 32). Job responds that his throne

---

[31] Especially curious is the way in which Satan rallies the locals against Job's family (17:1–18:1). He disguises himself as the king of Persia and reminds the people that Job is the one who tore down τὸν μὲν ναὸν τοῦ μεγάλου θεοῦ ("the temple of the great god") (17:3) and thus destroyed all the good things of earth. Because Job's children might be a similar problem to the neighbors in the future, says Satan, they should be killed. M. Delcor, "Le Testament de Job, la prière de Nabonide et les traditions targumiques," in *Bible et Qumran* (ed. S. Wagner, et al.; Berlin: Evangelische Hauptbibelschaftsgesellschaft, 1968), 72–73, says this supports dating the testament to 40 B.C.E. because it was then that Acorus of Persia invaded Egypt. But John J. Collins, "Structure and Meaning in the Testament of Job," *1974 SBL Seminar Papers* (ed. G. W. MacRae; Missoula: Scholars, 1974), 1.50, rejects that proposal, noting that Egyptians habitually vilified Persian monarchs in their literature.

[32] There is considerable discord over the translation of the wife's name. Some claim that the form that appears in the text, Σιτιδος, is the genitive of Σιτις; for a summary of the debate, see P. W. van der Horst, "Images of Women," 96–97. For the sake of convenience we use the name as it is written in the text.

[33] For a complete comparison see Spittler, "Testament of Job," 850 n. 25a.

and his wealth are in heaven before God (ch. 33). Eliphaz rebukes Job, implying that earthly goods are the proper measure of one's greatness (ch. 34). Baldad tests Job's sanity on the premise that Job, recalling his wealth, has gone mad (35:4). He asks Job in whom he trusts and who destroyed his goods, and to each query Job answers "God" (37:1–4).[34] Baldad ascribes to Job the view that God is unfair and admonishes him to eschew such a position. Finally, Baldad tests Job with a riddle regarding the setting of the sun in the west and its rising in the east (37:8). Job responds by riddling Baldad with the puzzle of why food and drink go into the same place within the body but emerge separately in the latrine. When Baldad cannot answer Job asks him why he should query him about heavenly things when he fails to understand earthly matters (38:1–5). Sophar next offers his physicians to heal Job, but Job refuses them, preferring the divine doctor (38:6–8). At this Sitidos reappears to ask the kings to use their forces to unearth her dead children from under the house that crushed them, but Job says there is nothing to find since her children were taken to heaven, and if Sitidos would only look upward she could see them. Sitidos does glimpse her offspring in their heavenly home and returns to her place of servitude at peace and dies (chs. 39–40). After Elihu appears long enough to insult Job for the claim that he possesses a heavenly estate that exceeds the goodness of earthly prosperity (ch. 41), Eliphaz rebukes Elihu and God tells Job to sacrifice for the sins of the other three friends (ch. 42). Then Eliphaz delivers a mocking dirge for Elihu who was possessed by Satan and who loses his wealth as a consequence (ch. 43). Finally, Job's wealth is restored by generous friends (ch. 44). Job concludes his account by urging his children to be generous to the poor and to avoid marrying foreign women. Then he distributes his wealth to his sons (ch. 45).

Lastly Job's daughters Hemera, Kasia, and Amaltheia's Horn complain that they have no inheritance and he gives them the sashes that God gave him to bind himself with when God commanded him to rise and gird his loins (Job 38:3; 40:2). Job tells his daughters that the sashes cured his physical and emotional distress and gave him other miraculous benefits. Each of the women has an ecstatic religious experience as she dons her sash (chs. 46–50).

---

[34] Some cite this shift from Satan as the destroyer to God as the troublemaker as evidence of the testament's composite character. For the general view that the *Testament of Job* underwent an extended compositional history see, for example, M. R. James, "The Testament of Job," Apocrypha Anecdota II, (TS 5/1 [Cambridge: Cambridge University, 1897]), lxxxix, xcvi; M. Philonenko, "Le Testament de Job, Introduction, traduction et notes," *Sem* 18 (1968): 1–75; van der Horst, "Images of Women," 106ff.; and Spittler, "Testament of Job," 834. Bernd Schaller, "Zur Komposition und Konzeption des Testaments Hiobs," in *Studies in the Testament of Job*, 46–92, would seem to have the last and best word on this topic; he shows by the repetition of catch-phrases throughout the work that, though it may contain disparate sources, it is the work of a single author-redactor.

Then Job dies, his daughters assist him into heaven with their songs, and his body is buried (chs. 51–53).

The contents of the work and its familiarity with LXX Job roughly establish its date and provenance. The reference to Job as a king of Egypt (28:7) suggests the country of origin. As for date, some precise suggestions have been put forward,[35] but familiarity with LXX Job and the theme of endurance suggest a first-century C.E. date – LXX Job was certainly available by then and the persecutions Jews experienced in first-century Egypt might have prompted exhortation to endurance and patience.[36] The debate regarding the testament's redactional unity confuses attempts to ascertain the work's date, but although some still defend the view that it underwent a long redactional process, most grant that a single composer, using disparate sources, created the received work sometime around the first century C.E.[37]

Regarding the theological perspective of the work, Spittler offers the suggestion that "the theological outlook of the *Testament of Job* aligns with Hellenistic Judaism."[38] He supports the suggestion with the following elements: the living God (37:2) is just (43:13) and the creator of all things (2:4); and God is the master of all virtues (50:2) and a healer (38:8; 52:1–2).[39] More helpfully Collins observes regarding its theological outlook that the *Testament of Job* contrasts "heavenly realities and earthly transience and illusion," an opposition that is "overcome by heavenly insight, and finally by transportation to the divine realm."[40] Shaller does not think the testament has any real theological significance, but was only meant to shape various aspects of its audience's religious life.[41] Cees Haas concludes that its goal, like other texts from the "Hellenistic-Jewish" literature, is to inculcate a spirit of endurance in the face of difficulties.[42]

What does understanding the *Testament*'s reliance on the Hebrew Bible and the LXX suggest about its theology? How might the dynamics of first-century Egyptian life have shaped that effort? What it takes over from the

---

[35] See, for example, Delcor's thesis cited in n. 30 above.

[36] See Spittler, "Testament of Job," 833–4, for a summary of the most important arguments regarding date and provenance. Note especially the view espoused by K. Kohler, "The Testament of Job: An Essene Midrash on the Book of Job Reedited and Translated with Introductory and Exegetical Notes," in *Semitic Studies in Memory of Rev. Dr. Alexander Kohut* (Berlin: S. Calvary, 1897) 264–338; and M. Philonenko, "Le Testament de Job et les Thérapeutes," *Sem* 8 (1958): 41–53, that the work comes from the Therapeutae. For the most careful approach to the question, see John J. Collins, "Structure and Meaning," 50.

[37] See also the works cited in n. 35.

[38] Spittler, "Testament of Job," 835.

[39] Ibid.

[40] Collins, "Structure and Meaning," 49.

[41] Schaller, "Zur Komposition," 91–92.

[42] Cees Haas, "Job's perseverance in the Testament of Job," in *Studies on the Testament of Job*, 117–54.

Hebrew Bible is obvious: probably the testamentary genre,[43] certainly the text of LXX Job,[44] and without a doubt much of the same biblical book's content.[45]

At the level of narrative strategy the "prosaic and occasionally humorous"[46] style aimed at entertaining the reader echoes *Joseph and Aseneth,* another work from Egyptian Jews from around this period. Thus it seems the *Testament* intends to lure its audience's interest and then teach them about a few small matters (the nature of Satan; funerary practices; the character of women; cosmological dualism; and eschatology), but ultimately it seeks to instruct them on one major point, the value of endurance or patience. This rhetorical strategy would have been familiar to Jews in Egypt.[47]

With regard to content the *Testament* provides a sharp contrast with the Book of Job, with its well-known story of the heavenly wager between God and Satan, Job's piety and patience in the narrative prologue, the rebellious and complaining Job of the speeches, and the restored and pious Job of the narrative epilogue.[48] Also, Cees Haas has convincingly demonstrated the text's reliance for its central theme of perseverance on a *topos* found in a number of Jewish-Hellenistic works of the era.[49]

What does the *Testament of Job* accomplish theologically with this genre, narrative strategy, and content? First, it blends the testamentary genre with the entertaining narrative strategy to illustrate the value of endurance and patience, a virtue well-known to a first century C.E. Diaspora audience. The surprise comes in the way the *content* of the story, produced within the testamentary framework and by means of the entertaining narrative strategy, varies from that encountered in the Book of Job. The *Testament of Job* boldly contradicts its biblical counterpart. While the Book of Job leaves in question

---

[43] But see the warning of Collins, "Structure and Meaning," 51–52, that is only superficially a testament, and may share more in common with "Jewish and Christian accounts of martyrdom." Nevertheless, it is still framed as a testament and is undeniably treated as such. See also the discussion of genre and the vigorous defense of the view that it is a testament in Spittler, "Testament of Job," 831–2.

[44] See n. 27 above.

[45] It also exhibits familiarity with other biblical and Hellenistic literary genres. For instance, *T. Job* 25 and 32 are laments that would have been situated in the funerary setting; taken together with the wider interest in funerary practices exhibited in the work, this suggests an expectation that an audience would understand something of related practices and literary forms. Job's psalm of affirmation in ch. 33 also points to a familiarity with certain liturgical forms, ones perhaps typical of the synagogue and its practices.

[46] Spittler, *ABD,* 3.869.

[47] In addition to *Joseph and Aseneth,* see 3 Maccabees.

[48] Thus many speculate that James 5:11 reflects on the *Testament,* not the biblical Book of Job; see Luke Timothy Johnson, *The Letter of James* (AB 37A; New York: Doubleday, 1995), 319–20, 324.

[49] Haas, "Job's perseverance," *passim.*

God's relationship to evil and innocent suffering, the *Testament* permits no ambiguity on the matter, nor is there any question regarding the value it attaches to notions of retribution. First, according to the *Testament* there is no innocent suffering: even if it is God who permits them to come to pass (8:1–3), Job knows that his difficulties befall him because of Satan's wrath at the destruction of his temple; anyway, Job is reassured that if he trusts God he will be restored to wealth, health and happiness twice over, and in the bargain will be raised from the dead (4:6–9).

The historical context for this refashioning of the Book of Job – the early Roman period in Egypt – illuminates the work's likely intention. The effects of Roman rule on Jews residing in Egypt are well known. Economic conditions could hardly have been worse. With the disbanding of the Ptolemaic army Jews recruited to Egypt as mercenaries, who had won substantial privileges and wealth through their service, were left without a profession or a means to support themselves and their families.[50] The coveted role of the civil servant was beyond the reach of most Jews who could not bear the cost of the associated Roman taxes.[51] Augustus' *laographia* was especially burdensome to Jews.[52] And Vespasian's escalated collection of the temple tax after the temple's destruction in 70 C.E. to pay for reconstruction of the temple of Jupiter Capitolinus (destroyed in 69 C.E.) drove many Jews, especially those in the *chora*, into even deeper fiscal woes.[53] Socially and culturally this was also a period of deep distress. Prior to Roman domination the Jews of Alexandria and the *chora* had made apparent their preference for the Ptolemaic leaders who were allied with Rome, so that when Rome took control they were natural targets for those who resented Roman rule, especially native Egyptians and Greeks.[54] There were also considerable tensions with Egyptians over the Jewish view of the animal cult practiced by the native peoples.[55] These accumulated strains led to the pogroms of 38 to 41 C.E., the questioning of Jewish privileges in Alexandria in particular, and eventually to the ruling of Claudius in 41 C.E. that Jews should retain the right

---

[50] E. Mary Smallwood, *The Jews Under Roman Rule: From Pompey to Diocletian* (SJLA 20; Leiden: Brill: 1976), 231.

[51] Ibid.

[52] Ibid., 231–2.

[53] Whereas the tax was levied against males 20 to 50 years of age before Vespasian's intervention, by his decree it was to be paid by all Jews between three and 62; see V. Tcherikover and A. Fuks, *Corpus Papyrorum Judaicarum* (3 vols.; Jerusalem: Magnes, 1957–64), 1.80–82; 2.204–5.

[54] Josephus, *Contra Ap.* 2.49–56, recounts Onias' support for Cleopatra II, the consequences of which "were to reach far into the future" (John M. G. Barclay, *Jews in the Mediterranean Diaspora: From Alexander to Trajan (323 B.C.E.–117 C.E.)* [Edinburgh: T&T Clark, 1996], 37–38).

[55] See Barclay, *Jews,* 33–34, and the primary sources cited there.

to practice their faith and preserve the culture of their ancestors, but should not have Alexandrian citizenship.[56] Amid such stresses the continuation of the temple tax by Vespasian, in the absence of the temple, served not only to impoverish Jews, but also to identify them as Jews for the purpose of public humiliation.

For all of these reasons – and more[57] – Egyptian Jews in the first century C.E. must have felt tremendous tension as they considered their future: should they remain faithful to the traditions of the past and to the God of their ancestors, and suffer the material and social consequences, or should they abandon the faith? That the latter route was taken on occasion is certain, as the astounding success of Philo's nephew, Tiberius Julius Alexander, in Roman administration proves.[58]

Against this backdrop it is not difficult to see what the *Testament of Job* intends with its use of the testamentary genre and an entertaining narrative style to contradict the views expressed in the canonical Book of Job: it argues for perseverance in the faith in anticipation of rewards from God. It makes clear that the struggles Jews face are not the fault of God, in spite of what the biblical Book of Job may suggest, but of demonic forces that take the shape of beggars, bread merchants, storms, and even foreign kings. And it insists that if one simply faces all the hardships such evil forces may bring with faithful endurance, not only will the material goods so important in this world be restored (access to which had been severely curtailed by Roman rule), but more important, God's promise of heavenly and spiritual rewards will also be realized. It is noteworthy that through all of this Job is aware of what is correct precisely through the illumination granted him by God.

Although there is a sense in which the *Testament* seems to accept the notion that God elects the faithful – in this case an Egyptian – and requires of them steadfastness in that relationship, the work's lack of interest in Jewish law as the means by which a relationship to God is sustained undercuts the degree to which the *Testament* may be said to exhibit Sanders's covenantal nomism. The piety that Job should practice as he awaits restoration of his prosperity is not governed by the keeping of laws; it is instead a simple matter of remaining faithful to the God of Israel who gave him the insight to do so.[59]

---

[56] See Barclay, *Jews,* 60–71, for a convincing analysis of the diverse and difficult evidence regarding Claudius' ruling.

[57] For fuller analysis see Barclay, *Jews,* 48–81.

[58] See especially Barclay, *Jews,* 105, for a description of Alexander's situation; see also Josephus, *Ant.* 18.159–160; 19.276–77; 20.100–103 for the tale of Alexander's success and connections in the imperial family. He is mentioned by Philo in *De Providentia* 1 and 2; and in *De Animalibus.*

[59] On the aspect of heavenly illumination, see the work by Collins, cited in n. 39 above.

4. Testaments of the Twelve Patriarchs[60]

The *Testaments of the Twelve Patriarchs* is a collection of valedictory speeches from Jacob's twelve sons. Because it is such a large work it is impossible to review all of its contents here. Instead we offer a summary of the structure to which each of the twelve testaments roughly adheres and a brief description of the general contents of each part of the structure.

Each testament begins with all or part of a standard introduction that states that the testament is a copy of the patriarch's final words, announces the patriarch's impending death, gives his age at the time of death, and indicates that his family gathers around him on the occasion of his speech. Finally, the patriarch commands his audience to heed his instructions.[61]

The main body of each testament usually includes three parts: a biographical account (hagiography), moral exhortation supported by ethical discourse (ethics), and predictions of the future (eschatology). Usually the biographical account is linked to the theme of the ethical section of the testament. So Reuben recalls aspects of his transgression with Bilhah (Gen 35:22) and exhorts his children to avoid the pitfalls of youthful foolishness, impurity and over-attachment to the beauty of women. Simeon says it was his envy of Joseph that led to an overweening desire to kill him, and so he warns his sons against falling into the same weakness, lest they too suffer consequences such

---

[60] The text of the *Testaments of the Twelve Patriarchs* is preserved in a number of Greek manuscripts of varying value, and in Armenian and Slavonic manuscripts of decidedly less help in establishing the best text of the work. For an overview of the text-critical worth of the various manuscripts and the general problems associated with them, see especially Marinus de Jonge, "Textual Criticism and the Analysis of the Composition of the *Testament of Zebulun*," in *Studies on the Testaments of the Twelve Patriarchs. Text and Interpretation* (SVTP 3; Leiden: Brill, 1975), 120–39. The original language of the work is almost certainly Greek, in spite of claims that there was an original Hebrew text, a claim based on the parallels for parts of *T. Levi, T. Naphtali,* and *T. Judah* located in various Semitic texts (see, for example, Anders Hultgård, *L'eschatologie des Testaments des Douze Patriarches*, vol. 2, *Composition de l'ouvrage textes et traductions* [Acta Universitatis Upsaliensis; Historia Religionum 7; Uppsala: Almqvist & Wiksell, 1982], 2.168–87; for a summary overview of the Semitic texts and their significance, see H. Hollander and Marinus de Jonge, *The Testaments of the Twelve Patriarchs. A Commentary* [SVTP 8; Leiden: Brill, 1985], 17–29; for the *editio princeps* of the Hebrew and Aramaic material from Qumran that has some relationship to *T. Levi* and *T. Naphtali,* see DJD XXII, 1–82; and for a recent study devoted in large part to the material related to *Testament of Levi,* see Robert A. Kugler, *From Patriarch to Priest: The Levi-Priestly Tradition from Aramaic Levi to Testament of Levi* [SBLEJL 9; Atlanta: Scholars, 1996]). However, it is more likely that the author composed his work in Greek while relying on these Semitic works as sources (or even on Greek translations of those texts).

[61] Some testaments preserve other elements in the introduction, noting, for instance, whether when he spoke the patriarch was well (*T. Levi* 1:2; *T. Naph.* 1:2a; *T. Ash.* 1:2) or ill (*T. Reub.* 1:2; *T. Sim.* 1:2), that some of his brothers were also present (*T. Reub.* 1:4), or that the context of the testament was a banquet (*T. Naph.* 1:2b).

as he experienced in being taken captive by Joseph in Egypt (Gen 41:38). Levi reminds his children of the zeal he had for the Lord around issues of purity (Gen 34) and exhorts his descendants to observe the law with the same intensity. Judah dwells on his love of money, impure desires, and predilection for strong drink and his concomitant marital and sexual troubles (Gen 38), and he encourages his children to be satisfied with what they have, and to be temperate and pure. Issachar focuses on his life as a farmer (LXX Gen 49:14–15) and how that made him a man of "simplicity," the virtue at the root of most other good character traits, and the one to be pursued by his children. Zebulun describes his life as a simple fisherman (Gen 49:13) and encourages mercy and warm-heartedness in his children. Like Simeon, Dan says it was envy that created in him a desire to kill Joseph and led him to engage in falsehood; against these he warns his descendants. Because Naphtali's natural fleetness of foot led to his contentment as the family messenger, he encourages his children to also lead a life in harmony with the natural order and to seek natural goodness. Gad reveals the substance of Joseph's bad report to his father (Gen 37:2a) saying that it had to do with an inaccurate claim that the sons of Zilpah and Bilhah were eating the lambs of the flock; because of this Gad became angry (Gen 37:4, 8) and suffered the consequences of inordinate anger, and so he exhorts his children to control their tempers. Asher says that he sought single-mindedly to keep the law of God; around this he builds an explanation of double- and single-mindedness and an exhortation to choose the latter lifestyle. Joseph recounts his difficulties with Potiphar's wife and his self-restraint with respect to his brothers even after they betrayed him, and exhorts his listeners to live similar lives of prayer, chastity, endurance and care for others. And Benjamin's brief biographical recollection focuses on Joseph and explains how Joseph told Benjamin in Egypt (Gen 45:14–15) the circumstances surrounding his sale to the Ishmaelites in such a way as to explain how even the brothers could have thought he had been killed by a wild beast; thus, says Joseph, they should not be blamed in the matter. From this memory Benjamin launches into a panegyric for Joseph that calls him a good man with a good mind, one whom Benjamin's children would do well to emulate.

The concluding eschatological sections predict the future of the ancestor's descendants using several kinds of future-oriented passages.[62] Sin-Exile-Return (S.E.R.) sections generally describe the future sins of the patriarch's descendants, the tribe's exile among the Gentiles as punishment for their sin, and God's restoration of the tribe.[63] A second type of eschatological material

---

[62] For the first identification of these, see Marinus de Jonge, *The Testaments of the Twelve Patriarchs. A Study of their Text, Composition, and Origin* (Assen: Van Gorcum, 1953).

[63] Testaments lacking S.E.R. passages include *T. Reuben*, *T. Simeon*, and *T. Joseph*; for a list of the passages, see Hollander and de Jonge, *A Commentary*, 53–56.

are Levi-Judah (L.J.) passages. In some of these (*T. Reub.* 6:5–7; *T. Sim.* 5:4–6) the patriarch bemoans his descendants' rebellion against Levi's descendants, as well as their certain defeat in such efforts (cf. *T. Dan* 5:4; *T. Gad* 8:2), and in others the patriarch looks forward to his descendants' loyalty and obedience to the tribes of Levi and Judah out of respect for their special roles.[64] A third type of future passage looks forward to the advent of an ideal savior.[65] A final group of future passages announce the resurrection of the patriarch to rule over his tribe in the future.[66]

After the section with future predictions each testament closes with all or some of the following elements: the patriarch says he has concluded his speech, gives instructions for the disposition of his remains, and dies. Lastly there is a report that his children followed his burial instructions.

Establishing the date and provenance of the *Testaments of the Twelve Patriarchs* is notoriously difficult, and is inextricably tied up in the question of their compositional history. A vast body of literature has been produced in the effort to ascertain whether the document ever existed as a Jewish work prior to its obviously Christian form, and thus whether it can be dated any earlier than around 200 C.E., the earliest certain appearance of the work.[67] Given the existence of the Jewish texts related to the testaments associated with Levi, Naphtali, and perhaps Judah, few deny that there were Jewish

---

[64] Testaments lacking L.J. passages include *T. Zebulun*, *T. Asher*, and *T. Benjamin*; for a complete list of the L.J. passages in the *Testaments*, see Hollander and de Jonge, *A Commentary*, 56–61.

[65] Texts that fit this description include *T. Levi* 18; *T. Jud.* 24; *T. Zeb.* 9:8 (connected with an S.E.R. passage); and *T. Dan* 5:10–13 (connected with a L.J. passage); see Hollander and de Jonge, *A Commentary*, 63–64.

[66] These include *T. Jud.* 25; *T. Zeb.* 10:1–4; *T. Benj.* 10:6–10; cf. *T. Sim.* 6:7; *T. Levi* 18:14; see Hollander and de Jonge, *A Commentary*, 61–63.

[67] The leading proponent of the Christian origin of the *Testaments of the Twelve Patriarchs* is Marinus de Jonge ("Christian Influence in the Testaments of the Twelve Patriarchs," *NovT* 4 [1960]: 182–235; "Once More: Christian Influence in the Testaments of the Twelve Patriarchs," *NovT* 5 [1962]: 311–19; "The Testaments of the Twelve Patriarchs: Christian and Jewish. A Hundred Years After Friedrich Schnapp," *NedTT* 39 [1985]: 265–75). Some still contest this view, holding to the notion that the *Testaments* are in their entirety of Qumran, or Essene, origin (see, for example, the work of M. Philonenko, *Les interpolations chrétiennes des Douze Patriarches et les manuscrits de Qoumrân* [Paris: Presses universitaire de France, 1960]). For a history of scholarship dealing with the *Testaments of the Twelve Patriarchs* in general, and with the question of their Jewish, Essene, or Christian origin, see H. Dixon Slingerland, *The Testaments of the Twelve Patriarchs: A Critical History of Research* (SBLMS 21; Missoula: Scholars, 1977); for developments since then, see Jarl Henning Ulrichsen, *Die Grundschrift der Testamente der zwölf Patriarchen: Eine Untersuchung zu Umfang, Inhalt, und Eigenart der urprsünglichen Schrift* (Acta Universitatis Upsaliensis; Historia Religionum 10; Uppsala: Almqvist & Wiksell, 1991): 15–20; and see also Robert A. Kugler, *Testaments of the Twelve Patriarchs* (GAP; Sheffield: Sheffield Academic Press, forthcoming).

predecessor documents.[68] But the mere existence of such works does not prove that there was a complete pre-Christian *Testaments of the Twelve Patriarchs*; it only confirms that the Christian form contains within it significant Jewish source material. Consequently, for our purposes it is best to assume that the *Testaments of the Twelve Patriarchs* were known to Christians and Jews by the second century C.E., although they were probably complete and available some time before that.[69] As for their provenance, little can be said with confidence, although a Palestinian or even Egyptian origin is not out of the question.[70]

As for views regarding their theological significance, perhaps because of the preoccupation with their compositional history and provenance, few have said much on the topic. The general view, however, is that as a Christian work, on the one hand, they address various moral issues using the authority of the developing Christian "Old Testament," and, on the other hand, they tie the fate of Israel under the new dispensation introduced by God in Jesus Christ to adherence to the God-given law.[71] Were one to accept the view, as do we, that Jews also read this, it would seem to argue that while the people had been chosen by God long ago, the preservation of that relationship depended on the people's faithfulness in that relationship through the keeping of the law.[72]

Is this judgment borne out by an examination of the genres, narrative strategies and content of the Hebrew Scriptures that are taken over in the *Testaments of the Twelve Patriarchs* in making a theological argument? We turn now to an examination of the *Testament of Simeon* as a means of answering that question.[73] The theme is Simeon's jealousy of Joseph that led

---

[68] See the material cited in n. 66 above.

[69] Hollander and de Jonge, *A Commentary*, 82–83. Note, however, that we add Jews to those who knew the text inasmuch as we cannot exclude that possibility. Indeed, one of the reasons the text's provenance among Jews or Christians has remained in dispute for so long is the fact that, apart from a very few clear Christian passages, the *Testaments of the Twelve Patriarchs* could just as easily have been composed and used in exclusively Jewish circles.

[70] On this question see the convenient summary of various views and the standard evidence cited in favor of each in Collins, "Testaments," 343–4.

[71] This view is most easily identified in the work of Marinus de Jonge; see, for instance, Marinus de Jonge, "The Transmission of the Testaments of the Twelve Patriarchs by Christians," *VC* 47 (1993): 1–28, esp. 21.

[72] For a sampling of this approach, see Jarl Henning Ulrichsen, *Die Grundschrift der Testamente der zwölf Patriarchen: Eine Untersuchung zu Umfang, Inhalt, und Eigenart der urpsrünglichen Schrift* (Acta Universitatis Upsaliensis; Historia Religionum 10; Uppsala: Almqvist & Wiksell, 1991). Ulrichsen expresses the rather typical view that there is behind the Christian form of the *Testaments* a much older Jewish document that also contained twelve testaments.

[73] Justification for this choice from among the *Testaments* lies in the "typical" character of the *Testament of Simeon*: it contains all three of the standard main parts and it presents no unusual or anomalous characteristics.

to his fratricidal inclination. Simeon tells of his envy, its fruits, and how his children and their descendants should avoid the same mistake lest they suffer the same consequences. The *Testament* goes about this in such a way as to evince Sanders's notion of covenantal nomism, but with an added twist that will soon be evident.

Though a testament, the *Testament of Simeon* includes within that genre's framework several other biblical and nonbiblical forms. The hagiographic section uses the Greco-Roman biographical genre that often illustrated a virtue or vice through the story of a well-known person's life.[74] The parenetic section parallels classical discourses on vices and virtues, addressing in this case envy.[75] And if we may stretch the definition a bit, the eschatological section resembles a biblical apocalyptic discourse with its thoroughly biblicizing rhetoric and its use of *ex eventu* prophecy and other devices typical of that genre.[76]

In addition to the genre-mixing just observed, the text employs some important narrative strategies. The biographical material is built from an exegetical midrash, an expansion and/or rewriting of the Bible that uses as its starting point contradictions, unexplained circumstances, and curious turns of phrase from the Bible.[77] In this case it is the question of why Joseph singled out Simeon for bondage in Egypt (Gen 42:24). Together the biography and the parenetic section show that it was Simeon's impassioned envy of Joseph that led to his imprisonment.

"Tropes of metalepsis," or echoes of biblical stories, are another rhetorical device used in *Testament of Simeon*.[78] These echoes call to the reader's mind, if even only subconsciously, the language of the passage of origin as well as its impression on a reader. As such this narrative strategy is intimately connected to the content of the work taken up in the *Testament*. So in addition to developing itself around references in the Hebrew Bible to Simeon that depict him as a violent man (Gen 34:25) and as the one taken captive by Joseph in Egypt (Gen 42:24), by its use of tropes of metalepsis the *Testament of Simeon* calls to mind Cain's fratricidal jealousy of Abel,[79] and perhaps even Saul's envy of David.[80]

---

[74] For a succinct description of the genre and the variety of its uses, see the articles "biography, Greek," and "biography, Roman," in *OCD*, 241–3.

[75] For more on envy as a Hellenistic *topos* and its importance in the testament, see below.

[76] E.g., Dan 7–12; 1 *Enoch* 1–36; *Jubilees* 23.

[77] For an extended treatment, with examples, of exegetical midrashim, see, for example James Kugel, *In Potiphar's House* (San Francisco: HarperSanFrancisco, 1990).

[78] For the notion of "tropes of metalepsis," see Richard Hays, *Echoes of Scripture in the Letters of Paul* (New Haven: Yale University, 1989).

[79] That the reader of the *Testaments* is meant to relate Cain to Simeon is clear from *T. Benj.* 7:1–5 where Cain is the only other individual named in the *Testaments* as having been afflicted with envy. Furthermore, among the many tropes that recall Cain, in 3:2–3 Simeon argues that

In addition to drawing into its orbit content of the Hebrew Bible, the *Testament of Simeon* clearly evokes the Hellenistic *topos* of envy. This was a popular *topos* in antiquity.[81] According to Socrates envy was a sickness of the soul;[82] Plutarch asserted that envy was the worst illness one could incur.[83] According to the moralists envy blinds the person to everything but the object of his or her jealousy: thus the envious person is prone to violence, killing, and war;[84] friendship, even with persons not associated with the cause of one's envy, withers;[85] and indulging in envious behavior spawns a surfeit of associated miseries.[86] Moralists deemed the cause of envy to be the weakness of an undisciplined human mind; thus Dio Chrysostom claimed that the absence of envy is found in the ideal philosopher, the person who has

---

envy rules the mind and stays one's power to *do well*. Similarly, God uses much the same language with Cain in Gen 4:7, saying that sin lurks at the door of one who does not *do well*.

[80] For instance in 2:6–7 Simeon says a spirit of deceit caused his jealousy that in turn motivated him to plan to kill Joseph. Although this recalls Gen 37:11, 18, 20, 26, it even more readily echoes 1 Sam 18:10; 19:9, where Saul is overcome by an evil spirit from God that drives him to take violent action against David. Again, Simeon notes that God withheld from him the use of his right hand for seven days after the sale of Joseph, and that it was on account of Joseph that that happened (2:12–13a). Hollander and de Jonge explain this as the standard approach in the *Testaments* to punishment for sinful actions (*A Commentary,* 114). *T. Gad* 5:10 does say that one is afflicted in the organ that transgresses, and according to *T. Reub.* 1:7 a sexual predator is plagued by God in the loins for seven months and Gad's liver is beset with illness for eleven months because he set it against Joseph so passionately that he took direct part in his brother's sale. Likewise, suggest Hollander and de Jonge, had Simeon acted against Joseph to kill him he would have used his hands to do so. There is a problem here though. Like Gad's transgression, Simeon's sin was seated in his liver (". . . and I set my liver against him to kill him" [2:7]), but he never did get to lift a hand against his brother, and he does report later that his liver pains him as a result of his anger against Joseph (4:1). Hence the affliction of the hand is difficult to explain; one is driven to consider other reasons for saying that Simeon's hand was stayed. We solve the problem by once more recalling Saul, who is all along ghosted into the narrative. *T. Sim.* 2:7–8 recalls Saul's spirit-induced will to kill David and David's escape from Saul's spear thrust; it is only logical that this reference to a hand denied its natural action would echo 1 Sam 18:10; 19:9, where it is said that Saul's spear, which was resting in *his hand* in David's presence failed to meet its target when he used that hand to throw the spear at David. Finally, it is worth noting that in similar fashion the parallel between Joseph and David is apparent elsewhere as well. For example *T. Sim.* 5:1 describes Joseph as "comely in appearance and beautiful to look at." This recalls not only Gen 39:6, but more closely parallels 1 Sam 14:42; 16:12 where David is described.

[81] For a lengthy treatment of the *topos,* see E. Milobenski, *Der Neid in der griechischen Philosophie* (Wiesbaden: O. Harrassowitz, 1964).

[82] *Stobaeus* III, 38, 48.

[83] *De Invidia et Odio* 537E.

[84] Plato, *Lysis* 215D; Plutarch, *De Capienda* 36C, 91B.

[85] Plato, *Philebus* 49D; Aristotle, *Politics* 1295B; Plutarch, *De Invidia et Odio* 536F.

[86] See especially Josephus, *Ant.* 1.56–66, for description of Cain's fate as a result of his envious fratricide.

submitted the mind to stern and consistent correction.[87] As for the man without envy, Pseudo-Phocylides and Dio Chrysostom observe that he seeks the good of the other and lives life in a spirit of generosity.[88]

In the *Testament of Simeon* these genres, narrative strategies, and biblical and Hellenistic themes are woven together to form a sophisticated argument against the classical view regarding the cause and remedy for envy. In the biographical section Simeon's affliction with envy is made clear, and already he and Joseph are likened by the language of the account to Cain and Abel and Saul and David.[89] Simeon's autobiographical comments and allusions to Saul and Cain illustrate that envy works as the classical moralists claimed it did: because of their envy Simeon, Saul and Cain were preoccupied with hatred, isolated from others, murderous, and weighed down by the consequences of such attitudes. But an important difference vis-à-vis the classical authors' is also introduced: instead of blaming the affliction on an undisciplined mind, Simeon attributes it to the influence of an evil spirit (2:7).

In the parenetic material, which is dressed in the garb of a classical moralist's discourse, the *Testament* further qualifies classical notions regarding envy. Simeon says that because of the evils of envy he repented in fear of the Lord for two years, and learned from the experience that one escapes from the emotion's effects only through *fear of God* (3:4). He follows this with a conditional statement of instruction in 3:5–6: if one flees to the Lord, then the evil of envy departs and the selfish behaviors conceived in envy give way to generosity, kindness, and enlightenment. This passage evokes nothing of the moralists' discourses, and in fact contradicts it on one central point: enlightenment comes from lack of envy (which in turn is given by God), not the other way around. Thus the testament drives home its point that the cause and remedy of envy has not so much to do with the state of the human mind, but with the battle between the God of Israel and evil spirits at work in the world.

Further along in the parenetic section the testament adjusts even more the classical notions regarding envy. In 4:1–4 Simeon notes that Joseph, who was without envy and was also kind and merciful, flourished in Egypt. Thus he says that his children should avoid envy and πορεύεσθε ἐν ἁπλότητι ψυχῆς καὶ ἐν ἀγαθῇ καρδίᾳ ("walk in singleness of heart, and with a good heart") by mimicking Joseph so that they too can experience *from God* the rewards for grace and glory Joseph received (4:5). Thus according to the testament

---

[87] Dio Chrysostom, *Seventy-Seventh/Eighth Discourse: On Envy*, 31–45.

[88] Pseudo-Phocylides 70ff.; Dio Chrysostom, *Seventy-Seventh/Eighth Discourse: On Envy* 39, 40–45.

[89] See nn. 79–80 above.

the rewards of being without envy, which the Greeks said were intrinsic, are from God who takes away the spirit of envy in the first place.[90]

The future-oriented section of the testament completes this partial reversal of classical notions regarding envy by suggesting that Simeon's descendants, should they follow his advice, can usher in a new age. Abandoning any attempt to mimic Greco-Roman genres, the text now resorts exclusively to language and forms from well-known passages in Hosea, Psalms, Song of Songs, Proverbs, Sirach, and the Psalms of Solomon that anticipate a glorious, messianic future for Israel.[91] *T. Sim.* 6:3–5 promises that if Simeon's descendants eschew envy they will one day flourish, Israel's foes will be defeated, there will be peace on earth, and Israel will be glorified by the Lord God. And 6:6 announces that the crowning glory of the new age will be the defeat of evil spirits, including those that cause envy in human hearts.

This pattern of taking on Hellenistic moral norms from a theocentric perspective is discernible in the other testaments of the *Testaments of the Twelve Patriarchs*.[92] It is difficult to say much regarding how this would have worked in its earliest historical context because we know so little of what that might have been. However, if we grant wide acquaintance with the classical *topoi* addressed in the individual testaments, it is imaginable that it was received by Jews (and Christians) who generally believed that human beings could manage their own moral foibles and create their own manageable, if not ideal, futures. As such the *Testaments of the Twelve Patriarchs* worked to contradict that popular view and replace it with one that called the individual and the community to dependence on the God of Israel in all matters. Failing that, warned the *Testaments,* people could expect the loss of the relationship which God had established with their ancestors.

It seems the implicit consensus that the *Testaments of the Twelve Patriarchs* express something of Sanders's covenantal nomism is supported by our investigation. However we have nuanced that perspective by demonstrating that the perceived threat to the covenantal relationship between God and Israel, at least in the case of the *Testament of Simeon,* came from the influence of classical culture. We have further nuanced that understanding by showing how the *Testaments* artfully weave together the genres, narrative strategies, and content of the Hebrew Scriptures and of Greco-Roman literature to counter the threat of assimilation to classical culture and

---

[90] And in 4:6 Simeon illustrates the claim that lack of envy makes one generous and merciful by remembering Joseph's kindness to his former oppressors and his largesse for his whole family when they arrived in Egypt (Gen 47:6, 12)

[91] See the specific biblical and extrabiblical texts cited by Hollander and de Jonge, *A Commentary,* 123–5.

[92] For more on this see my introduction to the *Testaments of the Twelve Patriarchs* (Sheffield: Sheffield Academic, 1999).

encourage a Jewish (or Christian) lifestyle shaped by the Hebrew Bible and its values.

5. Conclusion

These three testamentary works offer qualified support to the notion that covenantal nomism was pervasive in Jewish literature from around the turn of the era. The *Testament of Moses* seemed to favor the view that the people of Israel are indeed chosen, although their fate in relationship to God is not ultimately dependent on what they do, but on God's abiding decision for them. The *Testament of Job* does favor the view that one must remain faithful to the electing God of Israel to receive his benefits, but it does not require believers to keep particular laws to sustain their relationship with God. In like fashion the *Testaments of the Twelve Patriarchs* hold the view that God has chosen Israel for a special relationship, and seem to require mostly reliance on God and little in the way of specific law-keeping to sustain that relationship.

8. Wisdom

by

DONALD E. GOWAN

The five works that will be discussed in this chapter are generally labeled "wisdom literature" for various reasons. Sirach and Pseudo-Phocylides contain collections of proverbs, continuing the tradition to be found in the Old Testament book of Proverbs. That kind of literature does not appear in Baruch, Wisdom of Solomon, or 4 Maccabees. The development of a wisdom-theology, which begins in Prov 1–9, continues through Sirach, Baruch and Wisdom of Solomon. Fourth Maccabees does not use the traditional vocabulary of other Jewish literature, but most of what is said about "devout reason" corresponds to the wisdom-theology of the other books. There are relationships among the books, but it will be seen that only in limited ways do they represent the development of a tradition. Each is a response to a different situation. The subjects they take up and their treatment of them vary considerably.

There is little evidence to enable us to date these books, except for Sirach, which is probably the earliest. The order in which they are discussed here is thus rather arbitrary. It will be seen that it has not been chosen because development of thought can be traced in any significant way. The four books, other than Sirach, may be dated within a 200-year period, during the last century B.C.E. or first century C.E., according to most scholars. In keeping with the aims of this volume, the discussion of these books will focus on the relationship between God and Israel, rather than attempting to survey their entire content. Given the interests of the sages, the relationship between God and the individual Israelite will tend to predominate.[1]

1. Sirach

Jesus ben Eleazar ben Sira' wrote his book probably between 190 and 180 B.C.E.[2] He lived in Jerusalem, and as he describes himself as a man of long

---

[1] All quotations from Sirach, Baruch, Wisdom of Solomon, and 4 Maccabees are taken from the NRSV. Pseudo-Phocylides is quoted from *OTP*.

[2] I shall use the Hebrew form, Ben Sira', as the name of the author, and the Greek form,

experience, he must have spent most of his life under the rule of the Ptolemaic dynasty, and have seen the transition to control by the Seleucids in 199. The book makes no reference to these political affairs, but its lengthy exposition of Jewish wisdom is generally understood to be an attempt to uphold the superiority of Judaism over against the temptations of Hellenism, which had presented a new challenge to the traditional way of life.[3] He is a very traditional writer; although there is clear evidence of development beyond the wisdom literature of the Old Testament, what he says of the relationship between God and the Israelite differs little from that of the book of Proverbs.

The sovereignty of God, who is the creator of everything that exists, is emphasized throughout the book: "When he commands, his every purpose is fulfilled, and none can limit his saving power" (Sir 39:18). Ben Sira' does not shrink from saying that God has even created evil, but has his own way of defending God's essential goodness and justice: "Good things and bad, life and death, poverty and wealth, come from the Lord" (11:14). But God's good creations are for the righteous, and the bad are for the judgment of the wicked (39:22–31). According to 33:10–15, it would appear that Ben Sira' taught an absolute predestination ("Some he blessed and exalted, and some he made holy and brought near to himself; but some he cursed and brought low, and turned them out of their place," 33:12), but that is not in accord with the teaching of the book elsewhere, which emphasizes strongly that humans have the ability to choose good or evil.

> It was he who created humankind in the beginning,
> and he left them in the power of their own free choice.[4]
> If you choose, you can keep the commandments,
> and to act faithfully is a matter of your own choice.
> He has placed before you fire and water;
> stretch out your hand for whichever you choose.
> Before each person are life and death,
> and whichever one chooses will be given.
> . . . .

Sirach, as the name of the book.

[3] E.g. Alexander A. DiLella, "Conservative and Progressive Theology in Sirach and Wisdom," *CBQ* 28 (1966): 139–54; David A. deSilva, "The Wisdom of Ben Sira: Honor, Shame, and the Maintenance of the Values of a Minority Culture," *CBQ* 58 (1996): 433–55; Martin Hengel, *Judaism and Hellenism: Studies in their Encounter in Palestine during the Early Hellenistic Period* (Philadelphia: Fortress, 1974), 1:131–153. Collins describes the author's concerns not as opposition to Hellenistic culture as a whole, but as directed against those aspects of it that ran counter to the Jewish ethic: John J. Collins, *Jewish Wisdom in the Hellenistic Age* (OTL; Louisville: Westminster John Knox, 1997), 33, 41.

[4] The NRSV's "free choice" represents the Hebrew term *yetser* "inclination." "The term *'yeser'* gains its central anthropological significance in the sense of 'character', 'disposition' for the first time in Ben Sira; . . ." (Hengel, *Judaism and Hellenism*, 140).

He has not commanded anyone to be wicked,
and he has not given anyone permission to sin. (15:14–17, 20)[5]

The doctrine of reward and retribution in this book is like that found in Proverbs and elsewhere in the Old Testament. God rewards, in this life, those who love him and keep his commandments: "Do good to the devout, and you will be repaid – if not by them, certainly by the Most High" (12:2; cf. 34:14–20). He is also the stern and unfailing judge of unrighteousness: "Even if there were only one stiff-necked person, it would be a wonder if he remained unpunished. For mercy and wrath are with the Lord; he is mighty to forgive – but he also pours out wrath" (16:11). Although ideas concerning life after death must have been circulating within Judaism during his time, Ben Sira' still holds to the Old Testament view that reward and punishment are experienced in this life, and does not speculate about anything beyond death (cf. 11:26–28; 14:1–19; 17:27–28; 38:21). Thus, texts such as 11:26, "For it is easy for the Lord on the day of death to reward individuals according to their conduct," may mean that they will have a good death, rather than suggesting anything beyond (cf. 1:13).[6]

He shows a greater awareness than the book of Proverbs does of the hard fact that in real life reward and punishment does not work out as neatly as it should. He has a distinctive answer for that problem: Although present evidence seems to challenge his theory, at the right time it will be vindicated. God's time is an important theme for him.[7] It is the basis for his answer to those in his midst who evidently have been questioning the teachings of orthodox wisdom:

Do not say, "I sinned, yet what has happend to me?"
for the Lord is slow to anger.
Do not be so confident of forgiveness that you add sin to sin.
Do not say, "His mercy is great,
he will forgive the multitude of my sins,"
for both mercy and wrath are with him,
and his anger will rest on sinners.
Do not delay to turn back to the Lord,
and do not postpone it from day to day;
for suddenly the wrath of the Lord will come upon you,
and at the time of punishment you will perish. (5:4–7)

He will admit that the apparent delay of justice remains to some extent a mystery (cf. 16:17–22), but he holds firmly to the belief that in God's time all will be made right:

---

[5] ". . . remember that we all deserve punishment" (8:5b) is thus not to be understood as referring to original sin, but simply to the fact that everyone does sin.

[6] Collins also concludes the Hebrew text of Sirach is unlikely to have said anything about resurrection, although there are hints of it in the Greek version (*Jewish Wisdom*, 95–96).

[7] Gerhard von Rad, *Wisdom in Israel* (Nashville: Abingdon, 1972), 251–4.

All the works of the Lord are very good,
     and whatever he commands will be done at the appointed time.
No one can say, "What is this?" or "Why is that?" –
     for at the appointed time all such questions will be answered. (39:16–17)

Theodicy is thus an issue threatening to deconstruct the neat pattern of earthly reward and punishment that had been characteristic of orthodox wisdom, but Ben Sira' does not wrestle with it as the authors of Job and Ecclesiastes had done.[8]

God's best reward for those who love him is wisdom (1:10), which is both the reward for (e.g. 1:26; 15:1) and the way to achieve righteousness (e.g. 4:11–19). Ben Sira' continues the ambiguity to be found in the earlier wisdom writings. Wisdom is a divine attibute, and in that sense the possession of God alone (Sir 1:1–8), but can also be gained by humans through their obedience to the law (19:20). She should be sought because of the blessings she offers (4:11–12; 6:26–27; 51:13, 21), but is also the gracious gift of God, sent into the world without regard to human effort or merit (24:1–34). The ambiguities are probably to be accounted for by the focus on wisdom, in this literature, as the means of access to God, which has an immediacy about it but involves an encounter with mystery, so that completely straightforward language would be inadequate.[9] That wisdom is more than an intellectual construct is made abundantly clear in Sirach, since he associates it intimately with the fear of the Lord:

To fear the Lord is the beginning of wisdom; . . .
To fear the Lord is the fullness of wisdom; . . .
The fear of the Lord is the crown of wisdom, . . .
To fear the Lord is the root of wisdom, . . . (1:14, 16, 18, 20)

As in the Old Testament, fear of the Lord may be defined as "devout obedience." The connections regularly made among wisdom, fear of the Lord, and obedience to the law were thus natural ones for Ben Sira':

The whole of wisdom is fear of the Lord,
     and in all wisdom there is the fulfillment of the law. (19:20)
Whoever keeps the law controls his thoughts,
     and the fulfillment of the fear of the Lord is wisdom. (21:11)

In fact, the content (so to speak) of wisdom is the law, an equation made more explicit by Ben Sira' than by any earlier writer. He has "nationalized" wisdom, which had been international in character, making her the specific property of Israel.[10] As in Prov 8, this attribute of God has taken on a

---

[8] Cf. James L. Crenshaw, "The Problem of Theodicy in Sirach: On Human Bondage," *JBL* 94 (1975): 47–64.

[9] Cf. von Rad's discussion, *Wisdom in Israel*, 241–2.

[10] J. Coert Rylaarsdam, *Revelation in Jewish Wisdom Literature* (Chicago: University of Chicago, 1946), 27–39.

personality of its own in Prov 24. Wisdom, which held sway over every people and nation (24:6b), was given her resting place in Israel:

> He said, "Make your dwelling in Jacob,
>   and in Israel receive your inheritance."
> . . . .
> Thus in the beloved city he gave me a resting place,
>   and in Jerusalem was my domain. (24:8b, 11)

To Job's question, "Where shall wisdom be found?" (Job 28:12), Ben Sira' gave an explicit answer: "All this [i.e. wisdom] is the book of the covenant of the Most High God, the law that Moses commanded us as an inheritance for the congregations of Jacob" (24:23). There are mysteries that remain known only to the mind of God, surely, but there is no mystery about the way humans should live; that has been fully revealed in the Torah. It should be noted, however, that unlike later teachers, Ben Sira' does not explicitly quote the Torah as the basis for his teaching, in spite of the way he glorifies it.[11] It is evident that he assumes his task to be to transmit traditional wisdom, believing it to be fully in accord with the Torah (51:13–30).

It is assumed that people sin, and the remedies for sin offered by Ben Sira' are completely traditional.[12] Repentance is called for (17:24–26), because God is willing to forgive. The grace, compassion, and mercy of God exalted in the Old Testament are reaffirmed in Sirach:

> For the Lord is compassionate and merciful;
>   he forgives sins and saves in time of distress. (2:11)
> How great is the mercy of the Lord,
>   and his forgiveness for those who return to him! (17:29)
> Human beings are weak and short-lived,
> That is why the Lord is patient with them
>   and pours out his mercy upon them.
> He sees and recognizes that their end is miserable;
>   therefore he grants them forgiveness all the more. (18:11–12)

People are judged according to their works (16:12b), but that is no more a strict works-salvation scheme in Sirach than in the Old Testament (18:13–14).[13] There are human acts that have atoning value – honoring one's father and almsgiving are mentioned (3:3, 30) – and God forgives those who

---

[11] Johannes Marböck, "Gesetz und Weisheit. Zum Verständnis des Gesetzes bei Jesus ben Sira," *BZ* 20 (1976): 1–22; Collins, *Jewish Wisdom*, 55.

[12] Cf. E. P. Sanders's discussion of the distinction, in Sirach, between "the wicked" and the occasional transgressor. *Paul and Palestiniah Judaism: A Comparison of Patterns of Religion* (Philadelphia: Fortress, 1977), 342–6.

[13] Büchler comments on 28:1–7, "God takes note of all the sinful deeds of man, and keeps them collected, without yet punishing their author. Only when he presumes to revenge himself for any wrong done to him, and harbors hatred against his neighbor, does God remember his past sins." A. Büchler, "Ben Sira's Conception of Sin and Atonement," *JQR* 14 (1923–24), 55.

forgive the wrongs their neighbors have done (28:2; cf. Matt 6:14–15).
Offerings are important (7:31), but Ben Sira' re-emphasizes the prophetic
message that they are of value only when accompanied by a righteous life.
One cannot buy forgiveness:

Do not say, "He will consider the great number of my gifts,
  and when I make an offering to the Most High God, he will accept it."
  (7:9; cf. 35:14 "Do not offer him a bribe, for he will not accept it.")
Like one who kills a son before his father's eyes
  is the person who offers a sacrifice from the property of the poor.
  (34:24; cf. vv. 21–27)

Righteousness is an offering to God in itself (35:1–26); e.g., "The one who
keeps the law makes many offerings; . . . and to forsake unrighteousness is an
atonement" (35:1–5).[14] That does not mean, however, that sacrifices are not
also to be offered (35:6–15). Having equated righteousness with sacrifice, this
passage then moves to one of the most emphatic statements in Sirach of the
demand for social justice (35:16–26).

The prayer of the humble pierces the clouds,
  and it will not rest until it reaches its goal;
it will not desist until the Most High responds
  and does justice for the righteous, and executes judgment. (35:21–22)

Human responsibility is thus a major theme in Sirach, as in all the wisdom
literature. It always aims to teach one how to live the good life, and it is
always assumed that one can learn by paying attention to one's teachers, and
that the effort to live the righteous life will be rewarded by God with the
wisdom that can come from him alone. That wisdom is necessary, however,
not just a bonus. The effort to live the righteous life must, then, be accompanied by prayer, the sure means of access to the divine help. Prayer is not
only the way to appeal for help in time of trouble (e.g. 4:6; 35:13; 38:9;
51:9), but prayer for forgiveness (17:25; 21:1; 28:2) and for guidance is also
commended.

For our own mind sometimes keeps us better informed
  than seven sentinels sitting high on a watchtower.
But above all pray to the Most High
  that he may direct your way in truth. (37:14–15)

---

[14] The relationship between sacrifice and the righteous life had already been taken up in the
Old Testament in texts such as "The sacrifice acceptable to God is a broken spirit; a broken and
contrite heart, O God, you will not despise" (Ps 51:17); "To do righteousness and justice is more
accceptable to the LORD than sacrifice" (Prov 21:3); "For I desire steadfast love and not
sacrifice, the knowledge of God rather than burnt offerings" (Hos 6:6). These texts were later
used by the rabbis to commend repentance, justice, and mercy: e.g. *Lev. R.*, 7:2; *Deut. R.*,
5:1, 3; *'Abot R. Nat.* (vers. I), IV. 11a.

Ben Sira' thus shares the essential optimism of traditional Israelite wisdom. He indicates no sense of a need for radical change, as Jeremiah and Ezekiel did in their promises of the new covenant to be written on the heart (Jer 31:31–34) or a new heart and new spirit (Ezek 36:26).

His life within the Jewish community in Jerusalem may not have been very peaceful, for he speaks of personal enemies a remarkable number of times. Enemies seldom appear in the book of Proverbs, but they are referred to about thirty times in Sirach. He knows how to deal with them, however (e.g. 6:9, 13; 12:8–10, 16). The political situation was often precarious, but except for a prayer for divine victory over the nations, in 36:1–17, Ben Sira' shows little interest in that. Eschatology has not yet made its influence felt on the sages as it would later in the second century B.C.E. He remains confident in God's good intentions for Israel. "The days of a person's life are numbered, but the days of Israel are without number" (37:25). And he speaks of a close personal relationship with God that makes life good:

> The spirit of those who fear the Lord will live,
> for their hope is in him who saves them.
> Those who fear the Lord will not be timid,
> or play the coward, for he is their hope.
> Happy is the soul that fears the Lord!
> To whom does he look? And who is his support?
> The eyes of the Lord are on those who love him,
> a mighty shield and strong support,
> a shelter from scorching wind and a shade from noonday sun,
> a guard against stumbling and a help against falling.
> He lifts up the soul and makes the eyes sparkle;
> he gives health and life and blessing. (34:14–20)

In spite of turmoil during his lifetime, the essential optimism of traditional wisdom continued. Ben Sira' did not yet have to deal with the questions about God's power and justice, and the value of human righteousness, that were raised by the persecution of the Jews under Antiochus IV Epiphanes.

2. Baruch

Baruch is an anthology of compositions by different authors, combined because each of them deals with the problem of the continuing dispersion of the Jews.[15] It is included in this chapter because of the Wisdom poem in 3:9–4:4. Most of the book reflects the explanation of the exile offered by the Old Testament prophets, which makes the wisdom poem an original

---

[15] Carey A. Moore, *Daniel, Esther, and Jeremiah: The Additions* (AB 44; New York: Doubleday, 1977), 259.

contribution to the discussion. The whole book is problem-centered, offering varying approaches to the brokenness of the relationship between God and Israel which is felt because of the exile.

The first section (1:1–14) is full of historical inaccuracies, such as locating Baruch in Babylon (contrary to Jer 43:6), but by the time this book was compiled[16] the fall of Jerusalem in 587 B.C.E. and the ensuing exile in Babylonia had become the archetype of all subsequent disasters. Clearly the book was intended to offer help for dealing with those later problems, so the setting and the author had to be in the classic location, Babylon.[17]

The prophets' explanation of the exile as divine judgment for Israel's sins had become the orthodox explanation for all calamities to afflict the Jews in their later history,[18] so the book does not struggle with Israel's suffering, as 2 Esdras and 2 Baruch did later. "From the time when the Lord brought our ancestors out of the land of Egypt until today, we have been disobedient to the Lord our God, and we have been negligent, in not heeding his voice. So to this day there have clung to us the calamities and the curse that the Lord declared through his servant Moses . . ." (Bar 1:19–20a; cf. the confessions of sin in 1:15–21; 2:5, 8–10; 3:13; 4:12–13). The prophets' warnings are quoted (2:21–23), and it is acknowledged that they were not heeded (2:24–26). Baruch is in continuity with most of the Old Testament, in that the issue is communal rather than individual, namely the present and future relationship of Israel to the God who has chosen them to be his (1:20; 2:11, 15, 27), but whom they have perennially disobeyed.

God's justice has always been tempered with mercy, however (2:27), and the prayers of supplication and exhortations to repent and obey that appear throughout the book are based on the conviction that he is ready to forgive even the undeserving (4:28–29). Israel has no merit which might enable them to claim a continuing relationship with God: "For it is not because of any righteous deeds of our ancestors or our kings that we bring before you our prayer for mercy, O Lord our God. . . . we did not obey your voice" (2:19, 24a). Forgiveness is believed to be possible only because it is in keeping with

---

[16] Moore dates most of the book relatively early, before 168 B.C.E. (ibid., 260). Others date it after 70 C.E.

[17] Compare the prayer in Dan 9:1–19, located by the author in an exilic setting, but really concerned with the tribulation afflicting Jerusalem under Antiochus IV Epiphanes. Extensive use is made of the language of this prayer in Bar 1:15–2:19. See B. N. Wambacq, "Le prières de Baruch (1,15–2,19) et de Daniel (9,5–19)," *Bib* 40 (1959): 463–475. The use which Baruch makes of Old Testament materials has been traced elsewhere, and does not contribute significantly to this study.

[18] Cf. Jacob Neusner, *Self-Fulfilling Prophecy: Exile and Return in the History of Judaism* (Boston: Beacon, 1987), 41: "Judaism took shape as the system that accounted for the death and resurrection of Israel, the Jewish people, and pointed for the source of renewed life toward sanctification now and salvation at the end of time."

the character of God: "Hear, O Lord, our prayer and our supplication, and for your own sake deliver us, . . ." (2:14). "Do not remember the iniquities of our ancestors, but in this crisis remember your power and your name" (3:5). Although the exile was punishment for sin, God's intervention would make of it a cleansing experience, and so it can be said that he knew in advance that they would not obey without suggesting this was somehow unfair of God (2:30). Echoing Jer 24:6–7, Baruch has God take the initiative, bringing about an anthropological change which will make obedience possible: "I will give them a heart that obeys and ears that hear; they will praise me in the land of their exile, and will remember my name and turn from their stubbornness and their wicked deeds; . . ." (Bar 2:31b–33a). Repentance thus will become possible because of God's gracious act on their behalf. "You have put the fear of you in our hearts so that we would call upon your name; and we will praise you in our exile, for we have put away from our hearts all the iniquity of our ancestors who sinned against you" (3:7).

Among God's greatest gifts to Israel was wisdom, also neglected in the past, leading to their present distress (3:12–13). True wisdom belongs to God (3:29–36), and cannot be gained by human effort (3:15–23), but he "gave her to his servant Jacob and to Israel, whom he loved" (3:36b). Much of the wisdom poem (3:9–4:4) echoes Job 28's theme – Where shall wisdom be found? – but it ends with an explicit answer not found in Job, and very likely learned by this author from Sir 24:23. Divine wisdom is directly identified with the Law of Moses, here called "the book of the commandments of God, the law that endures forever" (Bar 4:1). The individual is alluded to here, with the repetition of the promise of life for those who hold fast to wisdom/law that appears many times in the Old Testament (Bar 4:2; cf. Lev 18:5; Deut 4:1; Ezek 20:11; Neh 9:29; etc.). The law is by no means a burden, but is a gift of grace, the source of life for Israel: "Happy are we, O Israel, for we know what is pleasing to God" (4:4).

The optimism of the Wisdom poem stands in some tension with the expressions of distress found elsewhere in the book, but it is in keeping with the promises that offer hope to those who appeal to God for help. The promise was already present in God's words to Moses: "I will make an everlasting covenant with them to be their God and they shall be my people; and I will never again remove my people Israel from the land that I have given them" (2:35). The latter parts of the book, with their strong dependence on Second Isaiah, contain assurances of deliverance in the future (4:21–24; 5:9), which are expected to be entirely the work of God, with no human prerequisites, as in the work of the exilic prophet. The Old Testament balance between divine initiative, which established and will renew the covenant, and human responsibility, which leads to punishment for sin, is thus maintained in Baruch, with an emphasis both on the justice of the sufferings Israel endures,

and on the mercy of God which makes possible the hope for future blessing
without expecting that it can be earned.

3. Wisdom of Solomon

There is general agreement that the book was written originally in Greek, by
a Jew who must have been living in Alexandria because of his familiarity with
aspects of Greek philosophy. Its aim has been identified as intending to
strengthen and deepen the faith of pious Jews, to bring worldly Jews back to
the faith, and to convince Gentiles of the foolishness of idolatry.[19] It is thus
a problem-oriented book, dealing not only with challenges to Jewish beliefs
and way of life, as in Sirach, but with severe pressures that might lead to the
endangerment of life itself. The assumption that it was written in Alexandria
has then led commentators to search for a time of persecution of the Jews
living there, which might explain the concerns of the author, but the language
is vague and does not point to any clearly identifiable event.[20] No credit has
been given to the possiblity that the author may have been influenced by the
earlier persecution of Palestinian Jews under Antiochus IV Epiphanes, but 2
Maccabees shows diaspora Judaism was profoundly influenced by that event,
and found it necessary to find a way to justify the miserable deaths of
precisely those who were most faithful to God. The author of Wisdom of
Solomon makes no reference to that period, but martyrdom had become a
part of the Jewish experience by his time, and the events of the mid-second
century may lie in the background of his description of the righteous sufferer
in chs. 2–3. Unlike earlier wisdom literature, but like 2 Maccabees and later
Jewish works, Wisdom of Solomon assumes that faithfulness will lead to
suffering.

The appearance of the suffering of the righteous as a major theme in the
earlier chapters seems odd given the addressees: rulers of the earth (1:1),
kings and judges (6:1). Reese has shown that this is not to be taken literally,
however, as it was a common literary device and stands in keeping with the

---

[19] Robert H. Pfeiffer, *History of New Testament Times, With an Introduction to the
Apocrypha* (New York: Harper & Row, 1949), 334.

[20] The date of the book has been variously estimated. It probably falls within the last half of
the first century B.C.E. and the first half of the first century C.E. Pfeiffer dated it a bit earlier,
between 100 and 50 B.C.E. (*New Testament Times*, 527; Winston follows Goodrick in locating
it during the reign of Caligula, 37–41 C.E.: David Winston, *The Wisdom of Solomon: A New
Translation with Introduction and Commentary* (AB 43; Garden City: Doubleday, 1979), 23;
A. T. S. Goodrick, *The Book of Wisdom, with introduction and notes* (The Oxford Church Bible
Commentary; New York: Macmillan, 1913), 13.

supposed authorship by Solomon.[21] It must have been written for Jews who knew the Torah well, since the author can retell the classic history from Adam to the occupation of Canaan without mentioning any names (chs. 10–11), and they probably were expected to know enough philosophy to be able to recognize the special uses being made of those terms and concepts in the light of the author's Jewish convictions.[22] After the introduction (1:1–15), which commends wisdom and righteousness, the author turns to the issue of theodicy, with the ultimate fates of the righteous and the wicked dominating the first main part of the book (1:16–5:23). Wisdom is not a major theme here; it occurs only once (3:11). It dominates chs. 6–10, but occurs only twice in an incidental way in chs. 11–19 (14:2, 5). Complementing this distribution of wisdom-vocabulary, justice (or righteousness; δικαιοσύνη, δίκαιος)[23] tends to dominate chs. 1–5 and 11–19, thus providing a rough division of the book into three parts, which will be useful for our purposes.[24] The contrast in chs. 1–5 between the fate of the righteous individual and that of the wicked who attack him has a certain parallel in chs. 11–19 which speak of the fates of Israel, during the classic period of its history, and Egypt, Israel's oppressor. While the author deals with Old Testament history, he chooses the useful parts, so his theology can be essentially traditional. God saved his chosen people and punished the Egyptians and Canaanites for their wickedness and idolatry. Election, covenant, and law are taken for granted and mentioned only a few times in passing (e.g. 12:21; 16:6, 26; 18:4, 22). Issues that perennially concerned other writers, such as the persistence of the exile and the status of Jerusalem, are of no interest. Neither do details about how to live righteously, dealt with at great length in Sirach, find any place in this book. Belief in Israel's special status and knowledge of what God requires seem to be assumed by the author. If he wrote for a community that was finding its beliefs and way of life to be under pressure, that is understandable. The pressure itself would have made obvious the distinctive nature of the community. The author's task would not be to define the community, but to extol the resources that would enable them to remain faithful. This would involve individual decisions, so wisdom's traditional address of the individual remained appropriate.

---

[21] J. M. Reese, *Hellenistic Influence on the Book of Wisdom and its Consequences* (AnBib 41; Rome: Biblical Institute, 1970), 146–51.

[22] For detailed comparisons of the book with Greek philosophical schools, see Winston, *Wisdom of Solomon*, 25–63, and *passim*.

[23] The root sometimes denotes an attribute of God or the good king, but is most often used in a polemical sense to designate those whom the wicked would oppress, but who are upheld by the power of God (even if it must be after death, as in 3:1; 4:7; 5:1, 15).

[24] For detailed discussions of structure, James M. Reese, "Plan and structure in the Book of Wisdom," *CBQ* 27 (1965): 391–9; A. G. Wright, "The Structure of the Book of Wisdom," *Bib* 48 (1967): 165–84.

The question about righteous individuals who suffer precisely because they are faithful to their God could no longer be dealt with in the traditional ways that were still essentially satisfactory to Ben Sira', however, and the persecutions under Antiochus probably have a good deal to do with that. The author imagines a conspiracy against an unnamed examplar of Judaism, who "professes to have knowledge of God, and calls himself a child of the Lord" (2:13, cf. vv. 16, 18). Aside from these terms, nothing explicit is said about the distinctive character of his life, except that he has reproached the unrighteous group for sins against the law (2:12). This suggests that the unrighteous in this part of the book are apostate Jews, although here, as at many other points, the author is not completely explicit about it.[25] That he has created a hypothetical case is suggested by the fact that the death of the individual is plotted, but not recorded, and instead the author moves to a general affirmation about the fates of righteous and wicked individuals after death (2:31–5:23). His contribution to the theodicy question is the promise of immortality, the major new element in the book.[26] It is not completely clear whether he believed in the pre-existence of an immortal soul (cf. 8:20), but that is not of great importance for our purposes, since the point he is concerned to make is that there is life after death, when the just treatment of righteous and wicked will be made manifest. Suffering in this life appears to be punishment (3:4), but that is explained by appealing to the old concept of discipline and testing (3:5–6; cf. Job 36:15). After death, the souls of the righteous are in the hand of God, and at peace (3:1, 3). "But the righteous live forever, and their reward is with the Lord; the Most High takes care of them" (5:15).

Death had been a minor subject for the sages who produced the wisdom materials in the book of Proverbs. For Job, it had become ambiguous. His "friends" advocated the traditional view that an early death was the fate of the unrighteous, but Job longed for death to bring an end to his suffering. He considered the possibility that life after death might lead to some sort of resolution of his problem, but decided one could not count on that (Job 14). It was a major problem for Koheleth; since one must die, the value of everything one might do in life was called into question. The agonies of Job and Koheleth do not appear in Sirach, who claims the righteous die a good death, while that is the moment of retribution for the wicked. The subject is dealt with in a new way in Wisdom of Solomon. Death is an enemy, as in

---

[25] Note 2:15b, which sounds more like what Gentiles would say about a Jew: ". . . his manner of life is unlike that of others, and his ways are strange."

[26] Vocabulary: Incorrupt/incorruption, 5 times; immortal/immortality, 6 times; eternal/eternity, 13 times.

Koheleth, not created by God, but by the devil (1:13; 2:24).[27] But the certainty of life after death, denied in Job and Ecclesiastes and of no interest to Sirach, gives Wisdom of Solomon a new way to deal with the old problems.

Whether the author believed in resurrection has been a debated subject. He never states it unequivocally, and many scholars think it would be inconsistent with his ideas concerning soul and body, but there are passages that suggest he knew of the belief and did not argue against it.[28] In 3:7–8 he wrote of the righteous after death: "In the time of their visitation they will shine forth, and will run like sparks through the stubble. They will govern nations and rule over peoples, and the Lord will reign over them forever." The language is reminscent of Dan 12:3 and 7:17, and the former text concerns the resurrection of the "wise." At the last judgment, "the righteous who have died will condemn the ungodly who are living" (Wis 4:16); these may be souls in heaven, but it is not explicit. The same vagueness appears in Wis 5:1: "Then the righteous will stand with great confidence in the presence of those who have oppressed them and those who make light of their labors." Evidently the *form* of life after death was not a subject on which the author had much to say, but the fact of it was essential. He is so satisfied with his solution to the theodicy question that he shows it to be the answer to a series of problems that had been sources of distress in Israel since earliest times. Those who died childless were thought to be truly dead, since one lived on in one's children, but Wisdom dares to say,

> . . . blessed is the barren woman who is undefiled, who has not entered into a sinful union; she will have fruit when God examines souls. Blessed also is the eunuch whose hands have done no lawless deed, and who has not devised wicked things against the Lord; for special favor will be shown him for his faithfulness, and a place of great delight in the temple of the Lord. (3:13b–14; cf. 4:1)

An early death had been called the punishment for wickedness, with a long and prosperous life the reward for righteousness, but Wisdom says, "the righteous man, though he die early will be at rest. For old age is not honored for length of time, nor measured by number of years; but understanding is gray hair for men, and a blameless life is ripe old age" (4:7–9).

The fate of the wicked after death is described as vaguely as that of the righteous, since the author's only concern is to emphasize the certainty of judgment. One might think, from 4:18b–19 that they will be annihilated:

> After this they will become dishonored corpses,
> and an outrage among the dead for ever;

---

[27] "The apparent metaphysical dualism of Wis. 2:24 seems inconsistent with the dominance of God and wisdom in the rest of the book." Collins, *Jewish Wisdom*, 190.

[28] P. Beauchamp, "Le Salut corporel des justes et la conclusion du livre de la Sagesse," *Bib* 45 (1964): 491–526; C. Larcher, *Études sur le Livre de la Sagesse* (Paris: Lecoffre, 1969), 321–7.

because he will dash them speechless to the ground,
  and shake them from the foundations;
they will be left utterly dry and barren,
  and they will suffer anguish,
  and the memory of them will perish.

Next, however, the wicked see the righteous vindicated and finally speak to acknowledge, at length, how wrong they had been (4:20–5:14). That the author is making no effort to be consistent, but simply offers a series of useful images, is evident from the passage that follows, a reuse of the divine warrior poetry of the Old Testament, which in its original settings was used to speak of Yahweh's judgment of the nations (5:16–23; cf. Isaiah 34; 63).

This first major section, with its emphasis on righteousness and immortality, seems to function in the following way: The book began with an address to the rulers of the earth, assuring them of the need for wisdom in order to be able to rule properly, and warning that unrighteousness is incompatible with that necessary quality (1:5, 8). The first subject to be developed, however, is righteousness rather than wisdom, with the introductory verse, "For righteousness is immortal" (1:15). The association between righteousness and immortality is then expounded in 1:16–6:8, when the author finally returns to the attribute they need in order to rule justly – wisdom (6:9). Wisdom is now also associated with immortality (6:17–19). "Because of her I shall have immortality, and leave an everlasting remembrance to those who come after me" (8:13; cf. v. 17).

God had been the direct agent of reward and punishment in the first major section, and it is only in the middle part of the book that wisdom appears as an intermediary. Earlier, God appeared as creator (2:23; 6:7), one who tests and examines (3:5, 13; 4:6), ruler (3:6), one who watches over, keeps safe, cares for, and shields the righteous (4:15, 17; 5:15, 16), and judges the wicked (4:18; 5:17–20; 6:5). With the second address to the rulers, beginning in 6:1, however, wisdom is introduced as a means of direct, personal contact with God. Reese comments, "Through his abstract method of presenting divine Wisdom Ps-Solomon has found a means of preserving the absolute transcendence of the unique God of revelation while at the same time offering in attractive imagery the possibility of intimate personal communion with him."[29]

The accessibility of wisdom is the first emphasis. The familiar tension between divine and human initiative is preserved in 6:12–16, for she must be sought by humans (v. 12b, 14–15), but she is already seeking out those who desire her (vv. 13, 16). The author now takes up the role of Solomon, with supposed autobiographical passages in chs. 7–9, but the interspersed descriptions of wisdom are of more importance for our purposes. Wisdom is

---

[29] *Hellenistic Influence*, 41–42.

now closely associated with the concept of the the Spirit of the Lord, with an explicit identification in 9:17 (cf. 1:5–7).[30] She is a breath of the power of God, and pervades and penetrates all things (7:24–25; 8:1). She is thus God's means of direct and perfect revelation of himself to humanity:

> For she is a reflection of eternal light,
>   a spotless mirror of the working of God,
>   and an image of his goodness.
>
> . . . .
>
> in every generation she passes into holy souls
>   and makes them friends of God, and prophets; . . .
>   (7:26, 27b; cf. 8:9–11)

Wisdom is the means by which God makes his will known (8:8–9; 9:10–11), and the only way fallible humans can discern the truth. "Who has learned your counsel, unless you have given wisdom and sent your holy spirit from on high?" (9:17). In the earlier tradition, wisdom was ambiguous in that it was both a divine attribute, which God shared with humans, and a quality that could be gained by human effort – study and observation. The human effort that is emphasized in this book is prayer, seeking the divine gift: "But I perceived that I would not possess wisdom unless God gave her to me" (8:21).

The emphasis of this central section of the book is on the possibility of obtaining an intimate relationship with God via Wisdom because of the grace and mercy of God, and these attributes appear in significant ways in what is said about God throughout the book. It is he who created all things (1:14, except death, 1:13) and as their maker, God loves everything and "you spare all things, for they are yours, O Lord, you who love the living" (11:24–26). Once again, the author is not being completely consistent, for he will have much to say about God as judge of the wicked, but his emphasis on the grace of God leads to somewhat extravagant statements: "But you are merciful to all, for you can do all things, and you overlook people's sins, so that they may repent" (11:23). Those who persist in sin will of course receive retribution after death, as noted earlier (e.g. 4:18–19), and the perfect justice of God's treatment of the incorrigible is spelled out by example in the retelling of the classic history in chs. 11–19: ". . . one is punished by the very things by which he sins" (11:16). The author's favorite examples are drawn from the account of the plagues in Egypt, and from his elaborate parody of idol-worship (13:1–15:19). He can even draw a lesson concerning mercy from the Bible's acknowledgement that the occupation of Canaan took a long time, which is variously explained in the Old Testament (e.g. Exod 23:29). Our author has a new explanation: It was to give the Canaanites time to recognize their sins and repent, even though he knew they would never do so:

---

[30] Rylaarsdam, *Revelation*, 99–118; Collins, *Jewish Wisdom*, 196–9.

> But judging them little by little you gave them an opportunity to repent, though you
> were not unaware that their origin was evil and their wickedness inborn, and that
> their way of thinking would never change (12:10)

He seems not to have been concerned about the apparent pointlessness of this kind of mercy. For him the point, as expressed in the poem praising God's justice that immediately follows, is to be found in v. 18:

> Although you are sovereign in strength, you judge with mildness,
>   and with great forbearance you govern us;
> for you have power to act whenever you choose.
> Through such works you have taught your people
> that the righteous must be kind,
> and you have filled your children with good hope,
> because you give repentance for sins. (12:18–19)

Of course the mercy of God is normally extolled for the ways he extends it to the righteous. Another of the more remarkable statements in Wisdom of Solomon puts the relationship between divine grace and human responsibility in an original way:

> But you, our God, are kind and true,
>   patient, and ruling all things in mercy,
> For even if we sin we are yours,
>   knowing your power;
> but we will not sin, because we know that you acknowledge us as yours. (15:1–2)

The divine choice of Israel and of the individual Israelite is thus primary, and able to prevail over human failure, but humans who know God will not presume on his mercy, and will take seriously their responsibility to live righteously. As noted earlier, the righteous life is not defined in any detail. Righteousness is associated with trust (1:2), with holiness (not further defined; 6:10), with kindness (12:19), and with the knowledge of God (15:3). The writer's concerns thus may be designated largely "spiritual," in keeping with his emphasis on life after death and on the possibility of achieving an intimate relationship with God through God's gracious gift of wisdom.

4. 4 Maccabees

This book is in many respects in a class by itself. It was little used in later Judaism, so it appears to represent a strand of thought that died out early. Like Philo, the author of this book attempted to express the truths of Judaism in terms of Hellenistic philosophy, but that approach was essentially ignored in later rabbinic teaching.[31] It is useful for our purposes as an illustration of

---

[31] R. B. Townshend, "The Fourth Book of Maccabees" in *APOT*, 657-8.

the variety of ways of expressing the Jewish faith to be found in the first century C.E.[32] Its closest relationships are with 2 Maccabees, from which the stories of the martyrdoms of Eleazar and the mother with her seven sons were taken, and Wisdom of Solomon, since both associate reward after death with the suffering of the faithful. The terminology is original; the opening sentence, "The subject that I am about to discuss is most philosophical," scarcely leads one to expect a first-century Jewish author, but the theology is familiar throughout.

Unlike the Wisdom of Solomon, which speaks of "law" without being very explicit about its content, 4 Maccabees cites a series of examples that make it clear the Torah lies at the heart of the argument. Restrictions on food that may be eaten (4 Macc 1:33–34; cf. Lev 11:1–31) are mentioned first, in keeping with the issue that led to Eleazar's death. The tenth commandment is quoted (2:5), as well as the laws concerning the seventh year, gleaning, fruit trees, and perhaps the neighbor's fallen ox (2:8–9, 14; cf. Lev 19:9–10; 23:22; Deut 24:19–24; Deut 20:19; Exod 23:4–5). Other than "law," the author uses few of the theological terms that are customary in other Jewish literature, having replaced them by his philosophical vocabulary. The challenge for one who wishes to compare his thought with that of other writings is thus to make the appropriate connections between those terms and the Jewish theology that lies behind them, and especially to explain his key term, ὁ εὐσεβὴς λογισμός, variously translated "devout reason," "religious reason," or "inspired reason."

Reason was not a purely intellectual quality, since modified by εὐσεβής, a standard term for religion in diaspora Judaism.[33] In attempting to determine what term or terms a more traditional writer would have used, we are guided by the author's own careful definition. It begins, "Now reason is the mind that with sound logic prefers the life of wisdom" (1:15). We must be careful not to assume immediately that by wisdom he means exactly the חָכְמָה of Proverbs and Sirach, for he has more to add: "Wisdom, next, is the knowledge of divine and human matters and the causes of law, by which we learn divine matters reverently and human affairs to our advantage" (1:16). This was a well-known Stoic definition of wisdom,[34] but it could just as well be said about wisdom as Judaism understood it. That point is reinforced by the next sentence: "This, in turn, is education in the law, by which we learn divine matters reverently and human affairs to our advantage" (1:17). Law will, in fact, be the most important part of the tradition for the author, and in this he

---

[32] Most scholars follow Bickermann in dating the book between 19 and 54 C.E. E. J. Bickermann, "The Date of Fourth Maccabees," in *Louis Ginzberg Jubilee Volume* (New York: American Academy for Jewish Research, 1945), English Section, 105–12.

[33] Townshend, "Fourth Maccabees," 666.

[34] Paul L. Redditt, "The Concept of *Nomos* in Fourth Maccabees," *CBQ* 45 (1983): 260.

is in continuity with the "mainstream" of Judaism. Wisdom is next divided into four kinds, which are the four virtues of Plato and the Stoics: rational judgment, justice, courage, and self-control (1:18). The last of these provides a useful transition for the author, for his discussion of self-control leads to a series of examples of the ability Jews have to obey difficult provisions of the law, citing the cases from the Torah mentioned earlier (1:33–35; 2:1–14).

> In fact, since the law has told us not to covet, I could prove to you all the more that reason is able to control desires. (2:6)
> If one is greedy, one is ruled by the law through reason so that one neither gleans the harvest nor gathers the last grapes from the vineyard. (2:9)

Certainly, there is a relationship between the "devout reason" of 4 Maccabees and the wisdom of which Wisdom of Solomon spoke, but the two should not be simply equated without careful consideration of the ways the former term is used. Traditionally, wisdom was both a human attribute and a divine gift. How could devout reason be obtained? Evidently it could be taught, as human wisdom could be, for the author speaks of "education in the law" (1:17). Eleazar's testimony, as he faced torture, contains a remarkable series of terms, perhaps not all to be equated:

> I will not play false to you, O law that trained me,
> nor will I renounce you, beloved self-control.
> I will not put you to shame, philosophical reason,
> nor will I reject you, honored priesthood and knowledge of the law. (5:34–35)

Here, as in the previous text, knowledge of the law seems to be prerequisite to the possession of devout reason. Later the author takes up the potential challenge to his main thesis, which is that devout reason is master of the passions. "Some perhaps might say, 'Not all have full command of their emotions, because not all have prudent reason'" (7:17). His reponse shows that "reason" is not purely intellectual:

> But as many as attend to religion with a whole heart, these alone are able to control the passions of the flesh, since they believe that they, like our patriarchs Abraham and Isaac and Jacob, do not die to God, but live to God. (7:18–19)

He has now introduced dedication based on the faith that, because they are Jews, they belong to God. A bit later, living as a philosopher is connected directly with trusting God (7:21). Once the biblical expression "fear of God" is used to refer to the source of strength that enabled the mother to witness the suffering of her sons without faltering, and that is used in a way parallel to the favorite word "reason." Compare 15:8, ". . . yet because of the fear of God she disdained the temporary safety of her children," with 15:11b, ". . . in the case of none of them were the various tortures strong enough to pervert her reason." That momentary use of traditional language may well have been due to the familiar proverb, "The fear of the Lord is the beginning of wisdom" (Prov 1:7; and elsewhere). The source of the mother's strength is also described as faith in God, in 15:24; 16:22; 17:2. The parallels to the way wisdom is used in the earlier literature are evident: It is available to those dedicated to living a righteous life (here defined explicitly as obeying the Law of Moses), and it is an essential possession if one is to live well. The special turn taken in this book is in making it an essential possession if one is to die well.

There is not as much emphasis on the devout reason as a divine gift as in the previous works, so what there is should be noted before taking up the prominent theme of human responsibility. It is stated in a roundabout way in 2:22–23:

> Now when God fashioned human beings, he planted in them emotions and inclinations, but at the same time he enthroned the mind among the senses as a sacred governor over them all. To the mind he gave the law; and one who lives subject to this will rule a kingdom that is temperate, just, good, and courageous.

The more religious vocabulary used elsewhere protects us from concluding from this that the divine gifts were simply the mind and the law, leaving humans on their own, to do the best they could with their intellects and a set of divine demands.[35] But more is said about the law than about reason as a gift of God. It is a good gift, as Eleazar emphasizes:

> Therefore we do not eat defiling food; for since we believe that the law was established by God, we know that in the nature of things the Creator of the world in giving us the law has shown sympathy toward us. (5:25)

Summarizing, the devout reason is obtained by study of and devotion to the law, and it then enables obedience to that same law under all conditions, even the most severe. The author's philosophical interests lead him to speak of devout reason in ways somewhat different from the tradional language about wisdom, so it does not play exactly the same role, but wisdom seems to be the closest parallel. "For only the wise and courageous are masters of their emotions" (7:23).

The devout reason makes it possible to obey the law, but why would one want to do it, especially when obedience may lead to terrible suffering and death? The old teaching that faithfulness to God will certainly be rewarded in this life is not even a matter for discussion, now that martyrdom has become a fact that has to be dealt with. The author had Antiochus himself put the question about obedience that leads to suffering and death in a very reasonable way. First, the law that prohibits Eleazar from eating pork does not make good sense; and second, even "if there is some power watching over this religion of yours, it will excuse you from any transgression that arises out

---

[35] "Reason, as seen above, does not operate in 4 Maccabees as an independent agent left free to follow its own devices." Redditt, "Concept of *Nomos*," 258.

of compulsion" (5:5–13; 8:14). Townshend's term "duty" fits the first part of Eleazar's explanation of his position.[36] "We, O Antiochus, who have been persuaded to govern our lives by the divine law, think that there is no compulsion more powerful than our obedience to the law" (5:16). There is a sense not only of obligation to the God who gave it, but of a duty toward both the ancestors in the faith and toward the present community. The seven brothers feel themselves to be representatives of the historic faith, and so they answer Antiochus, "For we are ready to die rather than transgress our ancestral commandments; we are obviously putting our forebears to shame unless we should practice ready obedience to the law and to Moses our counselor" (9:1b–2). When Eleazar was offered the opportunity to eat kosher meat, pretending it was pork, he refused indignantly, for that would set the wrong example for his community, who would think he had compromised, "and ourselves become a pattern of impiety to the young by setting them an example in the eating of defiling food" (6:18–19). So the author says Eleazar "strengthened our loyalty to the law through your glorious endurance," for "by your deeds you made your words of divine philosophy credible" (7:9). Obedience to the law is thus partly motivated by one's concern for maintaining the integrity of the community.

Love[37] and gratitude are not part of this author's vocabulary, but the duty to obey is so far different from an onerous burden that he can depict the martyrs dying almost gladly (with a predecessor in 2 Maccabees's quotation of Eleazar's last words; 2 Macc 6:30).

> What person who lives as a philosopher by the whole rule of philosophy, and trusts in God, and knows that it is blessed to endure any suffering for the sake of virtue, would not be able to overcome the emotions through godliness? (7:21–22)
> Let us with all our hearts consecrate ourselves to God, who gave us our lives, and let us use our bodies as a bulwark for the law. (13:13b)
> Remember that it is through God that you have had a share in the world and have enjoyed life, and therefore you ought to endure any suffering for the sake of God. (16:18)

There is no hint in the book of the idea that obedience is compelled by a fear of punishment in the afterlife. Antiochus and his people will certainly be judged for their crimes (9:8, 32; 10:11, 15; 12:19; 13:15; 18:5, 22), but the fear of punishment is not only absent from all the explanations of the martyrs' choices; it is explicitly denied. Antiochus had been right when he told Eleazar that he should not expect to be punished for transgressing a law under

---

[36] "Fourth Book of Maccabees," 666. Also, "The motive that actuated these heroes was not so much the hope of gaining eternal life as the steadfast purpose to perform their duty (12:12, cf. 5:16ff., 6:14ff., etc.)." C. C. Torrey, *The Apocryphal Literature* (New Haven: Yale University, 1945), 104.

[37] Except 15:3: "She loved religion more, the religion that preserves them for eternal life according to God's promises."

compulsion, but that is irrelevant to the Jews. The author imagines what the brothers might have said, had they been willing to give in: "Also, divine justice will excuse us for fearing the king when we are under divine compulsion." But they would not appeal to that excuse.

There is a strong conviction that God does reward his faithful ones in the afterlife, however.

> For if we so die, Abraham and Isaac and Jacob will welcome us, and all the fathers will praise us. (13:17)
> They knew also that those who die for the sake of God live to God, as do Abraham and Isaac and Jacob and all the patriarchs. (16:25)
> But the sons of Abraham with their victorious mother are gathered together into the chorus of the fathers, and have received pure and immortal souls from God, to whom be glory forever and ever. (18:23–24; cf. 5:37; 9:8; 17:11, 18)

Nothing is said of resurrection; the author seems to think of the righteous dead going immediately into the presence of God, where they will live eternally.

A special reason for obedience to the law when it leads to suffering and death is prominent in this book, but not regularly found in Judaism. The deaths of the martyrs are here said to have atoning value for their people. "Be merciful to your people, and let our punishment suffice for them. Make my blood their purification, and take my life in exchange for theirs," Eleazar prayed (6:28–29). The author, giving no credit to the Hasmoneans, asserts that it was the deaths of the martyrs that saved Israel from Antiochus:

> These, then, who have been consecrated for the sake of God, are honored, not only with this honor, but also by the fact that because of them, our enemies did not rule over our nation, the tyrant was punished, and the homeland purified – they having become, as it were, a ransom for the sin of our nation. And through the blood of those devout ones and their death as an atoning sacrifice, divine Providence preserved Israel that previously had been mistreated. (17:20–22)

The concept of vicarious suffering did not become widely accepted in Judaism, as it did in Christianity, so this book adds a relatively unusual positive reason for obedience to the law. It not only sets an example, but benefits the whole community by its acceptance in heaven, it seems, as atonement for others' sins.

The law (specifically, the Torah) is the gracious gift of God to Israel. Dedication to the law produces the "virtues" most prized in Hellenistic philosophy, and so this book is in part a defense of the reasonableness of Judaism. To disobey the law under any circumstances, even the most terrible, would be unworthy of those given so great a gift, and in fact the greatest of the virtues that comes from the law makes obedience in all circumstances possible. Possession of the virtues makes possible a life that would be prized by philosophy, as master of the passions. Even more, faithfulness to the law will lead to a blissful life after death. The initiative is entirely from God, who set a reasonable requirement upon the Jews (5:25–27), which is to be obeyed as a duty (5:28–30), and which can be obeyed. The truth of this has been demonstrated in the most dramatic way possible by the deaths of the martyrs.

The relationship of devout reason to suffering is different in this book from the ways wisdom and suffering are related in earlier literature. Elsewhere wisdom was often said to preserve one from suffering:

> In all that he does, he prospers. (Ps 1:3)
> Wisdom rescued from troubles those who served her. (Wis 10:9)
> You have forsaken the fountain of wisdom.
> If you had walked in the way of God,
>   you would be dwelling in peace for ever. (Bar 3:12–13)

Another point of view is that suffering produces wisdom by purging, disciplining, and testing:

> Before I was afflicted I went astray;
>   but now I keep thy word. (Ps 119:67)
> He delivers the afflicted by their affliction,
>   and opens their ear by adversity. (Job 36:15)
> My son, if you come forward to serve the Lord,
>   prepare yourself for testing.
> . . . .
> For gold is tested in the fire,
>   and those found acceptable, in the furnace of humiliation. (Sir 2:1, 5)

In 4 Maccabees, however, the devout reason, which in many ways parallels wisdom in the other literature, does not save one from suffering, and is not produced by suffering, but is the attribute faithful Jews may possess that will enable them to withstand suffering, no matter how severe.

5. The Sentences of Pseudo-Phocylides

This work may have been written during the same period as Wisdom of Solomon and 4 Maccabees, but it is completely different from either of them. It is a collection of maxims, with very little theology involved,[38] so it need not be discussed at length here. The attitude expressed is the optimism concerning human potential that tends to prevail in Prov 10–31. The author says it plainly at the end of the collection:

> These are the mysteries of righteousness; living thus
> may you live out (your) life well to the threshold of old age.

---

[38] Collins notes one verse of theological significance: "The one God is wise and mighty" (v. 54) may be an echo of Deut 6:4; *Jewish Wisdom*, 165.

The possibility of achieving the good life is thus apparently fully under human control. One value of the work is thus to serve as a reminder that in spite of all the theologizing of wisdom that had taken place in Judaism, popular proverbs, with no other intention than to give good advice on how best to live, continued to be produced and collected.

The author was certainly Jewish, although there were earlier debates over that.[39] He used much of Lev 19 (in vv. 9–41), and alludes to such unusual Old Testament laws as "One should not take from a nest all the birds together, but leave the mother bird behind, in order to get young from her again" (vv. 84–85; cf. Deut 22:6–7); "Eat no meat that is torn by wild animals, but leave the remains to the swift dogs" (147–148; cf. Exod 22:31); and "Strangers should be held in equal honor among citizens. For we all experience the poverty of much wandering" (vv. 39–40; Exod 23:9 and frequently). The intended readership of his work remains uncertain. The choice of the sixth century poet Phocylides as a pseudonym suggests the author may have been addressing hellenized Jews with the claim that an esteemed Greek author agreed with the basic principles of their faith.[40]

The occasional references to God tell us little about the author's understanding of the divine-human relationship. There are a few echoes of Jewish thought, but most of what is said about God can also be found in Hellenistic sources, as van der Horst has demonstrated. The human soul is the image of God (vv. 105–106), who set mortals apart from the other creatures by giving them speech and wisdom (vv. 128–129). God is called immortal (v. 17), wise, mighty and rich in blessings (v. 54), and he judges those who lie (v. 17) and judge falsely (v. 11). He is to be honored above all (v. 8).

Nothing is said about covenant or law, although the author alludes to six of the ten commandments in vv. 3–8, and no reference to Israel or its history appears. The work appears to have the intention of being generally useful for any reader. A distinctly Jewish belief that does appear is that of the resurrection of the body:

> It is not good to dissolve the human frame;
> for we hope that the remains of the departed will soon come to the
>   light (again)
> out of the earth; and afterward they will become gods. (vv. 102–104)[41]

---

[39] For a full history of research on Pseudo-Phocylides, see P. W. van der Horst, *The Sentences of Pseudo-Phocylides, with Introduction and Commentary* (SVTP 4; Leiden: E. J. Brill, 1978), 3–54.

[40] van der Horst, *Pseudo-Phocylides,* 71.

[41] The last part of v. 104 has raised questions about the author's Jewishness, but the glorification of resurrected ones could be described in various ways, as in Dan 12:3; Wis 3:7; 4 Macc 17:5; and *ᵉlohim* was used of angels. The NT says those in the resurrection will be like angels in heaven (Luke 20:36). Cf. P. W. van der Horst, "Pseudo-Phocylides and the New

The immortality of the soul is also affirmed in the same context, however:

> For the souls remain unharmed among the deceased.
> For the spirit is a loan of God to mortals, and (his) image.
> For we have a body out of earth, and when afterward we are resolved
>   again into earth
> we are but dust; and then the air has received our spirit. (vv.105–108)
> All alike are corpses, but God rules over the souls. (v. 111)
> But (our) soul is immortal and lives ageless forever. (v. 115)

The context of these sayings is different from that which produced the affirmations in Dan 12:3; 2 Macc 7:9, 14, 23; Wis 3:1–9; and 4 Macc 17:5, however. Life after death here is not an answer to the problem of the suffering of the righteous, but is introduced by advice concerning funeral customs (vv. 97–102), is interrupted by the reminder that we can't take it with us (v. 109), and affirms the equality of the dead (vv. 111–113), rather than reward and punishment. Belief in life after death, apparently in a vague form, appears thus to be taken for granted, rather than being part of serious wrestling with the issue of being Jewish in the midst of an alien culture.

6. Conclusions

With reference to Sanders's terms, "getting in" is clearly attributed entirely to the divine initiative in the first four of these works. They affirm the existence of a special relationship between God and Israel; and Sirach, Wisdom of Solomon, and 4 Maccabees base their teachings on the certainty that the sovereign and merciful God is faithful to that relationship. The author of Pseudo-Phocylides keeps his understanding of Israel as the people of God well-hidden. As to "staying in," Baruch is the only book in this group to consider the continuation of the covenant-relationship to be uncertain, because of the exile, but it uses the promises in the prophetic books and makes a new use of wisdom-material in order to offer reassurance. As in the other books, the Old Testament teaching concerning the grace of God is the basis for its message of hope. Staying in does not depend entirely on human obedience, but depends on mercy that transcends merit. Confession of sin and appeal for forgiveness play a larger role than in the other books. The need for repentance and forgiveness is also dealt with in Sirach, and this shows that the author does not operate with a strictly merit-based theology. The background of persecution in Wisdom of Solomon and 4 Maccabees leads to more interest in divine support for those suffering for their faithfulness than concern about what they may have done wrong. Facing the problem of survival, these

---

Testament," *ZNW* 69 (1978): 187–202; Felix Christ, "Das Leben nach dem Tode bei Pseudo-Phokylides," *TZ* 31 (1975): 140–9.

authors could call for faithfulness only because they were certain there was an active God ready to provide what humans could not hope to attain by their own efforts.

The law of God plays a major role in each of the first four books, but as a theme rather than as a set of statutes to be expounded. It is God's gift to Israel, making it clear what God wants of his people. There is no suggestion that works of the law are expected to prove anything to God, or that God counts up merits. Rewards for faithfulness are regularly assured. There is generally more interest in assuring those who would be faithful that "the wicked" will be punished – evidently groups or individuals who are enemies of the faithful – than in threatening punishment for individual sins, although that does occur, especially in Sirach. The books thus begin with the assumption that the readers are "in," and that there is another group, the enemies, who are "out." Given the hazardous nature of Jewish existence during these centuries, the most frequently expressed concern is not how to remain "in," but how to survive physically, both as individuals and as a community, and the Old Testament message that God preserves the righteous is reaffirmed in various ways for that reason. Two of the books, Wisdom of Solomon and 4 Maccabees, adopt the hope for life after death, when the righteous will finally be justified, as a new form of that message.

9. Josephus[1]

by

PAUL SPILSBURY

1. Introduction

In his magisterial volume entitled *Judaism: Practice and Belief 63 BCE–66 CE*, E. P. Sanders states, "The principal source for the history of the period, and for its social, political and religious issues, is the work of the Jewish author, Josephus."[2] Appropriately, therefore, in the study which follows, Sanders makes extensive use of the writings of Josephus in elucidating his topic.[3] However, it is noteworthy that the works of Josephus play practically no part at all in Sanders's earlier work, *Paul and Palestinian Judaism*.[4] There is no discussion of Josephus as an important source for our understanding of Palestinian Judaism in the pre-70 era, nor is there any engagement with his thought. According to the book's Index of Passages, Sanders cites the writings of Josephus only three times.[5] The reasons for this omission are not clear, though they might include the fact that at the time of writing Josephus was a resident not of Palestine but of Rome. Nevertheless, as Sanders himself affirms in *Judaism*, the works of Josephus are indispensable for the study of Judaism in the Second Temple period, whether in Palestine or in the Diaspora. Sanders's omission of Josephus in *Paul and Palestinian Judaism* means that there is yet need for an investigation into the nature of the relationship between God and human beings (especially the Jews) in Josephus' thought.

---

[1] An earlier draft of this paper was presented during the 1998 meetings of the Canadian Society of Biblical Studies in Ottawa. I am grateful for the input of my colleagues on that occasion. I also owe a debt of gratitude to the co-contributors to the present volume for numerous very helpful comments and criticisms. All quotations of Josephus are from H. St. J. Thackeray, R. Marcus, A. Wikgren and L. H. Feldman (ed. and trans.) *Josephus* (10 vols. Loeb Classical Library; Cambridge and London: Harvard and Heinmann, 1926–1965).

[2] E. P. Sanders, *Judaism: Practice and Belief 63 BCE–66 CE* (Philadelphia: Trinity Press International, 1992), 5.

[3] A perusal of the Index of Passages on 567–572 is enough to make this abundantly clear.

[4] E. P. Sanders, *Paul and Palestinian Judaism. A Comparison of Patterns of Religion* (London: SCM, 1977).

[5] *Paul and Palestinian Judaism*, 608. The passages cited are *J.W.* 2.162, 163 and *Ant.* 18.12 all of which relate to Josephus' description of the Pharisees. The book's Index of Names lists seven incidental references to Josephus.

We should state at the outset, however, that Josephus' interests were not primarily religious or theological. As is often, and rightly, pointed out by those who have studied Josephus' works at some length, his interests were of an historiographical and apologetic nature. While he was indeed concerned to provide his readers with an accurate portrayal of the laws of Moses, he described these in political terms as a "constitution."[6] Further, he was more concerned to win praise for Moses in particular and the Jews in general than he was to expound the theological profundities of his religion.[7] Thus we do not find in Josephus' works sustained explanations or discussion of such matters as "justification" or the relative importance for salvation of "faith" and "works," or a clear picture of "salvation" as a theological category. What we will find, rather, is interpretive historiography which, from time to time, yields insights into what Josephus, one particular late first-century Jew, thought on specific theological subjects.[8]

Further, it will not do simply to look for terms and modes of argumentation associated with particular subjects in other sources, whether they be the writings of Paul or any other ancient Jewish source. Rather, we will have to

---

[6] On Josephus' political thought, see Y. Amir, *"Theokratia* as a Concept of Political Philosophy: Josephus' Presentation of Moses' *Politeia," Scripta Classica Israelica* 8–9 (1985–88): 83–105; T. Rajak, "The *Against Apion* and the Continuities in Josephus' Political Thought," in *Understanding Josephus. Seven Perspectives* (ed. S. Mason; JSPSup 32; Sheffield Academic, 1998), 222–43; D. R. Schwartz, "Josephus on the Jewish Constitution and Community," *Scripta Classica Israelica* 7 (1983–84): 30–52; P. Spilsbury, *"Contra Apionem* and *Antiquitates Judaicae*: Points of Contact," in *Josephus'* Contra Apionem. *Studies in its Character and Context with a Latin Concordance to the Portion Missing in Greek* (ed. L. H. Feldman and J. R. Levison; AGJU 24; Leiden: E. J. Brill, 1996), 262–6.

[7] There is a significant body of literature on Josephus' portrayal of Moses. Some of the most significant contributions include J. Cohen, *The Origins and Evolution of the Moses Nativity Story* (SHR 58; Leiden; E. J. Brill, 1993), 46–59; L. H. Feldman, "Josephus' Portrait of Moses," *JQR* 82 (1991–92): 285–328; 83 (1992): 7–50; 83 (1993): 301–330; G. Hata, "The Story of Moses Interpreted within the Context of Anti-Semitism," in *Josephus, Judaism and Christianity* (ed. L. H. Feldman and G. Hata ; Leiden: E. J. Brill, 1987), 180–97; C. R. Holladay, *Theios Aner in Hellenistic Judaism: A Critique of the Use of this Category in New Testament Christology* (SBLDS 40; Missoula: Scholars, 1977), 47–102; P. Spilsbury, *The Image of the Jew in Flavius Josephus' Paraphrase of the Bible* (TSAJ 69; Tübingen: Mohr [Siebeck], 1998), 94–111; D. L. Tiede, *The Charismatic Figure as Miracle Worker* (SBLDS 1; Missoula: Scholars, 1972), 207–40.

[8] On whether Josephus might legitimately be thought of as a theologian, see H. W. Attridge, *The Interpretation of Biblical History in the Antiquitates Judaicae of Flavius Josephus* (HDR 7; Missoula: Scholars, 1976), 3–16 and L. H. Feldman, "Use, Authority and Exegesis of Mikra in the Writings of Josephus," in *Mikra: Text, Translation, Reading and Interpretation on the Hebrew Bible in Ancient Judaism and Early Christianity* (ed. J. Mulder; CRINT 2/1; Assen: van Gorcum/Philadelphia: Fortress, 1988), 503–4. On Josephus' "theology" in general, see A. Schlatter, *Die Theologie des Judentums nach dem Bericht des Josephus* (Gutersloh: C. Bertelsmann, 1932); and "Wie Sprach Josephus von Gott," in *Kleinere Schriften zu Flavius Josephus* (ed. K. H. Rengstorf; Darmstadt: Wissenschaftliche Buchgesellschaft, 1970), 65–142.

be open to new terminology, and perhaps quite different ways of addressing the issues for which we have come to the text of Josephus for illumination. Our examination of Josephus' corpus will yield fruit only insofar as we are willing to dialogue with his terms and at his level of engagement with theological subjects.

Before we tackle the main topic of this investigation, it is necessary to place our study in a broader context. The study of the works of Josephus is both aided and complicated by the fact that we know a good deal about him – a good deal, that is, in comparison with most of the other sources of ancient Judaism that have come down to us. Our information about Josephus enables us to set his works in their general context. We know that they are the work of a Jew of priestly stock living in Rome in the final decades of the first century. We know that this Jew was born and raised in Jerusalem and had first-hand knowledge of the city of Jerusalem and the temple in their final doom-laden years. And we know that in later life, as an expatriate in Rome, he took great pains to present to the citizens of that city a favorable picture of the Jews and their philosophy of life. Some of our knowledge of Josephus, though, is less certain and open to serious question.[9] For example, while his claim to have been a child prodigy, sought out at the age of fourteen by the leading figures of his day (*Life* 9), is harmless enough, his claim to have studied each of the three main sects of Judaism in depth (*Life* 10–11) presents more significant challenges. If we dismiss as a literary *topos* his claim to have investigated each of the sects of Judaism, as many scholars have, then how reliable is anything he says about the sects themselves?[10] And are we to take seriously his claim to have become a Pharisee after sampling each of the three main Jewish "philosophies" (*Life* 12)? It has often been pointed out that Josephus' portrayal of the Pharisees seems to change from the *Jewish War* to the *Antiquities*, and various theories have been put forward to explain the development.[11] In recent debate the question has been further complicated by S. Mason's argument that, in fact, Josephus did not claim to be a Pharisee at all, but only that he chose to follow their rulings bearing on public life, since they were the most influential sect in Palestinian society at the time.[12] These

---

[9] For a discussion of the numerous difficulties with Josephus' account of his own life, see P. Spilsbury, *The Image of the Jew*, 8–11.

[10] Cf. T. Rajak, *Josephus: The Historian and his Society* (Philadelphia: Fortress, 1984), 34–37. Rajak regards Josephus' claim as essentially truthful, despite the evidence that it is made in conventional terms. She writes, "That the search [for the best philosophy of life] becomes a *topos*, a literary formula, by no means implies that it was not carried out by the individuals who recount it" (36).

[11] See especially S. Schwartz, *Josephus and Judaean Politics* (CSCT 18; Leiden: E. J. Brill, 1990).

[12] S. N. Mason, *Flavius Josephus on the Pharisees. A Composition-Critical Study* (SPB 39; Leiden: E. J. Brill, 1991), 347–56. E. P. Sanders rejects the notion that the Pharisees were the

factors suggest that it is probably better not to assign a sectarian designation to Josephus' descriptions of Judaism not only because of the difficulties that have been raised, but also because he wrote at a time when such designations apparently no longer applied. Or, if they did apply, we are not in a position to say how, for in the last decades of the first century, Judaism throughout the Roman world had entered into a period of significant transformation as different groups responded to the destruction of Jerusalem and the temple by formulating new visions of the essential nature of Judaism and what it meant to be a Jew.[13] In this study, therefore, we will regard Josephus' account of the nature of the divine-human relationship as merely his own, and not apply to it the descriptive "pharisaic," or any other such term.

When we turn to the writings of Josephus, we are faced with one of the most important questions in Josephan studies, namely, the aims their author had in mind in writing them. On this question scholars tend to fall into two broad groups: those who view Josephus in an essentially positive light, and those who read almost everything he wrote with the utmost scepticism.[14] Those in the latter group tend to base their assessment of Josephus' worth as an historian on prior assessments of Josephus' morality drawn from what he himself tells us about his involvement in the Jewish war (see especially *J. W.* 3.350–91). How, it is often asked, can we trust someone on any significant matter when he has shown himself to be utterly unscrupulous and a traitor to his nation and religion? Those in the former group choose to reserve judgment about Josephus' morality, and to focus instead on the writings Josephus has left behind. These scholars attempt, insofar as it is possible, to read the works of Josephus on their own terms, and tend to have a more optimistic assessment of the historical worth of Josephus' writings. On the matter under discussion in this essay we have chosen to take Josephus as much as possible at his word. In other words, we will attempt to hear Josephus' own voice[15] as he presents his account of the functioning of

---

most influential sect; see *Judaism*, 448–51. In another context (532 n. 9) he remarks that if Josephus became a Pharisee in order to seek public office he would have been unique in this respect.

[13] For a discussion of Josephus' revisioning of Judaism at the end of the first century, see P. Spilsbury, *The Image of the Jew*. On the varying perceptions of Jewish identity throughout the diaspora, see J. M. G. Barclay, *Jews in the Mediterranean Diaspora from Alexander to Trajan (323 BCE–117 CE)* (Edinburgh: T & T Clark, 1996).

[14] See the discussion of these two approaches in P. Bilde's useful survey of scholarship in *Flavius Josephus Between Jerusalem and Rome. His Life, his Works, and their Importance* (JSPSup 2; Sheffield: JSOT Press, 1988), 123–71.

[15] Josephus' widely acknowledged use of both oral and written sources makes it difficult to differentiate his own "voice" from that of his sources. On this subject, with some suggestions for resolving the difficulty, see J. Sievers, "Josephus and the Afterlife," in *Understanding Josephus. Seven Perspectives* (ed. S. Mason; JSPSup 32; Sheffield: Sheffield Academic, 1998), 22–24, 30–31.

Judaism. Having said this, we are still faced with the question of Josephus' aims in the writing of his individual books. It is to this subject that we now briefly turn.

2. Josephus' Aims

2.1 *The* Jewish War

In the opening paragraph of this his first work Josephus writes: "I . . . propose to provide the subjects of the Roman Empire with a narrative of the facts [of the war of the Jews against the Romans], by translating into Greek the account which I previously composed in my vernacular tongue and sent to the barbarians in the interior" (*J.W.* 1.3). The reference to "the barbarians in the interior" reveals the *Jewish War* to be a piece of Roman-sponsored propaganda, intended to make clear to readers of Aramaic the invincibility of the Roman army and the futility of revolt. Here we have Josephus, the state historiographer.[16] Even in this guise, however, it is clear that Josephus also had things to say in defense of the Jewish people. In other words, in the *Jewish War* he is also an apologist for the Jews.[17] His main point in this regard would seem to be that *the Jews as a whole* did not revolt against the Romans (cf. *J.W.* 1.10). Rather, it was a small, misguided and unrepresentative group of brigands and religious hotheads who set in motion the tragic events that eventually embroiled the whole nation in a war which even God could not find a way to support (cf. *J.W.* 5.412).[18] Thus, while imperial propaganda is certainly one of the aims of the work, it is clear that a more significant aim is to distance the Jews as a nation from the war which had led to such public humiliations in the latter decades of the first century as the *fiscus Iudaicus* and Titus's arch of triumph in Rome.

2.2 *The Jewish* Antiquities

In this work, completed some twenty years after the *Jewish War*, Josephus is still writing apologetic history.[19] In the preface he indicates that the book's

---

[16] For a full discussion of this aspect of the work, see H. St. J. Thackeray, *Josephus, The Man and the Historian* (New York: Jewish Institute of Religion, 1929) 23–50. Important balance to this treatment is supplied by T. Rajak, *Josephus*, 174–184.

[17] For an excellent summary of the pertinent evidence here, see J. M. G. Barclay, *Jews in the Mediterranean Diaspora*, 351–6.

[18] We will discuss this point further below.

[19] Gregory Sterling (*Historiography and Self Definition*) classifies *Antiquities* generically as "apologetic historiography," a genre in which indigenous authors rewrite Greek ethnographic accounts of their nations in their own terms. Besides Josephus, other authors who composed such apologetic accounts were individuals such as Manetho and Berossus.

scope will cover "our entire ancient history and political constitution, translated from the Hebrew records" (*Ant.* 1.5). In his later work, *Against Apion*, Josephus further reveals that his intention in the *Antiquities* had been to demonstrate "the extreme antiquity of our Jewish race, the purity of the original stock, and the manner in which it established itself in the country we occupy today" (*Ag. Ap.* 1.1). Later on in that work he also gives evidence of a desire to counter the calumny that the Jews "have not produced any geniuses . . . inventors in the arts and crafts or eminent sages" (*Ag. Ap.* 2.135). He accomplishes this by asserting that "Our own famous men, who are entitled to rank with the highest, are familiar to readers of my *Antiquities*" (*Ag. Ap.* 2.136). A careful reading of the *Antiquities*, however, strongly suggests that Josephus was concerned with far more than an encomiastic rendering of his national history. Indeed, much of what he had to say was leveled as much at fellow-Jews as it was at his stated Gentile audience.[20] In the *Antiquities* Josephus spells out his program for refashioning Judaism in the aftermath of the failure of the Jewish war. This is done not so much by propositional statements as by a nuanced rewriting of the Jewish Scriptures complete with Hellenistic coloring and Jewish "midrashic" embellishments.[21] Indeed, as we have seen in *Antiquities* 1.5, quoted above, Josephus cast the entire work as an original translation of the Bible into Greek.

2.3 The Life

This work, which is taken up almost entirely with personal apologetic about a short period of time in which Josephus was involved in the Galilean phase of the Jewish war, has little bearing on the subject of the present study, and as such need not be considered here.[22]

---

[20] The audience Josephus intended for the *Antiquities* has been the subject of some debate. For some recent treatments, see S. Mason, "'Should any Wish to Enquire Further' (*Ant.*. 1.25): The Aim and Audience of Josephus' *Judean Antiquities/Life*," in *Understanding Josephus. Seven Perspectives* (ed. S. Mason; JSPSup 32; Sheffield: Sheffield Academic, 1998), 64–103; P. Spilsbury, *The Image of the Jew*, 16–22; G. Sterling, *Historiography and Self-Definition: Josephos Luke-Acts and Apologetic Historiography* (NovTSup 64; Leiden: E. J. Brill, 1992), 298–302.

[21] For a synthetic analysis of how Josephus accomplishes this, see P. Spilsbury, *The Image of the Jew*. More detailed analyses of individual pericopae are provided by the many studies of L. H. Feldman and C. Begg on Josephus' "portraits" of various biblical characters. A representative sample of these studies may be found in the bibliography of my *Image of the Jew*. See also L. H. Feldman, *Jew and Gentile in the Ancient World. Attitudes and Interactions from Alexander to Justinian* (Princeton: Princeton University, 1993).

[22] On the aims of the *Life*, see S. Mason, "Should Any Wish to Enquire Further," 101–3.

2.4 Against Apion

This is Josephus' attempt to accomplish in a more direct and propositional way what his indirect approach failed to do in the *Antiquities* (cf. *Ag. Ap.* 1.2–3).[23] After devoting three-quarters of the work to the refutation of specific literary calumnies against the Jews, Josephus eventually turns to a positive presentation of the strengths of Judaism, chief among which are the Law and the lawgiver, Moses.[24] This final section of the work is among Josephus' most important compositions, and will merit closer scrutiny in our study.

What emerges from this brief survey is that all of Josephus' works are aimed in one way or another at defending the Jews against various charges brought against them in Josephus' own time. This apologetic agenda colors everything Josephus wrote and must be taken into account in any analysis of his thought. With respect to his understanding of the relationship between God and the Jews, for instance, it is quite possible (even quite likely) that Josephus' apologetics caused him to express himself in a way that would cast the Jews in a positive light. Thus it comes as no surprise that there is in Josephus no substantial discussion of the shortcomings of the Jews, or of the inadequacies of the Law, as there is in the writings of Paul, for example. Be that as it may, there is still much to learn from the way Josephus did in fact depict the divine-human relationship, and it is to that subject we now turn.

3. God's Relationship with the Jews

God's relationship with the Jews in Josephus' writings is founded upon Jewish observance of the Law of Moses. This basic datum, though variously expressed, is affirmed in each of the major works of Josephus. We will look at each of these in turn, beginning with the *Antiquities* because it is there that we will find Josephus' most extended treatment of the subject.

---

[23] On the relationship between *Against Apion* and the *Antiquities*, see P. Spilsbury, "Points of Contact."

[24] For recent assessments of Josephus' powers of argumentation as they are expressed in *Ag. Ap.*, see J. M. G. Barclay, "Josephus v. Apion: Analysis on an Argument," in *Understanding Josephus. Seven Perspectives* (ed. S. Mason; JSPSup 32; Sheffield: Sheffield Academic, 1998), 194–221; A. Kasher, "Polemic and Apologetic Methods of Writing in *Contra Apionem*," in *Josephus' Contra Apionem. Studies in its Character and Context with a Latin Concordance to the Portion Missing in Greek* (ed. L. H. Feldman and J. R. Levison; AGJU 34; Leiden: E. J. Brill, 1996), 143–86.

3.1 The Jewish Antiquities

The Law in the *Antiquities* is the gift of God.[25] It is the means by which God governs his people[26] and, Josephus argues, it is obeyed by the Jews in every detail.[27] The Law is inherently good and it causes the Jews to be the most generous, hospitable and charitable of people.[28] It is also profoundly rational and in keeping with the natural laws of the universe.[29] As such it reflects not only its divine origin, but the extreme piety and sagacity of the lawgiver, Moses.[30] Further, in Josephus' view, piety is explicitly linked to observance of the Law, and law-observance results quite naturally in God's favor.

A significant aspect of Josephus' portrayal of God's relationship with the Jews in the paraphrase of the Bible is his notorious omission of all references to the covenant. That is to say, there is no explicit reference to a covenant between God and Abraham in Josephus' retelling of Abraham's departure from Ur (*Ant.* 1.154–157), or the sacrificing of Isaac (*Ant.* 1.222–236). Even the account of the institution of the sign of circumcision (*Ant.* 1.191–193) is devoid of any reference to a covenant between God and the people. The same remarkable pattern of omission is repeated throughout Josephus' account of the entire biblical story.

This is a subject that has been approached in various ways by Josephus scholars. Betsy Halpern-Amaru has argued that Josephus was concerned to drive a wedge between himself and the land-oriented covenantal theology of the zealot factions of the pre-70 period.[31] According to this suggestion, Josephus' omission of covenantal language was due to his discomfort with the militaristic messianism that it inspired in some of his compatriots. H. W. Attridge[32] has shown further that Josephus replaced the idea of covenant with the notion of divine providence (πρόνοια), in which God's support is seen to be a natural outworking of his retributive justice. This notion is expressed in Josephus' own words near the beginning of the *Antiquities*:

---

[25] E.g., *Ant.* 3.78, 223; 4.213, 316, 318.

[26] *Ant.* 4.223.

[27] *Ant.* 3.317–22.

[28] E.g., *Ant.* 4.231–39, 275, 276.

[29] *Ant.* 3.180–87.

[30] E.g., *Ant.* 3.179–87; 4.196, 331. For Josephus' treatment of the figure of Moses see the literature cited in note 7 above. For Josephus' treatment of the Law see especially B. Schröder, *Die "vaterlichen Gesetze". Flavius Josephus als Vermittler von Halachah an Grieschen und Römer* (TSAJ 53; Tübingen: Mohr [Siebeck], 1996); L. H. Feldman, "Use, Authority and Exegesis," 507–18; G. Vermes, "A Summary of the Law by Flavius Josephus," *NovT* 24 (1982): 289–303.

[31] B. Halpern-Amaru, "Land Theology in Josephus' *Jewish Antiquities*," *JQR* 71 (1980–81): 210–29.

[32] H. W. Attridge, *Interpretation*, 86–87.

Speaking generally, the main lesson to be learnt from this history by any who care to peruse it is that [those] who conform to the will of God, and do not venture to transgress laws excellently laid down, prosper in all things beyond belief, and for their reward are offered by God felicity; whereas, in proportion as they depart from the strict observance of these laws, things (else) practicable become impracticable, and whatever imaginary good thing they strive to do ends in irretrievable disasters. (*Ant.* 1.14)

According to Attridge's understanding, any benefits the Israelites derive from God are based not on any special relationship with God (as implied by the term "covenant," for instance), but on the Israelites' conformity to the will of God as spelled out in the Law of Moses. Building on this foundation, I have argued in another context[33] that the broad strokes of Josephus' portrayal of the God-Israel relationship may be accounted for by recourse to the patron-client system of social relations prevalent in the Roman empire during the late first century. In this system of relations unequal partners agreed to be linked together for mutual benefit. E. Badian describes the lesser partner in the relationship thus:

The client may be described as an inferior entrusted, by custom or by himself, to the protection of a stranger more powerful than he, and rendering certain services and observances in return for this protection.[34]

R. P. Saller defines patronage as "an exchange relationship" between parties of unequal status.[35] This system of relations, which is essentially a contractual one, not altogether unlike the biblical covenant, seems to be the best paradigm for understanding Josephus' account of the relationship between God and Israel. Israel is God's client and God is Israel's patron. In other words, in keeping with Josephus' tendency to hellenize his account of biblical history for his Gentile audience, Josephus seems to have translated the biblical picture of the covenant-based relationship between God and Israel into the system of relations most familiar to his Roman audience.

While I do not want to repeat here what I have argued elsewhere, it may be worthwhile to summarize the evidence for this position.

3.2 The Patron-Client Relationship between God and Israel in the Antiquities

A careful reading of the *Antiquities* seems to suggest that Josephus was indeed convinced of a special relationship between God and Israel. This is clear in such passages as *Antiquities* 4.114, 3.313 and 7.380, all of which

---

[33] P. Spilsbury, "God and Israel in Josephus: a Patron-Client Relationship," in *Understanding Josephus. Seven Perspectives* (ed. S. Mason; JSPSup 32; Sheffield: Sheffield Academic, 1998), 172–91.

[34] E. Badian, *Foreign Clientelae (264–70 BC)* (Oxford: Clarendon, 1958), 1.

[35] R. P. Saller, *Personal Patronage under the Early Empire* (Cambridge: Cambridge University, 1982), 4.

express God's esteem and care for the Hebrew race. Further, there are many passages which itemize the benefits which the Israelites enjoy because of God's favor. For example, God commits himself to be their ally (σύμμαχος, βοηθός), guaranteeing them freedom from slavery, and a land to possess (*Ant.* 2.268–69; 3.300). The Balaam episode is especially instructive in this regard because it portrays God's unwillingness to turn against his "favored" people on whom he has "zeal to confer . . . a life of felicity and everlasting renown" (*Ant.* 4.122). Even more important than God's alliance, however, is God's gift of the Law which is described as the greatest of all God's benefactions (*Ant.* 4.213). This point is developed further when Josephus makes it clear that gratitude for God's benefactions (which is the response required from humans) is most appropriately expressed by obedience to the Law. Thus, God's Law given through Moses evokes gratitude expressed in obedience.

In all of this Josephus had no need for the term "covenant" because the reciprocal nature of the relationship between God and Israel as he envisioned it could be expressed adequately in terms reminiscent of patron-client relationships in Roman society. In Josephus' view, God functions as Israel's patron by offering numerous benefactions including military alliance and, most importantly, the Law of Moses. As God's favored client Israel is required to express profound gratitude for this benefaction by a life of piety which is defined quite explicitly as obedience to the Law of Moses.

This reading of Josephus is further confirmed by those instances in which he seems to be opposing certain misunderstandings of the divine-human relationship among the Jews themselves. For example, in the aftermath of the people's failure to enter the promised land, when the people decide to try to enter Canaan by force, Josephus writes:

> They were accordingly bent on war with the Canaanites, declaring that it was from no favour for Moses that God succoured them, but because in general He had a care for their race out of regard for their ancestors whom He had taken under His protection (*Ant.* 4.2).

What is significant about this passage is that it seems to represent a misconstrual of the relationship between God and Israel. In the overall context of Josephus' aims in the *Antiquities* it would seem that Josephus is here refuting actual Jewish views of the nature of the "covenant." From a kind of "mirror reading" of this passage, we may conclude, firstly, that for Josephus the relationship between God and Israel is, in fact, closely connected to God's regard for Moses, and in context this implies specifically *the Law* of Moses. And secondly, we may deduce that membership in the group is not simply a matter of physical descent from illustrious and meritorious forebears.

Both of these elements are affirmed again later in another episode significantly embellished by Josephus, namely the affair of the erection of an altar beyond the river Jordan in Josh 22. In this episode a misunderstanding of motives leads to the brink of civil war as the tribes on the western shore of the Jordan prepare to punish the trans-Jordanian tribes for an alleged breech of the Mosaic code. At the heart of the matter is the connection between Abrahamic descent and obedience to the Law of Moses. In the preamble to the episode, Joshua reminds the tribes departing for their territories beyond the Jordan that Abrahamic descent carries with it the responsibility to fulfil Mosaic religious duties (*Ant.* 5.97), and that this responsibility is not negated by geographical considerations (see also *Ant.* 5.109). Observance of the Law will ensure God's alliance, while turning away "to imitate other nations" will result in God turning away from them (*Ant.* 5.98). When the western tribes hear of the alleged offenses of those on the east, they set out to punish them, "For they held that they should take no account of their kinship . . . but of the will of God and the fashion in which He delights to be honoured" (*Ant.* 5.102). The implication of this, which is made clear throughout the episode, is that ethnic descent from Abraham is subservient to obedience to the Mosaic Law when it comes to membership in the commonwealth of Israel. At the end of the affair the trans-Jordanian tribes affirm that, had they been guilty of "new-fangled ways that are perversions of our customary practice," their pedigree as the descendants of Abraham would have been insufficient defense against the punishment they deserved, namely to be extirpated (ἐξώλεις εἶναι) (*Ant.* 5.113).

It is likely that Josephus was primarily addressing his Jewish compatriots in Rome at this point. The position he is apparently countering here is one positing that outside of the land of Israel ethnic descent without detailed observance of the Law was a sufficient basis for continued Jewish identity. For Josephus, this view is anathema. Indeed, for him, Abrahamic descent makes the crime of disregarding the Law even more heinous. Thus, clearly, the Law is at the heart of Israel's relationship with God.

As I have already indicated, Josephus' depiction of the relationship between God and Israel may best be understood in terms of the patron-client system of relations prevalent in Roman society at the time. In Josephus' grand scheme it is the Law of Moses that is presented as God's most important benefaction. Gratitude for this gift is expressed primarily in due observance of the Law itself. Thus Josephus conceives of a situation in which God bestows his patronage on the Jews in the form of the Law of Moses. This wonderful gift, which enables them to live a life superior to any other people on earth, calls forth the gratitude of the people. This gratitude is expressed primarily in obedience to the Law. This obedience then secures God's continued favor.

At this point we should remember the overtly apologetic nature of Josephus' work. He is at great pains throughout the *Antiquities* to praise the Jewish people and especially their illustrious forbears. It is conceivable that his apologetic agenda led him to falsify his real understanding of the nature of the relationship between God and Israel. It might be argued that it simply would not have suited his overall purpose to say that the Jews were a small and insignificant nation who experienced God's blessing for no other reason than that God bestowed his love upon them (cf. Deut 7:7–8). Be that as it may, the impression with which Josephus actually leaves us in the *Antiquities* is that divine favor is based on human piety.

Further, given Josephus' non-use of the term "covenant," it is doubtful that Sanders's term "covenantal nomism" is the most appropriate one to describe Josephus' understanding of the fundamental shape of Judaism. This holds true even though there are significant points of contact between "covenantal nomism" as Sanders defines it and Josephus' hellenized account of the functioning of Judaism. I would suggest that because of Josephus' (apparently deliberate) omission of the term "covenant," and the importance of human piety in Josephus' understanding of the divine-human relationship, an alternative expression ought to be found to describe Josephus' view. Perhaps a term like "patronal nomism" could serve that purpose. Such a term would do justice both to the importance of the Law in the *Antiquities* and to the particular way in which Josephus has used patron-client language to translate the biblical concept of covenant. "Patronal nomism" is more than just "covenantal nomism" by another name. It is, in fact, a thoroughly Romanized translation of a biblical concept into a new idiom. As with any translation, some things are lost and others gained in the process. For Josephus, one of the great advantages of his formulation was the avoidance of any explicit link to the kind of militaristic messianism possibly associated with the term "covenant." Another benefit was the opportunity to praise both the contemporary Jews and their forebears for being of such caliber as to secure the protection of the most powerful patron in the universe.

3.3 *The* Jewish War

The key passage to consider in the *Jewish War* is Josephus' account of his own attempt to persuade his compatriots to surrender rather than face the inevitable loss to the Romans of all they hold dear (*J.W.* 5.362–419). Interestingly, in this episode Josephus styles himself as exhorting his compatriots to "salvation" (παρακαλῶν πρὸς σωτηρίαν) (5.393; cf. 5.361). While the salvation of which he speaks is escape from the prospect of death by the sword or through famine, the terms in which Josephus couches his argument indicate that his argument has a far wider application as well.

Central to Josephus' exhortation is his conception of God's relationship both to the nations of the world in general and to the Jews in particular. As far as the nations are concerned, Josephus implies that each has its turn to exercise supreme power, and that Rome presently enjoys that position. Thus he urges his compatriots to desist from kicking against the inevitable and God-ordained ascendency of Rome.

> Fortune, indeed, had from all quarters passed over to [the Romans], and God who went the round of the nations, bringing to each in turn the rod of empire, now rested over Italy. (*J.W.* 5.367)[36]

Previous generations of Jews, Josephus argues, had realized this fact and so had submitted without shame to the superior might of Rome, knowing that "God was on the Roman side" (*J.W.* 5.368). Those now engaged in reckless combat with Rome should be aware that they "are warring not against the Romans only, but also against God" (*J.W.* 5.378).

It is in this general context that Josephus places his understanding of God's relationship to the Jews in particular. For while God may rotate "the rod of empire" from one nation to another, the Jews nevertheless, even without being blessed with universal ascendency, are "beloved of God" (θεοφιλεῖς) (*J.W.* 5.381). Josephus makes this point in the process of a highly idiosyncratic review of Jewish history in which he recounts the record of God's dealings with the Jews and tries to persuade his compatriots that God has never rewarded military activism, but only submission to the will of God (*J.W.* 5.376–412). Thus, he asks, "When did God who created the Jews fail to avenge them if they were wronged?" (*J.W.* 5.377) For example, when Abraham's wife Sarah was carried off by Pharaoh,[37] Abraham did not mount a military expedition to secure her return. Rather, counting his army of three hundred and eighteen officers "each in command of a boundless army"[38] as nothing, he lifted pure hands to the temple site[39] to enlist the help of the invincible Ally (ὁ ἀνίκητος βοηθός) (*J.W.* 5.380) who fought his battle for him. The same pattern is repeated throughout the Jews' national history, Josephus argues. When the people trusted God rather than their own devices they succeeded against all odds.

In the course of this exposition of the lessons of history, two sets of terminology for describing God emerge. The predominant set describes God in military terms as an ally (σύμμαχος, βοηθός) and general (στρατηγός). In a number of cases, however, this description of God is supplemented by

---

[36] On Josephus' treatment of the Romans in the *Jewish War* generally, see M. Stern, "Josephus and the Roman Empire as Reflected in the *Jewish War,*" in *Josephus, Judaism and Christianity* (ed. L. H. Feldman and G. Hata; Detroit: Wayne State University, 1987), 71–80.

[37] The version of the story given here is significantly different from that in either Genesis itself or in Josephus' paraphrase of the story in *Antiquities.* Instead of having Abraham and Sarah go down to Egypt themselves, this version of the story has Pharaoh invade Canaan and kidnap Sarah.

[38] An embellishment of Gen 14:14.

[39] This reference to the temple site in a story set in a period long before the temple (or even the tabernacle) existed is fascinating. It may reflect a priestly origin for this story.

another kind of terminology which uses legal language to describe God. Thus, in *J.W.* 5.389–390 when Josephus describes Cyrus' decision to grant the exiles their liberty, he speaks of their returning to Jerusalem to re-establish the temple-worship of their Ally (σύμμαχος). Josephus then argues that this illustrates his point that the Hebrew forebears did not triumph by resorting to arms, but rather, "if they sat still they conquered, as it pleased their Judge (κριτής). . . ." He makes a similar point a little later when he writes,

> Thus invariably have arms been refused to our nation, and warfare has been the sure signal for defeat. For it is, I suppose, the duty of the occupants of holy ground to leave everything to the arbitrament (δικάζειν) of God and to scorn human hands, can they but conciliate the Arbiter above (ὁ ἄνω δικαστής). (*J.W.* 5.400)

This proves to be a pivotal point in Josephus' argument for it allows him to introduce the key criterion for conciliating the divine arbiter, namely obedience to the stipulations of the "lawgiver" Moses (*J.W.* 5.401). Josephus' point is precisely that the Jewish revolutionaries have no claim to the ear of God or to his alliance because they have disregarded the requirements of the Law both with reference to general morality and insofar as they touch upon the temple. In a fit of pique he asks, "And after all this do you expect Him, thus outraged, to be your ally? Righteous suppliants are ye, forsooth, and pure the hands with which you appeal to your protector" (*J.W.* 5.403)! Along the same rhetorical lines, he adds, "It is surely madness to expect God to show the same treatment to the just as to the unjust" (*J.W.* 5.407). The clear implication is that the revolutionaries cannot expect the kind of miraculous deliverance from their enemies experienced by the people of God in biblical times because they have offended the One they are claiming to serve. Indeed, the very fact that the Romans had not yet been destroyed by God proved that this generation of Jews had not been judged (ἔκρινε) by God to be worthy of freedom (*J.W.* 5.408; also 5.396). In a telling rhetorical flourish at the conclusion of this section Josephus asks, "Can you persuade yourselves that God still remains with his household in their iniquity . . ." (*J.W.* 5.413)? His own answer to that question is starkly clear:

> My belief . . . is that the Deity has fled from the holy places and taken His stand on the side of those with whom you are now at war. (*J.W.* 5.412)

This takes to a new level what has already been said about God being on the side of the Romans. What we have seen up till now is only that in the grand scheme of the ascendency of nations, God has granted Rome universal rule. What has happened here, though, is that God, the divine Judge, who is usually the protector of those who honor him, has deserted the temple and taken his stand decisively in a particular battle. The cause of the revolutionaries is thus hopeless.

Even in these dire circumstances, though, Josephus still holds out a means of escape. "Yet a way of salvation (σωτηρίας ὁδός) is still left for you, if you will," he writes, "And the Deity is easily reconciled to such as confess and repent" (*J.W.* 5.415). It is significant at this point that Josephus does not call on the revolutionaries simply to surrender. Clearly the salvation of which Josephus is speaking here is more than the deliverance of the city from destruction, though that aspect is, of course, present. What Josephus has in mind goes beyond physical survival to the re-establishment of relationship with God. And the primary basis of that relationship is piety expressed through observance of the laws of Moses. Thus this whole section evinces a similar view of the divine-human relationship as the one already seen in *Antiquities*. While God's purposes on the grand historical scale are not subjected to analysis, God's dealings with Israel, nevertheless, are clearly predicated upon the Law of Moses.

One further passage from a context much earlier in the *Jewish War* will reinforce what we have found so far. This time Josephus uses the voice of Agrippa to express his views:[40]

> The only refuge then left to you is divine assistance (συμμαχία). But even this is ranged on the side of the Romans, for, without God's aid, so vast an empire could never have been built up. Consider, too, the difficulty of preserving your religious rules from contamination, even were you engaging a less formidable foe; and how, if compelled to transgress the very principles on which you chiefly build your hopes of God's assistance (σύμμαχος), you will alienate Him from you. . . . [I]f . . . you transgress the laws of your ancestors, I fail to see what further object you will have for hostilities, since your one aim is to preserve inviolate all the institutions of your fathers. How could you invoke the aid of the Deity, after deliberately omitting to pay Him the service which you owe Him? (*J.W.* 2.390–394)

Here again there is an unmistakable link between the alliance of God and obedience to the Law. Disregard of the Law will alienate God and undermine any claim the Jews might otherwise have to his favor.

Once again, the apologetic context of Josephus' account is clear and pervasive. Significantly, in the passages we have considered here Josephus' rhetoric is addressed as much to the Jews themselves as to any Gentile readers. While it might be contended that Josephus was concerned only to portray himself as opposed to war (for narrowly personal and selfish reasons), it should be noted that many years later, in his paraphrasing of the book of Daniel, he would hold to a position still in harmony with his position in the *Jewish War* (cf. *Ant.* 10.208–210).

---

[40] On Agrippa's speech generally, see M. Stern, "Josephus and the Roman Empire," 75–77; H. Lindner, *Die Geschichtsauffassung des Flavius Josephus im Bellum Judaicum. Gleichzeitig ein Beitrag zur Quellenfrage* (AGJU 12; Leiden: E. J. Brill, 1972), 21–25.

3.4 Against Apion

Our analysis of *Against Apion* will focus on the final quarter of the work, in which Josephus extols the virtues of Moses and the Law. It is important once again to remember the overriding concern with apologetics in Josephus' presentation. He tells us in *Ag. Ap.* 2.145 that in order to counter the charges of the likes of Apollonius Molon, Lysimachus and others who have maligned Moses as a charlatan and his laws as lessons in vice, he will set out "a brief account of our constitution as a whole and of its details." Josephus' purpose is to make clear that the Jews "possess a code excellently designed to promote friendly relations with each other, and humanity to the world at large, besides justice, hardihood, and contempt of death." And again, as was the case with the *Antiquities,* he is anxious to refute the slander that the Jews "are the most witless of all barbarians, and are consequently the only people who have contributed no useful invention to civilization" (*Ag. Ap.* 2.148). In a rousing conclusion to the whole work Josephus summarizes his presentation of the Law thus:

> Upon the laws it was unnecessary to expatiate. A glance at them showed that they teach not impiety but the most genuine piety; that they invite [us] not to hate [our] fellows, but to share [our] possessions; that they are the foes of injustice and scrupulous of justice, banish sloth and extravagance, and teach [us] to be self-dependant and to work with a will; that they deter [us] from war for the sake of conquest, but render [us] valiant defenders of the laws themselves; inexorable in punishment, not to be duped by studied words, always supported by actions. For actions are our invariable testimonials, plainer than any documents. I would therefore boldly maintain that we have introduced to the rest of the world a very large number of very beautiful ideas. What greater beauty than inviolable piety? What higher justice than obedience to the laws? What more beneficial than to be in harmony with one another, to be a prey neither to disunion in adversity, nor to arrogance and faction in prosperity; in war to despise death, in peace to devote oneself to crafts or agriculture; and to be convinced that everything in the whole universe is under the eye and direction of God? Had these precepts been either committed to writing or more consistently observed by others before us, we should have owed them a debt of gratitude as their disciples. If, however, it is seen that no one observes them better than ourselves, and if we have shown that we were the first to discover them, then the Apions and Molons and all who delight in lies and abuse may be left to their own confusion. (*Ag. Ap.* 2.291–295)

This passage very neatly captures Josephus' apologetic strategy in the entire work. It also gives important clues concerning our central concern in the present essay. The passage alludes to the role of God as ruler of the universe. Josephus' description of the rule of God here is an important datum in Josephus' understanding of the divine-human relationship in that it closely parallels the depiction of God as patron in the *Antiquities* and the picture of God rotating universal rule among the nations in the *Jewish War*. Josephus explains that when Moses was drawing up the constitution by which the Jewish people were to live he was unimpressed by the various forms of government practiced by other nations. This led him to formulate a new form of government called "theocracy" which "plac[ed] all sovereignty and authority in the hands of God" (*Ag. Ap.* 2.165).[41] A little later in the treatise Josephus asks, "Could there be a finer or more equitable polity than one which sets God at the head of the universe, which assigns the administration of its highest affairs to the whole body of priests, and entrusts to the supreme high-priest the direction of the other priests?" (*Ag. Ap.* 2.185). And again later he asserts, "The universe is in God's hands" (*Ag. Ap.* 2.190).

It is in this context of the universal rule of God that Josephus wants his readers to understand the Jews' obedience to their Law. For, as he remarks in *Ag. Ap.* 2.184, "For us, with our conviction that the original institution of the Law was in accordance with the will of God, it would be rank impiety not to observe it." Thus, Josephus' logic is uncomplicated and compelling in its own terms: God is the ruler of the universe; the Law is the expression of the will of God; the Jews, who are a deeply pious people, are naturally committed to obeying the Law. This is why, Josephus claims, there are so few transgressors of the Law among the Jews (*Ag. Ap.* 2.178). In *Ag. Ap.* 2.277 he writes, "There is not a Jew so distant from his country, so much in awe of a cruel despot, but has more fear of the Law than of him." This also explains the inherent conservatism among the Jews, which in turn explains their alleged uninventiveness in crafts or literature. For, as Josephus puts it:

> In the eyes of the world at large there is something fine in breaking away from all inherited customs; those who have the temerity to defy them are credited with the possession of consummate ability. To us, on the other hand, the only wisdom, the only virtue consists in refraining absolutely from every action and every thought that is contrary to the laws originally laid down. (*Ag. Ap.* 2.182–183)

This conviction also explains why the Jews are so famous for their willingness to die rather than disobey the Law. Indeed, Josephus suggests that in some instances Jews have been persecuted by tyrants for no other reason than that people wanted to see the strange spectacle of "[people] who believe that the only evil which can befall them is to be compelled to do any act or utter any word contrary to their laws" (*Ag. Ap.* 2.233). In another place Josephus reveals that this willingness to die for the Law is animated in part by a belief in the resurrection.[42] He writes:

> Each individual, relying on the witness of his own conscience and the lawgiver's prophecy, confirmed by the sure testimony of God, is firmly persuaded that to those who observe the laws and, if they must needs die for them, willingly meet death, God has granted a renewed existence and in the revolution of the ages the gift of a better

---

[41] This formulation is itself a development of similar ideas found in *Antiquities*. On this subject, see P. Spilsbury, "Points of Contact," 362–6.

[42] For a fuller discussion of Josephus' descriptions of existence after death, see J. Sievers, "Josephus and the Afterlife."

life. I should have hesitated to write thus, had not the facts made all . . . aware that many of our [compatriots] have on many occasions ere now preferred to brave all manner of suffering rather than to utter a single word against the Law. (*Ag. Ap.* 2.218–219)

This is the only place in *Against Apion* where we find an explicit reference to the future content of "salvation," namely life in the age to come. This is a belief which Josephus already held at the time of writing the *Jewish War*, for there he wrote concerning those who have died naturally (as opposed to by suicide):

. . . their souls, remaining spotless and obedient, are allotted that most holy place in heaven, whence, in the revolution of the ages, they return to find in chaste bodies a new habitation. (*J.W.* 3.374)

In this passage the hope is clearly of bodily resurrection, a hope which in another context is associated with the beliefs of the Pharisees (*J.W.* 2.163; cf. *Ant.* 18.14). What is most significant for our purposes is to note that in *Against Apion* it is a hope that is predicated upon the conviction that God is in supreme control of the universe, and that, ultimately, unswerving loyalty to him expressed through obedience to the Law will have its reward. Josephus' understanding of "salvation", therefore, if we might be permitted the term, is profoundly theological. God is the ruler of the world, and the Law given by Moses is the "constitution" whereby the people are governed.

In this conception there is no explicit reference to a special status for the Jews, for God is the ruler of the whole world. The only advantage the Jews have is their association with Moses, who in his extreme sagacity discovered the truth about God and formulated laws in keeping with God's will. Those who experience God's blessing, therefore, will be those who accept the Law as their "standard and rule" and who live under it "as under a father and master" (*Ag. Ap.* 2.174).

4. Conclusion

We may now bring our study to a conclusion. It is clear throughout his works that for Josephus the divine-human relationship is predicated upon obedience to the Law of Moses. This is because the Law represents the will of God, and as such is a detailed account of the means by which people might gain favor with God and experience his blessing. Although God is the ruler of the universe who grants to each nation in turn the "rod of empire", the Jews are particularly well situated because of their close connection to Moses, the man to whom God granted knowledge of the Law because of his great piety. At this point the words of the apostle Paul approximate Josephus' position:

> Then what advantage has the Jew? Or what is the benefit of circumcision? Great in every respect. First of all, that they were entrusted with the oracles[43] of God. (Rom 3:1–2)

As far as Josephus is concerned, this trust gives the Jews privileged access to God's favor, but only to the extent that they obey the Law faithfully. The Jews may regard God as their divine patron who will stand by them in times of need and prosper them in times of peace. This patronage, however, is directly connected to the Law which represents God's greatest benefaction. In other words, remaining in God's favor is not simply a matter of ethnic descent, as if physical descent from Abraham or Moses ensured God's patronage. Rather, each generation is required to live with a gratitude to God expressed through scrupulous obedience to the Law. In Josephus' own lifetime this meant that the destruction of Jerusalem and the temple could be explained as God's disgust at the impiety of those who caused the war against the Romans. It also meant that if Jews were to re-establish their position of favor with their divine patron, the way forward was clear. They needed to re-affirm their commitment to the Law of Moses and do everything in their power to shape their day-to-day lives by its requirements.

I suggested earlier that the term "patronal nomism" might serve as a descriptive title for Josephus' understanding of the functioning of Judaism. On the basis of the study we have undertaken here we might define this term as an exchange relationship in which people enjoy the blessings of God's patronage to the extent that they display gratitude in the practice of their lives for the divine benefaction which is God's law. As Josephus himself put it in *Ag. Ap.* 2.192, "Him must we worship by the practice of virtue."

Finally, we have often noted the apologetic motivation of everything Josephus wrote. We are thus obligated to acknowledge that Josephus' depiction of Judaism and its way of functioning might be little more than a propagandistic ploy to convince Gentiles of the essential piety of the Jews. However, what is far more likely is that in these works Josephus was indeed reflecting his own deeply held understanding of God's relationship with the Jews. Significantly, the Jews themselves are depicted as a people among the nations of the world. Gone is the notion of an eternal covenant ensuring a perpetual and exclusive relationship between God and Israel. In its place we find a view well suited to the social and political climate of Josephus' Rome. It is a view also well suited to the Jewish dilemma at the end of the first century. Here, at least as far as Josephus was concerned, was not only the

---

[43] The meaning of the term "oracles" here has been the subject of much debate. I am taking it, with D. Moo, to mean "the OT as a whole, with special reference . . . to the promises [of God]" (*The Epistle to the Romans* [NICNT; Grand Rapids: Eerdmans, 1996], 182). For a range of other suggestions, see the literature he cites.

explanation of the terrible events of 70 C.E., but also a blueprint for the reestablishment of God's favorable regard for the Jews.

10. Torah and Salvation in Tannaitic Literature

by

PHILIP S. ALEXANDER

הכל צפוי והרשות נתונה
All is foreseen, yet freedom of choice is given
Mishnah *'Abot* 3:16

1. "Torah," "Salvation" and "Tannaitic Literature"

The purpose of this essay is to explore the concept of salvation in the Tannaitic literature. "Salvation" is a vague term and must at this stage remain so, its precise meaning being left to emerge from a study of the texts. However, broadly speaking it denotes the supreme good (the *summum bonum*) to which humanity, individually or collectively, can attain, the state of blessedness in which the trials and tribulations of this life are transcended and the highest perfection realized. It always implies a dualism, though this will be felt and expressed with varying degrees of intensity – a contrast between the present wretched state of affairs and a longed-for ideal future, or conversely between the present blessedness and the misery that has been overcome. Judaism is a religion of salvation, and its two most comprehensive terms for this concept are ישועה and גאולה. Neither of these, nor the cognate verbs, is common in Tannaitic texts, but this does not mean that salvation was of little interest to the Tannaitic rabbis. On the contrary, the themes of "salvation" and "redemption" are central to Tannaitic Judaism, and, arguably, the focus of much of its literature. The Tannaitic rabbis presuppose the stress on "salvation" already present in the Hebrew Bible, where the verb ישע and its derived nouns ישועה and מושיע are frequently used to denote the saving acts of God (Gen 49:18; Exod 14:13,30; Isa. 45:17; and elsewhere). Normally these terms are associated with saving acts whereby God delivers Israel from some specific distress (exile, oppression by enemies, famine, pestilence), but implicit in the term is a general notion of what constitutes Israel's ultimate blessedness: "salvation," therefore, embraces both the state of felicity itself and the means by which it is realized.

Much of our discussion will focus on the role of Torah in the process of salvation. This is inevitable. Rabbinic Judaism is theistic. That is to say, it

believes in a God who created the world and continues to govern it. His
purpose for the world is, therefore, central to the definition of its supreme
good. The Torah is the expression of God's purpose, and, consequently, to
put it in very simple terms, salvation is bound up with obedience to the Torah
which is the expression of God's will. But there are complications which will
have to be explored. Torah is not a univocal concept in rabbinic Judaism, as
we shall presently see: it embraces both the written Scriptures and the oral
tradition. Is obedience to the Oral Torah as important as obedience to the
Written? And are there any factors which would mitigate the mechanistic
operation of the nexus between disobedience and punishment, and obedience
and reward?

The study is confined very strictly to the Tannaitic literature. This denotes
a collection of texts which supposedly record the teachings of the rabbinic
Sages who lived in Palestine from the first to the early third centuries C.E. It
includes the Mishnah, the Tosefta, the Baraitot of the Jerusalem and
Babylonian Talmuds, the *Mekhilta* of Rabbi Ishmael (on Exodus), *Sipra* (on
Leviticus) and *Sipre* (on Numbers and Deuteronomy). It also, commonly,
includes fragmentary works such as the *Mekhilta* of Rabbi Simeon bar Yohai,
Sipre Zuta and *Midrash Tannaim* which have been, somewhat speculatively,
reconstructed from quotations in the great medieval compendia of biblical
interpretation, *Midrash ha-Gadol* and *Yalqut Shim'oni*.[1] It is important to
realize at the very outset of our inquiry that these texts do not represent the
sum-total of Judaism in the first few centuries of the current era, or even,
necessarily, Jewish "orthodoxy" at this time. This literature is the product of
one particular religious party or movement within Judaism. But there were
other forms of Judaism. There was the Judaism of the Diaspora: it was to be
many years before Palestinian Rabbinate was to stamp its authority
comprehensively on many Diaspora communities. And there was also
"popular" Judaism within Palestine itself, that is to say Judaism as it was
practice by "ordinary" Jews who were not affiliated to the rabbinic movement. It would be wrong to assume that the Tannaitic literature reflects the
beliefs or practices of either of these non-rabbinic groups.

2. The Rise of Rabbinism after 70 C.E.

The extensive and complex Tannaitic corpus was produced by the emerging
rabbinic movement and must be interpreted in the light of the circumstances
in which it came to birth. Serious misunderstandings have arisen because it
has been read in a vacuum without regard to its social and historical setting.
History must in this case define the parameters of exegesis. It is essential to

---

[1] For an overview of this literature see Günter Stemberger, *Introduction to the Talmud and
Midrash* (2nd ed.; T. & T. Clark: Edinburgh, 1996).

realize that these documents, though the product of a party within Judaism, are not narrowly religious or sectarian. Rather they are manifestos of a movement which was bidding for political power in Israel and which, by the end of the Tannaitic period, had effectively achieved its political goals.[2] In the aftermath of the great war against Rome in 66–74 C.E., during which the Second Temple was destroyed, the rabbinic movement made a concerted effort to gain control of the Jewish communities of Palestine. But there was no sudden triumph of rabbinism.[3] Though the rabbis aspired to spiritual and political leadership, and set about creating a comprehensive constitution for post–70 Israel, they were opposed. Rabbinic literature designates one group of their opponents "the peoples of the land" (עמי הארץ). This may have been a loose coalition of landowners and farmers, whose influence would have been strong in the predominantly rural, agrarian economy of Palestine. They were resentful of the rabbis' strict interpretation of the agricultural laws of the Torah, such as tithes, which would have involved them in considerable financial loss.[4] The rabbis were also opposed by other more ideologically orientated groups, dubbed "sectarians" (מינים), who offered to Israel an alternative religious vision. The most important historically of those groups was the Jewish Christians (the נוצרים), who may have been a more significant force in second-century Palestine than is sometimes supposed.[5]

---

[2] I find it hard to believe that rabbinism finally triumphed through chance or serendipity. The rabbinic literature is shot through with political will. The cosy image sometimes projected of the rabbis as wise teachers rather meekly offering their fellow Jews advice on a range of narrowly "spiritual" issues is misleading. There is a steely determination in the early rabbinic texts and everywhere the implicit claim that the rabbis have the exclusive right to lead all Israel. The following offer valuable discussions of the rabbinic movement after 70: Martin Goodman, *State and Society in Roman Galilee, A.D. 132–212* (Totowa: Rowman & Allanheld, 1983); Catherine Hezser, *The Social Structure of the Rabbinic Movement in Roman Palestine* (Tübingen: Mohr [Siebeck], 1997); Shaye J. D. Cohen, "The Rabbi in Second-Century Jewish Society," in *The Cambridge History of Judaism*, vol. III (ed. W. Horbury et. al. ; Cambridge: Cambridge University, 1999), 922–90.

[3] The precise relationship of the rabbis to the pre–70 Pharisees is a matter of dispute. Despite the cautionary arguments to the contrary (see e.g., Shaye J. D. Cohen, "The Significance of Yavneh: Pharisees, Rabbis, and the End of Jewish Sectarianism," *HUCA* 55 [1984]: 27–53), the traditional view that there was a close link between the post–70 rabbis and the pre–70 Pharisees is probably correct. However, it is unlikely that the Pharisees wielded much political power in the period immediately preceding the first revolt. They had been politically important back in Hasmonaean times, but had subsequently become effectively a sect within Israel, concerned with narrowly religious issues. The transformation of this sect into a national political party in the post–70 period was one of the most important developments in the history of early Judaism. See further Roland Deines, *Die Pharisäer* (Tübingen: Mohr [Siebeck], 1997).

[4] The best analysis of the *'ammei ha-'aretz* remains Aharon Oppenheimer, The *'Am Ha-Aretz: A Study in the Social History of the Jewish People in the Hellenistic and Roman Period* (Brill: Leiden, 1977).

[5] The term מינים is broader than the Jewish Christians, but certainly includes them. The importance of the Jewish Christianity in second century Palestine and its influence on the development of rabbinic Judaism is much disputed. The striking lack of explicit reference to

The decisive turning-point in the fortunes of the rabbinic party occurred at the end of the second century C.E. when its leader, Judah, became the Patriarch of the Jewish community in Palestine. Judah was not only a scholar but also a wealthy landowner, with retainers, who could, if necessary, impose his will by physical force. And he probably enjoyed the confidence of the Roman administration. Tradition, almost certainly correctly, attributes to Judah the promulgation of the Mishnah, the first great codification of rabbinic law, which became the basis of study in the rabbinic schools not only of Palestine but of Babylonia as well, to which rabbinism spread in the early third century C.E. rabbinic power was further consolidated by the fact that by the early third century the rabbis seem to have reached some sort of accommodation with the "peoples of the land" whereby they moderated their advocacy of a strict interpretation of the "commandments pertaining to the Land" in return for political support. And they decisively saw off the challenge of the Jewish Christians, whose influence had been terminally weakened by the growing rift between Jewish and Gentile Christianity.[6]

Rabbinism was promoted through a number of channels in the Palestinian Jewish community. One was the synagogue. The synagogue was not a rabbinic institution in origin. It arose in the Diaspora and was imported into Palestine. Synagogues were probably relatively rare in Palestine before the destruction of the temple but increased rapidly after 70 to fill an obvious spiritual need. The rabbis did their best to ensure that the worship and the liturgy of the synagogue reflected rabbinic values and ideas. The synagogue was probably the major public forum in which the struggle with the מינים took place. Echoes of this struggle can be heard in both the Jewish and Christian accounts of the rabbis' attempt to impose on the synagogue the distinctive rabbinic version of the *'Amidah* with its public "cursing of the sectaries" (ברכת המינים).[7] Another instrument for imposing rabbinic authority on the synagogues may have been a new insistence on the centrality of the public reading of the Torah and on reading it in Hebrew, even when a vernacular translation was available. This would have been a particularly

---

Jewish Christianity in early rabbinic literature might simply indicate that Jewish Christians were of little significance in the rabbinic milieu. There is, however, another way of reading the evidence, viz., that a bitter power struggle was going on within the Jewish communities and that the "loud" silence of rabbinic literature on Christianity is a polemical ploy linked to the rabbis' claim that they represent the true continuity of Torah. Christian writers of the same period (e.g. Justin Martyr) took a diametrically opposed line: they confronted the conflict with Judaism head on. The rabbis chose to ignore Christianity, but their stance was equally polemical. See further my essay "'The parting of the ways' from the perspective of rabbinic Judaism," in *Jews and Christians: The Parting of the Ways A.D. 70 to 135* (Tübingen: Mohr [Siebeck], 1992), 1–25.

[6] See further my "The Parting of the Ways," 1–25.

[7] See my "Parting of the Ways," 6–11.

effective policy in rabbinizing Greek-speaking Jewish communities, where the custom of reading the Torah in Greek may have been the norm.[8]

Rabbinism also spread into the community at large through the law courts. The application of Roman law to Palestine allowed the local ethnic communities considerable legal autonomy. The Romans had neither the political will nor the bureaucracy to impose Roman law on all aspects of life. They reserved for their own jurisdiction criminal matters or matters where a state interest (such as state security) was involved, and left civil and private disputes to the local communities. There is growing evidence that a system of ethnic courts flourished in Palestine throughout the Roman period. This created a need for legal experts and the rabbis were willing and able to offer their services. They put themselves forward as skilled adjudicators and there was nothing to stop individuals submitting disputes to their arbitration, provided all parties agreed. In applying Jewish law through their courts the rabbis extended and clarified it. They played a rather similar role in the development of Jewish law to that played by the early jurisprudents in the development of Roman law. The jurisprudents were originally men of good family and private means who made themselves expert in the interpretation and application of the Law of the XII Tables. In earliest times the jurisprudents were not state-appointed: they exercised influence because they were widely respected and because the quality of the justice which they administered was seen to be good. So the rabbis were able, by providing a good quality adjudication service, to exert increasing influence on the communities in which they lived.[9]

However, the most powerful instrument for the dissemination of rabbinism was the rabbinic school, the Beit Midrash. The rabbis' powerbase lay in their schools, which were scattered through the coastal plain of Palestine and the Galilee. The schools often comprised no more than a teacher and a small circle of students (תלמידי הכמים), and they did not necessarily possess a dedicated building in which to meet. Many were transitory, and did not survive the demise of the teacher. After his death the students scattered, some going back into secular life, some joining other schools, and perhaps a few attempting to set up school on their own account. Only in rare cases did one of the students succeed the teacher and continue the school into the next

---

[8] There seems to be little doubt that the Greek versions of Aquila and Symmachus were produced in Palestine under rabbinic auspices. The peculiarities of Aquila can be explained if the version was meant as "crib" to help Greek-speaking Jews to learn Hebrew. The rabbinic attitude to Bible translations was initially somewhat contradictory. In the end, however, the rule became that the Torah must be heard in Hebrew, whether or not a translation was also provided. By Byzantine times the Greek Diaspora seems to have been universally observing that rule – an indication of the spread of rabbinic authority

[9] See further my essay, "Quid Athenis et Hierosolymis? Rabbinic Midrash and Hermeneutics in the Graeco-Roman World," in *A Tribute to Geza Vermes* (ed. Philip R. Davies and Richard T. White; Sheffield Academic: Sheffield 1990), 101–24.

generation. Despite their tenuous existence and primitive organization the rabbinic schools showed enormous intellectual vitality. They were the distinctive rabbinic institution, the bastion of rabbinism within Palestinian Judaism. They devoted themselves to the study of Scripture and of tradition, and developed a worldview which was to become the basis of Judaism down to modern times. The Torah to which they applied themselves was seen as more than just the written text of the Books of Moses: it embraced also traditions passed down from former generations, as well as extensions and clarifications of the Mosaic writings which emerged from the discussions of the Sages. Study was a religious duty; indeed, rabbinically speaking, it was *the* religious duty: it formed the character, suppressed the evil inclination (יצר הרע) and was a pre-requisite for the fulfillment of the Torah on which salvation, individual and collective, depended[10].

The schools were religious associations of a type well attested in the Greco-Roman world of the time. They influenced the general community in a number of ways. They attracted young, idealistic men, formed them spiritually and intellectually and sent them back into the community, perhaps to act, when need arose, as arbitrators (דיינים), but certainly to live the rabbinic way of life. The rabbinic movement encouraged young men to study in their Batei Midrash and it was inevitable that this should sometimes have provoked opposition, because it deprived the young men's families for a time of their physical labor and support. While they were studying at the Beit Midrash, the young men were not economically active and the burden on their families would have been doubled, if the families were also expected to find the funds to support their sons while they were studying. The schools sought to mitigate this problem by eliciting voluntary donations to finance their students, and they promoted such support as a highly meritorious religious act. This call for funds was not only a financial necessity, but good psychology as well, since it provided a means by which the community at large could (quite literally) buy into the schools and feel that it had a stake in the success of the rabbinic enterprise.[11] The schools also influenced the community at large in another way. They were distinctive religious organizations, which lived a communal life within their host societies marked

---

[10] We shall return to these points in greater detail presently. The first clearly documented example of such schools in Judaism is the Qumran community. Though scholastically speaking it possesses some unusual features, within the typology of institutions the most satisfactory classification of Qumran is as a school. Indeed, it is arguably the first recorded Yeshivah. It was, however, much larger and more wealthy, and lasted longer, than the immediately post–70 rabbinic Batei Midrash. Only from the third century onwards do rabbinic schools emerge to rival Qumran in size and continuity.

[11] The story in *'Abot de Rabbi Nathan* A.6 of Eliezer ben Hyrcanus's conflict with his father over his determination to study in the school of Yohanan ben Zakkai, whether factual or not, surely reflects accurately the sort of tension which must have arisen within families when able-bodied young men decided to go off to Yeshivah.

by distinctive behavior and etiquette and, possibly, even distinctive dress. They followed a rabbinic code which marked them off to some degree from their fellow Jews as holy men. This was quite deliberate: the schools in general and the great Sages in particular were portrayed as embodiments of Torah, as Torah incarnate. They were exemplars whose every action lived out Torah. Just as the תלמידי הכמים were exhorted not only to listen to their masters' teachings but to observe their every act, so the community at large was exhorted to observe, respect and, if possible, emulate the way of life of the schools and their Sages.

3. The Tannaitic Literature and its Theology

It is against this historical background, which I have lightly sketched in, that the Tannaitic literature must be read. Recalling the history of the rabbinic party after 70 reminds us that the rabbis were fully engaged in the political and social life of their communities and that what they worked to achieve was a Jewish polity which was obedient, as far as was possible, to the *whole* Torah of Moses. For several centuries two broad forms of Judaism had, in effect, existed side by side – the Judaism of the Land of Israel and the Judaism of the Diaspora. The Judaism of the Diaspora did not observe the whole Torah, and, indeed, was not obliged to do so. The Judaism of "exile" was a restricted Judaism, which through social, political and historical circumstances had come to emphasize the more narrowly religious aspects of the Torah. This form of Judaism could have been imported into Palestine in the post–70 period: Jews could have lived an "exilic" existence even within the borders of the Land (many probably did so); but the rabbinic movement set its face against such a position and strove to maximize the application and observance of the Torah.

The Tannaitic literature in the form in which we now have it is all a product of the rabbinic schools. It falls into two broad types: codification and Bible commentary. Codification covers Mishnah, Tosefta and the Baraitot; Bible commentary covers the so-called Tannaitic Midrashim. One of the most vexed questions in the study of early rabbinic literature is the relationship, both literary and theological, between these two types of text. Codification as found in the Mishnah seems at first reading to stand in remarkable independence from Scripture. It has its own thematic arrangement and its own agenda which often make little explicit reference to Scripture. And yet there is clearly a strong underlying relationship. Mishnah seems to present itself essentially as a restatement and clarification of the Written Torah of Moses. Some have argued that it has emerged basically through exegesis of Scripture and that between its present free-standing form and Scripture we must interpose an exegetical phase of development, more directly linked to Scripture. The Mishnah took the results of this exegesis and rearranged them in a more systematic and topical way. Having come this far in the argument it is tempting to postulate the Tannaitic Midrashim, in whole or in part, as the exegetical bridge between Mishnah and Scripture. There are, however, problems with this hypothesis. It overestimates the exegetical component in the Mishnah and underestimates its customary element which has no, or virtually no, connection with Scripture.

The alternative, and rather less problematic, view is to take the Tannaitic Midrashim as basically post-Mishnaic in origin, as an attempt to read Scripture in the light of Mishnah and to provide were possible biblical justification for the Mishnaic rulings. The Mishnah can thus be seen as generative of all subsequent rabbinic literature. The fundamental form which rabbinic intellectual activity assumed after the promulgation of the Mishnah was commentating – commentating on the one hand directly on the Mishnah (which leads eventually to the Gemarot of the two Talmuds), commenting on the other hand directly on Scripture in the light of the Mishnah (which leads eventually to the Midrashim). That there is a strong relationship between the Tannaitic Midrashim and the Mishnah is not in dispute: *Sipra* and, to a lesser extent, *Sipre* Numbers, share large blocks of text in common with the Mishnah. Analysis of these blocks in their midrashic context usually shows that they are not in any meaningful sense exegeted out of Scripture. Rather they are more or less apposite quotations from the Mishnah which have been simply (and sometimes rather crudely) juxtaposed to Scripture in order to suggest their biblical bases, without any attempt being made to argue rigorously the nature of the link[12].

Whichever view we take, it is clear that the Mishnah and the Tannaitic Midrashim have emerged from the same literary and historical milieu and share a broadly similar worldview. However, we must be careful not to assume that they are all saying precisely the same thing. The questions regarding Torah and salvation which we shall address to this literature do not come easily to it. They are essentially theological questions but the Tannaitic writings are not systematic theological treatises. They are legal or homiletical. They do contain theological propositions and themes which they may profoundly explore and which in aggregate may be taken loosely to constitute the Tannaitic worldview, or the worldview of the document in which they are found, but these separate propositions are seldom considered together, and never synthesized into a coherent theology. They often stand in mutual tension, or even contradiction, with little attempt being made to recognize let

---

[12] For recent important discussions of this problem, with particular reference to *Sipra*, the key text in the debate, see Jacob Neusner, *Uniting the Dual Torah: Sifra and the Problem of the Mishnah* (Cambridge: Cambridge University, 1990), and Ronen Reichman, *Mishna und Sifra: Ein literarkritischer Vergleich paralleler Überlieferungen* (Tübingen: Mohr [Siebeck], 1998). Older literature is cited in Stemberger, *Introduction to Talmud and Midrash*, 247.

alone resolve the contradictions. The broad emphasis is homiletical and exhortatory rather than theological. Rhetoric predominates over philosophy. Sometimes one theological theme is vigorously pursued, sometimes another, with little regard to overall theological coherence.[13]

These tensions and contradictions faithfully mirror the theological tensions and contradictions of Scripture itself. This is particularly evident in the case of the Tannaitic Midrashim. The general impression one gets from reading these commentaries is how strongly they are running with the grain of Scripture.[14] They present few theological propositions which are not apparently to be found on the surface of Scripture itself. This is not to suggest that the rabbinic position is simply identical with biblical religion, whatever that may be. Rabbinic Judaism, historically speaking, has developed well beyond the Judaism of the Second Temple period, let alone the Judaism of earlier eras, but it is remarkably easy on the face of it to justify its principal theological positions from Scripture. Over large sections the Tannaitic Midrashim simply accept the agenda of the Scripture on which they are commenting. One does not get the impression that they are constantly bending Scripture to serve a radically different agenda. The stress in some modern study of midrash on the discontinuity between Scripture and midrash can be misleading, at least as far as Tannaitic midrash is concerned.[15] This close congruence between the Tannaitic Midrashim and Scripture raises the acute methodological question of how far the views of the underlying biblical text should be factored into the message of the midrash. There is no easy solution to this problem. On the one hand we should obviously be careful not to carry over biblical ideas wholesale wherever the midrashim appear to accept unquestioningly the biblical agenda. On the other hand a reading of the Tannaitic Midrashim based exclusively on a principle of dissimilarity or discontinuity with the Bible

---

[13] I have assumed throughout my analysis a traditional, scholastic definition of theology, such as one would find classically in Thomism. Such a definition would not, of course, be espoused by all theologians, and it is possible that the Tannaitic sources could be seen as fitting more successfully into modern paradigms which define theology in more contextual or narrative terms. My claim that the Tannaitic sources lack ultimate theological coherence does not, I think, conflict with Jacob Neusner's claim that the Mishnah should be read as a philosophical text. Neusner addresses the deep structure of the Mishnah as reflected in its taxonomical principles; I address its surface structures as expressed in its overt theological propositions. See J. Neusner, *Judaism as Philosophy: The Method and Message of the Mishnah* (Baltimore and London: Johns Hopkins University, 1999).

[14] The rabbis would have had no hesitation in claiming that one can and indeed should create a biblical theology. Indeed the Tannaitic sources can be seen as one of the earliest attempts to produce such a theological construction. They accepted the traditional Scriptures in their totality and assumed, as a fundamental hermeneutical principle, that those Scriptures were utterly coherent, whether or not this appeared on the surface to be the case.

[15] Starting with the Amoraic period, rabbinic Bible commentary does increasingly work against the grain of Scripture, till in the Middle Ages a reaction set in and there was a powerful reassertion of the simple (פשט) sense.

would be equally distorting. Each case has to be considered on its merits and judgment exercised. In general, however, it can be confidently affirmed that the theology of the Tannaitic Midrashim is broadly congruent with a biblical theology based on the assumption of the unity and coherence of Scripture.

Rabbinic Judaism was to bequeath the tensions and contradictions of its own position to the Jewish theologians of the Amoraic and post-Talmudic periods, who did their best with the material at their disposal to produce a coherent rabbinic theology. A truly systematic rabbinic theology, however, does not begin to emerge till the early Middle Ages.[16] This medieval theology is of great value for understanding the early sources. Indeed, a major weaknesses of many modern theologies of Tannaitic Judaism is that they have been constructed by scholars insufficiently acquainted with the Amoraic and early medieval developments. One must, of course, be very sensitive to problems of anachronism, but the Amoraic and medieval sages offer us a close and authoritative reading of the Tannaitic texts, from within the same ongoing rabbinic tradition, that we ignore at our peril. In trying to expound the Tannaitic views on Torah and salvation I shall naturally proceed more or less systematically, noting tensions and seeking for ways within the thinking of the texts to resolve them, but it should be understood at the outset just how speculative this approach can be. For didactic purposes it is inevitable that I should be somewhat systematic, but as a result my exposition will have a rounded, almost medieval feel to it that will be challenged the moment we return to the original sources. In the context of the present volume, it is impossible to set out a clear and consistent Tannaitic position on Torah and salvation which can be compared with the views of Paul (which also, of course, may not be systematic). Modern interpreters may join up (like dots scattered on a page) the discrete Tannaitic theologoumena in different ways to present quite different pictures of Tannaitic theology. Depending on where they start and how they prioritize the different elements, they may produce in the end either a theology of "works-righteousness" or of "grace," or of any number of mediating positions in between. There is absolutely no reason to suppose that the Tannaitic authorities when they stress that righteousness is determined strictly by the extent to which one keeps the commandments of the Torah expect the hearer mentally to qualify this with the idea that God is merciful and will not rigorously enforce the law. Conversely there is no reason to suppose that when they expatiate in glowing terms on the love, mercy and grace of God, they are expecting the hearer mentally to qualify this with the thought that actually God does expect his commandments to be obeyed and will assuredly punish the sinner if they are not. And when they do boldly juxtapose justice and mercy, law and grace, they make no serious

---

[16] One of the earliest and most influential of these systematic rabbinic theologies was the *Book of Beliefs and Opinions* of Saadya Gaon (882–942).

attempt to reconcile the tensions between them, but emphasize the one or the other according to their immediate homiletic purpose.

There have been a number of notable attempts to set out a theology of Tannaitic Judaism. It is probably no accident that in modern times some of the earliest and most influential of these were written by scholars from Christian background.[17] On the whole Jewish scholars have not been interested in constructing theologies of Tannaitic Judaism, and when they have shown interest it has generally been in response, directly or indirectly, to Christian efforts. Christians were the first in this field and have largely set its agenda. The most influential of these early theologies of classic rabbinic Judaism was F. Weber's *System der altsynagogalen palästinischen Theologie aus Targum, Midrasch und Talmud* (2nd ed. 1880).[18] There are numerous problems with Weber's work: his knowledge of the rabbinic literature is very derivative; he synthesizes ideas from diverse and incompatible sources; and in general his account is permeated by an anti-Jewish animus which is determined to depict Judaism as nothing more than a dry, legalistic works-righteousness. A much more informed and sympathetic account of Tannaitic Judaism was offered by Ed Sanders in his influential study *Paul and Palestinian Judaism: A Comparison of Patterns of Religion* (London: SCM, 1977). This too, however, is not without its problems. Sanders belongs to a line of interpreters of Tannaitic Judaism who have tended, often in conscious rejection of Weber, to stress its "liberal" side. It is surely significant that most of these scholars have either been Christians of liberal Protestant background or Jews arguably influenced by liberal Protestant ideas. One of the most impressive, and clearly a major influence on Sanders, is George Foot Moore.[19] Also apparently influential were the Jewish scholars Solomon Schechter and Claude Goldsmid Montefiore. Montefiore, one of the founders of Liberal Judaism in Britain, was educated at Balliol College, Oxford, where he was taught by Benjamin Jowett. Montefiore was deeply interested in Protestant theology. Schechter, who was later to become a leading light of

---

[17] This is not to deny that Jewish scholars produced important theologies of Judaism in the 18th, 19th and 20th centuries. Moses Mendelssohn, for all his avowed attempts to play down the role of dogma in Judaism, can be seen as a significant Jewish theologian (note his classic *Jerusalem,* published in 1783). One thinks also of the work of Nachman Krochmal (*Moreh Nevukhei ha-Zeman,* published posthumously in 1851 by Leopold Zunz), and Hermann Cohen (*Religion der Vernunft aus den Quellen des Judentums,* published posthumously in 1919). The Reform theologian Kaufmann Kohler issued his pioneering *Jewish Theology* in the 1918. In the interwar years we have Jewish theologians of the stature of Franz Rosenzweig (*Der Stern der Erlösung,* 1921) and Martin Buber (*Ich und Du,* 1923). None of these, however, offers a theology specifically of Tannaitic Judaism. They tend to take as their starting point, explicitly or implicitly, the medieval Jewish theologians, particularly Maimonides.

[18] A revised version appeared in 1897 under the title *Jüdische Theologie auf Grund des Talmud und verwandter Schriften* (Leipzig: Dörffling und Francke, 1897).

[19] *Judaism in the First Centuries of the Christian Era: The Age of the Tannaim,* vols. I–III (Cambridge: Harvard University, 1927).

Conservative Judaism in the States, was a protégé of Montefiore, who brought him to England to be his tutor in Talmud. Montefiore urged Schechter to write a theology of Judaism, and seems to have helped to educate him theologically. Montefiore probably regarded the creation of a theology of Judaism as a way of displaying Judaism to full advantage, of gaining respect for it in Christian eyes and of promoting Jewish-Christian dialogue. Schechter, though he struggled to meet Montefiore's wishes, never finished the work: he may have balked at the complexity of the task. His widely read and modestly titled little volume *Aspects of Rabbinic Theology*,[20] and a few other theological essays, are presumably fragments of the uncompleted *magnum opus*. It may have been disappointment at Schechter's failure to produce the *Theology* that stimulated Montefiore to compile his own *Rabbinic Anthology*, which presents the primary sources for a theology of classic rabbinic Judaism with comments.[21] It is not too difficult to demonstrate that all these works, to greater or lesser degree, have been influenced by liberal Protestantism. All seem tacitly to regard it as axiomatic that a religion of works-righteousness is inferior to a religion of grace. Weber had accused Judaism of legalistic works-righteousness. They set out to defend it against this charge, but nowhere does any of them radically question the premise that there is something wrong with a religion of works-righteousness. Though they are better informed about classic Judaism and write about it in a more respectful and sympathetic way, scholars such as Moore and Sanders may also be in danger of distorting it by forcing it into a typology which it does not fit. Where Weber overemphasized law, they may be overemphasizing grace.[22]

---

[20] First published 1909 (London: Macmillan) and often reprinted.

[21] Claude G. Montefiore and Herbert Loewe, *A Rabbinic Theology: Selected and Arranged with Comments and Introductions* (London: Macmillan, 1938). Montefiore and Loewe were anticipated, to some extent, by A. Cohen's *Everyman's Talmud*, in its way an exemplary work, which first appeared in 1931, was reissued in a revised edition in 1948 and reprinted several times since (e.g., New York: Schocken, 1975 and 1978). Cohen was a representative of enlightened English Orthodoxy, which nowadays would be closer to Conservative or even right-wing Reform Judaism. Again the idealizing and liberalizing slant of his interpretations are obvious. Schechter certainly did not endorse Montefiore's views (he famously described them as "not Liberal Judaism, but Liberal Christianity"), but that he too in some measure was influenced by liberalism seems beyond doubt. Montefiore also influenced another pioneering study of early Jewish theology, J. Abelson's *The Immanence of God in Rabbinical Literature* (London: Macmillan, 1912). On Montefiore see Daniel R. Langton, "Claude Montefiore and Christianity: Did the Founder of Anglo-Liberal Judaism lean too far," *JJS* 50 (1999): 98–119. Important though it is, we cannot here trace the complex history of these trends in modern Jewish thought. Suffice to note that the liberalizing tendency can be traced back at least to Abraham Geiger, on whom see Susannah Heschel, *Abraham Geiger and the Jewish Jesus* (Chicago and London: University of Chicago, 1998).

[22] Ephraim E. Urbach's *The Sages: Their Concepts and Beliefs* (Magnes Press: Jerusalem, 1975), is perhaps the most notable attempt by an orthodox Jewish scholar to write a theology of classic rabbinic Judaism. Though Urbach's mastery of the relevant sources is unquestionable, the

Ed Sanders's work was influential and for a time widely accepted. More recently, however, his conclusions have been challenged and the rabbinic evidence examined afresh. Among the more recent discussions Friedrich Avemarie's monograph *Tora und Leben: Untersuchungen zur Heilsbedeutung der Tora in der frühen rabbinischen Literatur*[23] deserves special mention. This is a highly competent and subtle analysis of the rabbinic texts, to which it is impossible to do full justice here. A few points must suffice. Avemarie correctly stresses the inconsistency of the rabbinic texts. He comes, in effect, to the conclusion that a dispassionate reading of these suggests that salvation can be either through law or through grace. The rabbis choose to emphasize one or other of these means depending on the situation which they are addressing. This comes very close to the position argued in the present paper. However, one should be very cautious how one interprets this inconsistency. There is a strong temptation to assume that it involves some profound theological strategy, or to postulate a worldview which makes such a contradictory position rational. I suspect that what lies behind it is simply fidelity to Scripture, which is just as inconsistent as the rabbis are on this point. The rabbis were perfectly capable of accepting two contradictory statements as equally "words of the living God," if both were derived by correct method from Scripture. The implication may be, if we really want a rationalization of such a paradoxical viewpoint, that the contradiction exists only at the level of human understanding, but presumably does not exist at the level of the mind of God.

4. Torah and Salvation in the Mishnah

Initially the correct way to proceed in analyzing the theology of the Tannaitic sources is document by document. Though all the texts emanate from the same small, closed circles, it should not be simply assumed, as we have already noted, that they are all saying exactly the same things and can be harmonized at will. We begin with the Mishnah, the central document of the Tannaitic corpus, which was edited, according to tradition, around 210 C.E. by Judah ha-Nasi. The Mishnah is essentially a law-code, but it contains one tractate, *m. 'Abot*, which is aggadic rather than halakhic in character.

---

work is somewhat disappointing. It displays a rather uncritical use of the sources and it lacks theological acumen. It also came late into the field and is largely content to follow the established agenda.

[23] TSAJ 55; Tübingen: Mohr (Siebeck), 1996; see also his essays, "Bund als Gabe und Recht. Zum Gebrauch von *berît* in rabbinischen Literatur," in *Bund und Tora. Zur theologischen Begriffsgeschichte in alttestamentlicher, frühjüdischer und urchristlicher Tradition* (WUNT 92; ed. F. Avemarie and H. Lichtenberger; Tübingen: Mohr [Siebeck], 1996), 176–224; and "Erwählung und Vergeltung. Zur optionalen Struktur rabbinischer Soteriologie," *NTS* 45 (1999): 108–26.

Mishnah *'Abot* is of particular relevance to the present inquiry since it contains numerous explicit theological propositions, in contrast to the rest of Mishnah, where the theology is largely implicit. The relationship of *m. 'Abot* to the rest of the Mishnah has long been a matter of debate.[24] It probably dates from around 250 C.E., somewhat later than the main body of the work. Its text, unlike the text of the rest of the Mishnah, is rather fluid. Three recensions of it are extant: one is found in the major manuscripts of the Mishnah; the other two are embedded respectively in the A and B recensions of the *'Abot de Rabbi Nathan*. And, of course, the sixth chapter, *Qinyan Torah*, is a medieval addition. Clearly whoever attached *m. 'Abot* to the Mishnah intended it to supplement the halakhic material of the Mishnah in some way. It is hard not to conclude that it is meant to state the ethical and theological principles that were perceived as undergirding the halakah. We shall treat it as being of one piece with the Mishnah and give it particular weight in our discussion, though strictly speaking it is post-Mishnaic and probably represents the earliest attempt to make explicit some of the theological premises of the Mishnah.

4.1 Salvation and the Summum Bonum in the Mishnah

First we must give some consideration to the question of what is the nature of salvation in the Mishnah. Salvation for the Mishnah seems first and foremost to be national rather than individual. This is implicit in its whole structure and program, and accords with the political aspirations of the rabbinic party. Salvation involves Israel living in peace and freedom in her own Land, following the Torah and reaping the rewards which come from obedience to God's law. The theocratic polity which the Mishnah describes in detail is an ideal polity which each Israelite must strive to realize. It postulates, therefore, as do all schemes of salvation, a certain dualism between "this world" and "the world to come," but that dualism is not strongly apocalyptic in coloring. There is little or no messianism in the Mishnah: the Messiah simply does not figure in its worldview. There may be historical reasons for this. After the disastrous Bar Kokhba war, during which Bar Kokhba had been hailed as Messiah, there was an understandable turning away from messianism. The emphasis in rabbinic Judaism moved towards constructing by peaceful means a righteous, civil and Torah-centered society here and now. Some elements of classic messianism (the resurrection of the dead, the concept of a world to come, the messianic banquet) do survive in the Mishnah,[25] but they are effectively residual. That they are there is hardly

---

[24] See Louis Finkelstein, *Mavo le-Massekhtot 'Avot ve-'Abot de-Rabbi Natan* (New York: Jewish Theological Seminary, 1950); Alexander Guttmann, "Tractate Abot – Its Place in Rabbinic Literature," *JQR* 41 (1950): 181–93. A useful overview of the problem is provided by Anthony J. Saldarini, *Scholastic Rabbinism* (Chico: Scholars, 1982).

[25] See note 51 below.

surprising: rabbinic Judaism came out of a Second Temple tradition so steeped in apocalyptic ideas that it would have been strange if it had lost all trace of this heritage. But the concept of "the world to come" seems to have weakened in the Mishnah to denote little more than the state of affairs which will result from the successful implementation of its religious and political program. And that program will be achieved by the obedience and piety of the individual Jew, not through some dramatic divine intervention in history, or through the agency of a messianic redeemer. These apocalyptic ideas were probably kept alive in the rabbinic milieu in synagogue prayers such as the *'Amidah* and in the Targum (neither of which is in origin a rabbinic text), but in the immediate aftermath of the Bar Kokhba debacle the rabbinic party seems to have had little truck with them. The seeds of apocalyptic and messianism which the Mishnah did preserve were to spring to life again in the late Talmudic period, and from then onwards messianism, in the full-blooded sense of the term, was to become one of the cardinal doctrines of rabbinic Judaism.[26] The Mishnah also speaks of salvation in individual terms. As we shall see the righteous are personally rewarded for observance of the Torah, but this individual salvation must be seen within the context of national salvation. Each Israelite is commanded to observe the Torah in all its fullness in order to bring in the kingdom of God. The ultimate reward for the individual is to have "a portion in the world to come," that is to say, to have a share in the blessings of that kingdom, and, if need be, to be brought back from the dead to enjoy Israel's future national felicity which he has helped to bring about. The Mishnah also speaks of the righteous being rewarded here and now (for example with a sense of the divine presence), but reward in the present is not guaranteed, and when it occurs it should be seen as an anticipation of the rewards of the "world to come."[27]

4.2 The Nature and Limits of Torah

Torah plays a central role in the soteriology of *m. 'Abot* and of the Mishnah as a whole. Torah in the Mishnah clearly means more than just the Five Books of Moses. This is implicit in the famous theologoumenon with which *m. 'Abot* opens:[28]

---

[26] See further my essay, "The King Messiah in Rabbinic Judaism," in *King and Messiah in Israel and the Ancient Near East* (ed. John Day; Sheffield: Sheffield Academic, 1998), 456–73. There I argue that messianism was always an element of "popular" Judaism in the Talmudic period, and it was under pressure of popular ideas that it was adopted into rabbinic Judaism in the late Talmudic period. However, the rabbis attempted to rabbinize it by making it an incentive for obedience to the Torah: the Messiah would come, if all Israel would keep the Torah. It was the apocalyptic revival of the seventh century (inspired largely by the rise of Islam) which entrenched messianism in rabbinic theology. Thus it plays a major part in the first great work of rabbinic theology, Saadya's *Book of Beliefs and Opinions*.

[27] See further below on reward and punishment.

[28] In quoting the Mishnah I have followed generally the translations of Herbert Danby, *The*

Moses received the Torah from Sinai and passed it on to Joshua, and Joshua to the elders, and the elders to the prophets; and the prophets passed it on to the men of the Great Synagogue. They said three things: Be deliberate in judgement, raise up many disciples, and make a fence around the Torah.

Traditional commentators gloss Torah here as "Oral Torah," but significantly this term is not actually used.[29] However, it is evident that what is in view cannot simply be the Written Torah. Torah here seems to mean a whole complex of tradition and teaching, both written and oral, which, it is claimed, was passed down from Moses through a secure line of tradents to the Tannaitic rabbis. Mishnah *'Abot* is offering a pedigree for the Mishnah: the Mishnah is Torah. When we turn to the content of the Mishnah itself for clarification as to what Torah means, we find that it embraces a number of distinct elements: there is biblical law, which in the Mishnah is restated in a more topical, systematic form; there are clarifications and extensions of biblical law; and there are traditional practices and customs. All three elements are woven in the Mishnah into a seamless fabric which *m. 'Abot* calls Torah.

Later rabbinic theology was to try to unpack this assertion, by formulating the doctrine of the Two Torahs – the Written and the Oral, which were both given to Moses on Sinai.[30] There was considerable dispute as to what exactly was the content of the Oral Torah which Moses received. According to one view it was the whole of the rabbinic tradition. This position was bolstered by the claim that the students simply passed on verbatim from their teachers the doctrine and tradition which they had received.[31] But this view of the content of the Oral Torah given to Moses on Sinai creates very obvious problems. The tradition as contained in the Mishnah clearly includes statements in the name of masters (Yohanan ben Zakkai, Eliezer ben Hyrcanus, Ishmael, Aqiva and a host of others) who lived long after Sinai. The natural assumption is that these Sages were the authors of the statements that are transmitted in their names. But then how can one claim that what they are uttering had been given as Torah to Moses on Sinai? One ingenious attempt to solve this problem was the suggestion that when Moses went up to receive the Torah he heard the Holy One reciting the traditions in the name of the masters who would later deliver them.[32] The assertion is intriguing and

---

Mishnah (Oxford: Oxford University, 1974), with modifications.

[29] The term "Oral Torah" (*Torah she-be 'al peh*) appears to have come into vogue only in the Amoraic period.

[30] See Peter Schäfer, "Das 'Dogma' von der mündlichen Torah im rabbinischen Judentum," in *Studien zur Geschichte und Theologie des rabbinischen Judentums* (Leiden: Brill, 1978), 153–97; David Weiss Halivni, *Revelation Restored: Divine Writ and Critical Responses* (Boulder: Westview, 1997), 54–75.

[31] For the idea that the whole content of both Torahs was given to Moses on Sinai see e.g., *Sipra* 269 [*Be-huqqotai* 8]; *y. Pe'ah* 10:4 [10a]; *b. Ber.* 5a. For the idea that the students repeated verbatim the traditions received from his teachers see e.g., *b. 'Erub.* 54b.

[32] *Pesiq. Rab Kah.* 4:7.

raises a host of questions which are not answered. It well illustrates how little the rabbis were interested in working out a theologically coherent position. Is the implication here that the Holy One in his omniscience foresaw (and endorsed?) what the rabbis were later to say by way of clarification and extension of the Torah? Whatever the rabbis working within the tradition were to deduce from the Torah had divine sanction. Or is the idea that the rabbis were present in soul at Sinai and heard these traditions, later to recall them by a kind of Platonic *anamnesis*?[33] An alternative view suggested that what was given to Moses on Sinai was only the correct principles (מדות) for the interpretation of the Written Torah and that the Oral Torah emerged over the generations through the application of these principles.[34] These subtleties are beyond *m. 'Abot* and the Mishnah which are content simply to assert that Torah is a complex entity consisting of both Scripture and Tradition, and that that Torah is in the Sages' possession and is transmitted by them.

Torah is seen by the Mishnah essentially as a system of "commandments" (מצוות), which as expressions of the will of God must be obeyed. It classifies these commandments topically under a number of heads: laws regarding agriculture (e.g. gleanings, tithes, sabbatical year, heave offerings, dough-offerings and first-fruits); laws regarding sabbaths and festivals; laws regarding women (e.g. betrothal, marriage and divorce); laws regarding legal procedure and punishment; laws regarding temple offerings (e.g. animal and meal offerings; firstlings; the daily whole offering); and laws regarding ritual purity (e.g. vessels; tents; leprosy-signs; the red heifer; immersion pools; the menstruant). Later rabbinic thought was to distinguish rather sharply between the מצוות which were actually contained in the Torah and the enactments of the Sages. A law could be classified as either *de-'oraita* , i.e. found in the Written Torah, or *de-rabbanan*, i.e. an enactment of the Sages. Six hundred and thirteen commandments were identified in the Written Torah, 365 positive and 248 negative. Classifying a law as an enactment of the Sages was not intended to suggest that it was less important or less binding, but it did in principle open the possibility of changing the enactment, which could not have been contemplated in the case of a commandment of the Written Torah.[35] Other distinctions among the laws were also formally recognized. For example, it was noted that laws could broadly be classified into those which govern the relationships between man and man and those which

---

[33] See Exod R. 26:6.

[34] See e.g. Joseph Albo, *'Iqqarim* III 23. A profound analysis of these questions may be found in A. J. Heschel, *Torah min ha-Shamayim*, vols. I–II (London: Soncino, 1965). See also my essay "'A Sixtieth Part of Prophecy': The Problem of Continuing Revelation in Judaism," in *Words Remembered, Texts Renewed: Essays in honour of John F. A. Sawyer* (ed. J. Davies, G. Harvey and W. G. E. Watson; Sheffield: Sheffield Academic, 1995), 414–33.

[35] See Menachem Elon, *Jewish Law: History, Sources, Principles*, vol. I (Philadelphia/Jerusalem: Jewish Publication Society, 1994), 207–23.

govern the relationships between man and God.[36] It was also noted that in the case of certain laws (some of them of the utmost gravity) punishment was "in the hands of heaven" and was not enforced through the courts.[37] However, at a theological level the Mishnah shows little concern for these distinctions: its system of commandments embraces both Torah laws and rabbinic enactments. All constitute Torah, and all must be obeyed. Even though the courts must naturally have distinguished between "light" and "heavy" commandments in the punishments they meted out, from the point of view of performance one was advised not to make this distinction, since one does not know the ultimate reward of any commandment in the reckoning of God[38].

It is evident from the Mishnah that it regards Torah as embracing all aspects of life. There is no attempt, as in the Diaspora, to restrict it to the narrowly religious sphere. In this the Mishnah simply follows the lead of the Written Torah itself, which, though it does distinguish between a realm of the "sacred" and a realm of the "secular," enacts laws to cover both. The מצוות relate to the "secular" as well as the "sacred." The Mishnah spends a great deal of time extending the Written Torah into all aspects of life and working out precisely how God's will is to be implemented in the most concrete, everyday situations. Its comprehensiveness can be breathtaking. Torah can be seen as embracing even etiquette and good manners (דרך ארץ).

M. B. Bat. 2:1–3 illustrates this process of extending the Torah:

> No one may dig a cistern [on his own land] close to a cistern of his neighbour; nor may he dig a trench, cave, water-channel, or laundry-pool unless he keeps it at least three handbreadths away from his neighbour's wall, and plasters its sides with lime. He must keep olive-refuse, manure, salt, lime, or stones at least three handbreadths away from his neighbour's wall, and he must plaster it with lime. He must keep seeds and furrows and urine at least three handbreadths away from the wall. Mill-stones must be kept at least three handbreadths from the wall measuring from the lower mill-stone, or four measuring from the upper mill-stone. An oven must be kept at least three handbreadths from the wall measuring from the belly of the oven, or four measuring from the rim.
>
> No-one may set up an oven inside a house unless there is an void of four cubits above it. If he sets it up in an upstairs room there must be a concrete floor at least three handbreadths thick beneath it, or, for a small stove, one handbreadth thick; and if it causes damage [to the floor] the owner of the oven must pay for the damage caused. Rabbi Simeon says: These measurements were stipulated so that if, [having observed them], damage ensues, he will not be liable to pay.
>
> No one may open a bakery or a dyer's workshop beneath his neighbour's food-store, nor [may he open] a cowshed. In fact, they allowed all these under a wine-store, apart from the cowshed. If someone wants to open a shop within a courtyard, his neighbour may stop him on the grounds that he would not be able to sleep because of the noise of the customers. However, if he is making articles to take out and sell in the market, his

---

[36] *m. Yoma* 8:9.

[37] *m. Ker.* 1:1.

[38] Cf. *m. Ḥul.* 12:5 with *m. 'Abot* 2:1, "And be as heedful of a light precept as of a weighty one, for you do not know the recompense of reward for each precept."

neighbour cannot stop him on the grounds that he would be unable to sleep because of the noise of the hammer, or the noise of the mill-stones. Nor can he protest about the noise of [school] children.

In modern western societies the laws listed here would not be seen as religious, but would come under municipal planning laws. For the Mishnah, however, they are Torah and expressions of the will of God. At first sight it is hard to see how this series of categorical rabbinic rulings is related to the Written Torah. There is no very obvious biblical law which is here being extended and applied. However, on maturer reflection it is not so difficult to derive these injunctions from biblical principles. There is clearly a general principle (a כלל) lying behind the precise rulings, viz., that no one, even when acting within his own domain, may cause harm to a neighbor. Once formulated more abstractly this underlying principle can readily be linked to some of the most fundamental injunctions of the Torah, such as the commandment "to love your neighbor as yourself" (Lev 19:18)[39].

4.3 Legalism and the Burden of the Law

M. B. Bat. 2:1–3 well illustrates the general character of the Mishnah as lists of detailed rules covering all areas of life. This interest in legal minutiae has led in the past to the accusation that rabbinic Judaism is legalistic. The charge takes various forms but two elements remain fairly constant. The first is that rabbinic Judaism has shown itself more concerned with the minutiae of the law than with broad moral principles, and sometimes sacrifices the latter in the interests of the former. The second is that by covering everyday life with a grid of precise rules and regulations the rabbis have imposed an intolerable burden upon their followers which has crushed out of religious life all spontaneity and joy. The charge of legalism, which has been classically articulated within Protestant theology and which picks up aspects of the thought of Paul, is usually formulated in terms of a contrast between the letter and the spirit of the law, or between bondage to the law and the freedom of the spirit. As normally articulated it is profoundly mistaken, but, as we have already noted, the grounds on which the rabbis have sometimes been defended may be hardly less mistaken and may run the risk of denying the absolute centrality of law to rabbinic Judaism and of turning rabbinic Judaism into a rather pale reflection of liberal Protestantism. It is important to try and clarify the matter.

The charge of legalism often ignores the fact that the rabbis inherited from the Bible a comprehensive system of law which was meant to serve as the

---

[39] On the discussion in early rabbinic jurisprudence of the principles behind the מצוות see my essay, "Jesus and the Golden Rule," in *Hillel and Jesus: Comparative Studies of two Major Religious Leaders* (ed. J. H. Charlesworth and Loren L. Johns; Minneapolis: Fortress, 1997), 363–88.

constitution of a people. It is true, as we have already observed, that for many
Jews in antiquity (as today) large areas of the law were inoperative. Many
lived outside the Land of Israel and could not implement parts of the law
because of their status as an ethnic minority. They were, in any case, not
subject to the "commandments pertaining to the Land." Even those who lived
within the Land could not for political reasons implement the whole Torah.
For all Jews, whether in Israel or the Diaspora, the laws relating to the temple
had perforce been in abeyance since 70 C.E. For many Jews, then, the content
of the Torah had effectively shrunk to cover only the more private and
religious aspects of life. But the Tannaitic rabbis were clearly not prepared
to concede such a restriction. They embraced the Torah as a whole, sought
to maximize its application to Jewish life and studied and codified even those
parts of it which through *force majeure* could not be implemented. Given
their view that Torah was from heaven and that Israel had solemnly accepted
it at Sinai, they could not do otherwise. Paul in largely ignoring the civil side
of the law, and in effect confining it to personal relationship between
individuals or between the individual and God, displays a deeply diasporan
mentality.

The casuistic presentation of the Mishnah can create a misleading
impression in the unwary modern reader. Because it formulates law in terms
of concrete cases and specific scenarios (some of which are patently
contrived and far-fetched), it can appear to display an obsessive interest in
pettifogging detail and to be neglecting larger matters of principle, morality
and religion. But casuistic formulation is a perfectly reasonable approach to
codification of law, especially in a work such as the Mishnah which appears
to have been aimed at teaching rabbis to think jurisprudentially. It is already
used in biblical law. Moreover it is has always been recognized in rabbinic
jurisprudence that the precise cases were meant to illustrate general
principles (כללים). From the late Second Temple period onwards there has
been a lively debate within Jewish jurisprudence as to the underlying
principles of the law. There was even speculation from time to time as to
whether the whole of the Torah could be seen as the multifarious expression
of one "great principle." Hillel was supposed to have answered a Gentile's
request to be taught the whole Torah while he stood on one foot by citing a
form of the Golden Rule: "what is hateful to yourself, do not do to others.
The rest is commentary, go and learn."[40] According to Matt 7:12 Jesus used
the Golden Rule in a similar way. Philo (*Decal.* 154; cf. *Spec.* 1.1), by
ranging each of the "special laws" of the Torah under one of the commandments of the decalogue, advocated the view that the principles embodied in
the concrete legislation were fundamentally moral. Some rabbinic authorities
were inclined to take a similar position. However, the standard rabbinic view
is that it is not the morality of a concrete law which in the end makes it

---

[40] *b. Šabb.* 31a.

obligatory but the fact that it is a command of God.[41] And classical rabbinic jurisprudence has always steadfastly resisted working from general principles, moral or otherwise, to the concrete מצוות, since this opens up the possibility of a radical critique of the מצוות, which may lead to their modification or even abolition.[42]

The accusation of legalism also fails to do justice to the role of much rabbinic jurisprudence in moderating the rigors of biblical law. Sometimes in creating "a fence around the Torah" the rabbis appear to be adding to its burdens, but their intention is just as often to mitigate its potential harshness. A case in point is the *prosbul* of Hillel (*m. Šeb.* 10:3–6). Biblical law had legislated that there should be a cancellation of debts every seventh year. The ruling was clearly motivated by a moral concern – to avoid the evil of debt-slavery. But in practice problems arose. As the sabbatical year approached it became increasingly difficult to obtain loans. In more complex economic systems than those envisaged in the original legislation, loans are an absolute necessity. Lack of a loan could reduce a farmer to destitution, just as readily as a debt. So Hillel devised the *prosbul*, which made a court responsible for collecting the debt during or after the sabbatical year. The court as a corporate agent was not subject to the restraint of biblical law which forbade the *individual* creditor to call in the loan. Significantly the device of the *prosbul* is seen by the Mishnah as a way of fulfilling the spirit of the biblical law as expressed in Deut 15:9, "Be careful that you do not harbor in your heart a mean thought by saying, 'The Seventh Year, the year of release, is coming.' You view with hostility your poor brother, and lend him nothing; and he cries out to the Lord against you, and you incur guilt."

The rabbis of the Mishnah were even willing in certain cases to allow, in effect, the abrogation of a law. When Christianity finally became dominant in the Mediterranean world, and even more so after the rise of Islam, which accepted the wholesale abrogation of biblical law, the rabbinic authorities, at least in apologetic contexts, steadfastly refused to admit to abrogation. The Torah had been given to Israel for all time: it would never be replaced by another Torah.[43] However, in some cases the Mishnaic authorities in effect

---

[41] Cf. the story Yohanan ben Zakkai and the rituals of the Red Heifer in *Pesiq. Rab Kah.* 4:7; Num. R. 19:8; *Tanḥ* Buber, *Huqqat* 26.

[42] See further my essay, "Jesus and the Golden Rule."

[43] The question of whether or not there will be a new Torah in the messianic age is raised in some rabbinic sources, but in general the idea is rejected. See W. D. Davies, *Torah in the Messianic Age* (Philadelphia: Westminster, 1952); Peter Schäfer, "Die Torah der messianischen Zeit," *ZNW* 65 (1974): 27–42; reprinted in Schäfer, *Studien zur Geschichte und Theologie des rabbinischen Judentums*, 198–213. The subject became important, however, in later Jewish mysticism. The Zohar raises the question whether the Torah, which, as it stands, addresses a broken, imperfect, sinful world, can apply to the world to come when the fractured state of the present world will be mended (see Isaiah Tishby, *The Wisdom of the Zohar: An Anthology of Texts*, vol. 3 [London: Littman Library, 1991], 1078–1121). It looks forward to a new Torah for the new age, as do, apparently, some forms of modern Hasidism (notably Habad, which stresses

allowed that a law had been at least *de facto* abrogated. A example of this is the law concerning the suspected adulteress, the שוטה (Num 5:11–31). Mishnah *Soṭah* discusses in exhaustive detail the implementation of this law only to reveal at the end of the tractate that it had been abolished by Yohanan ben Zakkai (*m. Soṭah* 9:9). The reason given is "because adulterers had increased," and, therefore, presumably, it was impractical to go on applying the procedures. But there were probably deeper reasons. The rabbis, sophisticated lawyers that they were, would hardly have been comfortable with the primitive custom of trial by ordeal, which negated the fundamental principle of rabbinic jurisprudence, that cases are to be decided by the majority vote of the judges after due deliberation of the evidence, a principle anchored in Exod 23:2, "after the majority opinion shall you incline" (cf. *b. B. Bat.* 59a-b).

The charge that in covering all aspects of life with rules and regulations the rabbis are imposing an intolerable burden on their followers and crushing all spontaneity and joy from the religious life ignores the very real experience of many Jews of "the joy of the law" (שמחת תורה).[44] Mishnah *'Abot* describes the Torah, not only as a burden, but also as a "precious instrument" and its revelation to Israel as an act of divine love.[45] And when it says that the "reward of a commandment is another commandment," it views this positively and not negatively.[46] The "burden of the law" is essentially psychological: it all depends on one's attitude. The rabbis of the Mishnah were very conscious of this when they interposed study between the commandment and its implementation. The Torah was not simply a list of rules and regulations to be blindly obeyed. It was a text to be studied intently and internalized. Study of the Torah is fundamental to Mishnaic Judaism, and *m. 'Abot* is full of lyrical praises of its benefits. It is a religious act, perhaps *the* religious act. There is more to this study than simply finding out exactly what one has to do. The act of studying has a formative power: it suppresses the inclination towards evil (the יצר הרע) and encourages the inclination towards good (the יצר הטוב, which according to rabbinic anthropology are constantly at war in the human personality.[47] Study of Torah is a precondition for correct fulfillment of Torah. The greatest perversion imaginable is to study and not fulfill. Mishnah *'Abot* claims that the Divine Presence (the Shekhinah) abides with even a single individual who studies the Torah, and

---

Isa. 51:4, "for Torah shall come from me," כי תורה מאתי תצא). I am indebted to my research student Max Kohanzad, who is working on antinomian tendencies in the thought of the Lubavitcher Rebbe, Menachem Schneerson, for discussing the Rebbe's messianic ideas with me.

[44] The classic essay on this subject remains Solomon Schechter's "The Joy of the Law" in *Aspects of Rabbinic Theology*, 148–69.

[45] *m. 'Abot* 3:15.

[46] *m. 'Abot* 4:2.

[47] See G. H. Cohen Stuart, *The Struggle in Man between Good and Evil: An Inquiry into the Origin and Rabbinic Concept of Yeser Hara* (Kampen: Kok Pharos, 1984).

by the Divine Presence it does not mean only the *objective* immanence of God in the world, but also the presence of God as *subjectively* perceived by humankind. The student of Torah will experience a benign sense of God's nearness.

This is the ideal. But the ideal was doubtless not always realized in practice. It is a simple fact that many Jews have throughout history testified to experiencing the law as a burden. This has certainly been the case in modern times and has led many to abandon traditional practices or to adopt liberal interpretations of the halakah. There are powerful antinomian currents within Judaism, which may be, at least in part, a reaction to the "burden of the law."[48] Human nature does not seem to change much, and it is reasonable to postulate that similar attitudes would have been found among Jews in the Tannaitic period.[49] The opposition of the עמי הארץ to the rabbis may have partly been based on objections to the rabbis' increasing the burden of the law. However, the lines of the rabbinic defense against the charge that they were adding to the burden of the law are clear. The Torah (and this, as we have seen, included all validly derived extensions and clarifications of the biblical injunctions) is God's gift to Israel, a sign of his love. It should be accepted as such and obeyed with love. Study is a fundamental religious duty which overcomes the sense of burden, and enables the Jew not only to fulfill the Torah fully but to fulfill it with joy.

4.4 God as Judge: Reward and Punishment

Since the Torah is essentially a system of מצוות which expresses God's will for Israel, obedience is a categorical imperative. God takes note whether or not his commandments are obeyed and rewards and punishes accordingly. The idea that God is unconcerned with what happens in the world (as in Epicureanism) or exhibits partiality in judgment is totally abhorrent to rabbinic Judaism. God's just governance of the world is a constant theme of *m. 'Abot.* "Consider three things and you will not fall into the hands of transgression: know what is above you – a seeing eye and a hearing ear and all your deeds written in a book" (*m. 'Abot* 2:1). "Know before whom you toil and who is your taskmaster who shall pay you the reward of your labour" (*m. 'Abot* 2:14). "Faithful is your taskmaster who shall pay you the reward of your labour" (*m. 'Abot* 2:16). "Consider three things and you will not come into the hands of transgression. Know from where you have come and

---

[48] For some remarks on this see my essay "'A Sixtieth Part of Prophecy': The Problem of Continuing Revelation in Judaism."

[49] It is interesting how often the rabbis themselves use the image of a burden in connection with the Torah. Note, e.g., *m. 'Abot* 3:5, "Whoever takes upon himself the yoke of the Torah, from him shall be taken away the yoke of the kingdom and the yoke of worldly care; but he who throws off the yoke of the Torah, upon him shall be laid the yoke of the kingdom and the yoke of worldly care."

to where you are going and before whom you are about to give account and reckoning. 'From where you have come' – from a putrid drop; 'and to where you are going' – to the place of dust, worm, and maggot; 'and before whom you are about to give account and reckoning' – before the King of the kings of kings, the Holy One, blessed be he" (*m. 'Abot* 3:1).

The overwhelming impression which one gets from the Mishnah is of God making a precise reckoning of the deeds of humankind and meting out exactly calculated reward and punishment: *m. 'Abot* 3:17, "All is given against a pledge, and the net is cast over all the living; the shop stands open and the shopkeeper gives credit and the account book lies open and the hand writes and every one that wishes to borrow let him come and borrow; but the collectors go round continually every day and exact payment of men with their consent or without their consent, for they have that on which they can rely; and the judgment is a judgment of truth; and all is made ready for the banquet." The impression of God's strict justice is further reinforced by the doctrine of "measure for measure" (מדה כנגד מדה) according to which the reward and the punishment are seen as matching the deed. This is the message of *m. 'Abot* 2:7, "He [Hillel] saw a skull floating on the face of the water and he said to it, 'Because you drowned [others] you yourself were drowned and at the last those that drowned you shall be drowned.'" It should be noted, however, that there appears to be no implication that in order to reap the ultimate rewards it is necessary to fulfill the whole Torah perfectly. The righteous person is not necessarily perfect: as *m. 'Abot* 3:16 puts it: "all is according to the *majority* of works (לפי רוב המצשה)."[50] It is the dominant characteristics of a person's life which categorize him as righteous or as wicked The צדיק (righteous man) does not seem to be generally equated with the חסיד (saint). Saintliness is a state beyond righteousness, one that is admired and to which all should aspire, but not one which all seemingly are obliged to attain.[51] Perfectionism of the sort that seems to affect some early Christian writers is not a feature of the Mishnah.[52]

---

[50] There is a famous textual crux here. I have little doubt that the standard text is original: הכל צפוי והרשות נתונה ובטוב העולם נידון והכל לפי רוב המעשה. The alternatives (e.g., אבל לא על פי [רוב] המעשה) have come about because copyists could not live with the stark contradiction of the text as it stands. But the paradox is deliberate, and is still there in the first stich (הכל צפוי והרשות נתונה), even if one accepts the alternative reading. See further Shmuel Safrai, "Vehakkol lefi rov hammaʿaseh," *Tarbitz* 53 (1983): 33–40.

[51] It is a moot point whether Tannaitic sources distinguish between the righteous man and the saint (see. e.g., *m. 'Abot* 5:10; 5:14; *m. Soṭah* 9:15). However, medieval Jewish thinkers, such as the Hasidei Ashkenaz, interpreted the classic sources as implying such a distinction.

[52] See e.g. Jas 2:10, "For whoever shall keep the whole law, and yet stumble in one point, he is become guilty of all." If this is meant literally, then I doubt if many rabbinic authorities would have subscribed to it. Note, however, *m. Qidd.* 1:10, "If a man performs but a single commandment it shall be well with him and he shall have length of days and shall inherit the Land; but if he neglects a single commandment it shall be ill with him and he shall not have length of days and shall not inherit the Land." See further the nuanced discussion of *4 Ezra* by

The Mishnah is somewhat vague about when and how God's judgment is exercised, and exactly what rewards or punishments are dispensed. Judgment, reward and punishment seem to take place both in this world and after death. Mishnah *'Abot* 3:17 implies that punishment is exacted continually, day by day, in this world. And *m. 'Abot* 5:8–9 treats certain categories of this-worldly event (famine, drought, pestilence, war, harmful beasts and exile) as retribution for certain types of transgression, in a broadly "measure for measure" way. The implication is that keeping the Torah leads to prosperity, plenty, peace and enjoyment of the Land (cf. *m. 'Abot* 4:9). There are other temporal benefits that flow from observing the Torah ranging from general worldly success to an individual sense of the presence of God.[53] But punishment and reward are also apportioned after death. Mishnah *'Abot* 4:22 contains a ringing affirmation that there will be a resurrection of the dead for judgment:

> Those that have been born [are destined] to die, and those that are dead [are destined] to be made alive, and those that live [again after death are destined] to be judged, that men may know and make known and understand that he is God, he is the Maker, he is the Creator, he is the Discerner, he is the Judge, he is the Witness, he is the Complainant, and it is he who shall judge, blessed be he, in whose presence is neither guile nor forgetfulness nor respect of persons nor taking of bribes; for all is his. And know that everything is according to the reckoning. And let not your [evil] nature promise you that the grave will be your refuge: for despite yourself you were formed, and despite yourself you were born, and despite yourself you live, and despite yourself you die, and despite yourself you shall hereafter give account and reckoning before the King of the kings of kings, the Holy One, blessed be he.

The rabbis were observant enough to realize that righteousness does not always lead to peace and prosperity in this life and, like many other theists, called into being another world to redress the inequities of this world and to justify the ways of God to men (צידוק הדין).

Richard Bauckham, and of the Qumran sources by Markus Bockmuehl, in this volume.

[53] *m. 'Abot* 2:4, "Do his [God's] will as if it was your will that he may do your will as if it was his will. Make your will of none effect before his will that he may make the will of others of none effect before your will"; *m. 'Abot* 3:2, "If two sit together and words of Torah [are spoken] between them, the Divine Presence rests between them, as it is written, *Then they who feared the Lord spoke one with another: and the Lord hearkened, and heard, and a book of remembrance was written before him, for them that feared the Lord, and that thought upon his name* (Mal. 3:16). Scripture speaks here of 'two'; from where [do we learn] that if even one sits and occupies himself with the Torah, the Holy One, blessed be he, appoints him a reward? Because it is written, *Let him sit alone and keep silence, because he has laid it upon him* (Lam. 3:28)." Cf. *m. 'Abot* 3:6. It is noteworthy, however, that the sense of the presence of God here as elsewhere is not the result of successful fulfillment of the commandment. It is granted earlier, as soon as one meets the fundamental precondition for the fulfillment of the מצוות by taking up the study of Torah. This ensures that the actual fulfillment of the commandment is done in love and joy, and not out of a grim sense of duty.

What happens to the wicked after the final judgment is far from clear.[54] The ultimate fate of the righteous is also not spelled out. They enjoy "the world to come," but there is a notable lack of definition as to what this means or the blessings which it entails.[55] This lack of precision about the eschatological rewards and punishments is all of a piece with the Mishnah's general lack of interest in eschatology, as we noted earlier. There may also have been another reason for the rabbis' vagueness, especially about eschatological rewards. It is that they were concerned to stress the notion that one should perform a commandment not with an eye to its reward, but "for its own sake" (לשמה) or "for the sake of heaven" (לשם שמים). "Be not," exhorts *m. 'Abot* 1:3, "like slaves who minister to the master for the sake of receiving a bounty, but be like slaves who minister to the master not for the sake of receiving a bounty; and let the fear of heaven be upon you."[56] It would hardly have been in keeping with such a stance to have dwelt in vivid detail on the rewards that await the righteous in the world to come.

4.5 God as Merciful: Repentance and Atonement

That God is merciful as well as just is one of the fundamental assertions of rabbinic Judaism. "All is foreseen," says *m. 'Abot* 3:16, "yet freedom of choice is given; and the world is judged by goodness (טוב = mercy), yet all is according to the majority of works." The tension between divine justice and divine mercy, already present in the Bible (note, e.g., Ps. 89:14), is dramatically represented in later rabbinic tradition by personifying the two attributes and depicting them as standing in dispute before God in the heavenly law court.[57] This tension is, perhaps, less prominent in the Tannaitic literature. There is a tendency, however, to see mercy as prevailing over strict justice. The rabbis of the Mishnah advocate inclining the scales of justice in human courts towards mercy, and doubtless they believed that in so doing they were simply imitating the merciful divine Judge.[58] It is doubtful that

---

[54] There are fleeting references to Gehenna at *m. 'Abot* 1:5 and 4:20.

[55] *m. 'Abot* 4:17 speaks of "the bliss (קורת רוח) of the world to come." *m. 'Abot* 3:17 states cryptically that "all is made ready for the banquet." This should be compared with 4:16, "This world is a vestibule before the world to come: prepare yourself in the vestibule so that you may enter into the banqueting hall." Even vaguer is 2:16, "the recompense of the reward of the righteous is for the time to come" (לעתיד לבוא). In later rabbinic usage לעתיד לבוא is synonymous with לעולם הבא, but it is not certain that this is the case in Tannaitic literature. The context here may be theodicy: do not worry if the righteous are not rewarded immediately; their reward will, in the end, come. *m. 'Abot* 4:20 refers fleetingly to "the Garden of Eden," but again no substance is given to concept. Cf. also *m. 'Abot* 3:12 and *m. Sanh.* 10:1 quoted below.

[56] Cf. *m. 'Abot* 2:2, "Let all who labour with the congregation labour with them for the sake of heaven."

[57] Cf. *b. Šabb.* 55a; *b. Sanh.* 97b, 103a; *b. Pesah* 119a. See further *Gen. R.* 8:4; *'Abot de Rabbi Nathan* A 37; *b. Ber.* 7a.

[58] See e.g., *m. 'Abot* 1:7, "And when you judge any man incline the balance in his favour." Cf. *m. Sanh.* 1:6 and 5:5.

God's "grace" or "mercy" in Tannaitic theology is ever totally free. God never simply overlooks wrongdoing. There are always grounds for the exercise of clemency, residing either in the behavior of the wrongdoer himself subsequent to his fault, or in the merits of his own or others' righteousness which cover his sin.

God's mercy is activated by repentance (תשובה, literally "returning"), in virtue of which he waives or mitigates the punishment due to the sinner. Without repentance there can be no exercise of mercy. The important rabbinic concept of תשובה is very inadequately represented by the English repentance, which rather stresses the change of heart or attitude. תשובה is the turning of the whole being back to God. It involves confession of sin and supplication of the mercies of God. "When you pray," says *m. 'Abot* 2:13, "do not make your prayer a fixed form, but a [plea for] mercies and supplications before God, for it is written, *For he is gracious and full of compassion, slow to anger, and plenteous in mercy, and repents him of evil* (Joel 2:13)." תשובה involves not only a change of heart and regret for the wrongdoing, but also restitution, if restitution is possible, or, if it is not, the performance of good deeds by way of compensation. It is unclear from Tannaitic sources whether or not the "good deeds" must be works of supererogation (to use a Christian term), or whether a return to the scrupulous performance of the commandments can atone. Possibly both are envisaged. The quintessential "good deeds" are acts of charity (צדקות) some of which are commanded by the law, but others above and beyond the call of duty. According to *m. 'Abot* 4:11, "He who performs one precept gets for himself one advocate; but he who commits one transgression gets for himself one accuser [when the final judgement is made whether on balance a man is righteous or wicked]. Repentance and good deeds are a shield against retribution." Intention is of immense importance in both rabbinic jurisprudence and rabbinic theology. If one applies a sort of calculus to one's deeds, doing wrong deliberately with a view subsequently to repenting and making atonement, then the repentance and the good deeds will not be accepted by God[59].

Punishment also atones: when punishment has been fully borne there remains no barrier to the restoration of communion with God. The criminal on the way to execution is exhorted to utter the confession, "May my death be an expiation for all my iniquities" (*m. Sanh.* 6:2). Punishment always seems to be limited in Tannaitic thought. There is little evidence for the idea that sins may be so heinous that they merit endless punishment and can never be finally expiated. Under the biblical dispensation the rituals of the Day of Atonement (the scapegoat and the holocaust) brought expiation for the sins

---

[59] Cf., e.g., *m. Yoma* 8:9, "If a man said, 'I will sin and repent, and sin again and repent,' he will be given no chance to repent. [If he said,] 'I will sin and the Day of Atonement will effect atonement,' then the Day of Atonement effects no atonement."

of all Israel, certainly for the deserving and perhaps for the undeserving as well. This idea persisted into Tannaitic thought: "For light transgressions, whether of commission or omission, repentance atones; for the serious transgressions repentance holds the matter in suspense until the Day of Atonement comes and brings expiation" (*m. Yoma* 8:8). The idea implicit here seems to be that if Israel as a whole fasts and prays on Yom Kippur then this will expiate the sins of the community as a whole. It is easy to extend this idea into a doctrine of the merits of the righteous covering the sins of the whole community. The truly righteous sustain the community, and indeed, the world in which they live. They are pillars of the world, and deflect the divine judgment. Particularly meritorious are the "sufferings of love" – the sufferings which the righteous apparently gratuitously undergo. Suffering expiates sin, and when the righteous suffer, apparently undeservedly, their sufferings may serve to make atonement for all Israel.[60] Nothing could be further from Tannaitic thought than the notion of an inexorable justice operating blindly or mechanistically. Israel has many means by which to call forth the divine mercy, to make atonement for sin and mitigate the rigors of divine justice. The texts, however, leave the strong impression that Israel must choose to exercise those means. Unless they are invoked justice will take its course. The demands of justice can never simply be ignored.

5. *Torah and Salvation in the Tannaitic Midrashim*

I will now turn to consider the Tannaitic Midrashim, highlighting for the most part only those ideas which are new or which supplement the theology of the Mishnah. The discussion will focus on *Sipre* Deuteronomy. The reason for proceeding in this way is that *Sipre* Deuteronomy out of all the Tannaitic Midrashim puts forward the clearest and most coherent theology. This is hardly surprising. The biblical book on which it comments provides the clearest and most coherent theology of all the Pentateuchal books. That theology, with its stress on Torah, covenant, Israel and the Land, was immensely influential in the late biblical and Second Temple periods and in broad outline became the fundamental theology of Judaism. Early rabbinic Judaism can plausibly be seen as a late development of Deuteronomistic thought. Much of the coherence of *Sipre* Deuteronomy is derived from the underlying biblical text whose agenda *Sipre* Deuteronomy addresses, attempting to clarify its ambiguities and resolve the problems that it raises. The other Tannaitic Midrashim, the *Mekhilta de Rabbi Ishmael*, *Sipra* and *Sipre* Numbers, are much more anthological in character, less tightly argued.

---

[60] Note *m. Ber.* 9:5 on giving thanks to God for suffering, and see further the long discussion of the value of suffering in *Mekhilta de Rabbi Ishmael, Bahodesh* X. On the sufferings of love, see Urbach, *The Sages*, 444–8.

Moreover in the case of the *Mekhilta* there is some doubt as to whether the work is truly Tannaitic.[61]

5.1 Salvation and the Covenant

The major element which *Sipre* Deuteronomy adds to the Mishnah's theology is the centrality of the covenant in defining God's relationship to Israel, and in defining Israel's supreme good. Doubtless the covenant is presupposed in the Mishnah, but little is said about it directly. *Sipre*'s emphasis on the covenant is hardly surprising given the importance of this idea in Deuteronomy. *Sipre* sees the covenant in legal-contractual terms as an agreement entered into freely by two parties in the presence of witnesses. The covenant is offered by God. That may be an act of grace on his part, since as Creator he was presumably not obliged to offer such terms, though *Sipre* Deuteronomy does not seem explicitly to make this point. What it does claim is that Israel freely entered into the covenant. Israel's choice of God is as important as God's choice of Israel. "We do not know whether the Holy One, blessed be he, chose Israel to be his own treasure, or whether Israel chose the Holy One; therefore Scripture says, *And the Lord has chosen you to be his own treasure* (Deut 14:2). And whence do we learn that Jacob also chose God? From the verse, *Not like these is the portion of Jacob* (Jer. 10:16)" (*Pisqa* 312).

Pisqa 343 contains an important pericope on the giving of the Torah:

A. *And he said: The Lord came from Sinai* (Deut 33:2).

B. When God revealed himself to give the Torah to Israel, he revealed himself not only to Israel but to all the nations.

C. He went first to the children of Esau and asked them, "Will you accept the Torah?" They replied, "What is written in it?" He said to them, *You shall not murder* (Exod 20:13). They replied that this was the very essence of these people, and that their forefather was a murderer, as it is said, *But the hands are the hands of Esau* (Gen 27:22), and *By your sword you shall live* (Gen 27:40).

D. He then went to the Ammonites and the Moabites and asked them, "Will you accept the Torah?" They replied, "What is written in it?" He said, *You shall not commit adultery*

---

[61] See especially Jacob Neusner's analysis of these works, e.g., *Sifre to Deuteronomy: An Introduction to the Rhetorical, Logical and Topical Programme* (Atlanta: Scholars, 1987); *Sifra in Perspective* (Atlanta: Scholars, 1988); *Mekhilta according to Rabbi Ishmael: An Introduction to Judaism's First Scriptural Encyclopaedia* (Atlanta: Scholars, 1988). B. Z. Wacholder, "The Date of the Mekilta de-Rabbi Ishmael," *HUCA* 39 (1968): 117–44, attempts to argue that the *Mekhilta* is a pseudepigraphon composed as late as the eighth century C.E. Though his arguments are far from conclusive, it should be noted that Neusner's analysis does suggest that the *Mekhilta* is somewhat later than *Sipre* Deuteronomy. In *Sipre* Deuteronomy one has a sense of a theological system in process of formation, in the *Mekhilta* of a theological system already well formed which the redactor shares with his audience and which can be presupposed. Quotations of *Sipre* Deuteronomy below follow, with minor modifications, Reuven Hammer, *Sifre: A Tannaitic Commentary on the Book of Deuteronomy* (New Haven and London: Yale University, 1986).

(Exod 20:13). They replied that adultery is their very essence, as it is said, *Thus were both the daughters of Lot with child by the their father* (Gen 19:36).

E. He went next to the Ishmaelites and asked them, "Will you accept the Torah?" They replied, "What is written in it?" He said, *You shall not steal* (Exod 20:13). They replied that theft is their very essence and that their forefather was a thief, as it is said, *And he shall be a wild ass of a man* (Gen 16:12).

F. And thus is was with every other nation – he asked them all, "Will you accept the Torah?" as it is said, *All the kings of the earth shall give you thanks, O Lord, for they have heard the words of your mouth* (Ps. 138:4).

G. One might think [from this verse] that they heard and accepted [his offer]; therefore Scripture states elsewhere, *And I will execute vengeance in anger and fury upon the nations, because they did not hearken* (Mic. 5:14).

H. It was not enough for them that they did not hearken – they were unable even to observe the seven commandments that the children of Noah had accepted upon themselves, and they cast them off.

I. When the Holy One, blessed be he, saw that, he gave them to Israel.

J. A parable: A man took his ass and his dog to the threshing floor and loaded the ass with a *letekh* (of grain) and the dog with three *se'ahs*. The ass went along [easily], but the dog began to pant, so the man took off a *se'ah* and put it on the ass, and so too with the second and the third *se'ah*. So all Israel accepted the Torah, with all its explanations and details, as well as the seven commandments which the children of Noah had not been able to observe and had cast off.

K. Therefore it is said, *And he said: The Lord came from Sinai, and rose from Seir unto them.*

The development of the argument here is somewhat unexpected. One anticipates by unit I that God having offered the Torah to the nations will then offer it to Israel, who will accept. This is how the parallel in the *Mekhilta de Rabbi Ishmael, Bahodesh* 5, puts the matter: "But when he came to the Israelites and *At his right hand was a fiery law unto them* (Deut 33:2), they all opened their mouths and said, *All that the Lord has spoken we will do and obey* (Exod 24:7). And thus it says, *He stood and measured the earth; he beheld and drove asunder the nations* (Hab 3:6)." Israel's eager acceptance of the Torah led to her separation from the other nations, in effect to her election. But this is not what *Sipre* Deuteronomy actually says. In the *Sipre* God simply commits the Torah to Israel. The parable hints why. He saw that Israel was fit to bear the Torah, as an ass is fit to bear a burden. The intrinsic merit of the sons of Jacob to receive the Torah is stated a little further on in the same *Pisqa*: "When our father Abraham came into the world, he had unworthy children, Ishmael and the children of Keturah, who were more evil than the previous generations. When Isaac came along, he had an unworthy child, Esau, and all the princes of Edom became more evil than the previous generations. But when Jacob came along, he had no unworthy children, for all the children born to him were worthy, as it is said, *And Jacob was a worthy man, dwelling in tents* (Gen 25:27). Whereupon the Holy One, blessed be he, said to him, 'To you shall I give the Torah.'"[62] The Torah may

---

[62] Cf. *Pisqa* 31, which notes the sin of Reuben, but exonerates him on the grounds that he

have been offered to all but once it was accepted by Israel it became, so to speak, her exclusive property. There is little suggestion that the nations are now or ever will be[63] obliged to keep the Torah. They are required only to keep the seven commandments to the sons of Noah[64].

Though God is the God of the whole world, the nations do not recognize his sovereignty but worship idols instead.[65] Only Israel recognizes the true God. Idolatry is the supreme sin, especially for Israel, since it blurs the distinction between Israel and the nations. Because of the nations' idolatry and because of her acceptance of the covenant, Israel has an exclusive relationship to God. In *Pisqa* 343 Israel claims that the nations have no share in God, quoting Song of Songs 6:3, "I am my beloved's and my beloved is mine, who feeds among the lilies."[66] If pushed to its logical conclusion this line of thinking would seem to weaken the concept of God's election of Israel. God may, in a sense, choose Israel, but would his choice have been frustrated if Israel had not accepted? Did God, in any way, compel or manage Israel's acceptance of the Torah? These questions are barely addressed, let alone answered, in Tannaitic literature. The tension between election and free choice is always present but never resolved[67].

5.2 The Rewards and Sanctions of the Covenant

The Torah, which *Sipre* Deuteronomy, like the Mishnah, sees as the expression of God's will,[68] contains the stipulations of the covenant. If Israel keeps the covenant certain benefits ensue; if she breaks it punishments follow. In line with Deuteronomy, *Sipre* stresses that there will be blessing

---

repented.

[63] However, the matter is not, it must be admitted, entirely clear. Certain texts do suggest that Gentiles can acquire merit by keeping the Torah. Thus *Sipra* 194 ['Aharei Mot 13] deduces from the use of the general term "man" in Lev 18:5, "You shall therefore keep my statutes and my judgements: which if a man do, he shall live in them," that "even a gentile who keeps the Torah is like the high priest."

[64] See *Pisqa* 343. The statement there that the Gentiles have "cast off" (פרקום) the Noachide laws does not mean that they are no longer obliged to obey them.

[65] See *Pisqaot* 43, 89, 96.

[66] See also *Pisqa* 31, "The name of God rests upon Israel in greatest measure"; *Pisqa* 344, God loved Israel more than the nations. Further *Pisqaot* 345 and 315, "I am going to make you dwell alone in the age to come, and none of the nations will benefit from you in any way." There is an ongoing tension in rabbinic thought over the role of Israel as an elect people within humanity as a whole. One chauvinistic strand of thought stresses the idea that Israel alone is benefitted by her election. Another strand, however, sees Israel's election as ultimately benefitting humanity as a whole. She plays a priestly role within humanity, bearing divine revelation and the knowledge of God. Tannaitic literature tends to take the more chauvinistic line.

[67] I shall return to this point later.

[68] The Torah is frequently defined as "the will of the Omnipresent" (see, e.g., *Pisqaot* 40 and 104).

if Israel obeys, and cursing if she does not.[69] And doubtless the redactor of *Sipre* would have approved of the Mishnah's insistence that the study of Torah is important and a precondition of the correct fulfillment of the terms of the covenant: "*That you may learn them, and observe to do them* (Deut. 5:1): This indicates that deeds are dependent upon learning, but learning is not dependent upon deeds. Hence we find that one is punished more severely for failure of learning than for failure of deeds" (*Pisqa* 41).[70] *Sipre* Deuteronomy itself stands as a monument to the redactor's belief in the importance of the meticulous study of the Torah.

In *Sipre* Deuteronomy the rewards of the covenant are essentially twofold: first, the gift of the Land and the establishment of the theocratic polity, and second, the sense of God's presence. These define for *Sipre* the condition of "salvation." *Sipre* Deuteronomy waxes lyrical about the glories of the Land of Israel, how it is the center of the world and the most fertile of lands, and it contrasts it favorably with Egypt and Babylonia.[71] As we noted earlier this emphasis on the Land separates early rabbinic Judaism from Diaspora Judaism. Jews in the Diaspora had effectively written the Land of Israel out of their Judaism. The Land may have remained a symbolic center to which Diaspora Jews had emotional ties, but their day-to-day religious life did not need to be nurtured by contact with it. They had, in a sense, universalized Judaism.[72] The Tannaitic rabbis continued to assert the importance of the Land, but their emphasis does not involve political activism: they are gradualists and their politics deeply pacifist. They do not view the Land primarily as the theater of Jewish political autonomy, to be seized by force from the colonial power, but rather as the sphere were the Torah can best be observed, since so much of the Torah comprises commandments pertaining to the Land. *Sipre* Deuteronomy, like the Mishnah, is generally vague about eschatology and remarkably un-messianic. It contains some references to "the world to come" but little messianism. What it does envisage is first and foremost the creation of a civil society here and now, rather than the dramatic intervention of God in history to create a messianic utopia. Though the

> Not surprising for Mosaic covenant

[69] See *Pisqaot* 40 and 54.

[70] See also *Pisqaot* 48 and 58.

[71] See especially *Pisqaot* 37–39.

[72] The role of the Land of Israel in early Judaism is ambiguous. Since the rise of modern Zionism and the re-establishment of the State of Israel it is natural to assume that the Land is absolutely central to Judaism and to see any lack of stress on it as, therefore, unusual and calling for comment. This is the line taken by W. D. Davies in *The Gospel and the Land* (Berkeley: University of California, 1974) and in *The Territorial Dimension of Judaism* (Berkeley: University of California, 1982). The fact is, however, that the Land has been of only marginal significance for large sectors of Judaism for long periods of time. Even for rabbinic Judaism it was not always central: it was of little importance for Babylonian Judaism in the Amoraic period and hence the Babylonian Yeshivot did not study the first order of the Mishnah. See further Isaiah M. Gafni, *Land, Center and Diaspora: Jewish Constructs in Late Antiquity* (Sheffield: Sheffield Academic, 1997).

messianic allusions in *Sipre* Deuteronomy are, perhaps, a little more numerous and insistent than in the Mishnah, it is broadly in line with Mishnah in de-emphasizing messianism.

The other reward of the covenant is the Presence of God (the Shekhinah), symbolized by the temple.[73] But *Sipre* Deuteronomy was written after the destruction of the temple. Is there then no possibility of experiencing the Presence of God while the temple is in ruins? *Sipre* Deuteronomy would doubtless have concurred with the Mishnah that there is: the Shekhinah abides with those who study the Torah. Part of that study of the Torah involves studying the laws of sacrifice and cult. Study of these laws is in some sense a substitute for fulfilling them. It is part of the rabbinic program of "full Torah" and demonstrates the reluctance of the rabbis to acknowledge any *de facto*, let alone *de jure*, limitation on the operation of the law.

If Israel breaches the terms of the covenant punishment follows. The blessings of the covenant are conditional. The gift of the Land is, apparently, not absolute. If the terms of the covenant are not fulfilled then Israel is handed over to the nations and exiled from her Land. God "hides his face" and withdraws his presence: "*And the Lord saw and spurned* (Deut 32:19): R. Judah says: They spurned him with the very things that he gave them for their own benefit. . . . *And he said: I will hide my face from them* – said the Holy One, blessed be he: I shall now remove my Presence from among them – *I will see what their end shall be* (Deut 32:20) – and I will know what will become of them. Another interpretation: I shall now deliver them into the hand of the four kingdoms, which will enslave them. *I will see what their end shall be* – I will inform them of their fate – *for they are a very forward generation*, [meaning that] they are fickle, they are perfidious – *children in whom is no faithfulness* (Deut 32:20). You are children who are not trustworthy. You stood at Mount Sinai and said, *All that the Lord has spoken will we do, and obey* (Exod. 24:7), [whereupon] *I said: You are godlike beings* (Ps. 82:6); but when you said to the [golden] calf, *This is your god, O Israel* (Exod 32:4), I said to you, *Nevertheless, you shall die like men* (Ps. 82:7). When I brought you into the land of your fathers, and you built for yourselves the Chosen House, I said that you will never be exiled from it; but when you said, *We have no portion in David* (2 Sam. 20:1), I said, *And Israel shall surely be led away captive out of the land* (Amos 7:17)" (*Pisqa* 320)[74].

---

[73] See *Pisqaot* 107 and 129. Note the remarkable gloss on Deut 33:27 in *Pisqa* 356, "*Happy are you, O Israel, who is like you? A people saved by the Lord* – a people whose salvation depends entirely upon the Shekhinah (עם שאין ישועתו אלא בשכינה)." There is a hint in *Pisqa* 37 of the idea that the temple is the navel of the earth. On the development of this idea in early Judaism see my essay, "Jerusalem as the *Omphalos* of the World: On the History of a Geographical Concept," *Judaism* 46 (1997): 147–58.

[74] Note also *Pisqa* 40 where the fertility of the Land depends on Israel doing the will of the Omnipresent. It is not, however, easy to square this with the idea that it was not Israel's own merit but the merit of the fathers that gained for her the Land (*Pisqa* 8). In *Pisqa* 184 the gift of

5.3 Mercy and Justice

Does God insist on strict justice in implementing the terms of the covenant? Here *Sipre* Deuteronomy, like the rest of rabbinic literature, struggles to reconcile the measure of justice and the measure of mercy. The conflict between these two great principles is carried back into the nature of God himself: as יהוה he is merciful, as אלהים he is just (*Pisqa* 26). The tension between justice and mercy runs through the whole of *Sipre* Deuteronomy. Sometimes justice is stressed,[75] sometimes mercy,[76] but the tension is never satisfactorily resolved. It was to prove fruitful for later Jewish theology.[77] However, the general impression one gets from reading *Sipre* Deuteronomy as a whole is that mercy wins out over strict justice. A number of important theological ideas moderate the conflict between these principles and contextualize the triumph of mercy over justice.

In the first place the relationship between Israel and God is conceived of in highly anthropomorphic terms. God loves Israel and Israel, in turn, is expected to love God (see especially *Pisqa* 32). The relationship between God and Israel is conceived of on the analogy of the relationship between father and son or husband and wife, relationships in which the affections and emotions are strongly engaged. This moderates the image of God as a stern and implacable judge, ruthlessly applying the letter of the law. Just as a

---

the Land is said to depend on both the merit of the fathers and on Israel's own merit.

[75] *Pisqa* 307: God is just, requiting each exactly as he deserves; he justifies the innocent and convicts the guilty. *Pisqa* 347: Merit is never replaced by guilt, nor guilt by merit, but one receives a reward for the performance of the מצות and punishment for transgressions. When the problem of the suffering of the righteous is raised a number of lines of response are developed. First, the principle that punishment follows sin may simply be reaffirmed, and the doctrine of measure for measure stressed. Second, arguing *ad hominem*, the testimony of the martyrs, a striking case of righteous suffering, may be cited to show that they justified God. Third, the doctrine of the world to come may be invoked to redress the imbalances in reward and punishment meted out in this world. See *Pisqaot* 49, 96, 307, 308.

[76] Note especially *Pisqa* 26: "Israel had two fine leaders, Moses and David, king of Israel. Their meritorious deeds could have sustained the whole world, yet they begged the Holy One, blessed be he, only on the basis of favour (חנם). Is it not a matter of inference from the minor to the major? If those whose meritorious deeds could have sustained the whole world petitioned the Holy One only on the basis of favour, how much more so should a person who is not even one thousand-thousandth or ten-thousand times ten-thousandth part the disciples of their disciples beseech the Holy One only on the basis of favour." Cf. *Sipre* Numbers §41. Hammer's note to *Pisqa* 26 catches well the inconsistency of the rabbinic position: "Cf. Deut. Rabbah 2:1: 'No creature has any claim upon its Creator.' The idea that it is God's compassion and grace rather than our merits upon which we must depend is found in Dan. 9:8 and is quoted in the daily prayers, as well as in the concluding service of the Day of Atonement. In Christianity this became the doctrine of grace; cf. Rom. 3:19ff." But he then goes on to note: "For a contrasting view, see *'Ab* 2:16, 3:19 [3:16], and 4:11" (*Sifre: A Tannaitic Commentary on the Book of Deuteronomy*, 400).

[77] In the medieval Kabbalah, for example, the tension between mercy and justice is a major theme for speculation.

merciful father will receive an erring son back into favor, or a merciful husband will pardon an erring wife, so God, in the end, will receive back Israel. The rabbis are not afraid of using highly anthropomorphic language of God, which goes well beyond the anthropomorphism of the Bible (cf. *Pisqa* 319). This was to cause problems later on for rabbinic theologians, but the problems which it creates are offset religiously by the problems which it solves or glosses over. Israel is exhorted to imitate God, particularly in showing mercy (see *Pisqa* 49). God is the exemplar whom Israel should follow. This idea, in fact, probably started out with what was perceived to be admirable behavior on the part of human beings and projected this onto God, only to turn round and reinforce the behavior in humans on the grounds that it involves an *imitatio dei*. Such a process of thinking is immeasurably helped by conceiving of the relationship between God and Israel in emotive and human terms. The same anthropomorphic context helps to explain the power of repentance. The harshness of the terms of the covenant is mitigated by the concept of atonement. Integral to atonement in Deuteronomy is the sacrificial system. But *Sipre* Deuteronomy was composed at a time when the sacrifices were no longer operative. So how does atonement now work? *Sipre* Deuteronomy probably sees repentance as in some sense taking its place (see *Pisqa* 43), though it also sees a correlation between the sacrifices and personal suffering (see *Pisqa* 32). This is in line with the prophetic thinking which prioritizes the personal virtues of obedience and mercy over sacrifice (see Hos 6:6 and 1 Sam 15:22). The tension between justice and mercy is also moderated by a doctrine of merits, especially the merits of the fathers. It was due to the merit of Abraham, Isaac and Jacob that Israel was granted the Land. The merits of the fathers avail for their descendants, satisfy the attribute of justice and allow the attribute of mercy to work in Israel's favor (see *Pisqaot* 8, 184, 319 and 325).

5.4 Is the Covenant Ultimately Conditional?

So far our exposition of *Sipre* Deuteronomy seems to leave open the possibility that the covenant can ultimately fail. Israel will simply not fulfill its terms and there will be little that God can do about it. *Sipre* Deuteronomy can hardly be said specifically to address this issue, but, in keeping with the general drift of rabbinic thought, it does not appear to envisage the covenant as finally coming to nothing, despite the ups and downs of God's relationship with Israel. God is the ultimate guarantor of the covenant and he will ensure that in the end it is fulfilled. Two points should be borne in mind here.

First, *Sipre* Deuteronomy states that the covenant cannot ultimately be revoked by the sins of Israel. When in *Pisqa* 96 Rabbi Judah explains that Deut 14:1, "You are the children of the Lord your God," means that Israel are God's children only if they conduct themselves like dutiful children, Rabbi Meir's opinion that they remain God's children whether they behave

righteously or not is immediately introduced by way of refutation.[78] And
Meir's view is reinforced in *Pisqa* 308, where a series of negative statements
about Israel in Scripture is skillfully turned to show that sin does not
ultimately break the bond between Israel and God. There is no final rejection
of the people. A polemical (possibly anti-Christian) intent may lie behind
this,[79] but it is also entirely in keeping with the general thrust of rabbinic
teaching. The rabbis may be here thinking primarily as lawyers. The
covenant is a fact: Israel and God entered into it at Sinai. That fact can never
be altered; there is no going back. This is not to say, however, that all Israel
will finally be saved, whatever they do. Early rabbinic sources regularly
categorize certain groups of Jews as excluded from the world to come. The
most important text is *m. Sanh.* 10:1:

> A. All Israel has a share in the world to come, for it is written, *Your people also shall
> be all righteous, they shall inherit the land for ever, the branch of my planting, the work
> of my hands that I may be glorified* (Is. 60:21).
> B. And these are they who have no share in the world to come: he who says that there
> is no resurrection of the dead prescribed in Torah, and he who says that the Torah is not
> from heaven, and an Epicurean.
> C. Rabbi Aqiva says: Also he who reads external books, or who utters charms over a
> wound and says, *I will put none of these diseases upon you which I have put on the
> Egyptians: for I am the Lord who heals you* (Exod 15:26).
> D. Abba Saul says: Also he who pronounces the Name with its proper letters.

It seems obvious that this unit has been built up in a number of layers, the
original sweeping assertion of A being steadily more and more qualified. The
broad categories of sin which exclude from the world to come are heresy,
witchcraft and blasphemy. Though it is implied that some will be excluded,
it is equally implied that some will be saved. The Tannaitic sources do not
speculate on the proportions of the saved to the damned. However, though it
would have been open to them to develop the remnant theology of Isaiah, the
impression one gets is that they expected most of Israel in the end to share
in the world to come. One way or the other the covenant would be fulfilled.

Second, it would be possible by linking the doctrine of God's election of
Israel with a certain understanding of God's power, his purposes in the world
and the nature of his love, to argue that the covenant cannot finally fail.

---

[78] Cf. *m. 'Abot* 3:15; *'Abot de Rabbi Nathan* A 39. It should be noted, however, that the view
that the covenant might ultimately fail is put in the mouth of a respected scholar. Normally such
sensitive questions are raised by outsiders (heretics, philosophers, Roman matrons, the Emperor
and so forth). The fact that the problem is not posed in this way may suggest that it was not seen
as all that embarrassing.

[79] One sin that caused particular concern to the rabbis was the sin of the Golden Calf. This
may, in part, have been due to the use of the story polemically by Christians to argue the rejection
of Israel. See L. Smolar and M. Aberbach, "The Golden Calf Episode in Postbiblical Literature,"
HUCA 39 (1968): 91–116; Pier Cesare Bori, *The Golden Calf and the Origins of the Anti-Jewish
Controversy* (Atlanta: Scholars, 1990). Smolar and Aberbach suggest that the sin of the Calf is
"the nearest Jewish equivalent to the concept of original sin" (p. 6).

God's choice of Israel is central to Deuteronomy. A key text is 7:6–8, "For you are a holy people to the Lord your God: the Lord your God has chosen you to be a peculiar people to himself above all the peoples that are on the face of the earth. The Lord did not set his love upon you, nor choose you, because you were more in number than any people; for you were the fewest of all peoples: but because the Lord loves you, and because he would keep the oath which he swore to your fathers, has the Lord brought you out with a mighty hand, and redeemed you out of the house of bondage, from the hand of Pharaoh, king of Egypt."[80] *Sipre* Deuteronomy, and the Tannaitic literature in general, certainly accept the doctrine of the divine election of Israel, but it is striking how little either Scripture or the Tannaitic sources state in clear and unequivocal terms that God's choice is unconditional. Those passages of Scripture (Deut 7:6ff. included; note 7:9–11) which speak so emphatically of Israel's election always introduce a note of conditionality. And the same is true of the Tannaitic sources. *Sipre* Deuteronomy *Pisqa* 312, which is sometimes quoted as a strong defense of God's continuing election of Israel,[81] in fact stresses the mutuality of the covenant. Having conclusively proved from Deut 14:2 that it is the Lord who has chosen Israel, the midrash immediately asks, "And whence do we learn that Jacob also chose God? From the verse, *Not like these is the portion of Jacob* (Jer. 10:16)." I suspect that if they had been directly challenged on this issue the Tannaitic sages would have maintained that God would see to it that the covenant would not ultimately fail,[82] but there were few who would seriously raise this issue in their milieu. This left them freer to stress the conditionality of the covenant as a way homiletically of encouraging their fellow Jews to observe the Torah. However, with the emergence in the Amoraic period of a triumphant Gentile Christianity which constantly preached the supersession of Israel they became more sensitive on this point and began to develop ideas of God's eternal and irrevocable election of Israel. God has a purpose in history. History will follow a foreordained pattern and will culminate in the messianic age when the covenant will finally reach fruition. Israel can co-operate in this process, and perhaps hasten or delay it, but the process will inevitably run its course and will reach its predetermined goal, because it depends ultimately on God and not on Israel.

---

[80] See also Deut 14:2, 26:18–19, 28:9; cf. Exod 19: 5–6.

[81] Possibly against the Christians: see Eugene Mihaly, "A Rabbinic Defence of the Election of Israel," *HUCA* 25 (1964): 103–35.

[82] Note, e.g., *Pisqa* 309: Israel is precious to God because he has acquired her. *Pisqa* 306: God, despite the divorce of Israel from himself through sin will restore the relationship; Israel has rejected God, but God has remained steadfast towards Israel.

6. Concluding Theses

I have tried to survey in this essay an extensive and complex body of rabbinic
literature, posing to it an agenda which has essentially been framed elsewhere
(in the study of Paul and of post-Reformation Christian theology), and asking
of it questions which it is reluctant to answer. I have been constantly troubled
by the feeling that I have, to some degree, been forcing the sources – reading
them somewhat against their grain, and imposing upon them a consistency
which they do not possess. It is important to remind ourselves constantly just
how incongruous is the comparison of the letters of Paul with the Mishnah,
the foundational document of rabbinic Judaism. The Mishnah is a large and
sophisticated corpus of law produced over approximately two centuries by
jurists. It is a collective effort, a deeply political document intended to be the
code by which a whole nation was to live and to constitute a civil society
here and now. Paul's letters are the product of a single, driven religious
genius, an itinerant preacher who believed that the end of the world was at
hand. They are deeply personal, idiosyncratic and sectarian and, in Jewish
terms, shot through with a diasporan mentality. The comparison of these two
collections of texts is about as easy and meaningful as the comparison of the
sermons of Chrysostom with the Code of Justinian, or the writings of John
Wesley and the Code Napoléon. However, in a spirit of co-operation with the
broader enterprise of this volume to set Paul in his early Jewish context, I
shall conclude by attempting to distill the results of the foregoing brief
analysis into ten useful and hopefully valid propositions.

1. Though there are numerous and important theologoumena scattered
across the Tannaitic corpus, no attempt is made within the corpus itself to
synthesize these into a coherent theology of Judaism. The nearest we come
to such a theology is in *m. 'Abot*, which is intended to articulate the broad
principles underlying the Mishnah. But *m. 'Abot* is patently not a theology
in any meaningful modern sense of the term, and it makes no effort to
reconcile the manifest tensions and even contradictions between many of its
propositions. Homiletics always predominates over theology in the Tannaitic
sources.

2. The Tannaitic sources do presuppose a worldview and therefore to
construct a theology of Tannaitic Judaism is probably a legitimate intellectual enterprise. It should, however, proceed initially on the basis of the
individual Tannaitic documents, analyzing first the ideas of each document
and not jumping too quickly to synthesize ideas from different documents
into a grand whole. We examined briefly the Mishnah and *Sipre* Deuteronomy as representing the two major genres of Tannaitic literature, law code
and Bible commentary. The ideas put forward in these documents are
compatible and complementary, which is hardly surprising since they arose
in the same small circles, but the emphases in each is rather different. The

concept of the covenant is central to *Sipre* Deuteronomy (in line with the underlying biblical text), but one could hardly claim that it is explicit in the Mishnah.

3. In constructing a theology of Tannaitic Judaism it is important to take into account how the Tannaitic theologoumena were interpreted and developed in later Jewish thought from the Amoraic period down to modern times. A very fine line needs to be trod here. On the one hand there is a danger of reading later ideas anachronistically into earlier texts: the principle of historical development must never be forgotten. The Judaism of the Mishnah should not be simply equated with the Judaism of Saadya or Maimonides. On the other hand the later developments should not be ignored. The later thinkers were involved in a close reading of the earlier sources and their insights are often highly suggestive as to the theological implications of the Tannaitic texts. Particularly valuable are the interpretations of the Amoraim, the generations of the Sages immediately after the close of the Mishnah. The alternative to reading the Tannaitic sources discriminatingly in the light of the later tradition is often naively to introduce modern agendas and ideas to the study of these texts, and then dress up one's findings as historical scholarship. It is somewhat disturbing to note the extent to which the systematic construction of Tannaitic theology has been dominated by Christian scholars who have a liberal Protestant agenda and little or no knowledge of the later rabbinic theological tradition, or by Jewish scholars who have been, arguably, theologically influenced by liberal Protestant thought.

4. There is a marked congruence between Tannaitic thinking and Scripture, at least to the extent that Scripture yields usable theological propositions. In particular Tannaitic Judaism aligns itself closely with the theological thought of the Deuteronomistic school. Broadly speaking, if there was a theology in early post-biblical Judaism it was the theology of Deuteronomy. That is not to say that Deuteronomy itself has a worked out, totally consistent theology.

5. Torah is central to Tannaitic theology. However, in sharp contrast to elements of Diaspora Judaism, the Tannaitic sources stress the totality of Torah. Torah embraces not only what the Pentateuch stipulates, but also the tradition which extends and clarifies the Pentateuchal laws. It includes the "laws pertaining to the Land" and the laws of sacrifice. Though the latter cannot be implemented since the temple has been destroyed they are still valid and must be studied. Tannaitic Judaism is a "full Torah" Judaism. Tannaitic Judaism is deeply anti-sectarian in the sense that it aspires to provide a national program for the whole of Israel. The Mishnah offers a constitution for a national community; it is the manifesto of a party which claims the right spiritually and politically to guide all Israel.

6. Torah is binding only on Israel. The nations are measured by a less demanding code, the commandments to the sons of Noah. A Gentile who

keeps that code is fully righteous. Israel, however, achieves righteousness by keeping the commandments of the Torah. There is no hint of perfectionism in the Tannaitic sources: righteousness is determined fundamentally by the preponderance of one's deeds. It is true that some may go beyond the demands of strict righteousness and become "saints" (חסידים) but, although חסידות is clearly admired and seen as a worthy aspiration, there seems to be no general obligation to achieve "sainthood."

7. Study of the Torah is a precondition for the proper performance of the Torah. Study of the Torah informs the mind, suppresses the inclination towards evil and encourages the inclination towards good, promotes love of God and a sense of his presence, and generally neutralizes the dangers of formalism.

8. Salvation for Tannaitic Judaism is essentially national – the nation's enjoyment of peace and prosperity in its own Land. It is not, however, overtly messianic: there is no hint in the Mishnah or in *Sipre* Deuteronomy of political activism, nor is any encouragement given to those who would work by violent means to overthrow Rome and establish full political independence. The individual who keeps the commandments will be rewarded by God, but ultimately his salvation consists of enjoying the blessings of the fulfilled covenant as a member of the Community of Israel. The rewards of righteousness are essentially this worldly. There are hints of eschatological rewards and punishments (whether in the days of the Messiah or the world to come), but eschatological dualism is not developed to any significant degree in the Tannaitic sources.

9. Tannaitic Judaism can be seen as fundamentally a religion of works-righteousness, and it is none the worse for that. The superiority of grace over law is not self-evident and should not simply be assumed. There is little hint in Tannaitic sources that God can simply forgive the sinner without any action whatsoever on the sinner's part. However, the rigors of divine justice are moderated by divine mercy. There are means of atonement which can stay or mitigate the application of strict justice. Repentance, which includes contrition, confession and supplication, amendment of life and (where possible) restitution, gives scope for the mercy of God. The merits of the fathers and of the righteous cover the sins of all Israel. And in general the relationship between God and Israel is depicted in such anthropological and emotional terms that one does not get the impression that it is governed by the operation of blind fate (ἀνάγκη) or inexorable justice (δίκη).

10. In dialectical tension with the basic works-righteousness of the Tannaitic worldview stands the doctrine of the election of Israel, which suggests that God has chosen Israel to fulfill his purposes in the world and that he will guarantee that, whatever Israel does, the covenant in his mercy and grace will not ultimately fail. This idea, which is biblical in origin, was probably sharpened by polemics and may have been directed against Christian claims that Israel had been rejected by God. It is, however,

nowhere clearly articulated in Tannaitic literature, nor are its tensions with the doctrine of works-righteousness ever deeply explored or finally resolved.

11. Some Targum Themes

by

MARTIN MCNAMARA

1. The Targums in Second Temple Judaism

1.1 Terminology

In the context of the present volume, as of biblical studies in general, the meaning intended by the term "targum" is a Jewish translation of the Hebrew Scriptures.[1] The quadrilateral Hebrew verb and noun תרגם seems to have the basic meanings of "translate"/"interpret," and "translation,"/"interpretation." The word itself appears early in the Semitic languages (for instance Akkadian *targumannu*, "translator"), and seems to have entered the Semitic languages from Indo-European, possibly Hittite.[2] In Hebrew the term can mean translation into any language, and in early rabbinic texts is also used to refer to the Greek Septuagint translation. In modern biblical and Jewish studies its usage is restricted to Jewish (and Samaritan) translations of the Tanak into Aramaic.

1.2 Admissibility of Targums in Study of Second Temple Judaism

We have Qumran Aramaic biblical translations which were composed during the Second Temple period – the Targum of Job from Qumran (4QtgJob and 11QtgJob), possibly from the second century B.C.E., and also fragments of a Targum of Leviticus (4QtgLev), from the first century B.C.E. Since these form part of the literature of the Second Temple no objection can be raised to their use in studies of the period.

Matters are different with regard to the "traditional" Targums known to us. We have texts of Jewish Aramaic translations of all the books of the Hebrew Bible with the exception of Daniel and Ezra-Nehemiah (portions of which books are already in Aramaic). For the Pentateuch we have Targum

---

[1] For a general introduction to Targums see P. S. Alexander, "Targum, Targumim," *ABD*, 6.320–31; M. McNamara, "Interpretation of Scripture in the Targums," in *History of Biblical Interpretation. I. The Ancient Period* (ed. A. J. Hauser and D. F. Watson: forthcoming). See also A. D. York, "The Targum in the Synagogue and in the School," *JSJ* 10 (1979): 74–86.

[2] See Ch. Rabin, "Hittite Words in Hebrew," *Orientalia* 32 (1963): 134–6.

Onqelos, the Targums of the Pentateuch (represented almost completely by
Targum Neofiti 1; partially by the Fragment Targums found in the four
manuscripts from Paris, the Vatican Library, Nuremberg and Leipzig – with
the sigla PVNL; by texts from the Cairo Genizah and by the numerous glosses
to Codex Neofiti 1 – given the siglum Nfmg). For the Pentateuch we also
have the Targum Pseudo-Jonathan, a later work which used both Onqelos and
a form of the Palestinian Targum (sometimes referred to as the Targum of
Jerusalem), and other sources as well. We have a full Targum of the Prophets
(Former Prophets, Major and Minor Prophets) and Targums for the individual
writings (two for Esther), with the exception as said of Daniel and Ezra-
Nehemiah. As is well known from the history of New Testament and Jewish
studies, much use was made of certain of these Targums (particularly that
known as the Palestinian Targum of the Pentateuch) in New Testament
studies, particularly of the Gospels and this because these Targums were
believed to pre-date the New Testament period and to represent in language
and thought the situation in New Testament Palestine.

Very serious objections have been raised against this position, in particular
after the discovery of the Aramaic texts from Qumran, dating from immediately before or from the New Testament period, and differing significantly
from the traditional Targums in language, in concepts and in the manner of
translating the Hebrew Text. Scientific study of the Aramaic language
strengthened this position. At best, while the language of Onqelos and the
Targum of the Prophets might be considered pre-132 C.E., the language of the
Palestinian Targum is considered to be somewhat later than this, say third
century at the earliest.[3] This, in the view of some of the specialists, does not
preclude the existence of a first-century C.E. Proto-Palestinian Targum, from
which both Onqelos and the Palestinian Targum of the Pentateuch are
separately descended.[4]

Together with this research on the language of the Targums there has over
recent years also been intensive examination of the interpretative tradition
enshrined in our present Targums, mainly in Targum Onqelos, the Targums
of the Prophets and in the Palestinian Targums of the Pentateuch. In many
instances the interpretation is regarded as not all of the same date; Targums
may have layers of interpretation from different periods. In fact some speak
of the tell-like structure of the Targum of the Twelve Minor Prophets, a
sensitivity to which tell-like character is required in our investigation of it

---

[3] See S. Kaufman, "Dating the Language of the Palestinian Targums and their Use in the
Study of First-Century Texts," in *The Aramaic Bible. Targums in their Historical Context* (ed.
D. R. G. Beattie and M. J. McNamara; JSOTSup 166; Sheffield: JSOT, 1994), 118–41, at 122.

[4] See Kaufman, "Dating the Language," 130.

since the extant text probably includes stratified elements representing as much as several centuries of targumic development.[5]

In a volume such as the present one, the position of E. P. Sanders regarding the use of the Targums in Judaism contemporary with Paul merits special attention. In the introduction to his work *Paul and Palestinian Judaism: A Comparison of Patterns of Religion* he regards it necessary to make a few comments about Palestinian Jewish sources for the years from 200 B.C.E. to 200 C.E. His general intention is to consider the entire body of material available from the period. The sources he lists are rabbinic (Tannaitic) literature (which he takes to be, on the whole, the latest body of literature to be treated in his work), then the Dead Sea Scrolls, and thirdly the apocryphal and pseudepigraphical writings, from Ben Sira' to IV Ezra. He then goes on to say:[6]

I have further left out of consideration the Aramaic Targums which are now sometimes dated to this period.[7] In part, I am not persuaded of the antiquity of the Targums as we have them.[8] Even if generally late, the Targums may, to be sure, contain early traditions, but these must now be sought out one by one. In general, the present state of Targumic studies does not permit the Targums to be used for our purposes. At present the Targums can be used in motif research, in which one can investigate a given theme or idea and attempt to date the Targumic material which is relevant. We are not at the stage, however, of being able to discuss the view of religion and the religious life in the Palestinian Targum to the Pentateuch, and especially not to date a coherent view of religion to the period which falls within our purview.

It must be conceded that scholarly opinion with regard to the dating of the Targums and targumic tradition has not changed considerably, if at all, since these words were written. Some would go even further, expressing the view that the conceptual world of the Targums depends on rabbinic views (and therefore late).[9] There has been no breakthrough that would prove that

---

[5] On this see R. Gordon, *Studies in the Targum to the Twelve Prophets. From Nahum to Malachi* (VTSup 51; Leiden: Brill, 1994), 152–3.

[6] E. P. Sanders, *Paul and Palestinian Judaism: A Comparison of Patterns of Religion* (London: SCM, 1979), 25–26.

[7] With reference to the present writer's *The New Testament and the Palestinian Targum to the Pentateuch* (AnBib 27A; 2d ed.; Rome: Biblical Institute, 1978), 35.

[8] With reference to J. Fitzmyer's reviews of the present writer's *The New Testament and the Palestinian Targum*, in *TS* 29 (1968): 321–6, and of A. Díez Macho's edition of *Neofiti* in *CBQ* 32 (1970): 524–5, as well as other essays by Fitzmyer; likewise J. Greenfield's review of the republication of Etheridge's translation of the Targum to the Pentateuch in *JBL* 89 (1070): 238–9; B. Z. Wacholder's review of the present writer's *Targum and Testament* (Shannon, Ireland: Irish Academic Press/Grand Rapids: Eerdmans, 1972) in *JBL* 93 (1974): 132–3, and A. D. York's essay, "The Dating of Targumic Literature," *JSJ* 5 (1974): 49–62.

[9] Thus, for instance, B. L. Visotzky, "Text, Translation, Targum," in *Fathers of the World* (ed. B. L. Visotzky; WUNT 80; Tübingen: Mohr [Siebeck], 1995), 106–12, esp. 107: "Finally, it must be remembered that the world of ideas found in the Targums are a watered down version

targumic tradition in whole or in part belongs to the Second Temple period, nor is there likely to be any unless we discover a Hebrew text of a rewritten Bible along the lines of the targumic paraphrase. We thus have currently three groups with regard to the use of the Targums in New Testament or Second Temple studies. Some regard the Targums as definitely later than the period in question; another group of scholars considers an early date unproven. A third group, while aware of the problems, believes that there are sufficient indications of the early origins or roots of the central group of Targums (Palestinian Targums of the Pentateuch; Onqelos; Targum of the Prophets) to warrant their being taken into consideration in the study of Second Temple Judaism.

A number of scholars regard the basic redaction of the Targum of the Prophets as having been made about the year 100 C.E., and Onqelos as from roughly the same period. While the basic redaction of the Palestinian Targum as we now have it (distinct from Onqelos) may be somewhat later (say late second or third century C.E.) the interpretative tradition it represents can be presumed to belong to the period of Second Temple Judaism.

If we accept these dates as probable, it is a justifiable assumption that the interpretative tradition which these Targums represent belongs to the Second Temple period of Judaism. While admitting the uncertainties involved, to exclude the targumic evidence would be to run a serious risk of not paying due attention to the complexities of Second Temple Judaism.

1.3 Origins and Early Development of Interpretative Biblical Tradition and of Targums

One of the phenomena revealed by modern biblical studies is inner-biblical interpretation. The Hebrew Scriptures reached the final and canonical stages of their development through evolution in law, in doctrine and in traditions. While still in the process of formation this development would be registered as part of Scripture. Even the first stage of a work such as the book of Jeremiah as translated into Greek could be developed to give us the longer and canonical Jeremiah of the Hebrew Masoretic Text. Once a work was regarded as canonical any further development could not be registered as part of the canonical text itself. The canonical text, however, gave rise to further reflection and would always present questions as to its precise meaning as

---

of rabbinic (and therefore late) theology held captive to the necessity of translating the biblical text (even loosely) in a synagogal-lectionary and late setting" (essay earlier in *Prooftexts* 9 [1989], 93–98). Likewise Visotzky in his introduction to this volume of collected essays (p. 21): "[In this essay] I take to task those scholars (particularly Christian) who fall prey to anachronism in their quest for recovery of some element (in this case, Aramaic language and literature) of the historical Jesus. I point out that targums as we have them are notably late, often post Islam. One may as well rely on Syriac literature to recover Jesus' Aramaic."

God's inspired word, or in the case of law codes as a practical guide for living.

We have a practical example of what is intended in the solemn reading and interpretation by Ezra and the Levites of the "law of Moses which the Lord had given to Israel," an event which took place in the seventh month of the seventh year of Artaxerxes (458 B.C.E. if Artaxerxes I is intended; 398 if Artaxerxes II). See Ezra 7 and Neh 8. On that occasion "they read from the book, from the law of God, with interpretation (?; מְפֹרָשׁ) and gave the sense, so that the people understood the reading" (Neh 8:8). Detailed exegesis of this passage is not required for our purpose here (for instance: Who read? Who gave the sense? What is the meaning of מפרשׁ?). What is important is the evidence the text provides of the existence of "the book of the law of God, given through Moses" (apparently identical in substance at least with our present Pentateuch), together with the concern that this be read to the covenant community, that the meaning of the book's message be put before the people and that the people he helped to understand. The book of the law was in Hebrew. The explanation would have been given in the language of the people. What the spoken language was at that time in Jerusalem is not altogether clear, but it probably was still Hebrew rather than Aramaic.

The concerns shown on that occasion can be presumed to have continued in the generations and centuries that followed. The book of the law of Moses would continue to be explained and the traditions it contained developed. One can only surmise the centers at which the study of, and reflection on, the law of Moses and the Tanak took place. In part it would have been at liturgical gatherings and at synagogues when these came into being. We know from the prologue to Ecclesiasticus that by the year 200 B.C.E. or so the Law, the Prophets and the other writings were studied and piously reflected on in the academies and schools of the wisdom tradition. The traditions that developed from and around the Law of Moses (and indeed the other books of the Tanak, we can presume) were not unilinear. With regard to Moses one line of development passed through the Qumran communities, another to and through early and later rabbinic tradition.

The traditions enshrined in the Targums (notably the Targums of the Pentateuch and of the Prophets) have been transmitted to us through the rabbis. There is also close connection between the interpretative tradition found in the Targum and in rabbinic tradition. A question arises as to whether the Targums depend on rabbinic tradition, or vice versa, and whether the Targums reflect the tradition of the synagogues or of the school (בית ה-מדרשׁ). It would seem unwise to set one over against the other. Both stand within a larger tradition, with a concern to understand the sense of the Bible and to bring its message to the general public. One can envisage a broad Jewish approach to the Bible (independent of that of Qumran) which is reflected in the Targums, rabbinic tradition and in other works such as the *Biblical Antiquities* of Pseudo-Philo.

When the language of the Jewish community in Palestine came to be Aramaic rather than Hebrew, instruction of the people in the Law of Moses, in the Prophets and in their religious tradition in general would have been in Aramaic. How early the change from Hebrew to Aramaic came cannot be ascertained with certainty, but Aramaic was at least the spoken language of a good portion of the Jewish population, if not of the majority, by 200 B.C.E. or so.

Some form of instruction on the Bible through the medium of Aramaic can be presumed to have originated at the same time. And the aim of the Aramaic instruction would be to give the sense of the biblical text, and have the people understand the import of the biblical message. Thus, an Aramaic translation or paraphrase, a Targum of some sort, can be presumed to have existed during the Second Temple period, at least for the Pentateuch and the Prophets. We can reasonably presume that the translation would not be haphazard, an ad hoc translation in the synagogue in keeping with the expertise of the member of the congregation called on, or volunteering, to do it. Translation is rather work for the school, requiring expertise in translation techniques. In point of fact, all our extant Targums of the Pentateuch and of the Prophets indicate that they are works of expert translators, even though these employ somewhat differing translation techniques.

We can say very little of the origins and early development of the Aramaic translations of the Pentateuch and of the Prophets. All we have to go on are the extant Targums of these biblical works, together with what conclusions we can draw from an analysis of the language of these texts and from their contents. As already noted, some scholars deduce from this evidence that within our present Targums there are layers of interpretative tradition, indicating a growth over some considerable time.

1.4 Some Questions of Methodology in the Use of Targums in Second Temple Studies

1.4.1 Targums as translation and expanded paraphrase

The Aramaic Targums of the Pentateuch and the Prophets are first and foremost translations of the Hebrew text. Their chief aim is to give the sense of the biblical text. Together with this they offer certain expanded paraphrase and some additional midrash. In our study of the Targums as witnesses of Second Temple Judaism we must take this whole evidence into account. The Targums as literal translations may at times have served as a counterbalance to some later popular opinions also to be found in these same Aramaic translations.

The translator may not always have held the same beliefs, or formulations of belief, as the text he has translated. Of course, there is ample evidence that the translation very often reflects beliefs and mind sets later than those of the biblical authors. In these interpretative translations, expansions and additions the Targums provide rich information on the language and beliefs and mind sets of later generations.

1.4.2 The Targums and Jewish rabbinic midrash and rabbinic biblical interpretation

It is quite clear that traditions found in the Targums are closely related to rabbinic tradition. It is a matter of debate as to which is dependent on the other, or whether the similarities are to be explained by dependence of both on a common earlier tradition. Studies in this area usually indicate the rabbinic parallels to targumic texts. I refrain from so doing in this study, in which I consider the targumic evidence alone. Detailed examination of any particular topic would require examination of all the relevant evidence from rabbinic and other sources, together with consideration of the probable date to be assigned to the tradition in question.

1.4.3 Choice of Targums used

Since consideration of the select topics in all the Targums would prove too difficult in a study of this nature, I have confined myself to the Targums of the Pentateuch (with the exception of the Targum of Pseudo-Jonathan) and of the Prophets. The Targum of Pseudo-Jonathan is commonly regarded as a late work, the product of a scholar's desk rather than representing an early living tradition.

2. Law (The Torah)

The Targums pass beyond the biblical text in particular by the added references to the Torah (in Aramaic אורייתה, אורייתא). The references appear to be ubiquitous. Reference to the Law is made where the biblical text being translated affords some basis for its introduction, and very often where it provides none. This holds true for the Targum of the Prophets as well as the Targums of the Pentateuch.[10] One's attitude to God is measured by one's

---

[10] What has been observed with regard to the Targum of Isaiah can be taken as true for the other Targums. J. F. Stenning notes with regard to Tg. Isaiah: "A noticeable feature of the translation is the frequent reference to the Law and the insistence on obedience to it as the basis of religion. In the majority of the passages cited the reference can be regarded as a legitimate, if narrow, explanation of the text, but in others the context affords no justification for such a limited interpretation" (*The Targum of Isaiah* [Oxford: Clarendon, 1949], xv, with examples

attitude to the Law. Conversion (תתובה) is turning or returning to the Law.
They are an indication of how central the concept of Law was in late Jewish
thought, how near to the hearts of those who produced the Targums. No
single definition can be given that will hold for Torah in all its uses in the
Targums. It seems to sum up God's revelation to Israel and expressed Israel's
response in obedience to God.[11]

Here I consider some aspects of the teaching of the Palestinian Targums
on Torah, seen especially against the biblical background.

2.1 Wisdom and the Torah in Ben Sira' (Late Judaism)

In their teaching on the Law (Torah) the Targums develop further what is
already very much present in late Second Temple Judaism, as evidenced for
instance in Ben Sira' and the Book of Baruch. In their approach to the Law
the Targums are heirs to the traditions of the school, the בית ה־מדרש (*bet
ha-midrash*), which by the time of Jesus ben Sira' (180 B.C.E. or so) was
meditatively reflecting on Israel's entire tradition, the Law (of Moses), the
Prophets and the Other Writings.

In singing her own praises, Wisdom personified, which came forth from the
mouth of the Most High (Sir 24:3), tells us that the Creator of all things gave
her a commandment, the one who created her assigned a place for her tent,
and he said: "Make your dwelling in Jacob, and in Israel receive your
inheritance" (Sir 24:8). Ben Sira' himself practically identifies wisdom with
the law of Moses: "All this is the book of the covenant of the Most High God,
the law which Moses commanded us as an inheritance for the congregation
of Jacob" (24:25). The Torah, or "the law which Moses commanded," is
brimful with wisdom, it runs over with understanding, it pours forth
instruction (παιδείαν) (24:25–27). A. A. Di Lella remarks on this text: "The
Torah, like wisdom in v. 3, is viewed as a spirit. Hence Ben Sira' can speak
of the Torah as being 'brimful, like the Pishon . . . with wisdom' . . .; it also
'runs over like the Euphrates . . . with understanding.'"[12] The central theme

---

from twenty-three of the chapters between ch. 1 and 63). Likewise, B. D. Chilton, *The Glory
of Israel: The Theology and Provenience of the Isaiah Targum* (JSOTSup 23; Sheffield: JSOT,
1983), 13: "The meturgeman is so convinced that law is the means offered God's people for
relating themselves to him that he frequently introduces the term when there is no analogue to
it in the Hebrew text," with as example Tg. Isa. 1:2–3: "Hear, heavens, which trembled when
I gave my law to my people . . . they have rebelled against my Memra . . . my people has not
had the intelligence to return to my law."

[11] For the concept and term in the Targum of the Prophets see L. Smolar and M. Aberbach,
Studies in Targum Jonathan to the Prophets, with *Targum Jonathan to the Prophets* by P.
Churgin (The Library of Biblical Studies; New York and Baltimore: KTAV Publishing House
and The Baltimore Hebrew College, 1983), 159–64 ("Torah and good deeds").

[12] A. A. Di Lella, *The Wisdom of Ben Sira. A New Translation with Notes* by P. W. Skehan.
Introduction and Commentary by A. A. Di Lella (AB 39; New York: Doubleday, 1987), 336.

of the book of Ben Sira' and the relationship of recurrent themes such as wisdom, fear of God and the Law has exercised the minds of scholars. Di Lella believes that R. Smend suggests the best approach to this question when he writes: "Subjectively, wisdom is fear of God; objectively, it is the law book of Moses (chap. 24)."[13] Di Lella continues: "Accordingly, I would argue that ben Sira's primary theme is wisdom *as* fear of God, and that the fundamental thesis of the book is the following: wisdom, which is identified with the Law, can be achieved only by one who fears God and keeps the commandments. Or, as Ben Sira' himself writes: 'The whole of wisdom is fear of the Lord; complete wisdom is the fulfilment of the Law' (19:20)."

2.2 *Summary of Targumic Position in Pal. Tg. Gen. 3:15, 24*

Sir 24:25–27 compares the Law, identified with wisdom, with the rivers of Paradise, spoken of in Gen 2:10–14, and goes on to say that the first man (in the Garden of Eden presumably) did not know wisdom fully. There was a tree of life in the middle of the Garden of Eden (Gen 2:9), a tree which could be regarded as capable of making one wise (Gen 3:6). In Prov 3:18 Wisdom is described as a tree of life for all those who lay hold of her; long life is in her right hand (Prov 3:16).

It is, then, not surprising to find the fullest Targum statement on the Law in the translation and paraphrase of Gen 2 and 3 in the Palestinian Targum, especially in Targum Neofiti.

After the naming of the rivers flowing from Eden the Bible says that the Lord God took the man (הֹאָדָם) and put him in the garden to till it and keep it (Gen 2:15). This is paraphrased in the Palestinian Targum as follows: "And the Lord God took Adam and had him dwell in the garden of Eden to toil *in the Law and observe its commandments.*"

That the Law already existed presents no problem. According to Prov 8:22–31 wisdom (for the targumic tradition identified with the Law) was present with God at creation, and according to Prov 8:30 was יוֹם יוֹם (generally translated as "daily") his delight. Now, according to a Jewish principle found in 2 Pet 3:8 (see also Ps 90:4) one day in the Lord's sight is as a thousand years. The Law was thus regarded in targumic tradition as created two thousand years before the world. The Palestinian Targum paraphrases the biblical account of the expulsion of Adam and Eve from the garden of Eden (Gen 3:22–4) as follows (italics indicate targumic expansions):

(3:22). And the Lord God said: "Behold, the *first* Adam *whom I have created is alone in the world as I am alone in the heavens on high. Numerous nations are to arise from*

---

[13] Di Lella, *The Wisdom of Ben Sira*, 75, citing R. Smend, *Die Weisheit des Jesus Sirach erklärt* (Berlin: Reimer, 1906), xxiii.

him, and from him shall arise one nation who will know to distinguish between good
and evil. *If he had observed the precept of the Law and fulfilled its commandment he
would live end endure forever like the tree of life.* And now, *since he has not observed
the precepts of the Law and has not fulfilled its commandment, behold we will banish
him from the garden of Eden* before he stretches out his hand and takes of *the fruit* of
the *tree of life* and eats and lives for ever. 23. And the Lord God banished him from
the garden of Eden to till the earth from which he had been *created.* 24. And he
banished *Adam*; and he had made *the Glory of his Shekinah* dwell *from the beginning*
to the east of the Garden of Eden, *between the two* cherubim.

> *Two thousand years before he created the world he had created the Law; he had
> prepared the garden of Eden for the just and Gehenna for the wicked. He had prepared
> the garden of Eden for the just that they might eat and delight themselves from the
> fruits of the tree because they had kept the precepts of the Law in this world and
> fulfilled the commandments. For the wicked he prepared Gehenna, which is
> comparable to a sharp sword devouring with both edges. He prepared within it darts
> of fire and burning coals for the wicked to be avenged of them in the world to come
> because they did not observe the precepts of the Law in this world.*

> *For the Law is a* tree of life *for everyone who toils in it and keeps the command-
> ments: he lives and endures like* the tree of life *in the world to come. The Law is good
> for all who labour in it in this world like the fruit of the tree of life.*

Twice in v. 22 Neofiti speaks of the fulfilling of a commandment (in the
singular) of the Law (פקודה, "its [feminine] commandment"*)* on Adam's part
in the garden of Eden. The commandment in question may be the single
prohibition regarding the eating of the forbidden fruit. Use of the singular may
be accidental, since elsewhere in the paraphrase of these verses in the
Palestinian Targum the plural form is used ("its commandments").

2.3 Earthly Reward for Keeping the Commandments of the Law

In the paraphrase of Gen 3:22–24 eternal life, on earth or in eternity, is
promised as the reward for keeping the precepts of the Law in this world.
Victory over enemies, or defeat by the enemy, is promised in some other
texts, for instance in the Palestinian Targum paraphrase of Gen 3:15 where
the biblical text speaks of the constant struggle between the woman, her seed
and the serpent. This is paraphrased as follows in Neofiti (italics indicate
targumic expansion):

> (3:15) And I will put enmity between you and the woman and between *your sons and
> her sons. And it will come about that when her sons observe the Law and do the
> commandments they will aim at you and smite you* on your head and *kill you. But when
> they forsake the commandments of the Law you will aim and bite him on his heel and
> make him ill. For her sons, however, there will be a remedy, but for you, O serpent,
> there will not be a remedy, since they are to make appeasement in the end, in the day
> of King Messiah.*

There is a similar presentation of the doctrine in the paraphrase of Gen
27:40 in Isaac's valedictory message to Esau ("By your sword you shall live,

and you shall serve your brother; but when you break loose, you shall break his yoke from your neck"), which is thus paraphrased in the Palestinian Targums:

> (27:40) And by your sword shall you live and *before* your brother shall you serve and *be subjected. And when the sons of Jacob toil in the Law and keep the commandments they will place the yoke of their burden upon your neck. And when the sons of Jacob abandon the commandments and withhold themselves from toiling in the Law you will rule over him and shall break the yoke of servitude from off your neck.*

Similar teaching is found in Nf Deut 32:14: "If Israel toils in the Law and keeps the commandments, from one bunch of grapes they will drink a kor of wine" (MT: "You drank fine wine from the blood of grapes"). Likewise in Nf Deut 32:30: "When Israel toiled in the Law and kept the commandments, one of them would pursue a thousand and two of them would put to flight ten thousand. Because they have sinned and provoked anger before him, the Strong One, he has forsaken them, and the Memra of the Lord has handed them over to the hands of their enemies" (NRSV: "How could one have routed a thousand, and two put a myriad to flight . . ."). Similarly in Nf Deut 33:29: ". . . And your enemies will be broken before you; and you, my people, children of Israel, shall tread on the necks of their kings when you toil in the Law and do the commandments" (NRSV: "Your enemies shall come fawning to you, and you shall tread on their backs").

In this point the Targums scarcely pass beyond biblical, especially Deuteronomic, teaching; see Deut 28:1ff.; 30:16–18; Ps 18:20–24, 37–42. Likewise Ps 81:14–15: "O that my people would listen to me that Israel would in walk in my ways! Then I would quickly subdue their enemies, and turn my hand against their foes. Those who hate the Lord would cringe before him, and their doom would last for ever. He would feed you (HT: 'he would feed them') with the finest of wheat, and with honey from the rock I would satisfy them."

2.4 Toiling in the Law

Targum Neofiti speaks on a number of occasions of "laboring (לעי) in the Law" (Gen 3:24; 27:40; Deut 32:4, 14, 30; 33:29; see also Nfmg Gen 3:15; 27:40), some of which texts we gave already cited. That the basic meaning of the Aramaic word לעי is "labor, work, toil" seems clear from its use in conjunction with the noun לעו, "work," e.g., Gen 3:18: "Let us arise now and let us toil (נלעי), and from the work (לעית) of our hands let us eat food." See also Nf Deut 28:33: "and your toil (לעותכון) a people whom you have not known shall eat." Mehetabel worked (לעי) with his hunting-spear (Nf Gen 36:38). The people of Sodom were laboring (לעין) to find the door of the house and did not find it (Nf Gen 19:11). It is used in the intransitive sense of "being weary" in Nf Exod 18:18 and Nf (and Nfmg) Deut 25:18.

When used in relation to the Law the term is used in conjunction with "keep the [or: 'its'] commandments," for instance Gen 3:24: "For the Law is a tree of life for everyone who toils in it and keeps the commandments." In words addressed to Esau we read: "And when the sons of Jacob toil (לעיין) in the Law and keep the commandments." Likewise in Nf Deut 32:14, 30; 33:29. The meaning to be attached to "toiling in the Law" does not appear to differ significantly from "observing the Law," and this is what we find in Nf Gen 3:15: ". . . when her sons [i.e., the sons of the woman] observe the Law and do the commandments."

Nf Deut 32:4 says Moses saw the Master of all ages, the Lord, dividing the day and making four portions of it: "three hours לעי in the Law" (three hours sitting in judgment; three hours binding the marriage bond between man and woman, raising on high and bringing low, and three hours sustaining the whole world). The meaning to be given to לעי in this context is not clear. Sokoloff[14] renders it as "study," as he also translates the word in Nf Deut 32:14; 33:29. This is doubtful with regard to Nf Deut 32:4. There is a diversity in the other witnesses of the Pal. Tg. for this particular verse with regard to the term used of God with relation to the Law. Three manuscripts of the Fragment Targums (VNL) have עסיק, "was occupied with," and the Paris manuscript (P) has the composite לעי ועסיק. In Neofiti and in P לעי can be presumed to have a meaning similar to עסיק, and is thus to be understood as "to labor/toil in" rather than "to study."

2.5 The "Instruction of the Law of the Lord"

A phrase that occurs frequently in the Palestinian Targums is "instruction (אולפן) of the Law of the Lord."[15]

---

[14] M. Sokoloff, *A Dictionary of Jewish Palestinian Aramaic of the Byzantine Period* (Jerusalem: Bar Ilan University, 1990), 284.

[15] A phrase occurring some thirty-two times in the margins of Neofiti (never in the text of Neofiti itself) is "the אחווייה [sometimes written וחווייה] (of the Law)," which term M. Sokoloff and S. Kaufman render as "instruction (of the Law)"; see M. Sokoloff, *A Dictionary*, 46; S. A. Kaufman, M. Sokoloff and Edward M. Cook, *A Key-Word-in-Context Concordance to Targum Neofiti* (Publications of the Comprehensive Aramaic Lexicon Project 2; Baltimore: Johns Hopkins University, 1993), 34. The term also occurs in the Fragment Targums, from whence we can presume it has come to the margins of Neofiti. This term חווייה / אחווייה, from the root חוי, in the Pail and Afel "to show," is the same as אחויה, "manifestation," of Dan 5:12. In the Fragment Targum and in the glosses of Neofiti the phrase occurs in places where Neofiti has "decree of the Law" (גזירת אורייתה), that is in places where the term *torah* of the Hebrew text is seen to refer to a specific regulation, not to the Mosaic dispensation as such. See McNamara, *Targum Neofiti 1: Numbers, 6; Targum Neofiti 1: Deuteronomy. Translated, with Apparatus and Notes* (Collegeville: Liturgical, 1997) 5. In these contexts the phrase "instruction (אחווייה) of the Law" is quite distinct from that expressed by the term אולפן.

Outside of this phrase, the term אולפן is used in contexts of personal contact, or encounter, of Israel's leaders with God. Its use seems part of the effort to avoid speaking of direct human contact with God. Thus the phrase "to seek" or "consult" (דרש) God is rendered "to seek instruction (אולפן) from before the Lord" (Exod 18:15). Somewhat similar is Nfmg (not Nf) 25:17. Without use of the word דרש, but in a context of encounter with God ("go up to God" and such like) the Pal. Tg. (Nf) renders in like fashion: "to seek instruction (אולפן) before the Lord" (Exod 4:16 "and you shall be for him as one seeking instruction before the Lord"; HT: "you shall be to him as *'elohim*"). Similarly in Exod 18:19 (MT: "be you for the people opposite God"; RSV: "you shall represent the people before God"); 19:3 (Nf, Frg. Tg. PVN; Cairo Genizah MS F, J, NN: "And Moses went up to seek instruction from before the Lord"; HT: "And Moses went up to God"); 24:1 (similar to Exod 19:3); 33:7 (Nf: "and everyone who sought instruction from before the Lord went out of the tent of meeting . . ."; MT: "everybody seeking the Lord"); 34:28 (Nf; "And he [Moses] was there seeking instruction from before the Lord"; MT: "And he was there with the Lord"). We have a variant in Nf Exod 23:17: "seeking instruction before the Lord of all ages." There is mention of "seeking instruction from the dead" in Nf Deut 18:11 (MT: "consult, דרש, the dead").[16]

2.6 "A People Hard (Difficult) with Regard to Receiving Instruction of the Law"

The phrase "a stiff-necked people" is rendered in the Pal. Tg. as "a people hard (difficult) with regard to receiving instruction of the Law" (Gen 26:35; Exod 32:9; 33:3, 5; 34:9; Deut 9:6, 13). In Nf Deut 31:27, however, the HT is rendered rather literally, but this section of Codex Neofiti 1 most probably does not represent the central Nf tradition.

2.7 "Instruction of the Law of" Inserted in Rendering of HT Expressions to "Love," "Hold Fast to," "Fear," "Listen to," "Forget," "Forsake," "Return to" the Lord God[17]

The phrase "instruction of the Law (of the Lord)" is found in Targum Neofiti in the rendering of the verbs "love," "hold fast to," "fear," "listen to,"

---

[16] Occasionally the phrase "instruction (אולפן) of the Law of the Lord" is used in other contexts, such as in Pal. Tg. Deut. 15:11 in free introductory paraphrase: "if the children of Israel keep the instruction of the Law and do the commandments there will not be any poor among them"; Israel neither rested nor reposed from the instruction of the Law, Pal. Tg. Deut. 33:3.

[17] See M. McNamara, *Targum Neofiti 1: Deuteronomy. Translated, with Apparatus and Notes* (Collegeville: Liturgical, 1997), 6.

"forget," "forsake," "return to," in instances where in the HT God is the object.

When God is the subject of these verbs Neofiti can render literally; the Lord loved Israel's fathers, and graciously chose their children after them (Nf Deut 4:37: if Israel obeys his ordinances, the Lord will love and bless them [cf. Nf Deut 7:13]). The same is true when the subject is a human being, with another human as object; thus for instance Jacob loved Rachel (Nf Gen 29:18); the Israelite is told to love his neighbor as himself (Nf Lev 19:18); the slave may love his master (Deut 15:16).

2.7.1 Love the Lord

In the context of the general principle of God's rewarding those who love him (Exod 20:6, "love him/me"; Deut 5:10, "love me"; Nf Deut 7:9, "love him"), Nf renders literally. Neofiti renders literally, with an expanded paraphrase, also in Deut 33:3, where MT (RSV) "Yea, he loved his people" is rendered in Nf: "Yet all this was to show that he loved his people, the children of Israel." The text goes on to paraphrase the remainder as follows: "myriads of holy angels descended; since although he brought numerous chastisements on them, they neither rested nor reposed from the instruction (אולפן) of his Law, and were led and came to the foot of his clouds, and set out and encamped according to his commandments" (RSV: "all those consecrated to him were in his [Hebrew text: thy] hand; so they followed in his steps, receiving direction from thee"). In the other cases where Yahweh, or the Lord God, is the object of "to love" Nf renders as "love the instruction of the Law of the Lord." Thus in Deut 6:5; 10:12; 11:1, 13, 22; 13:4; 19:9; 30:6, 16, 20.

2.7.2 The HT phrase "hold fast (cleave) to the Lord" is similarly treated

Thus Neofiti renders Deut 13:5 as: "obey the voice of his Memra, serve before him with a perfect heart, and hold fast to the instruction of his law" (RSV: "obey his voice, serve him and cleave to him"). Nf Deut does likewise in other texts: "before him you shall pray; and you shall hold fast to the instruction of his law" (10:20; RSV: "you shall serve him and cleave to him"); "loving the instruction of the law . . . and holding fast to the teaching of the law" (11:22 RSV: "loving the Lord your God . . . and cleaving to him"). Similarly in 4:4.

2.7.3 Likewise with regard to the places where the HT speaks of "listening to (שמע ל) me (to the Lord)."

In Neofiti this becomes "listen to the instruction of my Law" (Nf Lev 26:14, 18, 21, 27, and Neofiti margin in Lev 26:23).

2.7.4 Similarly with regard to the phrase "forget the Lord"

The verb with God as subject and the covenant as object is rendered more or less literally (4:31; also with Israel as subject, 4:9, 23). When the Lord is the object this becomes "forget the instruction of the law of the Lord." Thus in Nf Deut 6:12; 8:11, 14, 19. Nf Deut 32:18, however, does say of Israel: "You have forgotten the Memra of the Lord who perfected you," although (as already observed) these last chapters may not represent the central Neofiti tradition.

2.7.5 In Deut 28:20 the Lord speaks of the punishments to come "because you have forsaken me"

In Nf this becomes: "because you have forsaken the instruction of my law."

2.7.6 In Deut 30:2 Israel is invited to return to the Lord

In Nf this becomes: "Return to the instruction of the Law of the Lord your God."

A question arises as to whether this terminology of Neofiti represents an early form of the Palestinian Targum or is a later creation of the tradition that produced or transmitted Targum Neofiti. Unfortunately the other witnesses of the Palestinian Targums are of no help at all in this, since none of the texts in question (with the seven verbs mentioned) has been preserved either in the Cairo Genizah texts or in any of the Fragment Targums manuscripts (PVNL), although as noted in 2.5 above, the phrase "instruction of the Law" occurs in a number of all texts of the Palestinian Targums without association with these verbs.

The Targum of Onqelos does not have a uniform approach to the set of texts we have just studied. Onqelos renders literally the texts speaking of loving the Lord God. It translates "cleaving [staying close] to the Lord" (Deut 4:4; 10:20; 13:5) as "cleaving [staying close] to the reverence [or 'fear,' דחלתא] of the Lord (your God)." Likewise with regard to "forget the Lord" of the Hebrew Text. Onqelos paraphrases as "forget the reverence [or 'fear,' דחלתא] of the Lord." Similarly with regard to "forsaking the Lord." Onqelos renders as "forsaking the reverence [or 'fear,' דחלתא] of the Lord." Israel in Onqelos (Deut 30:2) is invited to return to the "reverence [or 'fear,' דחלתא] of the Lord." Finally, Onqelos paraphrases "listen to the Lord" as "listen to the Memra of the Lord."

This takes us to the meaning of the phrase "instruction of the Law" in Neofiti. It does not appear that study of the Law is what is intended. It has much more to do with the instruction for living (*paideia*) that comes from the law, the way of life in keeping with the Law, shown in the observance of the commandments, as is expressed in the phrase that generally accompanies it.

In a number of instances it is not far removed from the fear of the Lord, or reverence for the Lord, as Onqelos often paraphrases the texts in question.[18] In some instances it appears that "the instruction of the Law of the Lord" has become a kind of buffer word, much in the sense of Memra of the Lord, "the fear of the Lord," or "the reverence of the Lord."

A question arises as to whether Neofiti's paraphrase of "love the Lord" as "love the instruction of the Law of the Lord" is a later adaptation by the Neofiti tradition of an the earlier literal rendering "love the Lord" as is found in Onqelos. It seems clear from the Gospels that the "great commandment" as known to the Jews in the first century C.E. read as in the Bible, not as in Neofiti's paraphrase, that is "You shall love the Lord your God . . . " (Mark 12:30, 33; Matt 22:37; Luke 10:27). It is, however, conceivable that both the biblical phrasing as found in the Gospels and the paraphrase found in Neofiti could have existed side by side. In one context, or in a particular religious group, God could be made the direct action of the verb "to love," while in another context (such as the biblical paraphrases), or another group, people could have reservations with regard to speaking of humans loving directly the invisible God, and may have preferred to speak of love made manifest through behavior, through devotion to his Law. There may be a reflection of this attitude in 1 John 4:20: "We love because he [God] first loved us. (20) Those who say, 'I love God,' and hate their brother or sister, are liars; for those who do not love a brother or sister whom they have seen, cannot love God whom they have not seen. (21) The commandment we have received from him is this: those who love God must love their brothers and sisters also."

2.8 Summary and Conclusion

The emphasis on the Law in the Targums is indicative of the central place of the Law in Jewish life. The practical identification of wisdom with the Law led to the transferral to the latter of characteristics predicated of wisdom, such as being the tree of life, the source of life for those who observe the commandments. When interpreted otherwise than as figures of speech or metaphors this would almost of necessity lead to direct conflict with the Christian position where Christ, incarnate Wisdom, was seen as the sole source of life and healing. The positions taken up by both sides because of

---

[18] On this usage in Onqelos see B. Grossfeld, *The Targum Onqelos to Genesis* (The Aramaic Bible 6; Wilmington: Michael Glazier, 1988), 22. K. J. Cathcart and R. P. Gordon, *The Targum of the Minor Prophets* (The Aramaic Bible 14; Wilmington: Michael Glazier, 1989), 4: "Scarcely less important [than the Memra concept] from a Targumic operational point of view are the terms *pûlhana'* ('service', 'worship') and *dahl'ta'* ('fear'), whose surrogate role could be illustrated from a host of passages. Hos 14:2 ('Return, O Israel, to the fear of the Lord your God') and Hos 14:3 ('Return to the worship of the Lord') are especially useful in that they show the high degree of compatibility between the two terms."

this may have helped towards the Jewish accentuation of the central place of the Law of Moses and towards the formulation of the Christian position on salvation through faith in Christ, and Paul's emphasis on Christ being the end of the Law.

3. Righteousness and Divine Grace

3.1 Treatment of the Hebrew Terms צדק, צדיק, צדקה *of the Pentateuch in the Targums*[19]

3.1.1 צדק

The term צדק, generally with the sense of "true, just," occurs only rarely in the Pentateuch. Neofiti renders by the noun קושוט (in status emph. קושטא; with variants קשט, Lev 19:36; Deut 1:16), "truth." Thus in Lev 19:15; 19:36; Deut 1:16; 16:18, 20; 33:19, or the corresponding adjective קשיט (Deut 25:15). Thus also Onqelos (but with substantive קשוט in Deut 25:15).

3.1.2 צדיק

The term צדיק, adjective "righteous, just," of the Hebrew Text is reproduced with this same word in Aramaic in Neofiti Gen 6:9; 7:1, with reference to Noah, and in Exod 9:27 with reference to Yahweh. It also occurs in non-translational texts with reference to Noah (Gen 6:8), the "Fathers" (patriarchs) in general (Gen 38:25; Exod 17:12; Num 23:9), the "mothers" of Israel (Num 23:9); individual patriarchs such as Abraham, Jacob; in the plural of pious multitudes, pious nations; of the just in general in contrast with the wicked (especially with regard to eternal rewards).

Otherwise, in Neofiti, the other Palestinian Targums and in Onkelos the Hebrew word is translated by the Aramaic זכי (with the same meaning as צדיק).

3.1.3 צדקה

In Neofiti, the Palestinian Targums and Onqelos the Hebrew צדקה, "righteousness," is almost invariably rendered as זכו.

In the Pentateuch the sole exception is Gen 18:19 where in the HT phrase "(to perform) צדקה ומשפט" the Hebrew term is retained in Neofiti, Pseudo-Jonathan and Onqelos as צדקתה (Onq., Ps.-J.: צדקתא [ודינה]),

---

[19] For treatment of צדק זכה and related terms in Tannaitic literature, see E. P. Sanders, *Paul and Palestinian Judaism*, 183–205 ("Proper religious behaviour: *zakah* and *tsadaq*").

which Kaufman and Sokoloff[20] render as "charity (and justice)." (Nfmg has
‎זכו וסדר דן‎.)

In Neofiti Gen 35:9, in an added midrash, the term ‎צדיקן‎ occurs, and is
rendered by Sokoloff and Kaufman[21] as "righteousness": "God of the universe
– May his name be blessed for ever and for ever and ever – your meekness
and your rectitude and your *righteousness* (‎צדיקותך‎), and your power and
your splendour shall not come to an end for ever and ever. . . ."

Otherwise the almost universal translation of the Hebrew term ‎צדקה‎ in the
Targums of the Pentateuch (in the Palestinian Targums and in Onqelos) and
in the Targum of the Prophets is ‎זכו‎.

It is worthy of note that the Targum of Psalms renders with the cognate
Aramaic word ‎צדקא‎, as does occasionally the traditional (rabbinic) Targum
of Job (Tg. Job 33:26; 35:8; 37:23; not however on 27:6). It is also
noteworthy that in the sole occurrence of a section with the Hebrew noun in
the Qumran Targum of Job the Aramaic renders with the cognate Aramaic
word (‎צדקתך‎; 11QtgJob 26:3; Job 35:8).

3.2 The Righteousness of God in the Targums of the Pentateuch

In a text of Moses' blessing of the tribe of Gad Deut 33:21 says that some
unnamed person ("he") performed ‎צדקת יהוה‎ (‎עשה‎), "the righteousness of
Yahweh (and his ordinances with Israel). " The subject of the verb seems to
be Gad. Here Yahweh's righteousness seems to be what is righteous in
Yahweh's eyes, what Yahweh considers right, the ordinances he gave to
Israel – as the continuation of the text says. In Jewish tradition, as represented in the Targums and rabbinic literature, this section of Moses' blessing
is understood to speak of Moses, of his death and burial, and so the person
who did Yahweh's righteousness is consequently understood as Moses. After
an added paraphrase on Moses leading the people in this world and in the
world to come, Neofiti renders literally as: "he [that is: Moses] executed the
righteousness of the Lord (‎זכות ייי‎) and he taught his judicial ordinances
to the children of Israel." Onqelos has the same basic understanding of the
text as referring to Moses and translates: "He performed righteous deeds [or:
meritorious deeds, ‎זכוון‎] before the Lord. . . ."

3.3 The Righteousness of God in Targum Isaiah[22]

Both terms ‎זדק‎ and ‎זדקה‎ are of frequent occurrence in the book of Isaiah,
the latter sometimes in conjunction with ‎משפט‎ (Isa 4:4; 9:6; 33:5; 56:1; see

---

[20] See M. Sokoloff, *A Dictionary*, 458; S. A. Kaufman and M. Sokoloff, *A Key-Word-in-Context Concordance*, 1162.

[21] See M. Sokoloff, *A Dictionary*, 458; S. A. Kaufman and M. Sokoloff, *A Key-Word-in-Context Concordance*, 1162.

also 1:27). Before examining the value of the evidence from the theological point of view we must first consider the targumist's translation technique with regard to these terms. In general, as in the Pentateuch, צדק is rendered as קשוט, "truth."[23] In 11:5 צדק is rendered as צדיקיא, "the just/righteous ones," and at 45:8 by טוב, "goodness." In other occurrences ([42:21, לזכאותיה דישראל;] 51:5 – "my צדק"; 58:8; 62:2; 64:4/5), probably due to the context, צדק is rendered as זכו, "righteousness" (the usual rendering for צדקה).[24] As in the Pentateuch, in Tg. Isaiah צדקה is, with few exceptions, rendered by the Aramaic זכו.[25] In 32:16 and 56:1 (where in the Hebrew it occurs in conjunction with משפט) it is rendered as צדקתא (see Tg. of Gen 18:19) and also twice in 32:17 where there is no such connection. At 45:24 and 59:17 it is rendered as זכוון, "righteous (or meritorious) deeds."

Some dictionaries define the Aramaic term זכו as "merit, meritorious deed, acquittal, benefit."[26] However, within the Targum of Isaiah at least, the meaning of the term seems to be determined by the underlying term צדק /

---

[22] For the doctrine of Tg. Isaiah see in particular B. D. Chilton, *The Glory of Israel*; idem, *The Isaiah Targum. Introduction, Translation, Apparatus and Notes* (The Aramaic Bible 11; Wilmington: Michael Glazier, 1987). For the concept of righteousness in Targum Isaiah, see especially K. Koch, "Die Drei Gerechtigkeiten. Die Umformung einer hebräischen Idee im aramäischen Denken nach dem Jesajatargum," in *Rechtfertigung. Festschrift für Ernst Käsemann zum 70. Geburtstag* (Tübingen: Mohr [Siebeck]; Göttingen: Vandenhoeck & Ruprecht, 1976) 245–67. Koch studies the three Aramaic terms used as a rendering of the Hebrew root צדק, that is words from the Aramaic roots זכי, צדק (mainly as an adjective צדיקא, צדיקיא), and קושטא. He also notes the instances in which these terms occur in Targum Isaiah as additions, without a corresponding term in the Hebrew Text. He examines the question in greater detail than is called for in this present study. A fuller examination of the question of the use of these terms in the Targum of Isaiah will be greatly facilitated by the publication of the Bilingual Concordance of Isaiah in the project *A Bilingual Concordance to the Targum of the Prophets*, Project Director J. C. De Moor (Leiden: Brill), forthcoming.

[23] Thus 1:21, 26; 11:4; 16:5; 26:9; 32:1; 41:10 ("my צדק," God as speaker); 42:6; 45:13, 19; 51:1.

[24] In Isa 42:21, צדק in the biblical text is generally taken to speak of Yahweh's righteousness: MT: NRSV: "The Lord was pleased, for the sake of his righteousness (יהוה חפץ למען צדקו), to make [his] teaching great and glorious" (יגדיל תורה ויאדיר). Going apparently on the context immediately preceding, the Targum understands the suffix to refer to (the servant) Israel, and renders accordingly: "The LORD has good pleasure for the sake of the integrity (righteousness) of Israel (דישראל) [*l-zakka 'ûteh*] (בדיל לזכאותיה); he will magnify those who observe his law and will take hold of them" (Tg. Isa. 42:21).

[25] Thus in Tg. Isa. 1:27; 5:7, 16, 23; 10:22; 28:17; 33:5; 45:8, 24; 46:12, 13; 48:1, 18; 51:6, 8; 54:17; 58:2; 59:16; 60:17; 61:10, 11; 63:1; 64:6.

[26] See M. Sokoloff, *A Dictionary of Jewish Palestinian Aramaic*, 176; M. Jastrow, *A Dictionary of the Targumim, the Talmud Babli and Yerushalmi, and the Midrashic Literature* (1903; reprint New York: Pardes Publishing House, 1950), 399. J. Levy pays greater attention to the fuller Targumic evidence in *Chaldäisches Wörterbuch über die Targumim und einen grossen Theil des rabbinischen Schrifthums* (Leipzig, 1867–1868; 3d ed. 1881; reprint of 3d ed. Cologne: Melzer, 1959), 221: "zakû, zᵉkûta, zakûta 1. Gerechtigkeit, Tugend. 2. Sieg."

צדקה of the Hebrew Text, and by the parallel terms that accompany it such as redemption, vindication.

> Attend to my Memra, you stubborn-hearted who are far removed from righteousness (זכותא). My righteousness (זכותי) is near; it shall not be far off, and my redemption (פורקני) shall not be kept back. I will set a redeemer (פריק) in Zion for Israel my praise (תשבחתי) (Tg. Isa. 46:12–13).
>
> (MT: "Listen to me, you stubborn of heart who are far from צדקה [RSV, NRSV: "deliverance"]. I will bring near my צדקה [צדקתי; RSV, NRSV: "my deliverance"] . . . my salvation (ישעתי) will not tarry; I will put salvation [ישועה] in Zion, for Israel my glory.")
>
> . . . that they may know from the rising of the sun, and from the west, that there is none beside me; I am the Lord, and there is no other. . . . I the Lord do all these things. Let the heavens minister from above and let the clouds flow with goodness [MT: "rain down righteousness," צדק]. Let the earth open and let the dead come to life [MT: "that they may bring forth salvation"], and let righteousness (זכותא) be revealed at the same time: I the Lord have created them (Tg. Isa. 45:6–8).
>
> (MT, NRSV, v. 8: "Shower, O heavens, from above, and let the skies rain down righteousness [צדק], and let the earth open that salvation (ישע) may spring up, and let it cause righteousness [צדקה] to sprout up also. . . .")
>
> Attend to my Memra, O my people, and give ear to my service (פולחני), O my congregation; for a [the] law shall go forth from before me, and my judgment as a light. (5) The peoples shall be gathered together to it. My righteousness (זכותי; HT: צדקי) is near; my salvation [redemption; פורקני] is gone forth and by the strength of my mighty arm shall the peoples [nations] be judged (Tg. Isa. 51:4).
>
> (NRSV: "Listen to me, my people, and give heed to me, my nation; for a teaching [תורה] will go out from me, and my justice [משפטי] for a light to the peoples. (5) I will bring near my deliverance [צדקי] quickly, and my salvation [ישעי] has gone out. . . .)
>
> . . . my salvation (פורקני; HT: ישועתי) shall be for ever and my righteousness (זכותי: HT צדקי) shall not fail (Tg. Isa. 51:6).
>
> Hear this, O house of Jacob which are called by the name of Israel, and who are come forth from the family of Judah; with whom a covenant (קים) was made in the name of the Lord God of Israel; your remembrance (memorial; דוכרנכון) shall not cease. Does not his Memra stand firm in truth and in righteousness (בזכו) (Tg. Isa. 48:1).
>
> (48:1b NRSV: ". . . who swear in the name of the Lord, and invoke the God of Israel, but not in truth or right," [לא באמת ולא בצדקה])
>
> Jerusalem has said: I will greatly rejoice in the Memra of the Lord; my soul shall exult in the salvation (בפורקנא; HT: ישע) of my God; for he has clothed me with garments of salvation (פורקן); he has wrapped me with a robe of righteousness (זכו). . . . (Tg. Isa. 61:10).
>
> For as the earth brings forth flowers . . ., so shall the Lord God reveal the righteousness (זכותה) and the praise of Jerusalem before all the peoples (Tg. Isa. 61:11; HT: ". . . the Lord will cause צדקה and praise to spring up before all the nations").

One may legitimately ask whether this translation is due to the targumist's theological stance or is merely a consequence of his translation technique. It appears that in the Targum tradition as represented by the Aramaic translations of the Pentateuch זכו was the accepted rendering of the Hebrew צדקה. It could be that in the Aramaic translation of Isaiah the targumist is doing no more than abiding by this translation principle. However, even with the targumist's translation techniques, we can say that in the Targum of Isaiah the prophet's message on Yahweh's saving plan for his people Israel and humanity, his righteousness, his salvation/redemption, his vindication of his eternal purpose, come across clearly.[27] The Lord's righteousness is his saving plan. This comes from him; it is not any human doing. The meaning of the term used, זכו, "righteousness," is determined by its biblical context in the book of Isaiah, not by what it might mean in another setting (for instance "merit"). Given the general use of זכו as a rendering for צדקה in the Targums of the Pentateuch, one can legitimately presume that this was also the term used in the translation of the book of Isaiah in Second Temple times.

3.4 The Righteousness of God in the Targum of Psalms

The translation technique of Tg. Psalms with regard to the HT terms צדק and צדקה is quite different from that in the other Targums already examined. The usual rendering of the term צדק is צדקתא, or צדק, צדקא, צידקא. It is rendered as זכו in 7:9; 9:5; 50:6; 51:21; 52:7; 96:12(13) (which = 98:9 where it is rendered צדקתא); 119:7, 106, 138; 132:9. It is translated as קשוט ("truth") at 17:15; 45:5; 119:75. The term צדקה occurs thirty-three times in the Psalter. It is generally rendered as צדקתא. At Pss 72:3; 106:31; 111:3; 112:3, 9; 11:7 we have זכו (at 112:4 זכאי); at 69:28 צדיקיא.

While the Targum of Psalms has a certain amount of paraphrase and midrashic additions, in general its rendering remains close to the Hebrew original, and in general it conveys in Aramaic the sense and message of the original Hebrew. This holds for the usages of the Hebrew text in the matter of the meanings of צדק and צדקה.

Thus, for instance, for Ps 85:11–14 (in RSV rendering):

Steadfast love and faithfulness will meet;
righteousness (צדק) and peace will kiss each other.
(12) Faithfulness will spring up from the ground, and righteousness (צדק) will look down from the sky. . . .
(14) Righteousness (צדק) will go before him,
and make his footsteps a way.

In the Targum this reads:

---

[27] See Koch, "Die Drei Gerechtigkeiten," 256–7: "Von menschlichem Verdienst ist im Umkreis der Wurzel *zkj* im Jesajatargum weit und breit nichts zu entdecken. *Zakûta* ist Gottes zurechtbringende eschatologische Machttat, die auf Erden unter seinem Volk – der zu ihm gehörenden Gemeinschaft – durchsetz, was Jahwäs Wort verheissen und was in Gottes Umgebung seit jeher wirksam war!"

Goodness and truth have met;
righteousness (צידקא) and peace have joined together.
Truth has sprung up from the earth and righteousness (צידקא) has looked down from heaven.
Righteousness (צידקא) will walk before him and set his footsteps in a good path [way].

In Ps 96 (Ps 96:13) Yahweh's righteousness is mentioned in conjunction with the coming reign of God.

(96:10) Say among the nations, "The Lord reigns:
Yea, the world is established, it shall never be moved.
He will judge the peoples with equity . . .
(13) He will judge the world with righteousness (בצדק), and all the peoples with his truth." (RSV rendering)

This in the Targum reads:

Say among the nations, "The Lord reigns;
he has also established the world; it will not be moved.
He will judge the nations in uprightness. . . .
(13) He will judge the world in righteousness (בזכו) and the nations in uprightness."

As already noted, the last verse also occurs in Ps 98:9, where the Targum employs צדקתא instead of בזכו.

3.5 Israel's Election Not Due to Her Own Righteousness (or Merit – זכו)

In seeking to determine the position of the Targums on any particular point, it is important to examine the Targums as translation, to see how faithful they are to the message and teaching of the original biblical text. It may be that certain emphases within later Jewish tradition run counter, and depart from, the biblical text. On some occasions the Targum clearly rewrites the biblical text through what are known as "converse translations," which say the opposite to what the text itself says. Such texts have generally to do with marginal issues. Converse translations do not appear to be an issue with regard to God's election of Israel being due to God's free initiative, to divine grace, not to Israel's merits. The point is made in the Hebrew text of Deut 9:4–6:

Do not say in your heart, after the Lord your God has thrust them [the nations of Canaan] before you, "It is because of my righteousness (בצדקתי) that the Lord has brought me in to possess this land." . . . Not because of your righteousness (בצדקתך) or the uprightness of your heart are you going in to posses the land; but because of the wickedness of these nations the Lord your God is driving them out from before you, and that he may confirm the word which he spoke to your fathers, to Abraham, to Isaac, and to Jacob. Know therefore that the Lord your God is not giving you this good land because of your righteousness (בצדקתך); for you are a stubborn people.

The Palestinian Targum (Neofiti) renders this as follows:

> (9:4) At the time the Memra of the Lord your God blots them out before you, do not say in your hearts, saying: "It is because of our merits (בזכוותן) that his Memra has brought us in to possess this land," whereas it is because of the sins of these nations that the Memra of the Lord has driven them out before you. 5. It is not because of your merits (בזכוותכון) or the uprightness of your hearts that you are going in to possess their land; but because of the sins of these nations the Lord your God is driving them out before you, and that he may fulfil the word which the Lord swore to your fathers, to Abraham, to Isaac and to Jacob. 6. And you must know that it is not because of <your> [correcting text, which has "their"] merits (בזכוותהון) that the Lord your God is giving you this good land to possess, for you are a stiff-necked people for receiving instruction.

The translation of Onqelos is no different: "Do not say in your heart . . . . : 'It was because of my merit that the Lord brought me to possess this land. . . .' It is not because of your merit (בזכותך) and the truthfulness of your heart. . . ."

The same is true of Tg. Ezekiel 36:20–23. In the original biblical text Ezekiel is commanded by God to prophesy to Israel in exile that the Lord is to redeem her from exile, not for her sake but for the same of his own holy name, which has been profaned. The Targum is faithful to the biblical text, apart from brief expansions noted here in italics.

> And they came in among the nations to which they *had been exiled*, because they profaned my holy name, in that men said to them: *If these are the people of the Lord, how is it that they have been exiled from the land which is the abode of his Shekinah?* (21) But I had consideration for my holy name, which the house of Israel had profaned among the nations to which they *had been exiled*. (22) Therefore say to the house of Israel, "Thus says the Lord God: It is not for your sake (בדילכון) that I am acting, O house of Israel, but for my holy name, which you have profaned among the nations, which you have caused to be profaned among them, and the nations shall know that I am the Lord, says the Lord God, when I shall be sanctified through you before their eyes." (Tg. Ezek. 36:20–23)

Similarly in Isa 48:11 God says concerning the great deed of redemption soon to come: "For my own sake, for my own sake, I do it, for how should my name be profaned? My glory I will not give to another." The Targum remains faithful to the fundamental idea: "For the sake (בדיל) of my name, for the sake of my Memra, I will do (it), so that it is not profaned. And my Glory which I revealed to you I will not give to any other people." (Tg. Isa. 48:11). There is a similar idea in Isa 42:8: "I am the Lord, that is my name; my glory I give to no other." The Targum translates practically as at 48:11: "I am the Lord; this is my name and the glory I have revealed to you I will not give to any other people."

In Tg. Ezekiel 16 much of the Hebrew text is rewritten. The rewriting of 16:3 speaks of God's covenant with Abraham in Canaan. The rewriting of Ezek 16:6 speaks of the bondage in Egypt, and of God's intervention because of his covenant with Abraham: "And the memory of the covenant with your forefathers came in before me, so I revealed myself in order to redeem you, for it was revealed before me that you were oppressed by your servitude." At the end of the chapter (Ezek 16:60–62) God promises to make a new and everlasting covenant with Israel, a text rendered literally in the Targum: "Yet I, for my part, will remember my covenant with you of former days and I will establish an everlasting covenant with you" (Tg. Ezek. 16:60). The text goes on to speak of God (the HT says "you," i.e. Israel) taking Israel's older and younger sisters and giving them to her as daughters, "but not on account of the covenant with you" (Ezek 16:61). The Targum paraphrases of Israel waging war with countries that are mightier than herself as well as with weaker ones, and of God handing them over to her "even though you [i.e., Israel] did not observe the Torah."

3.6 The Merits (or: Righteousness – זכו) of the Fathers (and Mothers) of Israel

3.6.1 Views of scholars on the matter

In the course of their consideration of theological concepts of the Targum of the Prophets, M. Smolar and M. Aberbach write:

> The concept of ancestral merit aiding and preserving their offspring – even when the children do not measure up to the standards of their forefathers – is well established in both Biblical and rabbinic theology. In particular, it is the Patriarchs, Abraham, Isaac and Jacob, whose treasure-house of merit is an unfailing source of grace for their descendants, the children of Israel.
>
> Even when the latter are unworthy and sinful, they are saved from the full force of divine punishment and total destruction by the inexhaustible residue of ancestral merit. This concept is fully accepted by T[argum]J[onathan]. . . .
>
> Because of the good deeds of Israel's righteous and God-fearing ancestors, Israel's transgressions are forgiven, and they are delivered from divine wrath. Even when they are punished because of their sins, God's covenant with the Patriarchs protects them from annihilation, and ensures their ultimate redemption and restoration – a reward for the righteous acts of Israel's forefathers, who are called by God's name, and whom the Almighty created for his glory.[28]

A. Shinan writes in like vein in his doctoral dissertation on the Haggadah of the Palestinian Targumim:

> III.2.4. *The doctrine of inherited ancestral merit.* This notion is often mentioned in the Targumim. It appears both as a factor in explaining the flow of events in the biblical

---

[28] *Studies in Targum Jonathan to the Prophets* by L. Smolar and M. Aberbach and *Targum Jonathan to the Prophets* by P. Churgin (The Library of Biblical Studies; New York and Baltimore: KTAV Publishing House and The Baltimore Hebrew College, 1983), 219–21; with biblical, rabbinic and targumic (Targum of Prophets) references.

narrative, for example Num. 21:1 (PsJ, TN, PT) and as an assurance which the Meturgeman offers his audience, for example Gen 15:11 (PsJ, TN, FT, MTN). This complete and simplistic belief in the inheritance of ancestral merit as a constant shield for the people of Israel is characteristic of Jewish folk belief and rabbinic sources contain quite a few comments opposed to this belief.[29]

Similarly in other introductions to the Targums. Thus S. Levey in his introduction to the Targum of Ezekiel:

> The rabbinic principle of *zekut 'abot*, "the merit of the fathers," finds a favourable response in Tg. [Ezekiel]. The idea that the ancestral faithfulness to the covenant is sufficient for God to redeem their descendants is expressed in [Tg. Ezekiel] 16:6, which combines this idea with the observance of circumcision and the sacrifice of the Paschal lamb as the rationale for Israel's deliverance from Egyptian bondage.[30]

In his commentary on the words "my merit" (זכותי) in Targum Onqelos Deut 9:4 ["The Lord has brought me in to take possession of this land on account of my merits (בזכותי), . . ."] I. Drazin remarks:

> MT: *tdk*, "righteousness." The three Pentateuchal Targums have *zkwt*, merit. There is no implication here of the concept of proxy *Zachuth*, by which one can vicariously tap into the reward owed to others for their righteous acts. One aspect of this concept is *Zachuth Aboth*, whereby Jews were (or, according to some, are) able to reap the rewards of Abraham, Isaac and Jacob. The unofficial Targums contain many verses reflecting this concept, but it is not found anywhere in T[argum]O[nkelos]. The official Targum is simply rendering the Hebrew with an Aramaic equivalent.[31]

3.6.2 *The term and the concept*

(a) זכו in the singular, absolute, can mean "vindication," "innocence" in a legal case. Thus, for instance, Nf Lev 19:16 ("when you know he is innocent ['that there is innocence to him'] in the trial"); Lev 19:18; Lev 24:12. Likewise in Nf margin Gen 18:19 (Nfmg: "to perform זכו וסדר דן"; Nf: "צדקתה ודינא"; for Nf see 3.1 above).

In Nfmg in Gen 15:1 the term occurs twice with the meaning "meritorious deed," or "deed worthy of merit": "perhaps he did not find זכו in me the first time they [i.e. the foreign kings] fell before me . . . or perhaps he will not find זכו in me the second time. . . ."[32]

---

[29] A. Shinan, *The Aggadah in the Aramaic Targums to the Pentateuch* (Jerusalem: Makor, 1979 [Hebrew, with an abstract in English]), xiv (in English abstract).

[30] S. H. Levey, *The Targum of Ezekiel: Translated with a critical introduction, apparatus and notes* (The Aramaic Bible 13; Wilmington: Michael Glazier, 1987), 13.

[31] I. Drazin, *Targum Onkelos to Deuteronomy. An English translation of the text with an analysis and commentary* (New York: KTAV Publishing House, 1982), 125–6; with reference to his doctoral dissertation (St. Mary's University, Baltimore, Maryland) "Targumic Studies" for a full discussion of *Zachuth*.

[32] Pal. Tg. Gen. 15:1 cited in full below, section 4.2 (p. 335). The term זכו is used in connection with keeping the commandments in Nf Deut 6.25: "it will be זכו (=virtue; merit)

(b) (זכו(ת)ב) in sense of "for the sake of."[33] In Nfmg Gen 18:26 (בזכו(ת) has clearly this sense. Abraham says: "(shall you not) loose and forgive the city for their sake [i.e. of the fifteen righteous] –בזכוותהון," rendering HT בעבורם – a Hebrew word rendered in Neofiti here and elsewhere (apart from Gen 26:24) by מן בגלל or בגלל. In HT Gen 12:13 both terms are used: Abraham says to Sarai: "Say, I pray, that you are my sister so that it may be well with me because of you (בעבורך) and that my life may be spared on your account (בגללך)." Neofiti renders the first of these terms by בגללך, "because of you," and the second by בזכוותך ("by your merits"; possibly to be understood as singular; so also Nf Gen 28:14), clearly to be understood here as "on your account." In Gen 26:24, with reference to Abraham ("בעבור Abraham my servant"), Neofiti renders as בזכוותא דאברהם, "for the merits of Abraham." The word בגלל occurs, as just instanced, in Hebrew with the sense of "on account of, for the sake of." In Neofiti it is rendered by בזכות, "on account of, for the sake of" (or: "for the merit of?") in Gen 39:5 (בזכות of Joseph) and Gen 30:27 (Laban said to Jacob: I know that the Lord has blessed me בזכותך; "on your account;" or "by your merit?"). In Deut 18:12 Neofiti renders by the cognate Aramaic בגלל. We seem to have an indication of the practical equivalence of בגלל and בזכות, or rather the plural form – בזכוות, in Neofiti Num 22:30: ". . . the sons of Abraham, of Isaac and of Jacob because of whom (בגללהון) the world was created from the beginning and for whose merits (בזכוותהון; or: "for whose sakes"?) it is remembered [read:? being governed] before them."

Two questions arising from this evidence of Neofiti are made acute by the corresponding evidence of the other texts of the Palestinian Targums, in particular the glosses to Neofiti and the manuscripts (PVNL) of the Fragment Targums. These questions have to do with the exact meaning to be given to בזכות- in a number of texts, and whether there is any significant difference in this regard in the use of the singular (בזכות) or the plural (בזכוות). We have seen that in Gen 12:13 Neofiti uses both terms בגלל and בזכות (בזכוות) apparently with the same meaning, "for the sake of." That this is so seems confirmed by Nfmg, which corresponding to Neofiti's בזכותך has בגללך. In similar manner in Gen 12:16 corresponding to Neofiti's בגללה ("for her [Sarai's] sake"), Nfmg has בזכוותה ("for her merits," plural). Likewise for Gen 18:26, where for Neofiti's "(will you . . . pardon all the sinners of the place) because of them" (בגללהון), Neofiti margin has "for their merits" (בזכוותהון). Texts such as these possibly indicate that we

---

for us if we do all this precepts." The text is, however, not particularly significant since זכו renders צדלה of the HT.

[33] According to Sokoloff (*Dictionary*, 176) זכו, no. 2, "merit" is used especially in the phrase בזכוה, "for the sake of," with example in the singular (בזכוה), from Nf Num 23:9; 24:5, the midrashim; in the plural (בזכווה), Frg. Tg. MS P Gen 39:5; Nf Gen 39:5; 12:13; Deut 9:5.

should not press the singular or plural form or even a very clear distinction in at least some texts between the rendering "for the sake(s) of" and "for the merit(s) of."

3.6.3 The merit (זכות) of the Fathers and Mothers in Neofiti and Margins

In Neofiti Num 23:9 in the course of one of his oracular replies to king Balak Balaam says:

> (8) How can I curse when the Memra of the Lord (blesses)? How can I diminish them when the Memra of the Lord multiplies them? (9) For I see this people travelling and coming[34] for the merit (בזכות; or: merits?) of the just Fathers who are comparable to the mountains – Abraham, Isaac and Jacob; and for the merit (בזכות; or: merits?) of the just Mothers who are comparable to the hills – Sarah, Rebekah, Rachel and Leah. (The MT has: "How can I curse whom God has not cursed? How can I denounce whom the Lord has not denounced? For from the top of the mountains I see him; from the hills I behold him.")

It may be noted that in Nf Num 23:9 (as in Nf Num 24:5) Sokoloff[35] translates בזכו as "for the sake of": "for the sake of the righteous fathers."

Moses blessed Joseph "with the finest produce of the ancient mountains, and the abundance of the everlasting hills" (Deut 33:15). The mountains and the hills are given the same haggadic interpretation as in Num 23:9. The text is thus paraphrased in Neofiti: "[The land of Joseph is] (a land) producing good fruits by the merit (בזכות; or: merits?) of our fathers, who are comparable to mountains – Abraham, Isaac and Jacob; and by the merit (בזכות; or: merits?) of the mothers, who are comparable to the hills – Sarah, Rebekah, Rachel and Leah."

The text of Neofiti in Deut 33, as the various forms of the Fragment Targum (MSS VNL) go on, we may note, to use the term זכות ("of the land"), in the paraphrase of the verse that follows (viz. Deut 33:16), reads: "(a land) producing good fruits בזכות of the land (בזכות ארצא) and of its fullness, and which does the will of him who made the glory of his Shekinah dwell in the thorn bush." (The MT has: "with the best of the earth and its fullness and the favor of him that dwelt in the bush.") One writer[36] believes that זכות (found in all witnesses) seems out of place in verse 16, and may be an intrusion from the preceding verse. However, it may be original, and to be translated not by "merit(s)" but simply as "on account of."[37]

---

[34] Sokoloff, *Dictionary*, 139 renders as "travelling to and fro."

[35] Sokoloff, *Dictionary*, 176.

[36] B. Barry Levy, *Targum Neophyti 1. A Textual Study.* Vol. 2. *Leviticus, Numbers, Deuteronomy* (Studies in Judaism; New York: Lanham, 1987), 335.

[37] We may note here a somewhat similar case: "for the merits of the tents . . . for the merits of the school houses" in Nf Num 24:5.

Mention is often made of the merit (or merits) of Abraham alone. God promises Abraham that in (for) his merit (בזכותך; merits, בזכוותא, 18:18; HT in you) all the earth, peoples, etc., will be blessed: Gen 12.3; 18:18; 26.4. God promises Isaac: "I am with you, and I will bless and multiply your sons for the merits (בזכוותא; possibly to be understood as singular) of Abraham my servant" (Neofiti Gen 26:24). Although the HT has בעבור ("because of"; RSV: "for Abraham's sake") here the use of the plural (זכוותא) in the Aramaic indicates that Abraham's merits are intended. The "merit (זכותיה, VN; or merits, זכוותיה, PL, Neofiti) of their father Abra(ha)m" are mentioned in the Pal. Tg. Gen. 15:11 as protecting his sons against the schemes of the kingdoms of the earth.

The Pal. Tg. Gen. 39:5 says the Lord blessed the house of the Egyptian Potiphar for the merit of (בזכותיה) Joseph." Since the HT has here בגלל ("on account of") it may be that the Aramaic בזכות is to be understood in the same sense. Jacob blesses Joseph's sons Ephraim and Manasseh with the words: "By your merit (בזכותך; HT 'in you') shall Israel be blessed" (Gen 48:20).

In an added paraphrase Jacob tells Laban: "The Lord has blessed me for my merits" (בזכוותי, Neofiti Gen 30:30) and in another free paraphrase Jacob speaks of his own merits (בזכוותי, Neofiti, P; merit, בזכותי VN) and his own good works (Pal. Tg. Gen. 48:22). God also promised Jacob than in (or by) his merits (בזכוותך) all the families of the earth would be blessed (Gen 28:14).

Benefits were bestowed on Israel for the merits of Miriam and Aaron. When Miriam was struck with leprosy her brother Aaron said to Moses: "Pray her dead flesh. . . . Why should we lose her merit?" (Pal. Tg. Num. 12:13). The benefits conferred on Israel through Miriam's merits are noted in Tg. Neofiti: Israel became sixty myriads (Num 12:16); while she was leprous the clouds of glory did not move (Tg. Num. 12:16); for her merits the well used to come up.[38] The benefits of the merits of both Aaron and Miriam are recalled in Pal. Tg. Num. 21:1: "And the Canaanite, the king of Arad, who was dwelling in the south heard that Aaron, the pious man for whose merits (דבזכותיה) the clouds of glory used to lead Israel forth had been removed (i.e. had died); and that Miriam the prophetess, for whose merits (דבזכותיה) the well used to come up had been removed. . . ." We may note in passing that the tradition in this paraphrase of Num 21:1 is very old, already clearly attested in the *Biblical Antiquities* of Pseudo-Philo (*LAB* 20:7): "And these are the three things that God gave to his people on account of (=? בזכות; or: "for the merits of") three persons: that is, the well of water of Marah for

---

[38] See the text of Neofiti Num 12:12, with notes, in M. McNamara, *Targum Neofiti 1: Numbers. Translated, with Apparatus and Notes* (The Aramaic Bible 4; Collegeville: Liturgical, 1995), 78–79.

Miriam and the pillar of cloud for Aaron and the manna for Moses. And when these came to their end, these three things were taken away from them."[39]

3.7 Divine Grace

It is scarcely necessary to treat of this theme as a special section. The biblical teaching on this matter comes across in the Aramaic translation. Israel's election as God's chosen people is due to God's free choice, to God's goodness, not to any merit on Israel's part. Israel has sinned and deserves punishment. In the Targums, as in the biblical text, Israel acknowledges this. But the nation also knows of God's unbounded mercy and of the pardon he has promised for genuine repentance. Outside of passages that have direct translation there is abundant mention of divine mercy. In Israel, prayers of the nation and the individual were addressed to the merciful God. God was asked to listen to their supplications in his "good mercy"; they begged him to listen in the name of the "mercy that was before him." See further below under the heading "repentance."

3.8 Summary and Reflection on זכו, "Righteousness," "Merit" in the Targums and in Paul

It is clear that according to the Targum Israel's election was not due to her own merits. This cardinal point is clearly stated in the biblical text (Deut 9:4–6), a doctrine equally clearly expressed in the Aramaic translation. It is also clear from Ezekiel 36, in both biblical text and Aramaic translation.

The Targums also speak of merit (or merits) of the Fathers and Mothers of Israel, and also of Miriam and Aaron, but nearly always in the phrase בזכות (or plural בזכוות). Sometimes this phrase is to be translated simply as "because of," "for the sake of." On other occasions it is doubtful whether we should render as "on account of," or as "by/for/through the merit(s) of." From the evidence examined earlier, it is not at all clear whether we should see any significance in the use of the plural rather than the singular form.

Even if we do understand the phrase as "through the merits of" (the patriarchs in general, of an individual patriarch or mother of Israel, of Aaron, Miriam) the targumic evidence does not lead us to a doctrine of an inherited merit that of itself saves Israel, the descendants of these patriarchs. The belief must be taken in conjunction with God's covenant with the patriarchs, with his oath to them, with the biblical doctrine of prayer and intercession. The Bible speaks of God remembering his covenant with the patriarchs. Moses, a model for prayer and intercession before God on Israel's behalf, prays to God when the election and covenant were in danger: "Turn from your fierce

---

[39] Translation of D. Harrington, in *OTP*, 2 (London: Darton, Longman & Todd, 1985) 329. Further references in McNamara, *Targum Neofiti 1: Numbers*, 79 n. 8.

wrath; change your mind and do not bring disaster on your people. Remember Abraham, Isaac, and Israel, your servants, how you swore to them by your own self, saying to them, I will multiply your descendants, like the stars of heaven . . ." (Exod 32:12–13). The covenant was as a memorial before God. So too in later Jewish theology (but already well formulated by the first century C.E.) was the Akedah, the Binding of Isaac.[40] In the Palestinian Targums we have the following prayer of Abraham to God: "When his sons (i.e. the sons of Isaac) are in the hour of distress you shall remember the Binding of their father Isaac, and listen to the voice of their supplication, and answer them and deliver them from all distress. . . ." (Nf Gen 22:14).

It is doubtful that in the matter בזכות of the Fathers, the Targums are far removed from what Paul writes to the Romans concerning Israel: "They are Israelites, and to them belong the adoption . . . and the promises; to them belong the patriarchs (ὧν οἱ πατέρες)" (Rom 9:4–5). "As regards the gospel they [the Israelites] are enemies of God for your sake (δι' ὑμᾶς), but as regards election they are beloved because of the Fathers (διὰ τοὺς πατέρας)" (Rom 11:28). The phrase διὰ τοὺς πατέρας corresponds well to בזכות אבהתה (צדיקיה) of Balaam's oracle in the Palestinian Targum of Num 23:9.

The development of Paul's own specific theology on the revelation of God's justice and of justification by faith owes much to the theology of Deutero-Isaiah and the Psalms of the kingship of Yahweh. The Targums, had Paul known them, would not have come between him and the biblical text, since the basic message of the original authors comes through in the Aramaic translation.[41]

4. Good Works and Reward of Good Works

"Good works" and "evil works" are phrases which occur a number of times in the Palestinian Targums of the Pentateuch. Acceptance of God's plan for humans is shown in good works (or deeds; עובדין/עובדין טבין), rejection of this by evil works (or deeds; עובדין/עובדין בישין). Good deeds are rewarded in the next life (and occasionally in this); evil deeds are punished; retribution will be exacted by God for them. The occurrence and frequency of these phrases in the Palestinian Targums of the Pentateuch is all the more

---

[40] See Pseudo-Philo, *Biblical Antiquities* 18:5: "his [i.e. Isaac's] offering was acceptable before me, and on account of his blood I chose them," with references by D. Harrington, "Pseudo-Philo," in *OTP*, 2.302 n. 12.

[41] On the bearing of targumic evidence on the Pauline doctrine on justification see B. Chilton, "Aramaic and Targumic Antecedents of Pauline 'Justification,'" in *The Aramaic Bible. Targums in their Historical Context*, 378–97.

significant in that they are not found in the Hebrew Scriptures or in the Greek translation.[42]

4.1 Good Works

The relevance of good or evil works, the doctrine of reward or punishment, appears to have been a matter of debate in early Judaism. The conflicting viewpoints are put at some length in a debate between Cain and Abel in an added midrash on Gen 4:6–8. As preserved in Neofiti it reads (additional paraphrase noted by italics):

> And Abel also brought (his gift) from the first-born of his flock and from the fat ones among them. And the Lord *received* Abel and his offering *with favour*, (5) but he *did not receive* Cain and his offering *with favour* and Cain was greatly displeased and *his countenance changed.* (6) And the Lord said to Cain: "Why, I pray, are you displeased and why has your *countenance changed?* (7) Surely, if you make your work *in this world* to be good, *you will be remitted and pardoned in the world to come*; but if you do not make your work *in this world* to be good, *your sin will be kept for the day of great judgement* and at the door of *your heart* your sin crouches. *Into your hands, however, I have given the control over the evil inclination and you shall rule it, whether to be remain just or to sin.*" (8) And Cain said to Abel his brother: *"Come! Let the two of us go out into the open field." And when the two of them had gone out into* the open field, *Cain answered and said to Abel: "I perceive that the world was not created by mercy and that it is not being conducted according to the fruits of good works and that there is favouritism in judgement. Why was your offering received favourably and my offering was not received favourably from me?" Abel answered and said to Cain: "I perceive that the world was created by mercy and that it is being conducted according to the fruits of good works. And because my works were better than yours, my offering was received from me favourably and yours was not received favourably from you." Cain answered and said to Abel: "There is no judgement, and there is no judge and there is no other world. There is no giving of good reward to the just nor is vengeance exacted of the wicked." Abel answered and said to Cain: "There is judgement, and there is a judge, and there is another world. And there is giving of good reward to the just and vengeance is exacted of the wicked in the world to come." Concerning this matter the two of them were disputing in the open field.* And Cain rose up against Abel his brother and killed him.

God's will is that humans repent of the evil work, their evil deeds, and perform good works. For this reason he extended the age of his patience and gave his spirit to men to have them change before he sent the flood. In the paraphrase of Gen 6:3 in the Palestinian Targum God is made to say: "Behold I have put my spirit in the sons of man because they are flesh and their deeds are evil. Behold I have given them the span of one hundred and twenty years [in the hope that] perhaps they might do repentance, but they have not done it."

---

[42] On good deeds and rewards in the Targums see M. McNamara, *Targum and Testament,* 131–2.

In the terminology of the Palestinian Targums the just were characterized by good deeds, the wicked by evil deeds. The Hebrew words שלם ("whole," "perfect") and תמים ("perfect") in the Pentateuch when they refer to a sacrificial animal are paraphrased in the Pal. Tg. as "perfect without blemish"; when referring to humans as "perfect in good works."[43] Noah was perfect in good works in his generation (Gen 6:9); and so also others (Gen 17:1; 25:27; 33:18; 34:21).

Israel is to be different from those who seek direction from the dead. God tells them: "My people, children of Israel, you shall be *perfect in good work* with the Lord your God" (Nf Deut 18:13; the MT has תמים). Abram is told by God: "Serve before me in truth and be *perfect in good work*" (Nf Gen 17:1; MT: "Walk before me and be perfect"). Jacob was a man *perfect in good work* (Nf Gen 25:27). The dying Jacob called all his sons before him and blessed them; "each one *according to his good works* he blessed them" (Nf Gen 49:1).

4.2 The Reward of Good Works

As expressed in the profession of faith in Pal. Tg. Gen. 4:8 good works bear fruit in this world and in the next. They have their reward – in Aramaic אגר טב. The basic sense of the Aramaic (as of the Hebrew) word אגר is "payment for hire, wages, reward, profit." God tells the Levites that they may have the choice part of liturgical offerings; "for it is your wages (אגר; Hebrew שכר) in return for your work in the tent of meeting" (Nf Num 18:31). Jacob asks of Laban: "Where is the wage of my work?" (אגר לעותי) (Frg. Tg. MS V Gen 31:39). We hear of the wage (אגר) lost through enforced idleness (Nf Exod 21:19).[44]

The same term is used for the reward for deeds or actions: a good reward or a bad reward in keeping with the action. We have already cited the words of Cain and Abel in their discussion of the question: "the giving of good reward (אגר טב) to the just." In Lev 22:31 God tells Israel: "So you shall keep my commandments and do them: I am the Lord." This in the Pal. Tg. becomes: "And you shall keep the commandments of my Law and do them. I am the Lord who gives *a good reward* to those who keep the commandments of my Law."

The good reward is already there, stored up for the just in the world to come, or for the world to come (לעלמא דאתי). It is thus expressed in an oracle of Balaam, in a midrashic expansion of the biblical text: "Blessed are you, just ones! What a good reward is prepared for you before the Lord for

---

[43] On this see M. McNamara, *Targum Neofiti 1: Genesis*, 73 (note on Nf Gen 6:9).

[44] Further examples in Sokoloff, *A Dictionary*, 34–35.

[or: 'in'] the world to come" (Pal. Tg. Num. 23:23).[45] In another expansion of the Hebrew Text Balaam speaks of an eschatological divine intervention "when the Lord sets his mighty anger to take vengeance on the wicked, to give reward to the just ones . . ." (Pal. Tg. Num. 24:23).

All observance of the commandments has its reward, but some of the reward can be given by God in this life instead of being reserved for the world to come. In an expansion of the biblical text of Deut 7:10 the Pal. Tg. has Moses say of God:

(7:9). You shall know, then, that the Lord your God is God, the faithful God who keeps the covenant and steadfast love for a thousand generations for the just ones who love him and for those who keep the precepts of his law, (10) and who repays in this world the rewards of their good works to those who hate him, in order to take revenge on them in the world to come. And he does not delay the good reward for those who hate him: while they are still in this world he repays them the reward of the small precepts (אגר מצוון קלילן) that are in their hands.

Abram expresses this great fear of being rewarded in this life, with no reward stored up for him in the world to come. This is clearly expressed in an expanded introduction to Genesis ch. 15 in the Palestinian Targum, which is as follows (given in Neofiti's translation):

(15:1) After these things, after all the kingdoms of the earth had gathered together and had drawn up battle-lines against Abram and had fallen before him, and he had killed four kings from among them and had brought back nine encampments, Abram thought in his heart and said: "Woe, now, is me! Perhaps I have received the reward of the precepts [or: 'reward for (keeping) the commandments' – אגר מצוותה] in this world and there is no portion for me in the world to come. Or perhaps the brothers or relatives of those killed, who fell before me, will go and will be in their fortresses and in their cities and many legions will become allied with them and they will come against me and kill me. Or perhaps there were a few meritorious deeds (מצוון קליל)[46] in my hand the first time they fell before me and they stood in my favour, or perhaps no meritorious deed (מצוה) will be found in my hand the second time and the name of the heavens will be profaned in me." For this reason there was a word of prophecy from before the Lord upon Abram the just saying: "Do not fear, Abram, for although many legions are allied and come against you to kill (you), my Memra will be a shield for you; and it will be a protection for you in this world and although I delivered up your enemies before you in this world, the reward of your good works (אגר עובדיך טביא) is prepared for you before me in the world to come."

In Pal. Tg. Deut. 28:31 (in the text on the curses for violating the covenant) we find belief that good works could save from the enemy in this world. Here "there shall be no one to help you" of the MT is paraphrased:

---

[45] The Fragment Targums (MSS PVN) have s lightly different text: "How happy are you, O righteous ones, what good reward is prepared for you with your Father in heaven, for the world to come."

[46] Sokoloff, *A Dictionary*, 493 renders the Aramaic words מצוון קליל of this text as "light commandments" and of the Frg. Tg. of the text as "easy commandments" (*Dictionary*, 325).

"and you shall have no good works before the Lord your God which might deliver you from the hands of your enemies." Similar sentiments are expressed in Tg. Isa. 26:20: "Go, my people, make for yourself good deeds which will protect you in time of distress" (MT: "Go, my people, enter your chambers, and shut your doors behind you").

4.3 Summary and Reflection

These phrases "good works," "bad works," frequent in the Palestinian Targums of the Pentateuch, are found neither in the Hebrew Bible nor in the Greek Old Testament. It is the language we find in the Gospel of Matthew.[47] Christ tells his followers to let their light shine before others so that they see their good works (καλὰ ἔργα) and give glory to their Father in heaven (Matt 5:16). We also find mention of human good works in certain letters of the Pauline corpus: 2 Thess 2:17 (ἐν . . . ἐργῷ . . . ἀγαθῷ); 1 Tim 2:20; 5:10; 5:25; 6:8; 2 Tim 2:21; 3:17; Tit 1:16; 2:7; 2:14; 3:8; 3:14; Heb 10:24; 13:21.[48]

As in the Palestinian Targums, so also does Matthew's Gospel speak of reward. Blessed are those who suffer persecution for the sake of righteousness. Christ tells them to be glad and rejoice, for their reward is great in heaven (Matt 5:11).

Good works are to be done, but the glory is to be given to God. Christ tells his followers to beware of practicing their righteousness before men (ἔμπροσθεν τῶν ἀνθρώπων) in order to be seen by them; for then they have no reward from (παρά) their Father in heaven (Matt 6:1). They would already have received their reward on earth (Matt 8:2, 5, 16).

5. Covenants and Visions of the Future

In Rom 9:4 Paul, in his anguish of heart, reminds his readers that his people, the Israelites, are most beloved by God: to them belong the adoption, the glory, the covenants, the giving of the law, the worship and the promises. The covenants are principally two: the covenant with the Fathers and the covenant with Moses at Sinai. Because of the importance of the concept for Judaism and Paul, I here treat briefly of targumic evidence on covenant. This scarcely goes beyond the evidence of the biblical text, without denying or notably changing the biblical teaching. A vision of the future is connected with God's

---

[47] See M. McNamara, *Targum and Testament,* 131–2. "Mt. 6:19–21 = Lk. 12:33f. speak in current Jewish imagery" (H. Preisker, "μισθός," in *TDNT* 4.712–28, esp. 714, with reference to Str-B. 1.429–31).

[48] For the Pastoral Epistles see Preisker, "μισθός," 723–4; for Hebrews, 726.

covenant with Abraham (Gen 15). Here the Palestinian Targums expand considerably, and relate the text to later Jewish history and the rewards and punishments in the otherworld, retribution in keeping with observance or neglect of the precepts of the Law. Another person accredited with visions of the future is the patriarch Jacob. I also include treatment of his visions. There are a number of references to the revelation of the kingdom of God in the Targums, which I believe merit treatment here. The same holds true with regard to the expectation of the Messiah. In all these the Aramaic paraphrases go beyond the biblical text, and I believe that they are witnesses to the complexities of Second Temple Judaism.

5.1 Covenant with Moses (The Sinai Covenant)

As one would expect, the Targums transmit faithfully the biblical narrative of the covenant with Moses, as recounted in Exod 19[49] and 24, even though there are the usual changes in the Palestinian Targum texts. Moses is called to the holy mountain. God tells him: "If you hearken to the voice of my Memra and observe my covenant, you will be to my name a beloved people, as a special possession from all the nations, because all the earth is mine. And you shall be to my name kings and priests and a holy nation" (Pal. Tg. Exod. 19:5–6; Nf cited). In contrast with this sober narrative,[50] the account of the giving of the commandments in Exod 20 is highly colorful, following a lead given in the biblical text itself in 20:18.

The targumic rendering of the biblical account of the ratifying of the Sinai covenant (Exod 24) is also fairly literal: the sprinkling of the blood on the top of the altar; the people's profession of obedience ("All that the Lord has spoken we will do and we will obey"); Moses' sprinkling of the blood on the people with the words: "behold the blood of the covenant with the Lord established[51] with you, all these words" (Exod 24:6–8; Nf, only Pal. Tg. text extant).

5.2 Breaking of the Covenant

In a number of instances the Hebrew Bible speaks of breaking (הפר, *hip'il* from root פרר) the covenant with God or Yahweh.[52] The Targums have

---

[49] On Pal. Tg. Exod. 19 see A. Chester, *Divine Revelation and Divine Titles in the Pentateuchal Targumim* (Tübingen: Mohr [Siebeck], 1986), 110–18.

[50] Chester, *Divine Revelation*, 116, remarks on the Pal. Tg. Exod. 19: "Overall, again, it is striking that the Targumim develop the account of the Sinai theophany so little: this stands in marked contrast to their treatment of the giving of the Torah in the following chapter."

[51] On the terminology "establishing a covenant" in the Pal. Tg. see R. Hayward, *Divine Name and Presence: The Memra* (Totowa, NJ: Allanheld, Osmun, 1981), 59–63.

[52] Thus Gen 17:14; Lev 26:15, 44; Deut 31:16, 20; Judg 2:1; 1 Kgs 15:19; Isa 24:5; 33;8; Jer 11:10; 14:21; 31:32; 33:20; Ezek 16:59; 17:15, 18; 44:7; Zech 11:10; 2 Chron 16:3. The

nothing specific to add in this regard, apart from the manner in which the different traditions understand and translate the Hebrew term in these contexts. In the Pentateuch Neofiti renders throughout by a form of אפיס, the afel of the root פסס, "to desecrate."[53] Onqelos understands and translates differently in the Pentateuch, through a form of the verb שני, "to change." So, too, does the Targum of the Prophets, in all cases except Jer 33:20–21, where the context is somewhat different: "If you can break (אם תפרו) my covenant with the day and my covenant with the night . . . then also my covenant with David my servant may be broken" (תפר), a word which the Targum here renders as "abolish," from the root בטל. The terminology of "changing the covenant" may have entered Jewish religious vocabulary at an early date. In 1 Macc 1:49 we have a letter of king Antiochus to the Jews telling them that they "should forget the law and change all the ordinances" (ὥστε ἐπιλαθέσθαι τοῦ νόμου, καὶ ἀλλάξαι πάντα τὰ δικαιώματα).[54]

5.3 Promises of New Covenant

The Targums do not play down the threat made to the very existence of Israel by her unfaithfulness. Jeremiah prays to the Lord in Tg. Jer. 14:21: "For your name's sake, do not remove us afar off; do not make vile the place of the house of the throne of your Glory; let the memorial of the covenant of our fathers come I before you; do not alter your covenant with us" (NRSV: "Do not spurn us for your name's sake; do not dishonour your glorious throne; remember and do not break your covenant with us"). The Targum paraphrases the simple verb "remember" as letting the memorial (remembrance) of the covenant with Israel's Fathers (that with the patriarchs, and probably that with Moses) come before God.

Apart from phrasing in keeping with that of the Targum of Prophets, there is no significant difference in the targumic rendering of the promise of the new covenant in Jer 31:31–34. We may note 31:32: "'Not like the covenant which I made with their fathers on the day that I took them by their hand to bring them out from the land of Egypt, which covenant of mine they changed (אשנינו), although I took pleasure in them,' says the Lord."

---

verb הפר is used also with objects other than the covenant. These occurrences do not concern us here.

[53] See M. Sokoloff, *A Dictionary*, 440–1; Kaufman, *A Key-Word-in-Context Concordance*, 1141, with all occurrences (35) of the term in the text and margins of Neofiti.

[54] In the Prayer of Azariah in the Greek addition (in LXX and Theodotion) to Daniel, however, the verb used is διασκεδάννυμι ("disband, annul"): μὴ διασκεδάσῃς σου τὴν διαθήκην (Dan 3:34 – as in LXX Deut 31:16, 20; Judg 2:1; Isa 24:5; Jer 11:20; 14:21 [all with HT root פרר]).

The same can be said of the corresponding prophecy in Tg. Ezekiel, which remains faithful in substance to the biblical Hebrew text, apart from translating "new heart, new spirit" of v. 36 as "faithful heart, faithful spirit."[55]

5.4 Covenant with Abraham and Abraham's Vision of the Future

The covenant par excellence with the Fathers was that with Abraham. This is colorfully narrated, in two stages, in Gen 15. First a deep sleep (תרדמה) fell on Abram, during which the Lord told him of the sufferings his offspring were to suffer before coming into possession of the promised land (Gen 15:12–16). The Palestinian Targum introduces into its paraphrase mention of Abram's merits as a guarantee of delivery for Abram's children.

I here give the relevant portion of the text of the Pal. Tg. in Nf's version (noting in italics deviations from the biblical text):

> (15:8) And he [Abram] said: *"I beseech by the mercies that are before you,* how, I pray, will I *know* that I shall inherit it?" 9. And he [the Lord] said to him: *"Sacrifice before* me a heifer, three years old; a goat, three years old; and a ram, three years old; a turtle dove and the young of a pigeon." 10. And he sacrificed before him all these things, and he divided them in the middle and he placed each piece opposite the other, but the birds did not divide. 11. And *the birds* came down upon the pieces and the merit of Abram removed them. *When* the bird of prey came down it *hovered over the pieces. What is this bird of prey? This is the impure bird of prey. This is the impure bird. These are the kingdoms of the earth; when they plot evil counsel against the house of Israel, in the merits of their father Abram they find delivery.* 12. *The sun was at the time* to set and a *pleasant* sleep fell upon Abram; and behold *Abram saw four kingdoms rising against him.* DREAD: *that is Babylon;* DARKNESS: *that is Media;* GREAT: *that is Greece;* FELL UPON HIM: *this <is Edom, the wicked which will fall and will not rise again>.* 13. And he said to Abram: "Know of a surety that the descendants *of your sons* will be strangers *and sojourners* in a land that is not theirs; and they will enslave them and afflict them for four hundred years. 14. I, however, will *be avenged* of the nations that will *enslave* them. After that they will go out with great riches. 15. And *you shall be gathered* to your fathers in peace and you shall be buried at a good old age. 16. And the fourth generation, will return here, because the *sins of* the Amorites are not as yet complete."

The second part of the narrative (15:17–21) gives the ratification of the covenant, with mention of the "smoking fire pot and the flaming torch" that passed between the divided pieces of the covenant. The Pal. Tg. sees in this a vision Abram had of the end time, of the damnation of the wicked and of the salvation of the just. I here give the text of Nf, italics denoting expansions.

> (15:17) And behold the sun set and there was darkness, and behold Abram *looked while seats were being arranged and thrones were erected. And behold, Gehenna*

---

[55] In thus translating Tg. Ezek. differs from Tg. Psalms rendering of Ps 51:12: "Create a pure heart for me O God, and a spirit that is correct in the fear of [in reverence for] you renew (תחדית) within my body."

which is like a furnace, like an oven *surrounded by sparks of fire, by flames of fire,
into the midst of which the wicked fall, because the wicked rebelled against the Law
in their lives in this world. But the just, because they observed it, have been rescued
from the affliction. All was thus shown to Abram when he* passed between these parts.
18. <On that day> the Lord established a covenant with Abram saying: "To your *sons*
I will give this land, from the Nile of Egypt to the Great River, the river Euphrates, 19.
the *Salmites,* the Kenizzites and the *Orientals;* 20. the Hittites, the Perizzites and the
Giants; 21. the Amorites, the Canaanites, the Girgashites and the Jebusites."

5.5 Jacob's Vision of the End Times

The biblical narrative of Jacob's last words to his sons opens as follows (Gen
49:1–2): "Then Jacob called his sons and said: 'Gather around, that I may tell
you what will happen to you in the days to come (באחרית הימים). (2)
Assemble and hear, O sons of Jacob; listen to Israel your father.'" The
Palestinian Targums have an expansive paraphrase of the entire chapter 49,
with the blessings of Jacob, and in particular of verses 1–2 which interest us
here. These verses are extant in Neofiti, in the Fragment Targums, MS PVN
and in a Cairo Genizah targumic Tosefta (MS FF) for v. 1. A long history of
composition lies behind the Pal. Tg. paraphrase of Gen 49, some of it very
old. This is particularly true of verses 1–2. In these verses MSS VN are
practically the same as Nf. The paraphrase of these verses is particularly
interesting because of the eschatological concepts they contain.[56] A central
point in the introductory paraphrase in verses 1–2 is that Jacob intended, even
tried, to reveal to his sons the end time (variously called concealed secrets,
hidden ends, Gehenna, Eden, determined times of redemption and consolation, the mystery), but was prevented by God from doing so.[57] I here give the
translation of Neofiti's text.

> (49:1) And Jacob called his sons and said to them: "Gather together and I will tell you
> the concealed secrets, the hidden ends, the giving of the rewards of the just, and the
> punishment of the wicked, and what the tranquillity of Eden is." The twelve tribes

---

[56] For a detailed study of Gen 49, and of the opening verses in particular, see R. Syrén, *The
Blessings in the Targums. A Study of the Targumic Interpretation of Genesis 49 and
Deuteronomy 33* (Åbo: Åbo Akademi, 1986) (119–24 for eschatology); M. McNamara in the
notes to the chapter in *Targum Neofiti 1: Genesis,* 215–17 for verses 1–2; Y. Komlosh, "Ha-
Aggadah betargumê birkat Yaʿakob," in *Annual of Bar-Ilan University: Studies in Judaica and
the Humanities* I. *Pinkhos Churgin Memorial Volume* (ed. F. Z. Hirschberg and P. Artzl;
Jerusalem: Bar Ilan University, 1963), 195–206.

[57] According to a tradition transmitted in rabbinic writings, Jacob suspected that the reason
why the secret was not revealed was that one of his sons might be unworthy; he was however
reassured by their unanimous profession of the unity of God: "Hear, O Israel [i.e., Jacob], the
Lord our God, the Lord is one." This is also probably the reason for the inclusion of the opening
words of the Shema' in Pal. Tg. Gen. 49:2. For the rabbinic tradition see *b. Pes.* 56*a*; Genesis
R. 98 (99), 3, ed. J. Theodor and Ch. Albeck, *Bereshith Rabba* [Jerusalem: FLAG, 1965],
1251–2).

gathered together and surrounded the bed of gold on which our father Jacob was lying *after the end was revealed to him and that the determined end of the blessing and the consolation might be communicated to them. As soon as the end was revealed to him, the mystery was hidden from him.* They hoped that he would relate to them the determined end of the redemption and the consolation. As soon as the mystery was revealed to him, it was hidden from him and as soon as the door was opened to him, it was closed from him. Our father Jacob answered and blessed them: each according to his good works he blessed them.

(49:2) After the twelve tribes of Jacob had gathered together and surrounded the bed of gold on which out father Jacob lay, they were hoping that he would reveal to them the order of the blessings but it was hidden from him. Our father Jacob answered and said to them: "From Abraham, my father's father, arose the blemished Ishmael and all the sons of Keturah. And from Isaac, my father, arose the blemished Esau my brother. And I fear lest there should be among you one whose heart is divided against his brothers to go and worship before foreign idols." The twelve sons of Jacob answered together and said: "Hear us Israel, our father, the Lord our God is one Lord." Jacob answered and said: "Blessed be his name; may the glory of his kingdom be for ever and ever."

The section of Nf, given above in italics ("after the end . . . hidden from him"), not in VN, is probably an interpolation in Nf.

The opening section, "Gather together . . . he blessed them" shows dependence on apocalyptic texts, for instance Dan 2:18, 28, 30, 47–48; *2 Baruch* 81:4. Terms with an eschatological flavor are: "concealed secrets" or "hidden mysteries" (רזייא סתימייא); "hidden ends" (קיצייה גניזייא); "the rewards of the righteous" (אגריהון דצדיקייא); "the punishment [or: 'retribution'] of the wicked" (פורענותהון דרשיעא); "the tranquillity [or: 'security,' שלוותה) of Eden." Likewise such phrases as: "was revealed to him," "was concealed from him," "the end (קץ) with bliss and consolation," "each according to his good deeds."

We are not told what precisely "the determined end (קץ) of the blessing and consolation" is. The text has been compared with the Qumran pesher of Habakkuk (1QpHab 7:5–8): "*For still the vision awaits its time and hastens to the end* (קץ), *it will not lie.* The explanation is that the determined fixed end (קץ) will be of long duration, and it will exceed all that the prophets have said; for the mysteries of God (רזי אל) are marvellous. . . ."

The eschatology of the verses can be, and has been, compared with Tg. Isa. 24:14–16, 23, esp. 24:16:

(24:14) They will lift up their voice, they will sing in the name of the Lord; they will shout as they broke forth over the prodigies that were done for them at the sea . . . (24:16). From the sanctuary, whence joy is about to go forth to all the inhabitants of the earth, we hear a song for the righteous. The prophet said: "The mystery (רז) of the reward for the righteous is visible to me, the mystery of the retribution of the wicked is revealed to me! . . ." (24:23) for the kingdom of the Lord of hosts will be revealed on the Mount of Zion and in Jerusalem and before the elders of his people in glory.

(MT [NRSV]: 24:16. From the ends of the earth we hear songs of praise, of glory to the Righteous One. But I say: I pine away. I pine away. Woe is me! The treacherous deal treacherously The treacherous deal very treacherously . . . 24:23 . . . For the Lord of Hosts will reign on Mount Zion and in Jerusalem, and before his elders he will manifest his glory.)

The vision of the rewards of the righteous and the punishments of the wicked found in this text of Tg. Isaiah are in line with the eschatology of the Pal. Tg. Gen. 4:8 and 15:11.

5.6 "Blushing in the World to Come": The Patriarch Judah and the Afterlife

In keeping with the teaching on the final judgment and afterlife in the Pal. Tg. texts already cited we may add a text from Judah's profession of guilt in the affair of Tamar, in a lengthy paraphrase on Gen 38:25 in the Pal. Tg., a text that may be compared with Christ's words in Luke 9:26.[58] I cite the text of Nf:

> Judah immediately stood upon his feet and said: "I beg of you brothers, and men of my father's house, listen to me: It is better for me to burn in this world, with extinguishable fire, that I may not be burned in the world to come whose fire is inextinguishable. It is better for me to blush in this world that is a passing world, that I may not blush before my just fathers in the world to come. And listen to me my brothers and house of my father; In the measure in which a man measures it shall be measured to him, whether it be a good measure or a bad measure. Blessed is every man who reveals his works.

5.7 The Coming Kingdom of God

Reference to God's kingship, to the kingdom of God, to the kingdom of God to be revealed, is found in the Palestinian Targums of the Pentateuch and in the Targum of Prophets. In many of the cases the introduction of the expression can be explained through the description of God as king in the biblical text. It is not so always, however, and the occurrences of the phrase are an indication that it represents a once current religious terminology. We give the chief occurrences of the phrase here.

At the end of the Song of Moses (or of Miriam) in Exod 15:18 the biblical text says: "The Lord shall reign (יהוה ימלך) for ever and ever." Onqelos paraphrases slightly: "The Lord, his kingdom is [variants: endures] for ever and ever and ever." The Palestinian Targum texts are much more expansive, and so may Onqelos once have been.[59] Neofiti paraphrases v. 18 as follows: "The children of Israel said: 'How the crown of kingship become you, O Lord!' When your sons saw the signs of your wonders in the sea, and the

---

[58] See M. McNamara, *Targum and Testament*, 135–6.

[59] See B. Grossfeld, *The Targum of Onqelos to Exodus. Translated, with Apparatus and Notes* (The Aramaic Bible 7; Wilmington: Michael Glazier, 1988), 42.

might between the waves, at that hour they opened their mouths together and said: 'The kingship belongs to the Lord before the world and for ever.'"

The Song of Moses in the biblical text and Targum mainly concerns a past event. Yahweh was proclaimed king at the Exodus. There are other texts that speak of Yahweh as king (יהוה מלך, or מלך יהוה) with a future reference or in contexts that can be given such a reference. In these the Targums often render as the future kingdom of God, a kingdom to be revealed. Reference to the kingdom of God to be revealed can also be read into texts where no explicit mention of a kingdom is made in the biblical text. We give instances here.

Isa 24:23 ends a hymn with the words: "Then the moon will be astounded, and the sun ashamed; *for the Lord of hosts will reign* on Mount Zion and in Jerusalem and before his elders he will manifest his glory."

The last part of this is thus paraphrased in the Targum:[60]

for the kingdom of the Lord of hosts shall be revealed on the mountain of Zion, and in Jerusalem, and before the elders of the people in glory.

A little later in the same Targum we find mention of the kingdom of God in a context of divine intervention in favor of his people. The biblical text has: "As a lion or a young lion growls over his prey . . . so will the Lord of hosts come down to fight upon Zion and upon its hill like birds hovering, so the Lord of hosts will protect Jerusalem; he will protect and deliver it, he will spare and rescue it" (Isa 31:4–5).

This in the Targum becomes:

As the lion, even the young lion, roars over its prey . . . *so shall the kingdom of the Lord of hosts be revealed to dwell upon Mount Zion and upon its hill.* (5) And as a bird flies quickly so shall the might of the Lord of hosts be revealed over Jerusalem; he will protect and deliver, he will rescue and make free.

This revelation or manifestation of the kingdom of God to protect his people and avenge them of their enemies recalls the heavenly "epiphanies," appearances or manifestations for this same effect in 2 and 3 Maccabees (see 2 Macc 2:21; 3:24; 5:4; 12:22; 14:15; 15:27; see also 3 Macc 2:9; 5:8; likewise 2 Thess 2:8).

There is mention of revelation of the kingdom (by which the kingdom of God may be intended) in a somewhat similar context of punishment in Tg. Ezek. 7:7 (but this time against Israel), in the paraphrase of an obscure Hebrew word צפירה (MT צְפִירָה). The MT has: "(7:6) An end has come, the

---

[60] For the theme of the kingdom of God in Tg. Isaiah see B. D. Chilton, *The Glory of Israel*, 77–81; *The Isaiah Targum*, in index under "kingdom of God." On the use of the term "to be revealed" (אתגלי) in the Palestinian Targums see A. Chester, *Divine Revelation and Divine Titles*; M. McNamara, *The New Testament and the Palestinian Targum to the Pentateuch* (AnBib 27; 27A; Rome: Biblical Institute, 1966; second printing, with additions 1978), 239–82.

end has come. It has awakened against you; see, it comes! (7) Your doom (RSV; HT: צפירה) has come to you, O inhabitant of the land."

This in the Targum becomes:

> The end has come. The retribution of the end has come upon you, behold it comes. (7) *The kingdom has been revealed to you,* O inhabitant of the land! The time of misfortune has arrived.

Likewise in the same Targum in verse 10:

> "Behold, the day of retribution! Behold it is coming. *The kingdom has been revealed!* The ruler's rod has blossomed. (MT: "See, the day! See, it comes! Your doom [צפרה] has gone out. The rod has blossomed.")

It could be, of course, that in using the term kingdom these texts did not intend to refer to the kingdom of God, but to some other kingly rule, believed to be implied in the obscure Hebrew word צפירה. The term צפירה occurs again in Isa 28:5 where the Targum renders as "crown" but understands the passage messianically:

> At that time the anointed one [or: Messiah] of the Lord of hosts will be a diadem of joy and for a crown (לקטר) of praise for the remnant of his people. . . . (MT [NRSV]: "At that time the Lord of hosts will be a crown of glory and a צפירה of beauty for the remnant of his people").

Mention of the revelation of the kingdom of God is also made the Targum of Second Isaiah, in contexts of rejoicing.

> Get up to a high mountain, prophets who herald good tiding to Zion; lift up your voice with force you who herald good tidings to Jerusalem. Lift up, fear not. Say to the cities of the house of Judah: 'The kingdom of God is revealed.'"(Tg. Isa. 40:9). (For the final sentence the MT has: "Behold your God.")

Likewise in Tg. Isa. 52:7:

> How beautiful upon the mountains of the land of Israel are the feet of him who announces, who proclaims peace, who announces good tidings, who says to the congregation of Zion: "The kingdom of your God is revealed." (For the final words the MT has: "Your God reigns.")

In the vision of the restoration promised after the exile, in Mic 4:7 God says: "The lame I will make the remnant, and those who were cast off a strong nation; and the Lord will reign over them in Mount Zion now and for evermore." This in the Targum becomes: "I will make the exiled a remnant, and the scattered a mighty nation. The kingdom of the Lord shall the revealed upon them on Mount Zion for now and for ever."

The biblical text goes on (4:8) to promise that the former dominion, the sovereignty of daughter Jerusalem, shall come to the tower of the flock.

This is paraphrased in the Targum as follows:

And you, O anointed one of Israel, who have been hidden away because of the sins of the congregation of Zion, the kingdom shall come to you, the former dominion shall be restored to the kingdom of the congregation of Jerusalem.

There are two texts in the Targum of the Prophets that speak of the kingdom of God being revealed to all humanity. One is at the end of the book of Obadiah, where the biblical text says, "Those who have been saved shall go up to Mount Zion to rule Mount Esau; and the kingdom shall be the Lord's." This in the Targum becomes: "Liberators shall go up to Mount Zion to judge the citadel of Esau, and the kingdom of the Lord shall be revealed over all the inhabitants of the earth."

There is a text similar to this in Tg. Zech 14:9. After the prophecy on the living waters to flow out of Jerusalem (14:8) the biblical text has: "And the Lord will become king over all the earth; on that day the Lord will be one and his name one." The Targum paraphrases as follows: "And *the kingdom of the Lord shall be revealed* upon all the inhabitants of the earth; at that time they shall serve before the Lord with one accord, for his name is established in the world; there is none apart from him."

A question that arises from the above evidence is whether these references to the kingdom of the Lord are merely exegetical expansions, or are indicative of a particular theology, and if so what precise meaning is to be attributed to the expression "kingdom of the Lord." In their treatment of "the concept of God" in the examination of the theological concepts of Targum Jonathan to the Prophets (TJ) L. Smolar and M. Aberbach write:[61]

TJ also maintains firmly the eternity of God and of the kingdom of God. Hence the divine declaration, "I am the first and I am the last," which implies a beginning and an end – an impossible theological proposition, – is subtly altered by TJ into, "I am from of old, yea, the everlasting ages are mine." Similarly, a prediction such as Micah 4:7b (". . . and the Lord will reign over them"), connoting a *future* reign of God and its absence in the past and present, was unacceptable in TJ's orthodox theology. TJ, therefore, renders: ". . . and the kingdom of the Lord shall be revealed unto them." It follows that God *always* reigns, but his kingdom will be revealed to those who through ignorance are unaware of it.

The two authors go on to comment on the expansion in Tg. Obad. 1:21b in the same vein. The expansion "the kingdom of the Lord shall be revealed to all the inhabitants of the earth" is homiletic, because the MT "and the kingdom *shall be* the Lord's" could be misinterpreted to mean that only in the future would the kingdom be the Lord's, but not in the past or in the present.[62] It is doubtful that we can reduce the presence of the references to

---

[61] See L. Smolar and M. Aberbach, *Studies in Targum Jonathan to the Prophets* (note 7 above), 132.

[62] The Smolar and Aberbach viewpoint has influenced K. J. Cathcart and R. P. Gordon in their notes to the translation of the Targum of the Minor Prophets; see their work, *The Targum*

the kingdom of the Lord in these texts merely to an interest in bringing out homiletically or exegetically the implications of the biblical doctrine on the reign of God. It seems better to take the expression as an indication of a belief in a future intervention of God in history, one in which his rule and what this indicated would be made manifest. It seems impossible to define precisely what the expression kingdom of God means in the Targums. What it denotes in a particular instance seems to depend in part on the underlying biblical text (punishment for Israel or its enemies; salvation; vindication of God's glory).

It is worthy of note that no theological development of the theme is found in Targum of the so-called Psalms of Divine Kingship (Pss 47, 93, 96–99). For the greater part the Targum on these gives a rather literal translation of the biblical text.

5.8 Expectation of the Messiah

The messianic expectations in the Targums have been so often examined that here they need to be treated only briefly.[63]

In Pal. Tg. Gen. 49:1–2 we are not told that the end secrets which Jacob had intended to reveal were specifically about the coming of the Messiah, although we can presume a reference to him would be included. In any event the mysteries of the end time that Jacob was expecting to be able to reveal to his children were withheld from him. Not so for Balaam. What was hidden from the prophets was revealed to him (Pal. Tg. Num. 24:3, 15).[64]

The targumist does succeed in including a reference to King Messiah already in the Garden of Eden, as part of God's word on the enmity between the seed of the serpent and the seed of the woman. The paraphrase of Gen 3:15, already cited above (1.3) with regard to the Law, ends: "*For her sons, however, there will be a remedy, but for you, O serpent, there will not be a remedy, since they are to make appeasement* [or "peace," שפיותה, used only here in Pal. Tg.[65]] *in the end, in the day of King Messiah.*" Since in the

---

of the Minor Prophets (The Aramaic Bible; Wilmington: Michael Glazier, 1989), 102, 120 (in notes to Obadiah 21b and Mic 4:7, with references to Smolar and Aberbach, 132).

[63] See S. H. Levey, *The Messiah: An Aramaic Interpretation: The Messianic Exegesis of the Targums* (Monographs of the Hebrew Union College 2; New York: Hebrew Union College, 1974); M. Perez Fernandez, *Tradiciones mesianicas en el Targum Palestinense. Estudios exegéticos* (Institución San Jerónimo 12; Valencia-Jerusalem, 1981). See also Chilton, *The Glory of Israel*, 86–96, for Messiah in Targum Isaiah; 112–7 for Messiah in Prophetic Targumim other than Isaiah. For the "Messianic Night" of Pal. Tg. Exod. 12:42 see R. Le Déaut, *La Nuit Pascale: Essai sur la signification de la Pâque à partir du Targum d'Exode XII 42* (AnBib 22; Rome: Biblical Institute, 1963), esp. 264–303.

[64] See M. McNamara, *The New Testament and the Palestinian Targum*, 242.

[65] Sokoloff, *A Dictionary*, 563, understands שפיו(תא) as "peace"; the corresponding adjective שפי, "peaceful, pleasant," occurs in Pal. Tg. Gen. 22:8; 31:5; Num 23:3.

paraphrase of the first part of the verse victory for the woman's sons is through observance of the Law one may ask whether the peace promised for the end time, in the day of King Messiah, will also be through observance of the Law.

Gen 49:10–12 receives a messianic interpretation in the Pal. Tg., an understanding of the text that is apparently very old.[66] It reads (in the translation of Nf):

> Kings shall not cease from among those of the house of Juda and neither (shall) scribes teaching the Law from among his sons until the time King Messiah shall come, to whom the kingship belongs; to him shall all the kingdoms be subject. (49:11) How beautiful is King Messiah who is to arise from among those of the house of Judah. He girds his loins and goes forth to battle against those that hate him; and he kills kings with rulers, and makes the mountains red with the blood of their slain and makes the valleys white from the fat of their warriors. His garments are rolled in blood; he is like a presser of grapes. (49:12) How beautiful are the eyes of King Messiah: more than pure wine, lest he see with them the revealing of nakedness or the shedding of innocent blood. His teeth are purer than wine, lest he eat with them things that are stolen or robbed. The mountains will become red from his vines and the vats from wine; and the hills will become white from the abundance of grain and flocks of sheep.

In the blessing of Dan Jacob says: "I wait for your redemption, O Lord" (49:18). In the paraphrase of this in the Pal. Tg. the targumist says that his soul does not wait for the redemption of Gideon, which is short-lived ("of an hour"), or of Samson, which is transient. The paraphrase then continues: "Rather to the redemption of him does my soul look that you have promised [lit.: "said"] to bring your people, the house of Israel. To you, to your redemption, do I look, O Lord."

The Pal. Tg. understands Gen 49:10 as referring to a warlike Messiah to come. It gives a similar interpretation of Balaam's oracle on the star to arise from Jacob (Num 24:17–24), a messianic interpretation which is probably very old and may be the prophecy of a liberator and ruler which help fuel the 64–70 C.E. Jewish revolt against Rome.[67]

The messianic interpretation is carried through in the Targum of the Prophets. The topic has received detailed examination by various authors.[68]

---

[66] See P. Grelot, "L'exégèse messianique d'Isaïe, LXIII, 1–13," *RB* 70 (1963): 371–80; M. McNamara, *The New Testament and the Palestinian Targum,* 230–33.

[67] On the messianic interpretation of Num 24:17–24 see M. McNamara, "Early Exegesis in the Palestinian Targum (Neofiti 1) Numbers Chapter 24," *Proceedings of the Irish Biblical Association* 16 (1993): 57–79; also in *Targum Neofiti 1: Numbers,* 140–42 (notes on Ng Neofiti Num 24:17–24).

[68] See the works of Levey and Chilton referred to in n. 63 above; also K. J. Cathcart and R. P. Gordon in *The Targum of the Minor Prophets,* 6–7, and in the index under "Messiah."

6. Repentance

Repentance is so much part of the message of the Aramaic Bible that no extensive treatment of it is called for here. In fact, as Smolar and Aberbach remind us, both the Hebrew Bible and the Talmud provide numerous examples testifying to the concept of repentance as a cardinal principle of Judaism.[69] The Targums carry across in translation the biblical message of God's call to repentance, together with the doctrine of God's mercy and forgiveness to those who repent. They also constantly insert mention of obedience to the Law, but as well as this can expand on God's mercy, and insert mention of it in places not required by the translation. In the Pentateuch there are fewer mentions of repentance (with verb שוב) than in the Prophets, and this is also reflected in the Targums. In the Pal. Tgs. the Hebrew verb can at times be rendered through the cognate Aramaic תוב (or derived noun תתובה).

Mention of repentance through the verb תוב (in Nf Num 10:36) or noun תתובה (Gen 6:3; 18:21; Deut 30:3; Nfmg Deut 4:30) in the Palestinian Targums is relatively rare, but there are also occurrences through the other verb חזר, "come back." The text with use of the verb תוב reminds us that both God and humans are involved in repentance, the Lord "repenting" of the evil he had purposed to bring on sinners and "turning" from his anger. Israel prays to the Lord to turn in mercy towards them. Thus in Nf 10:36:

> When it (the ark) came to rest, Moses used to pray saying: "Return (תוב), now, O Lord, from the might of your anger and come back to us in your good mercies, and make the glory of your Shekinah dwell in the midst of the thousands and myriads; let the myriads be multiplied and bless the thousands of the children of Israel." (MT: "Whenever it came to rest he (Moses) would say: 'Return, O Lord of the ten thousand thousands of Israel.'")

The divine call to all to repent goes hand in hand with belief in God's patience, long-suffering and unbounded mercy, as well as in his truth and justice, and in his covenant with his people. Many examples could be given on this point. From the Palestinian Targum we may instance Pal. Tg. Gen. 6:3 where God is made to say of the generation of the flood: "Behold I have put my spirit in the children of man because they are flesh and their deeds are evil. Behold I have given them the span of one hundred and twenty years (in the hope that) perhaps they might do repentance, but they have not done so" (text of Neofiti).

---

[69] Smolar and Aberbach, *Studies*, 210; 212–17 for their treatment of forgiveness in the Targum of the Prophets. For the theme in Targum Isaiah see Chilton, *The Glory of Israel*, 37–46.

Sin, repentance and divine acceptance of repentance are central themes in the book of Deuteronomy, and the Aramaic translation is faithful to the biblical message, adding of course that the "return" is to the Law or the instruction of the Law.[70] Thus in (Pal. Tg. Deut. 30:1–3; text of Neofiti cited; expansions noted by italics):

> (30:1) And when these things come upon you . . . (2) and you return (ןורזחת) to *the instruction of the Law of the Lord your God* . . . (3) then the *Memra of* the Lord your God will *receive your repentance* and take pity on you. . . ."

In the Targum of the Prophets (as indeed elsewhere), repentance (אבותת; literally "return," that is, to God) is equated to a return to God's service (for a literal return to God would have anthropomorphic connotations) as well as to the Torah. It involves an undertaking not to sin in the future.[71] Texts from these Targums on repentance could be multiplied, especially from the prophets Jeremiah and Ezekiel.

7. The Intimacy of God

7.1 Anti-Anthropomorphisms and Divine Intimacy

The existence of anthropomorphisms in the discourse concerning God in the Hebrew Scriptures, and the targumic efforts to avoid those by anti-anthropomorphisms, are facts accepted by all and need not detain us here. They are treated in most introductions to targumic texts.[72] Such expressions as those that refer to the eyes, hands, mouth, face of God tend to be rephrased. There is a tendency to avoid making God the subject or object of actions relating to humankind or creation; actions are often said to be done "before the Lord" rather than by him or to him. Partly in keeping with this mentality, when speaking of humankind's relation to God rather frequent use is made of such terms and concepts as "glory," "Shekinah" ("Presence") of the Lord, or even of "the glory of the Shekinah of the Lord." The "Memra" ("Word") of the Lord," of course, is a well-known targumic expression, one which at least

[70] On this see above 2.7 (p. 315).

[71] See Smolar and Aberbach, *Studies*, 211.

[72] See M. Klein, *Anthropomorphism and Anthropopathisms in the Targumim of the Pentateuch* (Ph. D. diss., Hebrew University, Jerusalem [in Hebrew]); published Jerusalem 1982; *idem*, "The Translation of Anthropomorphisms and Anthropopathisms in the Targumim," *VTSup*, Congress Volume, Vienna 1980 (Leiden: Brill, 1981), 162–77; M. McNamara, in *Targum Neofiti 1: Genesis* (The Aramaic Bible 1A; Collegeville: Liturgical, 1992), 33–35.

very often is used to avoid putting God or at least the name God as the subject of a sentence.[73]

These designations of God are not to be taken as indicating intermediaries between God and humankind, nor do they in any way imply that the God of the targumists was a God out of reach. They are designed to protect the invisibility, the incorporeality and the spirituality of God. The God of the targumists is in fact very much a personal being – the God who has revealed himself to the Fathers and to Moses, the God of the covenant, the God whose lasting presence with his people was seen inherent in the divine name itself, a point clearly made in the various versions of the Palestinian Targums. Neofiti paraphrases Exod 3:14 as follows: "And the Lord said to Moses: 'I AM WHO AM' [left in Hebrew untranslated]. And he said: 'Thus shall you say to the children of Israel: The one who said and the world came into existence from the beginning; and is to say to it again: Be, and it will be, has sent me to you.'" A marginal variant in Neofiti and MS V of the Fragment Targums are practically identical with this. A further variant in Neofiti reads: "I have existed before the world was created and have existed after the world was created. I am he who has been at your aid in the Egyptian exile, and am he who will be (again) at your aid in every generation. And he said: Thus shall you say to the children of Israel: I AM [Hebrew אהיה] sent me to you.'"

God's presence in heaven, his dwelling with his people on earth, his omnipresence, are expressed through the term Shekinah, or, as in Neofiti, through the terms "the glory of his Shekinah." It dwells with them, is revealed to them, leads them, goes along with them, is among them.[74]

Direct contact and intimacy of the individual believer with God is evident in particular in the Targums when there is reference to prayer, or when examples of prayer are given. A notable feature of the Targums, of course, is the emphasis on prayer.[75]

A frequent expression in the Palestinian Targums is that a given person was "(praying and) beseeching mercy from before the Lord" (Nf Deut 3:35; 9:18, 20; Nf Gen 25:22 – to give a few references from among many). The presence of "from before" is a targumic and polite manner of saying "from"; its presence does not make the prayer any less direct. "I beseech by the

---

[73] On Glory, Shekinah, Memra, Dibbera, Holy Spirit, in the Palestinian Targums see M. McNamara, *Targum Neofiti 1: Genesis*, 35–9; also D. Muñoz León, *Gloria de la Shekina en los Targumim del Pentateuco* (Madrid: Consejo Superior de Investigaciones Científicas, 1977); D. Muñoz León, *Dios-Palabra. Memra em los Targumim del Pentateuco* (Institución San Jerónimo 4) (Granada, 1974); R. Hayward, *Divine Name and Presence: Memra*.

[74] For literature on the usage of the terms "glory," "Shekinah," "glory of the Shekinah" see preceding note.

[75] On this see M. Maher, "The Meturgemanim and Prayer," I, *JJS* 40 (1990): 226–46; II, *JJS* 44 (1993): 220–46; for the Targum of the Prophets, Smolar and Aberbach, *Studies in Targum Jonathan*, 164–9.

mercies before you, O Lord" is a very frequent manner of introducing direct prayer to God (Nf Gen 3:18; 15:2, etc.).

7.2 Intimacy with God

We have evidence of an intimate relationship with God in a beautiful targumic meditation on the significance of God's revelation to Jacob on the death of Rachel (Gen 35:7–9). I cite the text from Targum Neofiti:

> (35:7) And he built there an altar and called the place where the Lord was revealed to him Beth-El, because there the Lord had been revealed to him when he fled from before Esau, his brother. (8) And Deborah, the nurse of Rebekah, died and she was buried under the oak and he called the name of the oak "Weeping." (9) O God of eternity–may his name be blessed for ever and forever and ever–your meekness and your rectitude and your justice and your strength and your glory will not pass for ever and ever. You have taught us to bless the bridegroom and the bride from Adam and his consort. And again you have taught us to visit those who are ill from our father Abraham, the righteous one, when you were revealed to him in the Valley of the Vision while he was still suffering from circumcision. And you taught us to console the mourners from our father Jacob, the righteous one. The way of the world overtook Deborah, the foster mother of Rebekah his mother. And Rachel died beside him on his journey and he sat down crying aloud and he wept and lamented and wailed and was dejected. But you in your good mercies were revealed to him and blessed him; (with) the blessing of the mourners you blessed him and consoled him. For thus the Scripture explains and says: And the Lord was revealed to Jacob a second time when he came from Paddan-aram and blessed him.

8. Palestinian Judaism, Covenantal Nomism and Targumic Evidence

In this essay for the greater part I have kept to the evidence of Targums in those themes which I consider of importance as a background for issues discussed by E. P. Sanders in his work *Paul and Palestinian Judaism*. I have not entered into dialogue to any great extent with other writers on these topics. At the end of this study I can now give a summary of what has been said in the course of the essay on the main issues, briefly referring to Sanders's position, and conclude with a brief reflection on what bearing the targumic evidence may have on the entire discussion in any appraisal of the situation.

8.1 Summary of Chief Points of Targumic Teaching

It scarcely needs repeating that by the nature of the case it is well nigh impossible to arrive at a synthesis of practically any doctrine in the Targumim. The Targumim are primarily translations of the biblical text; later and nonbiblical concepts and doctrines are presented between the translation either as expansions of the translation or as inserted midrashim. By reason of the nature of the Targums as faithful translation of the biblical text and as containing expansive paraphrases, we may see in them a certain tension, with the central biblical message counterbalancing newer positions found in the expansive paraphrases or added midrashim.

Going on the evidence of the Targums of the Pentateuch and of the Prophets, it does not seem possible to associate the Aramaic paraphrases with one particular section within Judaism of the Second Temple period. The presence of the doctrine of resurrection indicates that they did not originate in Sadducean circles. This belief does not necessarily point towards Pharisaism, since in this matter the Pharisaic tradition was heir to apocalyptic teaching. In the matter of eschatological beliefs the Targums show a link with apocalyptic thought.

From the point of view of literary genres the Targums present a certain variety. There are passages belonging or similar to apocalyptic (for instance Pal. Tg. Gen. 49:1–2; Tg. Isa. 24:16). In its teaching on the afterlife, on the joys of paradise and on Gehenna, on the shame attending the revelation in the other world of one's personal sin, on rewards and punishment, on the revelation of the kingdom of God, the language of the Targums is similar to that of the Gospels.

The Law (Torah) is central to targumic translation, paraphrase and added midrash. As noted already, the Torah appears almost everywhere. And yet the targumic position on the Law is principally a development of the position in Late Judaism, as seen in particular in the Book of Ben Sira'. The Law is identified with wisdom, with the tree of life. Observance of the Law brings reward; it can be said to bring divine protection in times of trouble. Most of such statements on the Law may not go much beyond what the Bible says on rewards attendant on observance of the covenant and on keeping the commandments. What is new in the Targums (as in rabbinic literature) is the presence of the word Law – its centrality or even ubiquity. The Law, "instruction in the Law," observance of the Law, can even almost become a surrogate for God, somewhat like the Memra, the fear of God, the Shekinah.

The Targums remain faithful to the biblical teaching that election is of God's grace and free will, not because of Israel's righteousness. They also remain faithful to Isaiah's presentation of the future revelation of God's righteousness as a feature of his saving advent. God had promised to remember his covenant with the patriarchs, with the Fathers. The Targums (and in particular the Targums of the Pentateuch) often speak of God's doing something or other to Abraham's descendants בזכות of Abraham, the patriarchs, Aaron or Miriam. The phrase ב־זכות may be translated "for the merit(s) of," or simply as "on account of" "for the sake of." Even if we translate as "for the merits of Abraham, etc." it appears that we must consider this in conjunction with the covenant with the Fathers and promises made to them. It seems unwarranted to see in this phrase a doctrine of merit on the patriarchs' part at work independently of the covenant and promise, although there may be one or two instances in the Targums in which this is so (for instance Pal. Tg. Gen. 15:11). Given the teaching on the covenant as free gift of God, unmerited by Israel, as well as the emphasis on the mercy of God, on prayer, and on repentance, we may say that the Targums have retained the biblical doctrine of grace. The constant intrusion of the Law, and the presentation of the Law as the yardstick (if not the source) of proper relationship with God does not disprove the presence of the doctrine of grace. The presence of both is simply an example of the tensions one may observe in the Targums by reason of the nature as translation and expansive paraphrase.

The targumic position on good works, on evil works, and on the rewards or punishments for these either hereafter or here is in keeping with the language of the Gospels.

The Targums are faithful to the biblical teaching on the covenants with the patriarchs and with Moses. They contain traditions of a vision of the end time which Jacob believed he was to receive, but did not, and which was granted to Balaam. Among those is a doctrine on the Messiah and on the future revelation of the kingdom of God.

As in the Bible, a central targumic doctrine is human sinfulness, offences against the covenant, stress on divine mercy, on the call to turn from sin (repentance) and the assurance of divine mercy to those who do. But here again the Law takes a central place: repentance is return to the Law, to the observance of the Law.

Despite the centrality of the Law and the use of surrogates (such as Memra, Shekinah, fear of the Lord), the God of Israel remained a living God. The surrogates, though frequent, are not universal; they are on occasion dispensed with. The targumists and the people they served worshiped a living God. This is clearest in their practice of prayer. They prayed to a merciful God, one who listened and cared. His visitations of humanity, as recorded in the Bible, were taken as examples of how men and women should imitate him in his loving care for others in their trials and sorrows, and in their joys.

8.2 The Targums; Pattern of Religion; Covenantal Nomism

Two very important elements, two key concepts in fact, in E. P. Sanders's work *Paul and Palestinian Judaism*[76] are patterns of religion and covenantal

---

[76] E. P. Sanders, *Paul and Palestinian Judaism: A Comparison of Patterns of Religion* (London: SCM, 1977).

nomism. In the course of a lengthy "definition" of pattern of religion he writes:[77]

> 1. By "pattern of religion," I do not mean an entire historical religion – all of Christianity, Judaism, Islam, Buddhism and the like – but only a given, more or less homogeneous, entity. For our purposes, "Paulinism" is a religion. . . .
>
> 2. A pattern of religion does not include every theological proposition or every religious concept within a religion. The term "pattern" points toward the question of how one moves from the logical starting point to the logical conclusion of the religion. Excluded from the pattern proper are such speculative questions as how the world was created; when the end will come; what will be the nature of the afterlife; the identity of the messiah; and the like. A great deal of the research which has investigated the relationship of Paul and Judaism and the relationships among the various parties within Judaism has focused on just such questions. It is my hypothesis that the pattern of religion, the sequence from its starting point to its conclusion, does not necessarily vary according to the answers given to such speculative questions. . . .
>
> A pattern of religion, defined positively, is the description of how a religion is perceived by its adherents to *function*. "Perceived to function" has the sense not of what an adherent does on a day-to-day basis, but of *how getting in and staying in are understood*: the way in which a religion is understood to admit and retain members is considered to be the way it "functions.". . .

"A pattern of religion," Sanders writes a little later, "thus has largely to do with the items which a systematic theology classifies under 'soteriology.'"[78] However, he finds "pattern of religion" a more satisfactory term for what is described in this work, although he occasionally uses the other word. This he does when what he regards the rabbinic view on the essence of Jewish religion. Sanders puts it thus:[79]

> There does appear to be in Rabbinic Judaism a coherent and all-pervasive view of what constitutes the essence of Jewish religion and how that religion "works," and we shall, occasionally, for the sake of convenience, call this view "soteriology." The all-pervasive view can be summarized in the phrase "covenantal nomism." Briefly put, covenantal nomism is the view that one's place in God's plan is established on the basis of the covenant and that the covenant requires as the proper response of man his obedience to its commandments, while providing means of atonement for transgression.

As noted at the outset of this study, in his work Sanders left out of consideration the Aramaic Targums, in part because he is not persuaded of the antiquity of the Targums as we have them. We are not at the stage, he says a little later, of being able to discuss the view of religion and the religious life in the Palestinian Targum to the Pentateuch, and especially not to date a coherent view of religion to the period which falls within our

---

[77] Ibid., 16–17.
[78] Ibid., 17.
[79] Ibid., 75.

purview.[80] Even if one accepts that the Targums we have considered fall within the period 200 B.C.E. and 200 C.E., by the nature of the evidence it would still be difficult to reconstruct from them a coherent theology or a coherent view of religion. This, as just noted, is because of the close connection of the Targums with the Hebrew text. Nevertheless, we may compare the evidence of the Targums with what Sanders has to say of rabbinic and Palestinian Judaism.

Most of the points made in the preceding section would hold true also for rabbinic Judaism. Sanders says that we should pay special attention to the covenant conception in rabbinic literature. The covenant, especially on God's side, is more presupposed than directly discussed, but the very existence of the halakah, which discusses man's side, gives a first indication that God's side *was* presupposed, not forgotten or ignored.[81] The same holds true for the Targums. The Targums do not have their own idea of covenant, but transmit the biblical concept of both the covenants (with the Fathers and with Moses) and, in the main, of their implications.

Since both the covenant and the Law are as central to the Targums as they are to the biblical text which they translate, it may be permissible to describe the religious approach of the Targums, in so far as this can be reconstructed, as "covenantal nomism." To me, however, it is questionable whether "covenantal nomism" is an apt description of any form of Jewish religion. The term "nomism" tends to denote a static position, conformity to a defined set of rules. Covenant, on the other hand, has reference to a living God, who was and who is, and who will be, a God active in the past, the present and in the future. The covenant is not a term that describes a static religion. The covenant looks backward and forward: backward to the covenant with God and to God's promises, to what God has done; forward to what God will do again, as God sees fit. The prophets were the living witnesses of this special nature of the covenant. Covenant cannot be defined by law, be that law as it was understood by Qumran, by early or later rabbinic tradition, or by any other grouping. The proper response to covenant is obedience – a point amply made by Sanders[82] – obedience in response to covenant, obedience to commandments, but also obedience to the voice of the living God. Before the covenant with Moses, and the giving of the commandments, God spoke to the people: "Now therefore, if you obey my voice and keep my covenant, you shall be my treasured possession out of all the peoples" (Exod 19:5). The appeal continued through history: "O that today would listen to his voice" (Ps 95:7). At given times in history, his voice may have been made known in laws or traditions, yet could again speak in a self-revelation as God himself would

---

[80] Ibid., 25–26.

[81] Ibid., 236.

[82] See Sanders, *Paul*, index of subjects, p. 622, under "obedience."

see fit to make. This brings an element of faith, enlightenment, true knowledge (in Paul's words), into covenant obedience.

In his letter to the Romans (Rom 10:2–4) Paul expresses his deepest convictions concerning his own people and their refusal to accept the gospel message: "I bear them witness that they have a zeal for God (ζῆλον θεοῦ ἔχουσιν), but it is not enlightened. For, being ignorant of the righteousness that comes from God, and seeking to establish their own, they did not submit to God's righteousness. For Christ is the end of the law, that every one who has faith may be justified." Paul declared himself "a Hebrew born of Hebrews; as to the law a Pharisee, as to zeal a persecutor of the Church; as to righteousness under the law, blameless" (Phil 3:5–6) ('Εβραῖος ἐξ 'Εβραίων, κατὰ νόμον Φαρισαῖος, κατὰ ζῆλος διώκων τὴν ἐκκλησίαν, κατὰ δικαιοσύνην τὴν ἐν νόμῳ γενόμενος ἄμεπτος). These advantages Paul regarded as loss because of the surpassing value of knowing Christ Jesus as Lord (3:7).

12. Philo of Alexandria

by

DAVID M. HAY

1. The Philonic Corpus

The voluminous writings of Philo of Alexandria have been preserved quite well, although some have been lost and others survive only in fragments.[1] Most of his writings can be classified as works of biblical exegesis, and their author must be understood as a very productive and self-conscious interpreter of the Jewish Bible.

There are eight non-exegetical treatises. Four of these are organized around philosophical themes, though Philo's own Jewish viewpoint is generally made clear: *Every Good Man is Free* (arguing that thesis from many examples of individuals and groups, most non-Jewish), *On the Eternity of the World* (an assortment of philosophical opinions as to whether the world is eternal or had a beginning in time), *On Providence* (a two-volume work including a dialogue of Philo with his skeptical nephew, Alexander), *On Animals* (a dialogue between Philo and Alexander on the question if animals have reason).[2] Each of these works (with the possible exception of the treatise on the eternity of the world) makes Philo's own Jewish viewpoint more or less clear; but each emphasizes a variety of opinions, some opposed to that viewpoint. The other four non-exegetical works have a more overtly apologetic orientation. The fragmentary treatise called *Hypothetica* is a general defense of Judaism. *On the Contemplative Life* focuses on the Therapeutae, a group of Jewish men and women living in a monastic community near Alexandria in Philo's own time; the treatise implies that the Therapeutae surpass the highest non-Jewish ideals of spirituality, and it further stresses that scriptural interpretation is at the heart of their spirituality. The treatises *Against Flaccus* and *The Embassy to Gaius* recount respectively

---

[1] A detailed survey of the corpus with bibliography is offered by Jenny Morris in the new edition of Emil Schürer, *The History of the Jewish People in the Age of Jesus Christ (175 B.C.-A.D. 135)* (Edinburgh: T. & T. Clark, 1973–87), III.2.819–70. She lists the lost works (about twenty) and also describes the treatises now generally regarded as spurious.

[2] Full titles of Philo's works are given in English in the text. Abbreviations of the treatises, whether in the text or notes, follow the system of abbreviations in the *Studia Philonica Annual*.

the history of the persecution of Jews in Alexandria around 38 C.E. (launched or permitted by Flaccus, the city's governor) and the subsequent effort by a Jewish delegation to Rome in 39/40 C.E. to persuade the Emperor Caligula to protect the Alexandrian Jews from further violence (and, perhaps, to recognize their claims to Alexandrian citizenship).[3] Both treatises strongly assert the justice of the Jewish cause in Alexandria.

Philo's exegetical writings fall into three series or groups. The groups can be distinguished fairly clearly according to literary characteristics, but the relationships between the three in terms of sequence and methodology remain unclarified. First may be mentioned the seven treatises that form the Exposition of the Law: *On Abraham, On Joseph, On the Life of Moses, On the Decalogue, On the Special Laws, On Virtue, On Rewards and Punishments.* These treatises deal largely with the literal meaning of the biblical text, though allegorical interpretations are offered periodically. They are organized thematically, not by sequential passages in the Bible.

The second major set of commentaries is the *Questions and Answers on Genesis and Exodus* (hereafter abbreviated "QGE"). This little-studied but large work survives in fragments, mainly in an Armenian version; originally there may have been similar commentaries on Leviticus, Numbers, and Deuteronomy. For the most part the QGE presents concise questions about the interpretation of details in the biblical text, followed by pithy or extensive "answers" – usually on answer on the level of literal exegesis followed by another (or several) on the allegorical level.[4]

What most scholars consider Philo's chief body of work, however, is the *Allegorical Commentary*, a set of treatises which also offer both literal and allegorical explanations, most attention being given to the latter. Nineteen treatises are extant, but some are incomplete and other treatises in this series have been lost. The surviving ones deal with passages within Genesis 2–41.[5]

The treatise *On the Creation of the World* is *sui generis* among Philo's writings. Unlike the other treatises of the Exposition, it focuses on Genesis 1–3. Unlike those of the *Allegory*, it does not emphasize the individual's spiritual journey as much as it does metaphysical and cosmological issues, demonstrating how the opening chapters of Genesis agree with the best

---

[3] See E. Mary Smallwood, *Philonis Alexandrini – Legatio ad Gaium* (Leiden: Brill, 1961); Ray Barraclough, "Philo's Politics: Roman Rule and Hellenistic Judaism," *ANRW* II.21.1: 421–36.

[4] An anthology of recent essays by various scholars is D. M. Hay, ed., *Both Literal and Allegorical: Studies in Philo of Alexandria's "Questions and Answers on Genesis and Exodus"* (BJS 232; Atlanta: Scholars, 1991).

[5] The surviving books: *Leg.1–3, Cher., Sacr., Det., Post., Gig, Deus, Agr., Plant., Ebr., Sobr., Conf., Migr., Heres, Congr., Fug.,Mut., Deo,* and *Somn.* 1–2.

Hellenistic philosophy (especially the Middle Platonic tradition, building on the Timaeus).[6]

The order of chronology of Philo's writings has been studied by a number of scholars, without any strong consensus emerging.[7] Obviously the treatises on Flaccus and Gaius were written soon after the events they describe. A good case can be made that the *On Animals* and *On Providence* were also written late in Philo's career.[8] Occasionally one treatise seems to allude to something already written in another. It does not seem possible, however, to establish a definite order of composition for most of the treatises. It is altogether possible that Philo worked on the three different groups of exegetical writings (the QGE, the Exposition, and the *Allegorical Commentary*) not in a simple serial fashion but rather in a complex way, perhaps moving back and forth between these groups over a period of many years. In any case, it is hazardous to trace changes or development in Philo's thought across the treatises, given the lack of strong evidence for their sequence or the specific historical contexts within which most were written.[9]

2. Aims, Audiences, and Allegory

Having sketched the Philonic corpus, we may venture some judgments about Philo's intended audiences and literary purposes. Apart from his writings, which rarely mention specific events in his life, the only first-century report about Philo is by Josephus, who writes of the embassy to Caligula:

> Meanwhile, there was civil strife in Alexandria between the Jewish inhabitants and the Greeks. Three delegates were chosen by each of the factions and appeared before Gaius. One of the Alexandrian delegates was Apion, who scurrilously reviled the Jews, asserting, among other things, that they neglected to pay the honours due to the emperor. . . . Philo, who stood at the head of the delegation of the Jews, a man held in the highest honour, brother of Alexander the alabarch and no novice in philosophy,

---

[6] The standard work is now David T. Runia, *Philo of Alexandria and the "Timaeus" of Plato* (Philosophia Antiqua 44; Leiden: Brill, 1986). Papers from a symposium on the question of Philo's relation to Middle Platonism may be found in *Studia Philonica Annual* 5 (1993): 95–155.

[7] See David Winston, *Philo of Alexandria: The Contemplative Life, the Giants, and Selections* (CWS; New York: Paulist, 1981), 4 and 301 n. 7 (listing the most important secondary literature on the topic).

[8] See Abraham Terian, "A Critical Introduction to Philo's Dialogues," *ANRW* II.21.1: 272–94 (esp. 289–91); idem, *Philonis Alexandrini de Animalibus: The Armenian Text with a Translation and Commentary* (Chico: Scholars, 1981), 28–34.

[9] Cf. Samuel Sandmel (*Philo of Alexandria: An Introduction* [New York: Oxford, 1979], 81): "Can the treatises not related to events, such as Against Flaccus and Legation, be dated either absolutely or relatively, whether they are early in his career or late? The effort has been made, but not persuasively."

was prepared to proceed with the defense against these accusations. But Gaius cut him short, told him to get out of his way, and being exceedingly angry, made it clear that he would visit some outrage upon them. Philo, having thus been treated with contumely, left the room, saying to the Jews who accompanied him that they should be of good courage, for Gaius' wrath was a matter of words, but in fact he was now enlisting God against himself. (*Ant.* 18.257–60)[10]

Josephus thus identifies Philo as a man of high distinction, an expert philosopher, and a resolute advocate for the Jews of Alexandria whose faith in God enabled him to encourage others under circumstances that ordinary persons might judge appalling. This description fits well with the author revealed in Philo's own writings.[11]

Differences in ideas and terminology between different Philonic treatises may be partly explained on the hypothesis that they were written for different audiences.[12] The books making up the Exposition seem to presuppose an audience, probably including both Jews and Gentiles, which has limited knowledge of the Bible; these books explain issues on a fairly elementary level and emphasize the greatness of the Jewish religious tradition. Both the *Allegorical Commentary* and the QGE, on the other hand, seem to assume a readership consisting of Jews who know the Scriptures well, are familiar with literal and allegorical modes of interpretation, and share many of Philo's philosophical and religious concerns. All of his non-exegetical works have a literary style that might appeal to educated Gentiles as well as Jews, and it is likely that Philo wrote them with both audiences in mind, partly to encourage the latter to remain faithful to their religious heritage, partly to warn the former against contempt or violence directed against Jews (and probably to urge Gentiles to consider becoming proselytes).

An apologetic thrust can be found in certain passages of the commentaries – for example, Philo assails persons who criticize passages in the Scripture like the story of Abraham's willingness to sacrifice Isaac, claiming that many other people have made similar sacrifices (*Abr.* 178–91). Often his apologetic remarks seem aimed at Jewish readers tempted to abandon their ancestral faith.

The principal hermeneutical controversy of which Philo is aware concerns the distinction between literal and allegorical exegesis of the Bible. He himself

---

[10] Unless otherwise noted, translations of passages in Josephus and Philo are taken from the Loeb Classical Library.

[11] On the city of his residence, see now Dorothy I. Sly, *Philo's Alexandria* (London: Routledge, 1996). On Philo's sense of identity, see esp. Alan Mendelson, *Philo's Jewish Identity* (BJS 161; Atlanta: Scholars, 1988); Gregory E. Sterling, "'Thus are Israel': Jewish Self-Definition in Alexandria," *Studia Philonica Annual* 7 (1995): 1–18.

[12] This methodological idea is effectively exploited in Ellen Birnbaum, *The Place of Judaism in Philo's Thought: Israel, Jews, and Proselytes* (Studia Philonica Monographs 2; Atlanta: Scholars, 1996).

is an advocate of both literal and allegorical interpretation, but he knows literalists who oppose all allegorizing (e.g., *Conf.* 190; *Somn.* 1.39) and allegorists who repudiate the literal altogether (*Migr.* 89–92). Philo sometimes implies that he and other allegorists are an elite minority ("the few," in contrast to a majority of literalists).

Philosophical-religious concerns guide his writing in all genres. Although Philo is mainly a writer of biblical commentaries, what he writes indicates that he sought to explain not only selected pentateuchal texts but the meaning of Judaism in general as profoundly and as compellingly as possible. Many of Philo's allegorical interpretations use terms and concepts drawn from Hellenistic philosophy. Philo's driving concern, however, is not to "package" Judaism in the most appealing cultural dress or surreptitiously to equate the teachings of Moses with those of Plato and other renowned Greeks. The writings of Moses, properly interpreted, are simply for Philo the supreme and perfect statement of all religious and philosophical truth. And he is persuaded that the smallest details in the biblical text bear profound meaning (see, e.g., *Spec. Leg.* 1.212–215).

Philo should not be pigeonholed as a philosopher or a biblical exegete or an advocate of mysticism and spiritual journeys. It is just as misleading to play off these categories against each other as it is to try to decide if he is really Jewish or Hellenistic, really a defender of the Jewish people or an advocate of universalistic religious individualism. He is all these things, and more. For Philo the truest philosophy is to be found hidden in the teachings of the Pentateuch, and allegorical study is the appropriate tool to uncover it. His exegetical writings dwell on philosophical and spiritual themes, not simply on dutiful or mechanical plowing through biblical texts. His apologetic and philosophical works are permeated by his religious convictions, and these in turn are intimately connected with his exegetical labors. If near the end of his career he would write, "I always have time to philosophize, to which field of knowledge I have devoted my life,"[13] the most reasonable inference is that he saw all of his writings as expressions of his commitment to philosophy.[14]

In a sense, Philo offers a "postmodern theology" – he does not attempt to prove that Judaism is true by any general direct argument, e.g., from Platonic or other premises that might claim to provide criteria for truth that all reasonable persons would have to grant. Rather he uses Platonic ideas and arguments and everything else he thinks valuable in the pagan culture in the service of presenting Judaism as final truth.[15] He offers a view of Judaism

---

[13] *Prov.* 1.115 (cited in Terian, "Introduction to Philo's Dialogues," 292).

[14] David Winston writes, "Far from subordinating philosophy to Scripture, Philo is rather identifying the Mosaic Law with the summit of philosophical achievement" (*Philo of Alexandria*, 25).

[15] This is not to agree with Harry Wolfson, who thinks that Philo affirms a subordination

mainly "from the inside." Yet this "insider's exploration of the Bible" is so potent and multi-faceted that one could well imagine some Jews of Philo's day and later generations saying: this demonstrates that our religion is the best, indeed the final truth. One can also imagine pagan readers finding Philo's depiction of Judaism attractive. For Philo, the biblical world and its truths are the truths of reality – the law of nature, and the key to understanding events in the public arena of his own time. As Dawson astutely remarks, "Scripture provided the interpretative lens through which Philo viewed his world."[16] This need not be viewed as an act of deliberate cultural revision or "usurpation," however.[17] It seems more likely that Philo simply saw no fundamental conflicts between the best in pagan culture and the Mosaic revelation, and he used allegorical interpretation to make this plain.

What for Philo are fundamental criteria of religious truth? The text of the Bible is fundamental. Though he recognizes that different literal and allegorical interpretations of individual passages are possible, he regularly indicates that the Scriptures (primarily for him the Pentateuch) are perfect in teaching and expression. Further, Philo has certain general concepts of God and the world which define for him a kind of "orthodoxy." There are some interpretations of the Bible (notably anthropomorphic ones) that he utterly rejects, and he may have known of a strong tradition of "secular" or other allegorizing of the Bible that he found religiously offensive.[18]

In a passage that has been called "the first creed of history,"[19] Philo concludes his treatise on creation by summing up its lessons:

---

of philosophical reason to scriptural revelation (*Philo* [2 vols.; Cambridge: Cambridge University, 1947], 1.149–51). That is not the obvious implication of *Congr.* 79 or the other texts he cites. David Winston (n. 14, above) seems to express Philo's attitude more accurately.

[16] David Dawson, *Allegorical Readers and Cultural Revision in Ancient Alexandria* (Berkeley: University of California, 1992), 125–6.

[17] Dawson argues that Philo's interpretation of the Bible "revises Greek culture by subordinating it to Jewish cultural and religious identity; his interpretation is not a synthesis but a usurpation" (ibid., 113). A modern scholar may judge Philo a kind of usurper, but Philo's own statements do not show that he thought of himself and his aims in this way.

[18] Richard Goulet has argued that behind Philo's biblical commentaries one can discover a source that was a complete "secular" commentary on the Pentateuch, one that Philo attempts to "overcome" through pious revisions (*La philosophie de Moïse: Essai de reconstitution d'un commentaire philosophique préphilonien du Pentateuque* [Paris: Vrin, 1987]) This is a bold hypothesis, which depends on much speculation about the pre-Philonic exegetical traditions and on very questionable methods of disentangling sources Philo used from Philo's own statements. Still, Philo does clearly, if only occasionally, mention other allegorists whose interpretations of the Mosaic text seem decidedly non-religious (though, perhaps, not anti-religious). See D. Hay, "Defining Allegory in Philo's Exegetical World," *SBLSP* 33 (1994): 55–68.

[19] Erwin R. Goodenough, *An Introduction to Philo Judaeus* (2nd ed.; Oxford: Blackwell, 1962), 37. Cf. H. A. Wolfson, *Philo* 1.164–5 and Mendelson, *Philo's Jewish Identity*, 29–49.

By his account of the creation of the world of which we have spoken Moses teaches us among many other things five that are fairest and best of all.

Firstly that the Deity is and has been from eternity. This with a view to atheists, some of whom have hesitated and have been of two minds about His eternal existence, while the bolder sort have carried their audacity to the point of declaring that the Deity does not exist at all, but that it is a mere assertion of men obscuring the truth with myth and fiction.

Secondly, that God is one. This with a view to the propounders of polytheism, who do not blush to transfer from earth to heaven mob-rule, that worst of evil polities.

Thirdly, as I have said already, that the world came into being. This because of those who think that it is without beginning and eternal, who thus assign to God no superiority at all.

Fourthly, that the world too is one as well as its Maker, who made His work like Himself in its uniqueness, who used up for the creation of the whole all material that exists; for it would have been a whole had it not been formed and consisted of parts that were wholes. For there are those who suppose that there are more worlds than one, while some think that they are infinite in number. Such men are themselves in very deed infinitely lacking in knowledge of things which it is right good to know.

Fifthly, that God also exercises forethought on the world's behalf. For that the Maker should care for the thing made is required by the laws and ordinances of Nature, and it is in accordance with these that parents take thought beforehand for children.

He that has begun by learning these things with his understanding rather than with his hearing, and has stamped on his soul impressions of truths so marvelous and priceless . . . will lead a life of bliss and blessedness, because he has a character moulded by the truths that piety and holiness enforce. (*Opif.* 170–72)[20]

Philo of Alexandria wrote most of his works in the form of biblical commentaries or expositions of biblical themes. He must in large measure have thought of himself as an exegete, writing for the benefit of others seriously engaged in biblical interpretation.[21] Although the sheer bulk of his œuvre implies considerable self-assurance, he is certainly aware of a variety of viewpoints; and he does not claim to be supreme or infallible among exegetes. He is a scholar, conscious of some kind of community of interpreters existing around him and before him – a sort of "exegetical world" – including his intended readers (or hearers), but also predecessors and colleagues in the exegetical enterprise.[22]

---

[20] The idea that this is a "creed" implies that it was accepted by the Jewish community (or a particular Jewish community) as a kind of test of correct belief. Clearly Philo's text does not explicitly refer to any kind of communal standard or orthodoxy test; still, this statement is apparently a good indication (probably not an exhaustive indication) of things that he thought were essential to true religious belief. In *Dec.* 58 he says that to deny God's existence or his eternity is "profanity" (οὐ θεμιτόν), which does suggest something like sanctions.

[21] For a recent comprehensive interpretation of Philo from this perspective, going beyond the work of V. Nikiprowetzky, see Peder Borgen, *Philo of Alexandria: An Exegete for His Time* (NovTSup 86; Leiden: Brill, 1997).

[22] One important exploration of the exegetical tradition within which Philo worked is Thomas H. Tobin, S. J., *The Creation of Man: Philo and the History of Interpretation* (CBQMS

He writes within some considerable and long-standing tradition of Hellenistic Jewish thinking in Alexandria,[23] thinking that accepts the Septuagint as an inspired form of the Scriptures and is unembarrassed by study of Hellenistic culture, especially philosophy, finding in such studies not grounds for cognitive dissonance with Judaism but rather ideas and methods that can reveal new depths of meaning in the Mosaic texts.

It seems altogether likely that Philo's treatises were meant to be used in some kind of Jewish academy, perhaps one linked with a synagogue. The QGE in particular seem to breathe an atmosphere of open-ended discussion and consideration of alternatives for literal and symbolic interpretation. Philo's commentaries quite often mention other exegetes – never by name! – who work on literal or allegorical levels.[24] On the other hand, we have no certain evidence of ancient Jews who read Philo's works.[25] Yet it seems impossible to imagine that he did not write with a considerable number of Jewish readers in mind, persons with leisure and education who were sympathetic to his ideals and interests. The preservation of a large body of his writings itself testifies to the existence of Alexandrian Jewish readers who appreciated his works, reading and preserving them at least into the second century C.E.[26]

3. The Spiritual Journey of the Individual

At the heart of Philo's religious philosophy is a concern to portray the pilgrimage of the soul to God.[27] Marguerite Harl says that Philo represents an

---

14; Washington, D.C.: Catholic Biblical Association of America, 1983).

[23] Aristobulus and the *Letter of Aristeas* clearly precede Philo and anticipate some of his concerns. The Wisdom of Solomon and Fourth Maccabees may have been written during Philo's lifetime. Whether their authors knew Philo or were known to him is unknowable. Neither is philosophically as sophisticated as Philo, but both reflect an eagerness to appropriate some elements of pagan philosophy to define the meaning of Judaism for their readers.

[24] See D. Hay, "Philo's References to Other Allegorists," *SPhilo* 6 (1979–80): 41–76.

[25] Some scholars have argued that Josephus and Rabbi Hosha'ia of Caesarea (3rd cent. C.E.) used Philo. See David T. Runia, *Philo in Early Christian Literature* [CRINT 3; Minneapolis: Fortress, 1993], 13–14). The first indisputable reference to Philo from a later Jewish writer comes in the sixteenth century (Rabbi Azariah de Rossi of Venice); see Ralph Marcus, "A 16th Century Hebrew Critique of Philo," *HUCA* 21 (1948): 29–69.

[26] All the certain references to Philo's writings from antiquity come from Christian authors, beginning with Clement of Alexandria. See Runia, *Philo in Early Christian Literature*. One can only speculate about how Philo's works were preserved. For an insightful survey of Philo's relation to other ancient Jewish writings, see Gregory E. Sterling, "Recluse or Representative? Philo and Greek-Speaking Judaism Beyond Alexandria," *SBLSP* 34 (1995): 595–616.

[27] E.g., Valentin Nikiprowetzky, *Le commentaire de l'Ecriture chez Philon d'Alexandrie* (ALGHJ 11; Leiden: Brill, 1977) 239; Sandmel, *Philo*, 82–88; David Winston, "Philo's Ethical

"interiorization of the Jewish religion. . . . He is the first representative of a new type of religious man."[28] His allegorical explorations of Scripture can yield lessons about the nation of Israel, certain events in biblical history, about politics in Alexandria and elsewhere, epistemology, cosmology, and metaphysics – and in this he seems to be simply carrying on traditions of earlier allegorists. But "the allegory of the soul" is the chief object of his concern, especially in the numerous treatises composing the *Allegorical Commentary*. He was not the first Jewish allegorist to focus on this topic, but he develops it more fully than any other ancient Jewish writer known to us. Indeed, the allegorical option often seems to stimulate introspection and legitimate psychological investigations. Philo sometimes speaks of being heavily involved in outward affairs (*Spec. Leg.* 3.1–6), and there is no reason to doubt that he was keenly aware of public responsibilities and took the outward fortunes of the Jewish people very seriously. Yet he can speak of all the world of visible events as a kind of confused dream[29] in contrast to the enduring realities of God and the human soul.

In the *Allegorical Commentary* Philo seems to address persons committed to the Jewish religion and the Scriptures and eager to learn more about how they may approach God. In a sense he is "preaching to the converted." But the main theme of his preaching is not the need for conversion, in the sense of turning toward God, but rather the means of turning to God, the barriers people encounter when they try to grow closer to God, and the stages of spiritual progress. Quite often Philo introduces a hortatory passage with an interjection like "O my soul!" The sense seems to be that he writes as one who addresses himself – but the self being addressed is anyone who desires to draw close to the one God. The audience in view is composed of persons who individually aspire to deeper religious experience. In an important sense, these are the "insiders" Philo writes mostly in relation to, while the "outsiders" are all those who refuse to make their relationship to God their chief business in life.

Although, as we shall see, Philo is perfectly capable of writing about sins and forgiveness, he much more often in the *Allegorical Commentary* talks in terms of human weakness and the acquisition of virtue, about the inner conflict within each person between the powers of God-inspired reason and the power of the senses or the passions. In the Garden of Eden story, Eve represents the senses and their power to lure people into false judgments and

---

Theory," *ANRW* II.21.1, 376: the heart of Philo's concern is "the issue of man's ultimate spiritual goal, which involves his escape from the material world of contingent reality and his mystical attachment to God."

[28] In *Quis rerum divinarum heres sit* (Les œuvres de Philon d'Alexandrie 15; Paris: Cerf, 1966), 153.

[29] *Jos.* 125–47.

values. The serpent is interpreted as a symbol not of sin or the Devil, but of pleasure. Adam represents the corruptible mind, capable of following God but also prone to error because of its connection with the body. Philo's Platonic heritage leads him to speak of the body largely as a necessary evil and of the human soul as the true human self. To draw near to God, the soul must turn away from body and the senses.

In one passage Philo remarks that a true human being is not simply "a living creature endowed with reason and subject to death," but rather "a soul so constituted as to hope on the God that really is" (*Det.* 138–39). Good persons rely on God and they are optimistic because of that reliance – "he that is despondent is not man" (*Det.* 139). The "psychology" that matters to Philo is an understanding of the soul of the individual in relation to God. Sometimes his allegorical exegesis produces reflections on the components of the soul, sometimes accounts of its internal conflicts, but always his chief interest is the spiritual pilgrimage.[30]

The spiritual journey is elaborated very largely through Philo's interpretations of the stories of the patriarchs. Abraham is the great model of approaching God through true knowledge: he learns to abandon the Chaldean mindset of his ancestors, with its astronomy and polytheism, and gains faith in the one God who summoned him out of his homeland. He is the quintessential proselyte. Jacob is the great model of the Athlete or Practicer of virtue: his outward conflicts symbolize his struggles against the realms of the body and outward appearance, along with the struggle to gain God's blessing. Isaac and Moses are the great examples of the "self-taught," persons who from birth had perfect natures and unimpaired awareness of God. These last two biblical figures represent the ideal toward which everyone else should strive.[31] Sometimes Philo writes as though all biblical characters symbolize spiritual elements within every individual; at other times he suggests that people are of different spiritual types, or that persons of different spiritual types are able to reach different levels of closeness to God (e.g., *Fug.* 97–99).

The dominant role and direction of Philo's psychological allegory may be readily seen by a brief survey of one of the outstanding (but not atypical) treatises in the *Allegorical Commentary, On the Cherubim*, which deals with a few lines in Genesis:

> And he expelled Adam and set over against the Garden of Pleasure the Cherubim and the sword of flame, which turns every way so as to guard the way to the tree of life.

---

[30] This is explored in detail in my essay, "The Psychology of Faith in Hellenistic Judaism," *ANRW* II.20.2, 881–925.

[31] Although Philo sometimes seems to describe Isaac as too perfect to be imitated, at other times he mentions experiences of joy (*Cher.* 106) or of being self-taught (or taught by God) that are evidently possible for his readers (*Sacr.* 79).

And Adam knew Eve, his wife, and she conceived and bore Cain, and he said "I have gotten a man through God" (Gen 3:24–4:1).

Philo begins (§§1–10) by discussing different types of expulsions, emphasizing the two expulsions of Hagar (Gen 16 and 21) as indicating that she symbolizes secular education, while Sarah represents philosophy. He then examines the phrase "set over against," noting that in a judicial setting it can mean "reveal the real motives" (§§11–20). A longer discussion is then given to different possible allegorical interpretations of the cherubim and the flaming sword (§§21–39). Philo starts by mentioning two cosmological explanations: (a) the moving sphere of the planets balanced by the sphere of the fixed stars, the revolution of the whole heaven being the sword; (b) the two hemispheres of the heaven, with the sun as the sword. He then goes on to a metaphysical/psychological interpretation that he credits to "a higher voice in my soul": the two cherubim are the chief Powers of God, while the sword is the Logos (divine reason) uniting the two. Philo draws his existential conclusion in direct terms:

> O then, my mind, admit the image unalloyed of the two Cherubim, that having learnt its clear lesson of the sovereignty and beneficence of the Cause, thou mayest reap the fruits of a happy lot. For straightway thou shalt understand how these unmixed potencies are mingled and united, how, where God is good, yet the glory of His sovereignty is seen amid the beneficence, how, where He is sovereign, through the sovereignty the beneficence still appears. Thus thou mayest gain the virtues begotten of these potencies, a cheerful courage and a reverent awe towards God. When things are well with thee, the majesty of the sovereign king will keep thee from high thoughts. When thou sufferest what thou wouldest not, thou wilt not despair of betterment, remembering the loving-kindness of the great and bountiful God. And for this cause is the sword a sword of flame, because in their company reason, the measure of things must follow, reason with its fierce and burning heat, reason that ever moves with unswerving zeal, teaching thee to choose the good and eschew the evil. (§§29–30)

The second half of the treatise focuses on Gen 4:1. The physical union of Adam and Eve leads Philo to speak of the non-physical unions of God with the virtues, the latter being allegorically signified by Sarah, Rebecca, Leah, Zipporah (§§40–52). Another homiletic application comes at the end:

> Why then, soul of man, when thou shouldst live the virgin life in the house of God and cling to knowledge, dost thou stand aloof from them and embrace outward sense, which unmans and defiles thee? For this thou shalt bring forth that thing of ruin and confusion, Cain, the fratricide, the accursed, the possession which is no possession. For the meaning of Cain is "possession" (§§52).

The remainder of the treatise deals with false human claims to possession, notions that what we have is our own and not God's. Mind (Adam), mating with the senses (Eve), comprehends phenomena and is deluded into supposing this is its own doing (§53–64). Philo points out parallels to Adam's arrogance in words of Laban (§§65–71) and Pharaoh (74–76). True human passivity is not helplessness but active cooperation with God (§77–83). God alone truly keeps festival (§§84–97), and the human soul should prepare itself to be a residence for God, partly through secular education (§§98–105). Human beings who are thus fitted to receive God find their chief joy in acknowledging God's sovereignty and ownership (§§106–123). At the end of the treatise (§§124–30), Philo briefly argues that Adam was foolish to claim that he had "gotten a man through God" since God is not a means but the ultimate cause:

> For we are the instruments, wielded in varying degrees of force, through which each particular form of action is produced; the Craftsman it is who brings to bear on the material the impact of our forces, whether of soul or body, even He by whom all things are moved (§§128).

The treatise on the Cherubim thus illustrates some of Philo's primary convictions. There is an existential character to Philo's religion (despite his stout opposition to anthropomorphism[32]): he speaks about God and God's powers and actions primarily in relation to human experience and need. Wise and religious persons are so largely because they are followers of "a philosophy that cannot lie" (§§129–30) – the Mosaic injunction to "Stand fast and see the salvation from the Lord, which he will accomplish for you" (Exod 14:13). They therefore confess God's total sovereignty and goodness. The root of human wickedness, as symbolized by Cain, is not outward sinful behavior but a way of thought that claims for oneself what actually belongs to God. Finally, human beings should strive for mystical union with God.

The exact nature of Philo's ideas about, or personal experiences of, mysticism have been much debated.[33] In this treatise he speaks of it in several ways. He speaks of humans cooperating with God ("When God is with us all we do is worthy of praise; all that is done without Him merits blame" – §24).[34] He speaks of times of inspiration that he himself has known, not least in writing his commentaries:

> But there is a higher thought than these. It comes from a voice in my own soul, which oftentimes is god-possessed and divines where it does not know. This thought I will record in words if I can . . . (§27).

Philo's rather mysterious[35] discussion of virtues, represented by the wives of the patriarchs and Moses who are impregnated by God, applies in some fashion to human souls:

---

[32] Expressed frequently, as in *Sacr.* 94 (citing Num 23:19).

[33] See esp. Winston, *Philo of Alexandria*, 21–35; idem, *Logos and Mystical Theology in Philo of Alexandria* (Cincinnati: Hebrew Union College, 1985), 43–58; Erwin R. Goodenough, *By Light, Light: The Mystic Gospel of Hellenistic Judaism* (New Haven: Yale University, 1935), esp. 235–64. Cf. Sandmel, *Philo*, 124.

[34] Cf. *Spec. Leg.* 1.282: with God things impossible to us become possible.

[35] It is mysterious because Philo's meaning is not altogether clear in this passage. Perhaps this is intentional, or perhaps he finds his thoughts hard to express. At any rate he

But when God begins to consort with the soul, He makes what before was a woman into a virgin again for He takes away the degenerate and emasculate passions which unmanned it and plants instead the native growth of unpolluted virtues. (§50; cf. §106)[36]

Finally, the image of God taking up residence in the pious and prepared human soul is strongly expressed:

One worthy house there is – the soul that is fitted to receive Him. Justly and rightly then shall we say that in the invisible soul the invisible God has His earthly dwelling place. (§§100–101)

Most of these references to a divine-human union do not stress occasional feelings or emotions on the human side but rather settled patterns of religious thinking and living. Philo comes closest to emphasizing moments of ecstatic experience when he talks about his own times of sudden inspiration or intuition (when his soul is "god-possessed").

4. Israel, Jews, and Gentiles

Philo speaks often of the Jews as a nation (ἔθνος) or race (γένος) with a special closeness to God. Theirs is the right "commonwealth" (πολιτεία, see *Virt.* 219) or "mystery" (*Virt.* 178).[37] Philo does not use "Israel" and "the Jews" as identical terms, however. "Israel" seems regularly to denote the community of all who "see God," and Philo does not claim that all Jews are inside that circle or that all Gentiles are outside.[38] That closeness is based on their possession of and devotion to the Mosaic revelation. Philo uses the language of "covenant" (διαθήκη) only occasionally,[39] but he regularly

---

emphasizes that he is presenting a "divine mystery" that can be revealed only to "the initiated who are worthy to receive the holiest secret" – as opposed to those (Jewish literalists?) who measure piety by their own barren words and rituals (§42).

[36] Cf. *Abr.* 100–102; *Somn.* 1.199–200. Richard A. Baer, Jr., *Philo's Use of the Categories Male and Female* (Leiden: Brill, 1970), 55–64, rightly stresses that the primary implication of this sexual imagery is that God is the source of all good in the human soul.

[37] E. P. Sanders, "The Covenant as a Soteriological Category," in Robert Hamerton-Kelly and Robin Scroggs, ed., *Jews, Greeks and Christians: Religious Cultures in Late Antiquity* (Leiden: Brill, 1976), 31–32, 37–38. Cf. Erwin R. Goodenough, *An Introduction to Philo Judaeus*, 88–90.

[38] This is a major finding argued convincingly by Birnbaum, *Place of Judaism* (e.g., 225–6).

[39] A newly-published Index lists only 23 uses in all Philo's works (Peder Borgen, Kåre Fuglseth, and Roald Skarsten, *The Philo Index: A Complete Greek Word Index to the Writings of Philo of Alexandria Lemmatised & Computer-Generated* [Trondheim: University of Trondheim, 1997]). This is now the most complete guide to Philo's word usage available since it covers the main Greek fragments and includes all words except δέ, καί and ὁ. Of the twenty-three uses of διαθήκη, none refers specifically to the Sinai covenant or to a covenant given by

implies that the Jews have a unique relation to God established through Moses at Sinai. They serve as priestly intercessors on behalf of all humanity (*Abr.* 98; *Mos.* 1.149; *Spec. Leg.* 1.97; 2.162–67).

E. P. Sanders has argued that Philo's overall position generally fits into a pattern of thinking which he calls "covenantal nomism," which he defines as "the view according to which salvation comes by *membership* in the covenant, while obedience to the commandments *preserves* one's place in the covenant." This way of thinking focuses not on the individual's search for salvation but on the community as recipient of divine promises. Sanders admits that Philo does not emphasize "nomism" or offer clear ideas about the nation's future redemption or life after death; he also recognizes Philo's great concern with the individual's search for God. To these qualifications two others should be added: (1) Philo says very little about God's covenant(s) with Israel, and (2) his framework of religious thought is not soteriological (despite his frequent references to God as "savior"). Adding together all these qualifications, it would seem, after all, not very useful to speak of Philo as a representative of "covenantal nomism."[40]

Philo often writes as though every Jew in the world were dedicated to studying and living by the law of Moses (*Mos.* 2.216; *Somn.* 2.123–27; *Deus* 148–51; *Legat.* 210–11). In speaking of "the Jews," Philo does not directly mention the covenant but says that the people are θεοφιλής (beloved by God, or God-loving) and a special object of God's providential protection.[41]

In the *Allegorical Commentary*, however, he seems to assume that relationship but chooses to concentrate on teaching that God associates with all wise and virtuous individuals who seek him. This makes most sense if the intended audience for this multi-volume work consisted of philosophically-minded Jews already familiar with biblical claims about God's election of Israel as a people.[42]

God to all the people of Israel (but see *QE* 2.34). Philo most often uses the term to refer to the gifts of grace God gives to individuals like Abraham and Isaac (*Sacr.* 57; *Det.* 67; *Somn.* 2:223–24; cf. *QG* 3.40, 42). In *Mut.* 53 Philo says he will not enter into a detailed discussion of covenants because he has already written two (not extant) treatises on this topic. Of course it is possible that in those treatises he discussed the Sinai covenant. See Birnbaum, *Place of Judaism*, 132–5. Cf. Isaak Heinemann, *Philons griechische und jüdische Bildung* (1932; rep. Hildesheim: Georg Olms, 1962), 483: Philo knows nothing of a "covenant" between God and the patriarchs and Israel.

[40] Sanders, "Covenant as a Soteriological Category," 25–42 (the definition of "covenantal nomism," with Sanders's italics, is from p.41). Birnbaum is right, I think, in asserting that Sanders's soteriological framework does not really fit Philo (*Place of Judaism*, 36 n. 21).

[41] *Abr.* 98; *Mos.* 1.147, 255; *Hypoth.* 6.7.

[42] So, convincingly, Birnbaum, *Place of Judaism*, 144.

Philo does not say that mere physical descent from Abraham is spiritually significant, let alone sufficient. He writes in praise of a Gentile converted to Judaism:

> The proselyte exalted aloft by his happy lot will be gazed at from all sides, marveled at and held blessed by all for two things of highest excellence, that he came over to the camp of God and that he has won a prize best suited to his merits, a place in heaven firmly fixed, greater than words dare describe, while the nobly born who has falsified the sterling of his high lineage will be dragged right down and carried into Tartarus itself and profound darkness. Thus may all men seeing these examples be brought to a wiser mind and learn that God welcomes the virtue which springs from ignoble birth, that He takes no account of the roots but accepts the full-grown stem, because it has been changed from a weed into fruitfulness. (*Praem.* 152)

As the above-cited passage indicates, Philo clearly recognizes that some who are physical Jews have become apostates, liable to the severest punishment.[43] His own nephew Alexander apparently abandoned the Jewish religion (Josephus, *Ant.* 20.100). Still, even apostates may gain forgiveness if they repent:

> I have now described without any reservation the curses and penalties which they will deservedly suffer who disregard the holy laws of justice and piety, who have been seduced by the polytheistic creeds which finally lead to atheism and have forgotten teaching of their race and of their fathers, in which they were trained from their earliest years to acknowledge the One in substance, the supreme God, to whom alone all must belong who follow truth unfeigned instead of mythical figments. If however they accept these chastisements as a warning rather than as intending their perdition, if shamed into a whole-hearted conversion, they reproach themselves for going thus astray and make a full confession and acknowledgement of all their sin, first within themselves with a mind so purged that their conscience is sincere and free from lurking taint, secondly with their tongues to bring their hearers to a better way, then they will find favor with God the Saviour, the Merciful, who has bestowed on mankind that peculiar and chiefest gift of kinship with His own Word, from whom as its archetype the human mind was created. (*Praem.* 162–63)

Philo himself was a leader in the Alexandrian Jewish community, but he often writes as though he has a constant awareness of, and concern for, the world-wide community of Jews. He writes of the persecutions under Flaccus and Caligula as though they were threats to Jewish well-being in all parts of the Roman Empire.

Since all of his extant commentaries concentrate on the texts of Genesis and Exodus, however, most of his references to "Jews" pertain directly to the families of the patriarchs or to the people whom Moses led. Many of his

---

[43] *Spec. Leg.* 1.54–57, 315–18 specifies the death penalty for apostates. Some scholars have expressed doubt that Philo is describing actual Jewish practice in Alexandria; see Heinemann, *Bildung*, 223–30. The contrary view is argued strongly by T. Seland, *Establishment Violence in Philo and Luke: a Study of Non–Conformity to the Torah and Jewish Vigilante Reactions* (Biblical Interpretation Series 15; Leiden: Brill, 1995).

discussions of ancient times, however, contain veiled or not-so-veiled references to Jewish-Gentile tensions in his own day. When he speaks, for example, of Abraham turning away from "Chaldean" astronomy and materialism, he often seems to be urging his readers to reject first-century Stoicism. When he denounces the animal gods of Egypt in Moses' time, he often seems to be mocking the religion of native Egyptians of his own time.

There are a few Greek writers (Plato and Homer especially) whose writings and ideas Philo almost always cites with great respect. Yet he never suggests that their writings have an authority comparable to the Mosaic texts. Likewise he can praise certain pagan political leaders – notably Augustus and Tiberius – but he never suggests that their religious ideas are on the same level as Jewish ones.

Philo often interprets the word "Israel" to mean "the one who sees God." In some passages he seems to allow for the possibility that some non-Jews might belong spiritually to Israel, just as he can sometimes speak of pagans who possess genuine wisdom. Yet Philo's great hope for Gentiles appears to be that they might become proselytes to Judaism.[44] He generally speaks of persons authentically related to God as being committed to the Mosaic law inasmuch as it constitutes the most accurate reflection of natural law.[45]

Apocalyptic or nationalistic eschatology does not have a very conspicuous place in Philo's writings.[46] In one remarkable passage, however, he speaks of a future time when all Jews will return to the land of Israel and when at least some pagans who have mistreated Jews in the past will recognize their folly (*Praem.* 164; cf. 171). This falls short of a prophecy of the conversion of Gentile nations to the worship of the God of Israel, but it may point in that direction (cf. Isa 2:1–4; Tob 14:6–7). In another passage, however, Philo speaks more plainly of a future when the Jewish people will prosper as they have not prospered for a long time; "if they should do so," all the Gentile nations will be converted to honoring only the Jewish laws:

---

[44] Cf. Winston, "Philo's Ethical Theory," 398–400.

[45] E. P. Sanders argues persuasively that Philo in general sought conversion for Gentiles, though Philo would hardly have expressed his view by declaring that "outside the covenant . . . there is no salvation" ("The Covenant as a Soteriological Category," 27–30). See also Birnbaum, *The Place of Judaism,* 224–30.

[46] Recently Peder Borgen has analyzed the limited evidence with care and insight; see his "There Shall Come Forth a Man: Reflections on Messianic Ideas in Philo," in *The Messiah: Developments in Earliest Judaism and Christianity* (ed. J. Charlesworth; Minneapolis: Fortress, 1992), 341–61; Borgen, *Philo of Alexandria: An Exegete for His Time* (Leiden: Brill, 1997), 261–81. See also James M. Scott, "Philo and the Restoration of Israel," *SBLSP* 34 (1995): 553–75. For a very different view of the evidence, see Burton L. Mack, "Wisdom and Apocalyptic in Philo," *Studia Philonica Annual* 3 (1991): 21–39.

I believe that each nation would abandon its peculiar ways, and throwing overboard their ancestral customs, turn to honoring our laws alone. (*Mos.* 2.44)[47]

Despite occasional references to life after death, Philo's writings generally focus on life in this world. He does not speak of Jews or Gentiles being "saved" after death.[48]

5. The Law of Moses, Forgiveness and Merit

The new *Philo Index* lists 536 occurrences of the term νόμος ("law") in the Philonic corpus. This is his standard term for the Mosaic legislation, and he often uses it to refer to the Pentateuch as a whole (narratives as well as statutes). Philo is persuaded that all of the specific commandments of Moses have permanent validity, though his treatise (in four books) *On the Special Laws* shows that he was aware of problems of applying them in his own time. Philo never distinguishes between cultic and ethical laws in the sense of suggesting that one group is more important than the other. He calls the Ten Commandments the "Ten Words" (λόγοι) and says that they summarize the Special Laws (*Spec. Leg.* 1:1). When he goes on to interpret individual laws of the Pentateuch, Philo tends to emphasize their relation to the Law of Nature, on the one hand, and their manifestation of the primary Greek virtues, on the other.[49]

One of Philo's most remarkable ideas is that the Law of Moses is the Law of Nature (φύσις).[50] Hence Moses begins by recounting the creation of the world, which God shaped in accord with the Law revealed at Sinai:

[Moses'] exordium . . . is one that excites our admiration in the highest degree. It consists of an account of the creation of the world, implying that the world is in

---

[47] For discussion, see Ronald Williamson, *Jews in the Hellenistic World: Philo* (Cambridge Commentaries on Writings of the Jewish & Christian World 200 BC to AD 200, I.ii; Cambridge: University, 1989), 25–27; Dawson, *Allegorical Readers*, 122. In *Mos.* 2.41–44 Philo describes an annual celebration of the LXX translation on the island of Pharos, a celebration in which pagans as well as Jews take part.

[48] E.g., *Cher.* 114 speaks briefly and quite opaquely of life after death as bodiless but as leading to "our rebirth, to be with the unbodied, without composition and without quality." See also *Gig.* 12–16, 31. Cf. E. P. Sanders, "The Covenant as a Soteriological Category," 36–38, where he recognizes that "Philo is generally vague" on the issue of personal immortality. Cf. Wolfson, *Philo* 1.395–416; Erwin R. Goodenough, "Philo on Immortality," *HTR* 39 (1946): 85–108; Winston, *Logos and Mystical Theology*, 27–42. The descriptions of the proselyte gaining "a place in heaven firmly fixed" while the Jewish apostate is dragged down to Tartarus (*Praem.* 152) appear to be metaphorical.

[49] So Goodenough, *Introduction*, 122.

[50] Cf. Goodenough, *By Light, Light*, 48–94; Winston, "Philo's Ethical Theory," 381–8; Borgen, *Philo of Alexandria: An Exegete for His Time*, 144–8.

harmony with the Law, and the Law with the world, and that the man who observes the Law is constituted thereby a loyal citizen of the world, regulating his doings by the purpose and will of Nature, in accordance with which the entire world itself also is administered. (*Opif.* 3)

Helmut Koester has argued[51] "there can be little doubt that Philo has to be considered as the crucial and most important contributor to the development of the theory of natural law" and, further, that "only a philosophical and theological setting in which the Greek concept of nature was fused with the belief in a divine legislator and with a doctrine of the most perfect (written!) law could produce such a theory, and only there could the Greek dichotomy of the two realms of law and nature be overcome."[52]

To this theory of natural law, Philo adds another quite as striking: that the patriarchs were "living laws" –

for in these men we have laws endowed with life and reason (οἱ γὰρ ἔμψυχοι καὶ λογικοὶ νόμοι ἄνδρες ἐκεῖνοι γεγόνασιν), and Moses extolled them for two reasons. First he wished to shew that the enacted ordinances are not inconsistent with nature; and secondly that those who wish to live in accordance with the laws as they stand have no difficult task, seeing that the first generations before any at all of the particular statutes was set in writing followed the unwritten law with perfect ease, so that one might properly say that the enacted laws are nothing else than memorials of the life of the ancients, preserving to a later generation their actual words and deeds, for they were not scholars or pupils of others, nor did they learn under teachers what was right to say or do: they listened to no voice or instruction but their own: they gladly accepted conformity with nature, holding that nature itself was, as indeed it is, the most venerable of statutes, and thus their whole life was one of happy obedience to law. (*Abr.* 5–6)

Moses also was a "living law" long before he gave the laws at Sinai (*Mos.* 1.162). The idea that some human beings personify the law seems to be connected with Philo's broader ideas about authentic kingship (*Mos.* 2.4). But like his idea that the world is created according to the law of Moses, this one has a partly literary value: it explains why the Pentateuch, which as a whole is called "the Law," presents narratives about creation and individuals long before it reports the giving of the legislation of Sinai.

More fundamentally, however, the concept of unwritten laws in nature and in the chief human figures prior to Sinai leads toward an audacious but fundamental claim: the Mosaic Law is valid for all humanity. It is the law of

---

[51] "Nomos Physeos: The Concept of Natural Law in Greek Thought," in *Religions in Antiquity* (ed. Jacob Neusner; Leiden: Brill, 1968), 521–41. See also Sandmel, *Philo*, 119–22; Naomi G. Cohen, *Philo Judaeus: His Universe of Discourse* (BEATAJ 24; Frankfurt: Peter Lang, 1995); John W. Martens, "Unwritten Law in Philo: A Response to Naomi G. Cohen," *JJS* 43 (1992): 38–45.

[52] For criticism of Koester's view, see R. A. Horsley, "The Law of Nature in Philo and Cicero," *HTR* 71 (1978): 35–59; Markus Bockmuehl, "Natural Law in Second Temple Judaism," *VT* 45 (1995): 17–44; Borgen, *Philo of Alexandria: An Exegete for His Time*, 144–8.

everyone's nature, even for those who have never heard of Moses. And it is not beyond human strength since it has already been demonstrated in human lives. Those who live by the law of Moses are citizens of the world – and they only![53]

This is not to say that Plato's philosophy and the teachings of certain other pagan writers are altogether lacking in truth and value. Philo praises the "encyclical" or "preliminary" studies, indicating that Jews in Alexandria and elsewhere should pursue a solid grounding in the best pagan intellectual traditions and skills.[54] Philo can also employ language linked with pagan mysteries to describe the religious experiences he and some other Jews share. Still, he never suggests that any pagan religion can compete with Judaism in quality or truth.

All the laws of Moses are intended to be obeyed, with no additions or subtractions (*Spec. Leg.* 4.143). One cannot pick and choose, as though some laws were not binding. When he turns to interpret specific biblical commandments, Philo often uses allegory to explain their religious rationale; but he regularly interprets the laws on a literal level indicating that they are to be obeyed in the realm of the external world. In a famous passage (*Migr.* 89–93) he criticizes a group of allegorists who understand ritual laws (circumcision, observance of the Sabbath and other holy days) symbolically but disregard their literal meaning. Philo agrees with their symbolic interpretations but warns that "we shall not escape censure from the many" if "we" fail to practice these laws on the literal level. Allegory can reveal the inner meaning of the laws; it is not a substitute for literal observance.[55]

---

[53] Peder Borgen, "Philo. Survey of Research since World War II," *ANRW* II.21.1, 150: "Philo shared the common Jewish view that the Jewish nation was the center of the world" and thought of the Mosaic Law as "equally suitable for Jews and Greeks." Yet Borgen goes on to argue that "Philo's extreme form of particularism was on the point of ending up in a universalism where Jewish distinctiveness was in danger of being lost" (154).

[54] See Alan Mendelson, *Secular Education in Philo of Alexandria* (Cincinnati: Hebrew Union College, 1982).

[55] On this much-discussed passage, the *only* one in which he plainly refers to these "radicals," see D. Hay, "Putting Extremism in Context: The Case of Philo, *De Migratione* 89–93," in *Wisdom and Logos: Studies in Jewish Thought in Honor of David Winston* (ed. D. T. Runia and G. E. Sterling; *Studia Philonica Annual* 9 [1997]), 126–42. The passage does not clearly indicate if the "extremists" carried their opposition to literal practice to non-ritual portions of the Mosaic laws. Sandmel, partly on the basis of this passage and following the lead of Goodenough, argues that Philo essentially agrees with the "extreme allegorists" (*Philo's Place in Judaism* [New York: KTAV, 1971], 198). Sandmel also draws the possible (but not necessary) inference, "No matter how much Philo exalts the Law of Moses, no matter how with the Law of nature, the Law of Moses is at best a copy, and thereby inescapably secondary" (197). A convincing critique of this view is offered by V. Nikiprowetzky, *Commentaire de l'Ecriture*, 117–55.

Is Philo's understanding of the Law related to rabbinic Jewish literature, or to the teachings of his Palestinian contemporaries? This has been debated for generations.[56] One recent scholar, Naomi Cohen, argues that Philo is thoroughly Jewish in his basic attitude toward the Mosaic Law and obedience at the literal level, as shown in *Spec. Leg.* 4:132–50, and that indeed Philo was acquainted with Palestinian midrashic traditions (both halakhic and haggadic) which later were formulated in the surviving rabbinic literature.[57] She contends, further, that Philo's references to "unwritten laws," while alluding in part to a Platonic philosophical conception, also refer specifically to the rabbinic "Oral Law."[58] Cohen's detailed arguments strengthen the case that Philo regarded literal observance of the written laws of Moses as essential; but she does not make a compelling case for connecting Philo with Palestinian midrash and "Oral Law."[59]

Although he believes that human beings can actually fulfill the laws of Moses, Philo consistently indicates that all human beings are prone to error (see, e.g., *Mut.* 47–51; *Deus* 75). Even the patriarchs faltered:

> They committed no guilty action of their own free will or purpose, and where chance led them wrong they besought God's mercy and propitiated Him with prayers and supplications, and thus secured a perfect life guided in both fields, both in their premeditated actions and in such as were not of freely-willed purpose. (*Abr.* 6)

Human proclivity to wrong-doing is suggested already in the laws about ritual (but not moral) impurity connected with birth, requiring that the mother be purified as well as the infant. The impurities are removed through rites of purification and circumcision (*Dec.* 45; *Spec. Leg.* 3.63; etc.). Philo's theory of human development in stages views the child as "pure wax," inexperienced in both good and evil. Because of the early development of the passions and defects in education, however, a child turns to evil before it is attracted to virtue under the guidance of reason. The conflict between Jacob and Esau in Rebecca's womb symbolizes the twin tendencies of good and evil in every human being (*Praem.* 62–63).[60]

The law itself provides means of restoring those who have transgressed. God alone can forgive sins (*Somn.* 2.299) since sin is a violation of the Law of Nature, which is God's law. Still, human beings must do their part. Inner repentance is required, and this should be followed by some kind of public

---

[56] See Sandmel, *Philo*, 127–34; Borgen, "Philo," 124–6.

[57] Cohen, *Philo Judaeus*. She feels herself close to the views argued earlier by Samuel Belkin, maintaining that Philo was "a distinguished representative of the contemporary Alexandria version of 'normative Judaism'" (287).

[58] Ibid., 256–77, 284.

[59] See the review by Ellen Birnbaum, *Studia Philonica Annual* 8 (1996): 189–96.

[60] Jean Laporte, *Théologie liturgique de Philon d'Alexandrie et d'Origène.* (Liturgie 6; Paris: Cerf, 1995), 195–6.

confession (so that others will be deterred from sin). Repentance occupies the second place after perfection (*Abr.* 26) and is symbolized by Enoch (*Abr.* 17–25; *Praem.* 15–21; *QG* 1.82).[61] The sensitive conscience exposes the evil thoughts concealed in the soul and seeks divine judgment, forgiveness and aid in distinguishing good and evil for the future (*Leg.* 3.1–13, 42–48; *Cher.* 16–17; *Fug.* 116–18). Moses prescribes sacrifices for sin, and the most complete and appropriate means for pardon are certainly those sacrifices for sin carried out daily in the temple in Jerusalem[62] as well as during festivals and, above all, on Yom Kippur (*Spec. Leg.* 1.180–93, 234; 2.193–96). Philo declares that on the Day of Atonement forgiveness is granted for both voluntary and involuntary sins, not just for legal impurities.[63] The sacrificial laws of Moses are understood by Philo on a literal external level to be legitimate and necessary, though he also emphasizes that only an authentic inner intention on the part of persons offering sacrifices can make the sacrifices valid.[64] Pentateuchal references to the wrath of God and dire consequences of disobedience are designed to awaken the claims of conscience and prompt repentance (*Spec. Leg.* 2.170; *Legat.* 6–7; *Jos.* 170–74; *Cher.* 1–17). The true "cure" for sin lies in divine forgiveness on the one hand and, on the other, a sinner's conversion to a better life through the elimination of vice and acquisition of virtue.[65] Philo takes for granted God's love and willingness to forgive sinners who repent.

Repentance itself is grounded on the grace of God. The awareness of guilt depends on the human conscience, which Philo understands to be God's word or reason (Logos) within each individual (*Deus* 134–38).[66] Philo often speaks of the Powers of God, angels or metaphysical expressions of God insofar as God is knowable to human beings. Thus the divine visitation to Abraham in Gen 18 was sometimes "seen" by him as three and sometimes as one; the one was God, the three were God and his two senior Powers, the Power of Punishment and the Power of Mercy. Had the inhabitants of Sodom and

---

[61] See esp. David Winston, "Philo's Doctrine of Repentance," *The School of Moses: Studies in Philo and Hellenistic Religion* (ed. John P. Kenney; Studia Philonica Monographs 1; Atlanta: Scholars, 1995), 29–40.

[62] Philo mentions that he himself has traveled to Jerusalem to offer sacrifices in the temple at least once in his life (*Prov.* 2.64). Although Diaspora Jews could visit that temple only occasionally, their awareness of daily sacrifices there for sins may have given them a sense of God's mercy for themselves, wherever they lived.

[63] Laporte, *Théologie liturgique*, 93–95.

[64] *Spec. Leg.* 1.269–79. On the other hand, Philo criticizes those who perform ritual purifications and sacrifices with souls polluted by moral sins: their offerings, like those of a prostitute, are unacceptable in God's temple (Deut 23:18; *Spec. Leg.* 1.280–84).

[65] Laporte, *Théologie liturgique*, 97.

[66] See esp. Dieter Zeller, *Charis bei Philon und Paulus* (SBS 142; Stuttgart: Katholisches Bibelwerk, 1990), 63–65; Winston, "Philo's Ethical Theory," 389–91.

Gomorrah been willing to repent, they would have experienced mercy rather than destruction. Philo allegorizes the biblical legislation concerning cities of refuge to mean that God has appointed means of finding mercy to all who turn to God.

Does Philo think that human beings earn God's forgiveness and mercy? He certainly often stresses that human beings have free will and that they must cooperate with God in acquiring the virtues. Toil for spiritual ends is good (*Sacr.* 112–13). Yet Philo does not think of human free will as absolute and his concept of grace is not synergistic. Fundamentally Philo considers that human responsibility centers in thankfulness to the Creator, who is the source of all that is good within each soul.[67] Everything finally hinges on divine grace.[68]

Despite this emphasis on grace, Philo does not hesitate to affirm that there are rewards for the righteous and punishments for the wicked. In discussing the blessings and curses at the end of the Mosaic legislation in Deuteronomy, Philo mentions rewards and penalties experienced in this world.[69] He does not typically speak about life after death as the realm when divine sanctions come into effect.

6. Conclusions

Philo takes for granted the existence of a worldwide Jewish community to which he belongs and for which he writes, though he manifests special concern for the Jews of Alexandria, whom he represented on at least one diplomatic mission. Within the community of biblical interpreters, he is particularly conscious of literalists who reject allegorizing and allegorists who also accept the literal level of biblical exegesis. He identifies with the latter group, which he often describes as an elite minority. Still, he often writes as one who feels a profound spiritual kinship with all Jews. Nevertheless, his most profound commentaries focus on the individual's spiritual journey toward God.

One may speak of a certain tension between the corporate and the individualistic concerns in Philo, but hardly of a fundamental contradiction in spirit or intent. Philo assumes that the essential human problem is how each person can draw close to the God of Moses. Outward observance of the

---

[67] See Jean Laporte, *Eucharistia in Philo* (New York: Edwin Mellen, 1983), 172–8, 184–5.

[68] Zeller, *Charis*, 72. Zeller rightly points out the falsity and bias in W. Völker's assertion that Philo was "ein naiver Synergist, der sich keine Gedanken über das Ineinander von Gnade und Freiheit machte" (66–67).

[69] On the tensions in Philo's position, see now Alan Mendelson, "Philo's Dialectic of Reward and Punishment," *Studia Philonica Annual* 9 (1997): 104–25.

Mosaic laws is assumed to be obligatory, but the deepest understanding of those laws is possible only through allegorical interpretation. Philo writes mainly for other Jews who care most about their personal religious relationship with the God of Moses, but who also appreciate the achievements of Greco-Roman culture. Philo, especially in his allegorical commentaries, shows them how they can find anchorage in the Bible, remain connected with the Jewish people, and grow in wisdom and philosophical sophistication – all at the same time. Philo's aims are fairly complex, but we must assume that he thought his contemporaries' religious needs were also complex.[70]

---

[70] I am indebted to David Winston for his judicious comments on an earlier draft of this essay.

13. 1QS and Salvation at Qumran

by

MARKUS BOCKMUEHL

How did the Qumran community envisage the salvation of God's people? Before we can engage with the sources and with previous scholarship on this question, several preliminary issues require attention. These include the exponential growth of the available source material in recent years, the place of soteriology in the Qumran literature as a whole, and some consideration of the most suitable point of departure.

1. Preliminary Considerations

1.1 New Sources

After decades of delay at the hands of an exclusive coterie of specialists, free access to the photographs of the Dead Sea Scrolls was at last opened up to the scholarly community in the autumn of 1991. At the same time, the editorial team was significantly enlarged and re-organized under the new aegis of Emanuel Tov. Since then, there has been a dramatic acceleration in the official publication of the Scrolls, and numerous new university appointments, academic journals and monograph series have been created to cope with the increased pace of scholarly activity. One small but significant statistic may serve to indicate the scale of change: in the 35 years from its inception until 1990, the definitive Discoveries in the Judaean Desert edition had produced only eight volumes. Between 1992 and the end of 1997, however, a further thirteen volumes appeared. In the study of Jewish and Christian origins, no other area has in the 1990s seen such large-scale engagement with new sources as the study of the Dead Sea Scrolls.

Before embarking on our study of Qumran's view of human salvation, therefore, it is important to note that almost the entire body of secondary literature on this subject pre-dates the scholarly watershed of 1992. Since then, numerous literary and theological questions have come to be clarified, new issues have been raised, and a far greater sense has been gained of the religious complexity behind that vast collection of texts found at Qumran. Several of the new texts have received attention far beyond the scholarly world, not least because of their supposed relevance to Christian origins.[1] Well beyond the sensationalist and idiosyncratic arguments of recent years, however, it is clear that many of the "new" texts are of considerable interest for the understanding of Jewish life and faith around the beginning of our era.

1.2 Salvation and "the Qumran Pattern of Religion"

In one sense this dramatic development significantly complicates our attempt to study the texts in dialogue with earlier scholars. When E. P. Sanders, for example, devoted ninety pages of his celebrated work *Paul and Palestinian Judaism* to the Scrolls,[2] he could assume as largely unproblematic their Essene authorship *in toto* and, with only minor exceptions, their more or less homogeneous character as representative of *"the* Qumran pattern of religion."[3] What is more, his study was overwhelmingly concerned with just four main documents, the first of which was then accessible to the public only in two medieval copies from the Cairo Genizah, while the others could be studied solely from published fragments in Cave 1: the *Damascus Document* (CD), the *Community Rule* (1QS)[4] and related eschatological texts (1QSa, 1QSb), the *War Scroll* (1QM) and the *Hodayot* or *Hymns* (1QH).[5] The only other texts cited repeatedly are the Habakkuk Commentary (1QpHab), part of the Psalms Commentary (4QpPs[a], *olim* 4QpPs37) and the so-called *Midrash on Eschatology* (4QMidrEschat[a], *olim* Florilegium=4QFlor).[6]

---

[1] Of these, the "Messianic Apocalypse" 4Q521 and 4Q285 (at one time famously misread as referring to a "slain Messiah") are perhaps the best known.

[2] E. P. Sanders, *Paul and Palestinian Judaism: A Comparison of Patterns of Religion* (London: SCM, 1977), 239-328.

[3] Ibid., 239 n. 1, emphasis mine; cf. 316-21.

[4] There is also a single passing reference to 4QS[e] as cited in C. H. Hunzinger, "Beobachtungen zur Entwicklung der Disziplinarordnung der Gemeinde von Qumran," in *Qumran-Probleme: Vorträge des Leipziger Symposions über Qumran-Probleme vom 9. bis 14. Oktober 1961* (Deutsche Akademie der Wissenschaften: Schriften der Sektion für Altertumswissenschaft 42; ed. H. Bardtke; Berlin: Akademie-Verlag, 1963), 231–47 (cited in Sanders, *Paul and Palestinian Judaism*, 324).

[5] 1QH will here be cited according to the reconstructed order as proposed by Émile Puech ("Quelques aspects de la restauration du Rouleau des Hymnes [1QH]," *JJS* 39 [1988]: 38-55) and now widely adopted, e.g. in the translation of Florentino García Martínez, *The Dead Sea Scrolls Translated: The Qumran Texts in English* (trans. W. G. E. Watson; 2d ed.; Leiden: Brill/Grand Rapids: Eerdmans, 1996) – see esp. p. 302. Unfortunately their line numbering does not always coincide; but since most readers seem likely at present to find García Martínez the most accessible translation, I have chosen to adopt his referencing. For the same reasons, citations of 4QMMT are given according to the "composite text" in García Martínez's translation, with the alternative reference to Qimron and Strugnell's version in DJD vol. 10 in parentheses.

[6] For the proposed change in the nomenclature of 4Q174 (*olim* 4QFlor) see Annette Steudel, *Der Midrasch zur Eschatologie aus der Qumrangemeinde (4QMidrEschat[a,b])* (STDJ 13; Leiden: Brill, 1994). Sanders does also cite 1QpMic 7ff. on two occasions; several minor texts from

Even if it were possible, no serious student would today attempt to describe "the Qumran pattern of religion" without reference to the large number of additional texts that have become accessible since 1977. For present purposes we need mention only a few of the most familiar: the *Temple Scroll* (11QTemple; cf. the earlier exemplar 4Q524[7]), the *Halakic Letter from Qumran* (4QMMT) and the extensive new Cave 4 fragments of the *Community Rule, Damascus Document, War Scroll* and *Hymns* (4QS, 4QD, 4QM, 4QH), new apocalypses concerning a "son of God" figure and the ministry of the Messiah (4Q246, 4Q521; cf. 4Q541), various important prayers and liturgical texts (4QPrFêtes, 4QShirShabb, 4QBar*kîNapshî), etc. Numerous other texts could be listed, including biblical MSS as well as a large number of "para-biblical" apocrypha, halakic and wisdom texts (see e.g. DJD vols. 19, 20, 22).

Given this much larger text base, a contemporary treatment of Qumran's "pattern of religion" would probably not follow along the lines one might have chosen a quarter of a century ago. Indeed it is instructive to recall, for example, how Sanders's at first largely soteriological construction of ancient Judaism came in for criticism, as suspiciously dominated by Christian and Protestant concerns.[8] One wonders, too, about the extent to which both Sanders and some of his critics were guided in their perception of this topic by the desire to arrive at a large-scale systemic "comparison" with central aspects of Pauline theology.[9]

It would be possible, for the sake of the argument, to grant the heuristic utility of such a "Protestant" reading in the case of 1QS and CD with their penchant for sectarian questions of membership, covenant and eschatological identity – even though, as Otto Betz has rightly noted, the Scrolls seem to employ no noun or verb that could be said to correspond closely to the (Pauline) notion of justification.[10] However, even a more broadly soteri-

---

Cave 4 are cited once.

[7] See Émile Puech, "Fragments du plus ancien exemplaire du *Rouleau du Temple* (4Q524)," *Legal Texts and Legal Issues: Proceedings of the Second Meeting of the International Organization for Qumran Studies, Cambridge 1995* (*Fs.* Joseph M. Baumgarten; STDJ 23; ed. M. Bernstein et al.; Leiden: Brill, 1997).

[8] So Jacob Neusner, "The Use of Later Rabbinic Evidence for the Study of Paul," *Approaches to Ancient Judaism* (ed. W. S. Green; Chico: Scholars, 1980) 2.43–63, and passim. This criticism may be said to have been refuted by Sanders's later work: see his *Jewish Law from Jesus to the Mishnah: Five Studies* (London: SCM/Philadelphia: Trinity Press International, 1990); idem, *Judaism: Practice and Belief 63 BCE–66 CE* (London: SCM/Philadelphia: Trinity Press International, 1992); but note also his response at the time: "Puzzling Out Rabbinic Judaism," *Approaches* 2.65–79.

[9] Note the subtitle of Sanders's 1977 book (n. 2 above).

[10] Otto Betz, "Rechtfertigung in Qumran," *Rechtfertigung* (*Fs.* Ernst Käsemann; ed. J. Friedrich et al.; Tübingen: Mohr [Siebeck]/Göttingen: Vandenhoeck & Ruprecht, 1976), 17. His claim that the Scrolls never use the *hip'il* of צדק to denote God's act of justification (ibid.)

ological focus no longer adequately accounts for the great variety of textual genres and perspectives that the more recent texts have brought to light. Documents like 4QMMT or 11QTemple, and various texts of calendrical and ritual import demonstrate the extent to which concretely halakic interests lie at the very heart of the Qumran community's identity and self-understanding, quite in addition to any explicit preoccupation with gaining or maintaining status before God. Similarly, the importance of worship, prayer and liturgical developments at Qumran is something which might have been guessed from certain passages in the *War Scroll* and the *Hymns*, but which the recently published texts have clearly underscored. The group's sustained interest in non-sectarian, traditional eschatology and apocalyptic, too, has emerged in a considerable number of both known and previously unknown works from Cave 4. In all these respects, an explanation of Qumran's religion purely or even predominantly in classic soteriological terms seems today to be unacceptably narrow.

1.3 Purpose and Method of this Study

Having said all this, our brief here is of course at once more narrow than the one that E. P. Sanders set out to address, and yet more congenial to the methods and results he actually espoused than a comprehensive survey of the Qumran "library" would lead one to conclude. Sanders's results pertain to the problem of salvation in a covenantal relationship with God – in his own somewhat imprecise words, of "getting in" and "staying in" such a relationship.[11] It may well be that Jacob Neusner was right to query this orientation as a biased interest more characteristic of the interpreter's Christian concerns than those of the Judaism he is trying to understand.[12] Christian or not, however, the question of human salvation is clearly a legitimate one; and it happens to be one which a great many Jewish texts (and not just *these* ones) do from time to time prominently address.[13]

In this sense, therefore, a meaningful discussion of Qumran's soteriology is indeed well advised to take seriously the contributions of E. P. Sanders and other earlier contributors to the debate.[14] What is more, even the particular

---

needs to be slightly modified in light of the phrase צדיק יהוה in 4Q370 2:2 – though of course this still leaves the possibility that that text might have originated outside the sect. Note also 1QS 3:3.

[11] Sanders, *Paul and Palestinian Judaism*, 544–5.

[12] Neusner, "The Use of Later Rabbinic Evidence," 49–50 and passim.

[13] Even Neusner concedes this, ibid., 48, 50.

[14] In addition to Sanders, *Paul and Palestinian Judaism*, significant contributors include Jürgen Becker, *Das Heil Gottes: Heils- und Sündenbegriffe in den Qumrantexten und im Neuen Testament* (SUNT 3; Göttingen: Vandenhoeck & Ruprecht, 1964); Betz, "Rechtfertigung in Qumran"; William H. Brownlee, "Anthropology and Soteriology in the Dead Sea Scrolls and in the New Testament," in *The Use of the Old Testament in the New and Other Essays* (*Fs.*

emphasis on the major documents from Cave 1 turns out to be not far from the mark. In many ways it is still these documents which most clearly concern themselves with both the social and theological aspects of people's acceptance before God – even if a study of the Qumran community's constitutional documents must now take into account the very significant manuscripts from Cave 4.

Given the constraints of space, therefore, this narrower soteriological concern of our study still makes it appropriate to concentrate on the *Community Rule* as our base text – although taking into account the various newly published fragments from Cave 4.[15] Where relevant, reference will of course also be made to other leading sectarian documents such as CD, 1QH and 4QMMT.

William Franklin Stinespring; ed. J. M. Efird; Durham: Duke University, 1972), 210–41; John V. Chamberlain, "Toward a Qumran Soteriology," *NovT* 3 (1959): 305–13; Paul Garnet, *Salvation and Atonement in the Qumran Scrolls* (WUNT 2/3; Tübingen: Mohr [Siebeck], 1977); Walter Grundmann, "The Teacher of Righteousness of Qumran and the Question of Justification by Faith in the Theology of the Apostle Paul," in *Paul and Qumran: Studies in New Testament Exegesis* (ed. J. Murphy-O'Connor; London: Chapman, 1968), 85–114; Norbert Ilg, "Überlegungen zum Verständnis von ברית in den Qumrântexten," in *Qumrân: Sa piété, sa théologie et son milieu* (ed. M. Delcor; BETL 46; Paris: Duculot/Leuven: Leuven University, 1978), 257–63; Annie Jaubert, *La notion de l'Alliance dans le Judaïsme aux abords de l'ère chrétienne* (Paris: Seuil, 1963); H.-W. Kuhn, *Enderwartung und gegenwärtiges Heil: Untersuchungen zu den Gemeindeliedern von Qumran* (SUNT 4; Göttingen: Vandenhoeck & Ruprecht, 1966); A. R. C. Leaney, *The Rule of the Community* (NTL; London: SCM, 1966); Hermann Lichtenberger, *Studien zum Menschenbild in den Texten der Qumrangemeinde* (SUNT 15; Göttingen: Vandenhoeck & Ruprecht, 1980); idem, "Atonement and Sacrifice in the Qumran Community," *Approaches*, 2.159–71; idem, "Enderwartung und Reinheitsidee: Zur eschatologischen Deutung von Reinheit und Sühne in der Qumrangemeinde," *JJS* 34 (1983): 31–62; Helmer Ringgren, *The Faith of Qumran: Theology of the Dead Sea Scrolls* (trans. E. T. Sander; expanded ed.; ed. J. H. Charlesworth; New York: Crossroad, 1995); Siegfried Schulz, "Zur Rechtfertigung aus Gnaden in Qumran und bei Paulus: Zugleich ein Beitrag zur Form- und Überlieferungsgeschichte der Qumrantexte," *ZTK* 56 (1959): 155–85; Mark A. Seifrid, *Justification by Faith: The Origin and Development of a Central Pauline Theme* (NovTSup 68; Leiden: Brill, 1992); J. W. Semmelink, "Die verband tussen genade en werke in 1QS se reddingsbegrip," *Skrif en Kerk* 16 (1995): 102–24 (*non vidi*); Peter Stuhlmacher, *Gerechtigkeit Gottes bei Paulus* (FRLANT 87; 2d ed.; Göttingen: Vandenhoeck & Ruprecht, 1966); and others.

[15] Beyond this, the scroll containing 1QS also included the eschatological Rule for the messianic age (1QSa, somewhat confusingly entitled "Rule of the *Congregation*") and the eschatological *Blessings* (1QSb). It is of course true that aside from this one MS we have no evidence that 1QS was typically copied together with 1QSa and 1QSb. So also Sarianna Metso, *The Textual Development of the Qumran Community Rule* (STDJ 21; Leiden: Brill, 1993), 151, although she somewhat overstates the case in claiming to find "no indication" that the three documents were "*ever* copied together" (emphasis mine). In any case it seems that at least the latest text form of the *Community Rule* was produced, and presumably read, together with 1QSa and 1QSb.

One might of course wish to argue that *all* the material maintained in the Qumran "library"[16] is in some sense indicative of the sect's beliefs at different stages. Nevertheless, even on a comprehensive view it is still in *Serekh ha-Yahad* that we have the constitutional text that most clearly and explicitly sets out the sect's distinctive beliefs and religious self-understanding. Its great importance for the sectarians is evident from the fact that no fewer than twelve copies have come to light at Qumran, more than of any other non-biblical text except *Jubilees*.[17] Although the text underwent continual change and was perhaps never finalized in definitive terms, it is clear that in its explicit function as a leadership manual it was intended to encapsulate the community's self-definition in terms of both theological and practical distinctives.[18]

2. The Rule of the Community

The document entitled *Sefer Serekh ha-Yahad* (after 4QS^a 1:1, where the phrase occurs verbatim) is a quasi-catechetical manual governing life in the Qumran sect, possibly intended in the first instance for the use of the community leader known as the *Maskîl* ("Instructor," משכיל).[19] In addition

---

[16] I am aware of the difficulty in assessing whether the minor caves and the more remote Dead Sea finds actually belonged to the community "library" – or, for that matter, whether that widely used term adequately interprets even the collections in the major caves.

[17] Cf. also Geza Vermes, "Preliminary Remarks on Unpublished Fragments of the Community Rule from Qumran Cave 4," *JJS* 42 (1991): 251 ("the most copiously attested sectarian writing" – unless of course one considers Jubilees "sectarian"); James H. Charlesworth, ed., *The Dead Sea Scrolls: Hebrew, Aramaic, and Greek Texts with English Translations*. Vol. 1: *Rule of the Community and Related Documents*. Vol. 2: *Damascus Document, War Scroll, and Related Documents* (The Princeton Theological Seminary Dead Sea Scrolls Project; Tübingen: Mohr [Siebeck]/Louisville: Westminster John Knox, 1994–95), 1.2.

[18] Note the reconstruction of 1QS 1:1: ל[משכיל ללמד את א[נ]נשי לחיו ספר סרך היחד, "for the *Maskîl* [Instructor] to teach the men during his lifetime, the book of the order of the Community."

[19] Leaney, *The Rule of the Community*, 117–8, and a majority of writers have followed Jean Carmignac ("Conjecture sur la première ligne de la Règle de la Communauté," *RevQ* 2 [1959]: 85–87) in restoring the opening word ל[משכיל (cf. already A. Dupont-Sommer, *Les Écrits Esséniens découverts près de la Mer Morte* [Bibliothèque Historique; Paris: Payot, 1959], 88, or more recently F. du T. Laubscher, "The Restoration of 1QS 1:1A,"*JNSL* 16 [1990]: 85–90), not least with reference to the undoubtedly central role of the Instructor elsewhere (e.g. 3:13; 9:12, 21). Whether or not this reconstruction is correct, however (note the cautious remarks of Michael A. Knibb, *The Qumran Community* [Cambridge Commentaries on Writings of the Jewish and Christian World 200 BC to AD 200; Cambridge: Cambridge University, 1987], 79), any overly specific conclusion about the document's actual *Sitz im Leben* must be tempered with the realization that the clearly liturgical *Songs of the Sabbath Sacrifice* tend *also* to begin with the words למשיל: 4Q401 1–2:1; 4Q403 1:30; 2:18; 4Q405 20–22:6; 4Q406 1:6; 11Q17 2:8.

to an almost complete MS from Cave 1, the document survives in ten fragmentary MSS of different text types in Cave 4 (4QS[a-j]) and, it appears, one small fragment from Cave 5 (5Q11). In substance, the *Rule* concerns the beliefs as well as the rules of admission and conduct that govern the life of the Qumran sectarians, although we cannot be wholly sure about its precise setting and use (a liturgical *Sitz im Leben* at least of the opening covenant renewal text is clear from 1QS 1:20; 2:18).[20] A number of other unresolved questions about the *Rule* cannot be addressed here, including its possible status among Essenes outside Qumran as well as the likely role played by the Teacher of Righteousness in its composition.[21] After a brief survey of its contents, we shall examine its view of salvation in systematic topical fashion before turning to a closer textual investigation.

2.1 Overview of 1QS

Five separate sections can be discerned in 1QS, although the evidence from Cave 4 suggests that some earlier versions of this document may have comprised no more than the first part of section 4.

(1) An introductory paragraph (1:1–18a) offers a definition of the community's identity and solidarity in strongly theocentric and praxis-orientated terms: the community seeks God in everything, concerned "to love all that he has chosen, and to hate all that he has rejected" (1:3–4). Membership of the community is equivalent to membership of an open-ended but exclusive "covenant of mercy" (1:8), which is at the same time sharply demarcated in opposition to the "children of darkness" (1:10). Although this section does envisage people turning from their past ways and devoting themselves to the ways of God (1:6–9) within the Community, there is no indication of a developed soteriology.

Next, we find (2) an intriguing liturgy for admission to "the covenant" (1:18b–2:18), containing instructions for the annual renewal of this "entry" into the covenant and the exclusion of those who refuse to "enter" in this fashion (2:19–3:12). This is followed by (3) the exposition of the doctrine of the Two Spirits (3:13–4:26), evidently intended as a précis of the sect's central distinctive beliefs. The writer speaks in strongly predestinarian

---

Cf. similarly 4Q511 2.i.1.

[20] Cf. Sarianna Metso, "In Search of the *Sitz im Leben* of the *Community Rule*," in *The Provo International Conference on the Dead Sea Scrolls: Technological Innovations, New Texts, and Reformulated Issues* (ed. D. W. Parry and E. Ulrich; STDJ 30; Leiden: Brill, 1999), 314, who suggests a quasi-midrashic purpose of the *Rule*, "as a record of judicial decisions and an accurate report of oral traditions."

[21] Some have attempted to derive the distinctive Two Spirits discourse (1QS 3:13–5:1) directly or indirectly from the Teacher of Righteousness, but this must remain speculative.

language[22] and concerns himself with the nature and activity of the "spirit of light" and the "children of light" on the one hand, and the "spirit of darkness" and the "children of darkness" on the other. The children of light are the object of God's eternal pleasure (cf. 4:1) and their way meets with great blessings in both this life and the life to come,[23] while the spirit of falsehood and his followers will experience shame and afflictions, eternal destruction by God's wrath, and eternal annihilation "in the fire of darkness."[24]

The next section (4), which has also undergone considerable alteration and expansion over time, addresses the community's overall organization (5:1–9:11). Finally (5), we find regulations pertaining to the role of the *Maskîl* or Instructor in particular (9:12–11:22; note previously 3:13). The document as a whole culminates in the psalm of praise and dedication that the *Maskîl* is to recite on a regular basis (10:6–11:22), and which no doubt serves in paradigmatic fashion to express the theology of the community. It is here that the document reflects most explicitly on the standing and eschatological acceptance of human beings before God.

2.2 Elements of a Doctrine of Salvation

Practicalities of time and space prohibit a detailed exposition, so that we shall need to confine ourselves here to a brief examination of several key themes and passages. In order to facilitate discussion with earlier work on the subject, my outline here briefly addresses several of the themes highlighted by E. P. Sanders,[25] with particular attention to issues of theological anthropology. Although initially confining our discussion to 1QS, we shall also see later in this chapter that some of the most interesting observations arise out of certain textual developments between the various MSS of *Serekh Ha-Yaḥad*.

2.2.1 Election and the people of God: the corporate dimension

We begin by examining the Scroll's use of the biblical ideas of Israel's election and covenant with God (cf. e.g. Deut 7:6–12). This language is of course consistently echoed in 1QS as in other Dead Sea Scrolls. Nevertheless, one finds considerable tensions in the way it is handled.

Early Essene texts, including parts of the *Damascus Document* (e.g. CD 1:1–4; 16:1–2), the *War Scroll* (e.g. 1QM 10:9–10; 12:13–14; 13:7–9; 17:8)

---

[22] E.g. 1QS 3:15–16, "Before they came into being he established all their designs; and when they come into existence in their fixed times they carry through their task according to his glorious design. Nothing can be changed. In his hand are the judgements of all things."

[23] Cf. 4:7f.: "healing and great peace in a long life, multiplication of progeny together with all everlasting blessings, endless joy in everlasting life, and a crown of glory together with a resplendent attire in eternal light."

[24] Cf. e.g. 4:12–13; 4Q280 2:4–5; 4Q286 7.ii.5–11.

[25] Sanders, *Paul and Palestinian Judaism*, 230–328.

and certain non-sectarian liturgical documents (e.g. 4QDibHamᵃ 3:1–2.iii.3–1–2.iv.12 4QPrQuot 21–28.vii.8f.; 4QPrFêtes 97–98.i.5–7) seem to take for granted a universal call to repentance as well as the election and eventual salvation of ethnic Israel as the holy covenantal people of God.[26] Although some members of Israel are evidently lost, there is no suggestion that the eschatological conflict with the enemies of God will entail a radical and final limitation of Israelite membership in the covenant. The difference is simply "between the just and the wicked," between "those who repent from sin" to seek refuge in God and those who do not (e.g. CD 20:17–34).

Other sectarian texts, however, appear unambiguously restrictive, explicitly limiting covenantal membership and divine election to the righteous and devout and denying salvation to the wicked, to the adversaries of the Teacher of Righteousness and of the community, and sometimes to all Jews who are not part of the covenant. This is perhaps true particularly in the Cave 1 *Hymns*. The wicked and even the deceivers among Israel are not only excluded from the covenant but doomed to divine judgment and annihilation (e.g. 1QH 12[=4]:7–20) – a polarity whose effect is heightened by the eschatological tension of the opponents' persecution of the psalmist (e.g. 13[=5]:17–39). In that connection, the righteous gives thanks that his lot has not fallen "in the congregation of falsehood, nor . . . in the counsel of hypocrites" (15[=7]:34).

In fact, the same problem pertains within the argument of 1QS. The document's language and vocabulary of salvation are to a considerable extent traditional, and familiar from biblical and other Jewish sources. One central theme for this as for other key sectarian documents (notably CD, 1QH, 1QM) is that of the *covenant*, sometimes explicitly the "covenant of God."[27] However, unlike the biblical use of the term to denote a normative divine relationship with the whole nation, the divine "covenant" has here become the defining characteristic of the sectarian community or *yahad* in particular, *over against* the nation (and of course the nations) at large. In this sense the covenant, while still divinely established, is no longer sufficiently defined as God's pact of grace with Abraham and his descendants or with all Israel at Sinai, but has become more particularly the sect's own exclusive alliance devoted to Torah observance. This covenant is an arrangement which one cannot collectively inherit but must individually resolve to *enter* (בוא *qal* or עבר), both initially (1:16f.) and continually (e.g. 10:10), and *into* which the community undertakes to *bring* (בוא *hip 'il*, e.g. 1:7; cf. נגש *hip 'il*, 11:13) its novices. In other words, membership in the "covenant of God" has become

---

[26] Cf. similarly Armin Lange and Hermann Lichtenberger, "Qumran," *TRE* 28 (1997): 69.

[27] ברית אל: 2:26; 5:8; 10:10; cf. CD 20:12; 1QpHab 2:5; 1QH 2:21–22, 28–9. For the term "covenant of God" see also Hermann Lichtenberger and Ekkehard Stegemann, "Zur Theologie des Bundes in Qumran und im Neuen Testament," *Kirche und Israel* 6 (1991): 136–7.

virtually co-extensive with the *"yaḥad* of God,"[28] even though the two concepts are not identical.[29] Some scholars, indeed, have been led to argue that the very understanding of the term "Israel" has in the Scrolls been largely subsumed under the community's self-understanding as the "true" Israel (as perhaps in 1QS 5:5, 22).[30]

All of this evidence, however, is fraught with ambiguity and remains extraordinarily difficult to assess. Beginning with the last issue, it is important to note that the *Community Rule* in fact almost invariably applies the term "Israel" to the nation as a whole (e.g. 1QS 1:22f.; 6:13; 8:11; cf. 3:24 "the God of Israel"). Even 1QS 5:5 or 5:22 are by no means unambiguous evidence of a restriction of "Israel" to the chosen few; indeed their meaning may need to be assessed in the light of redactional alterations, as we shall see. Much as scholars continue to argue that the community sees itself, in discontinuity with the rest of Judaism, as the only or "true" Israel,[31] this assertion is in fact nowhere to be substantiated – let alone with the kind of explicit clarity that would surely need to underpin such an extraordinary claim. Instead, many Qumran writings use "Israel" in its natural inclusive sense; it is particularly worth noting 4QMMT in this regard, given that document's polemical function.

Instead, a strong case can be made that the community's self-understanding continues to be in some sense eschatologically *representative* (rather than substitutive) for the nation as a whole. There is clearly a sense in which the community regards itself as the spiritual heart of the chosen people, and indeed as the eschatological remnant out of all Israel. "Remnant" language is of considerable importance for the definition of the community in both the *Damascus Document* (e.g. 1:4; 2:12–14) and the *War Scroll* (e.g. 13:7–9; 14:8–9),[32] and it is this biblical *topos* which most adequately accounts for the sect's notion of itself as "laying a foundation of truth for Israel" (1QS 5:5) and as constituted of "the multitude of Israel" who are dedicated to return together (or "in the *yaḥad*": ביחד) to God's covenant (5:22).

In the absence of unambiguous evidence to the contrary, it seems incumbent on the interpreter to understand this material in the first instance in relation to the established remnant tradition of the Old Testament. For all

[28] Compare 1:7–8, 16 with 1:11–12: devotees of divine truth *bring* (בוא *hip'il*) into the *yaḥad* of God (יחד אל) their knowledge, strength and property. The phrase יחד אל recurs again in 2:22.

[29] So rightly Lichtenberger and Stegemann, "Zur Theologie des Bundes," 136.

[30] See e.g. Lichtenberger, *Studien zum Menschenbild in den Texten der Qumrangemeinde*, 186; Seifrid, *Justification by Faith*, 87–88.

[31] E.g. Leaney, *The Rule of the Community*, 74; Lichtenberger, *Studien zum Menschenbild in den Texten der Qumrangemeinde*, 186; cf. Seifrid, *Justification by Faith*, 88.

[32] Cf. e.g. 1QH 14(=6):8; 4Q163 4–6.ii.10–16.

its language of pruning, purification and even (in CD) of a "new covenant,"[33] post-exilic tradition nevertheless seems to imply that after extensive judgment on Israel will follow not replacement but restoration: the promises of God are not finally subject to revision. Though destruction may have overtaken even the majority along the way, the few who are now the faithful remnant represent the continuing core of the people of God, around whom all who survive will find their identity and the fulfillment of the promises.[34] The salvation of the survivors gathered from the four corners of the earth thus finally incorporates and constitutes the salvation of "the whole house of Israel."[35]

It is true that the Qumran sect generally had a narrower conception of God's faithful people in the here and now. Nevertheless, the Scrolls give no indication that a belief in this same basic continuity of the covenant promises has been surrendered. Even the *Damascus Document*'s notion of a "new" covenant (whose constitution in any case lies some way in the past: see above, n. 33) merely fulfils and validates, but does not displace, the old.[36] In other

---

[33] CD 6:19; 8:21=19:33f.; cf. 20:12 and 6:5; 7:15, 18f.; also 1Q34 3.ii.5,7; 1QpHab 2:3f. Lichtenberger and Stegemann, "Zur Theologie des Bundes," 135, following Hartmut Stegemann, "Das Gesetzeskorpus der 'Damaskusschrift' CD IX–XVI," *RevQ* 14 (1990): 427–9, rightly correct a widespread misunderstanding about this term. The actual phrase "new covenant" (as distinct from "covenant of God," etc.) does not occur outside CD; more importantly, even there it concerns not the Qumran community's *present* self-understanding, but denotes the prior (and arguably pre-sectarian) group constituted "in the land of Damascus." Perhaps a little overconfidently, H. Stegemann, "Das Gesetzeskorpus," 428 n. 79, proposes to find in 1QpHab 2:3–4 confirmation that the original "new covenant" was *succeeded* by "the covenant of God." It is in any case worth noting that CD 20:12 identifies the pact in the land of Damascus as "the first covenant."

[34] See e.g. Sir 47:22; Isa 10:19–23 and 10:24–11:11, 16; 37:31–2. This is where Israel's fate finally differs from that of Babylon, which is cut off without remnant or posterity (Isa 14:22).

[35] E.g. Isa 45:24ff., esp. 45:25; 46:3, 13; Jer 23:3–8; Ezek 11:13–20; Mic 2:12; 7:18, 20; Zech 8:6–15.

[36] Cf. Jaubert, *La notion de l'Alliance*, 222, who speaks of two "phases" of the same covenant; Sanders, *Paul and Palestinian Judaism*, 241; Shemaryahu Talmon, "'The Dead Sea Scrolls' or 'The Community of the Renewed Covenant'," in *The Echoes of Many Texts: Reflections on Jewish and Christian Traditions* (*Fs.* Lou Silberman; ed. W. G. Dever and J. E. Wright; BJS 313; Atlanta: Scholars, 1997), 135–40 (cf. idem, "The Community of the Renewed Covenant: Between Judaism and Christianity," in *The Community of the Renewed Covenant: The Notre Dame Symposium on the Dead Sea Scrolls* [ed. E. Ulrich and J. Vanderkam; Christianity and Judaism in Antiquity 10; Notre Dame: University of Notre Dame, 1994], 12–15; idem, "The Essential 'Community of the Renewed Covenant': How Should Qumran Studies Proceed?" in *Geschichte – Tradition – Reflexion* [*Fs.* Martin Hengel; ed. H. Cancik, H. Lichtenberger, and P. Schäfer; Tübingen: Mohr (Siebeck), 1996] 345–7); Lange and Lichtenberger, "Qumran," 71 ("'neu' bedeutet hier jedenfalls nicht, daß man sich im Gegensatz zum Sinai-Bund verstanden hätte"); *contra* Seifrid, *Justification by Faith*, 89 ("it is certain that the Qumran covenant was understood to displace the covenant with Israel as a salvific structure").

words, for God to "renew" the covenant is to "remember" it, and vice versa.[37] What is indeed "new" is the revelation to the community of hitherto unknown religious mysteries, pertaining both to eschatology (רזים) and to exegetical insights of a halakic nature (נסתרות).[38] It is this knowledge, and the distinctive corporate religious praxis that accompanies it, which endow the community with a tangible "remnant" identity and enable a clear distinction between faithful and unfaithful Israel. As in the Old Testament, that remnant is understood as the survivors and descendants of Israel, an eternal people. The *War Scroll* unmistakably stresses this element of genetic continuity: "You are the God of our fathers, we bless your name forever. We are the people of your inheritance. You established a covenant with our fathers and confirmed it with their offspring for times eternal . . . the remnant, the survivors of your covenant . . . you have created us for you, an eternal people."[39]

It is true that the sect does not hesitate to view itself as "Israel" (e.g. 1QS 2:22; cf. CD 12:22); and joining the Community does indeed mean to join the definitive "covenant of God" (e.g. 1QS 5:7–8; cf. "covenant of the *yahad*" in 1QS 3:11–12; 8:16–17). Nevertheless, the very fact that there are those "in Israel" (e.g. 1QS 6:13) or "of Israel" (e.g. CD 4:2; 6:4–5; 8:16) who repent implies without doubt that "Israel" must also include others who do not (or not yet) – and who are by the same token clearly regarded as outsiders or even adversaries.[40]

---

[37] See 1Q34 3.ii.5,7; cf. CD 1:2–8.

[38] See Markus Bockmuehl, *Revelation and Mystery in Ancient Judaism and Pauline Christianity* (WUNT 2/36; Tübingen: Mohr [Siebeck], 1990 [=repr. Grand Rapids: Eerdmans, 1997]), 42–44; cf. Sanders, *Paul and Palestinian Judaism*, 241–2; Joseph M. Baumgarten, *Studies in Qumran Law* (SJLA 24; Leiden: Brill, 1977), 29–32.

[39] 1QM 13:7–9. See also the interpretation of Isa 10:21ff. in the pesharim ("many will die . . . but they will be saved," 4Q161 2–6.ii.5–7; the survivors will be a small number, 4Q163 4–6.ii.5–15).

[40] Note, however, Sanders's observation (*Paul and Palestinian Judaism*, 249–50) that while 1QM and 1QSa envisage a straightforward battle between "Israel" and the Gentiles, 1QS and 1QH include among the enemies the non-sectarian Israelites. Sanders surmises that this is because 1QM and 1QSa concern the time of the eschatological war, when the sect will have become co-extensive with "Israel." The boundary lines then are drawn unambiguously: Jewish enemies will either have been converted in the last days (so 1QSa 1:1–3, 6–9; cf. also Sanders, ibid., 253–4 on 1QpHab 5:3–6) or else have become wholly absorbed among the Gentile enemies (so apparently 1QM 1:2, which contains the scroll's only mention of Jewish apostates as "those who assist them [the sons of darkness] from among the wicked of the covenant"). The eschatological Israel appears to be comprised only of the three tribes of Levi, Judah, Benjamin (1QM 1:2; 3:15 par. 4papQM[f] 4.x.5), although this is not consistently maintained (contrast 1QM 2:1–2 [par. 4QM[d] 1:4–5]; 3:14; 5:1; 6:11; *pace* Sanders, ibid., 248). In any case only "Israel" is saved, never any Gentiles. See further Katell Berthelot, "La notion de גר dans les textes de Qumrân," *RevQ* 19 (1999): 171–216, on Qumran's apparent exclusion of *gerim*, noting CD as a possible exception.

Qumran's restrictive definition of the covenant is in many ways typical of a sectarian mindset: despite their sometimes idiosyncratic and innovative beliefs and practices, embattled religious minorities not infrequently take the view that they themselves are the only surviving group that is faithful to the letter and the spirit of the original religious reality, and that they are the loyal standard bearers in a sea of apostates and renegades.

The *yaḥad* itself is indeed at the heart of the Covenant, while the adversaries even of their own nation are outside it and will be judged – a fate that awaits above all the Wicked Priest and his associates.[41] Moreover, as we shall see below, an extensive late sectarian gloss in 1QS 5:11–13 suggests that outsiders of any sort were perhaps increasingly consigned to eternal damnation "without remnant," a phrase reserved elsewhere for Gentile enemies and the more vaguely defined cohorts of Belial, Melkiresha' and the Spirit of Deceit.[42]

Despite such late sectarian tendencies, however, there is in fact no *systematic* questioning of the notion that the Community will be the vanguard of the nation, and that in it, or through it, God's promises to all Israel will come to fulfillment. In the same way, restrictive-sounding remnant language (e.g. Isa 10:22) and universal redemption language (e.g. 45:25) can happily co-exist within the biblical book of Isaiah; "all the house of Jacob" and "the remnant of the house of Israel" can be equated (46:3). As for every sectarian grouping (including early Christianity), the new movement's relationship with the majority is fractious and ambivalent, holding together a belief in the judgment of all apostasy with an expectation of the comprehensive eschatological realization of the promises for the greater whole – however that may turn out to be defined.[43]

Far from seeking to *replace* the "true" historic Israel, the sect saw itself as the vanguard of its final redemption, "the house of truth in Israel" (1QS 5:6) which would one day encompass all the sons of light. The beliefs and practices of the group are held to be true and valid not just for insiders; in the words of the *Damascus Document*, they are "the covenant *for all Israel* for an eternal law" (CD 15:5; cf. 15:8–9, "the covenant oath which Moses established with Israel"). Similarly, the remnant is instrumental for "the covenant for Israel," disclosing the laws in regard to which "all Israel" had gone astray (CD 3:13–14).[44]

---

[41] Note e.g. 1QS 5:7–8; on the fate of the Wicked Priest see e.g. 1QpHab 8:8–12; 9:9–12.

[42] See CD 2:6–7; 1QH 14(=6):32; 1QM 1:6; 4:2; 14:5; 18:3; 4Q280 2:5; 4Q374 2.ii.4; also 1QS 4:14.

[43] Cf. rightly Sanders, *Paul and Palestinian Judaism*, 245: the sect "did not simply appropriate the title 'Israel'. The members seems to have been conscious of . . . being *a forerunner of the true Israel*, which God would establish to fight the decisive war."

[44] As in Rom 11:25–6, one can only interpret the community's role here in strictly exclusivist terms by assuming that "Israel" must mean two contradictory things in adjacent lines.

Such a wider eschatological perspective on the community's relationship to "Israel" may even be in view in the *Rule of the Community,* as for example when the Community is described in representative terms as "a holy house *for Israel*" בית קודש לישראל, whose task it is "to atone *for the Land*" לכפר בעד הארץ (1QS 8:5, 6, 10;[45] cf. 5:6). Qumran's primary vision continues to be that the *yaḥad* is God's "remnant for the land," which will grow and grow until it "fills the face of the world" with its offspring (CD 2:11–12).

In short, it seems clear that exclusive and inclusive understandings of election operate side by side in 1QS and other Qumran writings. A similar situation pertains in relation to other soteriological topics.

2.2.2 *Voluntarism and predestination: the individual dimension*

In addition to its sectarian view of the chosen people as a whole being focused in the Qumran covenant, the Dead Sea Scrolls could be said to reflect a wider trend in late Second Temple Judaism (and the contemporary Mediterranean world) towards a more individualized understanding of religious affiliation and experience. Religious status and acceptance before God could no longer be simply taken for granted as a matter of course; instead, especially in the wake of the deeply divisive cultural and religious crisis of the Maccabean revolt and the increasing ethnic complexity of Palestine, a personal commitment to Jewish faith and praxis came to be of decisive importance (cf. e.g. 1 Macc. 1:11–15, 52–63; 2 Macc. 6:23; 8:1).

This is perhaps particularly evident in certain sectarian texts like the *Hodayot* (e.g. 1QH 13[=5]:5–13). The Qumran psalmist acknowledges that his righteousness is the gift of God's righteousness, pre-ordained from all eternity (note e.g. 4[=17]:18–22; 5[=13]:23; 6[=14]:23–5; 7[=15]:16–20). The writer freely confesses his own sinfulness and impurity (e.g. 9[=1]:21–3; 12[=4]:29, 34–6; 15[=7]:16–19), which is atoned only by the righteousness of God (12[=4]:37). At the same time, however, the concrete expression of piety and moral rectitude does appear to be a definitive mark that sets apart the believer from the unbeliever and, as a necessary token of covenant membership, is instrumental in his salvation: "I will not admit into the council [of your truth] someone distant from your covenant" (6[=14]:21f.). Inclusion and exclusion are not only clearly demarcated between people groups, but even within those categories they depend fundamentally on one's personal conversion, in faith and praxis, to the life of the Qumran covenant. Such personal commitment, or lack of it, singularly determines one's standing before God in the final reckoning. In the *Damascus Rule* this perspective may even determine the membership of children born to sectarians. No under-age

---

[45] Note that this second occurrence of לכפר בעד הארץ is an interlinear gloss.

child may enter the congregation (CD 15:18 = 4QD^b 17.i.8); the children of novices must, like other members, attain the appointed minimum age before they can "pass over to the mustered" (15:15–16).[46]

This dimension is also very clear in the *Rule of the Community*. Thus the opening two sections make the voluntaristic definition of covenant membership quite explicit. Qumran welcomes "into the covenant of mercy" those who leave all evil, forsake the stubbornness of their own hearts (2:25) and "freely devote themselves (הנדבים) to carry out the statutes of God" (1:7; cf. e.g. 3:8; 5:6, 13–14, 22). Qumran's adherents are quite clearly regarded in the first instance as individually responsible rather than as members of particular tribes or families. This is a perspective which finds confirmation in Josephus on the Essenes (e.g. *J.W.* 2.134) and in the Essene practice of individual burial, documented both at the Dead Sea and near Jerusalem.[47] Those who belong to the covenant are only those who "choose the path, each one according to his spirit" (1QS 9:17–18). No one is born into this covenant.[48] To become members, the sectarians are individually examined for two years as to the soundness of their understanding and lifestyle (6:13–23; cf. Josephus *J.W.* 2.137–8).

Just as individuals choose to become members of the Community, so individuals can become apostate from it. This is evident as early as the *Damascus Document*, where the problem of backsliding *within the sect* seems consistently to concern individuals rather than the group as a whole.[49] In the *Rule of the Community* backsliders are still viewed as a phenomenon of willful individual disobedience. Thus, in discussing the annual ceremony of covenant renewal the document states quite categorically, "anyone who declines to enter [the covenant of Go]d in order to walk in the stubbornness of his heart . . . shall not be righteous לוא יצדק" (2:25–3:3). Such persons will be

---

[46] Cf. 1QSa 1:8–9, where that minimum age is set at twenty. I am grateful to Dr. C. Hempel for drawing my attention to the significance of these passages.

[47] See e.g. R. Hachlili, "Burials," *ABD* (1992), 1.792–3; Amos Kloner and Yosef Gat, "Burial Caves in the Region of East Talpiyot," *Atiqot* [Hebr. series] 8 (1982): 76; Hanan Eshel and Zvi Greenhut, "Hiam el-Sagha, A Cemetery of the Qumran Type, Judaean Desert," *RB* 100 (1993): 256–8; cf. further Markus Bockmuehl, "'Let the Dead Bury their Dead' (Matt 8:22/Luke 9:60): Jesus and the Halakah," *JTS* 49 (1998): n. 31. On the subject of the afterlife, the silence of the *Rule* and other sectarian texts leaves uncertain to what extent the Qumran community believed in a general resurrection: 4Q385 and 4Q521, if sectarian, seem to be somewhat exceptional in this regard. Nevertheless, the Community clearly did affirm a belief in some form of heavenly life after death. See e.g. John J. Collins, *Apocalypticism in the Dead Sea Scrolls* (London/New York: Routledge, 1997), 110–29; Philip R. Davies, "Death, Resurrection, and Life after Death in the Qumran Scrolls," in *Judaism in Late Antiquity*, Part 4: *Death, Life-after-Death, Resurrection and the World-to-Come in the Judaisms of Antiquity* (HO 1.49.4; ed. A. J. Avery-Peck and J. Neusner; Leiden: Brill, 2000), 189–211.

[48] So rightly Sanders, *Paul and Palestinian Judaism*, 260.

[49] See e.g. CD 8:1–2, 19; 19:13–14.

rejected as unclean, and excluded from divine atonement until they repent and turn from wickedness (3:4–9; 5:14; cf. 10:20–21; CD 2:4–5).[50] In the *Hodayot*, the psalmist takes for granted that God "forgives those who turn away from sin and . . . punishes the depravity of the wicked" (1QH 6[=14]:24); 1QH 25.v.13 offers an even more laconic description of the final judgment as intended to "pronounce the righteo[us man right]eous and sent[ence the guilty. . . .]."[51] This clear emphasis on the condemnation of the wicked also recurs in some texts of less evidently sectarian origin. The so-called *Hymn to Zion* seems to deny the possibility of being saved in iniquity (11QPsᵃ 22:9–10=4QPsᶠ8:3–4), while the apocryphal Psalm 154 affirms that "the Lord's eyes have pity on good people" (11QPsᵃ 18:16).

A casual observer might be tempted to conclude from all this individualism that the Qumran community held to a straightforwardly merit-based understanding of salvation, not unlike the strictly legalistic position sometimes assumed to lie behind *4 Ezra*, where only perfect individual righteousness will ensure salvation at the judgment (e.g. 7:104–15, 127–31) and God is unconcerned about those who sin (7:20–22; 8:37–39).[52]

As E. P. Sanders rightly notes, however, Qumran's assumptions about election are remarkably complex and do not necessarily lend themselves to a systematic analysis.[53] Against its starkly voluntaristic dimension must be set a number of balancing considerations, including a strong doctrine of predestination.[54] According to the *Rule of the Community*, the fate of both the just and the wicked is foreordained in detail by God himself (1QS 3:21–4:1; cf. e.g. CD 2:7–11); "before they existed he made all their plans and . . . they will execute all their works . . . according to his glorious design without altering anything" (3:15–16). God's dual predetermination of both the good and the evil governs Qumran's soteriology: salvation is for his chosen ones and judgment for the others. Nothing happens outside his control and purpose (e.g. 1QS 11:11, 17–18). This doctrine of predestination is one of the features highlighted in Josephus' account of the Essenes (e.g. *Ant.* 13.172), and it comes into its own especially in the Qumran *Hodayot* (e.g. 1QH 9[=1]:8, 19–20; 18[=10]:9; 7[=15]:13–19).

---

[50] See further 1QS 2:12–18; 7:18–21; 8:16–25; etc.

[51] Cf. similarly the *Song of the Sage*, 4Q511 63–64.iii.3–4; 4QDᵇ 18.v.11–14.

[52] For an assessment of *4 Ezra* as nevertheless located in some relation to the mainstream of the Yavnean rabbinic movement, see recently Bruce W. Longenecker, "Locating 4 Ezra: A Consideration of its Social Setting and Functions," *JSJ* 28 (1997): 271–93.

[53] Sanders, *Paul and Palestinian Judaism*, 265–6.

[54] Cf. e.g. Armin Lange, *Weisheit und Prädestination: Weisheitliche Urordnung und Prädestination in den Textfunden von Qumran* (STDJ 18; Leiden: Brill, 1995); idem, "Wisdom and Predestination in the Dead Sea Scrolls," *DSD* 2 (1995): 340–54; Eugene H. Merrill, *Qumran and Predestination: A Theological Study of the Thanksgiving Hymns* (STDJ 8; Leiden: Brill, 1975).

Salvation, on this view, could never be a matter of human merit. The covenanters do not know themselves elect by their works but, on the contrary, their works bear witness to their election. God has "caused them to inherit the lot of the Holy Ones" (1QS 11:7–8), "caused them to draw near" to the covenant (so 1QS 11:13; cf. 1QH 6[=14]:13). It is his agency that supremely determines a person's standing, and which underwrites human choice in the first place. Although Josephus suggests that it was the Pharisees who held divine providence and human free will in a fine balance (*J.W.* 2.162f.; *Ant.* 13.172; cf. *m. 'Abot* 3:19), in these texts we do in fact find a comparable co-existence of these two theological *topoi* in tension. Here lies the paradox of Qumran's view of salvation: although the sons of light *freely choose* to belong to the covenant and thus to be saved, the very fact that they do so is itself an expression of the overruling grace of God, whose sovereign design disposes over both the saved and the damned. At the same time, even the sect's evident determinism in relation to historical and cosmological events serves fundamentally only to reinforce and confirm this eternal predestination of the elect.[55]

2.2.3 "Righteousness" and justification

Our remarks thus far have taken a deliberately broad approach, so as not to tie our understanding of Qumran's view of salvation too closely to the terminology of "righteousness" and "justification" that has dominated the debate about Pauline and early Christian notions of grace and salvation at least since the Reformation.

Nevertheless, the *Rule of the Community* and other texts do repeatedly employ the forensic terminology of justice and righteousness in such words as צדקה, צדק, and משפט, all of which describe different nuances of a quality that is ultimately defined in relation to the character of God. Thus צדק is here best viewed as the quality of that which is right and pleasing to God, while צדקה is an action in keeping with that quality.[56] At the same time, however, the notion of "the righteousness of God" describes a quality that characterizes God, is exclusively constituted by him, and comes to be revealed in his historic and eschatological acts of salvation.[57] This common Qumran

---

[55] Hermann Lichtenberger, *Studien zum Menschenbild in den Texten der Qumrangemeinde*, 186–7.

[56] Cf. further Betz, "Rechtfertigung in Qumran," 18–19, with numerous references, which could now be extended in view of the newly published texts: see especially 4QMMT 117 (=C 31). Cf. also 11QTemple 57:13,19 of a human judge.

[57] See e.g. 1QH 6(=14):15–16; CD 20:19–21; cf. e.g. 1Q27 1.i.5–7 par. 4Q300 3:5–6. Despite the almost "metaphysical" role played by God's righteousness in the eschatological narrative of salvation, and poetic texts like 1QM 17:7–8 notwithstanding, I remain to be persuaded of the argument (e.g. of J. M. Baumgarten, "The Heavenly Tribunal and the

conviction also corresponds closely with Deutero-Isaianic views, where divine righteousness and salvation are similarly linked (cf. e.g. Isa 51:5–8; 56:1).[58] In particular, the "righteous deeds of God" (צדקות אל) are his saving actions in Israel's past (1QS 1:21; 10:23; cf. 1QH 4:17), but the manifestation of his righteousness also characterizes the eschaton. God's eschatological victory brought about by his "righteous acts" past and future is the key to the sect's understanding of salvation, as O. Betz among others has carefully documented.[59]

Perhaps the clearest account of what one might call Qumran's "doctrine of justification" appears in 1QS 10–11, which is partly paralleled in 4QS[j]. It is remarkable to note how this passage presumes a consistently forensic context with an emphasis on the individual – i.e. perhaps the *Maskîl* in the first instance, although the language seems clearly intended to be read in paradigmatic fashion. Here, then, the individual offers a forthright confession of his own sinfulness and inadequacy – qualities that he accepts as characteristic of the human condition and altogether outside his power to change. "Man cannot establish his own steps, for to God belong judgement (משפט) and perfection of way" (1QS 9:10; cf. 1QH 7[=15]:16); "no-one is righteous in your judgement, or innocent at your trial" (1QH 17[=9]:14f.).

This appeal to the human condition is employed not in order to excuse the believer's sin but rather to underscore the exclusively divine constitution of righteousness and forgiveness. In fact, it is specifically through God's righteous character and righteous acts that sins can be forgiven:

As for me, in God is my judgement (משפט); in his hand is the perfection of my path and the uprightness of my heart; and by his righteous acts (בצדקותו)[60] he will cancel

---

Personification of Sedeq in Jewish Apocalyptic," *ANRW* II 19.1 [1979]: 219–32; and of Roy Rosenberg, "*Sedeq* as Divine Hypostasis in Qumran Texts and its Link to the Emergence of Christianity," in *Mogilany 1993: Papers on the Dead Sea Scrolls* [*Fs. Z. J. Kapera*; Kraków: Enigma Press, 1996], 109–127) that צדק at Qumran is best viewed as a personified "hypostasis."

[58] Cf. Betz, "Rechtfertigung in Qumran," 23–24.

[59] See ibid., 20–25.

[60] We would expect בצקותיו. The unusual defective spelling is most likely due to a simple error of omission, perhaps parablepsis due to what would have been a triple succession of *waw* and *yod*, letters which are almost identical here, as frequently in 1QS (but cf. P. Wernberg-Møller, "Waw and Yod in the 'Rule of the Community' (1QS)," *RevQ* 2 [1960]: 223–36). Seifrid's proposed reading צדקותי (*Justification by Faith*, 100–103), by contrast, somewhat implausibly introduces the otherwise unattested idea of an individual atoning for his own sins by acts of righteousness (cf. also ibid., 94–95, and passim). The proposed form is not attested either at Qumran or in the Hebrew Bible. What is more, the context repeatedly denies human righteousness, and stresses instead that it is only *God's* righteousness (צדק) and righteous acts (צדקה sg. and pl.) that are *instrumental* to salvation (e.g. 10:11, 23 וצדקות אל], 25; 11:5, 6, 12 בצדקת אל], 14, 15); contrast the prayer that God will subsequently go on to establish the justified psalmist's own ways in that same righteousness (צדק, 11:16). The notion of *God's*

my transgression. . . . From the fountain of his righteousness is my judgement (וממקור
צדקתקו משפטי). . . . And if I stumble, the mercies of God are my salvation for ever
(חסדי אל ישועתי לצד); and if I fall in guilt of the flesh, my judgement is by the
righteousness of God (בצדקת אל) which endures eternally. (1QS 11:2–3, 5, 12)

God's righteousness and his righteous acts, therefore, constitute the salvation
and justification of the individual. This is a notion which finds an explicit
parallel in the apocryphal psalms appended to the biblical Psalter of Cave 11
(11QPsᵃ 19:5, 7, 11 par. 11QPsᵇ frag. a 6), and which recurs in a variety of
different forms elsewhere. The *Hodayot* psalmist, for example, repeatedly
makes the point that righteousness to cleanse from sin is solely in God's gift
to bestow, and cannot be attained by human effort (e.g. 1QH 4[=17]:17–20;
7[=15]:16–20; 12[=4]:37; 19[=11]:30–32).[61]

Thus, the *Serekh*'s view of justification clearly rides on a cosmic order of
God's righteousness whose revelation constitutes both the final salvation of
his people and the final destruction of the forces of darkness.[62] The revelation
of that righteousness, moreover, does not depend on either the predicament
or the achievements of believers,[63] but is determined solely by God himself.

2.2.4 Sin and atonement

In keeping with what we have discovered thus far, it is clear that the Qumran
sect combined a remarkable recognition of the universality of sin with a keen
awareness of the fact that atonement rests with God alone. "All the sons of
your truth you take to forgiveness in your presence, you purify them from

---

saving righteous acts (צדקות) as instrumental in averting his wrath over human sin appears
in very similar fashion e.g. in 11QPsᵃ 19:5,7 par. 11QPsᵇ frag. a 6. In each of these cases the
psalmist pleads with God to perform again his definitive saving works in keeping with his past
acts. (Cf. e.g. Dan 9:16 and note the analogous eschatological revelation of God's δικαιώματα
in Rev. 15:4.) It is worth pointing out that the Scrolls nowhere use the plural צדקות of actual
human deeds of righteousness. An interesting counterexample to prove the rule may be present
in 1QH 15(=7):17–18: "I have no fleshly refuge, nor righteous deeds (צדקות) to be delivered
from s[in, ex]cept through forgiveness." See further Isa 64:5; Dan 9:18 (cf. Isa 45:24) for the
inadequacy of human צדקות (pl.), although some OT texts at least imply a somewhat more
positive usage (e.g. Isa 33:15; Jer 51:5; Ezek 18:24; 33:13 [both *Qere'*, *v.l.*]).

[61] The same idea may have remarkably concrete implications for the eschatology of the *War
Scroll*, where "God's righteousness" (אל צדק) is among the slogans written on the battle
standards of the Sons of Light (1QM 4:6). The Sons of Light are also called "sons of
righteousness" (e.g. 1QM 1:8), and 1QM 17:8 may suggest that this should be understood of
the divine צדק personified: "righteousness will rejoice in the heights, and all the sons of his
truth will have joy in eternal knowledge." Cf. 4Q163 23:8, "This is why the Lord waits to take
pity on you, this is why he rises to be lenient with you. For YHWH is a god of righteousness."

[62] Cf. similarly 1QH 25.v.1–13.

[63] So rightly Betz, "Rechtfertigung in Qumran," 21, who further notes the close relationship
between God's "righteousness" and God's "truth" (p. 23). See e.g. 1QS 4:20; 1QH 19(=11):7;
etc.; cf. *T.Gad* 3:1; Rom 3:4–5.

their sins by the greatness of your goodness, and in your bountiful mercy, to make them stand in your presence for ever and ever" (1QH 15[=7]:30f.). And in keeping with what we discovered in the previous section, God himself here atones for sin through his righteousness (1QH 12[=4]:37). Within the *Serekh ha-Yaḥad*, too, atonement is initially said to be the work of God (1QS 11:3,[64] 14) or of his Spirit (1QS 3:6–8); and while CD usually also makes God the agent of atonement,[65] there is one significant passage in which the Messiah will atone for sin.[66] What is more, as Garnet and Lichtenberger have pointed out, the language of atonement varies considerably and its implied setting can be either cultic or non-cultic.[67]

At the same time, however, we have already seen the tendency in many of these same texts to make it quite clear that atonement for sin is not available for the unrepentant and for those outside the Community. Thus, atonement for sins is an act of God *for believers*: God does *not* atone for the sins of Belial's lot (2:8). Sanders rightly points out that where it applies to members of the Covenant, sin is always understood in terms of human actions rather than as a power that holds people in bondage. Sinfulness as such is merely part of the universal condition of human frailty, to which the believer also belongs; the sins of repentant believers do not affect their standing within the covenant.[68] Even members of the community are led astray by the angel of darkness (1QS 3:21–3), and they are liable to sin as long as they live: "we are in sin from the womb, and from the breast in gu[ilt . . .]. And while we exist, our steps are impurity" (4Q507 1:1–3; cf. 1QH 12[=4]:29f.; 1QS 11:9f.). The difference is that they have access to atonement for their sins, while outsiders do not.

This being so, however, it seems understandable that *Serekh ha-Yaḥad* should come to view priestly atonement for sin as located exclusively within the remit of the sect. As we shall see below, one can in fact document an increasing trend in this direction in the development of salvation language at Qumran. For now, it may suffice briefly to indicate the full-fledged affirmations to this effect in 1QS. The *yaḥad* atones for all those who join it (5:5–6);

---

[64] See, however, n. 60 above on the alternative reading of this passage proposed by Seifrid, *Justification by Faith.*

[65] E.g. CD 2:4f.; 3:18; 4:6–7; 20:34.

[66] 4QD[b] 18.iii.12 has supplied the lacuna in CD 14:19. Cf. also Joseph M. Baumgarten, "Messianic Forgiveness of Sins in CD 14:19 (4Q266.i.12–13)," in *The Provo International Conference on the Dead Sea Scrolls: Technological Innovations, New Texts, and Reformulated Issues* (ed. D. W. Parry and E. Ulrich; STDJ 30; Leiden: Brill, 1999), 535–44, who sees this as part of a Qumran tendency to assign divine functions to "surrogate personifications" like the Messiah, Melchizedek, etc.

[67] Garnet, *Salvation and Atonement in the Qumran Scrolls*, 57–80; Lichtenberger, "Atonement and Sacrifice in the Qumran Community;" with references.

[68] Sanders, *Paul and Palestinian Judaism*, 275–6, 278–9.

it will be accepted to atone for the land (8:10), "for all the fault of transgression and the guilt of sin" (9:3). The notion of an atonement for the land that has been polluted may already be anticipated in Num 35:33 and Deut 32:43.[69] More interestingly, perhaps, the penitential liturgy entitled "Words of the Luminaries" suggests that as Moses atoned for rebellious Israel in the desert, so now "we atone for our sin and the sin of our fathers" (4Q504 1–2.ii.9–10, vi.5–6; 4:5–7).

This atonement is explicitly said to operate outside the sacrificial cult; it serves either to replace it or, perhaps more likely in view of 11QT and 4QMMT, to function in deliberate analogy to it.[70] The community's worship here becomes the "pleasant aroma of righteousness"; its perfection of behavior will be as a freewill offering; and some scholars have gone so far as to see two disputed passages (1QS 9:3–6; cf. 8:5–6) as evidence of the *yaḥad* itself taking on the role of the temple's inner sanctuary or "Holy of Holies."[71] This important link between repentance and atonement also emerges in the sect's characteristic observance of the Day of Atonement (Yom Kippur) as a penitential festival marked by self-mortification.[72]

Finally, it is also interesting to note Qumran's significant connection of ritual purity with atonement for sins. This is quite clear in 1QS 3:3–9, where ritual washing is said to take place in the sanctifying "waters of repentance,"

---

[69] Cf. further Josh 22:19; Zech 13:2; Ezra 9:11; Ps 106:38.

[70] Non-cultic or quasi-cultic atonement for sin, especially through contrition and repentance, seems to have biblical antecedents in passages like Num 25:13; Isa 27:9; Ps 50:23; 51:17; 65:3; 78:38; 79:8–9; Prov 16:6; Dan 9:24.

[71] So e.g. Bertil Gärtner, *The Temple and the Community in Qumran and the New Testament* (SNTSMS 1; Cambridge: Cambridge University, 1965), 26–27, 29; Georg Klinzing, *Die Umdeutung des Kultus in der Qumrangemeinde und im Neuen Testament* (SUNT 7; Göttingen: Vandenhoeck & Ruprecht, 1971), 55, 69; and more recently Otto Betz, "Jesus and the Temple Scroll," in *Jesus and the Dead Sea Scrolls* (ed. J. H. Charlesworth; ABRL; New York: Doubleday, 1992), 95; Johann Maier, *Die Qumran-Essener: Die Texte vom Toten Meer* (3 vols.; Munich/Basle: Reinhardt, 1995–96), 1.190 and n. 517; and Hartmut Stegemann, *Die Essener, Qumran, Johannes der Täufer und Jesus: Ein Sachbuch* (4th ed.; Freiburg: Herder, 1994). This identification is, however, disputed, and most recent translations rightly avoid it. For the theme of the *yaḥad* as Temple see e.g. Gärtner, *The Temple and the Community in Qumran*; Klinzing, *Die Umdeutung des Kultus in der Qumrangemeinde*; Devorah Dimant, "*4QFlorilegium* and the Idea of the Community as Temple," in *Hellenica et Judaica* (*Fs.* Valentin Nikiprowetzky ל'ז; ed. A. Caquot et al.; Leuven/Paris: Peeters, 1986), 165–89; Michael O. Wise, "4QFlorilegium and the Temple of Adam," *RevQ* 15 (1991): 103–32, although it is clear from 11QTemple and 4QMMT that the sectarians continued to envisage the eventual restoration of the temple and even held specific halakic views on current practices in the existing temple. See also 1QM 2:3; 7:11; and cf. Lichtenberger ("Atonement and Sacrifice;" idem, "Enderwartung und Reinheitsidee") on the eschatological expectation; and note the more positive statements about the temple cult in CD 9:13–14; 11:17–21; 16:13–14.

[72] See Joseph M. Baumgarten, "Yom Kippur in the Qumran Scrolls and Second Temple Sources," *DSD* 6 (1999): 184–91.

and through the Holy Spirit to be effective for the atonement of sins. For the unrepentant, by contrast, these washings and acts of atonement remain ineffectual (3:3–4; cf. 5:13f.). The liturgical application of these beliefs can be seen in 4Q414 and 4Q512; the latter in particular explicitly links purification with atonement (29–32.vii.9–10).

For the Qumran Community, therefore, atonement for sin remains the prerogative of God himself. Its appropriation, however, is possible only to repentant members of the sect, since its sacrificial locus comes to be situated very specifically in the worship and praxis of the *yaḥad*.[73]

2.3 Developments in the Soteriology of Serekh Ha-Yaḥad [74]

Almost all our deliberations up to this point have proceeded on the assumption that 1QS represents for all practical purposes the complete and definitive version of the *Rule of the Community*. This assumption certainly simplifies interaction with previous scholarship on Qumran's view of salvation, which almost universally took it for granted.

It has long been recognized, however, that 1QS as it stands must be the result of a considerable textual development. As long as thirty years ago scholars were proposing and debating elaborate theories about the document's textual genesis.[75] These tended to revolve around the suggestion that 1QS 8–9 represents the original pre-sectarian core of the *Rule*, to which other material, including the liturgical columns 1–4 and the concluding Psalm of columns 10–11, was added later. No clear resolution of this question was achieved at the time, and the composition and redactional history of the *Community Rule* continue to be debated in contemporary scholarship. However, the public release of ten additional manuscripts and fragments from

---

[73] It is worth briefly noting 1QS 8:1–4, which mentions the Community Council's "paying for guilt": ‏ולרצת עוון בעושי משפט וצרת מצרף להתהלך עם כול‎. One popular reading has been to assume that the Council members atone for the sins of the community by means of their suffering (see e.g. Sanders, *Paul and Palestinian Judaism*, 326–7. and the scholars cited there; Seifrid, *Justification by Faith*, 95; Charlesworth, *The Dead Sea Scrolls*, 1.35). However, the Hebrew of this passage (paralleled in 4QSᵉ 2:10) is by no means clear, and García Martínez's translation of the following phrase seems equally possible: "doing justice and undergoing trials in order to walk with everyone. . . ." It certainly seems precipitous to see here positive evidence of a "suffering servant" motif, as Sanders does.

[74] For a more detailed version of the redactional analysis offered in this section, see Markus Bockmuehl, "Redaction and Ideology in the *Community Rule* (1QS/4QS)," *RevQ* 18 (1998): 541–60.

[75] See esp. J. Murphy-O'Connor, "La genèse littéraire de la Règle de la Communauté," *RB* 76 (1969): 528–49; and J. Pouilly, *La Règle de la Communauté de Qumrân: son évolution littéraire* (CahRB 17; Paris: Gabalda, 1976), who closely follows the former's literary analysis of four stages in the genesis of 1QS. For a survey of scholarship prior to the public availability of the Cave 4 fragments, see Robert A. Gagnon, "How did the Rule of the Community Obtain its Final Shape? A Review of Scholarly Research," *JSP* 10 (1992): 61–79.

Cave 4 (along with one from Cave 5, previously published) has helped in the 1990s to shed a good deal of fresh light on this ongoing debate, which turns out to have significant consequences for our perception of Qumran's view of human redemption.

2.3.1 Notes on the redaction history of Serekh Ha-Yaḥad

The manuscript containing 1QS was most probably copied in the first half of the first century B.C., although subsequent scribal corrections especially in 1QS 7–8 suggest further textual developments in the later first century. Considerable further copying continued throughout the Herodian period, including the important MSS 4QS[b,d]. None of the Cave 4 MSS, however, has produced any evidence that columns 5–7 and/or 8–9 ever existed as separate entities;[76] indeed it has recently been suggested that far from being early, most of 1QS 8 and 9 are secondary additions.[77]

One of the most difficult questions is the relative dating of 1QS especially vis-à-vis 4QS[b,d], and this turns out to be of some significance for our topic. Did the *Rule of the Community* develop from a text resembling 4QS[b,d] in the direction of that represented in 1QS, or vice versa? Simply put, the implication would be either that of a relatively lay-oriented renewal movement becoming increasingly authoritarian under explicit Zadokite governance, or else a development in the opposite direction. The soteriological implications are not insignificant.

An answer to this question, however, is complicated by the fact that the two key Cave 4 MSS represent a considerably shorter text type, but have been paleographically dated by F. M. Cross[78] about fifty years *later* than 1QS (a date which is widely accepted, and seems to be confirmed by Carbon 14 testing[79]).

The present study has no space and indeed no need for a detailed assessment of this complex subject matter, which I have attempted to address more fully elsewhere.[80] Suffice it to say that three main options have been proposed. (1) The texts may not be directly related, and perhaps served

---

[76] So also Metso, *The Textual Development of the Qumran Community Rule*, 108.

[77] Ibid., 117–9.

[78] Cf. F. M. Cross, "The Palaeographical Dates of the Manuscripts," in *The Dead Sea Scrolls: Hebrew, Aramaic, and Greek Texts with English Translations*. Vol. 1: *Rule of the Community and Related Documents* (ed. J. H. Charlesworth et al.; Tübingen: Mohr [Siebeck]/Louisville: Westminster John Knox, 1994), 57; cf. idem, "The Development of the Jewish Scripts," in *The Bible and the Ancient Near East* (ed. G. E. Wright; London: Routledge, 1961), 132–202.

[79] Cf. Philip S. Alexander, "The Redaction-History of *Serekh Ha-Yaḥad*: A Proposal," *RevQ* 17 (1996): 437–56.

[80] See Bockmuehl, "Redaction and Ideology of the *Community Rule*."

different purposes.[81] If there was some sort of development between them, this could presuppose either (2) the relative priority of 1QS over 4QS[b,d], in keeping with the chronological sequence of the MSS,[82] or else (3) the opposite development of 1QS out of an earlier text form represented in 4QS[b,d].[83] (Option 1 could in theory be held in conjunction with either one of the other two, although obviously not both.)

On balance, the most likely solution seems to be (3), which is in some ways the simplest reconstruction and would recognize the likelihood that constitutional texts of this kind tend, rather like the Pentateuch and certain rabbinic or gospel traditions, to undergo successive emendation and augmentation rather than simplification and cutting.[84] The question as to why earlier text forms such as 4QS[b,d] should continue to be copied after the completion of 1QS is obviously far from trivial;[85] but it is worth bearing in mind that the same phenomenon of authoritative writings preserved in multiple text types is very clearly present in the biblical manuscripts from Qumran. In practice, of course, day-to-day authority for the sect ultimately resided not in a given text form but in the person of the *Maskîl*.

If we take the view that 1QS is indeed the later text form, textual comparison suggests some interesting observations on the community's development, as apparently having originally been a relatively democratic renewal movement that grew more authoritarian and also came increasingly under the direct governance of its Zadokite priestly members.

The notion of a period of heightened Zadokite emphasis may find indirect support in a number of other texts, including the so-called *Midrash on*

---

[81] So e.g. Philip R. Davies, *Behind the Essenes: History and Ideology in the Dead Sea Scrolls* (BJS 94; Atlanta: Scholars, 1987); James H. Charlesworth and Brent A. Strawn, "Reflections on the Text of *Serek Ha-Yaḥad* found in Cave IV," *RevQ* 17 (1996): 403–35.

[82] So esp. Alexander, "The Redaction-History of *Serekh Ha-Yaḥad*;" cf. Paul Garnet, "Cave 4 MS Parallels to 1QS 5.1–7: Towards a *Serek* Text History," *JSP* 15 (1997): 67–78. Note that Philip S. Alexander and Geza Vermes, ed., *Qumran Cave 4*, vol. 19: *Serekh Ha-Yaḥad and Two Related Texts* (DJD 26; Oxford: Clarendon, 1998), 9–19, do not reach an agreed solution (see p. 9 n. 22).

[83] Geza Vermes, "Preliminary Remarks"; idem, "Qumran Forum Miscellanea I," *JJS* 43 (1992); 300–301; idem, "The Leadership of the Qumran Community: Sons of Zadok – Priests – Congregation," *Geschichte – Tradition – Reflexion* (*Fs.* Martin Hengel; ed. H. Cancik et al.; Tübingen: Mohr [Siebeck], 1996), 1.375–84; Charlotte Hempel, "Comments on the Translation of 4QS[d] I,1," *JJS* 44 (1993): 127–8; idem, "The Earthly Essene Nucleus of 1QSa," *DSD* 3 (1996): 253–69; Metso, *The Textual Development of the Qumran Community Rule*, 146; cf. also A. I. Baumgarten, "The Zadokite Priests at Qumran: A Reconsideration," *DSD* 4 (1997) 137–56.

[84] I am indebted to Dr. W. Horbury for this observation. In gospel studies, the so-called Griesbach hypothesis of Mark as an abbreviator of Matthew and Luke has once again been much discussed in recent years, but without winning many converts.

[85] So rightly Alexander, "The Redaction-History of *Serekh Ha-Yaḥad*," 448.

Eschatology,[86] which distinguishes between those who originally "turn aside from the council of the wicked" and "the sons of Zadok and the men of his council . . . who will come *after them* to the council of the community."[87] So also we find in the scroll containing 1QS (5:2, 9) along with the *Messianic Rule* (1QSa 1:2, 24; 2:3) and *Blessings* (1QSb 3:22) consistent signs of a preoccupation with Zadokite authority. The opposite hypothesis of a secondary *removal* of Zadokite primacy would need to account for the absence of any *anti-*Zadokite sentiment in the later documents.

The Zadokite emphasis, therefore, is likely to be a later superimposition.[88] It may have plausibly arisen in the aftermath of the Hasmonean usurpation of the Zadokite high priesthood: the archaeological record at Qumran certainly suggests that the settlement appears to have expanded precisely during the ruthless persecutions under Alexander Jannaeus (103–76 B.C.),[89] just when our scroll from Cave 1 was most likely copied. It seems in any case plausible that a renewal movement of Qumran's convictions might increasingly stress the importance of Zadokite status the more a succession of illegitimate incumbents in Jerusalem was perceived to degenerate into corruption.

My argument here will tentatively proceed on this assumption of 1QS as the latest form of the text, but in view of the uncertain evidence the conclusion will also indicate the implications that the opposite view would have for Qumran's understanding of salvation.

---

[86] See above n. 6 for this nomenclature.

[87] 4Q174 1–3.i.14–17; cf. the reference in the Isaiah pesher 4Q163 22:3.

[88] So also Davies, *Behind the Essenes,* 56–72, although he then concluded, as yet without access to the Cave 4 MSS, that scholarship "must stop talking Zadokite" altogether (p. 71). He would also appear on pp. 64–65 to dismiss somewhat hastily the evidence for a consistent redaction of 1QSa and 1QSb in the same scroll.

It is worth noting the possibility that this heightened Zadokite emphasis may have gone hand in hand with the group's increasingly sectarian self-perception. Thus, Charlotte Hempel, *The Laws of the Damascus Document: Sources, Tradition and Redaction* (STDJ 29; Leiden: Brill, 1998), 71–72 points out that unlike the specific rules governing the community, the wider halakah in CD appears to be traditional and does not as yet show any signs of redactional activity or polemics against outsiders. Pre-sectarian halakah is similarly suggested for 4QMMT by Miguel Pérez Fernández, "4QMMT: Redactional Study," *RevQ* 18 (1997): 191–205. In 1QS, as we shall see, the Zadokite takeover appears to be accompanied by the development of a more stringently sectarian soteriology as well as principles of governance and discipline. Cf. further the suggestion of Émile Puech, review of Metso, *The Textual Development,* in *RevQ* 18 (1998): 448–53, that the Teacher's death may have occasioned the group's reinforcement of its Zadokite identity and governance as a result of renewed reflection on its own history and origins.

[89] Cf. e.g. John J. Collins, "Essenes," *ABD* 2.626.

2.3.2 Redaction in 1QS 5

1QS 5–8 is now widely held to form part of the earliest core of the *Community Rule*,[90] a section which is well attested in the two important manuscripts from Cave 4 (4QS[b,d]), mentioned earlier. Some of the most significant textual changes for our purposes affect column 5 of 1QS, a passage that now opens a major new section and at one time may well have constituted the beginning of the whole document, outlining the central principles around which the community is organized. A number of observations in the handling of this section suggest that the group's self-understanding may have changed in a more clearly sectarian direction, stressing Zadokite authority and more rigorously enforced compliance with the ideals of the community. Within the confines of our present assignment, therefore, it seems justifiable to concentrate on 1QS 5.

Beginning in 1QS 5:1, the original description of the "men of the Torah" (אנשי התורה) in 4QS[b,d] has become the more technical "men of the *yaḥad*" (אנשי היחד).[91] Similarly, in 5:2–3 the simple term "the many" (הרבים) of 4QS[b,d] has been changed to "the multitude of the men of the *yaḥad*"(רוב אנשי היחד). While one should not over-interpret these changes, it is interesting that the self-identifications of the community in these crucial opening lines have both been altered to reflect the more clearly sectarian term *yaḥad*[92] – a word which in 4QS[b,d] does not in this context occur until line 5.[93]

---

[90] 4QS[d] clearly begins with the text of 1QS 5:1. See further Metso, *The Textual Development of the Qumran Community Rule*, 37, 108–9; Alexander, "The Redaction-History of *Serekh Ha-Yaḥad*," 443–6; more cautiously, Puech (see n. 88), 450.

[91] The contrary position, viz. that 4QS[d] here carries the later reading, sometimes seeks support (so e.g. Garnet, "Cave 4 MS Parallels to 1QS 5.1–7," 78) in the twofold omission in 1QS 5:23–24 of the words "in the Torah" after the phrase "and his works." Although not likely due to a technical scribal error, this change seems hardly intelligible in terms of systematic redactional activity, since the full phrase ומעשיו בתורה is happily used in 1QS 5:21 (cf. 6:18, etc.) and the words "of the Torah" are, for example *added* to "his counsel" in 1QS 9:17. It would be worth considering whether the absolute use of the term "works" might serve as a sort of technical term interchangeable with "works of the Law," in which case the difference may have seemed inconsequential to a scribe working in haste. That, at any rate, is how the terminology seems to function in texts like 4QMMT (5[=B 2] "the works," 109 [=C 23], 113 [=C 27] "the works of the Torah"), in Paul (e.g. Rom 3:20, 27–38; 4:2, 6), and in *4 Ezra* (7:24, 77; 8:32–3). Cf. also the term "doers of Torah" עושי התורה in 1QpHab 7:11; 8:1; 12:4–5. On the subject of "works of the Law" at Qumran as a halakic concept important for the study of Paul, see David Flusser, "Die Gesetzeswerke in Qumran und bei Paulus," in *Geschichte – Tradition – Reflexion* (*Fs.* Martin Hengel; ed. H. Cancik et al.; Tübingen: Mohr [Siebeck], 1996), 1.395–403; James D. G. Dunn, "4QMMT and *Galatians*," *NTS* 43 (1997): 147–53; Michael Bachmann, "4QMMT und Galaterbrief, מעשי התורה und ΕΡΓΑ ΝΟΜΟΥ," *ZNW* 89 (1998): 91–113.

[92] Note that although 1QM repeatedly uses the word *Yaḥad* (e.g. 1QM 13:11–12), it does not yet carry a sectarian meaning: cf. Jean Duhaime in Charlesworth, *The Dead Sea Scrolls*, 2.84.

Although we shall see in line 9 that the pattern of redaction is not wholly consistent, the Cave 1 redactor's general *Tendenz* throughout is to enhance the sectarian flavor of the passage.[94] Elsewhere in the *Rule*, the same words are, for example, twice inserted in 1QS 9:5–7.

Still in line 2, 1QS adds the phrase "and acquiesce to the authority of the sons of Zadok, the priests who keep the covenant" (על פי בני צדוק הכוהנים שומרי הברית). Here, then, to belong to the eschatological covenant now means to submit to the authority of the Zadokite priests within the sect.[95] Although this change is unlikely to imply a definite change in the community's authority structure, there can be little doubt of the implied change of emphasis.[96]

Further on this subject, an additional insertion in 5:5–6 suggests that this priest-centered sectarian *yahad* has now acquired for 1QS the status of an

---

Ostracon 1 (KhQ 1), found at the perimeter wall of Khirbet Qumran in 1966, may well provide an important missing link between the sectarian Scrolls and the settlement itself. I appears to describe a novice's transfer of his property to the *yahad* (line 8; see Frank Moore Cross and Esther Eshel, "Ostraca from Khirbet Qumran," *IEJ* 47 [1997]: 17–28). Although the initial reading of the ostracon was repeatedly questioned (e.g. P. R. Callaway, "A Second Look at Ostracon No. 1 from Khirbet Qumran," *QC* 7 [1997]: 145–70; Norman Golb, "*Qadmoniot* and the 'Yahad' Claim," *QC* 7 [1997]: 171–3; F. H. Cryer, "The Qumran Conveyance: A Reply to F. M. Cross and E. Eshel," *SJOT* 11 [1997]: 232–40; and Ada Yardeni, "Breaking the Missing Link," *BAR* 24 [1998]: 44–47), Cross has more recently issued a careful rejoinder: see F. M. Cross and E. Eshel, "1. Khirbet Qumran Ostracon (Plate xxxiii)," in *Qumran Cave 4: XXVI* (DJD 36; ed. S. J. Pfann et al.; Oxford: Clarendon, 2000), 497–507.

[93] Note, however, the unexpected change in 1QS 5:9 from "the men of the *Yahad*" אנשי היחד to "the men of their [sc. the Zadokites'] covenant" אנשי בריתם. But since the contextual stress on the *yahad* is already unmistakable, the reference to the Zadokite covenant simply reinforces the redactional *Tendenz* of 1QS (cf. similarly 9:2–3). The word "covenant" (ברית) is in any case another favorite word of this redactor, which he also inserts, for example, at 1QS 5:22.

[94] Similarly see 5:21–22, where (compared with 4QS^d) the Cave 1 redactor introduces an additional reference to the *yahad* (המתנדבים ביחד, 5:21) and to the covenant (המתנדבים לשוב ביחד לבריתם; 4QS^g here may read even more simply לשבת יחד [i.e. lit. "to dwell together"]). There are numerous other instances in this column and elsewhere in 1QS 5–9.

[95] Charlesworth, *The Dead Sea Scrolls*, 1.19, suggests that this could in theory be a case of parablepsis in 4QS^d. Instead, however, it agrees with other redactional trends in 1QS and should be seen as a clear *Tendenz*. Cf. also Metso, *The Textual Development of the Qumran Community Rule*, 84.

[96] See further Vermes, "Preliminary Remarks," 254–5, and Metso, *Textual Development*, 78; also Robert A. Kugler, "A Note on 1QS 9:14: The Sons of Righteousness or the Sons of Zadok?" *DSD* 3 (1996): 315–20 (on the apparent redaction of 1QS 9:14); idem, "The Priesthood at Qumran: The Evidence of References to Levi and the Levites," in *The Provo International Conference on the Dead Sea Scrolls: Technological Innovations, New Texts, and Reformulated Issues* (ed. D. W. Parry and E. Ulrich; STDJ 30; Leiden: Brill, 1999) 465–79 (on the Scrolls' elevation of the Levites following the Zadokites' alienation from the Jerusalem temple). Cf. further Frans du T. Laubscher, "The Zadokite Element in the Qumran Documents in the Light of CD 4:3," *JNSL* 24 (1998): 165–75.

"*eternal* covenant" that inherently "atones" for its members (ברית עולם לכפר, lacking in 4QS[b,d]).[97] This insertion further reinforces the desert community's isolation from the central temple cult, in confirming that theirs is the divinely appointed, definitive covenant for the eschaton[98] which provides effective and sufficient atonement for all who join (cf. similarly 1QS 8:3–4, 9–10; 3:11; etc.). It is of course true that the Cave 4 MSS do offer hints both of the priestly emphasis and of atonement in the community elsewhere (e.g. 4QS[d] 2.ii.4–5, 7); and so the redactor's intention may be merely to make more explicit what is already there. Nevertheless, it remains the case that 1QS 5:5–6 must represent a further redaction in this direction.[99]

In relation to our earlier discussion of the meaning of "Israel," this same passage in 1QS 5:5–6 also shows signs of a potential narrowing in the definition of this term. Whereas 4QS[b,d] seem to assume that the community is in the process of formation *within* and on behalf of Israel ("a foundation of truth for Israel, for all who devote themselves"), 1QS 5:5 has begun to shift the perspective in the direction of making the one co-extensive with the other: in apposition to "Israel" we now find "the *yahad* of an eternal covenant, in order to atone for all who devote themselves." We argued above that this absolute identification of "Israel" with the *yahad* has still not been made explicit, and that the text of 1QS as it stands does not admit of clear conclusions. Nevertheless, close observation of the redactional changes does suggest a trend in an increasingly narrow and exclusivistic direction. Similar insertions of references to the *yahad* and to its atoning significance occur in 8:10, 12, 16.

Following a further insertion in lines 6b–7 concerning penal discipline in the *yahad*, the scroll turns to the oath of entry into the "council of the *yahad*" (=1QS 5:7–9). In 4QS[b,d], this is described primarily as a penitential act of returning to all that has been revealed to the "men of the *yahad*" from the Torah. In 1QS this repentance has become an act under *public scrutiny* of the community (לעיני כול המתנדבים); it has become an explicit oath (שבועת אסר) and is set in a more comprehensively commandment-oriented context (ככול אשר צוה[100]) as well as a more clericalized concept of community authority and interpretation. The revelation from the Torah is now said to have been given not to the community at large (the אנשי היחד) but –

---

[97] Cf. the apposite observation of Sanders, *Paul and Palestinian Judaism*, 241, on the phrase "their covenant" as applying to the priestly leaders both here and in 1QS 6:19 (which has no extant parallel MS).

[98] Note similarly 1QS 3:11–12; 4:22; and see below on 5:22.

[99] Metso, *The Textual Development of the Qumran Community Rule*, 79, rightly surmises that while the addition of this highly charged theological phrase is understandable, its removal would be difficult to account for.

[100] But see similarly 1QS 1:3, 17; 3:10; 5:1, 22; 8:15, 21; 9:15, 24.

consistent with 5:2–3 – to "the sons of Zadok, the priests who keep the covenant and seek his will."

Lest there be any uncertainty about the identity of the outsiders, lines 11–13 clearly reinforce the sectarian perspective by means of a long gloss on the instruction "to separate (להבדל) from all the men of deceit" (l. 10). These people are identified as "those who walk in the way of wickedness," who as such "will not be accounted in his [God's] covenant" (לוא החשבו בבריתו). They have failed to seek God through his laws in order to know both his "revealed" will and the "hidden" halakic regulations, i.e. those that are specifically known to the sect; instead, they have sinned wantonly against the former and ignorantly against the latter.[101] As a result, they incur God's wrath and judgment in the curses of the covenant; his great eschatological judgments (משפטים גדולים) will result in their "eternal destruction without a remnant" (לכלת עולם לאין שרית). Given our earlier observations about the view of the remnant at Qumran, this gloss may document a further hardening of perspectives vis-à-vis outsiders: instead of seeing itself as the remnant in Israel, around which others will rally in the eschaton, here the community seems to assert that there will be no remnant at all among the outsiders from whom they have separated. It is particularly worth contrasting this assertion with the more liberal attitude in 4QMMT, which still envisages an outside readership able to recognize and be persuaded by the truth of the sectarian position, obedience to which will reckoned to them as righteousness – "for your good and that of Israel."[102]

Finally, the tightening sectarian position is further illustrated in lines 13–16. A reference in 4QS[b,d] about the outsider's (?) exclusion from the purity and the food of the community is extended by the redactor to apply to the sect's concern for ritual washing, in a parallel to 1QS 3:3–6 (par. 4QS[h], 4QpapS[c]): he asserts that ordinary ritual washing is ineffectual against impurity unless it is accompanied by repentance from wickedness. More specifically, 1QS asserts that to maintain its purity the Community must keep far from the wicked, in explicit accordance with Exod 23:7 and Isa 2:22, and goes on to deny them any legal authority and any contact. Throughout this passage 1QS shows a heightened concern with the exclusion of unrepentant outsiders and perhaps of novices whose conversion is not genuine.[103]

---

[101] הנסתרות/הנגלות: see Deut 29:28 and cf. n. 38 above.

[102] 4QMMT 117 (=C 31). See also above, p. 393 and n. 42 on the changing identity of those condemned "without remnant."

[103] So Metso, *The Textual Development of the Qumran Community Rule*, 114. A trend towards harsher corporate discipline recurs elsewhere, too. 1QS 9:1–2 laboriously underscores that inadvertent offenders against the Torah must be banned from serving on the council of the community for two years, as if to ensure that no *deliberate* sinner shall be restored in this fashion. Note also the interlinear gloss at 7:8 which raises the original penalty for an unjustified grudge from "six months" to "one year." We seem here to have solid textual evidence of the

The expansions in the remainder of column 5 primarily fill in the picture of observant, humble and truthful conduct within the community. Although generally illustrative of the enhanced emphasis on corporate discipline, the details do not add substantially to the present argument.

A number of significant changes are found in columns 6–9. Here, it is worth noting just one more in 1QS 8:10, where an interlinear insertion explicitly affirms that the community "will be accepted to atone for the land and to decide judgment over wickedness; and there will be no more iniquity." The notion that the community "atones for the land" is previously found in 8:6; but since neither of the two parallel manuscript fragments from Cave 4 (4QS[d,e]) has extant attestation of the text here, we cannot be absolutely certain what was in the *Vorlage* of 1QS.[104] Nevertheless, the interlinear additions here do underline the trend towards an enhanced sectarian emphasis, including the desert community's self-conscious independence from the official temple cult in Jerusalem.

I have attempted to document these and other changes in 1QS 5–9 more fully elsewhere.[105] The remainder of 1QS, too, contains material of considerable relevance to our topic, above all in column 11. Unfortunately the only available parallel to 1QS 11 is MS 4QS[j], which deviates from the Cave 1 text primarily in showing a preference for defective rather than *plene* orthography. On balance it seems clear that the final psalm appended to the *Rule* was originally separate, as was perhaps 9:12–26a.[106]

2.3.3 Implications for Qumran's view of salvation

In the end, the significance of these observations should not perhaps be overrated: they are based on relatively limited evidence and do not greatly alter the picture of Qumran soteriology that we presented earlier. Although the priority of 4QS[b,d] seems to this writer a sound hypothesis, future research may still question it on the basis of superior argument or evidence, and thereby reverse the conclusions we must draw. It certainly remains the case that 1QS is a composite document which, when taken at face value, manifests signs both of a lenient theology of grace and of a strongly authoritarian vision of the covenant, and a tension between milder and stricter penal regulations.

---

sorts of developments in penal legislation which Murphy-O'Connor ("La genèse littéraire") once postulated on the basis of more limited sources. At least in these cases, the co-existence of stricter and more lenient legislation in 1QS (compare 6:24–5; 8:16b–19 with 8:22–3; 9:1–2) seems then to be resolved in terms of a development in the direction of greater strictness.

[104] But contrast Charlesworth, *The Dead Sea Scrolls*, 1.35 n. 205, who makes the implausible claim that these supralinear additions are really just corrections of faulty copying.

[105] See Markus Bockmuehl, "Redaction and Ideology."

[106] See Metso, *The Textual Development of the Qumran Community Rule*, 119.

At the same time, what has become quite clear is that the manuscript tradition of the *Community Rule* did undergo significant changes, and that these changes may attest developments in Qumran's overall understanding of theology and membership in the people of God. This alone is a significant correction of earlier views. Scholars in the past tended to "take their pick" from this complex evidence, alternately stressing either the elements of grace or those suggesting a strict legalism. Sanders merely contemplated the possibility of development in passing, but then seemingly dismissed its relevance to the interpretation of 1QS in order to read discrepancies within the penal code as simultaneously valid for two different groups.[107] As late as 1992 Seifrid, though largely critical of Sanders's interpretation, explicitly declined to consider literary developments as indicative of changes in the sect's soteriology.[108]

While such judgments were understandable in the absence of the evidence from Cave 4, the situation has now changed to the point where flat, achronic readings of doctrine can no longer be justified. If our redactional analysis of 1QS is correct, it suggests a tightening religious practice in which atonement and forgiveness were increasingly limited to the sect itself, and religious authority was concentrated in the hands of Zadokite priests. The same point is reinforced by the eschatological vision of the *Messianic Rule* 1QSa (1:1–3, 23–25; 2:2f.) and in the *Blessings* of 1QSb (3:22–25), both of which were deliberately linked with 1QS by being included in the same Scroll, and arguably subjected to a comparable pro-Zadokite redaction.[109]

Several caveats are in order. First, with the obvious exception of the Zadokite emphasis, the effect of the redactional changes in 1QS is not so much to innovate as to reinforce and make more explicit certain tendencies of community doctrine and discipline that are already present in the earlier text forms. In most cases, the text bears witness to underlying trends and emphases rather than to radical change. Secondly, the redaction of 1QS is in any case rather haphazard; an emphasis on divine grace, for example, continued to co-exist side by side with the more stringent views. In this respect Sanders's observation that the Qumran sect's views of predestination remain unsystematic[110] must profitably be extended to its overall understanding of salvation.

---

[107] Sanders, *Paul and Palestinian Judaism*, 324–5. He assumes that, since it is a *Rule*, 1QS must be both consistent and valid in its entirety.

[108] Seifrid, *Justification by Faith*, 82, who writes with reference to Murphy-O'Connor, "La genèse littéraire," and Pouilly, *La Règle de la Communauté*, "It is not clear that the progressive stages of the community . . . involve shifts in the basic soteriology adopted by the group."

[109] On this point cf. also Alexander, "The Redaction-History of *Serekh Ha-Yaḥad*," 438. Hempel, "The Earthly Essene Nucleus of 1QSa," 256–60 and passim, argues the case for a Zadokite recension of 1QSa.

[110] Sanders, *Paul and Palestinian Judaism*, 265–6.

3. Conclusion

In this study we have approached Qumran's understanding of salvation from the relatively narrow perspective of its development in the constitutional *Rule of the Community*. A fuller treatment of the subject would certainly need to offer systematic treatments of several other key texts. In particular, it would be worth conducting a similar redactional analysis for the soteriology of the Cave 1 and Cave 4 fragments of both the *Damascus Document* and the *War Scroll*, documents which have been thought to reflect a somewhat earlier stage of the Qumran Community. The *War Scroll* in particular seems in its Cave 1 version to manifest a clear sectarian redaction in several respects, as was already observed by C.-H. Hunzinger.[111]

Overall, our findings are not fundamentally incompatible with those reached in E. P. Sanders's famous study of 1977: Qumran manifests an eschatological faith in which salvation and atonement for sins are not humanly earned but divinely granted by predestined election and membership in the life of the observant covenant community. Here, too, we might wish to question the heuristic usefulness of his philosophically and psychologically infelicitous bifurcation between "getting in" and "staying in";[112] but this is a query best addressed to his project as a whole, rather than to his treatment of Qumran in particular.

The major points of disagreement between Sanders's treatment and mine may be said to arise from more extensive primary sources and, partly as a result, from the availability of more discriminating analytical methods. The text base at our disposal has increased significantly over that available to Sanders twenty-five years ago; this in turn has led to greater clarity on some questions and cast doubt on others that once seemed clear. Sanders himself already recognized theological diversity in the Qumran material, but dismissed the notion of legal or theological development. Since then, however, scholars have discovered positive evidence for precisely such development in 1QS and other sectarian texts, while at the same time beginning to realize that a great many of the newly released Dead Sea Scrolls are in no significant sense sectarian at all. Much of what was found at Qumran turns out to be far more widely indicative of the diversity of Palestinian Judaism in the later Second Temple period.

Herein hangs the suggestion that "Qumran religion" may be at once less coherent and more peculiar than Sanders thought. First, the texts themselves

---

[111] Claus-Hunno Hunzinger, "Fragmente einer älteren Fassung des Buches Milhama aus Höhle 4 von Qumran," *ZAW* 69 (1957): 131–51; cf. Sanders, *Paul and Palestinian Judaism*, 251; J. Duhaime in Charlesworth, *The Dead Sea Scrolls*, 2.84. See also n. 88 above on the halakah of the *Damascus Document*.

[112] Cf. again, *Paul and Palestinian Judaism*, 320.

manifest a number of fundamentally unresolved tensions. As it stands, salvation is on the one hand "legalistic" both in its individualistic voluntarism and in its closely regimented corporate life; and yet it is the gift of divine grace alone, both objectively in regard to predestination and subjectively in the experience of the believer. The evidence itself now confirms that the intrinsically unsystematic soteriology of a central document like 1QS is due at least in some part to textual developments over a considerable length of time. Secondly, however, while the fact of diversity in the Scrolls in some ways invites more ready comparison with other elements in Palestinian Judaism, it also makes it more questionable to distill "the Qumran pattern of religion" and then proceed to find, as Sanders does, that it is fundamentally the same as that of rabbinic literature.[113] To be sure, Sanders is quite right to observe important particular similarities as well as a number of "striking differences and special emphases"[114] between major sectarian texts and central documents of the later normative rabbinic Judaism. What is less clear today is whether such grand systemic comparison is still appropriate at least to the Qumran sources – and, perhaps more importantly, whether the parties concerned would have found it not just true in generalities but meaningful in practice to speak of "the same basic pattern of religion."

Time and space prevent the pursuit of several other interesting questions. It is particularly poignant that several sectarian documents stress the community's existence "without a mediator" between it and "the holy angels in their midst."[115] This consciousness of direct participation in angelic worship is considerably strengthened by the redemptive role of Melchizedek in 11QMelch, by the function of Michael and other angels in 1QM, and by the *Angelic Liturgy* 4QŠirŠabb. Such a sense of "unmediated" contact with the angels, however, would be worth assessing in view of the apparently contrary move of concentrating power in Zadokite hands.

Our study is therefore only a beginning, and limited in scope. Nevertheless, it has served to show that the Qumran community had a strongly covenantal understanding of the salvation of Israel as centered in its own covenant community. Membership in the covenant of God was characterized both by a sustained individual voluntarism and by an all-embracing doctrine of divine predestination. The community combined a strong sense of the sinfulness of all humanity with a belief in divine grace to the believer as the only means of salvation. The texts manifest an uneasy co-existence of the belief that atonement for sins remains emphatically an act of God with other statements that the faith and life of the community, and of its priestly leaders in particular, is in some sense instrumental to that atonement.

---

[113] Ibid.
[114] Ibid.
[115] 1QH 14(=6):13, אין מליץ; CD 15:17 par.; cf. e.g. 1QM 10:11; 11QBer (=11Q14) 12f.

If the direction of my redactional analysis is correct, we may have in Qumran a developing example of the sort of exclusivistic preoccupation with "works of the law" against which Paul of Tarsus subsequently reacts in his letters to Gentile Christians.[116] If, by contrast, it could be shown after all that 4QS[b] and 4QS[d] represent the later recension of the *Serekh*, the conclusion would have to be that Paul was not alone in his reaction against narrow religious exclusivism.[117] Either way, the soteriology of the scrolls is clearly not a monolithic theological construct but remained subject to flux and development over an extended period of time.[118]

---

[116] The motif of religious "exclusivism" in the *Rule of the Community* and Qumran texts is usefully surveyed in George W. E. Nickelsburg, "Religious Exclusivism: A World View Governing Some Texts Found at Qumran," in *Das Ende der Tage und die Gegenwart des Heils: Begegnungen mit dem Neuen Testament und seiner Umwelt* (*Fs.* Heinz-Wolfgang Kuhn; ed. M. Becker and W. Fenske; AGAJU 44; Leiden: Brill, 1999), 45–67 and *passim*. James Dunn has variously explored the possibility of finding here a foil for Pauline theology (so e.g. James D. G. Dunn, "4QMMT and Galatians," *NTS* 43 [1997]: 147–53).

[117] He himself of course sometimes counsels separation from outsiders and exclusion of insiders: compare e.g. 1 Cor 5:9–13 with 2 Cor 6:14–7:1.

[118] Parts of this chapter were presented at the Oxford Qumran Forum (Nov. 1997), the Cambridge Seminar on Hebrew, Jewish and Early Christian Studies (Jan. 1998), and the Congress of the European Association of Jewish Studies in Toledo (July 1998). I am grateful for comments and suggestions from members of these seminars, Professors P. S. Alexander of Manchester and M. A. Knibb of London, and the editors and contributors of this volume.

14. Righteousness Language in the Hebrew Scriptures and Early Judaism

by

MARK A. SEIFRID

For obvious reasons, the various terms for "righteousness" (or "justice") in the Hebrew Bible associated with the root צדק have long been the focus of theological interest. The biblical understanding of God's dealings with the world is linked fundamentally to their interpretation. Moreover, Paul's conception of "righteousness" and "justification" clearly depends upon antecedent biblical themes. If we are to interpret him rightly, we must come to grips with the Jewish background of his thought on this topic. Although we do best to study the historical development of concepts such as "righteousness" by treating larger units of discourse, lexical studies remain indispensable to proper exegesis. In addition, because interpreters generally have linked the biblical conception of righteousness too closely with the noun צדקה a survey of scholarly treatment of the biblical terminology is necessary and relevant.[1]

One very influential line of interpretation of "righteousness" in the Hebrew Bible has construed the word-usage as consistently salvific, at least as it relates to God. As Gerhard von Rad has memorably put it, "der Begriff einer strafenden צְדָקָה ist nicht zu belegen; er wäre eine contradictio in adiecto."[2] Despite the wide assent which this reading has commanded, there remains a small but conspicuous group of texts in which a punitive form of divine righteousness appears. To dismiss them as late and secondary, as von Rad and others have done, remains questionable. A more definite explanation must be found for the instances in which a punitive conception appears, particularly since not all of them may be counted as post-exilic. At the same time, those who have asserted that the biblical conception of divine righteousness includes a retributive aspect run into another problem.[3] How does one

---

[1] I wish to thank Prof. Dr. Peter Stuhlmacher, Dr. Friedrich Avemarie, Dr. Markus Bockmuehl, and Dr. Peter O'Brien for their helpful comments on earlier forms of this essay.

[2] Gerhard von Rad, *Theologie des Alten Testaments* (2 vols.; 6th ed.; München: Chr. Kaiser, 1969), 1.389 = *Old Testament Theology* (2 vols.; trans. D. M. G. Stalker; New York: Harper & Row, 1962), 1.377.

[3] See, e.g., Friedrich Nötscher, *Die Gerechtigkeit Gottes bei den Vorexilischen Propheten:*

account for the fact that we find more than four times the number of occurrences of a "saving righteousness" of God than we do those involving a punitive divine justice? It is one matter to assert that the biblical conception is two-sided. It is another matter to explain satisfactorily the nature of the evidence.[4]

In a related way, there has been a continuing debate as to whether it is proper to speak of the vocabulary of righteousness in the Hebrew Bible as generally bearing the sense of "accordance with a norm" or, alternatively, "fidelity to a relationship." Obviously, theological issues related to the first question are present here. If "righteousness" involves correspondence to a standard, we may readily account for passages in which a punitive righteousness appears. If "righteousness" is regarded solely as descriptive of a "right relation," the way is open to interpreting divine righteousness in purely salvific terms: God's righteousness consists in his fidelity to his people in saving them.[5] There are theological issues just below the surface here, which for a considerable period have influenced interpreters in one way or another, not only in the answers that they have found, but in the questions they have put to the biblical texts.

In regard to both of these questions, it is instructive to turn to Hermann Cremer, whose century-old study of the language of righteousness in the Hebrew Bible has shaped both the content and method of a large part of modern study.[6] His lengthy treatment of the theme of righteousness came in response to Albrecht Ritschl's monumental work on justification and reconciliation. Relying upon the work of Diestel and Kautzsch, Ritschl construed divine righteousness as the consistency of God's action in relation to his aim of bringing salvation to the world. The "righteousness of God" therefore is

---

Ein Beitrag zur Alttestamentlichen Theologie (Alttestamentliche Abhandlungen 6.1; Münster: Aschendorff, 1915). Nötscher, although calling attention to several texts in which he discerns a punitive righteousness, appeals primarily to the prophetic description of divine judgment and wrath as a basis for his claim that the biblical conception of righteousness includes a retributive aspect. In doing so, he overlooks the actual language and usage in the prophetic literature.

[4] Although generally dismissed, Alfred Dünner's work is remarkably well-balanced, and takes into account both the contexts in which God's righteousness is salvific as well as those in which it appears in retributive form. He lacks only the insights of lexical semantics, which would have allowed him to draw more definite and persuasive conclusions. See *Die Gerechtigkeit nach dem Alten Testament* (Schriften zur Rechtslehre und Politik 42; Bonn: H. Bouvier, 1963).

[5] Note, however, that even this formulation cannot escape the idea of a norm (in this instance, "fidelity") which is to govern God's action.

[6] Hermann Cremer, *Die paulinische Rechtfertigungslehre im Zusammenhange ihrer geschichtlichen Voraussetzungen* (Gütersloh: Bertelsmann, 1899).

die "Rechtbeschaffenheit Gottes", die Congruenz seines Handelns mit seiner inneren Normalität und mit dem was die Israeliten von der Leitung ihrer Geschicke durch Gott zu erwarten haben.[7]

According to Ritschl, the idea of a retributive righteousness and its connection with a courtroom judgment is a product of the pagan world. Not the mechanical relation between worthiness and reward (or punishment), but the organic relation between beginning and result determines the biblical conception. God acts righteously in the sense that his deeds serve his ultimate purpose of bringing justice and salvation to his people. In response, Cremer insisted that the usage of righteousness language in the Scriptures is concrete, arguing that "God's righteousness" does not have to do with a future goal of salvation, but with his present activity in establishing and protecting justice.[8] Consequently, despite a certain proximity in their thinking, for Cremer the punishment of the wicked represented an essential element of the salvation of the righteous, while for Ritschl retribution remained a matter secondary to God's larger saving purpose.[9] In other words, while Ritschl (along the lines of Grotius) insisted that God acts as *rector* and not *iudex* in his saving acts, Cremer insisted that in biblical thought the roles of "ruling and judging" belong together, and that the Scriptures regularly speak of concrete acts of divine judgment. Here he was entirely correct, and his insights must not be overlooked.

At the same time Cremer draws a significant, although questionable conclusion regarding the language of "righteousness" as it appears in the Scriptures. In Cremer's view, while the judging activity of God is two-sided, including both the punishment of the oppressors and the salvation of the oppressed, the biblical terminology for "righteousness" always expresses the saving aspect of God's action. The punitive aspect of the divine action remains implicit, although presupposed. Cremer's formulation, which in fact lies behind von Rad's view, is equally memorable as the statement of von Rad:

An eine Herabdrückung dieses Begriffs zu dem der *justitia distributiva* ist nicht zu denken. Im ganzen Alten Testament ist und bleibt die Gerechtigkeit Gottes *justitia salutifera*.[10]

Cremer further regards it as improper to ascribe the concept of a norm to the biblical usage. "Righteousness" does not have to do with the relationship between a person and an idea, but between a personal subject and object:

---

[7] Albrecht Ritschl, *Die christliche Lehre von der Rechtfertigung und Versöhnung* (3 vols.; 4th ed.; Bonn: A. Marcus & E. Weber, 1903; original edition, 1874), 106.

[8] Cremer, *Rechtfertigungslehre*, 24.

[9] Cremer, *Rechtfertigungslehre*, 42: "Es ist namentlich nach Jes. 59,17.18 klar, daß der Begriff der Gerechtigkeit den der Vergeltung nicht ausschließt sondern einschließt."

[10] Cremer, *Rechtfertigungslehre*, 33. He acknowledges that several passages speak of a punitive righteousness, but argues that in those cases the very righteousness which punishes

צדק ist durchaus Verhältnisbegriff, sich auf ein wirkliches Verhältnis zwischen zweien, zwischen Subject und Object beziehend, zwischen zweien, zwischen einem Subjekt, welches Ansprüche macht und hat, und einem Objekt, welches demselben gerecht wird, nicht aber auf das Verhältnis eines Objektes, das der Beurteilung unterzogen wird, zu einer Idee oder zu seiner Idee.[11]

In making this claim, Cremer both preserves the concept of retribution and turns Ritschl's charge against him. Not the concept of punitive judgment, but the idealistic understanding of righteousness as the highest of all the virtues in human society, on which Ritschl's thesis depends, is characteristic of the Hellenistic (and therefore, pagan) world. Biblical language and patterns of thought are decisively different.[12]

Here, however, a fundamental weakness of Cremer's work emerges. The close and direct connection between thought and language which he assumes simply does not exist. It is this approach to the study of biblical vocabulary which plagued Cremer's earlier *Biblisch-theologisches Wörterbuch* and Kittel's subsequent *Theologisches Wörterbuch des Neuen Testaments*, and which James Barr so trenchantly criticized. We have no need here to rehearse the details of that critique, which are well-known. There are, however, at least two fundamental errors in Cremer's treatment of the vocabulary of righteousness from which scholarship in large measure has yet to free itself, and which therefore deserve some discussion.

The first consists in Cremer's obvious quest for a *Grundbegriff*, a fundamental conception of "righteousness," which may be applied to any and all appearances of צדק terminology. In one sense, it is perfectly appropriate to search for a general sense attached to a word-root, a sense which may help to clarify the use of terms in obscure or ambiguous contexts. There remains an important place for etymological study, an aspect of lexical semantics for which Barr in his famous work perhaps did not leave sufficient room. Yet the notion of a *Grundbegriff* becomes problematic when it is given priority over or used apart from description of context in determining the meaning of words. Such confusion is obvious not only in the citation of Cremer above, but in von Rad's claim regarding the salvific sense of divine righteousness in the Hebrew Scriptures which we have cited above.

Cremer's first error leads to a second. In accord with his construal of the *Grundbegriff* of צדק, he insists that the word-usage is always "social and forensic," having to do with a relationship between persons.[13] This conclusion is problematic, of course, since צדק is applied to various objects of commerce

---

Israel also prepares for her salvation (*Rechtfertigungslehre*, 31). Despite the conceptual attractiveness of this argument, it does not account for actual word-usage.

[11] Cremer, *Rechtfertigungslehre*, 34.

[12] Cremer, *Rechtfertigungslehre*, 23.

[13] Cremer, *Rechtfertigungslehre*, 23.

and cult, and sometimes is used metaphorically in an impersonal sense.[14] Although this misstatement in itself represents only a mild linguistic fault, it is symptomatic of Cremer's more serious error of supposing that every (personal) relationship itself somehow serves as its own "norm":

> Das Verhältnis zu dem Anspruch, den jemand hat, das Verhältnis des mit צדק gewerteten Objektes zu den Ansprüchen des Subjektes ist der Grundgedanke. . . . Sie (die Ansprüche) sind einfach mit dem bestehenden Verhältnisse gegeben, welches als solches ganz bestimmte Forderungen einschließt. Es liegt also auch nach dieser Seite hin kein Anlaß vor, an eine objektive, sei es in dem mit צדק gewerteten Objekt liegende, sei es in der Idee Gottes oder des Menschen enthaltene Norm zu denken. Das Verhältnis selbst ist die Norm.[15]

Beyond the obvious conceptual difficulty of applying this claim to impersonal objects, such as, say, "paths of righteousness" (Ps 23:3), it is nearly impossible to imagine how demands can be entirely internal to a relationship. The very fact that one party might have a claim upon another entails (at the very least) the idea that rectitude (in some sense) ought to be maintained in that relation. In other words, the relation is at minimum subject to a principle of rectitude, otherwise contentions regarding rights and duties could not arise. Undoubtedly, Cremer's concern to refute Ritschl's appeal to an inner divine norm or human ideal in defining "righteousness" leads him to this overstatement. Unfortunately this description of צדק language continues to appear in the literature without qualification.[16]

A brief glance at Gen 38:26, a passage to which frequent appeal is made in this regard, reveals the significant misstep which the statements above represent. Judah, informed of the illegitimate pregnancy of his daughter-in-law Tamar, orders that she be brought out of her father's house to be burned. The setting is clearly that of a trial or contention.[17] The narrator intentionally focuses upon the patriarch by framing the report in the passive voice ("it was reported to Judah"), but presupposes that the broader community informed Judah of Tamar's condition and became observers of the proceeding. Upon the proof that he was responsible for Tamar's pregnancy, Judah confesses, "[S]he is more in the right than I, since I did not give her to my son Shelah" (NRSV). What she had done conformed to community standards regarding the preservation of the familial line of the deceased husband (cf. Gen 38:8, Deut 25:5–10), and was necessitated by his refusal to give her to his last son as

---

[14] E.g. Lev 19:36 (balances, weights, ephah, hin); Ps 23:3 (paths).

[15] Cremer, *Rechtfertigungslehre*, 36.

[16] E.g., Elizabeth Achtemeier, "Righteousness in the Old Testament," *IDB* 2.80; von Rad, *Theologie des Alten Testaments*, 1:383; Alister E. McGrath, *Iustitia Dei: A History of the Christian Doctrine of Justification* (2 vols.; Cambridge: Cambridge University, 1986), 1.8.

[17] See Keith W. Whitelam, *The Just King: Monarchical Judicial Authority in Ancient Israel* (JSOTSup 12; Sheffield: JSOT, 1979), 39–42.

wife (Gen 38:26). Tamar escapes punishment *not* because Judah was complicit in the sexual act and therefore equally guilty – the narrative is tellingly silent in this regard – but because her action, as unusual as it was, was legitimated by community standards, leaving Judah without a claim. *Therefore* (the basis is clearly stated in the narrative) Judah could not condemn Tamar of "whoredom" (NRSV, Gen 38:24). As Cremer observes, the context is "social and forensic," so that one must regard the rendering, "She is more righteous than I" (NIV), as misleading. The narrative depicts justice in a concrete form, as a matter of competing claims between two parties. In this respect Cremer makes an important observation. Yet it is simply not the case that the relationship between Judah and Tamar served as a norm or contained a norm within itself. The (*qal*) verb צָדְקָה here signifies "she is in the right (more than I)," and entails applied justice, behind which stands a previously-fixed norm of the community, which governed Judah and Tamar's roles.[18]

We have used this text because it is supposed to represent a strong case for the view that the צדק root is relational *and not* reflective of a norm. A number of recent studies have concluded on the basis of both etymology and usage that the concept of a standard or norm is generally associated with the צדק word-group.[19] The work of Hans Heinrich Schmid has been very important in this regard. Although we would wish to qualify somewhat his thesis that the concept of a *Weltordnung* stands behind all biblical usage of righteousness language, his claim basically seems well-established.[20] The root צדק is associated with concepts of legitimacy and normativity throughout the

---

[18] We may note in passing that the parallel usage of the verb צדק with the preposition מִן in Jer 3:11 and Ezek 16:52 may perhaps reflect conflict between Judah and Israel and, respectively, Jerusalem and her neighbors, not a contention with God as might appear on first reading.

[19] See, e.g., David Hill, *Greek Words and Hebrew Meanings: Studies in the Semantics of Soteriological Terms* (SNTMS 5; Cambridge: Cambridge University, 1967), 82–86; Josef Scharbert, "Gerechtigkeit I: Altes Testament," *TRE* 12.404–11; Bo Johnson, "צָדֵק," *ThWAT* 6.898–924; Ahuva Ho, *Sedeq and Sedaqah in the Hebrew Bible* (American University Studies, Series VII, Theology and Religion 78; New York, Peter Lang, 1991); J. J. Scullion, "Righteousness: Old Testament," *ABD* 5.724–36. Somewhat grudgingly, Klaus Koch "*sdq*," *THAT* 2.515.

[20] Hans Heinrich Schmid, *Gerechtigkeit als Weltordnung: Hintergrund und Geschichte des alttestamentlichen Gerechtigkeitsbegriffes* (BHT 40; Tübingen: Mohr [Siebeck], 1968). See also Hans Heinrich Schmid, *Altorientalische Welt in der alttestamentlichen Theologie* (Zürich: Theologischer Verlag, 1974). Alfred Jepsen, commenting on the historical books, observes, "Zu allermeist wird deutlich, daß צדק etwas mit Gott zu tun hat. . . . Wenn also auch die Wurzel zunächst ein innermenschliches Verhalten meint, so ist dieses in Israel doch nie dem Urteil Gottes entnommen," "צדק und צדקה im Alten Testament," in *Gottes Wort und Gottes Land* (ed. H. Reventlow; Göttingen: Vandenhoeck & Ruprecht, 1965), 81–82. See also Albrecht Dihle, "Gerechtigkeit," in *RAC* 10.281–98.

entire Northwest Semitic language group,[21] and often appears in the Hebrew Bible in parallel with such terms as אמת,[22] ישר,[23] משרים.[24] Schmid has also in a general but very helpful way distinguished between contexts in which צדק signifies correspondence to a norm (such as cult, nature, war, and the description of material things) and those in which it *also* signifies faithfulness to a relation (*Gemeinschaftstreue*).[25] The use of צדק-terms in contexts having to do with "relationships" represents a certain concretion of the general sense.

Schmid's study entailed etymological work and the tracing of theological traditions rather than the elucidation of word-meanings, leaving much territory unexplored. Franz Reiterer's 1976 dissertation provides a further step in the analysis of צדק terminology.[26] With an appreciation for Barr's work, he engages in a basic componential analysis of the contexts in which צדק-terms appear, grouping them into three categories: juridical, ethical-social and conflictual-military. Due to the dimensions of the undertaking, he prescinds from a more precise description of usage which might have been gained through the plotting of equivalent and opposing terms.[27] Further useful work therefore remains to be done.[28] Moreover, despite these advances in interpretation, which have in an initial way made their appearance in dictionary articles,[29] confusion in the study of "righteousness" terminology is

---

[21] See Moshe Weinfeld, *Social Justice in Ancient Israel and in the Ancient Near East* (Publications of the Perry Foundation for Biblical Research in the Hebrew University of Jerusalem; Jerusalem/Minneapolis: Magnes/Fortress, 1995), 25–26.

[22] 1 Kgs 3:6; Isa 48:1; Jer 4:2; Zech 8:8, Ps 85:11–12.

[23] Deut 9:5; 1 Kgs 3:6; Hos 14:10; Ps 45:7–8; 119:137; Prov 2:9; 16:13.

[24] Isa 33:15; 45:19; Ps 9:9; 17:1–2; 58:2; 96:10–13; 98:9; Ps 99:4; Prov 1:3; 2:9.

[25] Schmid, *Gerechtigkeit als Weltordnung*, 184–6.

[26] Friedrich Vinzenz Reiterer, *Gerechtigkeit als Heil:* צדק *bei Deuterojesaja, Aussage und Vergleich mit der alttestamentlichen Tradition* (Graz: Akademische Druck- und Verlagsanstalt, 1976).

[27] Reiterer, *Gerechtigkeit als Heil*, 213.

[28] Ahuva Ho, *Sedeq and Ṣedaqah in the Hebrew Bible*, despite her awareness of lexical semantics breaks no new ground here. Nor does Jože Krašovec, *La Justice (Sdq) de Dieu dans la Bible hébraïque et l'interprétation juive et chrétienne* (OBO 76; Freiburg (Switzerland)/Göttingen: Universitätsverlag/Vandenhoeck & Ruprecht, 1988). Despite his appeal to lexical semantics, he limits his study to "God's righteousness," provides no real contextual analysis of synonyms and antonyms, and seems to operate from the start with a fixed notion of God's righteousness as his promise to save the people of God, which only the righteous receive. Similarly, despite his title, David Hill *Greek Words and Hebrew Meanings: Studies in the Semantics of Soteriological Terms*, 82–162, engages in no real semantic analysis. Frank Crüsemann begins with important lexical insights, but then shifts to analysis of blocks of tradition, "Jahwes Gerechtigkeit (*ṣᵉdāqā/ṣädäq*) im Alten Testament," *EvT* 36 (1976): 427–51. We have nothing comparable to John Sawyer, *Semantics in Biblical Research: New Methods of Defining Hebrew Words for Salvation* (SBT 2/24; London: SCM, 1972). And Sawyer's work represents only a start.

[29] See Scharbert, "Gerechtigkeit I: Altes Testament," *TRE* 12.404–11; Bo Johnson, "צדק,"

far from a relic of the past.[30] All too frequently, scholars investigating צדק-
terminology continue to overlook the semantic insight that any proper
definition of a word or word-group must describe the contexts which call
forth the various meanings of the terms.

We may take John Ziesler's influential work as illustrative of the problems
that continue to plague the study of righteousness language in the Hebrew
Scriptures, since his treatment succumbs in a fundamental way to the
temptation of imposing modern categories on word-usage.[31] In analyzing the
nouns צְדָקָה and צֶדֶק, and the adjective צַדִּיק, he begins by providing his
own definition of "forensic" usage, i.e. righteousness which has to do with
"status" and not activity or behavior.[32] This judgment, formed by traditional
Catholic-Protestant debates, turns out to be arbitrary and highly misleading
when the pattern of biblical usage comes into view. We need only to recall the
case of Tamar. She obviously was accorded a "status" by Judah's pronouncement, but that pronouncement had very much to do with her actions, so that
an absolute distinction between "status" and "behavior" is illegitimate.
Likewise, the charge brought against Tamar reveals an ethical interest, not
merely a "forensic" one: "to play the whore" (זנה), as she is said to have done
(Gen 38:24), is no mere legal description![33] Furthermore, especially from the
start of the monarchical period, legislative and executive decisions appear to
have been effected primarily in the judicial setting. In such instances one
cannot legitimately separate "status" from the vindicating act of the king, nor
should one, as Ziesler does, treat "legal activity" and "governing, ruling
activity" as separate categories.[34] More errors of this nature could be
catalogued.[35] Consequently, the resulting statistics in which Ziesler makes a
distinction between "forensic" usage and that having to do with "activity"
(legal and non-legal) are virtually worthless. Unfortunately, it is these data
which he brings to bear upon the language of righteousness in the New
Testament.[36]

ThWAT 6.898–924; J. J. Scullion, "Righteousness: Old Testament," *ABD* 5.724–36.

[30] Contrast the following articles, with those cited in the previous note: Klaus Koch, "*sdq*,"
THAT 2.507–30; Elizabeth Achtemeier, "Righteousness in the Old Testament," *IDB* 2.80–85.

[31] John A. Ziesler, *The Meaning of Righteousness in Paul: A Linguistic and Theological
Enquiry* (SNTMS 20; Cambridge: Cambridge University, 1972).

[32] Ziesler, *The Meaning of Righteousness*, 22.

[33] Note how it stands in contrast to the earlier description of Tamar incognito as a "cultic
prostitute" (קדשה; Gen 38:22).

[34] Ziesler, *The Meaning of Righteousness*, 23–24.

[35] E.g., since divine acts of vindication are part of the metaphor of God's kingly rule, it is
incorrect to create an independent category to describe "Gracious, Saving Activity" on God's
part, as does Ziesler, *The Meaning of Righteousness*, 29.

[36] Ziesler, *The Meaning of Righteousness*, 32–36.

Ziesler is hardly alone in imposing his own theological categories on the biblical usage. Interpreters often render references to "God's righteousness" in biblical contexts as God's "covenant-faithfulness," expressed in his saving acts on behalf of his people.[37] This way of understanding the biblical language presupposes that the idea of a promissory covenant is both fundamental and pervasive within the Hebrew Scriptures, a matter which is highly debated but into which we cannot enter in this essay.[38] In any case, it seems intuitively obvious to many that concepts of "righteousness" should be associated with those of "covenant" in the Hebrew Scriptures. But in what way is this so? Here we can speak only in the most general way: when one examines word-usage, it becomes clear that to speak of "righteousness" as "covenant faithfulness" is to invert the actual semantic relation between the terms. Only rarely do ברית and צדק-terms appear in any proximity to one another, despite their considerable frequency in the Hebrew Scriptures.[39] "Covenant" (ברית) occurs 283 times, צדק-terminology some 524 times, and yet in only seven passages do the terms come into any significant semantic contact.[40] This lack of convergence in usage is all the more striking when we take into account that both ברית and the צדק word-group have fields of meaning having to do with relationships, and both have ethical and juridical dimensions.[41] Other issues come into view with this observation, particularly the question, which goes back at least to Wellhausen, as to why ברית appears so infrequently in the prophetic materials and the psalms, where righteousness terminology is rather frequent. A full explanation for the infrequency of collocation would be quite detailed, and obviously may be approached from historical and theological perspectives rather than from that of lexical semantics. These matters lie beyond the scope of our concern.[42] Here we wish

---

[37] So, for example, Hill, *Greek Words and Hebrew Meanings*, 93–98.

[38] See Ernest W. Nicholson, *God and His People: Covenant and Theology in the Old Testament* (Oxford: Clarendon, 1986), esp. pp. 3–117.

[39] It is completely mystifying that Johnson, "צָדַק," *ThWAT* 6.919, says, "*ṣdq* steht in einer engen Verbindung mit ברית, und zwar als bundesgemäßes Verhalten." Nothing could be further from the truth. See the comment by Koch, n. 41, below.

[40] Making generous allowance, we may point to Isa 42:6; 61:8–11; Hos 2:16–20; Ps 50:1–6; 111:1–10; Dan 9:4–7; Neh 9:32–33. It is possible that further widely-separated appearances of ברית and צדק-terms which bear some narrative relation to one another might be added to this list, but none that reveals a close relation of the lexemes.

[41] Koch, "*ṣdq*," 2.516, comments, "Schwierig ist außerdem, daß zwar die Wurzel *sdq* häufig auf das rechte Verhalten des Menschen zu seinem Gott (und umgekehrt) angewandt wird, aber kaum je mit dem für das Gottesverhältnis grundlegenden Begriff *bᵉrît* zusammengestellt wird." See also Schmid, *Gerechtigkeit als Weltordnung*, 167.

[42] For representative views and bibliography see *inter alia* Nicholson, *God and His People*; Dennis J. McCarthy, *Treaty and Covenant* (AnBib 21A; 2d ed.; Rome: Pontifical Biblical Institute, 1978); idem, *Old Testament Covenant: A Survey of Current Opinions* (Oxford: Blackwell, 1972); G. E. Mendenhall and G. A. Herion, "Covenant," *ABD* 1.1179–202; E.

to make only two observations relevant to the understanding of righteousness language in the Hebrew Scriptures.

First, if we may continue to speak in the most general way, the word ברית signifies a distinct relationship, which often calls forth quasi-forensic and familial language. In biblical terms one generally does not "act righteously or unrighteously" with respect to a covenant. Rather, one "keeps," "remembers," "establishes" a covenant, or the like. Or, conversely, one "breaks," "transgresses," "forsakes," "despises," "forgets," or "profanes" it. Charges of covenantal infidelity appear in the prophetic materials in the form of familial metaphors (usually without the use of the word ברית), e.g. "I have reared children and brought them up, but they have rebelled against me" (Isa 1:2, NRSV); "Go and take for yourself a wife of whoredom and have children of whoredom, for the land commits great whoredom, by forsaking the Lord" (Hos 1:2, NRSV). Expressed positively, a covenantal relation demands love (חסד) and loyalty (אמונה): "For I desire steadfast love, and not sacrifice, the knowledge of God rather than burnt offerings" (Hos 6:6). To act in faithfulness and love in a covenant is to act righteously, of course, so that it is not surprising to find righteousness language in occasional connection with חסד and אמונה.[43] Quite understandably, the demand for faithfulness and love appears at times with "righteousness" in reference to social relations.[44] Nevertheless, righteousness language is more often found in parallel with terms for rectitude or in opposition to terms for evil, expressing approbation or condemnation.[45] Contrastingly, terms such as חסד and אמונה, which carry associations of enduring friendship, appear with special prominence when a covenantal relation is in view. Just as a covenant is a particular kind of relation, righteousness takes the particular form of love and loyalty in a covenantal relation. All "covenant-keeping" is righteous behavior, but not all righteous behavior is "covenant-keeping." It is misleading, therefore, to speak of "God's righteousness" as his "covenant-faithfulness."[46] It would be closer to the biblical language to speak of "faithfulness" as "covenant-righteousness."

The common inversion of the biblical word-relations is not without its misleading effects. Once the further step is taken to reduce biblical usage of "covenant" to a simple promissory covenant, the characterization of God's

---

Kutsch, "Bund," *TRE* 7.397–410; M. Weinfeld, "ברית," *ThWAT* 1.782–808.

[43] E. g. Ps 40:11; 88:12–13; 103:17; 143:1–2.

[44] E.g. Isa 11:5; 16:5; 59:4; Jer 9:23; Hos 10:12.

[45] See the references above in footnotes 22, 23, 24. Note the frequent contrast between the צדיק and the רשע.

[46] As does, again, Ziesler, *The Meaning of Righteousness*, 28. The German expression "Gemeinschaftstreue" is a bit better, because it is broader, but it tends to suggest Cremer's confused notion of a relation which provides its own norm.

saving action as "righteousness" is fully explicable in a syllogistic manner.[47] God is "righteous" because he has promised to save, a promise which he has fulfilled or yet will fulfill.[48] This reading comes remarkably close to Ritschl's idealistic conception, and ignores Cremer's insight into the implicit involvement of punitive action in God's "ruling and judging," not to mention the instances in which God's righteousness is associated with retribution.

Secondly, a more fundamental explanation of the infrequent collocation of righteousness and covenant language emerges from the work of Schmid to which we have referred. If, as he argues, righteousness language in the Hebrew Scriptures has to do in the first instance with God's ordering of creation, its relative distance from covenantal contexts is entirely explicable. In favor of this conclusion, we may point not only to the infrequent collocation of "righteousness" with "covenant," but also to the remarkable frequency with which "righteousness" is associated with the vocabulary of "ruling and judging," especially the root שפט. The צדק-root and the שפט-root are found in close proximity (i.e. within five words of one another) in 142 contexts, a dramatic contrast with the usage of ברית. Since kingship obviously includes the making of "covenants," it is not surprising that "ruling and judging" sometimes has to do with a covenant with Israel (and with David, in particular): occasionally "righteousness" and "covenant" appear together in larger literary units (e.g. Ps 50; Ps 89). At root, however, the biblical conception of kingship bears a universal dimension, as is apparent in its various aspects and developments: in the connection between ruling and wisdom, in the hope for all-embracing justice by means of God's rule, and in the messianic ideal.[49] The frequent association of "righteousness" language with "ruling and judging" therefore strongly supports Schmid's claim that in biblical thought "righteousness" has to do with creational theology.

This view receives obvious support from a number of biblical ascriptions of righteousness to human beings. In Genesis, righteousness is attributed to Noah and to Abraham prior to God's establishing a covenant with either of them.[50] Likewise, God might have found a few righteous ones in Sodom and

---

[47] The term ברית is thereby subject to the same abstract treatment that is imposed upon צדקה. When scholars speak of "God's covenant faithfulness" do they make reference to the Sinaitic, Abrahamic, Davidic, or Noachic covenant, or something else? Is it historically and theologically legitimate to collapse all of the biblical covenants into one? One can hardly overlook the fact that in three of the seven contexts in which צדק-terms appear with ברית a retributive divine righteousness seems to be in view (Ps 50:1–5; Dan 9:4–7; Neh 9:32–33).

[48] This interpretation of "God's righteousness" has become a commonplace among New Testament scholars. For only one example among many see James D. G. Dunn, "The Justice of God: A Renewed Perspective on Justification by Faith," *JTS* 43 (1992): 16–17.

[49] E. g. Ps 2; Pss 93–100; Isa 2:1–22; Prov 31:1–9.

[50] Gen 9:8–17; 15:7–21. Their "righteousness" is described in different ways. Noah is a צדיק, blameless in his generation (Gen 6:9), while Abraham has righteousness (צדקה)

Gomorrah (Gen 18:22–33). Neither Job nor Noah are Israelites, even though they are named along with Daniel as exemplary righteous ones who might deliver themselves from divine judgment by their righteousness (Ezek 14:14, 20). And, of course, the running contrast between the righteous and the wicked in Proverbs is tied to universal wisdom, rather than to a covenant with Israel. It seems quite clear that the biblical understanding of righteousness has to do in the first instance with the context of creation, not that of covenant.[51]

This creational context of the administration of justice in the Hebrew Scriptures both illumines and delimits Cremer's claims regarding the concreteness and salvific character of righteousness language. For the biblical writers, the demand for social justice derives from God, the divine king, who has determined to secure the good and beneficial order of creation.[52] We might more properly say that the biblical writers again and again anticipate God's intervening to reinstate right order in a world in which evil for a season prevails.[53] Perhaps because of the prevalence of oppression and injustice in the world, and because of underlying notions of the goodness of the proper created order, "righteousness" language takes on a positive or salvific sense in juridical settings, including the well-known references to a saving "righteousness of God," Cremer's *iustitia salutifera*.[54] Furthermore, administration of justice in the biblical contexts, as in the ancient world

---

"reckoned" to him (Gen 15:6).

[51] On the current discussion of creation theology, see the thoughtful survey by Patrick D. Miller, "Creation and Covenant," in *Biblical Theology: Problems and Perspectives* (ed. S. Kraftchick, et al.; Nashville: Abingdon, 1995), 155–68.

[52] E.g. Ps 72:1–3; 85:9–13; 89:14; 97:1–2, and Isa 40–66 passim. See also Weinfeld, *Social Justice in Ancient Israel*, 19, who points to three foundational loci where divine kingship is celebrated: the creation, the exodus, and the time of universal redemption.

[53] See on this theme Hans Heinrich Schmid, "Schöpfung, Gerechtigkeit und Heil: 'Schöpfungstheologie' als Gesamthorizont biblischer Theologie," *ZThK* 70 (1973): 1–19 = Schmid, *Altorientalische Welt*, 9–30. Here we would wish to add a significant element to Schmid's thesis. The establishment of justice at points in the "apocalyptic" sections of the Hebrew Scriptures transcends the restoration of order to the world: there is a reduction *ad nihilum* in which Yahweh's role as God and Creator is reasserted (e.g. Isa 51:6). It is unlikely that the theme of Yahweh's transcendence entered into Israel's understanding of "righteousness" only at a late period (e.g. Exod 9:27). As a consequence, the uniqueness of Israel's faith stands out far more clearly than Schmid allows. At the same time it must be said that Nicholson's thesis, that an earlier Israelite nationalistic understanding of world order came to be corrected by and reconciled with broader conceptions of moral order in the world in the concept and (eventually) the language of "covenant" is not convincing (*God and His People*, 191–217). Righteousness language is too strongly attached to the righting of social injustice from the start to suppose that it represented a confirmation of the *status quo* which required subsequent correction.

[54] E.g. Isa 41:10; 46:13; 48:18; 51:5–6; 56:1; 58:8; 59:16–17; 60:17; 61:10–11; 63:1; Ps 98:2.

generally, is simultaneously judicial, legislative and executive.[55] This joining of the judicial and executive functions, with the salvific associations that we have noted, goes a long way toward explaining much of the biblical usage, as may been seen, for example, in the use the *hip 'il* stem of the verb צדק, which usually signifies the act of vindication, e.g.:

> . . . act and judge your servants, condemning the guilty (להרשיע), by bringing his conduct upon his head, and vindicating (להצדיק) the righteous, by rewarding him according to his righteousness (1 Kings 8:32).[56]

Here the pronouncement and execution of justice are joined, as is the case for the antonym הרשיע.[57] Likewise, the expression "to do justice and righteousness" (עשה משפט וצדקה, 13x), which usually describes the governing activity of kings, has to do with the restoration and preservation of social justice, in a positive and active sense, and not merely with personal piety or the avoidance of evil deeds.[58] Since the execution of justice comes into view in contexts where "judging and ruling" are in view, it is also understandable that ideas of power and authority, and even battle, are associated with צדק-terminology, as is the case with one of the earliest references to divine righteousness in the song of Deborah:

> They shall recount the vindicating acts of Yahweh (צדקות יהוה), vindicating acts (צדקות) of his peasantry in Israel (Judg 5:11; NRSV).[59]

The task of establishing justice belonged first and foremost to Yahweh, then to the king (or "judge" in the premonarchical period),[60] and then in other ways to all the people, especially the socially powerful.[61] Consequently, this

---

[55] In addition to Weinfeld, *Social Justice in Ancient Israel*, and Whitelam, *The Just King*, see Herbert Niehr, *Herrschen und Richten: die Wurzel špt im Alten Orient und im Alten Testament* (FB 54; Würzburg: Echter, 1986).

[56] Exod 23:7; Deut 25:1; 2 Sam 15:4; Ps 82:3; 2 Chr 6:23.

[57] For further examples of this use of הרשיע see 1 Sam 14:47; Isa 50:9; 54:17; Ps 37:33; 94:21; 106:6. On this account, the suggestion that הצדיק is a "delocutive verb," meaning roughly "to say that someone is in the right" is not adequate. Cf. Delbert R. Hillers, "Delocutive Verbs in Biblical Hebrew," *JBL* 86 (1967): 320–24.

[58] E.g. "deliver the one who has been robbed, do not mistreat the stranger, orphan or the widow, do not shed innocent blood" (Jer 22:3; cf. Jer 23:15–16; Ezek 18:5–6). The social dimensions are inherent in the specifically royal settings, e. g. David ruled (מלך) over Israel and "did justice and righteousness for all his people" (2 Sam 8:15; cf. 1 Kgs 10:9; 1 Chr 18:14; 2 Chr 9:8).

[59] Cf. Deut 33:21, and see other instances in which authority or power is in view, e.g. Isa 9:6–7; 41:10; 50:8–9; 51:6–8; 54:11–17; Prov 31:9; Ps 45:3–5.

[60] It is Whitelam's burden to show that Israelite kings exercised *legislative* power, precisely by their judging, e.g. 1 Sam 30:22–25.

[61] E.g. Gen 18:19; Ezek 18:5–9; Isa 58:1–12; Prov 31:9.

juridical background substantially explains the frequent association of the vocabulary of "salvation" or "deliverance" with that of "righteousness."

The feminine noun צדקה appears especially frequently in these instances, most likely due to a slight difference between its semantic field and that of the masculine form צדק. The feminine tends to refer to a concrete thing such as a righteous act or vindicating judgment. The masculine usually signifies the more abstract concept of "right order," or "that which is morally right." Although some scholars have expressed doubt about the validity of this distinction, or have underplayed its significance, there are strong reasons for preferring it unless a particular context should dictate otherwise. In the first place, as Jepsen has observed, it is unlikely that two different words should bear the same sense.[62] Or, to qualify this statement slightly, it is highly improbable that two words will have exactly the same field of meaning: in some contexts they will differ from one another. Bo Johnson has given precision to this claim, by observing that in Hebrew feminine nouns often represent some concretion of a corresponding masculine substantive, and sometimes bear a (concrete) individualized sense in relation to a corresponding collective masculine form.[63] Certain features of the usage of צדק and צדקה reinforce these considerations, particularly the use of צדק as a "characterizing genitive," a function which צדקה never performs.[64] Likewise, צדק appears 14x immediately following שפט ("to judge righteously"), but never צדקה. Conversely, עשׂה צדקה occurs 24x ("to do righteousness"), while עשׂה צדק only twice. Further משפט וצדקה appears 26x ("righteousness and just judgment"; also צדקה ומשפט 3x) but צדק is found with משפט only in the formulation משפט צדק (9x, "righteous judgment"). These variations in collocation suggest that צדק usually functions as an abstract, while צדקה as a concrete. We may add the further observation that often צדקה signifies an "act of vindication" and in these instances most likely represents a nominalization of the *hip'il* stem of the verb.[65] Individual contexts may vary, and there might be a tendency for צדק to take on a concrete sense in the later writings (anticipating the shift of צדקה to the

---

[62] Alfred Jepsen, "צדק and צדקה im Alten Testament," *Gottes Wort und Gottes Land* (ed. Henning Graf Reventlow; Göttingen: Vandenhoeck & Ruprecht, 1965), 78–79.

[63] Bo Johnson, "Der Bedeutungsunterschied zwischen ṢĀDĀQ und ṢEDAQA," *Festschrift Gillis Gerleman* (ASTI 11; ed. Sten Hidal, et al.; Leiden: Brill, 1978), 31–39.

[64] E.g. Lev 19:36 (balances, weights, ephah, hin); Deut 25:15 (weight, measure); Deut 33:19 (sacrifices); Ezek 45:10 (scales, ephah, bath); Job 31:6 (scales); Prov 16:13 (lips); Ps 118:19 (gates).

[65] Note that the verb is relatively infrequent (44x) in comparison with the nominal forms, particularly צדקה (157x). A similar relation appears to exist between the verb הרשׁיע and some of the usage of its nominal counterpart רשׁעה. See Deut 9:4–5; Isa 9:17; Ezek 5:6; Mal 1:4; Prov 13:6.

sense of "almsgiving"),[66] but apart from definite evidence to the contrary the distinction between צדק (abstract) and צדקה (concrete) may be assumed.

This distinction in usage sheds light on the debated matter of a punitive divine righteousness. Despite the inevitable exegetical debates associated with some of these texts, in my judgment there are approximately 15 instances in the Hebrew Scriptures in which God's righteousness is conceived in retributive or punitive terms.[67] Not surprisingly, all these occurrences appear in juridical contexts.[68] Nine of these 15 examples involve confessions in which God is described with the adjective צדיק.[69] Six of these nine have basically the same form: a guilty party who has suffered divine punishment confesses, "Yahweh is righteous" (יהוה הצדיק).[70] The examples from the biblical literature are familiar: Pharaoh's confession after the plague of hail takes this form (Exod 9:27), as does the lament after the destruction of Jerusalem (Lam 1:18). Rehoboam and the "princes" likewise make this confession after Shishak captures the cites of Judah (2 Chr 12:6). The same confession appears concerning the exile in Neh 9:33 and Dan 9:7, 14. Although this usage is concentrated in the later biblical writings, the language and form cannot be said to be late, since we find it already in Exod 9:27. It appears that we here have to do with a *Gerichtsdoxologie*, comparable to Achan's confession of guilt in Josh 7:19–21.[71] Three further texts in the Psalms describe God as righteous (צדיק) in his role as judge who rewards the righteous and punishes the wicked.[72] Once the abstract noun צדק appears (Ps 50:6). The concentration of the adjective צדיק in these examples is highly instructive, particularly in light of the judgment that צדקה generally refers to a concrete act or thing and may often represent a nominalization of the verb. In fact, it is precisely the texts which speak of righteous deeds of God (צדקה

---

[66] So Jepsen, "צדק and צדקה im Alten Testament," 80.

[67] Exod 9:27; Ps 7:10; 7:12; 11:5–7; 50:6; Isa 1:27; 5:15–16; 10:22; 28:17; Lam 1:18; 2 Chr 12:1–6; Neh 9:33; Dan 9:7; 9:14; 9:16. There are approximately 64 instances in which a saving righteousness of God appears. The usage is obviously weighted, but not overwhelmingly so.

[68] At least two of the contexts are cultic-forensic: Ps 11:5–7 and Isa 5:15–16.

[69] See Pietro Bovati, *Re-Establishing Justice: Legal Terms, Concepts and Procedures in the Hebrew Bible* (trans. Michael J. Smith; JSOTSup 105; Sheffield: JSOT, 1994), 103. Bovati fails to note, however, that the confession of God's righteousness often appears subsequent to the divine punishment meted out.

[70] Exod 9:27; Lam 1:18; 2 Chr 12:1–6; Neh 9:33; Dan 9:7. Dan 9:14 takes a different form, but should be understood in the same way. See also Isa 41:26. The legal papyri found at Elephantine contain similar usage of the adjective and the aphel verb. See A. Cowley, *Aramaic Papyri of the Fifth Century B.C.* (Oxford: Clarendon, 1923), 22–23, 30–31, 147–8 (Papyrus 8, line 22; Papyrus 10, line 19; Papyrus 44, line 6).

[71] On this form see Christian Müller, *Gottes Gerechtigkeit und Gottes Volk: Eine Untersuchung zu Römer 9–11* (FRLANT 86; Göttingen: Vandenhoeck & Ruprecht, 1964), 58–59; von Rad, *Theologie*, 1:355 = *Old Testament Theology*, 1:357–358.

[72] Ps 7:10; 7:12; 11:5–7.

or צְדָקוֹת) in which a punitive sense might be debated, since God or his
purposes are vindicated in the action contemplated.[73] We find then a lexical
distinction: the biblical writers often use צְדָקָה when speaking of a vindicating act of God (probably a nominalization of the verb), and the adjective צַדִּיק
(derived from the abstract) when signifying a retributive justice of God. It
may be that Cremer, von Rad and others failed to find a punitive divine
righteousness because they too closely associated the concept of righteousness with the feminine noun. The difference in meaning between the noun and
the adjective should not be unexpected: in the Hebrew Scriptures in all but
one instance צַדִּיק is used of persons,[74] while, as we have observed, the use
of צְדָקָה is weighted toward description of action.

We may also conjecture that the relative frequency of the idea of a *iustitia
salutifera* stems in part from the concreteness which characterizes much of
the biblical usage: promises of God's intervention to "right" the wrongs in
this fallen world stand at the center of biblical interest. This perspective does
not exclude the divine recompense of the wicked, it rather presupposes it, as
Cremer saw. Consequently it is not surprising that in certain biblical narratives
of divine contention with human beings, those who experience retribution
confess not merely God's triumph over them, but his righteousness. For this
reason, too, it is possible for biblical writers to speak of God as a righteous
judge who punishes the wicked (Ps 7; 11).[75]

When we turn to extrabiblical Jewish writings from the period of the return
from exile until the promulgation of the Mishnah, the task of analyzing the
terms for "righteousness" becomes exceedingly complex. In the first place,
Aramaic becomes the common language. Hebrew itself takes on new usages,
including significant ones in the relational and forensic realms. To complicate
matters further, a number of important witnesses to Hebrew or Aramaic usage
from this period are preserved only in Greek, Latin, or perhaps Syriac or an
Ethiopian dialect. In brief, Judaism and Jewish writings become exceedingly
diverse. The Aramaic of the Elephantine papyri is not the Hebrew of the
Qumran community (nor of the Aramaic writings preserved there), which
again is different from Mishnaic Hebrew. In so far as it is possible, the word-
fields of parallel and opposing terms must be plotted for each body of

---

[73] Isa 1:27; 5:15–16; 10:22; 28:17; Dan 9:16.

[74] The single exception is the plural form found in Deut 4:8.

[75] Accordingly an inner-biblical tension emerges between "saving justice" and "retributive
justice." Divine promises of saving righteousness *for* his people must somehow be squared with
his contention *with* his people. In some measure this tension is reflected in the rabbinical
description of God as צַדִּיק, which sometimes reflects his strict justice and sometimes his mercy
(following the traditional rabbinic description of God's attributes). On this theme see Benno
Przybylski, *Righteousness in Matthew* (SNTSMS 4.1; Cambridge: Cambridge University, 1980),
42–43.

writings. We cannot ignore, either, the continuing influence of the Scriptures themselves upon the language of the communities which used them. It is no wonder then, that we lack basic work in lexical semantics on the terms for righteousness in these materials. It is impossible in the scope of this essay to remedy this situation. Here we hope only to point out some deficiencies of some of the work that has been done in this field, and to make some general observations about the relation of this usage to that of biblical Hebrew. In doing so, we shall not make reference to Greek translations of Jewish writings, saving discussion of those for another essay (in the second volume of this set).

The failure to execute substantial lexical semantic work has meant that studies of righteousness language generally have been guided by the theological or ethical questions of the interpreters. David Hill's 1967 treatment of righteousness language in the early Jewish materials is exceedingly limited, a mere eleven pages beyond his discussion of the LXX. This brevity is facilitated by Hill's presupposition of an immediate connection between thought and word-usage. His comments on Jastrow's description of the Aramaic noun זכות are indicative of this approach:

> The noun possesses four main senses: (i) acquittal, favorable judgment; (ii) doing good, blessing; (iii) the protecting and atoning influence of good conduct, merit; (iv) advantage, privilege, benefit. The pattern of thought suggested by this development of meaning would seem to be as follows: in order to win the favour of God, right conduct is essential; one's own righteousness may be supplemented by the merit achieved by others, which thus becomes a source of benefit or advantage to them.[76]

There is no attempt here to trace the development of language, simply theological speculation.

As we have indicated, Ziesler's 1972 discussion of the early Jewish materials is shaped by the misleading question as to whether verbal or nominal and adjectival forms are "ethical" or "forensic." His discussion leads prematurely to questions of righteousness and justification and merit, which cannot be decided on the basis of word-usage alone.[77] Granted, there is a certain tendency in early Jewish writings to use righteousness language generally, that is, apart from a specific instance of "ruling and judging." There might be more ground here than in the biblical writings for drawing a distinction between ethical and forensic usage. But particularly in the Qumran writings the boundary between the two seems indistinct, as for example in 1QS 10:11:

> And I will affirm his judgment (משפטו) according to my perversity, and my transgressions are before my eyes as an engraven statute. And to God I will say "My

---

[76] Hill, *Greek Words and Hebrew Meanings*, 117.
[77] Ziesler, *The Meaning of Righteousness*, 70–127.

righteousness (צדקתי)!" and to the Most High, "Well of my good, spring of knowledge, spring of holiness!"

Here "righteousness" is associated with the "gift" of obedience and true knowledge of God, and at the same time stands in a clearly forensic context. Verdict and vindication are joined, as in biblical contexts.[78]

In his 1977 *Paul and Palestinian Judaism*, E. P. Sanders, too, is concerned primarily with particular theological questions rather than actual description of the usage of צדק-terms.[79] Only one of the several claims he makes in this context is related to word-meaning.[80] At the same time, although his approach bypasses linguistic questions regarding the field of meaning of צדק-terms, it must be said that he displays greater sensitivity to actual word-usage than does Hill or Ziesler.[81] One of his burdens is to show that the usage of זכה/זכא is differentiated, and that the word may not simply be translated by "merit" in every instance. He assumes, however, that at least in some instances זכה/זכא, in contrast to the צדק word-group, expresses the notion of a claim upon divine benefit or reward (if we may so characterize his usage of "merit").[82] This distinction over against צדק seems questionable, since we

---

[78] Cf. the admonition from the story of *Aḥikar*, "Bend not your bow and shoot not your arrow at the righteous (צדיק), lest God come to his help and turn it back on you" (line 126). See Cowley, *Aramaic Papyri*, 224. We leave aside here the question about a technical use of the expression "the righteousness of God" to signify "God's saving power," since we have discussed this matter elsewhere and current scholarship has largely moved away from the view that there was such a usage. Seifrid, *Justification by Faith*, 99–108. See John Reumann, "Righteousness: Early Judaism," *ABD* 5.739–740.

[79] E. P. Sanders, *Paul and Palestinian Judaism: A Comparison of Patterns of Religion* (Philadelphia: Fortress, 1977).

[80] With reference to זכה Sanders wants to show that 1) the rabbis did not regard "merits" as transferable to other persons, 2) that the "merits" of another "never counterbalance demerits at the (final) judgment." See *Paul and Palestinian Judaism*, 183. With reference to צדק-terms, he wishes to show 1) that righteousness is not ascribed to persons on the basis of their righteous deeds outweighing their evil deeds, 2) and that righteousness is not "equated" with earning or securing salvation. See *Paul and Palestinian Judaism*, 198. Although his treatment of righteousness language in early Jewish materials appears under two separate headings (he quite legitimately separates his discussion of the Tannaitic literature from that of the Qumran materials), he treats Qumran writings with the same basic questions he has in view in his discussion of צדק-terms in the Tannaitic materials. See *Paul and Palestinian Judaism*, 305–13.

[81] He raises the question, for example, of the meaning of זכה when it appears in opposition to חובה, and questions whether Marmorstein's translation of the former as "merit" is correct. Sanders prefers "innocence" (*Paul and Palestinian Judaism*, 187–8), since he takes חובה as "guilt." Yet Marmorstein discusses in far greater detail the terms which oppose זכות: a) חטא, b) עבירה, c) חובה. See A. Marmorstein, *The Doctrine of Merits in Old Rabbinical Literature* (Jews' College Publications 7; London: Jews' College, 1920) 5–11. Jastrow likewise glosses חובא/חובה as "debt" as well as "guilt" (citing Tg. Yer. I Deut 29:15; Tg. Isa 3:12). Further work is clearly necessary.

[82] See *Paul and Palestinian Judaism*, 188–90.

have quite early examples of צדק-terms used in the sense just suggested. Perhaps the most significant of these is the Aramaic petition to Bigvai, the Persian governor of Judea, for the construction of the temple in Elephantine, dating to the late fifth century B.C.:

> They shall offer the meal-offering and incense and sacrifice on the altar of God יהו on your behalf, and we will pray for you at all times, we, our wives, our children, and the Jews, all who live here. If they thus do (עבדו) in order that the temple might be built, it will also be righteousness to you (צדקה יהוה לך) before יהו the God of Heaven, more than one who offers burnt-offerings and sacrifice worth in value according to the value of a thousand talents.[83]

Here we have צדקה itself used at an early date in the sense of an acquired standing or benefit. A similar sense attaches itself to the use of צדקה in the now-famous 4QMMT C, line 31 (= 4Q398; to which, of course, Sanders did not have access):[84]

> And it shall be reckoned to you as righteousness, when you do what is right and good before him (i.e. God) . . .

In fact, in some instances the pairing of זכות and צדקה in the Tannaitic materials indicates that the latter was understood in terms of a claim to divine blessing, as for example in *m. 'Abot* 2:2:

> And all who work with the community – let them work with them for the name of Heaven, for the merit (זכות) of the fathers supports them (the community), and their [fathers'] righteousness (צדקתם) endures forever. And as for you (pl.) I confer upon you (pl.) great reward as if you (pl.) had done it (trans. by Neusner, slightly modified).

There is an obvious parallelism between זכות and צדקה here, צדקה most likely appearing for the sake of a biblical allusion (e.g. Ps 112:9).[85] It is clear, then, that from an early date the idea of a "saving benefit" is not simply associated with זכה/זכא but also with צדקה.[86] Apparently, the use of צדק-language for divine intervention and judgment became increasingly general-

---

[83] Cowley, *Aramaic Papyri,* 113 (Papyrus 30 line 27), 114, 117–118. On his transliteration of יהו as "Ya'u" see p. xviii. This text bears further significance in that it shows that at least in this period, "righteousness" was not restricted to the Jewish people. Even a pagan governor could enjoy righteousness before God. This conferral of righteousness is primarily due to the petition of the Jewish people, which functions more effectively than lavish sacrifices.

[84] Elisha Qimron and John Strugnell, *Qumran Cave 4: V, Miqsat Ma'ase Ha-Torah* (DJD 10; Oxford: Clarendon, 1994), 62–63.

[85] See also *m. Mak.* 3:16.

[86] We here leave open the question as to whether the "merit" of the patriarchs derives from their deeds or God's grace, or (more likely) both. Klaus Koch's article on the terms for righteousness in the Isaiah Targum give an indication of the amount of work yet to be done, "Die drei Gerechtigkeiten: Die Umformung einer hebräischen Idee im aramäischen Denken nach dem Jesajatargum," *Rechtfertigung: Festschrift für Ernst Käsemann zum 70. Geburtstag* (ed. J. Friedrich, W. Pöhlmann and P. Stuhlmacher; Tübingen: Mohr [Siebeck], 1976), 245–67.

ized, more attached to the expectation of universal final judgment, and perhaps for this reason came to overlap with terms for innocence and purity (זכה/זכא), which themselves underwent semantic change.

The single linguistic claim which Sanders makes deserves some consideration. He argues that both in the Tannaitic materials and the Qumran writings, righteousness does not have to do with earning or securing salvation. Instead, being "righteous" means that one is "in the covenant." Righteous behavior preserves one's status, but does not obtain it.[87]

Although Sanders's proposal relates to early Judaism and not to the Hebrew Scriptures, it is worth noting the considerable distance from the biblical usage which his claim involves. While early Jewish usage of "righteousness" language underwent considerable development, it is not clear that it changed uniformly nor that it changed in the way that Sanders argues. As we have seen, in the Hebrew Scriptures ברית is only rarely associated with righteousness language, and where it does appear notions of retribution for disobedience also frequently appear.[88] In terms of the biblical usage, it is not appropriate to speak of being "in the covenant" as in a metaphorical "sphere" of salvation. The expression בברית is relatively infrequent. Where it does appear it signifies the entrance into covenant responsibilities, not the enjoyment of saving benefits, e.g.:

> (You stand here) so that you might enter into covenant with Yahweh your God, and into the oath which Yahweh your God is making with you this day (Deut 29:11).[89]

We may freely grant that the Qumran writings frequently associate ברית with righteousness terminology.[90] Moreover, in the Qumran writings the covenant of the Community is regarded as salvific.[91] It is not clear, however, that Sanders's framework of interpretation holds even here. The Community regarded the covenant into which they had entered as the true will of God, which one was obligated to perform:

> . . . in order to receive all those who devote themselves to do the statutes of God into the covenant of faithful love (בברית חסד) for the Community in the counsel of God (להיחד בעצת אל) to walk perfectly before him . . . (1QS 1:7–8).

Salvation, although it comes from God alone, is found in obedience to God's requirements:

---

[87] See Sanders, *Paul and Palestinian Judaism,* 204–205, 312.

[88] Ps 50:1–6; Dan 9:4–7; Neh 9:32–33. See n. 40, above.

[89] See also 1 Sam 20:8; 1 Kgs 20:34; 2 Kgs 23:3; Isa 56:4, 6; Jer 34:10; Ezek 16:8; Ps 78:37; 2 Chr 15:12.

[90] See, e.g., 1QS 1:1–2:24; 10:1–11:22; 1QSb 3:23–24; 1QM 17:7–8; 18:8; CD 1:19–20; 3:15; 8:14; 19:27–31; 20:11; 20:29.

[91] E.g. 1QS 1:1–2:24; 1QS 10:1–11:22. Cf. CD 1:19–20; 3:15; 20:11; 20:29. Of course, the Damascus Document frequently speaks of the transgression of the former covenant.

> May he establish his steps to walk perfectly in all God's ways, just as (God) commanded the appointments of his appointed times, and not turn aside to the right or the left, and not transgress against any one of all his words. Then he will be pleasing with an atonement of soothing sacrifice (ניחוח) before God. And it shall be for him a covenant of eternal Community (1QS 3:9b–12).[92]

Even though saving divine intervention is still anticipated, the Qumran covenant does not save as a promise prior to and independent of obedience, but precisely *as* the "perfection of way" in which righteousness is found.[93]

Here we may call attention to an indication of such thinking which has been overlooked. Contrary to the usual transcription, there are strong reasons for reading 1QS 11:2–3 in the following way:

> For I belong to the God of my vindication and the perfection of my way is in his hand with the uprightness of my heart. And *with my righteous deeds* (צדקותי instead of צדקותו "his righteousness") he blots out (or shall blot out) my transgression(s), for he opened his light from the well of his knowledge and with his wonderful deeds he caused my eyes to see . . .[94]

Waw and *yodh* are indistinguishable from one another in 1QS so that some decision has to be made concerning the pronominal suffix. Orthographically, the first-person reading clearly is to be preferred: 1) the Qumran copyists generally preserve the distinction between the ‎ו‎- and ‎וי‎- endings, the latter being expected here for a third-person suffix;[95] 2) the next feminine plural noun in the same line has the full ending (נפלאותיו), so that the reading "his righteousness" involves the unlikely assumption that the copyist changed spelling practices midline; 3) since various nouns with first-singular endings appear in context, a full spelling seems necessary, if the copyist wished to avoid ambiguity (given the identical appearance of *waw* and *yodh*).[96]

---

[92] Jürgen Becker misses this idea in his treatment of 1QS, but comes closer to recognizing it in his discussion of the *Hodayoth, Das Heil Gottes: Heils- und Sündenbegriffe in den Qumrantexten und im Neuen Testament* (SUNT 3; Göttingen: Vandenhoeck & Ruprecht, 1964), 115–26, 149–55. With regard to the connection between righteousness and Torah (which Becker denies) see 1QS 1:3–5; 1:13; 1:26; 8:2 and the citation of 1QS 11:3 below. The inwardness of righteousness and its character as a gift do not diminish the connection to obedience.

[93] See also 1QS 1:1–20; 10:10–12. We must leave unaddressed the interesting question as to why the articular forms of the nouns צדק and צדקה appear with such frequency in the Qumran writings. The articular forms are rare in biblical Hebrew: only 3x each for צדק and צדקה, 4x of 6x in the construct state.

[94] See Mark A. Seifrid, *Justification by Faith: The Origin and Development of a Central Pauline Theme* (NovTSup 68; Leiden: Brill, 1992), 100–103.

[95] See Elisha Qimron, *The Hebrew of the Dead Sea Scrolls* (HSS 29; Atlanta: Scholars, 1986), 33–35, 59.

[96] 1QS 11:2: משפטי, דרכי, לבבי; 1QS 11:3: פשעי. Note the difficulty in deciding the reading of איריו in the same line. In light of the following נפלאותיו ("his wonders") it is probably to be taken as a third-person suffix.

The usage of the plural צדקות in the Qumran writings and the Hebrew Scriptures likewise favors the first-person singular reading. As we have seen, the feminine form noun צדקה generally signifies an action. Like the biblical authors, the Qumran writers remember and retell God's (past, plural) saving deeds of righteousness. This usage appears in the immediate context of our passage:

> My tongue shall continually recount the righteous deeds of God and the iniquity of human beings (1QS 10:23).

In contrast, when "God's righteousness" is a matter of present action or future hope, the singular form appears, expressing the particular act of divine judgment which the author awaits or already experiences.[97] Correspondingly, although the Qumran authors speak of the present experience or hope of cleansing by God's righteousness,[98] there is no instance in the Qumran writings (or Hebrew Scriptures) in which God's (plural) saving deeds of righteousness are said to purify from sin.[99] The wording of 1QS 11:3 probably reflects certain passages in Ezekiel (Ezek 3:20; 18:24; 33:13), where God says that he will not remember the righteous deeds (צדקותיו) of the righteous so as to forgive them.[100] The thought here comes very close to that of 1QS 11:3, since the inference lies close at hand, that God would forgive if he did remember these righteous deeds.

The idea that God would cleanse the Qumran psalmist with the psalmist's righteous deeds fits both the immediate context and the broader thought of the *Community Rule* very well. The removal of transgression (ימח, imperfect) for which the psalmist hopes is based upon what God has already done for the psalmist:

> For from the well of his knowledge, he has opened his light. And with his wonderful deeds he caused my eyes to see. And the light of my heart is in the mystery of that which shall be. . . . (1QS 11:3–4a)

---

[97] See for example, 1QS 11:14–16. 11QPs[a] is no exception to this claim. The author here repeatedly appeals for help from God "according to your mercy and your deeds of righteousness" (כרוב רחמיכה וכצדקותיכה; line 4–5; 10–11; cf. 7–8), *recalling* what God has done. Note, too, that the author uses the full ending including *yodh* with the plural, but not with the singular form in line 3 (צדקתכה), precisely in line with our observations on orthography above. The same may be said for 11QPs[b] frag. a 4, 6.

[98] E. g. 1QS 11:14; 1QH 11:30–31; 4Q370 2:2.

[99] Again 11QPs[a] is no exception. The psalmist remembers that God delivered him from death, not from the sin which brought him near to it. In fact, he subsequently appeals for forgiveness of sin (11QPs[a] 9–11, 13–14).

[100] The plural reading צדקותיו in these texts which the Masoretes adopted is *clearly* early, since it is attested by manuscripts from the Cairo Geniza (Ezek 18:24) and by the Septuagint, Vulgate and Targums.

This revelation of the divine mystery gives the psalmist support and strength (1QS 11:4–5). It is this present possession which serves as the basis of his confidence of cleansing: *"For* from the well of his knowledge. . . ."

The wording with which the author introduces the statement in 1QS 11:3 is of considerable significance:

> For I belong to the God of my vindication and the perfection of my way is in his hand with the uprightness of my heart. And with my righteous deeds he blots out my transgression(s). . . . (1QS 11:2–3a).

On account of the working of God, the psalmist possesses "perfection of way" and "uprightness of heart." These expressions are not general references to piety. "Perfection of way" represents the essence of the life and worship of the Community.[101] It is this characterization of conduct which elsewhere in 1QS is named as a cultic offering:

> The offerings of the lips for judgment are a righteous, soothing sacrifice (כניחוח), and perfection of way a pleasing free-will offering (1QS 9:4–5).

These offerings, moreover, serve as atonement for "the guilt of transgression and the evil of sin" (1QS 9:4). In place of the temple cult, the praise of the Community and its "perfection of way" remove sin.[102] The hymn in which 1QS 11:3 appears begins with a reference to the sacrificial nature of praise: "With the offering of the lips I shall praise him" (1QS 10:6; see also 1QS 10:14). Given this setting and the connection between "perfection of way" and atonement, it is not at all surprising that the author speaks of "his righteous deeds" as the means by which God will cleanse him, particularly since elsewhere "doing righteousness" is associated with the atonement effected by the Community.[103] The author's statement in 1QS 11:3 represents nothing more than the conception of atonement which appears elsewhere, expressed in terms of righteousness. The influence of the book of Ezekiel on the reinterpretation of the cult in the Qumran community may explain why the language here comes close to texts in Ezekiel which speak of the possibility of forgiveness by means of righteous deeds.[104]

The thought of 1QS 11:3 remains firmly grounded in the saving action of God. The righteousness of the psalmist is given to him by God, in the life and worship of the community. It is no contradiction to this thought, that the

---

[101] See 1QS 3:10; 5:24; 8:25; 9:2; 9:4–5.

[102] On atonement by obedience in the Qumran community, see Georg Klinzing, *Die Umdeutung des Kultus in der Qumrangemeinde und im Neuen Testament* (SUNT 7; Göttingen: Vandenhoeck & Ruprecht, 1971), 93–106; Bernd Janowski, *Sühne als Heilsgeschehen: Studien zur Sühnetheologie der Priesterschrift und zur Wurzel KPR im Alten Orient und im Alten Testament* (WMANT 55; Neukirchen: Neukirchener, 1982), 259–65.

[103] 1QS 8:1–4.

[104] See Ezek 20:41; Klinzing, *Umdeutung des Kultus*, 106–42.

Qumran writers also speak of human beings as having no righteousness.[105]
The righteousness which they have is not theirs, but is found in the community which God founded.[106] Likewise, the various references to hope in or the
experience of God's righteousness (singular) in the context of 1QS 11:3 do
not make the reading we have offered less likely.[107] The point to be taken
from this reading of 1QS 11:3 is simply that for the Qumran community
covenantal forgiveness is found in the doing of God-given deeds of righteousness, not apart from them, as Sanders has claimed.

When we turn to the rabbinic materials, it becomes clear that ברית is used
in a far more complicated manner than Sanders's formulation might suggest.
Friedrich Avemarie recently has shown that the rabbis associate Israel's
election with the ברית given to Abraham and with circumcision, not with the
Sinai ברית and the Exodus.[108] Furthermore, the usage of ברית is exceedingly
diverse, and extends not only to the promise to Abraham (and Israel), but also
to Torah itself and its individual demands.[109] In addition, the rabbis most
frequently use ברית to signify "circumcision" as an act of obedience in
association with the Abrahamic covenant.[110] Consequently, Sanders's use of
the phrase "being in the covenant" to convey the idea of "participating in
salvation," does not fit the nature of rabbinic usage, since here again the idea
of obedience is often attached to ברית, as in the Scriptures.[111]

The same may be said concerning Sanders's assumptions concerning
"righteousness" language in the rabbinic materials. As is well-known, צדקה

---

[105] See, for example, 1QH 1:26–27; 4:29–32. The context of 1QH 7:17 (where the plural
form appears) contains too many lacunas to draw any firm conclusions about what it says.

[106] The *Rule of the Community* directly and unambiguously speaks of its members doing
righteous deeds (1QS 1:5, 4:9; 8:2) and names them as "sons of righteousness" בני צדק (1QS
3:20 – in this instance not 'Zadok').

[107] 1QS 11:5; 11:14. The psalmist also recounts God's righteous deeds according to 1QS
10:23.

[108] Friedrich Avemarie, "Bund als Gabe und Recht," *Bund und Tora: Zur theologischen
Begriffsgeschichte in alttestamentlicher, frühjüdischer und urchristlicher Tradition* (ed. F.
Avemarie and H. Lichtenberger; Tübingen: Mohr [Siebeck], 1996), 163–216.

[109] Avemarie, "Bund," 187–91.

[110] See, e.g. *m. 'Abot* 3:11; *m. B. Qam.* 1:2; *m. Ned.* 3:11.

[111] Furthermore, when Sanders speaks of the obligation of the righteous as "faithfulness to
the *covenant*," he has deviated from the rabbinic perspective, which placed emphasis on
submission to "the yoke of heaven," i.e. love and fear toward the one true *God*. See Urbach, *The
Sages*, 400–419; Friedrich Avemarie, *Tora und Leben: Untersuchungen zur Heilsbedeutung der
Tora in der frühen rabbinischen Literatur* (TSAJ 55; Tübingen: Mohr [Siebeck], 1996),
162–219. This faithfulness to God is to be manifest in actual obedience, which (it was assumed)
the human being had the ability to perform, not a mere "obeying the Law to the best of one's
ability." Cf. Sanders, *Paul and Palestinian Judaism*, 205, "Being righteous in the sense of
obeying the law to the best of one's ability and repenting and atoning for transgressions
preserves one's place in the covenant (it is the opposite of rebelling), but it does not *earn* it."

generally came to signify "almsgiving."[112] More relevant for our concern is the adjective צדיק, which the rabbis apply to those who give alms or who keep the commandments of Torah in other ways.[113] Sanders somewhat softens the standard of obedience thereby implied by describing צדיק as "the general term for one who is properly religious," preparing the way for his later statement that "the righteous are those who are saved."[114] It quickly becomes apparent, however, that the concept of a צדיק functions more narrowly than Sanders suggests. The term sets forth the ideal of obedience for the community, as is evident from its exceedingly rare application to contemporaries, and more frequent association with notable figures from the past.[115] From this perspective, the rabbis were able to speak occasionally of "the righteous among the Gentiles,"[116] and even to describe the animals who entered Noah's ark as righteous.[117]

Furthermore, it is quite clear that the rabbis could view God's righteousness in terms of a retributive justice applicable to all creation, as for example in *Sipre* Deut 307, where in various ways Deut 32:4 is applied to the final judgment, e.g.:

> *And without iniquity:* When one departs from this world, all his deeds will come before him one by one and say to him, "Thus did you do on such-and-such a day, and

---

[112] It is difficult to judge precisely why צדקה came to take the sense of "charity," or "almsgiving" in early Judaism. As Donald Gowan has observed, Ps 112:9 may have provided one of the sources for this usage. The early development of this usage is indicated by its occurrence in Tobit and Sirach, e.g. Sir 3:14; 3:30; 12:3; 16:14; 40:17; 40:24; Tobit 4:10–11. See also Klaus Berger's collection of references in "Almosen für Israel: Zum historischen Kontext der paulinische Kollekte," *NTS* 23 (1977): 180–204. This use of צדקה along with the association of צדק-terms with divine leniency in judgment reflect the salvific connotations of the biblical usage, but without the concrete juridical context.

[113] E.g. *Sipre* Deut. § 49; *m. 'Abot* 6:1; *m. Sanh.* 8:5; *m. Neg.* 12:5; *m. Mak.* 3:16. See Rudolf Mach, *Der Zaddik in Talmud und Midrasch* (Leiden: Brill, 1957), 14–31, 86–90.

[114] Sanders, *Paul and Palestinian Judaism*, 201, 204.

[115] See Asher Finkel, "Gerechtigkeit II: Judentum," in *TRE* 12:413–14. Saul Lieberman's observation is highly significant, "The old tombstones of Palestine do not crown their inhabitants with the title צדיק or δίκαιος. It is very instructive to note that the inscription on the tomb of one of the Rabbis in Jaffa reads זיכרונו לברכה ("His memory unto blessing") and does not quote Prov. X.7: זכר צדיק לברכה ("The memory of the righteous unto blessing")," *Greek in Jewish Palestine: Studies in the Life and Manners of Jewish Palestine in the II-IV Centuries C.E.* (New York: Jewish Theological Seminary, 1942), 69. There is an example of a diaspora tombstone with δίκαιος, but, neither צדיק nor δίκαιος has been found on the tombstones of Beth She'arim (Lieberman, *Greek*, 69, 71). See also Rudolf Mach, *Der Zaddik*, 242–5. In the Tannaitic material only Simeon, one of the members of the Great Synagogue is called צדיק (*m. 'Abot* 1:2; *t. Sotah* 13:7). Cf. Sanders, *Paul and Palestinian Judaism*, 201–2. Cf. CD 1:20, 4:7, in (probable) reference to the Teacher of Righteousness.

[116] Job, in particular, is named. See Ephraim E. Urbach, *The Sages: Their Concepts and Beliefs* (trans. Israel Abrahams; Jerusalem: Magnes, 1975) 412–413.

[117] See Mach, *Der Zaddik*, 14.

thus did you do on such-and-such other day – do you acknowledge these matters?" And he will reply, "Yes." He will be told, "Sign!," as it is said, *The hand of every man shall seal (it), so that all men may know his deeds.*

Just and upright is He: The man thereupon will justify the verdict and say, "Well I was judged," as it is said, *That Thou mayest justify (the judgment) when Thou speakest.*[118]

In the same section, the story of the martyrdom of Rabbi Ḥanina b. Teradion appears, a story which is paralleled in *b. 'Abod. Zar.* 18*a*. Sentenced to death by Rome for the study of the Torah, the rabbi, his wife and his daughter, acknowledge the justice of God's judgment upon them (את עליהם צידקו הדין) by quoting Deut 32:4 and Jer 32:19. In the account which appears in the Talmud, the idea of retributive justice is obviously at work. The rabbi had pronounced the divine name. His wife did not stop him. The daughter was guilty of enticing the attention of some noble Romans. As a result, the husband was burned, the wife put to death, and the daughter consigned to a brothel. It is likely that we have to do here with a traditional form, or even technical terminology.[119] We therefore have evidence of the continuing existence of the *Gerichtsdoxologie* which we saw in the biblical materials. Furthermore, it is clear that the rabbinic conception of "righteousness" could include personal conduct judged in terms of retributive justice.[120]

These uses of צדק-terminology make it quite clear that Sanders's description of "righteousness" as "(Israel's) covenant status" is inadequate. The rabbinic application of the title of צדיק to Gentiles indicates that for them, just as in biblical usage, righteousness terminology has to do with creational thought, not merely God's covenant with Israel. "Righteousness" obviously can be used with reference to conformity to divine demands, and not merely membership within Israel.[121]

---

[118] *Sifre: A Tannaitic Commentary on the Book of Deuteronomy* (trans. Reuven Hammer; New Haven: Yale University, 1986), 312.

[119] See the entries in Marcus Jastrow, "צדק" *A Dictionary of the Targumim, the Talmud Babli, and Yerushalmi, and the Midrashic Literature* (2 vols.; P. Shalom: New York, 1967), 2:1263.

[120] Sanders himself recognizes this usage, although he does not make anything of it (*Paul and Palestinian Judaism*, 198–9). I am indebted to Dr. Friedrich Avemarie for the reference to these passages, and to the theme of "confession of God's righteousness" in the context of the death of martyrs. Clearly this theme, and the associated conception of retributive justice in rabbinic thought deserves further exploration.

[121] In his monograph on the topic of righteousness, originally written as a dissertation under E. P. Sanders, Benno Przybylski is concerned to show that in both the Qumran writings and the Tannaitic literature "righteousness" is conceived as obedience, independent from and subsequent to the gift of salvation: *Righteousness in Matthew and His World of Thought* (SNTSMS 41; Cambridge: Cambridge University, 1980). He assumes that words represent "concepts," and consequently seeks for a "unified concept" from mere examination of the terms. See Przybylski, *Righteousness in Matthew,* 74–75. Consequently, he fails to see that Torah

As we have indicated above, the task of plotting the semantic field of righteousness terminology in the Hebrew Scriptures and early Jewish writings lies far beyond the scope of our study, and perhaps is not even feasible, owing to its complexity. Nevertheless, the works of Hill, Ziesler, and Sanders (along with others) are indicative of the need for greater sensitivity to the distinction between concepts and word meanings in the treatment of righteousness terminology.

More significantly, our observations call for a reassessment of recent interpretation of Paul's understanding of "the righteousness of God" and "justification" as God's "covenant-faithfulness" to Israel. The associations from the Psalms and Isaiah which Paul evokes by speaking of the "revelation of God's righteousness" (Rom 1:17) belong to creational thought. God appears in such texts as creator, lord, and king, who "rules and judges" the entire earth.[122] Naturally, he acts in faithfulness toward his people, contends with their enemies, and executes judgment on their behalf. Yet his acts of "justification" do not represent mere "salvation" for Israel, or even merely "salvation." They constitute the establishment of justice in the world which Yahweh made and governs. Indeed, they may be seen to entail his own justification as the true God over against the idols.[123] The nations are to anticipate that Yahweh will bring about justice for them, even as he has brought it about for Israel.[124] This perspective is apparent, for example, in Psalm 98:1–3, which speaks of Yahweh revealing his "righteousness" to the eyes of the nations. The psalm continues by calling on creation (the sea, the inhabitants of the earth, the rivers and mountains) to rejoice before Yahweh, the king, and to await joyfully his judgment of the earth "in righteousness and equity" (Ps 98:4–9). We have seen, too, that both in the Hebrew Scriptures and early Judaism the usage of righteousness language includes the idea of

---

itself, i.e. its very commands, could be regarded as the source of life, so that from the very start the dichotomy which he draws between "obedience" and "gift" is a false one: "the more Torah, the more life" (*m. 'Abot* 2:7). On this theme, see Avemarie, *Tora und Leben*, 376–445. The "gift of righteousness" need not simply mean, as Przybylski supposes, "imputed righteousness." The criticisms which we raised concerning Sanders's thesis above apply here as well.

[122] E.g. Ps 98:1–9; Isa 51:4–8. See also the references in n. 52 above.

[123] See Isa 41:10; 46:13.

[124] Consequently, in speaking of "God's righteousness" Paul does not correct a "covenantal" concept from the Old Testament or Jewish thought by making it universal, as Käsemann proposed. He rather takes up "creational" thought, which was already present. See Ernst Käsemann, "Gottesgerechtigkeit bei Paulus," *Exegetische Versuche und Besinnungen* (Göttingen: Vandenhoeck & Ruprecht, 1964), 181–93 = "The 'Righteousness of God' in Paul," *New Testament Questions of Today* (Philadelphia: Fortress, 1969), 168–82. Stuhlmacher has long recognized the creational context of righteousness language in Paul. See Peter Stuhlmacher, *Biblische Theologie des Neuen Testaments 1: Grundlegung, Von Jesus zu Paulus* (2d ed.; Göttingen: Vandenhoeck & Ruprecht, 1997), 327–41.

retributive justice. There are reasons for supposing that Paul's understanding of justification, too, involves notions of retributive justice. We must leave this topic, however, for the second volume.

15. The Pharisees Between "Judaisms" and "Common Judaism"

by

ROLAND DEINES[*]

1. Introduction

The fact that within the framework of the first volume of *Justification and Variegated Nomism*, an independent chapter on the Pharisees has been

---

[*] This essay developed during the time I was an assistant at the "Deutsches Evangelisches Institut für Altertumswissenschaft des Heiligen Landes" in Jerusalem. It is dedicated with heartfelt thanks to its Director, Professor Dr. Volkmar Fritz on the occasion of his 60th birthday, February 12, 1998. I am grateful to friends and colleagues Hans Bayer, D. A. Carson, Andreas Köstenberger, Eckhard Schnabel, Mark Seifrid, and Robert Yarbrough for the translation.

planned alongside the articles on the individual literary corpora (and none on the Essenes and Sadducees), shows that they continue to hold a special place within theological scholarship. The reason for this interest is readily understandable, precisely in the present work: Paul characterizes himself in Phil 3:5 as κατὰ νόμον Φαρισαῖος and thereby raises the question as to the meaning of this self-description. Yet the investigation of Paul the Pharisee is no isolated phenomenon of Pauline research. It rather forms an important link between him and Jesus, whose most significant interlocutors and opponents, according to the witness of all four Gospels, were the Pharisees.[1] Furthermore, the inquiry into the Pharisees and their place in Jewish society decides whether and what kind of a connection exists between them and a portion of the literature treated in this volume.

Anyone who understands Judaism in the period of the rise of Christianity as a conglomeration of many conflicting "Judaisms," can hardly attribute a dominating role to the Pharisees. Each represents then simply *one* form of "Judaism," which stood in competition with numerous others, but on the whole remained without a significant effect beyond its own circles. That is in large measure also the picture of the Pharisees presented by E. P. Sanders. But in contrast to most of the other representatives of this view, he proceeds from a unified "Common Judaism," yet one that is decidedly not shaped by Pharisaism.[2] It is however striking that his remarks concerning the relative lack of influence of the Pharisees appear, as a rule, in the summarizing sections of his works, that only qualifiedly correspond to the statements which appear in the historical overviews.[3]

---

[1] Cf. J. D. G. Dunn, "Mark 2:1-3:6: A Bridge between Jesus and Paul on the Question of the Law," *NTS* 30 (1984): 395–415 = *Jesus, Paul, and the Law: Studies in Mark and Galatians* (London: SPCK, 1990), 10–36; R. Deines, *Die Pharisäer: Ihr Verständnis im Spiegel der christlichen und jüdischen Forschung seit Wellhausen und Graetz* (WUNT 1/101; Tübingen: Mohr [Siebeck], 1997), 16–18.

[2] For debate with the image of the Pharisees as it is presented in *Jewish Law from Jesus to the Mishnah* (London/Philadelphia: SCM/TPI, 1990) and *Judaism: Practice and Belief: 63 B.C.E.–66 C.E.* (London/Philadelphia: SCM/TPI, 1992), see D. R. de Lacy, "In Search of a Pharisee," *TynB* 43 (1992): 353–72; J. Neusner, *Judaic Law from Jesus to the Mishnah: A Systematic Reply to Professor E. P. Sanders* (SFSHJ 84; Atlanta: Scholars, 1993); R. Deines, *Jüdische Steingefäße und pharisäische Frömmigkeit* (WUNT 2/52; Tübingen: Mohr [Siebeck], 1993) 19–21, 269–272, 280–282; R. Deines and M. Hengel, "E. P. Sanders' 'Common Judaism', Jesus, and the Pharisees: A Review Article," *JTS* 46 (1995): 1–70. A longer German version of the latter appeared in M. Hengel, *Judaica et Hellenistica: Kleine Schriften I* (WUNT 1/90; Tübingen: Mohr [Siebeck], 1996), 392–479.

[3] Cf. e.g. Sanders, *Practice*, 380–412. In this chapter the historical statements of Josephus are repeatedly relativized by questionable interpretations. Although in this section Sanders points to the important distinction between "the popularity of the Pharisees and their ability to control official and public events" (*Practice*, 389), he does not connect their "popularity" with a corresponding influence. The reason for this lack, in my estimation, is a contrived and overdone hostility to the position that "the Pharisees controlled all public activities" (so Sanders,

In this contradictory relation between Sanders's overviews and his summaries, a phenomenon from the older history of interpretation appears in a new form. In the traditional presentations of Jewish history of the Second Temple period, the Pharisees frequently were first described comprehensively together with the Sadducees and the Essenes (in dependence on Josephus, *Ant.* 13.171–3) in the framework of the reign of Jonathan (at the latest in the time of John Hyrcanus [on account of *Ant.* 13.288–98]), for which Josephus' summarizing reports of the groups provided the basis.[4] The report that was thereby obtained – particularly because of the use of *Ant.* 18.15, 17)[5] – led to ascribing to the Pharisees an uninterrupted, comprehensive influence upon the broad populace, the temple cult, and – in connection with *Life* 12[6] – also the political shaping of the Jewish community. It was thereby overlooked that through his reports of the groups, which he always fit into the context of situations of political transitions[7], Josephus wished to make clear that there

---

Jewish Law, 101). Similarly imbalanced, it seems to me, is A. J. Saldarini, *Pharisees, Scribes, and Sadducees in Palestinian Society: A Sociological Approach* (Wilmington: Glazier, 1988), 87–98, 90–91, 93–95, 102–3, 119–22, 155–6, 188.

[4] Along with *Ant.* 13.171–173, also 18.4–25; *J. W.* 2.117–166.

[5] *Ant.* 18.15: "As a result of these teachings [interpretation of the Law, predestination, continued existence after death, see 18.12–14] they counted with the people as the most persuasive, so that all the arrangements of divine worship, prayers as well as offerings, must be presented only according to their 'exegesis.' The inhabitants of the cities gave them such a glorious testimony, since they believe that they desire only the best in word and deed. The teaching of the Sadducees . . . nevertheless, has as good as no effect, and when they are required to fulfill an office, . . . they join with the Pharisees, since the masses otherwise would not endure them." On the exegesis of this and all other passages concerning the Pharisees in Josephus, Steve Mason, *Flavius Josephus on the Pharisees: A Composition-Critical Study* (StPB 39; Leiden: Brill, 1991) is to be closely consulted.

[6] "In the nineteenth year of my life I began to lead a public/political life, whereby I joined with the program of the Pharisees, which is comparable to that which the Greeks call Stoicism."

[7] First during the reign of Jonathan Maccabeus in the context of the Jewish sovereignty which had been regained (*Ant.* 13.171–3), then with the transformation of Judea into a Roman province after the deposing of Archelaus in A.D. 6 (*J. W.* 2.117ff. and *Ant.* 18.1ff.), in connection with the depiction of the rise of the "Fourth Philosophy" founded by Judas the Galilean (according to *Ant.* 18.4, 9–10 together with Zadok the Pharisee), which was the cause of the political destiny and the destruction of Jerusalem in A.D. 70. The new party is distinguished from the other three in such a manner that it is clear that with them Josephus describes the *main currents* among the people. The biographical notice of *Life* 9–12 has a different character, which points to the period between A.D. 51 and A.D. 55. A. J. Saldarini, *Pharisees,* 84–85, 119 presents these data in a somewhat reductionistic manner: "The Pharisees and Sadducees are mentioned at times of change, crisis, or transition in government because when power shifted they and many other social and political forces in Jewish society became active in the competition for power and influence." Similarly Sanders, *Jewish Law,* 101, when he presents the thesis, "The Pharisees were predominant *only* when Josephus says they were" (emphasis mine). It is solely the presupposed "dogma" of "many other social and political forces in Jewish society" alongside the ones named by Josephus, that requires that the Pharisees (and

was *no* monolithic, united Jewish society, that, on the contrary, the internal tensions could be understood only when one took into account these distinctions.

In the historical presentations that were constructed according to this pattern, that which Morton Smith insisted upon with respect to Josephus himself was repeated,[8] namely, that Josephus' following report of history did not provide support for his insistence upon almost complete dominance by the Pharisees.[9] He did, however, give evidence of an ongoing striving for influence by the Pharisees, which in the long run was not without success – a matter with which Smith and his disciples did not deal sufficiently. The perspective of Josephus, who stood at the end of this development and formed his summaries from this standpoint, became the *stumbling-block of modern historiography*, in that it allowed itself to be misled by the framework of Josephus to define summarily the Pharisees and their place in society at the latest by the time of John Hyrcanus. The break with the subsequent presentation is thereby programmed in advance, since in reference to the Pharisees the heading for the period beginning at the end of the second century B.C. can only be: *the ever-changing struggle for social significance*, and recognition of the form of Judaism that they propagated. This form of Judaism may be summarized as the view that the holy Scriptures and the traditions of the fathers formed a unity. Both together constituted the precondition for a God-pleasing life in conformity with the covenant for the whole people.[10]

Sadducees) be regarded finally as a "minor factor, or better, one of a large number of forces which made up Jewish society" (Saldarini, *Pharisees*, 120). For Josephus, clearly, there were apart from the mentioned three (or four) groups together with the official authorities (the Romans, the high priests, and the leading representatives of the people, of which the last two groups are strongly influenced by Sadducean and Pharisaic interests) no socially influential groups that determined the spiritual and political climate of Palestine lastingly and enduringly.

[8] M. Smith, "Palestinian Judaism in the First Century," *Israel: Its Role in Civilization* (ed. Moshe Davis; New York: Seminary Israel Institute of the Jewish Theological Seminary of America; distributed by Harper, 1956), 67–81 (esp. 77). Also in *Essays in Greco-Roman and Related Talmudic Literature* (The Library of Biblical Studies; ed. Henry A. Fischel; New York: Ktav, 1977), 193–7 (esp. 193).

[9] Whereby Smith likewise misinterprets the reports of Josephus, in that he presupposes that *Ant.* 18.15–17 serves as a sort of bracket for the entire span of Pharisaic activity. Furthermore *Ant.* 18.15–17 does not have to do with political power, rather with influence upon society in the formation of the national religion: Josephus mentions only "prayer and offering," which according to his reports the Sadducees practiced in agreement with Pharisaic teaching.

[10] Cf. *Ant.* 13.296–7, 408; Mark 7:1–5 par. Matt 15:1–11; 23:2–3; *m. 'Abot* 1:1ff. In this respect it has to do with a fullness of traditions, which had grown out of centuries-long practice and interpretation of the Law. They represent what appeared important to the Pharisees beyond the actual biblical words themselves. The sources for this tradition are the close study of the Scripture *(J.W.* 2.162) as well as thoughtful reflection upon it *(Ant.* 18.12; in my estimation that is an indication of the presence of the wisdom tradition within Pharisaism), and the prior model of the teachers *(Ant.* 18.12; cf. in contrast the Sadducees, *Ant.* 18.16). On παράδοσις as the

In the most recent history of interpretation, however, precisely the opposite portrait has emerged: the Pharisees are defined *a priori* as one of many groups competing with one another.[11] Nevertheless, when the historical course of events is presented, the Pharisees appear as the most clearly recognizable and socially active group over the entire span of time.[12] The matter is decided, however, in favor of the *a priori* assumption of their marginal position in society. A break in the presentation results, which has as its point of departure not the sources themselves, but rather at the very best a theory about the sources, or alternatively, a theory about the sociological structure of traditional societies.[13] With E. P. Sanders this new approach expresses itself in *Judaism: Practice and Belief*, in which he first presents all the shared forms of "Common Judaism," and intentionally postpones the

---

decisive characteristic of the Pharisees see Günter Stemberger, *Pharisäer, Sadduzäer, Essener* (SBS 144; Stuttgart: Katholisches Bibelwerk, 1991), 84–86, 89–90 [English edition: *Jewish Contemporaries of Jesus: Pharisees, Sadducees, Essenes* (trans. Allan W. Mahnke; Minneapolis: Fortress, 1995)]; J. Neusner and C. Thoma, "Die Pharisäer vor und nach der Tempelzerstörung des Jahres 70 n. Chr.," *Tempelkult und Tempelzerstörung (70 n. Chr.)* (JudChr 15; ed. S. Lauer; Bern/New York: Peter Lang, 1994), 71–104, esp. 77, 96–98; M. Hengel and R. Deines, "Common Judaism," 17–41; furthermore, as fundamental to this topic, J. M. Baumgarten, "The Unwritten Law in the Pre-Rabbinic Period," *JSJ* 3 (1972): 7–29; A. I. Baumgarten, Korban and the Pharisaic Paradosis, *JANESCU* 16–17 (1984/85): 5–17; idem, "The Pharasaic Paradosis," *HTR* 80 (1987): 63–77; D. R. Schwartz shows the importance of tradition in the Hillel tradition, "Hillel and Scripture: From Authority to Exegesis," in *Hillel and Jesus: Comparative Studies of Two Major Religious Leaders* (ed. J. H. Charlesworth and L. L. Johns; Minneapolis: Fortress, 1997), 335–62 (esp. 337).

[11] A. J. Saldarini, *Pharisees*, 10.

[12] Here also there is a misunderstanding to be avoided: Josephus did not compose annals, in which were recorded for every year the more or less important events, together with the persons involved, their official positions, and their social connections. Over long stretches of time, precisely in the first century A.D. he reports only summarily, or restricts himself to individual episodes. He has no interest in a continuous presentation of the Pharisees or other groups (with the exception of the "Zealots" in *J.W.*). Therefore it is wrong to conclude on the basis of the absence of mention of the Pharisees, in particular sections, that they had no influence on that period or had given up their struggle for influence. It is rather to be noted *where* Josephus says anything at all about social influences and forces. Here the Pharisees always stand in the foreground: in a punctiliar manner, to be sure, in agreement with his entire presentation, but nevertheless throughout the entire span of time. (Josephus' historical conception is, as is rightly emphasized again and again, oriented to the *official* authorities, that is, in this respect he writes out of a Roman perspective, to which the Pharisees belonged only through individual representatives.)

[13] It finally has to do with A. J. Saldarini's influential and important book. It appears problematic to me in any case, that here the structure of Jewish society is nearly without exception sorted out in sociological categories ("honor and shame"; "patron-client relations"), which are distilled out of various cultures ("agrarian empires"). It is not sufficiently taken into account in this all-encompassing model the extent to which the Jewish people had a particular history, tradition, and religion, *along with* that which they shared in common with others. This particularity of Judaism was apparent and noteworthy already to the ancient authors.

chapter concerning the parties. In the concluding chapter, "Who ran what?" he again stresses his introductory thesis: certainly not the Pharisees. As he says, "I have argued extensively that the Pharisees governed neither directly nor indirectly" (p. 459).[14]

A further characteristic of the current research on the Pharisees, which likewise is to be understood as a reaction against the older history of interpretation, is the rejection of all attempts to attribute individual texts from the area of apocryphal and pseudepigraphic literature to the Pharisees or other known groups, and correspondingly to depict their theology or piety.[15] On the contrary, it is stressed that every document must be treated and understood in itself, since every text contains its own form of "Judaism," which must not be brought into connection with one of the three groupings known from Josephus[16] too hastily (mostly the highly disparaging words "naive" or "uncritical" are used).[17] The *methodological* objection is entirely justified, since every text is in fact always to be investigated for itself. To remain at this point means, however, to refrain from understanding the context of the text, and thereby, in the end, from historical understanding itself.[18] None of these texts arose in surroundings free from history or tradition. Each, in its own way, participates in the religious struggle in the centuries before and after Jesus' birth. This judgment applies especially to texts with a polemic or appelatory aim. It places these texts in a relation to one another, and thereby

---

[14] One must agree with this statement, of course, since Sanders understands "governed" in the sense of official, politically-anchored exercise of power, which is not what Josephus and the other sources mean. It is always a favorite method of treatment to overstate the opposing position, in order to refute it the more easily. In this not only is Sanders a master, but also his counterpart J. Neusner, who caricatures Sanders's position with the words, "Sanders really thinks that any and every source, whoever wrote it, without regard to its time or place or venue, tells us about one and the same Judaism" (*Judaic Law*, 289). To this unjustified assertion he adds (here I can say only, to my greatest amazement) an objection against "Sanders's pan-Pharisaism" (*Judaic Law*, 279, and again 280). As a mere reminder of Sanders's actual view see *Practice*, 490: "Palestinian Judaism was a rich, diverse, multifaceted society, with a good deal of restless change."

[15] On the altered state of research see R. A. Kraft and George W. E. Nickelsburg, "Introduction," in *Early Judaism and its Modern Interpreters* (The Bible and its Modern Interpreters 2; eds. Kraft and Nickelsburg; Atlanta: Scholars, 1986), 1–30 (13–14). As an example of the continuation of this method into the present, see R. T. Beckwith, "The Pre-History and Relationship of the Pharisees, Sadducees and Essenes," *RevQ* 11 (1982): 3–46, and the justified criticism of G. Stemberger, *Pharisäer*, 97–98.

[16] See, e.g., L. Cansdale, *Qumran and the Essenes: A Re-evaluation of the Evidence* (TSAJ 60; Tübingen: Mohr [Siebeck], 1997), 194.

[17] On the usage of *Unworte* in the history of interpretation, by which differing approaches are defamed as not belonging to the standard of research, see R. Deines, *Pharisäer*, 9–13.

[18] This procedure appears to me like the attempt to comprehend the content of a mosaic solely by describing each little stone as carefully as possible. A colorful variety indeed results from this venture, but no comprehensive picture.

to the Pharisees, Sadducees, and Essenes as the most influential groups, which to Josephus seem alone worthy of mention (alongside the Zealots) – unless one wishes to proceed from a complete fragmentation of Judaism and a total isolation of the individual "Judaisms" of that period.[19]

The designation of the Pharisees and other groups as "sects" – which in recent literature is again current – strengthens this tendency to speak of individual Judaisms. For as a rule, "sect" is defined as a group that is largely closed off from outsiders; it is represented as having "a common, perhaps arrogant presupposition of being the true community of God in practice and belief."[20] In his "Glossary of Sociological Terms," Saldarini defines a sect as "a religiously based group which is either actively involved against society or withdrawn in reaction to it."[21] Neither possibility, in my view, fits the Pharisees, if sects are understood to be always "reacting against . . . society."[22] In his understanding of sect, Saldarini joins Bryan R. Wilson, who distinguishes seven different types of sects, "based on the group's relationship with its *host* society."[23] The expression "host society" already implies a distanced relationship that makes it impossible to understand a "sect" thus defined as an *integral part* of that society. Even if, as Saldarini does, one understands the Pharisees as "reformist," they were a solid element of Jewish society in which they sought to set in place certain convictions and goals. But they did not thereby react *against* the society, but helped to *shape* the society, and agitate *in* it and *for* it.[24] Albert I. Baumgarten fully explained this matter when he asked the question, "What Is a Sect?" His own comprehensive definition of a sect is at least broad enough to be suitable as well for

---

[19] See the basic and very good statement by E. P. Sanders, *Practice*, 8–9, "I think that the description of first-century Judaism according to the categories of surviving literature (apocalyptic, rabbinic, philosophical, mystical and the like) is an error" (p. 9). Nevertheless, he ascribes the *Pss. Sol.* and the *As. Mos.* to an "otherwise unidentifiable pietist or group of pietists" (p. 455).

[20] Th. R. Hatina, "Jewish Religious Backgrounds of the New Testament: Pharisees and Sadducees as Case Studies," in *Approaches to New Testament Study* (JSNTSup 120; ed. S. E. Porter and D. Tombs; Sheffield: Sheffield Academic, 1995), 46–76 (esp. 47). On the problem of the concept of "sect" with reference to the Pharisees, see A. J. Saldarini, *Pharisees*, 70–75, 123–7, 285–7.

[21] A. J. Saldarini, *Pharisees*, 309ff. (esp. 313).

[22] Ibid., 71.

[23] Bryan R. Wilson, *Magic and the Millennium: A Sociological Study of Religious Movements of Protest Among Tribal and Third-World Peoples* (London: Heinemann, 1973), 71 (emphasis mine).

[24] Cf. E. P. Sanders, *Jewish Law*, 240–42; *Practice*, 387, who likewise expresses himself against the classification of the Pharisees as a "sect." In this he is especially reacting against Neusner's understanding of the Pharisees as a "pure food club." So also K. G. C. Newport, "The Pharisees in Judaism Prior to A.D. 70," *AUSS* 29 (1991): 127–37 (esp. 137). Cf. also M. Hengel and R. Deines, "Common Judaism," 43–44.

describing the Pharisees: "I would therefore define a sect as a *voluntary association of protest, which utilizes boundary marking mechanisms – the social means of differentiating between insiders and outsiders – to distinguish between its own members and those otherwise normally regarded as belonging to the same national or religious entity.*"[25] So far as this applies to the Pharisees, I would replace "protest" with "reform," thereby pointing out (as Baumgarten in his book repeatedly says) that the "boundaries" were very unimposing compared to the other groups. The purpose of the associations of Pharisees was not to fence themselves off, but to mark themselves as a reform group within the society.

2. The Contested Place of the Pharisees in Current Research

This foregoing argumentation regarding the relationships among Pharisees, Sadducees, and Essenes can be rejected, however, by contesting the basic reliability of the portrait drawn by Josephus. In my estimation, one can distinguish three tendencies in this matter. First, the place of the Pharisees in society is reduced contrary to the witness of Josephus.[26] Second, the Sadducees – again in contrast with the witness of Josephus[27] – are increasingly shifted to the center of prominent focus,[28] not only as a politically but

---

[25] Albert I. Baumgarten, *The Flourishing of Jewish Sects in the Maccabean Era: An Interpretation* (JSJSup [earlier StPB] 55; Leiden: Brill, 1997), 5–15 (esp. 7).

[26] The starting point for this reduction is the already mentioned essay by M. Smith (see n. 8, above). It has been developed and popularized by J. Neusner, "Josephus's Pharisees," *Ex Orbe* Religionum (*Fs.* G. Widengren; SHR 22; Leiden: Brill, 1972), 224–44; Jacob Neusner, *From Politics to Piety* (2d ed.; New York: Ktav, 1979), 45–66; also L. H. Feldman and G. Hata, eds., *Josephus, Judaism, and Christianity* (Detroit: Wayne State University, 1987), 274–92 (now as: *Josephus' Pharisees: A Complete Repertoire*); also D. Goodblatt, "The Place of Pharisees in First Century Judaism: The State of the Debate," *JSJ* 20 (1979): 12–30. For criticism of this position see S. Mason, "Josephus on the Pharisees Reconsidered: A Critique of Smith/Neusner," *SR* 17 (1988): 455–69 (largely identical with S. Mason, *Pharisees*, 246–59, see also 193–5, 307–8; A. J. Saldarini, *Pharisees*, 128–32; G. Stemberger, *Pharisäer*, 22–23; P. Schäfer, "Der vorrabbinische Pharisäismus," in *Paulus und das antike Judentum* (WUNT 1/58; ed. M. Hengel and U. Heckel; Tübingen: Mohr [Siebeck], 1992), 125–72, esp. 148, 153–4, 163–4, 169–70; D. S. Williams, "Morton Smith on the Pharisees in Josephus," *JQR* 84 (1993/94): 29–42. Sanders's portrait of the Pharisees is strongly dependent upon M. Smith, to which is added a forced description of the statements of Josephus, which then are much more easily refuted: see, e.g., Sanders, *Jesus and Judaism* (Philadelphia/London: Fortress/SCM, 1985), 315, where he attributes to Josephus the opinion "that the Pharisees were leaders in the government of Israel." This idea cannot rightly be read out of *Ant.* 18.17 (see n. 9, above).

[27] A. J. Saldarini, *Pharisees*, 298–308; G. G. Porton, "Sadducees," *ABD* 5.892–5.

[28] E. P. Sanders, *Jesus and Judaism,* who identifies the Sadducees largely with the "chief priests" (p. 312), and attributes to them the sole political and religious authority (p. 197–8, 289, 315–6 and then constantly in *Practice,* 317–40); see also D. R. Schwartz, *Agrippa I: The Last*

also religiously dominating group. Third, the three- or four-fold division of Judaism that Josephus presupposes and describes is presented as a misleading simplification that does not do justice to the complex, variegated reality of Judaism.[29] By means of such arguments comes the claim that the majority of the Jewish people of Palestine belonged to none of the groups named.[30]

Decisive changes for the understanding of the Pharisees is the result. If for a long time they were reckoned without question to be the representatives of the mainstream of Jewish piety as it had developed from the days of the Hasmoneans, and the connecting element between the time prior to A.D. 70 and the subsequent beginnings of rabbinic Judaism, currently they are marginalized or thought to be a nearly indescribable entity.[31] In recent research a consensus certainly has not yet formed concerning their position within the Jewish people. The breadth of the opinions represented extends from modifications of the received *communiis opinio*[32] to a far-reaching denial

---

King of Judaea (TSAJ 23, Tübingen: Mohr [Siebeck], 1990), 116–30, on the time of Agrippa's reign.

[29] G. G. Porton, "Diversity in Postbiblical Judaism," in *Early Judaism and Its Modern Interpreters* (see n. 15), 57–80; K. Keith, "The Background of the New Testament: Diversity in First-Century Judaism and its Contemporary Implications," *LS* 17 (1992); 121–51; G. Boccaccini, "Middle Judaism and its Contemporary Interpreters (1986–1992): Methodological Foundations for the Study of Judaisms, 300 B.C.E. to 200 C.E.," *Henoch* 15 (1993): 207–33.

[30] Cf., *inter alios*, K. Keith, *Background*, 143; E. P. Sanders, *Jesus and Judaism*, 289; *Practice*, 11–12, 14, 29. If one thereby understands "solid" membership, that is naturally correct. Behind this argument frequently stands the image of the Jewish "sects" (see n. 19, above), which had at their disposal a firm internal structure. In contrast, I hold it far more probable that the Pharisees had no formal membership. Moreover, adherence to a political or religious program does not automatically mean "membership." Only a minority of the voters who elect political parties are formally members of those parties, although the degree of identification can be very high even among those who only vote.

[31] See A. J. Saldarini, *Pharisees*, 1; L. Gaston, "Pharisaic Problems," in *Approaches to Ancient Judaism* (SFSHJ 56; ed. J. Neusner; Atlanta: Scholars, 1992), 85–100; S. Mason, "The Problem of the Pharisees in Modern Scholarship," *Approaches to Ancient Judaism*, 103–140; K. Keith, *Background*, 143: "To embark upon a discussion of the contemporary study of the Pharisees is to solve a riddle which has no solution. The questions are so diverse, the methods employed so divergent and the opinions so divided, that one feels confident in stating only the minutest of conclusions."

[32] Marcel Pelletier, *Les Pharisiens: Histoire d'un parti méconnu* (Lire la Bible 87; Paris: Editions du Cerf, 1990); S. Mason, "Pharisaic Dominance Before 70 C.E. and the Gospels' Hypocrisy Charge (Matt 23:2–3)," *HTR* 83 (1990): 363–81; K. G. C. Newport, *Pharisees* (see n. 19); F. Siegert, "Le Judaïsme au premier siècle et ses ruptures intérieures," in *Le déchirement: Juifs et chrétiens au premier siècle* (MdB 32; ed. D. Marguerat; Genève: Labor et Fides, 1996), 25–65; H.-F. Weiss, "Pharisäer I.–II.," *TRE* 26.473–85. More strongly influenced by Sanders and Saldarini is C. Tuckett, "Les Pharisiens avant 70 et le Nouveau Testament," in *Le déchirement: Juifs et chrétiens au premier siècle* (MdB 32; ed. D. Marguerat; Genève: Labor et Fides, 1996), 67–95. E. Rivkin goes his own way when he sees in the Pharisees a party of scribes ("teachers of the Law") which revolutionized the Jewish religion:

of Pharisaic influence on the world it shared with other Jews.[33] Further, it is contested that the Pharisees elevated their form of religion to a norm for other Jews, and that consequently they were concerned that as many as possible live according to their injunctions.[34]

3. "Judaisms" or "Common Judaism"?

The discussion related to these matters took a turn through Sanders's much respected works concerning Judaism in the New Testament period. On the one hand, he proceeded from the critical stance of research into the Pharisees. On the other hand he attempted to place in the center of his presentation of Judaism that which was shared, rather than that which divided. The shared basis of Palestinian Judaism, which Sanders in a summary manner describes as "Common Judaism" in his large work on *Practice and Belief*, extends to the temple cult, and in connection with this, to the payment of taxes and tithes to the temple and the priests, as well as to the observance of the commandments, which are bound up with the ministry of the temple and the Sabbath. Beyond this, he treats circumcision, purity, food laws, benevolence and deeds of charity. Two shorter chapters present the "common theology" of early Judaism and "hopes for the future." Already this brief overview shows that Sanders presents Judaism in his self-chosen framework of time 63 B.C.–A.D. 66 (the boundaries of which certainly are not persuasive)[35] in the first place as a religion of the priesthood and temple. The connecting element among all the groups is the knowledge of the divine establishing of the priesthood and the temple cult in the Torah.[36] Sanders's basic conviction therefore is "that a

---

A Hidden Revolution: The Pharisees' Search for a Kingdom Within (Nashville: Abingdon, 1978); cf. R. Deines, *Pharisäer*, 184, n. 144 and the literature cited there which debates with Rivkin.

[33] See n. 26, above.

[34] According to E. P. Sanders, *Jewish Law*, 35, and passim, this is decidedly not the case. The Pharisaic tradition, as Sanders understands it, concerned matters internal to the group, which had no soteriological relevance for Israel as a whole. Whoever did not keep them, did not on this account become a "sinner." J. D. G. Dunn in particular has especially expressed himself against this view: "Pharisees, Sinners, and Jesus," *Jesus, Paul, and the Law*, 61–88 (see n. 1).

[35] R. Deines and M. Hengel, "Common Judaism," 52–53.

[36] My criticism and that of M. Hengel of his understanding of "Common Judaism" – in dependence on Morton Smith, "what the priests and the people agreed on" – need not be repeated here (see n. 2, above). We need only remind the reader that the Judaism of the Hasmonean period took an entirely different form from that of the Persian epoch, for which much less reservedly one might claim a priestly rule. Precisely the *miqva'ot* and stone vessels to which Sanders appeals are here characteristic: naturally they are found in priestly households, but their usage is not limited to them. Both give indication, as also the emerging institution of the synagogue and the burial practices in ossuaries, of a change in religious practice that goes

broad agreement on basic theological points characterized Judaism in the Graeco-Roman period" (p. ix). With this position he stands in opposition to the dominant tendency to split up the Judaism of this period into many "Judaisms" or "Judaic systems," which fought with one another, separated from one another, and were no longer in the position to communicate with one another. Sanders rightly calls into question this splintered portrait of Judaism, which in my view derives its persuasive power less from the ancient sources than from the current state of research, which is devolving into disparate, increasingly isolated, and numerous specialized disciplines.[37] He is therefore to be thanked for placing the concept of what was "common" to Judaism so prominently in the center of his works. What Sanders has persuasively shown is that Judaism is to be understood as *one* religion, and was perceived as such by outsiders. When Greek and Roman (and later also Christian) authors wrote about Jews or the Jewish religion, they and their readers associated concrete conceptions with it: at the visible level of "practice" (which therefore was more readily perceptible to outsiders) were Sabbath, circumcision, food laws, and the temple cult. At the level of matters more difficult to understand (and therefore more easily misunderstood) of "belief" were monotheism, exclusivity, and a particular ethic.[38] This outward

---

well beyond that which may be demonstrated for the period before A.D. 164. Those responsible for this new development were, however, not the priests, but in the first place, the Pharisees (and this presupposes a strong priestly element even within Pharisaism).

[37] S. J. D. Cohen, "The Modern Study of Ancient Judaism," in *The State of Jewish Studies* (ed. S. J. D. Cohen and E. L. Greenstein; Detroit: Wayne State University, 1990), 55–73, esp. 58–66, has described the course of more recent research, at the end of which stand "Judaisms" in place of "Judaism": "The argument that ancient Judaism was diverse and multiform has led to a readiness to read each document of ancient Judaism independently, to emphasize its distinctive characteristics, and not to homogenize it with other, related documents. Documents that previously had been read in the light of one another are now read as autonomous works endowed with their own peculiar viewpoint. Not only have the documents been separated one from the other, they also have been dissected" (p. 59). The increasing specialization of research has doubtlessly contributed to this atomization within the discipline of Judaic studies. Immediately at the outset of his essay, Cohen points to the "explosive growth" (p. 55) which the contributions to research have seen in the past 20 years, which makes it impossible for the individual to read everything. This dilemma – that currently alongside the established disciplines of the Old and New Testament and the rabbinic literature, a Qumran discipline, disciplines for the study of the apocrypha and the pseudepigrapha, and further for the study of Philo, Josephus and others, have emerged – is made into a virtue by the "separators," in that they interpret a partial aspect as a whole.

[38] E. A. Judge, "Judaism and the Rise of Christianity: A Roman Perspective," *TynB* 45 (1994): 355–68: Christianity was never viewed as Judaism, that is, there were clear conceptions and clear divisions. On the other hand, on the level of daily life, there was very much in common: see J. Lieu, "'The Parting of the Ways': Theological Construct or Historical Reality?" *JSNT* 56 (1994): 101–19; and idem, *Image and Reality: The Jews in the World of the Christians in the Second Century* (Edinburgh: T. & T. Clark, 1996).

appearance of Judaism changed only non-essentially in the course of the centuries. Nevertheless, it is not appropriate to see therein only a "transformed Israelite legacy," from which the various individual "Judaisms" constituted themselves.[39]

If therefore it is granted that Sanders is right that there was a common, effective, and binding element to early Judaism, which held all the currents together and enabled communication among them (and here in the first instance the temple cult is to be named), then the question presents itself as to what the roots of this "Common Judaism" are.[40]

A few of the main lines might be named here. Next to the composition of a whole series of Old Testament books, the sifting, collection, and final redaction of the books of the Old Testament canon took place in the post-exilic period. There must have been circles, therefore, in which these traditions were preserved and edited: one might name priestly, prophetic, wisdom, nomistic, and apocalyptic traditions as the main currents, without thereby indicating that segregation of these traditions from one another or opposition of these traditions to one another is intended. Especially the Deuteronomistic history shows the close association of prophetic and "nomistic" elements.[41] The Deuteronomistically inspired theology and piety continue in the post-canonical literature in such a manner that the main themes of Deuteronomistic thought are to be counted among the decisive roots of "Common Judaism," which then were especially cultivated by the Pharisees.[42] In contrast, the tradition of the priestly literature and the

---

[39] W. S. Green, "Ancient Judaism: Contours and Complexity," in *Language, Theology, and the Bible* (*Fs.* James Barr; ed. S. E. Balentine and J. Barton; Oxford: Clarendon/New York: Oxford University, 1994), 293–310; cf. also G. Boccacini, *Middle Judaism*, 209: "What Sanders discovers through his common-denominator analysis are the common cultural elements: the raw matter shared and used by different types of Judaism to build their different ideological systems."

[40] Cf., *inter alios*, M. Smith, who extends his presentation into the second century A.D., *Palestinian Parties and Politics that Shaped the Old Testament* (2d cor. ed.; London: SCM, 1987); previous ed.: New York/London: Columbia University, 1971). On the background of the Persian epoch, see the contributions in *Introduction: The Persian Period, CHJ* 1; further, J. J. Scott, Jr., "Crisis and Reaction: Roots of Diversity in Intertestamental Judaism," *EvQ* 64 (1992): 197–212.

[41] As an overview, cf. N. Lohfink, "Deuteronomistisch," *NBL* 1.413–4; and S. L. McKenzie, "Deuteronomistic History," *ABD* 2.160–68.

[42] Cf. O. H. Steck, *Israel und das gewaltsame Geschick der Propheten* (WMANT 23; Neukirchen-Vluyn: Neukirchener, 1967), 205–12: "Es muß neben der essenischen Gemeinschaft im palästinischen Spätjudentum zwischen 150 v. Chr. und ca. 100 n.Chr. *eine in sich durchaus komplexe, eschatologisch ausgerichtete und am vorfindlichen Israel im ganzen orientierte Umkehrbewegung* gegeben haben, in der die asidäischen Traditionen und so auch das dtr GB [= Geschichtsbild, picture of history] fortlebten" (212; emphasis original). To this movement he reckons *Pss. Sol., As. Mos., L.A.B.,* 4 *Ezra,* and 2 *Baruch,* therefore primarily texts that are frequently connected with Pharisaism (see Section 5.4, below). According to my

historical work of the chronicler appear to have developed no comparable strong, integrating, effect, although their significance for the general portrait of "Common Judaism" cannot be called into question. It appears, however, that the priestly-levitical theology that predominates in these texts represented rather an exclusive-elite tendency. To this strongly priestly-oriented tradition, however, the Qumran writings and the Essenes in their description by Josephus may be ascribed, and with qualification also the Sadducees.[43]

A decisive change took place, nevertheless, at least from the time of Antiochus IV Epiphanes, in which for the first time the common foundation of the Jewish people was placed in question through the responsible aristocratic and priestly circles.[44]

---

observations, Pharisaism was the primary factor in the repentance movement, which had as its goal the whole of Israel. Cf. on this topic also O. H. Steck, "Zum Problem theologischer Strömungen in nachexilischer Zeit," *EvT* 28 (1968): 445–58; J. Maier, *Zwischen den Testamenten: Geschichte und Religion in der Zeit des zweiten Tempels* (NEB.EAT 3; Würzburg: Echter 1990) 260ff.; also T. Gorringe, "Job and the Pharisees," *Int* 40 (1986): 17–28: here the interesting attempt is undertaken to question Pharisaic piety on the basis of its own *ratio*. Basing themselves upon Deuteronomistic thinking (p. 22), the Pharisees represented a piety found also in the friends of Job and later in the Judaizing opponents of Paul.

[43] Also within the apocryphal-pseudepigraphic literature, a decidedly priestly-levitical tradition is recognizable, to which *Jubilees*, the *Testaments of the Twelve Patriarchs*, and *As. Mos.* may be counted. Cf. on this topic, A. D. Slingerland, "The Levitical Hallmark within the Testaments of the Twelve Patriarchs," *JBL* 103 (1984): 531–7; U. Glessmer, "Leviten in spätnachexilischer Zeit: Darstellungsinteressen in den Chronikbüchern und bei Josephus," *Gottes Ehre erzählen* (*Fs.* H. Seidel; ed. M. Albani and T. Arndt; Leipzig: Thomas, 1994), 127–51: Glessmer stresses the decidedly anti-levitical stance of Josephus, which comes to a head in *Ant.* 20.216–18; in contrast he is supposed to have had a pro-Pharisaic and pro-priestly perspective. Cf. also R. C. Stallmann, "Levi and the Levites in the Dead Sea Scrolls," *JSP* 10 (1992): 163–89, also in *Qumran Questions* (The Biblical Seminar 36; ed. J. H. Charlesworth; Sheffield: Sheffield Academic, 1995); J. Kugel, "Levi's Elevation to the Priesthood in Second Temple Writing, *HTR* 86 (1993): 1–64; R. A. Kugler, *From Patriarch to Priest: The Levi-Priestly tradition from Aramaic Levi to Testament of Levi* (SBLEJL 9; Atlanta: Scholars, 1996); C. Werman, "Levi and Levites in the Second Temple Period," *DSD* 4 (1997): 211–25.

[44] Cf. 1 Macc 1:11–15, 43–55; 2:16; 2 Macc 4:10–15, 19 (otherwise, Josephus, *J.W.* 1.31, 34–35; cf. also *Ant.* 12.251–6) and M. Hengel, *Judentum und Hellenismus* (WUNT 1/10; 3d ed.; Tübingen: Mohr [Siebeck], 1988), 503ff.; J. Sievers, *The Hasmoneans and Their Supporters: From Mattathias to the Death of John Hyrcanus I* (SFSHJ 6; Atlanta: Scholars, 1990), 19–20. Whether behind the politics of hellenization there was royal pressure (so 1 Macc 1:41–51; 2 Macc 6:1–9; *J.W.* 1.34), or if the initiative to do away with the Mosaic order proceeded from the Jewish Hellenists themselves, is contested. It may remain outside our consideration here. Decisive is the fact that numerous Jews actively participated in these proceedings. The contrarily rising resistance in holding firm to Yahweh-monotheism, the Yahweh-offering-cult, the food laws, circumcision, the Sabbath, and the festivals, expressed itself correspondingly, so that these aspects of "practice" gained a greater significance for Jewish identity. Concomitantly to this hellenization program, it came about that for the first time Jewish men and women suffered martyrdom for their fidelity to the Law (cf. 1 Macc 1:57–64; 2 Macc 6:10–11; 4 Macc). According to 1 Macc 1:49, the intent of the religious prohibitions and forceful measures was

4. The Subduing of the Hellenistic Reform Attempt by the Proponents of the Previous "Common Judaism"

In overcoming this crisis, which threatened Judaism's existence, various parties united to take common action:[45] the priestly clan of the Hasmoneans; the party of the Hasideans[46] with their ties to the scribes; in addition segments of the people who held dear the traditional forms of religion. Common to this insurgent movement, though in variegated distribution, is the fact that it carried on its struggle driven primarily not by political but by religious motives. That is why the correct exercise of defended religion plays such a large if not even decisive role in the reports of 1 and 2 Maccabees. Victory over the enemy is not due solely to their own military valor but to God's assistance.[47] The presupposition for this help, however, was adherence to the Torah, to the extent that this was possible for the combatants.[48] Here the

---

to make the Law forgotten. It is clear, however, that as a result the greatest possible value was placed precisely on these things, so that they might not be forgotten. To this belongs among other things the development of the associated customs.

[45] Cf. J. Sievers, *Hasmoneans*, 37–40, 57–67, 70–71, and elsewhere; J. Kampen, *The Hasideans and the Origin of Pharisaism. A Study in 1 and 2 Maccabees* (SBLSCS 24; Atlanta: Scholars, 1988), 65–150.

[46] Cf. 1 Macc 7:12–13: the γραμματεῖς mentioned here belong to the 'Ασιδαῖοι and obviously comprise their leadership group; cf. M. Hengel, *Judentum und Hellenismus*, 148. J. Kampen, *Hasideans*, 115–22 even goes a step farther: "From vv. 12 and 13 we learn that the Hasideans were scribes, leading citizens who were willing to respond to the threat of Greek force by means other than military resistance" (122; he sees in the Hasidim the forerunners of the Pharisees: 209–22). On the other hand J. Sievers, *Hasmoneans*, 38, does not see a complete identification: "Similarly, the connection between the *Asidaioi* and the Scribes or Pharisees is unprovable because 1 Macc 7:12–13 which speaks first of Scribes and then of Asidaioi should probably be read as distinguishing between the Scribes assembled by Alcimus and Bacchides to restore the Law (?), and the *Asidaioi* who, *because* of this demonstration of concern for the Law, *thereupon* sought peace with Alcimus" (emphasis Sievers'). With this however Sievers does not contradict but confirms the assumption that the *Asidaioi* oriented their conduct in keeping with the scribes (cf. ibid. 64–65), in the same way that later texts do regarding the Pharisees in their relationship to the scribes. Cf. also G. Stemberger, *Pharisäer*, 94–95.

[47] Cf. 1 Macc 3:18–22 and the significance of prayer, before and during the battle, and the resulting help from God: 1 Macc 4:8–11, 29; 5:33; 7:40ff.; 9:46; 11:71; 13:48, 51; 16:3; 2 Macc 1:8, 11–12, 17; 2:22; 3:15, 18ff.; 8:2–5:18ff.; 10:16, 25ff.; 11:6ff.; 12:6, 11, 15, 28, 36–37; 13:9ff.; 14:15, 34–35; 15:7ff., 21ff. The Maccabean priest-generals operate here precisely in line with the regulations in Deut 20:1–4.

[48] Cf. 1 Macc 2:45–46. (destruction of the sacrificial altars; forced circumcision); 3:5 (punishment of those who misled the people); 3:43–60 (fasting, repentance, first-fruits, tithe, stirring up of the Nazirites, readiness for battle in keeping with Deut 20:5–8); 5:54 (burnt offering on Zion, yet lacking is a report regarding purification in the wake of the impurity caused by contact with the dead, v. 52); 2 Macc 8:26–27 (Sabbath), 28 (mercy); 12:31–32 (Feast of Weeks), 38 (Sabbath), 42–46 (offering for the slain). It was difficult to keep the Sabbath commands during the battles (cf. 1 Macc 2:34–40), yet there appear to have been efforts to

purity laws take on a significance that is in this respect unique in the literature that Israel handed down. The high point and culmination of this first epoch of religious reconstitution was the reintroduction of the Yahweh cult in the purified Jerusalem sanctuary.[49] Although much regarding this era remains unclarified, it seems evident that the newly established temple cultus contained (and probably also emphasized) all the elements that the combatants thought to be decisive. But that meant accentuating questions surrounding sacrificial and priestly procedure, purity, food laws, and circumcision.[50]

---

observe them whenever possible (2 Macc 15:1–5). But sin and idol worship brought defeat and death to the people: 2 Macc 5:16–18; 6:12–17; 12:40–42. General admonitions about keeping the law are likewise found; cf. 1 Macc 2:21, 50ff. The Qumran *War Scroll* and other texts, some of which stretch back into the second century, testify to this understanding of purity as facilitating the presence of God.

[49] Rededication of the temple: 1 Macc 4:36–39; 2 Macc 10:1–9 (1:18; 2:16, 19–20; 1 Macc 14:36); cleansing of the Acra citadel: 1 Macc 13:50–51; 14:7; for the cleansing of other Judean cities: 1 Macc 13:47–48; 14:7; 2 Macc 12:38–39. Yet the roots for this lie, as one would expect, in Old Testament tradition: cf. Deut 23:10–16 (also Num 31:19–25). Cf. J. Sievers, *Hasmoneans*, 114–5: the cleansing of the Acra citadel by Simon is described in 1 Maccabees in conjunction with the temple purification, so that the work begun by Judas Maccabee is brought to completion. As Sievers likewise notes, to Simon's time belongs possibly also the *miqwa'ot* found in Gezer (see R. Reich, "Archaeological Evidence of the Jewish Population at Hasmonean Gezer," *IEJ* 31 [1981]: 48–52); its expansion from this time on becomes an important index of Jewish piety. The oldest proof that is datable with certainty comes from the Hasmonean palaces in Jericho: cf. E. Netzer, "Ancient Ritual Baths (Miqvaot) in Jericho," *The Jerusalem Cathedra* 2 (1982): 106–19. This topic subsequently drew considerable attention: cf. D. Small, "Late Hellenistic Baths in Palestine," *BASOR* 266 (1987): 59–74; E. P. Sanders, *Practice*, 222–9. Sanders attempted to distinguish between Pharisaic and Sadducean *miqwa'ot* in order to be able to demonstrate the relative insignificance of the Pharisaic traditions. But this argumentation comports with neither the archaeological nor the literary sources: cf. R. Reich, "The Great Mikveh Debate," *BAR* 19/2 (1993): 52–53; E. Regev, "Ritual Baths of Jewish Groups and Sects in the Second Temple Period," *Cathedra* 79/3, [Jerusalem] (1996): 3–21 (Heb.); A. Grossberg, "Ritual Baths in Second Temple Period Jerusalem and How They Were Ritually Prepared," *Cathedra* 83/4 [Jerusalem] (1997): 151–68 (Heb.); E. Regev, "More on Ritual Baths of Jewish Groups and Sects: On Research Methods and Archaeological Evidence – A Reply to A. Grossberg," *Cathedra* 83/4 [Jerusalem] (1997): 169–76 (Heb.); B. G. Wright III, "Jewish Ritual Baths – Interpreting the Digs and the Texts," in *The Archaeology of Israel* (ed. N. A. Silberman and D. Small; Sheffield: Sheffield Academic, 1997), 190–214. The foundational work on this subject was written by R. Reich, but this Jerusalem dissertation (*Miqva'ot* [Jewish Ritual Baths] *in the Second Temple Period and the Period of the Mishnah and Talmud*, Hebrew University, 1990) remains unpublished in either Hebrew or English. Only a series of essays has appeared; of these the most important seems to be "The Hot Bath-House (balneum), the Miqweh and the Jewish Community in the Second Temple Period," *JJS* 39 (1988): 102–7.

[50] Here circumcision proves to be of no import for subsequent development: its practice is in fact "common" for the whole of post-Maccabean Judaism. Proceedings like those described in 1 Macc 1:15 do not crop up thereafter. Circumcision was a question only in the context of coming over into Judaism (cf. *Ant.* 20.41, 44–46) and again at the beginning of the Christian mission. Cf. O. Betz, "Beschneidung II. Altes Testament, Frühjudentum und Neues Testament,"

In this connection John Sievers has pointed out that the role played by Judas Maccabeus in the reintroduction of the Yahweh cultus in the Jerusalem temple is presented in a strikingly understated fashion:

> According to both 1 and 2 Macc, Judas Maccabeus initiated the cleansing and rededication of the Temple. In 1 Macc, however, where we would expect this to be emphasized, he is only said to have selected suitable priests to cleanse the Temple (4:42) and, after its dedication, to have decided together with "his brothers and the whole assembly of Israel" to commemorate the event every year for eight days (4:59). In the best manuscripts, there is no reference to Judah in 1 Macc 4:43–58, i.e., during the cleansing and rededication of the Temple. This fact is particularly significant if we compare it with the active role assigned to Simon in the conquest and cleansing of the *Akra*.

He therefore concludes that at that time the priesthood did not yet stand under the control of the Maccabean priest-generals: "Jerusalem priests cooperate with him, but maintain relative independence" (47).[51] Other passages that bear this out include 1 Macc 7:33–38 and 2 Macc 14:31–36. The influence of the Maccabees on the temple cultus decreased still more when the high priest Alcimus took office. Allying themselves with him was a number of past Maccabean supporters whose concern was "to seek what is right" (ἐκζητῆσαι δίκαια[52]), by which Sievers (*Hasmoneans*, 65) understands "legal concerns":

> Among the most pressing problems may have been practical ones, such as property rights of refugees, compensation for damages, amnesty, calendar adjustments, etc., as well as the more general questions of Torah observance. Several new customs had been introduced by the Hellenizers before the Torah was outlawed as a whole (2 Macc 4:11). Also, a decision about the lawfulness of Hasmonean innovations concerning Sabbath, Temple, and holidays may have been considered urgent (cf. 1 Macc 2:41; 4:42–59; 2 Macc 10:2–8). It is possible but not certain that the "assembly of scribes" influenced the decision of the Asidaioi to recognize Alcimus as high priest.

TRE 5.716–22.

[51] In contrast to this Josephus, who as a priest and Hasmonean descendent had a fine sense for priestly competencies, wrote that it was Judas himself who cleansed the temple, brought in new vessels, hung up new veils, took down the old altar, and built a new one (*Ant.* 12.318). Yet the concentration on Judas or other "chief personalities" is a typical literary characteristic; cf. L. Feldman, "Josephus' Portrayal of the Hasmoneans compared with 1 Maccabees," in *Josephus and the History of the Greco-Roman Period* (*Fs.* M. Smith; ed. F. Parente and J. Sievers; StPB 41; Leiden: Brill, 1994), 41–68 (on Judas Maccabeus see 50–59).

[52] The root δικ- is for both Josephus and the New Testament a characteristic vocable in describing the Pharisees: cf. *Ant.* 13.289; 14.176; *J.W.* 2.163; Matt 5:20; Luke 16:15; 18:14; 20:20 (the Lucan passages all pejorative, as also CD 1:18–19). See also *Ps.Sol.* 1:2–3; 2:15; 3; 13:6–11; etc.; on this see J. Schüpphaus, *Die Psalmen Salomos. Ein Zeugnis Jerusalemer Theologie und Frömmigkeit in der Mitte des vorchristlichen Jahrhunderts* (ALGHJ 7; Leiden: Brill, 1977), 83–107.

There is therefore good reason to conclude that an anti-Hellenistic, reform-minded priesthood had gained the upper hand in the Jerusalem temple. Scribal and hasidic concerns were in evidence, but the priesthood remained independent of the Maccabees.[53] The demolition of the wall of the inner court, associated with Alcimus in 1 Macc 9:54–56, could have been part of this reform program, one which aimed to involve the people more intensively in the temple proceedings.[54]

But speaking against such an interpretation, which adopts as starting point a cooperative action on the part of Alcimus, the Hasideans, and the scribes, is the entire report of 1 Macc 7:5–25, in which Alcimus is portrayed in the most sinister light (cf. also 2 Macc 14:3–27). But this may show the pro-Hasmonean standpoint of the author.[55] In any case it is striking that after the murder of sixty Hasideans nothing is reported of direct opposition to him from other Hasideans or from the scribes. In 2 Macc 14:31–36 the priests of the Jerusalem temple decline to help Nicanor in the struggle against Judas Maccabeus, and they ask God to protect the temple from renewed defilement (which presupposes that the purity of the temple since its rededication was not imperiled in spite of Alcimus being high priest).[56] When Judas had defeated Nicanor, he had his head brought to Jerusalem and organized with the priests and the people a sort of victory celebration, because God had not

---

[53] Cf. L. H. Feldman, *Josephus' Portrayal of the Hasmoneans*, 49–50: Josephus' lack of mention of the Hasideans serves the purpose of passing over the splitting of the revolutionary movement. That he is aware of these developments is shown in *Ant.* 12.284, where the dying Mattathias counsels his son Judas to incorporate the δίκαιοι καὶ θεοσεβεῖς into his ranks, among whom would be included the Hasideans. Here too the initiative for the coalition is ascribed to Judas.

[54] Cf. J. Sievers, *Hasmoneans*, 75: "Apparently he wanted to ease access to the inner court of the Temple." But Josephus, like the author of 1 Maccabees, sees in this an illicit act (*Ant.* 12.413). See also J. A. Goldstein, "The Hasmonean Revolt and the Hasmonean Dynasty," *CHJ* 2.292–351 (esp. 312).

[55] Josephus in *Ant.* 12.393ff. keeps very closely to the version in 1 Macc but diverges at the decisive point: he neither mentions the Hasideans and scribes under this designation, replacing them instead with τινὲς . . . τῶν ἐκ τοῦ δήμου (but he cites the number of sixty slain; see n. 53 above); nor does he make Alcimus responsible for the killing: Bacchides thought nothing of his promise and carried out the bloodbath. By this, according to Josephus, he kept still more Hasideans or scribes from aligning themselves with Alcimus (12.396). After Alcimus, with Bacchides' help, came to power, he pursued a two-fold goal, according to Josephus: he sought to win the population with friendliness (12.398), and at the same time he waged a civil war against Judas. In this he leaned for support on the godless (ἀσεβεῖς) and renegades (φυγάδες) from among his people (i.e., the Hellenists: 12.399). This seems to deal with the Jewish occupants of the Acra: cf. J. Sievers, "Jerusalem, the Akra, and Josephus," in *Josephus and the History of the Greco-Roman Period* (see n. 51 above), 195–209 (199–200); see also J. A. Goldstein, "Hasmonean Revolt," 308–9

[56] Cf. also Josephus, *Ant.* 12.406–7. It is to be noted that Josephus in 12.406 mentions the elders in the temple next to the priests.

permitted the temple to become unclean (2 Macc 15:30–34). This victory is
also recalled in the Pharisaic festive calendar *Megillat Taanit* (number 30, see
below 5.4). The last two passages appear to make it plausible that Alcimus
did possess the title of high priest, but that he exerted no direct influence on
the priesthood and the organization of the temple cult; he rather let it carry
on in the manner established after the rededication. In Alcimus we are
certainly not dealing with a radical Hellenist, at least as far as the temple is
concerned.

5. The Battle for the Proper Form of the "Common Judaism" Needing Reformulation

The broad anti-Hellenistic coalition had therefore dissolved very quickly after
the first successes. There begins the phase that can be described as "trifur-
cation of Judaism." Josephus (*Ant.* 13.171–2) writes relatively unexpectedly
in his report about the time of Jonathan:

> During this time there were three Jewish streams which with respect to human affairs
> championed various and contrasting positions. One was called the Pharisees, the other
> the Sadducees, but the third the Essenes.

The common starting point of these three groupings is their rootedness in
the traditional, pre-Maccabean form of "Common Judaism," for the preservation of which the insurgents had fought. It was however precisely the
unexpected success that led immediately thereafter to dissension.[57] For if the
victory was due primarily to the keeping of the commandments (a "Deuteronomistic" insight, classically formulated above all at the beginning of the Book
of Judges[58]), then no efforts must be spared in this regard in the newly
forming commonwealth so that God would not once more turn away from his
people. But that could only be prevented by the entire people keeping the
entire law. That means, in turn, that now an extensive exchange set in – based
on a common foundation, be it noted – over how the people as a whole were

---

[57] Cf. 1 Macc 7:12–18 and on this text J. Kampen, *Hasideans*, 114–35, 148–50: for the
author of 1 Maccabees (written near the end of the reign of John Hyrcanus or during the regency
of Alexander Jannaeus [209]) the Hasideans present a danger for the new state. In contrast to
this the author of 2 Maccabees sees in them "well-known people, renowned for their purity in
the time of Hellenization and for their piety" (149). By situating them in relation with Judas
Maccabee, he attempts to enhance Judas's prestige (cf. also 213–14).

[58] Judges 2:10ff. Overall, the biblical Judges provide an important element of the Hasmonean
legitimization: cf. 1 Macc 5:61–2, 14:27ff. This understanding of the Hasmoneans as a line of
deliverers chosen by God may conceivably have made possible the Pharisees' initial recognition.
Yet when they strove for the kingly title along with that of the high priest (cf. also Judges 9 and
Ant. 5.234), relations were broken off: cf. R. Deines, *Pharisäer*, 274–5.

to comply with the commandments, both in the domain of the official cult in Jerusalem as well as in the private sphere. For after all, during the Hellenistic reform attempt it was not only the public cult that was placed in question but also the practice of personal piety. There came about, and this also for the first time in the history of Israel, a persecution of the individual on the basis of his religious practice. Further, it is noteworthy that women were often presented as objects of persecution and at the same time as martyrs for the ancestral faith.[59] That evidences an individual (in connection with children also a familial) understanding of religion which no longer restricts itself, not even in the public estimation, to the world of men or priests.

That shows how powerfully personal praxis of religion has surged alongside the official form of religion, to some measure as the result of hellenization.[60] It was therefore no longer sufficient to regulate the cult; rather, everybody, men and women, must contribute their part to make possible the deliverance of the country. They were to do this by knowing and doing the commandments, each in his own individual sphere.

5.1 4QMMT as a Document of Party Formation within Palestinian Judaism

It is accordingly no happenstance that in 4QMMT we have from a very early time period a document that is at pains to preserve the newly acquired purity of the temple by keeping 4QMMT's specially listed "Torah observances"[61] and hewing to its calendar.[62] At the same time, the tone it sounds shows the

---

[59] Cf. 1 Macc 1:63; 2 Macc 6:10; 7:20–23, 28–29, 41; 4 Macc 14:11–17, 20; on account of her piety (εὐσέβεια see 4 Macc 15:1, 2, 3, 14, 17, 29; 16:13, 14) the mother of the seven sons received the exalted title of a νομοφύλαξ (15:28–29). Love for their mother caused the sons "to observe the precepts unto death" (μέχρι θανάτου τὰ νόμιμα φυλάσσοντας; 4 Macc 15:10).

[60] Julius Wellhausen was the first to make reference to this: cf. R. Deines, *Pharisäer*, 44–47, 56–57, 546–7. (with additional literature).

[61] מעשי התורה C 27, cf. B 2. On the meaning of this phrase see Exod 18:20 LXX and E. Qimron/J. Strugnell, *Qumran Cave 4*, vol. 5: *Miqsat Ma'ase Ha-Torah* (DJD 10; Oxford: Clarendon Press, 1994), 139 (hereafter cited as: Qimron/Strugnell); F. García Martínez, "4QMMT in a Qumran Context," in *Reading 4QMMT. New Perspectives on Qumran Law and History* (SBLSyms 2; ed. J. Kampen and M. J. Bernstein; Atlanta: Scholars, 1996), 15–27 (23ff.). García Martínez shows decisively that the phrase can be understood only in the sense of "works" or "deeds" and not, as Qimron/Strugnell read it, as "precepts" or "commandments." On the importance of this phrase for the understanding of the Pauline expression ἔργα νόμου (Rom 3:20; Gal 2:16; 3:2, 5, 10; cf. also Rom 2:15 and 3:28) see D. Flusser, "Die Gesetzeswerke in Qumran und bei Paulus," in *Geschichte – Tradition – Reflexion (Fs. M. Hengel,* vol. 1: *Judentum,* ed. P. Schäfer; Tübingen: Mohr [Siebeck], 1996), 395–403; J. Kampen, "4QMMT and New Testament Studies," in *Reading 4QMMT* (see above), 129–44 (138–43).

[62] The question whether the calendar fragments were originally part of this document (only HS A contains the calendar too) is disputed; cf. J. Kampen/M. J. Bernstein, "Introduction," in

determination with which struggles about these questions were carried out. For at stake was nothing less than blessing or curse for the people. In the third part of MMT, which possesses a paranetic tone,[63] reference is made to Deut 30:1-3,[64] and immediately thereafter follows (C12-15):

> And it is also written that you will depart from the way, and evil will befall you. And it is written that he will bring these things upon you at the end of the days, the blessing and the curse. . . .[65]

It is clear, moreover, that in the conflict priestly concerns (which however affect the people and their "practice") are expressed, so that one must assume that both the senders as well as the recipients of the writing were priests. The critical interactions took place, accordingly – also at the very least – within the priesthood, which should prevent understanding it as a unified entity.[66]

The dating of 4QMMT cannot be cleared up beyond question, even if a majority have gone along with the dating furnished by the editors Qimron and Strugnell between 159 and 152 B.C., a time during the reign but previous to the high priesthood of Jonathan.[67] This yields the following spectrum of

---

Reading 4QMMT (previous note), 1–7 (4). According to J. Strugnell this part does not belong to the original document; cf. "Appendix 3: Additional Observations on 4QMMT," in Qimron/Strugnell, 203; so also L. H. Schiffman, "The Place of 4QMMT in the Corpus of Qumran Manuscripts," in Kampen/Bernstein, 81–98 (82–86). On the other hand, with good reasons H. Eshel sees it as an original comment in "4QMMT and the History of the Hasmonean Period," in Kampen/Bernstein, 53–65 (56 n. 12).

[63] Cf. Qimron/Strugnell, 111, "Homiletical-Paraenetic Section C."

[64] Cf. Qimron/Strugnell, 59.

[65] Cf. also C 19–20. On the text and supplements see Qimron/Strugnell, 58–61.

[66] Against Sanders and others, who use it to argue that according to Josephus 20,000 priests opposed only 6000 Pharisees, which is supposed to show the limited importance of the latter group. On the problematic nature of this argumentation see M. Hengel/R. Deines, "Common Judaism," 61–62.

[67] Qimron/Strugnell, 118–121, 175. The interpretation heavily depends on 4QpPs^a 4:7–9, where it is reported that the Teacher of Righteousness has sent back to the "Wicked Priest" a set of Torah regulations. If these דברי החוק והתורה are identical with 4QMMT (so among others H. Eshel, "4QMMT and the History of the Hasmonean Period," in Kampen/Bernstein, 54–55; P. A. Rainbow, "The Last Oniad and the Teacher of Righteousness," *JJS* 48 [1997]: 30–52 [50]), then the dating must be in agreement with the identification of the "Wicked Priest," who as a rule is viewed as the Maccabean Jonathan: cf. G. Jeremias, *Der Lehrer der Gerechtigkeit* (SUNT 2, Göttingen: Vandenhoeck und Ruprecht, 1963), 36–78; O. Betz, "The Qumran Halakhah Text Miqsat Ma'áse Ha-Torah (4QMMT) and Sadducean, Essene, and Early Pharisaic Tradition," in *The Aramaic Bible. Targums and Their Historical Context* (ed. D. R. G. Beattie and M. J. McNamara; JSOTSup 166; Sheffield: Sheffield Academic, 1994), 176–202 (196–7). Against this interpretation see among others G. J. Brooke, "The Significance of the Kings in 4QMMT," in *Qumran Cave IV and MMT: Special Report* (ed. Z. J. Kapera; Cracow: Enigma, 1991), 109–13; S. Medala, "The Character and Historical Setting of 4QMMT," *QC* 4 (1994): 1–27 (in my view too hypothetical in its identifications; cf. also in pp. 3–4 the overview of previous proposals); J. Kampen, "4QMMT and New Testament Studies," 130–32.

parties for this time. The "we"-group, which appears as the originator and sender of 4QMMT,[68] advocates a strictly priestly oriented theology, with ties to the Deuteronomistic traditions. With their writing they address a "you"-group ("you" in either plural or singular), whom they seek to convince and to win over by their distinctive interpretation of Scripture and the praxis that results from it, especially as regards the temple cult. The tone is solicitous, in spite of the obvious undercurrent of criticism. A third party is seen in a "they"group, to which the "we"-group stands in opposition. They determine the actual temple ritual, against which the "we"-group takes a stand, and for which it wants to win the "you"-group.

5.2 The Pharisees and 4QMMT

The editors of 4QMMT were not content to stop their analysis with a formal description of the three recognizable groupings. They attempted rather to integrate these into the partisan landscape suggested by the other sources.

Qimron/Strugnell understand the "we"-group as the "Dead Sea Sect" (116.175), for which the primary author of the writing *could* have been the "Teacher of Righteousness" (114).[69] There are, to be sure, differences over against the later Qumran writings, which are seen as genuine writings of the Qumranites. But these can be explained by the early historical location of 4QMMT (cf. Qimron/Strugnell, 113 [4.i.5.2], 115–6 [4.ii.5], 121 [4.ii.8]).

The "you"-group is addressed in such a way that those who produced it clearly ascribe to the addressees' knowledge of particulars regarding the priesthood and the people (cf. 114 [4.ii.3], 136 [5.ii.4 D]), yet without making them directly responsible for the deplorable state of affairs discussed.[70] Based on the thrice-used phrase, "For the sons of the priests/

---

[68] Cf. Qimron/Strugnell, 114, 116–7.

[69] Cf. however J. Kampen, "4QMMT and New Testament Studies," 132: "That this anonymous author is the Teacher of Righteousness is sheer conjecture." On the other hand his article furnishes an important argument for the identification he denies when he refers to the fact (133–4) that the closest parallel to the formulation "and you know" (B [46], 68, 80; C [7], 8) is the ἠκούσατε of the antitheses found in the Sermon on the Mount (Matt 5:21, 27, 33, 38, 43). Here he cites approvingly the formulation of David Daube regarding the differences between rabbinic controversy dialogues and the antitheses: "The tone [of the antitheses] is not academic but final, prophetic, maybe somewhat defiant. Nor is there any reasoning" (*The New Testament and Rabbinic Judaism* [London: Oxford, 1956], 57–58). But if this expresses something about the tone of 4QMMT, then it makes reference to an authoritative personality who takes it upon himself to decide "with fullness of power." But who would better fit this description than the "Teacher of Righteousness"?

[70] Cf. B 46: "And you know that some of the people . . ." (obviously dealing with marriage ties considered by the senders to be illegitimate); cf. in addition B 68; B 80: "and you know that some of the priests and the people intermingled . . ."; C 7: "and you know that we separated ourselves from the majority of the people . . ."; cf. on this J. Kampen, "4QMMT and New Testament Studies," 135–6.

Aaron should pay heed to this matter so they do not bring guilt upon the people" (B 11–13, 16–17, 25–27; cf. B 82), it appears that the "you"-group stood close to priestly circles or perhaps consisted of priests to a substantial degree. At the same time there is recognizable here a reserved yet clear criticism that the priests are not dealing with these things in the proper manner.[71]

Not until the switch from second person plural to second person singular in C 10 (cf. C 23, 25–32) does it become clear that the actual addressee of the writing is an individual.[72] He should be convinced that the doctrine advanced by the senders is in agreement with law and prophets and the rest of the Scriptures. The "you"-group assumes a distinctive place because only here within the group does an individual person emerge prominently into the foreground. The "we"-group credits it with the potential of exerting influence on the praxis in the temple.[73] The "people" or "Israel" are related with this individual figure; cf. C 26–32:

> And for this reason we have written to you a few of the Torah-practices that we think serve you and your people well (לטוב לך ולעמך), since we have seen that there is shrewdness and Torah-knowledge among you. Reflect on all this in his presence and request from him that he strengthen your resolve and keep far from you thoughts of evil and the counsel of Belial, so that you can rejoice in the end time, by finding some of our concerns to be well-founded. And it will surely be reckoned to you as righteousness, if you do what is right and good before him for your own well-being and that of Israel (לטוב לך ולישראל).

In my view, in 4QMMT there is a difference between the use of "people" (עם) and "Israel." The latter refers to an ideal entity (often as a people consisting of twelve tribes),[74] in which the senders include themselves. In

---

[71] For that reason the explanation of the connection between the "we"-group and "you"-group proposed by Kampen seems to me hardly correct: "The supposition that the addressee is part of the same movement as the writer, but geographically and/or theologically somewhat removed from the author's is much more likely, given that the addressee is recognized for his prudence and knowledge of Torah" ("4QMMT and New Testament Studies," 131). In my view the sole possible commonality is the priestly ancestry and the knowledge of the law related to it, along with the use of that law in the cult. The overall focus (see n. 88), however, contradicts Kampen's interpretation, and so does the implicit criticism of the addressee/s.

[72] Cf. Qimron/Strugnell, 175: "It appears that he was one of the Hasmonean kings." The designation "kings" is however false, since the first to assume the royal title was, at the earliest, Aristobulus, and more probably Alexander Jannaeus. Jonathan, whom Qimron/Strugnell regard as the actual addressee, was only high priest (see also 117–119).

[73] So also S. Medala, "The Character and Historical Setting of 4QMMT," 16, who then however wants to see in the priest being addressed the high priest Alcimus, whom the senders (representatives of a "pre-Pharisaic Hasidean group") wanted to warn about the machinations of Judas or Jonathan Maccabeus (17).

[74] Cf. B 53, 61–62, 63, 76; C 21, 32, cf. a. B 33, 48. Reference is made to the past only one time, in the phrase "kings of Israel" C 23.

contrast "the people" designates that part of the population which offers sacrifices in the temple in accordance with the repudiated halakah (B 13, 27), enters into illegitimate marriage bonds (B 46, 75), or brings condemnation on itself via other defiling acts or temple sacrilege (C 7; relating in general to all the preceding C 27 [see inset quote above]). It seems clear to me that the priests (cf. B 11–13, 16–17, 25–27, 46, 82) or the individually addressed recipient (C 27) are made responsible, at least partially, for this culpable behavior. True, there is explicit criticism only of the people. But implicitly it applies also to the priests who permit or facilitate the people's involvement in proscribed practices.

5.2.1 The identification of the "they"-group with the Pharisees or their predecessors by Qimron and Strugnell

On the basis of halakic agreements, Qimron/Strugnell identify the "they"-group with the Pharisees or their forerunners.[75] In addition, in their view this group should be linked with the רוב העם (C7), from which the "we"-group separated: "The implication is that it refers to the 'they' group which either composed the רוב העם or of whom the רוב העם formed a part. The erroneous halakic traditions of the 'they' group in section B were in all probability the same traditions that provoked the separation from the רוב העם in section C" (115). In the composition of its personnel the "they"-group remains very nebulous, but in any case it is clear that they have the authority over the cult praxis in the temple, and the people follow their interpretation of the rite. Based on the demand to the *priests* (already repeatedly mentioned) to pay attention to these things, it can possibly be concluded that behind this "they"-group stands a non-priestly tradition.[76]

---

[75] Cf. 115, 175, 177; this identification is confirmed by Y. Sussmann, "The History of the Halakha and the Dead Sea Scrolls. Preliminary Talmudic Observations on *Miqsat Ma'ase Ha-Torah* (4QMMT)," *Tarbiz* 59 (1989/60): 11–76 (Hebrew), now (shortened) in Qimron/Strugnell, 179–200; L. H. Schiffmann, "Qumran and Rabbinic Halakhah," in *Jewish Civilization in the Hellenistic-Roman Period* (JSPSup 10; ed. S. Talmon; Sheffield: Sheffield Academic, 1990), 138–46; idem, "Place of 4QMMT," 86–94; A. I. Baumgarten, "Rabbinic Literature as a Source for the History of Jewish Sectarianism in the Second Temple Period," *DSD* 2 (1995): 14–57. The identification is also upheld by D. J. Schwartz, "MMT, Josephus and the Pharisees," 77 and elsewhere; H. Eshel, "4QMMT and the History of the Hasmonean Period," 61 (n. 28 cites additional relevant works); J. Kampen, "4QMMT and New Testament Studies," 132. The critical report of Y. Elman, "Some Remarks on 4QMMT and the Rabbinic Tradition: or, When Is a Parallel Not a Parallel," in *Reading 4QMMT* (see n. 61 above), 99–128, likewise does not question this consensus, as far as I can determine.

[76] By which it is clear that the temple ritual was of course performed by the priests. But this clear differentiation between "they"-group and priests is in my opinion striking and is evidence for a connection of this group with the Pharisees, among whom the priestly element did not play such a dominating role. Possibly the influence of the Συναγωγή 'Ασιδαίων (1 Macc 2:42), or

Qimron/Strugnell relate the picture sketched above with the statement of Josephus in *Ant.* 18.15[77]: "It is interesting to note that we find a similar *early association* of the Pharisee group with the רוב העם attested also by Josephus, at a time which, we will shortly suggest, is about as early as MMT" (115; italics mine).

5.2.2 D. R. Schwartz and H. Eshel: The identification of the "you"-group with the Pharisees

Above all it has been Daniel R. Schwartz who has argued against such an understanding of 4QMMT and its application in discussion over the placement of the Pharisees. In his essay "MMT, Josephus and the Pharisees,"[78] he refers to the possibility, much discussed in recent decades, that Josephus' position on the placement of the Pharisees is an exaggeration. In his view this possibility exists regardless of whether one takes any of three lines of argumentation: the Smith-Neusner;[79] his own, which traces the texts back to Nicolaus of Damascus;[80] or that of Mason, according to whom Josephus adopts a hostile stance toward Pharisaic influence, yet nonetheless presupposes just such an influence.[81] With respect to 4QMMT his objection centers on the understanding of C 7 and the presupposed relation between רוב העם and the "Pharisees." He gives three points to consider:

1. The originally proposed translation of רוב as "majority" must be changed to the biblical term "multitude."[82] Schwartz concedes that this is only "a minor point" (75), to which must be added that he is not sure of it. For the meaning "majority" cannot be ruled out, though no decisive weight rests on it even for those who champion Pharisaic influence.

---

of the scribes associated with them (1 Macc 7:12), on the current temple praxis is reflected in the "they"-group.

[77] For the text see n. 5 above.

[78] In *Reading 4QMMT*, 67–80. His colleague H. Eshel adopts a similar stance against the historical interpretation of Qimron/Strugnell. To the extent that his argumentation runs parallel to that of Schwartz, this section refers also to it. In a separate section I subsequently discuss his proposal for interpretation.

[79] See notes 8 and 26 above.

[80] D. R. Schwartz, "Josephus and Nicolaus on the Pharisees," *JSJ* 14 (1983): 157–71; cf. idem, "MMT, Josephus and the Pharisees," 74 n. 19.

[81] S. Mason, *Flavius Josephus on the Pharisees* (see n. 5 above). For critical response to his position see the reviews by L. H. Feldmann, *JSJ* 23 (1992): 122–5; Rebecca Gray, *JTS* 43 (1992): 216–20; L. L. Grabbe, *JJS* 49 (1994): 134–6.

[82] Cf. already Qimron/Strugnell, 59: "The word רוב has here its biblical meaning 'multitude' rather than its mishnaic meaning 'majority'; there is no certain attestation of the M[ishnaic] H[ebrew] meaning of this word in Q[umran] H[ebrew]." H. Eshel lets both possibilities stand ("the majority of the people" or "a significant part of the people" ["4QMMT and the History of the Hasmonean Period," 60 n. 21]).

2. Between sections B and C Schwartz sees a clear difference, which he attaches to the switch from the second-person plural ("you [plural]-group" in section B) to the second-person singular ("you"-group [singular]).[83] He views the halakic details that are passed along to the "you"-group [plural] as priestly privileged knowledge that relates only to the temple cult: "They hardly serve to reflect popular practice" (76). This is to be *distinguished* from the reproaches found in the first part of section C (lines 4–5) regarding והמעל ‏‏[החמ]ס . . .][84] and החמס והזנות.[85] He sees in this such weighty

---

[83] Cf. 77: "Section B, the main, halakhic, part of the text is addressed to a group denoted by the second person plural, which the writer assumes to be interested in the details of Jewish law; section C, however, is addressed to a ruler of the Jewish people." Yet on the same page Schwartz writes, with reference to C 7: "The writer of MMT says that 'you' (plural), the recipients, know that 'we' separated ourselves from the multitude of the people, for the latter are involved in such terrible crimes" – by which he makes clear that he knows that the use of the second–person singular and plural cannot simply be ascribed to section B and C. In C 7 the editors supply "and you [plural] know that . . ."; however, in C 8 what is attested is [. . .]י ואתם which is then restored to ש ‏‏ יודעים‏‏[ו‏ ‏ ואתם.

[84] Qimron/Strugnell translate with "[. . . the malice] and the treachery" (59), while Schwartz wants a "more literal" understanding in the sense of "misappropriation of holy property" (76). So also H. Eshel, who refers to Lev 5:15 as decisive evidence: the reason for the separation is "misappropriation of the property of the Temple. . . . This accusation fits the priests of Jerusalem and not the Pharisees" ("4QMMT and the History of the Hasmonean Period," 60 n. 24). Both pay too little attention to the fact that Lev 5:15 deals with a מעל-transgression not by the priests but by some Israelite! Cf. also B. A. Levine, *Leviticus* ויקרא (The JPS Torah Commentary; Philadelphia: Jewish Publication Society, 1989), 30, who gives for the meaning of מעל the additional information: "It may also refer to betrayal of trust, involving marital infidelity; to acts of deceit; and to violation of the covenant between God and Israel by the worship of foreign gods." In Old Testament passages מעל can be the sin of the people (Josh 22:16; Lev 26:40; Deut 32:51; Ezek 15:8; 39:23), of the land (Ezek 14:13), or of an individual (Josh 22:20; Ezek 17:20, 1 Chr 10:13, 2 Chr 28:19). In addition adultery by a married woman is so designated (Num 5:12, 27), likewise in Ezra marriage with foreign women (9:2, 4; 10:2, 6, 10). מעל causes impurity which the priests are to remove (cf. 2 Chr 29:6–15); however, the priests too can commit מעל (2 Chr 36:14). Restricting the meaning of מעל to the parallel provided in Lev 15:5 as Schwartz and Eshel do is in my view unfounded. On the contrary, the context suggests much more readily some reference to illegitimate sexual relations, if one absolutely must arrive at such specificity. For in the other Qumran texts מעל has "simply become one of the many expressions for sin"; so H. Ringgren, "מעל," *ThWAT* 4 (1984) 1038–1042 (1041), with reference to 1QS 9:4; 10:23; 1 QH 4:30, 34; 11:11; cf. also CD 7:1, 9:16f. Cf. the next note.

[85] Qimron/Strugnell: "malice and fornication" (59). Both lines are very fragmentary; the preceding lines 1–3 consist only of unconnected words. The חמס attested twice in C 4–5 likewise cannot be restricted to cultic abuses. We are dealing with a term redolent of prophetic judgment language in which the ethical-social aspect comes to the fore. Cf. H. Haag, "חמס," in *ThWAT* 2 (1977): 1050–1061. But priests too could run afoul of the חמס-charges: cf. Zeph 3:4. The same goes for זנות in C 5 and שקר ורעה in C 9. In view of such a framework the understanding of מעל should not be too narrowly conceived.

reproaches of priestly misbehavior[86] that he thinks it impossible for the recipient of the writing to have been tied with it: "To accuse someone of זנות, מעל and חמס is not the same as to list one's arguments with him on points of legal detail.[87] Rather, the author of MMT is telling his addressees, with whom he has various legal arguments, that – as opposed to the 'multitude of the people' – they and he are all serious in their religion" (77).[88]

According to Schwartz, the formulation פרשנו suggests that the recipients (!) of the document were Pharisees, and that the group sending it wanted to let them know: we too have separated ourselves.[89] This results for him in the following scenario: the senders convey to the "you (plural)-group" of section B what they think is wrong in the present cult praxis.[90] Section C is, in contrast, addressed "to a ruler of the Jewish people" (again, the plural address in section C is ignored [see n. 83 above]). Between the addressees of sections B and C there must therefore have been a close relationship – which is also not contested (for Qimron/Strugnell they are one group, namely the "you"-group).

---

[86] He refers to CD 3–5, where likewise, as in the section under consideration, priestly misbehavior is presented by referring back to Eli's sons (1 Sam 2:12–17). The meaning of this text as a parallel need not be disputed here. It is however nevertheless obvious that none of the decisive terms חמס, מעל, and זנות is to be found in the biblical text, and only זנות in CD 4, 17:20 as a sin of *Israel*, caused by the priests' wrong Torah-exegesis.

[87] From the extant text it cannot be determined who is accused of this transgression. Whether the you [singular] addressee is intended, as Schwartz presupposes, is extremely improbable; see below n. 93.

[88] So also H. Eshel, "4QMMT and the History of the Hasmonean Period," 60–61. With this Schwartz and Eshel regard as negligible the criticism which the document, despite its solicitous tone, contains. Cf. O. Betz, "The Qumran Halakhah Text" (see n. 67 above), 180: with all the stress on the Torah-knowledge of the "you [singular]" addressee (cf. C 29–30), the purpose of the document is "to show that this knowledge of the Torah has to be improved; a better understanding and deeper insight into the book of Moses are required" C 10, 30–31). If the historical classification given above (see n. 67) is correct, then it follows that we are not dealing here with an innocuous doctrinal treatise but possibly with the deception of a presiding or newly installed high priest!

[89] Regarding the positive understanding of separation in sectarian groups he refers to A. I. Baumgarten, "Qumran and Sectarianism during the Second Temple Period," in *The Scrolls of the Judean Desert: Forty Years of Research* (ed. M. Broshi et al.; Jerusalem: Bialik Institute, 1992), 142–3 (Hebrew). Likewise H. Eshel, "4QMMT and the History of the Hasmonean Period," 65–66, regards the recipients of the document as Pharisees.

[90] The "you"-group, for Schwartz therefore the Pharisees, are accordingly credited with being able to alter the cited temple practices. That means therefore, even if one accepts the interpretation of Schwartz, that "Pharisaic" influence in this period can be assumed, which Schwartz then explicitly states: "In conclusion, MMT shows us a view of three major groups, termed 'us,' 'you' and 'them.' It indicates that the Pharisees were in power subsequent to a priestly group" (80), who in his view were the Hasmoneans.

It is nevertheless questionable who their opponents were once the "they"-group of section B is eliminated. Schwartz answers: the Sadducees, understood as a Zadokite party of priests who rejected the Hasmonean high priesthood. He thereby divides – and on this depends his main point – the authors *and* recipients from "the mass/majority of the people" whom he has pronounced to be Sadducees/Zadokites: "Who is that so-called 'multitude of the people,' viewed here as sinful, from whom the writer and his community have separated themselves? If they are not the Pharisees, the recipients, nor the Qumran Essenes, who wrote the letter, then they may be the Sadducees – the Temple establishment of the pre-Hasmonean period" (79–80). In this way the "multitude of the people" become "the multitude of bad priests" (80).

But that seems to me to be a forced interpretation which is already ruled out just by the use of עם in 4QMMT. There is no way to show that this likely refers to the priesthood (even if he assumes, as he decidedly does not, that reference was to the people who adhere to the Sadducean-Zadokite priesthood[91]), since the text clearly ties the "you (singular)" addressees in section C with the people in a positive fashion. It is in my opinion very improbable that עם in C 7 refers to another "people" than in C 27 (cf. the parallel usage in C 32 [see citation on p. 464 above]. Moreover it is unconvincing when Schwartz relates the statement about the separation of the senders (C 7) exclusively to the abuses named in C 4–5 (and does not like Qimron/Strugnell relate them to the entire list in B[92]). The beginning lines of section C are too fragmentary to yield such a comprehensive understanding. Possibly we are dealing with an additional point of complaint as in section B, with C 4 being introduced with [. . . הנשי]ם ועל[93] and closing with the reference to Deut 7:26 (C 6).[94] Given the link with Deut 7:25–26 it is possible but not certain that the passage is dealing with the temple cult;[95] in any case it is not the priests who are charged – of them there is no explicit mention in

---

[91] So H. Eshel, "4QMMT and the History of the Hasmonean Period," see below pp. 473–4.

[92] If I understand Schwartz correctly, he thinks that the critical exchange is related twice: the complaints in B, which presuppose a "Pharisaic" temple praxis, are virulent beginning with Jonathan's high priestly office; the abuses cited in C 4–5 refer back to the time of the Sadducean-Hellenistic priests. For criticism of this position see also E. Tigchelaar, review of *Reading 4QMMT* (see n. 61 above), *JSJ* 28 (1997): 331–3 (332).

[93] Cf. the introductions in section B (partially restored) ועל in 3, 5, 36, 37, 70, 75, 76, 77 along with נאף ועל in 9, 13, 17–18, 21, 22, 24, 49, 52, 55, 64, all clearly laid out in Qimron/Strugnell, 137; cf. also 135. I do not understand however why Qimron/Strugnell fail to see that there is in C a continuation of the complaint list. The demarcation of parts B and C proves to be too schematic; cf. M. J. Bernstein, "The Employment and Interpretation of Scripture in 4QMMT: Preliminary Questions," in *Reading 4QMMT* (see n. 61 above), 29–51 (46–47) and E. Tigchelaar (previous note), 333.

[94] For an example of the use of כתוב to conclude halakic argumentation see B 38, 76–78.

[95] Cf. Qimron/Strugnell, 58: "the restored word ביתכה may refer to the Temple."

the whole of Deut 7. It deals rather with God's blessing in the promised land, which survives through the *separating of the peoples* of the land. The Israelites are not to enter into marriage with them, for the result of this (i.e., the result of the forbidden sexual relations) is the worship of foreign gods "in your [singular] house" (cf. Deut 7:3–4, 25–26), which could also be understood as referring to the private household.

As in section B, the *participants* of temple worship are being criticized for their wrong doing. And in both instances the priests are accused (if indeed it is an accusation) of taking insufficient measures against this. Corresponding to section B, then, the focus lies on "popular practice" (76; contra Schwartz).

The senders presuppose a priestly elite-mentality and solidarity *against* the people and its teachers, who apparently were not priests.[96] The senders hope, therefore, to win over the priest Jonathan from the order of Jehoiarib to their agenda. This hints, I believe, at a time immediately prior or following Jonathan's acceptance of the high-priestly office. At that point, his approach towards the current "Pharisaic" character of temple worship had not been formulated. The shift from "people" (C 7) to "your people" (C 27) may then be understood in the following way: Concurrent with assuming the high-priestly office, "*the* people" becomes the people entrusted to Jonathan; consequently, Jonathan must be aware of his responsibility and duty (according to the views of the senders), to form "Israel" out of it. He is thus basically confronted with the following alternative: either to break with the temple reform which had been introduced at the time of the rededication of the temple and thus to join in with the "we"-interpretation, or to get along with the majority of the people, the latter of which he probably did. Contrary to Schwartz, the connection between רוב העם and the "Pharisees" (the "they"-group) turns out to be a likely and plausible interpretation.

C 7b–9 concludes the section and serves as a transition, regardless of the correctness of the editorial restorations that cannot be verified with certainty.

> [But you know that] we have separated from the peop[le and from all its impurities], from the mixing with these things and from joining with them[97] with regard to these

---

[96] From 159–152 B.C., after the death of Alcimus, there was *no* high priest; contra H. Stegemann, *Die Essener, Qumran, Johannes der Täufer und Jesus* (Freiburg: Herder, 1993) 205–6, who argues that in this time the "Teacher of Righteousness" was acting as high priest. See *Ant.* 20.237; J. Sievers, *Hasmoneans*, 76–77; P. A. Rainbow, "Teacher of Righteousness," 48–49; the "Scribes" and with them the Hasideans, did follow Alcimus and had thus distanced themselves from further political goals of the Hasmoneans. They may have exploited the uncertain circumstances after 159 to shape and develop temple worship according to their designs. Once a new high priest had been appointed, the renewed question arose how the successor would view the given situation.

[97] The text ולבוא ע[מהם] in C 8 is hard to understand. Qimron/Strugnell translate: "and from participating with [them]," taking בוא עם as a parallel expression to התערב. It is possible that sexual relations are in view here; see *m. Ker.* 1:1, where בוא על is to be

things. And you kn[ow that] on our hands there is [not] found guilt and deception and evil (מעל ושקר ורעה). For on [this] [w]e set [our hearts . . .].

In this revised catalogue of vices which is found only a few lines after C 4–5 (which is so decisive for Schwartz) only מעל is repeated, but this time it is applied to the senders. This raises the question whether מעל in C 4 is to be limited to the transgressions of the priests only. By way of conclusion, the senders emphasize in C 8–9 against the "you"-group [plural] that they themselves have not engaged in any wrong doing that has been mentioned thus far, and for which the people and the "they"-group are made responsible. Only from C 10 onwards is the "you" [singular] addressee spoken to and this change in the addressee marks in my opinion the cedisive break in the text.

An interpretation similar to that of Schwartz is offered by Hanan Eshel, who sees three groups as well, namely the "we"-group as senders, the "you"-group as recipients and the "multitude of the people." The latter is a distinct group that is neither addressed nor identical to the associates of the "you"-recipients (לטוב לך ולעמך [see citation above, p. 464]) mentioned in C 27.[98] Assuming this tripartite division, the "you"-group later turns into the Pharisees (see Schwartz) while the רוב העם-group, as the associates of the priestly group, become the Sadducees.[99] Eshel takes the "multitude" to refer

---

understood as "to have sexual connections" (Jastrow 1.143). In B 43 Qimron/Strugnell complements and translates: "[. . . and one must not coha]bit with them" (51; see 89, where they refer to a further instance of this phrase in the QH-fragments). Concerning the Old Testament usage of בוא על in the sense of "to have sexual relations," see Gen 19:31; Deut 25:5. The emendation of the text as ולבוא על[הם] is equally as possible as the rendering suggested by Qimron/Strugnell. Since B 80ff. concerns illegitimate sexual relations between priests and non-priests, such an emphasis is not impossible, especially since the *hitpa'el* התערב is used in section B 80 with this meaning (see also Ezra 9:2 with regard to mixed marriages). The negative image of marriage in Qumran may have one of its roots here.

[98] "4QMMT and the History of the Hasmonean Period," 59. His argumentation regarding C 7 is unconvincing: "Both grammatically and rhetorically the 'you' group, the target of persuasion, indicates a group distinct from רוב העם." It is clear that the "you"-group is still in view here. Otherwise, if עם with suffix were used, it would mean "your people," which is otherwise not documented. Furthermore, already the ם of עם is an emendation of the editors, which renders unanswerable the question whether a personal suffix was connected with it. Rhetorically it is certainly plausible not to use a suffix at this point (even if "your" people and the "majority of the people" were identical) since the entire document displays the tendency to fault the people rather than its priests (see above, p. 469). Furthermore, if the "majority of the people" is not connected in some way with the "you" addressees, then it would be uncertain what is meant in C 27+32, since there, "your people" is placed side by side with "Israel." Eshel sees here the followers of Jonathan in the time prior to his assuming high priesthood (60).

[99] See "4QMMT and the History of the Hasmonean Period," 60 n. 23: "This section of MMT indicates that when this text was composed this majority [= עם הארץ in the rabbinic texts] followed the hellenized priests, i.e. the ancestors of the Sadducees." I consider it unlikely that the Sadducees evolved from the Hellenist party in Jerusalem. It also appears unlikely that the

to the hellenized Jerusalem which followed the unknown high priest who reigned from 159–152 B.C., while Jonathan merely ruled in Michmash as judge over the loyalists of the Hasmonean cause (1 Macc 9:73).[100] When Jonathan then became high priest, the remaining priests would still have enjoyed the support of a majority of the people.[101] According to Eshel, the document MMT was penned shortly prior, or subsequent, to Jonathan's assuming the high priesthood from the unknown Hellenistic priest. While Jonathan did not, according to Eshel, possess any noteworthy influence (which still lay in the hands of the Hellenistic Jerusalem priests), it could be assumed that he would gain his influence sooner or later: "In either case, when this composition was written, the opponents of the Hellenistic priests had already realized that the leadership of that priestly group was temporary and would not last long, and that it was likely that Jonathan would be the next high priest" ("4QMMT and the History of the Hasmonean Period," 63).

This very hypothetical reconstruction does not appear convincing in any way, since it rests on the unlikely assumption that temple worship was dominated by Hellenistic priests even after the rededication of the temple by Judas Maccabeus. I have shown above that this assumption can hardly be

---

hellenistically inclined priests shaped temple worship between 159 and 152 B.C. (see above, section 5).

[100] At first glance, 1 Macc 9:23ff. could support Eshel's interpretation in which "the lawless and unrighteous" regain the upper hand after the death of Judas. However, in this context there is no mention of the temple or the high priest, which means that these battles concern political struggles and not the independence of temple worship. See also 9:61: Jonathan (or Bacchides, whose chance for success had been frustrated; the subject of the sentence is unclear) has fifty men "from the people of the land" taken captive and killed who had been the "leaders of the rebellious" (καὶ συνέλαβον ἀπὸ τῶν ἀνδρῶν τῆς χώρας τῶν ἀρχηγῶν τῆς κακίας . . . καὶ ἀπέκτειναν αὐτούς). It is crucial to observe here that priests are not in view, i.e. the Hellenistic party (the "rebellious") is not, as Eshel purports, led by the priests. Furthermore, 1 Macc 9:58, 69, 73 hardly states that the majority of the people sided with the Hellenists (see concerning this also J. Sievers, *Hasmoneans*, 58–59, 62–66).

[101] See "4QMMT and the History of the Hasmonean Period," 63. I consider this to be a correct interpretation, only that it was not the Hellenistic priests who served in the temple. There is no indication in the sources that there was a conflict between the priests or the people when Jonathan took office. Rather, Jonathan arrives in Jerusalem some time prior to his assuming his duties and lives there; in other words, he must have felt safe there (1 Macc 10:10; see 10:66, 87). He initiated building projects (1 Macc 10:11–12) and accepted the call to being high priest from Alexander Balas (1 Macc 10:20–21). Balas's choice of Jonathan against Demetrius occurred, at least according to 1 Macc, with the consent of the people (1 Macc 10:46; see 10:7). Even the capture of the Acra in Jerusalem, the last bastion of the "rebellious," was attempted, albeit unsuccessfully, by Jonathan in conjunction with the people (1 Macc 11:20; see also 11:30, 42). Furthermore, he enjoyed the support of at least part of the "elders" and "priests" (1 Macc 11:23). Even later, he rules in conjunction with the elders, the priests, and the people (see 1 Macc 12:6, 35–37) who deeply lament his imprisonment and murder (1 Macc 12:52; 13:26). His eulogy includes that he "brought the people together again" (1 Macc 14:30: καὶ ἤθροισεν Ιωναθαν τὸ ἔθνος αὐτῶν καὶ ἐγενήθη αὐτοῖς ἀρχιερεὺς . . .).

derived from the extant sources. Furthermore, the assumption that an unknown priest with Hellenistic inclinations ruled as high priest from 159–152 B.C. is untenable. And even if such a high priest existed and enjoyed the support of the רוב העם, we ask why there is not the slightest hint in the sources of a conflict, power struggle, or the like (and for the senders of MMT to anticipate such a drastic change), as Jonathan becomes high priest. This holds true especially since the Acra, the center of the Hellenists in Jerusalem, was besieged and "cleansed" only by Jonathan's brother and successor Simon (1 Macc 13:49–51; 14:36–37). It is unlikely that the Hellenists would surrender such a significant office without resistance, as long as they still possessed a military stronghold in the city. Furthermore, if Hellenistic priests controlled activities in the temple up to the rise of Jonathan, then it is difficult to imagine that the senders of the letter did not have more important matters to discuss with the new high priest than those raised in MMT. In addition, it appears that the noted deficiencies at the temple do not merely furnish a topic for theoretical discussion but arise from present practices of temple worship. It would also follow that the Hellenistic priests who later became the Sadducees were engaging in a practice that corresponded to that of the later Pharisees. The approach of both Eshel and Schwartz (always assuming that I have understood them correctly) is thus filled with hypotheses and hardly convincing.

3. The only well-argued point of Schwartz is the fact that the Josephus-section adduced by Qimron/Strugnell cannot be taken as "a similar *early* association" (115; emphasis mine) of the Pharisees with the majority of the people. The *Antiquities* of Josephus were only written towards the latter quarter of the first century A.D. and the context of Book 18 points to the beginning of the procuratorial rule in Judea in A.D. 6. Irrespective of this even Schwartz emphasizes:

> Just as the sectarian author of Pesher Nahum sees two major groups, Ephraim and Manasseh, corresponding to the Pharisees and Sadducees,[102] and just as the Gospels apparently show us another sect viewing its competitors as being mainly varieties, so too MMT shows us a Jewish world divided mainly into three camps: Qumranites, Pharisees and a Temple establishment which we associate, generally, with the Sadducees (80).

In my view, one fact is most decisive here. Beginning with 4QMMT, the oldest account, until the composition of the *Antiquities* by Josephus towards

---

[102] Likewise and emphatically H. Eshel, "4QMMT and the History of the Hasmonean Period," 63 n. 34: "It is important to note that when we read Pesher Nahum which describes the situation in Judea in the middle of the first century BCE, the situation is completely different. Then the majority of the people were the followers of Ephraim (the Pharisees) and they are called פתאי אפרים ('simple of Ephraim') (4QpNah 3–4.iii.5); Jerusalem is called עיר אפרים ('the city of Ephraim') (3–4.ii.2)."

the end of the first century A.D., three major divisions within Judaism are consistently portrayed.

What speaks against Schwartz and Eshel is the lack of evidence in support of their linking the "multitude/majority of the people" with the "temple establishment" of the Sadducees (which probably did not yet exist at that time). Therefore, 4QMMT remains an important, early and decisive piece of evidence for the popularity of that position which generally is identified as Pharisaic. Furthermore, the impression we glean from 4QMMT supports the reliability of Josephus' tripartite characterization of Judaism prior to A.D. 70.

5.3 Josephus' threefold division of Judaism into Pharisees, Sadducees, and Essenes

Josephus stresses that not all Jews directly belonged to one of the three parties (to which the Zealots must be added as a fourth party, having split off from the Pharisees); nevertheless, together they represented the *attitudes* of the majority of the people (see *J.W.* 2.166; *Ant.* 18.11; *Life* 10).[103] In my view this is also the reason why Josephus describes both the respective group's internal relationships *and* their contact with the outside world.

The *Essenes* form closed groups. No person of "other convictions" has access to their meetings (μηδενὶ τῶν ἑτεροδόξων; *J.W.* 2.129; see also *Ant.* 18.19). Josephus mentions particular rites of initiation and expulsion that are unique to the Essenes (*J.W.* 2.137–144). While he mentions nothing concerning goals or purposes outside the community (see, however, *J.W.* 2.139), life inside the community is spelled out in detail. Their teaching is secret, accessible only to those who are full members and have gone through a three year trial period (*J.W.* 2.142), or children who have been taken in by the sect[104] (*J.W.* 2.120).[105] There is, furthermore, no hint in Josephus that the

---

[103] See *J.W.* 2.118, where he mentions Judas the Galilean as σοφιστής of a separate αἵρεσις which was dissimilar to other Jewish groups. This is followed by the report concerning the Pharisees, Sadducees, and Essenes which are thereby presented as a standard, from which Judas deviates. In *Ant.* 18.4, 9–10, 23 he does, however, point to the proximity between Judas and the Pharisees. Also the term αἵρεσις suggests that he views the Pharisees, Sadducees, and Essenes as religious groups, among whom there existed different possibilities of identification: see A. J. Saldarini, *Pharisees,* 123–7: "A *hairesis* was a coherent and principled choice of a way of life, that is, of a particular school of thought" (123). Saldarini emphasizes, however, that "school of *thought*" does not imply a theoretical system. See also S. Mason, *Pharisees,* 125–8.

[104] In this context the term appears to be appropriate; see also E. P. Sanders, *Practice,* 341ff.

[105] Concerning parallels to Qumran, see I. Knohl, "The Revealed and Hidden Torah," *JQR* 85 (1994/95):103–8: "In summary, the widespread use in Qumran literature of terms of concealment and disclosure vis-à-vis Torah and the law, reflects the community's separatist nature, and served its leaders in justifying and establishing the ever-widening gap between their community and the rest of Israel (108)." See also A. Shemesh and C. Werman, "The Hidden Things and Their Revelation," *Tarbiz* 66 (1996/97): 471–82 (Hebrew, English summary).

internal laws (*J.W.* 2.122, 143) and purity practices of the sect (*J.W.* 2.123, 129, 138, 147, 150, 159, 161) were communicated to those outside the community.[106] Also, a priestly tendency is noticeable (*J.W.* 2.131). Their number is given by Josephus in the context of the "group-reports"[107] as 4000 (*Ant.* 18.20). Although he describes them in more detail than the other groups, he does not mention their following among the people. In *J.W.* 2.119 he even appears to criticize their position: δοκεῖ σεμνότητα ἀσκεῖν 'Ιουδαῖοι μὲν γένος ὄντες, φιλάλληλοι δὲ καὶ τῶν ἄλλων πλέον ("While they are Jews, they love each other more than they love others"[108]).

Concerning the *Pharisees*, Josephus points to a similar closeness within the group as that among the Essenes, albeit not mentioning a requirement for formal membership (*J.W.* 2.166).[109] Here, again, the parallel to the above-mentioned fellowship among the Essenes is conspicuous:[110] καὶ Φαρισαῖοι μὲν φιλάλληλοί τε καὶ εἰς τὸ κοινὸν ὁμόνοιαν ἀσκοῦντες ("Also the Pharisees love one another and strive to labor harmoniously for the communal good"). Once more, the question arises as to what τὸ κοινόν denotes. If one views the Pharisees as a sect with strong internal ties, it follows that here internal codes of conduct are in view.[111] Since Josephus emphasizes elsewhere the high popularity that the Pharisees enjoy, τὸ κοινόν could refer, however,

---

[106] Conversely, the Qumran texts display, as far as I know, no concern to actively communicate their convictions to Jews outside their community.

[107] This has not been sufficiently noticed. It is misleading merely to compare the number of 6000 Pharisees with that of 4000 Essenes, and to take them as absolute figures to arrive at the conclusion that the Pharisees had only a slightly higher number of members than the Essenes. The reference to the fact that 6000 Pharisees refused to swear the oath to Augustus and Herod does not say anything about their absolute number. See R. Deines and M. Hengel, "Common Judaism," 66; concerning the history of interpretation of this number, see R. Deines, *Pharisäer*, 638 (Index, see under "Pharisäer, Zahl der").

[108] There is a question what τῶν ἄλλων refers to: Is it a comparison with the other two groups, so that Josephus might want to say: they love each other more than the Sadducees and Pharisees do respectively; or does it refer to the non-Essene Jews? The conspicuous parallel in *J.W.* 1.110 (here the Pharisees are introduced with . . . Φαρισαῖοι, σύνταγμά τι 'Ιουδαίων δοκοῦν εὐσεβέστερον εἶναι τῶν ἄλλων καὶ τοὺς νόμους ἀκριβέστερον ἀφηγεῖσθαι) suggests that τῶν ἄλλων in both 2.119 and 1.110 refers to those outside the respective group. The introductory δοκέω would then refer to the self-understanding of the group, perhaps with a critical undertone on the part of Josephus. Also, the μὲν . . . δέ in 2.119 points to an emphasis on the contrast between Essenes and non-Essenes.

[109] See, however, H.-F. Weiss, art. "Pharisäer," 477, who sees here a proof for the organization of the Pharisees into so-called "fellowships" (חבורה). See e.g. *m. Dem.* 2:3; 6:6, 9, 12; *m. Toh.* 7:4; *m. Hag.* 2:7; concerning the conditions of membership, see *b. Bek.* 30*b*; the relevant references are collected in Str-B, 2.501ff.

[110] The strong connection between 2.119 and 2.162ff. suggests that Josephus may have used a source concerning the Essenes in 2.120–161, which he inserted at this point.

[111] So S. Mason, *Pharisees*, 170–73.

to the Jewish society at large.[112] In support of this latter interpretation I want to draw attention to the structure of presenting the three parties: first Josephus mentions internal characteristics of each group, then their contact with their fellow Jews. In the report concerning the *Sadducees* this structure is especially clear: amongst them "exist raw forms of treating each other, and relationships to each other are as unfriendly as to those outside" (. . . αἵ τε ἐπιμιξίαι πρὸς τοὺς ὁμοίους ἀπηνεῖς ὡς πρὸς ἀλλοτρίους, *J. W.* 2.166). He further states that they are only a small group which does not shy away from internal arguments. Neither special social contacts among themselves (see *Ant.* 18.16), nor positive elements concerning their goals are mentioned. In their public religious practices they are dependent on the Pharisaic influence upon the people. Here, again, it is quite noticeable which areas Josephus mentions and which he is silent about (see above, n. 5).

There is a correspondence between Josephus' threefold division of Judaism with regard to its religious life and its influence on the behavior of the people (besides its socio-political effects) and that of Qumran. As mentioned above, the polemical, inner-Jewish situation is clearly described in Qumran. Even if one is skeptical towards – or rejects – the plausible correspondence between "Judah," "Ephraim," and "Manasseh" on the one hand, and Qumran, the Pharisees, and the Sadducees on the other,[113] the identical and conspicuous tripartite religious differentiation remains intact. Furthermore, Qumran sees itself as inferior in the battle for religious influence upon the people, for the "simple people" (and not only they) are under the influence of "Ephraim."[114]

---

[112] This is also suggested by the comparison with the Stoics (see *Life* 12); see concerning this F. Hauck, art. κοινός κτλ., *TDNT* 3 (1938): 789–809 (794ff.).

[113] See e.g. A. J. Saldarini, *Pharisees*, 278–80 (see also art. "Pharisees," 301); G. Stemberger, *Pharisäer*, 104–5; J. Sievers, *Hasmoneans* 90–93. The identification of the concealed Qumran terms with the known Jewish groups was first undertaken by D. Flusser ("Pharisäer, Sadduzäer und Essener im Pescher Nahum," in *Qumran* [ed. K. E. Grözinger, N. Ilg, H. Lichtenberger, B.-W. Nebe and H. Pabst; WdF 410; Darmstadt: Wissenschaftliche Buchgesellschaft, 1981], 121–66) and has since been confirmed and further developed. See the recent works by L. H. Schiffman, "Pharisees and Sadducees in *Pesher Nahum*," *Minḥah le-Naḥum*, (*Fs.* N. M. Sarna; ed. M. Brettler and M. Fishbane; JSOTSup 154; Sheffield: Sheffield Academic (1993), 272–90; S. Goranson, "The Exclusion of Ephraim in Rev. 7:4–8 and Essene Polemic Against Pharisees," *DSD* 2 (1995): 80–85.

[114] Concerning the אפרים פתאי see 4QpNah 3–4.iii.2–9; but also "Ephraim" itself can be counted as the פתאים among the misguided (ibid. 3–4.ii.7–9); this means that concerning "Ephraim" there is a certain inconsistency which corresponds, however, to the phenomenon of the Pharisees: as scribes they are those who mislead the people, and as party-members they are the misguided; see also 1QpMic frag. 10, line 5. To teach the "simple" and to join (להחביר) them together in the יחד is the expressed purpose of the Qumran-community (see 11QPs^a 18:3–4 [=syrPs 2]). Only in an eschatological context do we find finally a reference to פתאי יהודה (1QpHab 12:4–5, see also 1QH 2:9–10). The passages 1QSa 1:19–21 and CD 15:15 (also 4 Q266 17.i) do not pertain here; there the "simple" refer to people with modest mental abilities side by side with other handicaps.

Flusser has pointed out that the reference to the "simple people of Ephraim" corresponds to the rabbinic עם הארץ. He concludes that the פתאי אפרים refers to "the great majority of the entire Jewish people who support Pharisaic teaching."[115]

It is important to note that this picture is not questioned by any early source. Furthermore, the New Testament assumes merely a bipartite division into Pharisees (whereby their closeness to the people is again apparent) and Sadducees, and the same applies to rabbinic tradition.[116] The latter knows of further separate groups and heretical teaching, but little of it points to a time before A.D. 70 or to major movements.

We therefore submit that these facts have clear consequences concerning the question of the *provenance of Jewish-Palestinian literature which arose after 4QMMT* and which does not contain any references to parties. If the division of Judaism into three major religious movements is correct, it follows that individual texts probably belong to one of these three basic movements. Otherwise they must be viewed as individual writings, representing individual religious personalities (with a certain following) which do not exert any significant influence on the people at large. To postulate multiple sects on the basis of individual texts thus misses the point. This means that a differentiated and individually demonstrated link between these texts to the Pharisees or, in a wider sense, a link with Pharisaic Judaism, may not be rejected out of hand.[117] More than hitherto, the halakic label should be considered, for it lends identity to the texts.

5.4 Jewish Writings from Hellenistic-Roman Times and the Division of Judaism into Three Primary Movements

While it is not possible to go into details, I would like to point out texts that qualify as possible sources. For this it is necessary to ask which texts were written in the time between 150 B.C. and A.D. 70/100[118] and whose Palestinian

---

[115] D. Flusser, "Pescher Nahum," 162; see also 158–62.

[116] In both cases we must add the Samaritans. In rabbinic literature the Boethuseans are linked with the Sadducees (Y. Sussmann, "History of the Halakha," 193–6 and others link them to the Essenes). In the New Testament the Herodians are mentioned. See S. J. D. Cohen, "The Significance of Yavneh: Pharisees, Rabbis and the End of Sectarianism," *HUCA* 55 (1984): 32–36.

[117] Contra J. Neusner/C. Thoma, "Pharisäer," 71, who state categorically: "Attempts to link the Scroll of Fasting, *Jubilees*, Qumran (esp. 1QpHab and 4QpNah), the Testaments, the Enoch-tradition, the 7th chapter of [1] Macc, the Psalms of Solomon etc. with the Pharisees, have led to exaggerated speculations concerning the Pharisees but not to historically defensible theses." A bit more cautious, but in the same direction, cf. G. Stemberger, *Pharisäer*, 8, and passim.

[118] A good number of texts arose out of a direct reaction to the destruction of the temple and thus belong in this setting. Neither Pharisaic Judaism nor other movements ceased immediately

provenance can be reasonably well assumed.[119] We note the problem that the dating of many texts is controversially debated as well as the possibility and extent of later Christian interpolations. What follows thus begins with the generally accepted standard.[120]

The oldest document for the chosen time-frame is most likely *Jubilees*, which may be dated in the middle of the second century B.C.[121] Some scholars date it even slightly earlier since it does not appear to presuppose the split among the priests.[122] The calendar presented therein, the text-fragments of Qumran, and the significance attributed to the calendar question since the discovery of these text-fragments, all point to a proximity to the Essenes and renders a connection with the Pharisees highly unlikely. Furthermore, the

---

after A.D. 70. The transition to rabbinic Judaism occurred gradually in these decades. Literature from these three decades may thus still reflect the character of the time before A.D. 70.

[119] For our purposes we may exclude the question to what extent Pharisaic Judaism exerted its influence on the Diaspora. The crucial fact is that it was shaped in Palestine and maintained its center there. Concerning Jewish-Hellenistic literature and its intention, see M. Hengel, "Anonymität, Pseudepigraphie und 'literarische Fälschung' in der jüdisch-hellenistischen Literatur" (now revised in: idem, *Judaica et Hellenistica* [see n. 2], 196–251), originally in *Pseudepigrapha I: Pseudopythagorica, lettres de Platon, littérature pseudépigraphique juive* [ed. K. v. Fritz; EnAC 18; Geneva: Fondation Hardt pour l'Etude de l'Antiquité Classique, 1972], 231–308): the individual works "seek to glorify its own people, its holy history, to serve its faith in the one God and his law, whereby the law was often interpreted in a generally relevant, ethical fashion. . . . Their goal was not primarily to serve as a missionary means of reaching the Greeks, but rather to satisfy the literary needs of the Greek-speaking Jews themselves, namely to strengthen their commitment to the tradition and the faith of their fathers and their religious and national identity" (249–50). The marks their basic difference from those texts that refer to *internal* conflicts of the Jewish Society.

[120] The standard views are found in classical presentations: E. Schürer, *The History of the Jewish People in the Age of Jesus Christ (175 B.C.–A.D. 135)*, Vols. I–III/2 (rev.; ed. G. Vermes, F. Millar, M. Black, M. Goodman; Edinburgh: T & T Clark, 1973–1987); R. A. Kraft and G. W. E. Nickelsburg, *Early Judaism and its Modern Interpreters* (see n. 15).

[121] See Schürer/Vermes/Millar 3.313; D. J. Harrington, "The Bible Rewritten," in Kraft/Nickelsburg, 239–47, esp. 243–4; K. Berger, *Das Buch der Jubiläen* (JSHRZ 23; Gütersloh: Mohn, 1981), 300: between 167 and 140 B.C., more specifically 145–140 B.C. See also J. C. VanderKam who dates *Jubilees* between 161 and 152 B.C. (*Textual and Historical Studies in the Book of Jubilees* [HSM 14; Missoula: Scholars, 1977]). *Jub.* 23:14–21, concerning the desecration of the Holy Place, may refer to Antiochus IV or the same period as 4QMMT. Especially 23:21 appears to point to the latter possibility: "And those who survived will not return to the path of righteousness from their evil ways. Rather, they will all engage in deceit and rise to riches, that one takes all that belongs to his neighbor. And the great name they will neither name in truth nor in righteousness. And the Holy of Holies they will desecrate through the impurity of their sin (transl. K. Berger; already M. Hengel, *Judentum*, 411 saw in this text a reference to the beginnings of the Maccabean rule; now, however, we are in the position to date even more precisely). *Jub.* 30:14–16 is also noteworthy: as in 4QMMT it is the people who desecrate the Holy Place and the sacrifice (and the priests?) by illegitimate sexual unions.

[122] Schürer/Vermes/Millar 3.314. I do not consider this argument to be very convincing.

different view concerning life after death (*Jub.* 23:31) is notable. Simultaneously, *Jubilees* does testify to a strong awareness concerning questions of purity and halakic issues, which can be documented from the time of the attempted Hellenistic reform onward. Above all, sexual conduct and contact with Gentiles are linked with concerns for purity (e.g. *Jub.* 30:1–16), a fact that places the text near 4QMMT.[123]

Judith may be dated toward the last third of the second century B.C., or at the latest in the first quarter of the first century A.D.[124] Also 1 and 2 Maccabees stem from that time.[125] Especially Judith reflects a piety akin to Pharisaic features: the heroine is a woman,[126] the significance of purity is assumed, the goal of her efforts is the salvation of her entire people.[127] All in all it is, however, not a political document but rather religious and devotional encouragement and admonition, in the best sense of the word, seeking to address as many people as possible.[128] Likewise, 2 Maccabees has been linked to Pharisaic circles, while 1 Maccabees may be close to the Sadducees.[129] Even these two works may not be identified as political documents in a literal sense. Rather, they are part of mainstream "Common Judaism" which includes

---

[123] Concerning the halakic categorization of *Jubilees* see J. Neusner, *The Idea of Purity in Ancient Judaism* (SJLA 1; Leiden: Brill, 1973), 55–58; K.-H. Müller, "Die hebräische Sprache der Halacha als Textur der Schöpfung. Beobachtungen zum Verhältnis von Tora und Halacha im Buch der Jubiläen," in *Bibel in jüdischer und christlicher Tradition* (Fs. J. Maier; ed. H. Merklein and others; BBB 88; Frankfurt/M.: A. Hain, 1993), 157–76. K. Berger, *Jubiläen*, 298, describes the community of *Jubilees* as an "anti-Hellenistic, priestly and restorative group of reformers who stand in close historical proximity to the Asideans as well as to the slightly later Qumran community."

[124] Schürer/Vermes/Millar 3.219.

[125] 1 Macc: Schürer/Vermes/Millar 3.181; H. W. Attridge, "Jewish Historiography," in Kraft/Nickelsburg, 311–43 (esp. 317); J. Sievers, *Hasmoneans*, 3; 2 Macc: Schürer/Vermes/Millar 3.532; H. W. Attridge, "Jewish Historiography," 321–2; 2 Macc belongs, strictly speaking, to Jewish-Hellenistic literature: see M. Hengel, "Anonymität," 207–8.

[126] Concerning the Pharisaic influence on women, cf. T. Ilan, "The Attraction of Aristocratic Women to Pharisaism During the Second Temple Period," *HTR* 88 (1995): 1–33.

[127] Cf. Jdt 12:7–9, 19 (cf. 10:5): note the emphasis on keeping purity- and dietary-laws. Indirectly, the message corresponds to that of 1 and 2 Maccabees: God saves his people through those who keep his commandments in every way, even in difficult situations. See also Jdt 11:13: the inability to keep the purity-laws is seen as a threat; cf. also R. Deines and M. Hengel, "Common Judaism," 48–49.

[128] It is nevertheless conspicuous that no copy of this document was found in Qumran. This may be accidental. On the other hand, it may be significant, since the view of women in the known texts is generally very negative.

[129] See R. Deines, *Pharisäer*, 123, 145, concerning 1 Macc; also J. Sievers, *Hasmoneans*, 2–3. There exists the less successful attempt to ascribe 1 Maccabees to a Pharisaic author: see K.-D. Schunck, *1. Makkabäerbuch* (JSHRZ 1/4; Gütersloh: Gütersloher Verlagshaus, 1980), 292. Concerning 2 Macc, cf. R. Deines, *Pharisäer*, 58, 72, 75, 145, 522; J. Sievers, *Hasmoneans*, 7–8.

at times a more Pharisaic, at times a more Sadducean tendency, without placing themselves outside this broad center.[130]

Written in the middle of the first century B.C., the *Psalms of Solomon* are usually regarded as an authentic source for a description of Pharisaism.[131] A decisive factor for understanding *Ps. Sol.* is the perspective from which they describe processes in Jewish society. Some psalms display a strong contrast between "we" and "they." The implied critique is directed against parts of the priesthood (cf. 1:7–8; 8:9–12), but also against the inhabitants of Jerusalem (2:3, 13). The deeds of sinners are opposed to the deeds of the righteous (3:6–12; 4:8; 12–16); resurrection is promised to those who fear God (3:16). The standpoint of the author(s) is Jerusalem; the ideal is the pious man who knows how to protect his house from sin (cf. 3:7–8; 6:5). The "righteous" or "pious" are not a community closed up (17:16); rather, they live in the midst of the nation, suffering under the sins that the sinners commit. There are numerous allusions to Qumran texts, but there is a complete lack of orientation towards the priesthood. The temple plays a relatively minor role, despite the polemic against its pollution; the same holds true for the priesthood, the festivals, the calendar, the Sabbath and the sacrifices. We find no "halakic" passages in *Ps. Sol.*, but this may be due to the genre of the psalms.

The perspective and the polemics of *Assumption of Moses*, dated to the first quarter of the first century A.D.,[132] has led to rather divergent ascriptions:

---

[130] I agree with M. Simon, *Die jüdischen Sekten zur Zeit Christi* (Zürich: Benziger, 1964), who states that all those groups belonged to "official Judaism" which were represented in the Sanhedrin (16); similarly already H. Graetz; cf. R. Deines, *Pharisäer*, 172.

[131] For the date cf. Schürer/Vermes/Millar 3.194: 63–48 B.C.; the revised English edition still detects "Pharisee ideology" in *Ps. Sol.* For older ascriptions to Pharisaic circles see R. Deines, *Pharisäer*, 49 n. 26 (Wellhausen); 74 with n. 81 (Schürer), 122–3 (Bousset); 231 n. 102 (Elbogen), 275 n. 109 and 282 n. 129 (Schlatter), 302 (Prince, Eaton); 306 n. 18 (Ryle, James); 353 (Herford); 370 (Abrahams); 418 n. 36 (R. Kittel); 470 (C. Schneider); 473–4 n. 185 (Preisker); 485 n. 218 (E. Meyer). E. P. Sanders rejects a link with the Pharisees, basing his position mainly on the essay of J. O'Dell, "The Religious Background of the Psalms of Solomon (Re-evaluated in the Light of the Qumran Texts)," *RQ* 3 (1961): 241–57. More recent studies of *Ps. Sol.* have confirmed their Pharisaic perspective, however; cf. J. Schüpphaus, *Die Psalmen Salomons* (see n. 52), and now M. Winninge, *Sinners and the Righteous. A Comparative Study of the Psalms of Solomon and Paul's Letter* (ConBNT 26; Uppsala: Almqvist & Wiksell), 1995. Differently J. H. Charlesworth, "Jewish Hymns, Odes, and Prayers" (in Kraft/Nickelsburg, 411–36) 415–6; J. L. Trafton, "The Psalms of Solomon in Recent Research," *JSP* 12 (1994): 3–19 (7–8), who, however, could not take into account the study of Winninge. Several scholars argue for an Essene provenance of *Ps. Sol.* Of course the possibility of ascribing *Ps. Sol.* to the Pharisees, or, more generally, to early Judaism as influenced by Pharisaic ideas, is dependent upon one's definition of the Pharisees or of Pharisaic Judaism.

[132] Cf. Schürer/Vermes/Millar, 3.283; D. J. Harrington, "The Bible Rewritten," in Kraft/Nickelsburg, 244; J. Priest, *OTP* 2.921; E. Brandenburger, *Himmelfahrt Moses* (JSHRZ 5/2; Gütersloh: Mohn, 1976), 59–60: shortly after A.D. 6. Occasionally scholars assume a two-

many have assumed a Pharisaic author,[133] but others have argued for a Sadducean, Zealot, Essene or Samaritan, or for an unknown provenance.[134] In the light of this diversity of opinions it is advisable to be cautious. At the same time we see that the perspectives common to the various groups were evidently so extensive that it is not easy to decide the question of provenance. However, the polemical demarcations of *As. Mos.* represent a milieu which is familiar from Josephus and, even more, from the New Testament. Thus this text is at least indirectly a confirmation of their picture of Judaism. The text 4QMMT may possibly lead to a new interpretation of *As. Mos.*, particularly of 5:4–5:

> For they will not follow the truth of God, but certain of them will pollute the high altar by [four to six letters are lost] the offerings which they place before the Lord. They are not (truly) priests (at all), but slaves, indeed sons of slaves. For those who are the leaders, their teachers, in those times will become admirers of avaricious persons, accepting (polluted) offerings, and they will sell justice by accepting bribes. (Translation J. Priest)

The interpretation of this passage has proved to be difficult since the actions of the Hasmonean priest-kings are not mentioned until 6:1ff. In the context of the interpretation of 4QMMT which I suggested earlier (see above 5.2), this polemic may refer to the time of or after Alcimus during which the scribes who were associated with him exerted decisive influence on the organization of the temple cult. The following ch.6 relates *inter alia* the suppression of the riots by Varus in 4 B.C. and the beginning of the rule of the sons of Herod. Chapter 6:7–8 appears to presuppose the deportation of Archelaus and the transformation of Judea into a Roman province. In ch.7 the author begins to describe the "end times," i.e. his own times. He characterizes his opponents

---

stage redaction: the older text was written between 175–167 B.C., with chs. 6–7 being a later interpolation; at that later stage chs. 8–9, which originally referred to Antiochus IV, were reinterpreted in eschatological terms. See J. Tromp, *The Assumption of Moses. A Critical Edition with Commentary* (SVTP 10; Leiden: Brill, 1993); he dates the work in "the first quarter of the first century C.E." (117). An unusually late date is assumed by A. Schalit, *Untersuchungen zur Assumptio Mosis* (ALGHJ 17; Leiden: Brill, 1989), xv: shortly before A.D. 66. Schalit does not give sufficient reason for his position, as his commentary remains a sketch.

[133] For older representatives see R. Deines, *Pharisäer*, 231 n. 102 (I. Elbogen); 370 (I. Abrahams); 474 n. 185 (H. Preisker); also J. Tromp, *Assumption* 101–2 (Charles, Clemen).

[134] Cf. E. Brandenburger, *Himmelfahrt Moses*, 65–66, who leaves the question open, as does J. Tromp, *Assumption*, 118–9 (cf. 107–109). Schürer/Vermes/Millar, 3.284, see the author as being "sympathetic to Essene ideology." The correlation of the predetermined course of the stars and the keeping of the commandments in 12:9–10 could be linked with the calendar piety of the Essenes. In contrast, *Ps. Sol.* end with the assertion that the eternal course of the stars can change when God directs them by the command of his servants (18:10–12).

in a highly polemical manner. The closest parallels are to be found in Jesus' accusations against the Pharisees and scribes:[135]

> Then will rule destructive and godless men, who represent themselves as being righteous, but who will (in fact) arouse their inner wrath, for they will be deceitful men, pleasing only themselves, false in every way imaginable, (such as) loving feasts at any hour of the day – devouring, gluttonous. [Seven lines of the text are either totally missing or are so broken as to permit no translation.] But really they consume the goods of the (poor), saying their acts are according to justice, (while in fact they are simply) exterminators, deceitfully seeking to conceal themselves so that they will not be known as completely godless because of their criminal deeds (committed) all the day long, saying, "We shall have feasts, even luxurious winings and dinings. Indeed, we shall behave ourselves as princes." They, with hand and mind, will touch impure things, yet their mouths will speak enormous things, and they will even say, "Do not touch me, lest you pollute me in the position I occupy. . . ." (7:3–10; translation J. Priest)[136]

After a new period of tribulation, depicted against the background of the Seleucid persecution, deliverance is eventually won by "a man from the tribe of Levi" (9:1).[137] This interpretation establishes for this document a point of view that is to be located in the context of priestly-levitical traditions from which the author polemicizes against the influence of the Pharisaic-scribal movement that was evidently strong.[138]

The second part of the Ethiopic *Book of Enoch*, the "Book of Parables" (or Similitudes) in chs. 37–71, dates with some certainty in the period before A.D. 70,[139] as do the *Vitae Prophetarum*.[140] Also to be mentioned is the *Megillat*

---

[135] But see Tromp, *Assumption*, 207–13, who points out that the text follows mostly the usual polemical patterns.

[136] It is surprising that Sanders does not refer to this passage in his brief section on *As. Mos.* (*Practice*, 455–7).

[137] Assuming that 10:1ff. is to be read as continuation of ch. 9. If this is correct, the text says: the time of salvation begins when the Levites are prepared to die rather than breaking the commandments; thus also E. Brandenburger, *Himmelfahrt Moses*, 63; J. Tromp, *Assumption*, 228.

[138] Cf. also A. Schalit, *Untersuchungen*, whose position is described by H. Schreckenberg in his "Preface" (vii–xvii) as follows: *As. Mos.* "seems to have been written in circles which distanced themselves from official Pharisaism, diverging in some respects from it" (xvi). Schalit interprets *As. Mos.* as a sectarian document ("Sektenschrift") whose author belonged to an unknown group. J. Tromp, in an earlier study, similarly linked the author with a "Levitical schismatical group" ("Taxo, the Messenger of the Lord," *JSJ* 21 [1991]: 200–209); his position in his subsequent study is more cautious (*Assumption*, 119 n. 2).

[139] Cf. Schürer/Vermes/Millar 3.259: between A.D. 0–70, but perhaps more towards the end of the first century. In contrast S. Uhlig, *Das Äthiopische Henochbuch* (JSHRZ 5/6; Gütersloh: Mohn, 1984), 574–5 (cf. 494) argues for a multi-stage origin during Maccabean rule with a final redaction in the first century A.D.; P. Sacchi, art. "Henochgestalt/Henochliteratur," *TRE* 15 (1986): 42–54: between the middle of the first century B.C. and the middle of the first century A.D. (47). The other parts of the *Enoch* literature are considerably older; only the "Book of Dream-Visions" (chs. 83–90) dates to the beginning of the Maccabean period (ca. 160 B.C.).

Taanit (Scroll of Fasting), a text which has been neglected in the recent discussion, unjustly in my opinion. Some assume a pre-70 date for the *Liber antiquitatum biblicarum* (Pseudo-Philo).[141]

The Book of Parables, the second Book of the "Enoch Pentateuch," is the only section of which no fragments have been found at Qumran. Nevertheless there is a clear terminological relationship with the Qumran texts,[142] so that the composition of the Book of Parables in the context of the Qumran community and thus the Essenes is most probable. The Parables are characterized by a dichotomy between the "congregation of the righteous"[143] and the "sinners"[144] (see 38:1 etc.); their main subject, however, is the eschatological conquest of the nations of the world who harass the people of God. There are but few traces of internal Jewish controversies; only the

---

Slavonic *Enoch*, written in the Alexandrian diaspora during the first century A.D. probably before 70, does not contain parallels to this part, even though its author knew the text: cf. Chr. Böttrich, *Das slawische Henochbuch* (JSHRZ 5/7; Gütersloh: Gütersloher Verlagshaus, 1995), 807–13. For an English translation see F. I. Andersen, *OTP* 1.91–221.

[140] See now A. M. Schwemer, *Studien zu den frühjüdischen Prophetenlegenden. Vitae Prophetarum* I/II (TSAJ 45/49; Tübingen: Mohr [Siebeck], 1995/1996) and idem, *Vitae Prophetarum* (JSHRZ 1/7; Gütersloh: Gütersloher Verlagshaus, 1997). She argues that Vit.Proph. was written in Jerusalem before A.D. 70. For an English translation see D. R. A. Hare, *OTP* 2.379–99.

[141] But see Schürer/Vermes/Millar 3.328: "written probably after the destruction of Jerusalem"; thus also Chr. Dietzfelbinger, *Pseudo-Philo: Antiquitates Biblicae* (JSHRZ 2/2; Gütersloh: Gütersloher Verlagshaus, 1975), 91, 95: between 73 and 132 A.D. A date between 135 and 150 A.D. is assumed by H. Jacobson, *A Commentary on Pseudo-Philo's Liber Antiquitatum Biblicarum with Latin Text and English Translation* (2 vols.; AGJU 31; Leiden: Brill, 1996), who argues for an origin in Galilee (1.999–210). R. Hayward argues for a date before 70 in his review of Jacobson, cf. *JJS* 38 (1997): 363–6 (365–6), as does D. J. Harrington, "The Bible Rewritten," in Kraft/Nickelsburg, 245.

[142] Cf. J. C. Greenfield and M. E. Stone, "The Enochic Pentateuch and the Date of the Similitudes," *HTR* 70 (1977): 51–65 (56–57); S. Uhlig, *Henochbuch*, 574.

[143] Also called "the righteous," "the elect," or "the holy ones": 38:2, 4; 39:4–7; 40:5; 41:2, 8; 43:4; 45:6; 46:8; 47:1–2, 4; 48:1, 4; 48:9; 50:1–2; 51:2, 5; and frequently.

[144] Also called "the wicked ones" or "those who have denied the name of the Lord of the Spirits": 38:2–3; 41:2, 8; 45:1–2, 6; 50:2. They are linked with "the kings and the mighty ones": 38:5; 46:4–5; 48:8. A clear description of this part of humankind is found in 46:7–8: "And they have become the judges of the stars of heaven; they raise their hands (to reach) the Most High while walking upon the earth and dwelling on it. They manifest all their deeds in oppression; all their deeds are oppression. Their power (depends) upon their wealth, and their devotion is to the gods which they have fashioned with their own hands. But they deny the name of the Lord of the Spirits. Yet they like to congregate in his houses and (with) the faithful ones who cling to the Lord of the Spirits" (translation by E. Isaac, *OTP* 1). This description shows in my opinion that the author does not refer to inner-Jewish enemies, although the meaning of the last sentence is questionable.

description of "those who dwell upon the earth"[145] implies an internal Jewish separation which, however, is not described in terms of enmity.

The *Vitae Prophetarum* focus on the origins of the prophets and on their graves. The evident parallels in Luke 11:47 and Matt 23:29 (a Q tradition that clearly indicates a date before A.D. 70) already caused Joachim Jeremias to explain the *Vitae* against the background of popular religion heavily influenced by Pharisaism.[146] Anna Maria Schwemer confirms this ascription. She argues on the basis of anachronisms that can be found in the later rabbinic tradition (e.g. that Nathan was David's teacher in matters of the law) and on the basis of the natural use of Deuteronomistic "standard theology," that the author belonged to the "Pharisaic-Scribal milieu."[147]

The *Scroll of Fasting* (Hebr. מגלת תענית), mentioned repeatedly in rabbinic texts (*m. Taan.* 2:8), is a list of thirty-five days of joy during which fasting is prohibited.[148] The Aramaic text is extremely concise which occasionally makes it difficult to link the reason for abstaining from fasting with a specific historical event. The historical value of a scholion written in Hebrew which fills these gaps is disputed.[149] Nevertheless, the *Scroll of*

---

[145] Cf. 37:5: The group of "those who dwell upon the earth" are the real addressees of the Parables; however, not all of them seem to belong to the righteous or the holy ones, see 43:4; 46:7; 48:8. The earth is being afflicted (40:6–7) and experiences the eschatological intervention of the Son of Man (45:5; cf. 51:5), after which he is recognized and worshiped by all (48:5). The prerequisite is repentance and forsaking the wrong path (50:2–3).

[146] J. Jeremias, *Heiligengräber in Jesu Umwelt* (Göttingen: Vandenhoeck and Ruprecht, 1958).

[147] A. M. Schwemer, *Vitae Prophetarum* 1997, 547–8; vgl. idem, *Studien I*, 70–71: "Man wird den Verfasser bei dem Pharisäismus nahestehenden νομικοί zu suchen haben." For Nathan as teacher of the law cf. Vit.Proph. 17:1 and Schwemer, *Vitae Prophetarum*, 638: "Der Verfasser . . . stellt sich das Verhältnis von Nathan und David vor wie das zwischen einem pharisäischen Gesetzeslehrer und seinem prominentesten Schüler." See also *Ant.* 13.289 where John Hyrcanus is similarly described as μαθητής of the Pharisees. For Pharisaic "students" see further *Ant.* 15.3; Mark 2:18 par Luke 5:33; Matt 22:15–16; also Acts 22:3. There are no comparable statements about students of the Essenes or the Sadducees (except the very general statement in *Life* 11) in either Josephus or the New Testament.

[148] Cf. K. Beyer, *Die aramäischen Texte vom Toten Meer* (Göttingen: Vandenhoeck und Ruprecht, 1984), 354–8, for the text, a short commentary and recent literature (in what follows I rely on his explanation of the festival days); for an English translation see A. Edersheim, *The Life and Times of Jesus the Messiah* (2 vols.; 3d ed.; London: Longmans, Green, 1886; repr. Peabody: Hendrickson, 1993) 2.698–700. See further H. Mantel, art. "Fastenrolle," *TRE* 11 (1983): 59–61, whose explanations differ occasionally from Beyer's; he dates the text to A.D. 64 (with several later additions) and assumes Pharisaic authorship. For various interpretations during the history of research see R. Deines, *Pharisäer*, 54 (Wellhausen); 73 (Schürer); 168, 186 (Graetz). The Scroll of Fasts plays hardly any role in the recent discussion (see above n. 117).

[149] Cf. Stemberger, *Pharisäer*, 61–62; also idem, *Einleitung in Talmud und Midrasch* (8th ed.; München: Beck, 1992), 44–45. The evidence of fasting during joyful commemorative days is also mentioned in Judith 8:6, and hints at the age of this practice.

Fasting is an indispensable document in that it reveals the events that are to be remembered as important hallmarks of history driving the Hasmonean and early Roman period. The arrangement of the days is diverse and the type of the memorial days clearly changes from the second to the first century B.C. Of the thirty-five memorial days four cannot be linked with any otherwise attested occurrences (No. 21, 25, 28, 34), and three are related to Old Testament events (No. 1, 4, 31). Of the remaining twenty-eight days a total of fourteen remember the success of the Maccabean revolt in the period between 164 and 108 B.C.[150] Five of these fourteen days are related to the restoration of freedom of worship and the restitution of the Jerusalem cult (all during the time of Judas Maccabeus), two remember the attainment of political sovereignty (No. 6, 12, during the time of Judas and of Simon Maccabeus), with the rest of the days linked with military successes and conquests. Only four events of the first century B.C. are mentioned. In striking contrast to the previously mentioned days these are exclusively related to internal Jewish conflicts. The opponents whose defeats are remembered with joy are the Sadducees (No. 10 [?], 19, 24) and Alexander Jannai (No. 33); these "victories" over the Sadducees all took place during the first phase of the reign of Salome Alexandra.[151] There is another change in the orientation of the days mentioned in *Meg. Taan.* for the first century A.D.: No. 20 remembers the successful resistance against the Roman standards in Jerusalem in A.D. 26 at the beginning of Pilate's reign as governor; No. 26 remembers a similar event in A.D. 41 when the emperor Caligula wanted to have his statue placed in the temple; No. 32 remembers the construction of the third wall during the reign of King Agrippa I. The text evidently refers again to national successes that are remembered. The other memorial days (No. 9, 10 [?], 13, 14, 15, 16) are all related to initial successes in the struggle against Rome in the years A.D. 66/67. The days that cannot be described more specifically (because the text does not give a reason why they should be remembered) are also dated to this period. It is assumed that the events commemorated had happened in the not too distant past so that the rationale

---

[150] The distribution is striking: seven days are linked with Judas Maccabeus (No. 2, 12, 17, 23, 27, 30, 35), only one with his successor Jonathan (No. 3: the rededication of the city walls of Jerusalem in 152 B.C.). Three days each are linked with Simon Maccabeus (No. 5, 6, 7) and with John Hyrcanus (No. 8, 18, 22).

[151] The interpretation of these passages is very much disputed. See e.g. S. Zeitlin, *Megillat Taanit as a Source for Jewish Chronology and History in the Hellenistic and Roman Periods* (Philadelphia: n.p., 1922), 78–79, 82, rejects any anti-Sadducean tendency of the text; cf. idem, "Nennt Megillat Taanit antisadduzäische Gedenktage," MGWJ 81 (1937): 351–5. We should note, however, that Zeitlin's arguments are tied to questionable premises about the relationship between Pharisees and Sadducees. H. Mantel, however, art. "Fastenrolle," TRE 11 (1983): 60, relates six days to the memory of the change from Sadducean halakah to Pharisaic halakah (No. 2, 10, 19, 21, 24, 33).

for these days was generally known during the time of the final redaction of *Meg. Taan.* (between A.D. 67 and 70).[152] The perspective of this list is rigorously nationalistic and anti-Sadducean and can thus be seen as a document of the nationalistic Pharisaic wing (of the Shammaites and/or of the Zealots).[153]

The *Liber antiquitarum biblicarum* belongs to the genre of "rewritten Bible," retelling the story from the time of Adam until Samuel. The book does not contain internal Jewish polemics. It may best be characterized as a book of consolation in the time between the two revolts which seeks to encourage the nation to wait for God's intervention. Divine intervention and help are not expected to come in military terms. In retelling the conquest and the time of the judges, military matters are noticeably pushed into the background, whereas prayer and empowerment through God's Spirit become central motifs. The appropriate manner for facing danger is not flight or resistance but unshakeable trust in God's intervention and rescue.[154]

The retelling of the Red Sea episode illustrates this emphasis in an impressive way. When the "sons of Israel" could not go any further and saw the Egyptians approaching from behind, they were "split in their opinions according to three strategies" (10:3). Some recommended voluntary death in the sea, others suggested voluntary return and subjection to the Egyptians, whereas a third group wanted to fight. Moses, however, prays and reminds God of his promises, thus rescuing the people. This division of the nation into three "strategies" may point to the three parties that Josephus mentions for the time before A.D. 70: the first party could be identified with the Essenes, the second party with the Sadducees or the mediatory party that included the most respected Pharisees, and the third party could be identified with the "Zealots." The position of the author (who adopts an attitude like that of the praying Moses) recalls the speech of Gamaliel in Acts 5:38–39: it is up to God either to help or to judge, the task of man is to trust God and to keep his law. The aims of the author are characteristically expressed, in my opinion, in an insight of the nation formulated after God had defeated the army of the enemy through a single person: "Now we know that the Lord has decided to save his people; he does not need a great number but only holiness" (*L.A.B.*

---

[152] No. 29 mentions the day of Trajan, but the passage is missing in the better manuscripts. This indicates that there were efforts to continue the calendar, possibly in the context of the Bar Kokhba revolt.

[153] The link with the Pharisees is confirmed by the importance of fasting for the Pharisees. The practice of fasting twice a week, well attested in Luke 18:12 (cf. *Ps.Sol.* 3:7–8; *b.Git.* 56a where fasting is said to have atoning power), could well have made a calendar such as *Meg. Taan.* necessary.

[154] See e.g. *L.A.B.* 6:2ff., 15–17: Abraham; 9:2–14: Amram; 38:3: seven men who refuse to sacrifice to Baal. The following translation follows D. J. Harrington, *OTP* 2.297–378.

27:14). This is the traditional Pharisaic program, formulated under the new conditions after the destruction of the temple.[155]

The despondency of the people after the destruction of the temple, which is portrayed in the description of the Egyptian bondage, may be seen as foreshadowed in the decision no longer to procreate:

> And now we are lost, and let us set up rules for ourselves that a man should not approach his wife lest the fruit of their wombs be defiled and our offspring serve idols. For it is better to die without sons until we know what God may do (9:2).

This attitude can be compared with a similar decision of the *Perushim* described in *t.Sotah* 15:11–12.[156] The author of *L.A.B.* responds by letting Amram, the father of Moses, say:

> It will sooner happen that this age will be ended forever or the world will sink into the immeasurable deep or the heart of the abyss will touch the stars than that the race of the sons of Israel will be ended. And there will be fulfilled the covenant that God established with Abraham when he said, "Indeed your sons will dwell in a land not their own and will be brought into bondage and afflicted 400 years" (9:3).

Amram thus accepts judgment but trusts, at the same time, that it will be limited and that it is not sent for the extermination of the entire nation. This corresponds to the way in which R. Yehoshua argues the *Perushim* out of their extreme position with regard to the destruction of the temple. This indicates in my opinion that *L.A.B.* belongs into the context of emerging rabbinic Judaism, expressing the mood in these circles, which was composed and hopeful despite the destruction of the temple.[157]

---

[155] The story of the defeat in the war against the Philistines with the capture of the ark of the covenant is another example of this attitude. While the dying Eli cries: "Behold, Israel perishes utterly, because the statues have been taken away from it" (54:5; cf. 54:6; 55:1), Samuel receives God's promise: "I will bring it back" (55:2). The author highlights the failure of the sons of Eli (52:1–4) and of the priests of Nob (63:1); this seems to point to a position that was critical of the priests. Samuel is described as savior of the nation, without being linked with a priestly genealogy (contra 1 Chr 6:1–13).

[156] A parallel is also found in *b.B.Bat.* 60*b*. This text is often cited as evidence that not all *Perushim* texts in rabbinic literature can be linked with the Pharisees; see e.g. P. Schäfer, "Der vorrabbinische Pharisäismus," 127–8; G. Stemberger, *Pharisäer*, 44. It seems to be possible, however, to take these *Perushim* to be very scrupulous Pharisees who refused to take any food because the prescribed dues for the temple and the sacrifices were no longer possible. In this context, the position of R. Yehoshua who overcame their scruples reflects the success of the generation of teachers after the destruction of the temple who helped the people and/or the pious to live a life according to the law without the temple.

[157] The *Martyrdom of Isaiah*, the first section of the Christian text called *Ascension of Isaiah*, is also dated into the final decades of the first century A.D. However, the text is almost devoid of contemporary historical references. The flight of the prophet to the desert (2:7–9) and the description of the ascetic life-style (2:10–11) are partly reminiscent of Qumran; several scholars have therefore attempted to link *Mart.Isa.* with the history of the Qumran group: cf. D. Flusser, "The Apocryphal Book of Ascensio Isaiae and the Dead Sea Sect," *IEJ* 3 (1953): 30–47, who

The *Ezra-Apocalypse* demonstrates that there were also much more somber sentiments in the circles to which *L.A.B.* belongs.[158] The Syriac *2 Baruch*, written slightly after *4 Ezra* and influenced by it, has a more optimistic outlook concerning the future and resembles in this respect *L.A.B.*[159] We will exclude *2 Baruch* from our discussion as it was written in the second century; the same holds true for *Paraleipomena Jeremiou* which has been dated in the recent study of Jens Herzer to A.D. 125–132.[160]

The *Fourth Book of Ezra*, has repeatedly received attention as evidence for Pharisaism in its final phase.[161] The text was written around A.D. 100, but the

---

sees the author as a member of the Qumran group (31); more cautious is E. Hammershaimb, *Das Martyrium Jesajas* (JSHRZ 2/1; Gütersloh: Gütersloher Verlagshaus, 1973), 19; see also R. Doran, "Narrative Literature," in Kraft/Nickelsburg, 287–310 (293–4): not wanting to assume the composition of the text in Qumran, "it is probably safer to say that the work emanates from a group with ideas similar to those found in the Qumran literature."

[158] Material parallels between *L.A.B.*, *4 Ezra* and *2 Baruch* make such an assumption more likely than the possibility of direct literary dependence. See J. Schreiner, *Das 4. Buch Esra* (JSHRZ 5/4; Gütersloh: Gütersloher Verlagshaus, 1981), 300–301.

[159] Cf. particularly 77:1–16: the transgression of the commandments (which is limited, however, to a small group: see 70:1–10: the description reminds us of Josephus who attributed the confusion of the entire people to a small group as well; again, 70:5 where the silence of the "sages" reminds us of the time before the outbreak of the war when the united efforts of Pharisees and Sadducees to achieve peace remained unsuccessful) has been forgiven by the time of tribulation. When the people lament: "For the shepherds of Israel have perished, and the lamps which gave light are extinguished, and the fountains from which we used to drink have withheld their streams" (77:13), Baruch responds by saying: "The shepherds and lamps and fountains came from the Law and when we go away, the Law will abide. If you, therefore, look upon the Law and are intent upon wisdom, then the lamp will not be wanting and the shepherd will not give way and the fountain will not dry up" (77:15–16; translation of A. F. J. Klijn, *OTP* 1.615–52). See also G. W. E. Nickelsburg, *Jewish Literature*, 287: "The author is still deeply grieved by the events of the year 70. Unlike the author of *4 Ezra*, however, he has not produced studied speculations on theodicy. His interest is primarily 'pastoral' and practical. His own grief has given way to consolation. His admonitions to 'prepare your souls' are part of that consolation, and together with his exhortations to heed God's sages and teachers they focus on the practical task of reconstruction."

[160] J. Herzer, *Die Paralipomena Jeremiae* (TSAJ 43; Tübingen: Mohr [Siebeck], 1994), 191. He characterizes the author as a Palestinian scribe who knew both the Old Testament and the post-biblical traditions of his people, particularly the apocalyptic and the Pharisaic traditions. Herzer suggests that the intellectual *Sitz im Leben* of the author may be identified with those circles of early Jewish society which were critical of the political-messianic movement, belonging rather to the rabbinic milieu that was consolidated after A.D.70 as represented by R. Johanan ben Zakkai and his school.

[161] Linked with this issue is the question of the relationship between apocalypticism and Pharisaism. It was particularly the older Jewish research that attempted to separate the two movements. As a result, *4 Ezra* and *2 Baruch* were regarded as secondary movements as scholars attempted, if at all possible, to separate them from Pharisaism (which was described exclusively from the standpoint of the rabbis); for various positions see Deines, *Pharisäer*, 117 (Bousset), 128 (Perles), 285, 287 (Schlatter), 353 n. 153 (Herford), 380–81 (Moore), 545

author evidently used material that was much older. His radical understanding of the sinfulness of man (3:5–26; 7:45–48, 62–69, 116–126; 8:35) links him with Paul. On account of the author's radical position Sanders however excludes him from the mainstream of "Common Judaism."[162] But if one reads *4 Ezra* in the context of *2 Baruch* and *L.A.B.*, one recognizes that his position is not as enigmatic as Sanders wants us to believe: in the context of this movement the author of *4 Ezra* is a warning voice admonishing his readers not to rely too quickly on God's mercy but to take the way of righteousness with greater seriousness than was the case in the past. In the fourth of the seven sections of the book (9:27–10:59), i.e. right in the middle of the sequence of seven sections, comes the turning-point, in which in his vision Ezra comforts with the hope of the resurrection a woman grieving for her son (10:15–17:24). The woman is Zion, and the resurrection of the individual is the model for the new Zion (10:55–57). The description of the fate of the ten tribes in exile illustrates that the study of the law makes a new beginning possible (cf. 13:54):

> But they formed this plan for themselves, that they would leave the multitude of the nations and go to a more distant region, where mankind had never lived, that there at least they might keep their statutes which they had not kept in their own land (13:41–42).[163]

As regards his own generation, "Ezra" receives the following commission: "Now therefore, set your house in order, and reprove your people; comfort the lowly among them, and instruct those that are wise . . ." (14:13). Finally he receives the new revelation of the "law of life" (14:30) in 94 books, of which he shall make public 24, referring to the books of the Masoretic canon. The other 70 books shall be kept, "in order to give them to the wise among your people" (14:45–47). It is thus the wise, among them Ezra himself, who have been given the responsibility for the nation. The priests and the temple, on the other hand, have no significance for the future, even though Ezra deplores their loss in moving terms (10:21–22). The author places his hope

---

(Steck); S. Mason, "Problems," 109–11. A first step towards overcoming this artificial separation was made in an essay by W. D. Davies, "Pharisaism and Apocalyptic" (1948), in idem, *Christian Origins and Judaism* (London: Darton, Longman & Todd, 1962), 19–30; see now S. E. Robinson, "Apocalypticism in the Time of Hillel and Jesus," in *Hillel and Jesus* (see n. 10), 121–136: "To seek the foundation of apocalypticism in only one sect is to adopt a reductionist view which cannot do justice to the pervasive influence of apocalypticism as a common cultural background to all the sects, including Pharisaism, before 70 C.E." (131). Also B. W. Longenecker, "Locating 4 Ezra: A Consideration of its Social Setting and Functions," *JSJ* 28 (1997): 271–293 (esp. 280–284).

[162] Cf. E. P. Sanders, *Paul and Palestinian Judaism* (2d ed.; Philadelphia: Fortress, 1983) 409–18. Recently, however, B. W. Longenecker has successfully attempted to establish a "Yavnean context" for *4 Ezra* (see previous note).

[163] Translation B. M. Metzger, *OTP* 1.517–60.

solely in a superior adherence to the law that has been placed into the hands of the sages. In view of the religious and national crisis after the destruction of the temple, the author of *4 Ezra* shows what is indispensable to "covenantal nomism" (and/or to Pharisaism): the law, given as statutes of the covenant, serves life *if* the law is obeyed. Therefore it is the primary task of the people of the covenant to know the law and live according to it. Necessary for such behavior are those who teach the law. Ezra and his "colleagues" Baruch, Pseudo-Philo and Pseudo-Jeremiah present themselves as teachers of this kind, who are able to interpret the pressing situation through an apocalyptic scenario. Their common aim, however, is to encourage the people to keep God's commandments (and in doing this, the covenant) in a renewed and strengthened devotion.

As we survey the texts which we have discussed briefly, the following observations may be made. The *oldest group* of texts that were written in the immediate context of the Maccabean uprising do not yet contain clear controversies between parties, even though the authors take divergent positions. Further, we see a consistent endeavor to keep the law properly and in better ways. Numerous elements that will have an important function in Judaism generally and in Pharisaism in particular become more noticeable. The *middle group* of texts is characterized by vehement internal Jewish conflicts in which questions of correct purity and holiness in cult and personal life play a central role. The *last group* of texts, written after A.D. 70, has basically left these internal Jewish controversies behind, as they attempt to convince the nation of the necessity to turn back to the law. The readers are presented with better times whose realization will be a gift of God's mercy, as it will be due to the keeping of the law. The authors of these texts do not discuss priestly matters and calendar questions. The issues they discuss and the theology they represent may be characterized as Pharisaic: they are oriented towards the people and the law, and they strongly emphasize the future on the basis of a certain hope regarding the resurrection of the dead. They recognize that the initiative for ushering in these better times lies solely with God, while the people are called upon to accept the judgment over Jerusalem as judgment for their own sins. Despite terminological differences many ideas remind us of Josephus' theology of history.[164]

The purpose of this survey was to demonstrate that the diversity of Judaism that is often referred to, i.e. the "Judaisms," do not go beyond Josephus' description of the religious movements of his people. Of course the

---

[164] Cf. R. Deines, *Pharisäer*, 286–91 (on Schlatter). Josephus' interpretation of biblical history partially resembles *L.A.B.*; cf. D. J. Harrington, "The Bible Rewritten," in Kraft/Nickelsburg, 245; see also the important study by H. W. Attridge, *The Interpretation of Biblical History in the Antiquitates Judaicae of Flavius Josephus* (HDR 7; Missoula: Scholars, 1976).

picture that Josephus draws is limited in scope, as the selection of the matters he includes depends on his intended readers, leading him to omit much which in other places receives extensive attention. But the texts we surveyed never relate a polemical demarcation or a group context that would go beyond that which we know from Josephus. What we do learn, however, is the fact that these major movements were diverse and contained a vast treasure of "practice and belief."[165]

6. "Pharisaic" and "Pharisees": Conceptual Clarification

The assigning of a given text to a Pharisee or a pharisaically shaped milieu depends to a significant extent on one's definition of "Pharisee" or "Pharisaic." Clearly the more narrowly these definitions are conceived, the more difficult, if not entirely impossible, it is to link these texts to Pharisaism. In the following discussion a view of "Pharisee" and "Pharisaic" is therefore proposed that emphasizes the movement's open, Israel-wide, non-sectarian character that makes it possible to investigate whether or not the above mentioned texts can be assigned to a Jewish milieu shaped by Pharisees.

6.1 The Term "Pharisee"

A survey of the history of research[166] indicates that the expression "Pharisee" cannot be precisely delimited, because it is not defined in the sources. A Pharisee is whoever calls himself a Pharisee[167] or is called such by others.[168] However, one's self-designation as Pharisee or one's designation of Pharisee by others is no absolute necessity in a person's characterization.[169] Rather, it

---

[165] Cf. O. Betz, "Qumran Halakhah," 199–200; K. Keith, "Background," 143: "Although Josephus' picture is too narrow, it serves as the best argument against a Palestine overrun by rampant sectarianism."

[166] Cf. R. Deines, *Pharisäer*, 638 (Index s.v. "Pharisäer, Name der"); and S. Mason, "Problems," 133–9.

[167] Phil 3:5; cf. Acts 23:6, where Luke has Paul say, ἐγὼ Φαρισαῖός εἰμι, υἱὸς Φαρισαίων; Josephus: *Life* 12. A good survey of all named Pharisees is now provided by J. Sievers, "Who were the Pharisees?" in *Hillel and Jesus* (see n. 10), 137–55.

[168] Luke 7:36–37, 39–40 (Simon); John 3:1 (Nicodemus); Acts 5:34 (Gamaliel); Josephus, *Ant.* 15.3 (Pollion); *Ant.* 18.4 (Zadok the co-founder of the Zealots; cf. *m. Soṭah* 9:9, where the epithet "ben Perisha" is supplied for the Zealot Techina); *Life* 190 (Simon ben Gamaliel); *Life* 197 (Jonathan, Ananias, the priest Joazar); in *Ant.* 13.289, John Hyrcanus is called a μαθητής of the Pharisees. Cf. S. J. D. Cohen, "Significance," 36 n. 20; J. Neusner and C. Thoma, "Pharisäer," 74.

[169] This is made clear by a comparison of Acts 22:3 ἐγώ εἰμι ἀνὴρ Ἰουδαῖος and Acts 23:6 (see n. 167 above); precisely parallel Phil 3:5 and Gal 1:13–14; cf. further: Acts 5:34: Gamaliel is introduced by Luke as a Pharisee and νομοδιδάσκαλος τίμιος; in Acts 22:3 only his name

is apparently used only where the designation of someone as Pharisee helps clarify a certain issue. The self-designation as Pharisee clearly serves the purpose of establishing one's close affinity to Judaism in its "best" form,[170] a proof that was apparently necessary particularly when a person had to justify himself within Judaism. It therefore depends to a certain extent on a respective author's preference whether he identifies himself as Pharisee or calls others such. *However, this is certainly not the rule.* This also helps explain why in the rabbinic literature, for example, none of the rabbis is called a Pharisee (see also the texts referred to in 5.4, which all constitute "inside literature"). In the internal discussion of a group, this could provide no additional information beyond the name itself. What was more telling, however, was alignment with a school (Hillel or Shammai) or a particular teacher (such as the circle surrounding Yohanan ben Zakkai). Occasionally, the expression is used in order to distinguish the Pharisees from the Sadducees as a group, but even there it varies with other designations.[171] Moreover, controversies between the Pharisees and the Sadducees were at that later time already a thing of the past.

Another fact that is attested unequivocally in the sources is that the term "Pharisee" designates primarily a *particular relationship to the Law*.[172]

---

is given; Luke 7:39–40 (par. Matt 26:6; Mark 14:3); Nicodemus is called a Pharisee in John 3:1; in 7:50 his identity as a Pharisee is mentioned as well, but not in 19:39. Conversely, Caiaphas, e.g., is in the NT always mentioned in conjunction with his title. The same can be observed in Josephus: cf. *Life* 191–2 with *J.W.* 4.159 and *Life* 197 with *J.W.* 2.628 (on which see M. Hengel/R. Deines, "Common Judaism," 35, n. 89). To this may be added in Josephus a whole list of individuals whom he does not expressly designate as Pharisees but whom he characterizes as such through certain descriptive vocabulary. This includes: Sameas, the student and colleague of Pollion (*Ant.* 14.172; 15.3, 370); the two Jerusalem teachers who called for the destruction of images at the temple (*J.W.* 1.648ff.; *Ant.* 17.149ff.); Simon, the expert in the Law (*Ant.* 19.332ff.); Eleazar the Galilean (*Ant.* 20.42ff.); those who protest against the judicial murder of James (*Ant.* 20.200–201).

[170] Cf. *Life* 10: Josephus wants to choose the best one (αἱρήσεσθαι τὴν ἀρίστην), therefore he deals with the three movements within his nation. The same is true for all of Paul's mentioned self-designations as a Pharisee. Thus also A. J. Saldarini, *Pharisees*, 136: "Paul's reference to Pharisaism in Philippians implies that it is well known and accepted as a legitimate and strict mode of living Jewish life."

[171] Another explanation is offered by S. J. D. Cohen, "Significance," 40–41: the Pharisees after 70 were no longer interested in referring to their "sectarian past" (regarding the Pharisees as sect, see ibid., 29–31; for a critique of this view, see n. 24), since the divisions were on the one hand considered responsible for the catastrophe of the year 70, and on the other hand had their point of reference in the temple and its cult (see 43–46). With its demise, a major point of conflict had fallen by the wayside as well. In my view, this explanation overestimates the function of the temple within Pharisaism.

[172] This is also the reason why "Pharisee" can be used as a synonym for "scribe." It is evident particularly in Josephus (as pointed out by Schlatter), that the individuals designated Pharisees by him were exclusively scribes; the same can be said for the language of John's Gospel, where

Someone becomes a Pharisee or can call himself a Pharisee who is κατὰ νόμον (Phil 3:5). One thing entailed by this Pharisaic *nomos* concept is the "tradition of the fathers." The repeated characterization of the Pharisees as transmitters, preservers, and developers of the tradition of the Law in its *written and its traditional form* ("custom") cannot be disputed.[173] In this regard it is largely immaterial whether this way of dealing with the Torah in its fixed and its living forms can be documented already through the theoretical model of the dual Torah which Moses received at Sinai or whether this took place only in the period after 70.[174] It seems clear to me that according to the Pharisees the tradition possessed normative character already prior to 70, so that it was understood by them not as "Pharisaic" tradition but ultimately as Mosaic and thus *Jewish*. The entire nation was charged to observe it, not merely a group within the nation.[175] The acrimonious dispute regarding individual issues pertaining to observance of the Law, which is already apparent in 4QMMT, results from this Pharisaic conviction which, in my opinion is hared by the other groups as well. What is at stake in the proper observance of the Law is the nation's standing with God and thus its future. It is the Law's *soteriological relevance* (which is inseparably linked with its traditional application) that requires its "precise" interpretation and observance. This Sanders does not adequately take into account.

Pharisaism's *non-exclusive understanding of tradition* is also the reason why traditions are found in rabbinic literature that cannot be a priori classified as Pharisaic (whereby, of course, one's preconceived notion of what is or is not Pharisaic is decisive). The Pauline maxim of 1 Thess 5:21, πάντα δὲ δοκιμάζετε, τὸ καλὸν κατέχετε, in my opinion also reflects a Pharisaic

---

likewise the term "Pharisee" is used when "scribe" may be expected on the basis of the Synoptics (in the place of the Synoptic expression "Pharisee," John frequently uses οἱ 'Ιουδαῖοι, cf. John 7:11–13; 10:19–20 and the passages where some [τινες] or many [πολλοί] of them believe in Jesus: 8:30; 12:9, 17–18; from their circles come also the informants of the Pharisees [11:45–46]). The Φαρισαῖοι are clearly presented as the leading group of the 'Ιουδαῖοι, just as in the Synoptic portrait the γραμματεῖς are the leading group of the Φαρισαῖοι; on this cf. A. J. Saldarini, *Pharisees,* 187–98, who considers it possible that the passages on the Pharisees in John's Gospel "may partly reflect the Palestinian situation in the middle of the first century" (196); cf. now also U. C. Von Wahlde, "The Relationships between Pharisees and Chief Priests: Some Observations on the Texts in Matthew, John and Josephus," *NTS* 42 (1996): 506–522 (513–518).

[173] See above n. 10.

[174] Cf. S. J. D. Cohen, "Significance," 37. The concept of an "oral *law*" is found only with the Tannaitic rabbis, but is nowhere in the Greek sources attributed to the Pharisees. However, it is the *validity* of tradition, not the rationale for it, that is decisive.

[175] When stressing "tradition," it is important not to see in this a "traditionalism." To the contrary, "tradition" enabled the Pharisees to adapt their use of the Law to changing circumstances.

disposition.[176] The Pharisees' interest in Jesus (and previously in John the Baptist), which is attested by the Gospels, can be explained by their essentially open understanding of tradition: they are prepared to listen to Jesus, even to learn from him, as long as he establishes his teaching in continuity with Torah tradition. The ways part, however, as soon as Jesus places his authority *above* that of Torah tradition. For this reason Jesus cannot be called a Pharisee, because he is *not* one at the decisive point, i.e. κατὰ νόμον.[177] Conversely, everyone who recognizes the Torah and its tradition as handed down by the Pharisaic teachers as normative can call himself a Pharisee (which, however, as suggested above, was not customary). A lot of what Sanders calls "Common Judaism" can thus be labeled in a wider sense as pharisaic influenced Judaism.

6.2 What is Pharisaic Judaism?

If the above discussion is accurate, it is the Judaism of Torah-tradition that should be characterized as Pharisaic Judaism. It emerged when the prevalence of Torah tradition, as it had developed in the time after the exile, was threatened both from within and from the outside. This made it necessary to provide an explicit formulation and defense of the conception of Torah that had up to that point existed and been presupposed subconsciously.[178] Thus the Pharisaic ἀκρίβεια was born, which includes both the study of Scripture and the cultivation of tradition.[179] The Pharisees emerged approximately between 160 and 140 from the scribes and the associated *Asidaioi* as the proponents of these efforts. This also seems to have been the time when the movement received its name, although the meaning of the term "Pharisee" cannot be determined with certainty. The statement in 4QMMT, Part C (transl. see pp. 470–1),

7 . . . [ואתם יודעים ש]פרשנו מרוב העו[ם ומכול טמאתם]
8 [ו]מהתערב בדברים האלה ומלבוא ע[ומהם] לגב אלה . . .

---

[176] S. J. D. Cohen, "Significance," 42, 50, on the other hand, limits the non-exclusive character of the Pharisees to the period after 70.

[177] This indicates that the *distinct teachings* of the Jewish parties (resurrection, freedom of the will, etc.) did not constitute the decisive boundary markers; for here Jesus and the Pharisees have a lot in common (resurrection, messianic expectations, angels and demons). It is therefore not primarily doctrine ("belief"), which provides Pharisaism with its identity, but acceptance, at least in principle, of the validity of halakah.

[178] Cf. M. Stern, "The Hasmonean Revolt and its Place in the History of Jewish Society and Religion," *CHM* 14 (1968): 92–106 (99, 102–104); Y. Sussmann, "History of the Halakha," 196: "The Hasmonean victories brought in their wake not only a great national awakening and devotion to the Jews' ancestral land, but also (and perhaps especially) a great religious awakening and *revival and devotion to the ancestral traditions*" (emphasis mine).

[179] For the terminology used in Josephus, see S. Mason, *Pharisees*, 89–96; cf. 75–79, passim (see Index, 420 s.v. ἀκρίβεια).

however, seems to indicate that the name was coined at that time and that it was initially disputed who could legitimately call himself a "separated one."[180] This suggests that the term possessed at that point positive connotations.[181] The separation should in this case be understood as a separation from all that is pagan, since it was after all precisely Hellenism that threatened the nation's religious existence. The later conflict with the house of the Hasmoneans would then have one of its roots in the Hasmoneans' close association with pagan nations which was considered to be *too* close by the "Separated Ones." The sources' indication of a possible rape of the mother of John Hyrcanus (*Ant.* 13.292) in pagan imprisonment may at least constitute a hint regarding *one* of the possible reasons for the conflict.

In this, the Pharisaic movement stands for the tradition of the Deuteronomistic view of history:[182] obedience to the revealed will of God brings salvation and blessing; disobedience, on the other hand, leads to exile and loss of the land. Nevertheless, additional tradition beside the written Torah was necessary to establish a legal observance that was as comprehensive as possible. In this regard priestly[183] and ancient scribal traditions[184] made a

---

[180] For the text, see Qimron/Strugnell, 58–59. Since this terminology does not correspond to the conventional delimination of the Qumran community (cf. e.g. CD 8:16; 19:29), they consider the possibility "that our text here reflects the terminology of the sect's opponents" (99; cf. 111, 114–5).

[181] This may be due to the material agreement with the *Nibdalim*, who likewise had separated from the גויי ארץ (Ezra 6:21; 10:11; cf. Neh 9:1; 10:29), so that a division arose among the people as well (cf. Ezra 9:1). On the other hand, the saying attributed to Hillel, אל תפרוש מן הציבור (*m. 'Abot* 2:4), reads like a rejection of the cited 4QMMT passage. *A separation from the national community* (in mishnaic Hebrew, ציבור frequently replaces עם; see Qimron/Strugnell, 86) is therefore rejected in the rabbinic texts, but not a *separation for holiness' sake*. It is rather expressly commanded, and this for the entire nation! See further 4QMMT B 76–79: Israel as a whole is "holy" (this is the purpose of halakah), but even holier are the priests. This priestly-elitist mindset is absent from the Pharisees and rabbis.

[182] See above n. 42.

[183] Regarding the strong priestly roots of Pharisaism, which influenced particularly its striving for purity with regard to the temple and the cult as well as the private sphere, even by non-priests, cf. the treatment of older positions in R. Deines, *Pharisäer*, 46, 56–57 (Wellhausen); 271, 273–4, 298 (Schlatter); 314–5 (K. Kohler); 474 (Preisker). With appeal to Schlatter and Joachim Jeremias, it was especially Rudolf Meyer who emphasized the priestly origin of the Pharisaic "separation": cf. "Die Bedeutung des Pharisäismus für Geschichte und Theologie des Judentums," *TLZ* 77 (1952): 677–84, now in idem, *Zur Geschichte und Theologie des Judentums in hellenistisch-römischer Zeit* (ed. W. Bernhardt; Neukirchener Verlag, 1989), 63–70 (63–65), and his essay "Tradition und Neuschöpfung im antiken Judentum. Dargestellt an der Geschichte des Pharisäismus" (SSAW.PH 110/2; Berlin: Akademie Verlag, 1965); now in ibid. 130–87 (137–8). A summary of the Akademie-treatment is found in "Φαρισαῖος: A. Der Pharisäismus im Judentum," *ThWNT* 9 (1973): 11–51 (11–36). This still controversial Pharisaic characteristic – cf. e.g. Neusner (*Judaic Law*, 263–70) and Sanders (*Jewish Law*, 131–252: "Did the Pharisees Eat Ordinary Food in Purity?") – provides the background for the continuing discussion of whether the Pharisees practiced the eating of common food (*Ḥullin*)

decisive contribution, just as the temple represented the model par excellence of holiness that was pleasing to God. Since the threat of Hellenism found its most visible expression in the syncretistic transformation of the Yahweh cult, its renewal must begin at the same place. Yet the most effective protection of the temple was that the entire nation was obliged to keep ordinances regarding purity analogous to the priestly requirements. In this way the nation guarded the purity of the temple by being given a share in its holiness (and presumably an understanding of it as well). At the same time the priests in the temple were compelled to take holiness very seriously themselves, if they did not want to lose their position of pre-eminence in public consciousness. This is why the Sadducees (and the Qumran community) offered more severe judgments in matters of halakah when dealing with issues of priestly and temple purity than the Pharisees. The dispute regarding the payment for regular temple sacrifices is part of that issue. Should it be taken from the half-shekel tax (thus the Pharisees) or from private contributions (permitted by the Sadducees, cf. b. Men. 65a)? As the Pharisees contended, the cult and its financial support are the obligation of the entire nation, not merely that of the priests or a few rich people.[185]

---

in analogy with the priestly use of pure food (thus Neusner). The custom of washing one's hands prior to eating is considered evidence for this. Cf. in this regard H. K. Harrington, "Did the Pharisees Eat Ordinary Food in a State of Purity?" *JSJ* 36 (1995): 42–54 (also in idem, *The Impurity Systems of Qumran and the Rabbis: Biblical Foundations* [SBLDS 143; Atlanta: Scholars, 1993], 267–81); J. C. Poirier, "Why Did the Pharisees Wash their Hands?" *JJS* 47 (1996): 217–33. The archaeological finds, particularly *miqwa'ot* and stone vessels, confirm Harrington's conclusion: "In no way do the Pharisees think of themselves as priests, but they do strive for a holiness above and beyond what the Torah prescribed for the lay Israelite" (54; thus also D. R. de Lacey, "Search," 370). Regarding the archaeological evidence, cf. R. Deines, "Steingefäße," 243–6, 266–75, and E. Regev, "The Use of Stone Vessels in the Late Second Temple Period" (Hebr.), in: דברי הכנס השישי ומחקרי יהודה ושומרון (ed. J. Eshel, 1996; Qedomim–Ariel, 1997), 79–95. D. R. Schwartz, in his essay "'Kingdom of Priests' – a Pharisaic Slogan?" in idem, *Studies in the Jewish Background of Christianity* (WUNT 1/60, Tübingen: Mohr [Siebeck], 1992), 57–80 (orig. Hebr. in: *Zion* 45 [1979/80]: 96–117), rightly pointed out that, as far as can be determined from the available sources, the Pharisees did *not* appropriate this motto taken from Exod 19:6 as a programmatic statement, since their aim was not "priesthood" but "holiness"!

[184] Cf. the schematic but nevertheless helpful formulation by J. Neusner, *Judaism: The Evidence of the Mishnah* (BJS 129; 2d ed.; Atlanta: Scholars, 1988), 230–56, where he distinguishes between "the Scribes," "the Priests," and "the Householders" as shapers of the Mishnaic tradition. What is decisive beyond Neusner's schematization, however, is that these were primarily *Pharisaic* scribes, priests, and heads of households.

[185] Cf. now A. I. Baumgarten, "Rabbinic Literature," 20–22. To this context belongs the division of popular representatives deputed from the towns of Israel to accompany the *tamid* sacrifice in the temple with prayer (*Ma'amadot*) required by the rabbinic literature as well as the promotion of pilgrimage and participation in the temple festivals. Again, the Qumran texts provide a plethora of material for comparison, which indicates that all these issues were already debated vigorously long before 70 and that the rabbinic controversies can be traced back to

What was in the earlier history of research frequently termed *democratization* of (temple) piety through Pharisaism is the expansion of the relevance of Torah to *the entire life of all of Israel.* This prevented the Law from losing its significance in shaping people's lives. The price for the practice of priestly oriented purity as the obligation of all Israel was the *reduction* of the calamitous power of ritual impurity and its sources. In her study "The Impurity Systems of Qumran and the Rabbis. Biblical Foundations" (see n. 183), Hannah K. Harrington has shown that both the Qumran and the rabbinic concepts of purity are anchored firmly in the written Torah. What differs, however, is the way in which these groups dealt with biblical commandments that were in need of fleshing out.

> Thus, it is my conclusion that the sectarians utilize Scripture's silences *to increase contamination or purification rulings* in order to safely avoid transgression of Scripture. . . . The Rabbis, by contrast, take advantage of Scripture's ambivalence *to ease the life of the community* rather than to lay unnecessary burdens upon it (264; emphasis mine).

Harrington perceives the implications of this divergent concept in the sociological development: the extension of purity led to the separated existence in the desert, while the ancestors of the rabbis remained in the community of the people and thereby shaped it and through their efforts preserved it after 70.

Of fundamental importance for an appreciation of the Pharisaic influence on religious practice is the linkage (first established by Wellhausen) between the genesis of Pharisaism and the emerging *individualism* of Hellenistic culture, which expresses itself as a *personal decision* for a particular form of piety.[186] This dual phenomenon must be credited with preserving the national religious heritage of Judaism in a cosmopolitan and increasingly individualistic environment. To this end, its creators formed a type of religion in which *national and individual religion entered into a symbiotic relationship that was mutually beneficial and where both elements made an impact on the*

---

events surrounding the temple. Cf. I. Knohl, "Post-Biblical Sectarianism and the Priestly Schools of the Pentateuch: The Issue of Popular Participation in the Temple Cult on Festivals," in *The Madrid Qumran Congress: Proceedings of the International Congress on the Dead Sea Scrolls, Madrid 18–21 March, 1991* (ed. J. Trebolle Barrera and L. Vegas Montaner; vol. 2; STDJ 11/2; Leiden: Brill, 1992), 601–609 (esp. 607); E. and H. Eshel, "4Q471 Fragment 1 and *Ma'amadot* in the War Scroll," ibid. 611–620; cf. the survey by M. Broshi, "Anti-Qumranic Polemic in the Talmud," ibid., 589–600.

[186] This idea is entirely absent from the current discussion regarding the Pharisees. An exception is Ellis Rivkin, but this part of his argument has thus far hardly received any attention. Cf. idem, "The Internal City," *JSSR* 5 (1966): 225–40; idem, "Pharisaism and the Crisis of the Individual in the Greco-Roman World," *JQR* (1970/71): 27–53; also in *Essays in the Greco-Roman and related Talmudic Literature* (ed. H. A. Fischel; New York: Ktav 1977), 500–526; idem, *Hidden Revolution,* 296–311; see also R. Deines, "Steingefäße," 279–283.

other. These founders thus made it possible for Judaism to retain the character of an essentially national religious community whose center was the temple and whose external characteristics were circumcision and the Sabbath, but which at the same time advanced universal truth claims by appealing to the one true God. It was made up of *all members* of the Jewish people (cf. *m.Sanh.* 10:1; Rom 11:25–26). But at the same time Pharisaism offered those who were religiously interested the opportunity to practice their piety within the framework and for the *benefit* of this national religion virtually as *intensely, individually,* and *as part of one's everyday life* as desired. Pharisaism did not lead one out of the nation (this is the fundamental error of a view of Pharisaism that conceives of the Pharisees as the "true Israel" or as an exclusive "sect"), it rather only made *being truly Jewish* possible (cf. Gal 1:13–14). Conversely, it is no accident that the demise of the ancient national temple religions coincides with the simultaneous emergence of "savior cults" with individual appeal. Pharisaism succeeded in combining temple and house, as well as national, universal, and personal eschatology.

This focus on the temple also has entailments for the *Pharisaic punctiliousness regarding the tithe and priestly contributions* (and in a later stage [?] also punctiliousness regarding the purity of profane foods). This is where the individual could and should prove his obedience to God. This is where the individual household[187] decided for blessing or curse for land and nation. And this is where a gradual differentiation emerged between the punctilious and the negligent, whose extremes are represented in the *Haberim* on the one hand and in the *Am ha-Aretz* on the other. Between these two groups stand in my opinion the "Pharisees," as they encounter us in the Synoptic Gospels. They are the pious ones par excellence who are devoted to Law and tradition. They are the adherents of the scribes (and priests) committed to Torah and tradition. They are doers of their word.[188] They are the exemplary pious ones who command respect and influence in the towns and villages and who took religious action where they had the opportunity.[189] In this context one may

---

[187] Cf. above n. 184 and J. Neusner, *Evidence of the Mishnah,* 250–256 regarding the share of "heads of households" in the Mishnah (see also 240).

[188] In this regard one finds a varying terminology in the different sources: frequently Pharisees and scribes are identical (Josephus, John's Gospel [see above n. 172], rabbinic lit.); at other times they are carefully distinguished. But this means that "Pharisee" may denote both the scribe of the Torah tradition and the common adherent to this movement.

[189] Cf. in this regard particularly A. J. Saldarini, *Pharisees,* 284–5: Only a minority belonged in his opinion to the "governing class," while "most Pharisees were subordinate officials, bureaucrats, judges and educators" (ibid.). This explains in his view also their (limited) influence, although they were numerically rather insignificant (he assumes the number 6000). What is interesting is that this assessment of the Pharisees is based significantly on the Gospels (cf. 151, 154–7 [on Mark]; 157–73 [on Matthew]; 174–87 [on Luke and Acts]), and in particular also on John's Gospel and Josephus. In my view, the problem is that he conceives of

recall the *connection between Pharisaism and the synagogue*,[190] which urgently requires a radical reappraisal. Also related is the question of liturgical developments: the setting of firm, universally normative times and formulas of prayer, etc. To what extent is it also here that the Pharisees are the agents of democratization and individualization of older forms?[191]

This open definition of Pharisaism makes it possible to detect within this total movement apocalyptic groups and circles that followed a Pharisaic line of thought in the halakic sphere – which, as far as personal identification and soteriology are concerned, was, after all, decisive. Messianic expectations and eschatological conceptualities, on the other hand, belonged to the sphere of "teaching," which was kept much more open; here a certain amount of diversity was possible. Beyond this, it should be noted that there is no evidence for *a purposeful circulation of eschatological teachings*, while the halakah was spread by way of schools, and it was *the people's obligation* to know the Law (cf. 4QMMT B 49b–54[192]; John 7:49). Knowledge regarding the last things, on the other hand, was limited to the scribes (cf. Dan 12:3–4; Matt 2:4; Mark 12:35–37 par. Matt 22:41–46; Luke 20:41–44; *4 Ezra* 14:26; *m.Hag.* 2:1). The "Zealots" can be viewed as one of these inner-Pharisaic groups which had a strong apocalyptic orientation and which – albeit probably at least in part only through terrorism – became a national movement.

6.3 What is the Relationship between Pharisaic Judaism and Palestinian Judaism as a Whole?

If it is correct that it was particularly halakah that constituted Pharisees as Pharisees, it is also true that it constituted Essenes as Essenes and Sadducees as Sadducees. The same can be said regarding the other Jewish groups that existed prior to 70.[193] This explains why the differences and even antagonism

---

the Pharisees primarily as a "political interest group" (see 79–133, 281) and that he equates their influence with political clout, so that he is able to see in them merely "a minor factor" in society (132). The particular form of religious authority, which was possible in Judaism independent of social status, can thereby not be grasped.

[190] Cf. regarding this M. Hengel/R. Deines, "Common Judaism," 32–33, 60–61; R. Deines, *Pharisäer*, 639, Index s.v. Pharisäer and Synagoge.

[191] Cf. J. Neusner/C. Thoma, "Pharisäer," 91, 98–102, who, however, deal only with liturgical changes after 70.

[192] Whoever was blind or deaf was excluded from the temple and from holy food, because he could not know or observe the necessary halakah in this regard. The rabbis judged similarly, albeit less exclusively: cf. *m.Ter.* 1:1 and *t.Ter.* 1:1, on which Qimron/Strugnell, 160–61.

[193] I think here particularly of the Samaritans. Cf. Qimron/Strugnell, 175–6, who clearly point to halakah as grounds for the division of Judaism into "sects": "From MMT we learn the reasons for the schism. Up to now we have had no explicit evidence on this subject. Josephus gives the impression that the sects were primarily divided over theological questions, for instance those relating to the resurrection of the dead or the role of Divine Providence. He was

between these three basic movements (which included diverse elements within themselves[194]) did not lead to the complete suspension of religious association within Judaism, whereas the association with early Christians broke off quite soon. All three Jewish movements oriented themselves basically around the Torah as the center of individual and national Jewish existence. In this system the Messiah was subordinated to the Torah. For Christians, on the other hand, Christ became the center of individual as well as *communal* existence. In him, a person's profound relationship with his own nation was expanded to an eschatological and thus at the same time universal horizon. The final breakdown came when the soteriological marginality of the Torah in relation to Christ could no longer be overlooked in the course of generational change. Even where Torah was observed with sincerity in the Jewish-Christian congregations, it had still lost its absolute, eschatological dimension. It had, even in these congregations, reached its τέλος in Christ.

But if the Pharisees were throughout their entire history *not* an exclusive party, this may also be the reason why there is no clear delimitation over against the Essenes nor an essential distinction over against the Sadducees (perhaps with the exception of *m.Sanh.* 10:1 where, however, precisely *no* "party" designation is found), but only against Christians and other *minim*, who likewise replace Torah with another principle. As a movement within the nation and for the nation the Pharisees were apparently not interested in exclusive boundaries. In this way they were able to find a modus vivendi with the Sadducees, because, and as long as, these remained committed to the Torah. To the extent that they were able, the Pharisees also sought to transform, or at least influence, the Sadducees' conception of Torah, because they considered it to be too narrow and thus deficient. However, the Pharisees did not declare the cult illegitimate, when it was not carried out according to their own tradition. There seemed to be even less of a need to distinguish the Pharisees from the Essenes, since the latter group's aspirations pointed essentially in the same direction as those of the Pharisees (albeit in exaggerated form, which is precisely why the Pharisees considered them ill-suited to be elevated to the level of universal norm).

---

concerned to produce an explanation that would make sense to his Greek (and Roman) readers. But the fact that only matters of practice are mentioned in MMT confirms the view that it was not dogma, but law that was apt to produce lasting schisms in Judaism. It can be seen once again how important the laws of purity were to all parties of that period." Thus also Y. Sussmann, "History of the Halakha," 196–9.

[194] The Qumran community may be distinguished from the Essenes described by Josephus (he himself distinguishes between a married and a celibate group, cf. *J.W.* 2.160) as a particular development. Likewise, halakic, apocalyptic, and mystical elements coexist in the broader Essene movement. Among the Sadducees the Boethusians represent a somewhat special group which is at least known by name. The Pharisees consist of various schools and rabbinic circles, apocalyptic and zealot groups, as well as the "co-operatives."

Another striking feature associated with the question of inner-Jewish differentiation is the similar dynamic operative in the New Testament. For the New Testament authors, too, differentiate themselves solely over against Pharisaism, while there seems to be no need whatsoever to mention the Essenes. The Sadducees are distinguished solely on the basis of their one basic doctrinal difference pertaining to the resurrection of the dead. This indicates that their teaching found virtually no echo or support in the circles which Jesus (and among the Gospels at least that of Matthew) sought to attract. The same thing can be said regarding the Essenes. The basic dispute rather took place with Pharisaism, and this is grounded in their position vis-à-vis the *Am ha-Aretz*. In my view, George Foot Moore was correct when he characterized the *Am ha-Aretz* as the majority of the Jewish population, which, as far as its values were concerned, belonged to Pharisaic Judaism, even though they lived these ideas *in reality* only to a very limited extent.[195]

Rudolf Meyer, the author of the article on "Pharisees" in Kittel's dictionary, also advocated such a connection in one of his early essays, even though he did not incorporate this view in his later studies (see n. 183), in which he wanted to see the Pharisees more strongly as a self-contained sect analogous to the group at Qumran. He wrote at that time:

> In the end, the *Am ha-Aretz* was still dependent on the religious thought world of the Pharisees. This is already apparent from the fact that we have absolutely no evidence, not even a hint, of a dogmatic difference, however small, between Pharisees and *Am ha-Aretz*. The *Am ha-Aretz* differs from the adherents to the Law merely by his unwillingness to draw the final consequences of nomism.[196]

If, then, the difference between the Pharisees and the *Am ha-Aretz* is "merely a gradual rather than a fundamental one," this means "that the term *Am ha-Aretz*" does not represent "a final verdict when pronounced by the adherents to the Law" (ibid., 34). Rather, it is at all times possible to follow the Pharisaic-rabbinic interpretation of the Law. In my view, this yields a significant insight regarding Pharisaism: it is a separate movement *within* the nation *for* the nation, whose legitimacy was indeed *accepted* by large parts of the people, even though its requirements were not *observed* to an equal extent. This provides us in my opinion also with justification to consider Pharisaism as normative Judaism, not because all *lived* according to Pharisaic halakah, but because Pharisaism was by the majority acknowledged as legitimate and authentic interpretation of the divine will for the chosen nation.

---

[195] Cf. R. Deines, *Pharisäer*, 385–8.

[196] "Der 'Am ha-'Ares. Ein Beitrag zur Religionssoziologie Palästinas im 1. und 2. nachchristlichen Jahrhundert," *Jud* 3 (1947): 169-99, now in idem, *Geschichte und Tradition* (see n. 183), 21-39 (33). With this view, the following are in general agreement: A. Oppenheimer, *The 'Am Ha-Aretz* (ALGHL 8; Leiden: Brill, 1977); A. Kovelman, הזמון ל"חז בספרות, in: *Jewish Studies* 36 (1996): 111–32 (Hebr.).

On the other hand, the Pharisees (appealing to *m.Sanh.* 10:1) never disputed that those who were negligent in matters of the Law nonetheless shared in the election of God's people (even though such election always also entailed certain obligations).

In other words, *when* the members of this class stated their religious views, they would do so in terms of Pharisaism, which they accepted (as representatives of Torah tradition) as the normative form of Judaism. This explains why the Pharisees had people's support in political and official religious questions, while they clashed with the people in the realm of personal piety and legal observance. Indeed, this conflict shows the proximity and mutual interest between both groups. If therefore Jesus' controversies with the Pharisees should be taken as evidence of his closeness to them, the same conclusion may be drawn regarding the relationship between the Pharisees and their scribes and the *Am ha-Aretz*. The same can emphatically *not* be said regarding the Sadducees and Essenes.

This is where, in my view, future research should resume, taking its point of departure with the above mentioned line of thought not further pursued by Meyer. The comparison with the group in Qumran seems particular promising to me. For it can be used as a paradigm for a group that considers itself to be the way in the desert. It is an example of the conception of "holy remnant," in which the separating group considers itself as the only true Israel. I consider following this route promising especially because such a comparison precludes the drawing of analogous conclusions regarding Pharisaic conceptions. After all, the Essenes in Qumran charge their Pharisaic opponents as דרשי חלקות, not with separation but with seduction of the people, the "simple-minded of Ephraim" (see nn. 102 and 113), on account of their easier interpretation of the Torah. The guiding thought of the Qumran community is the *substitution* of the old covenant people through a new one, which must be prepared for its new task by another time in the desert. Apparently, the end-time spiritual leaders no longer considered it possible to lead the nation in its entirety back to the path of true worship. The Pharisees, however, should be distinguished from this approach. Their theological stance in relation to the nation should be understood as *restitution*, which was to be realized by way of *representation* and *participation*.

The Pharisees thus did not conceive of themselves as the *holy*, but as the *sanctifying* remnant (cf. Rom 11:16), which, analogous to leaven, leavens the entire dough.[197] Their righteousness was oriented toward the nation, and it

---

[197] The Jesus logion (still not adequately explained) regarding the leaven of the Pharisees (Mark 8:15 par. Matt 16:6), in which the Pharisees are tellingly linked respectively with the Herodians (in Mark) and the Sadducees (in Matthew), could then be interpreted as a polemic word against the Pharisees' positive self-understanding. Their willingness to compromise, which enables them to cooperate with the Herodians and the Sadducees, then means also in

remains the subject of further investigation to what extent their thought was controlled by the notion of representation. Their remaining efforts likewise were oriented toward the entire nation, whom they sought to show the path to righteousness. This is the impact they strove to make, through the synagogues and schools, in the Sanhedrin and temple, and assuredly everywhere where people opened themselves up to their influence. That they were successful in this effort is indicated by the polemics of the Qumran texts, but also later the Gospels, the Book of Acts, and Paul. Their successful restitution of the Jewish community in Palestine (which was totally in shambles after the first Jewish War) as a result of this effort, constitutes the crowning historical achievement of this theological agenda.

7. Pharisaism as the Shaping Force of a Transformed "Common Judaism"

The essentially accurate threefold division of Judaism, which is confirmed by the Qumran texts, as well as the just described non-exclusive definition of Pharisaism, make it possible to understand Pharisaism in a new way as *the fundamental and most influential religious movement within Palestinian Judaism between 150 B.C. and A.D. 70.* It includes everything that belongs to the Torah tradition, and everything that is new can be integrated by the representatives of this movement, as long as it does not conflict with the principle of the normativity of Torah tradition as understood by the Pharisees.

Pharisaism can be called *normative*, because whatever was *integrated and thus legitimated* by its recognized representatives (generally probably its scribes and priests) over time became the possession of all of Israel. In the consciousness of the majority of the people, the Pharisees were the religious group that determined the boundaries of what was still and what was no longer Jewish.[198] This is why the Pharisees and their rabbinic successors

---

Jesus' mouth, comparable to the Qumran polemic, a recoiling from the new reality which has begun with the kingdom of God. O. Betz, *Offenbarung und Schriftforschung in der Qumransekte* (WUNT 1/6; Tübingen: Mohr [Siebeck], 1960), 96–97, already pointed to the connection with anti-Pharisaic polemic in Qumran. In Luke 12:1, the leaven is interpreted as hypocrisy, but the basic idea is also here "an invisible but highly effective influence which is permeating the crowds of Israel with a darkening malaise"; thus D. P. Moessner, "The 'Leaven of the Pharisees' and 'this Generation': Israel's Rejection of Jesus According to Luke," *JSNT* 34 (1988): 21–46 (31). Regarding this logion, cf. further R. C. Newman, "Breadmaking with Jesus," *JETS* 40 (1997): 1–11.

[198] Where "determined" should not be understood in terms of conciliar decrees, formal discipline, or the like. These may be *processes* of dealing with new ideas and views, which involves considering them, observing their implications, and weighing their compatibility with already recognized Torah tradition. This could, in due course, result in an increasing rejection,

increasingly pursued the isolation of Jewish Christians. This, however, also explains their interest in Jesus from the days of his ministry. It was part of people's expectation that they must take a position regarding the new teacher from Galilee.

This formative power can be called normative for Judaism to the extent that the Jewish majority recognized in the Pharisaic ideals the authentic expression of Jewishness.[199] "Recognized" does not mean that this majority practiced it to the fullest extent. For the majority of the people, the "Pharisaic ideals" remained an elusive ideal. For the interpretation of the New Testament and for the history of Jesus and of early Christianity, this means that Jesus and Paul engaged the dominant religious movement of their nation (which was at the same time the one closest to them). This is where it must come to light what both had in common and where they differed.

---

possibly even polemic refutation, that became part of the Pharisaic doctrine.

[199] To what extent this is also true for Diaspora Judaism requires separate investigation. The influence of the motherland was in any case very strong, and thus also the influence of pharisaically inspired piety.

16. Summaries and Conclusions

by

D. A. CARSON

Despite the variation of approaches and theological conclusions lumped together under one rubric, the "new perspective" on Paul customarily identifies one work above all others as the seminal volume that called so many other studies into being, viz. E. P. Sanders's 1977 book.[1] Central to that volume was Sanders's contention that the literature of Second Temple Judaism displays a pattern of religion that he labeled covenantal nomism. Because subsequent exegeses of Paul, especially of passages dealing with δικαιοσύνη and δικαιόω, have been heavily influenced by Sanders (not least where scholars have sought to go beyond him or to modify his views in some way), the cogency of Sanders's reconstruction of Second Temple Judaism is important not only for the study of Judaism but also for the study of Paul. At least in the Anglo-Saxon world, it is not going beyond the evidence to say that the new perspective is the reigning paradigm.

The first volume of this two-volume set provides a number of independent analyses of the relevant literature of Second Temple Judaism. In this final chapter, I propose, first, to summarize the arguments of the preceding chapters; second, to draw attention to two or three pieces of secondary literature that have appeared so recently they could not be included in these studies; and finally, to weave together the arguments advanced so far, in preparation for the second volume.

1. Summaries

One of the strengths of the essay by *Daniel Falk*[2] is that it recognizes the difficulty of attempting to read the theology of psalms and prayers. The language is conventional; moreover, the collections are scattered in highly diverse materials whose dating and *Sitze im Leben* are frequently disputed. Nevertheless, they do provide insight into the forms of piety that were

---

[1] *Paul and Palestinian Judaism: A Comparison of Patterns of Religion* (Philadelphia: Fortress, 1977).

[2] "Psalms and Prayers," 7–56.

practiced, and, approached with caution, they may disclose the presupposed and sometimes articulated theology of those who are praying. Having set forth his warnings, Falk briefly surveys several penitential prayers, all of them definitely pre-Christian (viz. *Words of the Luminaries, Communal Confession, Psalm 154, Psalm 155, Plea for Deliverance,* and *Prayer of Manasseh*). This is followed by a discussion of various series of petitions that have apparently drawn upon the *Amidah* – including examples drawn from Diaspora Judaism. Then, at greater length, Falk evaluates three larger collections: the *Hodayot* from Qumran, the *Psalms of Solomon,* and the *Odes of Solomon.*

Arising as they do out of "reflection on classic covenantal texts to understand and remedy the travails of the exile,"[3] the penitential prayers, Falk finds, often deploy language and motifs that nicely reflect the pattern of covenantal nomism described by Sanders. But that does not mean that these prayers do not stretch on occasion into fresh territory. *Prayer of Manasseh* raises the prospect of sinlessness. The patriarchs did not sin, and neither do their true offspring: these righteous persons do not need repentance, nor, apparently, grace, to enjoy the covenant. Sinners who repent will also enjoy the covenant. Throughout the penitential prayers, God's righteousness is a common theme, but it functions in diverse ways. Sometimes it is simply set over against the people's guilt. At other times, however, both God's mercy (or grace) and his righteousness can be appealed to when forgiveness is needed. But such appeals can take on forms that stretch the categories of covenantal nomism. When lenience is what is required, the appeal may be to mercy and grace; but when the appeal is to God's righteousness, the righteousness that removes transgression and purifies from sin may be more than simple help and forgiveness. In 4Q504 (*Words of the Luminaries*), there are two "circles of action"[4]: on God's side, he has sent "tests and blows" (4Q504 1–2.vi.7) and poured out his holy spirit on them so that they might pray to him "in the distress of [their] correction" (4Q504 1–2.v.15–17); on the people's side, they have humbled themselves and submitted to God's discipline, such that they can aver, "[W]e have atoned for our iniquity and the iniquity of our fathers" (4Q504 1–2.vi.4–9). God, then, is declared righteous for accepting the repentance and submission of the people in the context of his purifying discipline.

Falk traces many of the petitions in the *Amidah* (the so-called "Eighteen Benedictions") back to a variety of petitionary prayers in the period of Second Temple Judaism. Although much of the language of these petitionary prayers is conventional, he finds that they can be divided into two distinctive patterns. Always God is willing and able to answer the prayers of his people,

---

[3] Ibid., 16.
[4] Ibid.

who approach him on the basis of his mercy and often of his covenant. But in the first pattern, the focus is the nation, the evil is primarily foreign oppressors, and the harm that Israel suffers is either persecution for being faithful or punishment for sins of the nation. In the second pattern, the focus tends to be the individual, and the evil from which people need to be delivered is internal: individual or community sin, and sometimes demonic attack. That means that the problem is bound up with (fallen) humanness, not military "others."

It is the latter pattern that comes to the fore in *Hodayot*. Falk works through the intricacies of the debate regarding their style, form, vocabulary, and theology. In the end, however, he argues that these psalms must not be evaluated without constantly recalling that they cannot provide a picture of the overall piety of the sect, and that they serve sectarian purposes. Liturgical psalms in such a context function primarily "to confirm one's place in the covenant and to reinforce the boundaries between insider and outsider."[5] That is why, despite the emphasis on human sinfulness and unworthiness in *Hodayot*, these psalms are not so much penitential cries or petitions for help as hymns of thanksgiving for mercy received. They "reinforce one's standing in the covenant."[6] But because this is a sectarian community, into which one enters only by individual action (unlike the election of Israel) and submission to the authority and laws of the community and its Teacher, it is "meaningless in this context to make a theoretical separation between adherence to sectarian law and entrance to the community"[7] (which of course lies at the heart of Sanders's pattern of "covenantal nomism"). Falk concludes that the category of covenantal nomism is simply unsatisfactory for this literature.

After a thorough probing of the *Psalms of Solomon*, Falk offers an equivocal evaluation. There is nothing of classic "merit theology" in these *Psalms*, and in many respects Sanders's covenantal nomism would doubtless be a congenial category to the psalmists. But in one respect, at least, Falk finds the category rather awkward. When one focuses on the rhetorical function of the *Psalms of Solomon*, one must conclude that their preoccupation is "to reinforce community boundaries and one cannot escape that religious conduct is central to their group distinction."[8] The opponents are excluded as sinners. "This does not at all necessarily add up to a system of entitlement to God's mercy based upon one's actions, but to designate this restricted group-centered soteriology 'covenantal nomism' is ultimately not very helpful."[9] By contrast, the *Odes of Solomon*, a later Jewish Christian

---

[5] Ibid., 34.
[6] Ibid.
[7] Ibid.
[8] Ibid.
[9] Ibid.

work, have been so influenced by Christian eschatology and universalism that they prove of little help in analyzing Second Temple Judaism.

Craig A. Evans[10] examines four Scripture-based pseudepigrapha, viz. *Martyrdom and Ascension of Isaiah*, *Joseph and Aseneth*, *Life of Adam and Eve*, and *Lives of the Prophets*. In each case, Evans summarizes enough of the story that it becomes irresponsible to offer generalizations about the stories where they diverge from one another in tone or emphasis. Thus *Martyrdom and Ascension of Isaiah* (in the parts that are certainly Jewish and untouched by later Christian redaction) makes a contribution to demonology. Good and evil are sharply dualistic. There is no hint that for the original Jewish author of the book, the death of Isaiah had atoning value. By contrast, the conversion of Aseneth in *Joseph and Aseneth* imparts a rather different flavor to that story. Her confession, prayer, fasting, and self-abasement have been observed, the angel tells her (15:2–3), and she may now "eat blessed bread of life, and drink a blessed cup of immortality, and anoint [herself] with blessed ointment of incorruptibility" (15:5). Eating the bread of life nullifies her idolatrous past. Although one can draw partial parallels between this story and various biblical antecedents, the central emphases cannot be overlooked: "one is left with the impression that the change of lifestyle, not least the change of diet, plays a vital role in the redemption of Aseneth. God's grace is the presupposition, to be sure, but apart from wholesale adoption of Jewish food and purity laws, the conversion of Aseneth could not have taken place."[11]

The *Life of Adam and Eve* is a highly embellished and expanded version of Gen 3–4. It tells how Eve was deceived by Satan (twice), and how Adam and Eve, after falling into sin, were driven from earthly paradise, repented, and qualified for entry into the paradise of heaven. The focus of interest is on the effects of sin, and on "the elaborate penance performed by Adam and Eve."[12] "[T]he pardoning of Adam and Eve was not entirely the result of God's grace; it was in response to their vigorous penance."[13] If this is the Adamic equivalent of *entering* the covenant, it is not quite in line with the pattern summarized by Sanders's covenantal nomism. As for *Lives of the Prophets*, considerable emphasis is laid on the intercessory role of the prophets. It is not as if there are no biblical antecedents: one thinks, for instance, of the intercessory prayers of Elijah and Elisha. Still, in part it is the balance of things that is at issue; in part, the bits that find no biblical counterpart (e.g. Isaiah plays a post-mortem intercessory role in providing water at the pool of Siloam, 1:8). Perhaps no less important, though more difficult to assess, are the changes introduced in two of the stories. (1) The account of David and

---

[10] "Scripture-Based Stories in the Pseudepigrapha," 57–72.

[11] Ibid., 66.

[12] Ibid., 67.

[13] Ibid., 68.

Nathan is recast so that David's sin is somewhat mitigated. Beliar hindered Nathan from coming to David when the prophet was preparing to warn the king. (2) In the account of Daniel and Nebuchadnezzar, the king's repentance has certainly been heightened, and becomes bound up with diet (4:14).

Evans thinks these stories are broadly "consistent" with what one finds in early Christianity and in emerging rabbinic Judaism. The biggest divergence concerns the unique place in Christianity given to the atoning significance of the death of Jesus. Even so, Evans avers, there are elements in this literature (such as the way Aseneth becomes a member of the people of God) that reflect the sort of works-righteousness with which the apostle Paul would have disagreed.

The various expansions of Scripture evaluated by *Peter Enns*[14] are extraordinarily diverse, making generalizations inappropriate. Enns focuses on 1 Esdras, the Additions to Daniel, the Additions to Esther, *Jannes and Jambres*, Pseudo-Philo, and especially *Jubilees*. Of these, only *Jubilees* received much attention from E. P. Sanders in his 1977 volume.

1 Esdras (known as 3 Esdras in the Vulgate) covers approximately two hundred years, retelling the biblical stories from Josiah's celebration of Passover to Ezra's reforms (Neh 8:12). Nehemiah's importance is down-graded, that of Ezra increased. But by and large the pattern exhibited in 1 Esdras is in line both with Tanakh and with Sanders's covenantal nomism. "God has chosen a people for himself. If they sin, he will punish but not forsake them. They are his by election and they, or at least a 'root' or remnant, will remain so. Their own efforts, whether they are confession, oaths, or sacrifice, pertain to those who are already in, not the outsiders seeking entrance."[15] Nevertheless, Enns argues, it is important not to read this text at a personal or individualistic level. It is not about the way individual Jews have their sins expiated, for instance. Central to the book is the restoration of the temple, which is linked with "the relationship between an elect people and a saving God in their own land."[16]

By contrast, the Additions to Daniel are set on enemy turf, and the faithfulness of the individual is very much to the fore. Both through complex story-telling and through interweaving plainly anachronistic allusions to biblical texts, readers are exhorted to worship God regardless of the circumstances. They must remain true to him; in due course, he will deliver them – a common theme in Hellenistic Judaism. "The implicit message is that *God's* faithfulness to his people remains intact, and that provides the proper perspective from which to view the *people's* faith which God demands of

---

[14] "Expansions of Scripture," 73–98.
[15] Ibid., 77.
[16] Ibid.

them."[17] Once again, the emphases are at least in line with covenantal nomism, though there is one theme that draws the reader away in a slightly different direction. Perhaps it is seen more clearly in the Additions to Esther.

The six Additions to Esther aim to add religious content to a canonical book that is surprisingly reticent along these lines. Enns works through them, and shows that, as with the Additions to Daniel, the focus is on faithfulness in a hostile land. But Enns argues that there is much more at stake for the people of God than merely "staying in," remaining faithful in a difficult time. The personal level is not ignored, of course, but Esther's behavior symbolizes the conduct that the covenant people as a whole ought to have among the nations: "They are to be a holy and pure people in order to proclaim to the world the true God."[18] To God, the continuing existence of Israel is bound up with his intentions for the nations. That the covenant people of God will continue to exist does not come into serious question. "In other words, God's election of a people (getting in) must succeed for the sake of God's honor, which will be ultimately vindicated when the world at large, like Artaxerxes, acknowledges him."[19] This theme is no less present in the Additions to Daniel.

Turning to the pseudepigraphical texts, Enns finds that *Jannes and Jambres* is of little help, not only because the text is fragmentary but because the date of origin for both the tradition and the written text are highly disputed. By contrast, Enns finds the Pseudo-Philo's *L.A.B.* is much more relevant. Many parts of Old Testament history are omitted or disproportionately abbreviated in order to emphasize the period of the Judges. The repeated pattern of rebellion, punishment, repentance, and deliverance under the leadership of the judges provides examples of covenant (in)fidelity. The negative flavor (the book ends with Saul's death) bequeaths the message, "Don't let this happen to you."[20] That means this book is a book for insiders. Moreover, despite these stern warnings and the reiteration of Israel's obligations to God, God himself will never abandon his people utterly. In that sense, Enns writes, "Covenant precedes law."[21]

As for *Jubilees*, when Enns interacts with Sanders's treatment he finds himself in basic agreement with him, but at one crucial point offers a corrective. *Jubilees* greatly emphasizes God's elective grace in choosing the nation, and equally emphasizes Israel's responsibility to keep the commandments. So far, then, the pattern of covenantal nomism is explicit in this book. But Sanders himself finds there is a tension here between election and

---

[17] Ibid., 83.
[18] Ibid., 87.
[19] Ibid.
[20] Ibid., 92.
[21] Ibid.

obedience. Although obedience is necessary to remain in the covenant, God's election seems to carry the people through. Enns cites Sanders:

> It thus appears that the author's view that there is no atonement for forsaking the covenant, when it conflicts with the *historical reality of the continuation of Israel* and with his *conviction that Israel is elect and will ultimately be cleansed and saved*, yields. It must be confessed that we cannot achieve complete clarity on this matter.[22]

But Enns thinks that God's elective promise in *Jubilees* is with respect to Israel as a people. God is faithful, and therefore Israel as a people will never finally be destroyed. But that does not mean individual Israelites will not lose their covenant status and perish. On the other hand, certain individuals cannot be treated as mere individuals. Thus when an individual *patriarch* breaks an "eternal command," the *individual* transgression has *national* consequences, and so once again must be forgiven.[23] Thus, while Enns thinks that Sanders's assessment of *Jubilees* is fundamentally sound, he judges it important to nuance the discussion by a distinction between individual falling away and national preservation.

That brings Enns to his final musings and demurrals, not unrelated to the distinctions he has drawn. They have to do with the very categories that Sanders deploys. If "salvation" is by grace, how precisely is "staying saved" a matter of strict obedience? If obedience is an absolute condition of "preserving" salvation, in precisely what sense may we speak, with Sanders, of salvation depending on the grace of God? If election is the basis of salvation, how can there be sins unto death? Is part of the problem that Sanders is equating salvation with election? "Is salvation the best word to describe one's *initiation* into the covenant wholly apart from the final outcome?"[24] Insofar as the pattern of covenantal nomism is found in *Jubilees*, Enns writes, "It might be less confusing to say that *election* is by grace but *salvation* is by obedience."[25] And even this may not do justice to these Second Temple sources, for the categories of "getting in" and "staying in" are slightly misleading. According to *Jubilees*, election belongs exclusively to Israel. But because it is the beginning point, for the Israelites for whom *Jubilees* is written there is little point in talking of "getting in" at all: we might be wiser to speak of "being in," which is by birth. It is the "staying in" that requires individual effort. Enns concludes:

> Now, to be sure, that individual effort must be seen within the context of the individual's self-understanding and confidence as a Jew, a confidence that rests on God's faithfulness in calling a particular people to himself, and that he is predisposed to forgive transgression, an obvious fact seen in the biblical institution of a system of

---

[22] Ibid., 96, quoting Sanders, *Paul and Palestinian Judaism*, 378 (Sanders's emphasis).
[23] Ibid., 97.
[24] Ibid., 98.
[25] Ibid.

atonement. The point still remains, however, that the final outcome is based on more than initial inclusion in the covenant.[26]

These straightforward reflections demand more pondering (see below, pp. 543–548).

The stories covered by *Philip R. Davies*[27] include Tobit, Judith, Letter of Aristeas, 3 Maccabees and 4 Maccabees, all written in Greek (though Tobit, it appears, and probably Judith, had a Semitic original). Davies begins by reflecting on the ways that these stories "teach" – for failure to do so leads to interpretive errors. Stories entertain, but they also construct a world into which the reader is drawn. Inevitably, matters of genre come to the fore, raising questions of both content and form. But these stories, Davies avers, are sufficiently diverse that there is no single genre of "Jewish didactic story." Rather, several generic backgrounds feed into the stories under consideration. These include the court tale (which belongs to the scribal class, and not, for instance, to the village or the school), which stretches back into the wisdom tradition. By the time of Second Temple Judaism, wisdom is increasingly tied to Torah; thus it is tied to obedience rather more than to understanding in the modern sense. In this literature, God increasingly is the one who comes to the rescue, while there is more and more concern over the identity of Israel. "In Jewish didactic stories, being a good *person* is not the issue, but being a good *Jew*."[28]

Nevertheless, the diversity from story to story must not be underestimated. Sometimes the call is to live patiently, even under appalling suffering; sometimes God dramatically intervenes; sometimes an individual takes initiative, and God does not so much intervene as work behind the scenes. The resolutions can be highly varied: in Aristeas, there is a friendly exchange between the foreign king and the pious Jew; in 3 Maccabees, the foreign king is won over; in 4 Maccabees, the king is destroyed. In this literature, only 4 Maccabees reflects on theodicy in individualistic terms.

For each of the stories, then, Davies surveys the content, and discusses particular questions of genre, links with Scripture, and the pattern of relationships between God and the human beings on which these stories focus. In the case of Tobit, Davies argues that the traditional problem of the wisdom tradition is not the fate of the non-pious but of the exceptionally pious. The suffering of the exceptionally pious threatens the goodness of God in the world of monotheism. Tobit's piety is stressed "almost to the point of absurdity."[29] But at the end of the day, the book gives the traditional answer: Tobit dies well, Tobiah dies wealthy, witnessing the destruction of Nineveh

---

[26] Ibid.
[27] "Didactic Stories," 99–133.
[28] Ibid., 104.
[29] Ibid., 111.

and the return of the Assyrian prisoners. Yet this is not simply a rational-empirical system. Everywhere the question of the fate of the exiled Jewish people underlies the discussion (after all, Tobit himself is a member of one of the "lost" tribes), and in this context the sheer Jewishness of Tobit is critical: the son must marry a Jewish wife, must bury the dead according to Jewish law, and so forth. Fulfillment of the life of one Diaspora Jew somehow entails national restoration. How then are Tobit and Tobiah rightly related to God? On the one hand, the piety of these men is interwoven with the divine intervention, symbolized by God's agent Raphael. A mechanical theory of simple retribution is overtaken by divine intervention. On the other hand, the corporate element must never be overlooked: the heroes behave righteously not as human beings, but as Israelites, members of the covenant community.

Judith again stresses "the need for both individual initiative and self-reliance and also for piety and strict obedience to the law."[30] The question of suffering is largely corporate, however, rather than individual. "God can be trusted to protect his chosen people so long as they do not sin, though he will test them for their trust"[31] – and this trust is not passive, but issues in appropriate initiative, and responses of fasting and prayer. Indeed, even non-Israelites may trust God and become Israelites, though the enemies of Israel may suffer eternal torment. Davies suggests that both Daniel and Judith "perhaps reflect the beginnings of a considered theological approach to the question of a full divine recompense after death. The most a commentator on Judith can say is this regard is that like Daniel, Judith earned her own earthly reward."[32]

The *Letter of Aristeas* purports to give a non-Jewish account of the Law; it is an apology for Judaism to non-Jews. Little insight is offered as to how Jews were seen to be justified by God. Nevertheless, the extensive descriptions of temple and land, in the seven days of conversation between the king and the translators/delegates, carries the brunt of the argument, viz. the rationality and superiority of Judaism as a system. The Law is revealed and perfect, and accords with the best Greek philosophy. "One is justified, whether Jew or Gentile, by obedience to the Law, but also by obedience to reason, which is the same thing."[33] God is essentially Providence. There is no emphasis (against Sanders) on getting in by God's elective grace, and "staying in" is not quite the right category either, when what it means to be "in" is so broad. So Davies criticizes Boccaccini's thesis that this story develops a "true

---

[30] Ibid., 119.
[31] Ibid.
[32] Ibid., 118–9.
[33] Ibid., 121.

theology of grace" – for what we have in reality in this text is a theistic providence that makes God the source of all things.[34]

The presenting issue in 3 Maccabees is whether or not to adopt the pagan city's religious rites. The initial trigger is the conflict over the profanation of the temple. What part the temple plays in the "justification" of the people, however, is entirely unclear. There is little interest in what Judaism actually means to a Jew, other than the importance of not capsizing to paganism. This is so important that there is a stunning reversal: the pagan king is won over and finally honored, while the apostate Jews are executed by their own people. The account is finally a contrived story to warn against apostasy.

By contrast, 4 Maccabees has a philosophical agenda, as the opening lines make clear: "whether pious reason is the absolute control of the passions." The martyrdom of Eleazar and the seven brothers, narrated in 2 Maccabees, is repeated here. But whereas 2 Maccabees turns the account into a matter of personal vindication, the value of the martyr here is twofold: first, example, in which the supremacy of reason is demonstrated (rather than achieving glory in the eternal world); and second, in two crucial passages (6:27–29; 17:19–22), it is difficult to deny that the martyrs' death achieves benefit for others, apparently atoning for the sin of others. Perhaps, Davies suggests, this is in line with 1QS: there we find that good deeds could atone, and here the ultimate good deed of martyrdom proves especially efficacious. On the whole, Davies thinks the exemplary function of martyrdom is more important than the atoning function. But insofar as the atoning function of the martyrs' death is present, it stands outside the heritage of the Hebrew Bible, where the sacrificial system prescribed in the Law deals with sin, not the self-offering of martyrs. The entire focus of 4 Maccabees is on reason/Law: i.e. one could say that the focus of interest is on "staying in" and not "getting in" at all.

Davies concludes: "But all of these narratives make it clear that it was as a member of the Jewish people that each individual had to relate to God, and that equally the fate of that people depended on the allegiance, resourcefulness, reliability and honor of every single member. In these stories, no Jew is an island, and in the fate of every Jew lies, potentially, the fate of the Jewish people."[35]

The treatment of apocalypses by *Richard Bauckham*[36] focuses on those that are non-canonical, indubitably or probably non-Christian Jewish, and written before 200 C.E. Bauckham begins by insisting that the apocalypses are "a literature of revelation in which seers receive, by heavenly agency, revelations of the mysteries of creation and the cosmos, history and eschatol-

---

[34] Ibid., 122, with respect to G. Boccaccini, *Middle Judaism: Jewish Thought 300 B.C.E. to 200 B.C.E.* (Minneapolis: Fortress, 1991), 171.

[35] Ibid., 131.

[36] "Apocalypses," 135–88.

ogy."[37] The spectrum of approaches in this literature to such matters as law, covenant, and salvation reflects the range found in other bodies of Second Temple Jewish literature. Thus it is crucial to recognize that apocalyptic is a genre, not an ideology. Those who read apocalypses doubtless read other Jewish literature; probably a similar thing could be said about those who wrote them.

Bauckham begins his evaluation of individual apocalypses by unraveling the Enoch tradition. This tradition embraces originally discrete works that can be dated from the third century B.C.E. to (in the case of *2 Enoch*) the end of the first or the beginning of the second century C.E. The Book of Watchers (*1 Enoch* 1–36) is perhaps more concerned with the judgment of evil than with the origin of evil. The wicked and the righteous are divided exclusively: there does not appear to be any possibility of forgiveness for the wicked, any more than for the "paradigm apostates,"[38] the fallen angels, the Watchers. The righteous are assumed to be living righteously; what they need is assurance that justice will finally be served. There is no indication as to how the two attributes "righteous" and "elect" relate to each other: "it is simply assumed that the elect are those who are loyal and obedient to God. This is generally true of the rest of the Enochic literature also, though exhortations to the righteous not to be deflected from the path of righteousness sometimes occur (e.g. 91:3–4,19)."[39]

The Epistle of Enoch (*1 Enoch* 91–105), including the Apocalypse of Weeks, similarly maintains the connection between the elect and the righteous. But the contrast between the righteous and sinners is now given social definition: the latter are rich, powerful, arrogant; they oppress the poor. They are not Gentiles, but Jewish apostates. They will finally be judged according to their deeds (95:5; 100:7) – but this sort of expression is not grounded in a merely mechanical calculation of guilty deeds. Rather, such expressions "are consistent with the holistic sense of judgment on a whole way of life, and the main rhetorical function is to stress that the wicked will not escape judgment."[40]

Since Sanders does not include the Parables of Enoch in his study, Bauckham says that this is a good place to compare Sanders's findings on (at least these parts of) Enoch with his own. Even though Sanders's work represents an early stage of the study of *1 Enoch*, dominated by R. H. Charles and largely unaffected by the Qumran evidence, Bauckham and Sanders are in broad agreement so far. The righteous are the true Israel; sinners are either Jewish apostates or Gentile oppressors. The classifications are holistic; an

---

[37] Ibid., 135.
[38] Ibid., 144.
[39] Ibid.
[40] Ibid., 147.

individual totting up of merits and demerits is not in view. Obedience to the Law is here tied with "staying in," not "getting in." On the other hand, Bauckham argues that Sanders does less than justice to these texts by claiming that they exhibit "much the same pattern of religion" as he finds in the Rabbis.[41] Sanders reaches this conclusion, Bauckham contends, by focusing so narrowly on the particular questions he is studying, that he overlooks material differences between larger and narrower definitions of the true Israel in favor of a merely formal treatment. The Enoch literature deals with righteousness and salvation "in the context of a vision of a world presently dominated by evil. Evil on a cosmic and universal scale is the inescapable problem to which the solution is eschatological judgment."[42] This vision generates two tensions. On the one hand, the righteous are assured of their election, while being encouraged to remain loyal and implicitly being warned against apostasy; on the other, the Enochic tradition not only anticipates the vindication of the righteous but retains the prophetic hope that the nations will one day acknowledge the God of Israel.

The Parables of Enoch (*1 Enoch* 37–71) "seems in many respects a less coherent version of the Book of Watchers."[43] Probably the sinners here are pagans, since they can be characterized as idol-worshipers (46:7). Nevertheless, in general Gentiles are extended much more hope. When they witness the victory of the elect over all their oppressors, they will have opportunity to repent, renounce their idols, and trust the God of Israel, who will have compassion on them.

In many respects, *2 Enoch* has much in common with other Enochic works, and probably presupposes at least the Book of Watchers. Thus Enoch witnesses the places of eschatological judgment (a dominant theme), reward and punishment. On the other hand, the readers of *2 Enoch* do not seem to be troubled by widespread apostasy or oppression. As a result, the eschatological judgment does not function so clearly as encouragement to the faithful. Exceptionally, there is more ethical exhortation (accompanied by eschatological sanctions of reward and punishment), but also cultic requirements, including animal sacrifice. The universalistic features of the book do not annul its Jewish features, but are merely part of the antediluvian setting. But this means there are no explicitly covenantal elements in *2 Enoch*; there is no emphasis on election or on covenantal promises, "only God's commandments and rewards and punishments for observance or neglect of them."[44] One may be able to find formal parallels to much of this in the Hebrew Bible, but the balance of things is in consequence skewed in favor of this sort of schema.

---

[41] Ibid., 148; citing E. P. Sanders, *Paul and Palestinian Judaism*, 361.

[42] Ibid., 148.

[43] Ibid., 149.

[44] Ibid., 152.

More difficult to evaluate, and more important, is the image of weighing people or their deeds in the scales of justice (44:5; 49:2; 52:15). This motif is known elsewhere, of course (*1 En.* 41:1; 61:8; *Apoc. Zeph.* 8:5), but its most influential source is biblical: God is the one who weighs the heart and repays all according to their deeds (Prov 24:12; cf. 16:2; 21:2; Job 31:6; Dan 5:27). This biblical text links the image of weighing with paying back according to deeds; *2 Enoch* extends the formula by speaking of the weighing of deeds, but almost certainly in a similar sense. But a further extension comes in *2 En.* 44:5, which uses the image of scales in a marketplace to enrich this emphasis on "weighing" deeds. Unique to *2 Enoch* is the notion that a weighing scale is already prepared for each person, along with the place of that person's judgment, even before the person exists (49:2–3) – which is a way of saying that just judgment is an integral part of God's universe.

Yet it is probably going beyond the evidence to see here a simple arithmetical totting up of merits and demerits. Even when the *Testament of Abraham* (A12–14; B9) assigns people according to whether their sins outnumber their righteous deeds, this may not be intended crudely and literally, so much as a way of saying that there is a judgment on the person's whole quality and direction of life. In *2 Enoch* 30:15J this is easily seen in the treatment of Adam, whose free will enabled him to choose a good path or a bad; and for *2 Enoch*, Adam's descendants have the same freedom as their forebear. Yet one cannot deny that there is in this book a profound merit theology. There is no mention whatsoever of the mercy of God. As F. I. Andersen puts it, "A blessed afterlife is strictly a reward for right ethical conduct."[45] Bauckham notes that Sanders finds in *4 Ezra* a unique exception to the pattern of covenantal nomism, because (Sanders says) it lacks the notion that "the basically righteous but not always obedient members of Israel require God's mercy to be saved."[46] But if Sanders had included *2 Enoch* in his study, Bauckham insists, he would have found a work still more worthy of the description, "the closest approach to legalistic works-righteousness which can be found in the Jewish literature of the period."[47]

Bauckham treats the *Apocalypse of Zephaniah* cautiously, because a Christian origin cannot be entirely ruled out. The dominant concerns of the book have to do with postmortem judgment on the basis of the deeds done in this life, and also on the possibility of divine mercy after death. This *Apocalypse* deploys the common image of the book of life. Usually, however, when that image appears it coheres with covenantal nomism, in that it views all Israelites as belonging to the elect unless they apostatize. By contrast, the

---

[45] "2 (Slavonic Apocalypse of) Enoch," in *OTP* 1.96; cited by Bauckham, "Apocalypses," 156.

[46] *Paul and Palestinian Judaism*, 422; cited by Bauckham, "Apocalypses," 156.

[47] Sanders, *Paul and Palestinian Judaism*, 418.

Apocalypse of Zephaniah asserts that the righteous qualify by their righteousness to be included in the people of God and thus receive eschatological salvation. Here, however, one must be cautious about too sweeping a conclusion. The patriarchs are pictured pleading to God for sinners among their descendants, apparently as those sinners find themselves in a gap between death and the final judgment (after which there is no repentance) – and the presence of the patriarchs may suggest that the plea is offered on the basis of the covenant that God made with them.

Bauckham next considers several apocalypses written in the wake of the fall of Jerusalem, which projected such an enormous challenge to Jews who wanted to believe in the inviolability of the covenant. Perhaps the most important of these works, for our purposes, is *4 Ezra*. Here, ironically, Bauckham does not see quite the exception to covenantal nomism that Sanders himself sees. Bauckham denies that God's mercy is entirely excluded from God's dealings with the righteous, that the righteous are saved solely on the basis of their good deeds; rather, it is in mercy to the righteous that God finally saves them (12:34; 14:34). This might mean that God overlooks the relatively minor failings of those who generally keep the law, so as to reward their faithfulness. More plausibly, however, it refers to the grace by which God promised salvation to the covenant people in the first place. In *4 Ezra*, the covenant is understood as "God's promise to give the eschatological reward to those who themselves keep the covenant by observing the Law."[48] That means that salvation for the righteous is both a matter of God's grace (in that he chose to make the covenant with Israel) and a matter of reward (within the terms that God himself had laid down). "To suppose that for *4 Ezra* God gives the righteous eschatological salvation not because they are members of his elect people but because, regardless of their corporate affiliation, they have individually merited salvation, is to pose a false alternative. God gives salvation to those members of his elect people who have kept the terms of the covenant and so merit the salvation promised in the covenant."[49]

Of course, even this result lays strong emphasis on the urgent need "to merit eschatological reward by difficult obedience to the Law."[50] At a certain formal level, the structure of covenantal nomism is preserved. "But *4 Ezra* does rather importantly illustrate how the basic and very flexible pattern of covenantal nomism could take forms in which the emphasis is overwhelmingly on meriting salvation by works of obedience to the Law, with the result that

---

[48] Ibid., 173.
[49] Ibid.
[50] Ibid.

human achievement takes center-stage and God's grace, while presupposed, is effectively marginalized."[51]

All acknowledge strong links between *4 Ezra* and *2 Baruch*; nevertheless the latter, unlike the former, is not designed for "the wise" but for all the people. The moral wrestlings are less deep. Baruch quickly urges that since God has not abandoned his covenant with Israel, Israel must keep the law in order to benefit from the promises of the covenant. Accordingly, Sanders contrasts the two works in support of his view that *4 Ezra* embraces a unique "legalistic perfectionism" while *2 Baruch* nestles comfortably within the embrace of the categories of covenantal nomism.[52] "God punishes the wicked *for their deeds*, while bestowing *mercy on the righteous*."[53] But Bauckham remains unconvinced by this simple contrast between *2 Baruch* and *4 Ezra*. "With respect to *2 Baruch*, it would be more accurate to say not simply that God bestows mercy on the righteous, but that God has mercy on the righteous *because of their good works*."[54] Salvation does not depend on some narrowly arithmetical calculation of merit and reward, but salvation is certainly made dependent on deep adherence to God and his law. As with *4 Ezra*, the notion of salvation as a reward for righteousness is not necessarily utterly antithetical to the notion of salvation as a function of God's covenantal grace. After all, it is God's grace that has inaugurated the covenant and laid down the requirement of obedience as the condition of receiving the covenant's benefits. "Within this general framework it is possible to emphasize the need for human achievement to the point of marginalizing grace, as *4 Ezra* does, and it is possible to stress the need for human achievement at the same time as assuring people who adhere to the Law that God will be merciful to them, as *2 Baruch* does."[55]

The state of the debate over *3 Baruch* is still so fluid that more than a little caution must be exercised. Bauckham concludes, however, that this apocalypse is solely concerned with the corporate destiny of the people of God, not with the destiny of individuals.

Finally, Bauckham briefly assesses the Sibylline tradition, some of it, at least, written after the fall of the temple. Perhaps the most striking feature of some of the Sibyllines is the assumption that God's law is for Gentiles as well as for Jews, sometimes cast in a "two ways" mold.

Robert A. Kugler's treatment of testaments[56] finds diverging results in the literature he examines. The *Testament of Moses*, Kugler argues, for a large

---

[51] Ibid., 174.
[52] *Paul and Palestinian Judaism*, 427.
[53] Ibid., 421; cited by Bauckham, "Apocalypses," 181–2.
[54] Ibid., 182.
[55] Ibid.
[56] "Testaments," 189–213.

part of its body preserves several tensions; their resolution, however, moves the argument away from covenantal nomism. The testamentary character of the document leads one to expect that there will be reflection on future realities, and moral exhortation based on those realities: the people of God will either be rewarded or terminally punished. Certain passages (1:9; 2:7) refer to a covenant and oath, echoing Deut 29:9–14, and reinforce such an expectation. But as early as *T. Mos.* 1:6,9 those expectations are put into question: this *Testament* predicts "the people's corporate failure and God's remedial action *in place* of repentant and rectifying human activity."[57] A third factor is introduced in 1:14, where Moses himself has been determined from the beginning of the world to be God's covenant mediator, with the implication that Moses' mediation and intercession are necessary for the people's continued right standing with God and consequent blessing. Thus Moses' impending death threatens to jeopardize the people's good. Kugler argues that these various ways of conceiving of the relationship between God and his people continue in tension through much of the book, until in ch. 12 Moses resolves the tension. Although he was chosen from the beginning of time and his intercession is effective, it is effective only in accordance with the will of God (12:6–7). The people cannot do what only God can do (12:8). Although in this life they will suffer the consequences of their good and bad actions (12:10–11), nevertheless from the beginning God made creation for Israel (12:4–5,9) and will not let Israel be vanquished. Thus the stance adopted by this *Testament* is in line with Gen 15; 22; Exod 32; Deut 31–32, and this for understandable historical reasons – but it means that in this case one of the pegs of covenantal nomism does not fit. True, the people "get in" by grace, but here they do not "stay in" by obedience. They stay in by God's determined sovereign grace.

Although the *Testament of Job* is clearly modeled on the biblical Book of Job, the difference in theological outlook is very substantial. It combines the testamentary genre with an entertaining narrative strategy to illustrate and commend the importance of perseverance. The historical reasons are reasonably clear. Written for Diaspora Jews, probably in Egypt, after the Romans have taken over, this book addresses Jews whose situation was painful, economically depressed, uncertain. Whatever the historical reasons, however, the result is dramatically at odds with the biblical Job. There, the relationship of God to evil and innocent suffering remains mysterious; in the *Testament*, there is no such thing as innocent suffering, there is no doubt about the place and value of retribution, and although God may permit certain things to come to pass (8:1–3) the testamentary Job "is reassured that if he trusts God he will be restored to wealth, health and happiness twice over, and

---

[57] Ibid., 195 (emphasis his).

in the bargain will be raised from the dead (4:6–9)."[58] Theodicy is thus reduced to formulaic answers, and anguished questions to God are correspondingly reduced.

In one sense, of course, this corresponds to Sanders's "staying in" by obedience. Yet this obedience is not so much a matter of obeying a body of law so much as rather abstractly remaining faithful to the God of Israel in immensely troubled times.

The *Testaments of the Twelve Patriarchs* is large, complex, and notoriously difficult to date. Most recognize that there are at least segments of some of these *Testaments* that stretch back to entirely Jewish provenance, but there is no certain appearance of the finished document, heavily overlaid with Christian themes, until about 200 C.E. Kugler tentatively argues that the document was known and read by both Christians and Jews by the second century C.E. If the work is set within that framework, the usual reading understands the thrust of the argument to be that while the Jews were chosen by God long ago, their fate under the new, Christian dispensation that God has now introduced depends on their adherence to the God-given law. Kugler tests this theory by a close examination of *Testament of Simeon*. He argues that Sanders is right: covenantal nomism is a useful category for describing the importance of obedience if the people of God are to "stay in" their relationship with God. Nevertheless he nuances this perspective by showing that the perceived threat to the Jews (at least in the case of the *Testament of Simeon*) is from classical culture, and the *Testaments* respond by artfully weaving together "the genres, narrative strategies, and content of the Hebrew Scriptures and of Greco-Roman literature to counter the threat of assimilation to classical culture and encourage a Jewish (or Christian) lifestyle shaped by the Hebrew Bible and its values."[59] In short, the *Testaments of the Twelve Patriarchs* hold that God has chosen Israel, "and seem to require mostly reliance on God and little in the way of specific law-keeping to sustain that relationship."[60]

The treatment of wisdom literature by *Donald E. Gowan*[61] recognizes that fine dating of the relevant documents is impossible, so that one cannot trace development within the genre. Nevertheless the five works he treats (Sirach, Baruch, Wisdom of Solomon, 4 Maccabees, and the Sentences of Pseudo-Phocylides) all spring from the period between 200 B.C.E. and 100 C.E.

After careful and detailed inductive survey of these five works, Gowan concludes that "getting in" is attributed to God's initiative in the first four, and Sirach, Wisdom of Solomon and 4 Maccabees "base their teachings on

---

[58] Ibid., 203.
[59] Ibid., 212–3.
[60] Ibid., 213.
[61] "Wisdom," 215–39.

the certainty that the sovereign and merciful God is faithful to that relation-ship."[62] The author of Pseudo-Phocylides simply does not disclose his understanding of Israel as the people of God. As for staying in, Baruch is the only one that suggests the continuation of the covenant relationship is uncertain, but even this book deploys the promises of the prophetic books and makes new use of wisdom-material in order to offer reassurance. Here, staying in "does not depend entirely on human obedience, but depends on mercy that transcends merit. Confession of sin and appeal for forgiveness play a larger role than in the other books."[63] Sirach's emphasis on repentance and forgiveness likewise demonstrates that the author "does not operate with a strictly merit-based theology."[64] Because Wisdom of Solomon and 4 Maccabees are written against the background of persecution, there is more emphasis on God's support for those who suffer for their faithfulness, than on their sins.

In the first four of these five books, the law of God plays an important role (for instance, Sirach ties it to wisdom), "but as a theme rather than as a set of statutes to be expounded."[65] There is no hint that God counts up merits based on the works of the law. The threat of punishment is largely reserved for "the wicked" rather than for individual sins, though Sirach includes the latter theme as well. "The books thus begin with the assumption that the readers are 'in,' and that there is another group, the enemies, who are 'out.' Given the hazardous nature of Jewish existence during these centuries, the most frequently expressed concern is not how to remain 'in,' but how to survive physically, both as individuals and as a community, and the Old Testament message that God preserves the righteous is reaffirmed in various ways for that reason."[66]

The essay on Josephus by *Paul Spilsbury*[67] begins by pointing out that in his seminal volume *Paul and Palestinian Judaism*[68] E. P. Sanders makes passing reference to Josephus only three times. It is in his later work, *Judaism: Practice and Belief 63 BCE–66 CE*[69], that Sanders devotes substantial space to Josephus, and frankly acknowledges, "The principal source for the history of the period, and for its social, political and religious issues, is the work of the Jewish author, Josephus."[70] It is not entirely clear why this fact did not play into the earlier work.

---

[62] Ibid., 238.
[63] Ibid.
[64] Ibid.
[65] Ibid., 239.
[66] Ibid.
[67] "Josephus," 241–60.
[68] London: SCM, 1977.
[69] Philadelphia: Trinity Press International, 1992.
[70] Ibid., 5.

Spilsbury gives the usual warnings: Josephus is not primarily a theologian, so it is all the more urgent that readers respect his categories on their own terms. Spilsbury says we cannot be certain that Josephus was a Pharisee, so that what we learn from his writings must be taken to reflect his own opinions, and not necessarily those of Pharisees. Moreover, Josephus' apologetic interests ensure that he has no interest in detailed consideration of the shortcomings of the Jews.

In *Antiquities* Josephus lays considerable stress on the Law. God rules his people through the Law, which is profoundly rational and is in keeping with the natural laws of the universe. It is obeyed by Jews everywhere and in every detail, which makes the Jews the most generous, hospitable, and charitable of people. To observe the Law results in God's favor. With this emphasis on the Law, however, it is all the more stunning that *Antiquities* nowhere mentions the covenant. Various theories have been advanced to account for this remarkable omission. Betsy Halpern Amaru argues that Josephus was intentionally driving a wedge between himself and the land-oriented covenant theology of the Zealots in the pre–70 period.[71] Josephus omits covenant language to dampen down the militaristic messianism that inspired the rebels. H. W. Attridge argues that Josephus replaces the notion of covenant with the notion of divine providence (πρόνοια): God's support is the outworking of his retributive justice.[72] This means that whatever benefits the Israelites derive from God are not grounded in any special relationship ("covenant") with God, but in their conformity to his will as set forth in the Law of Moses. Spilsbury himself argues further that the broad strokes of the God/Israel relationship in *Antiquities* are best accounted for by recourse to the patron/client system of social relations, common in the Roman Empire in the late first century C.E. Unequal partners agree to be linked together for various kinds of mutual support. Thus Josephus could avoid the term "covenant" because the reciprocal relationship between God and his people was adequately expressed in patron/client categories. It follows, then, that Sanders's "covenantal nomism" is a particularly inappropriate category for Josephus. Spilsbury suggests that "patronal nomism" might be better – but that whatever the label, and whatever the points in common with covenantal nomism, this is not covenantal nomism by another name. "It is, in fact, a thoroughly Romanized translation of a biblical concept into a new idiom. As with any translation, some things are lost and others gained in the process."[73] It does not take much imagination to see how much such categories sidestep or even transmute traditional notions of the grace of God in covenantal election.

---

[71] "Land Theology in Josephus' *Jewish Antiquities*," *JQR* 71 (1980–81): 210–29.

[72] *The Interpretation of Biblical History in the Antiquitates Judaicae of Flavius Josephus* (HDR 7; Missoula: Scholars, 1976), 86–87.

[73] "Josephus," 252.

In *Jewish War*, Josephus defends the position that God is on the Roman side. Rebellion against Rome is therefore also rebellion against God. This leads to an original rereading of Jewish history. God has never sanctioned arms; Jews have never won by resorting to arms, but only by trusting God, who has won for them. Failure to submit to Rome is rebellion against God, and God cannot be expected to honor such rebellion, since he does not help the just and the unjust equivalently. Proper submission to God, along with the blessings that flow from such submission, turns on observance of the Law of Moses. Similarly, in *Against Apion* God is the ruler of the universe, the Law is the expression of God's will, and the Jews, deeply pious, are committed to obeying the Law, which explains why there are so few transgressions among them (especially in the Diaspora). "To us . . . the only virtue consists in refraining absolutely from every action and every thought that is contrary to the laws originally laid down" (2.182–3).

Both *Against Apion* and *Jewish War* make it clear that Jews who obey the Law and who die naturally enjoy the hope of the resurrection. This hope is "predicated upon the conviction that God is in supreme control of the universe, and that, ultimately, unswerving loyalty to him expressed through obedience to the Law will have its reward."[74] Thus, although such an understanding of "salvation" is profoundly theological, it is not set forth in a context in which there is a special status for Jews grounded in election. God rules the entire world. "The only advantage the Jews have is their association with Moses, who in his extreme sagacity discovered the truth about God and formulated laws in keeping with God's will. Those who experience God's blessing, therefore, will be those who accept the Law as their 'standard and rule' and who live under it 'as under a father and master' (*Ag. Ap.* 2.174)."[75]

In some ways, of course, this assessment of the Jews' relationship to the Law parallels what Paul writes in Rom 3:1–2. But Paul's question is set in a rather different framework. As far as Josephus is concerned, being entrusted with the Law meant that Jews knew how to obey God, and for the most part did so very admirably.

Philip S. Alexander explores the concept of salvation in the Tannaitic literature.[76] Restricting himself exclusively to the Tannaitic literature (texts that reportedly record the teaching of rabbinic Sages living in Palestine from the first to the third centuries C.E.), Alexander warns at the outset that he is not arguing that these texts represent all of Judaism during that period, nor even, necessarily, Jewish "orthodoxy." Moreover, he prefers to let the meaning of "salvation" emerge from the study of the texts.

---

[74] Ibid., 258.

[75] Ibid.

[76] "Torah and Salvation in Tannaitic Literature," 262–301.

Not a few errors in the interpretation of these texts spring from reading them in an historical vacuum. They are neither narrowly religious nor sectarian. Rather, they are primarily "manifestos of a movement which was bidding for political power in Israel and which, by the end of the Tannaitic period, had effectively achieved its political goals."[77] As they set about the task of creating a comprehensive constitution that responded to post–70 realities, they were opposed by "peoples of the land" (probably a coalition of landowners and farmers) and various sectarians (מינים), including Jewish Christians. Rabbinism was promoted through the synagogue, the law courts, and the Beit Midrash, the rabbinic schools.

Judaism of the Diaspora did not observe the whole Torah, nor was it required to do so; it was necessarily a restricted Judaism. Probably this form of Judaism was imported back into Palestine in the post–70 period. The rabbinic movement opposed the import. It resolutely set out "to maximize the application and observance of the Torah."[78] The Tannaitic literature, a product of the rabbinic schools, can usefully be divided into codification (Mishnah, Tosefta, and the Baraitot) and Bible commentary (the Tannaitic Midrashim). The relation between these two corpora is hotly disputed. But however we understand that relation, both come from a broadly similar worldview, though it is important to recognize that they do not all say the same thing. Because these texts are legal and homiletical, extracting answers to questions about the nature of salvation from them is not an easy or obvious enterprise. Indeed, Alexander asserts that a truly systematic rabbinic theology "does not begin to emerge till the early Middle Ages."[79] That means that, w.r.t. the themes that concern this present volume, the Tannaitic literature is quite capable of espousing mutually contradictory positions. Alexander insists:

> Depending on where they start and how they prioritize the different elements, they may produce in the end either a theology of "works-righteousness" or of "grace," or of any number of mediating positions in between. There is absolutely no reason to suppose that the Tannaitic authorities when they stress that righteousness is determined strictly by the extent to which one keeps the commandments of the Torah expect the hearer mentally to qualify this with the idea that God is merciful and will not rigorously enforce the law. Conversely there is no reason to suppose that when they expatiate in glowing terms on the love, mercy and grace of God, they are expecting the hearer mentally to qualify this with the thought that actually God does expect his commandments to be obeyed and will assuredly punish the sinner if they are not. And when they do boldly juxtapose justice and mercy, law and grace, they make no serious attempt to

---

[77] Ibid., 263.
[78] Ibid., 267.
[79] Ibid., 270.

reconcile the tensions between them, but emphasize the one or the other according to their immediate homiletic purpose.[80]

Modern attempts to synthesize a Tannaitic theology may be usefully placed into three groups. Older entries like that of F. Weber's *System der altsynagogalen palästinischen Theologie aus Targum, Midrasch und Talmud* (2nd ed. 1880) were permeated by a deep anti-Jewish animus, and were especially insistent that Judaism is characterized by legalistic works-righteousness. More recently there has been an array of works that have culminated in Sanders's seminal tome.[81] These works have been much more informed than the earlier studies, and certainly more sympathetic to Tannaitic Judaism. But they are not without weakness. Alexander argues that all of the writers in this group have either been Christians of liberal Protestant background, or Jews influenced by liberal Protestant ideas. He goes on:

> All seem tacitly to regard it as axiomatic that a religion of works-righteousness is inferior to a religion of grace. Weber had accused Judaism of legalistic works-righteousness. They set out to defend it against this charge, but nowhere does any of them radically question the premise that there is something wrong with a religion of works righteousness. . . . Where Weber overemphasized law, they may be overemphasizing grace.[82]

Now, however, there is a rising third group, best exemplified by the work of Friedrich Avemarie.[83] This "highly competent and subtle analysis of the rabbinic texts"[84] argues for the inconsistency of these texts: salvation can be either through law or through grace. Alexander agrees, but warns against improper inferences regarding this inconsistency. In Alexander's view, when the rabbis emphasize one side or another in response to particular situations they are addressing, in both cases they are drawing from Scripture itself.

At this point Alexander embarks on a careful study of Torah and salvation in the Mishnah and in the Tannaitic Midrashim. In a concluding section, he confesses he has been constantly troubled by the fear that in conducting this analysis he has been reading the sources against the grain, forcing them into a consistency they do not have, requiring them to speak to issues that are not theirs. To compare the writings of Paul with the writings of the Tannaim "is about as easy and meaningful as the comparison of the sermons of Chrysostom with the Code of Justinian, or the writings of John Wesley and the Code Napoléon."[85] Nevertheless, he ventures to distill the results of his

---

[80] Ibid., 270–71.

[81] Viz. *Paul and Palestinian Judaism.*

[82] Alexander, "Torah and Salvation," 272.

[83] See especially his *Torah und Leben: Untersuchungen zur Heilsbedeutung der Tora in der frühen rabbinischen Literatur* (TSAJ 55; Tübingen: Mohr [Siebeck], 1996).

[84] Alexander, "Torah and Synagogue," 273.

[85] Ibid., 298.

analysis into ten propositions.[86] In brief: (1) The Tannaitic corpus does not attempt a coherent theology of Judaism. The closest thing to an exception is *m. 'Abot*, but here too homiletics triumphs over theology. (2) Nevertheless the Tannaitic sources do presuppose a worldview, and so the construction of a theology of Tannaitic Judaism "is probably a legitimate intellectual enterprise."[87] Even so, such an enterprise should begin with the individual sources, since they are not all of a piece. Thus *Sipre* Deuteronomy, in line with the biblical text on which comment is being offered, makes the concept of covenant central, which can certainly not be said of Mishnah. (3) In constructing a theology of Tannaitic Judaism, one should take into account the interpretations and developments in later Judaism, especially from the Amoraic period but even beyond. There are two competing dangers: on the one hand, one must avoid mere anachronism, since Judaism changes with time; on the other hand, failure to take into account those in the line of Judaism who have read these texts most closely does not guarantee a more objective reading, but opens up interpreters rather uncritically to their own biases. "It is somewhat disturbing to note the extent to which the systematic construction of Tannaitic theology has been dominated by Christian scholars who have a liberal Protestant agenda and little or no knowledge of the later rabbinic theological tradition."[88] (4) There is a congruence between Tannaitic thinking and Scripture, especially the Deuteronomistic school. (5) Torah is central, but Tannaitic theology is a "full Torah" Judaism (unlike Diaspora Judaism). Torah embraces not only all that the Pentateuch stipulates, but the oral tradition that extends and clarifies those stipulations. It includes laws relating to the Land and to the sacrificial system even after the temple has been destroyed: all must be studied. Above all, it is anti-sectarian in the sense that it "aspires to provide a national program for the whole of Israel. The Mishnah offers a constitution for a national community; it is the manifesto of a party which claims the right spiritually and politically to guide all Israel."[89] (6) This Law is binding only on Israel; the nations are bound to obey the less demanding code given to the sons of Noah. Gentiles are fully righteous if they obey the latter; "Israel, however, achieves righteousness by keeping the commandments of the Torah."[90] The Tannaitic sources do not hint at perfectionism, though some who go beyond the demands of strict righteousness become "saints" (חסידים). (7) "Study of the Torah is a precondition for the proper performance of the Torah."[91] (8) In these sources,

---

[86] Here I am summarizing pp. 298–301.
[87] Ibid., 298.
[88] Ibid., 299.
[89] Ibid.
[90] Ibid., 300.
[91] Ibid.

salvation is essentially national; it is not overtly messianic. There are hints of
eschatological rewards and punishments, but they are not highly developed.
(9) "Tannaitic Judaism can be seen as fundamentally a religion of works-
righteousness, and it is none the worse for that. . . . There is little hint in
Tannaitic sources that God can simply forgive the sinner without any action
whatsoever on the sinner's part."[92] Nevertheless divine justice is moderated
by divine mercy, and there are means of atonement that "stay or mitigate the
application of strict justice."[93] Moreover, the "merits of the fathers and of the
righteous cover the sins of all Israel."[94] This is not a crude arithmetical
counting, however: the relationship between God and Israel is portrayed in
anthropological and emotional terms that rule out notions of blind fate or
inexorable justice. (10) "In dialectical tension with the basic works-
righteousness of the Tannaitic worldview stands the doctrine of the election
of Israel, which suggests that God has chosen Israel to fulfill his purposes in
the world and that he will guarantee that, whatever Israel does, the covenant
in his mercy and grace will not ultimately fail."[95] The tensions between this
outlook and the doctrine of works-righteousness are never "deeply explored
or finally resolved."[96]

Martin McNamara leads us through the Targums.[97] After preliminary
discussion of the nature, provenance, and dating of the Targums (all to some
extent disputed matters), McNamara restricts himself to the Targums of the
Pentateuch (with the exception of the Targum of Pseudo-Jonathan) and of the
Prophets.

Detailed examination of what the Targums say on defined subjects follows.
The emphasis on Law is a reflection of the central role of the Law in Jewish
life. "The practical identification of wisdom with the Law led to the transferral
to the former of characteristics predicated of wisdom, such as being the tree
of life, the source of life for those who observe the commandments."[98] Indeed,
if these identifications were interpreted as other than figures of speech or
metaphors, it is not hard to see how conflict would arise with the Christian
position in which Christ is incarnate Wisdom, the sole source of life and
healing. "The positions taken up by both sides because of this may have
helped toward the Jewish accentuation of the central place of the Law of
Moses and towards the formulation of the Christian position on salvation

---

[92] Ibid.
[93] Ibid.
[94] Ibid.
[95] Ibid.
[96] Ibid., 301.
[97] "Some Targum Themes," 303–56.
[98] Ibid., 318.

through faith in Christ, and Paul's emphasis on Christ being the end of the Law."[99]

As for righteousness, merit, and grace, the Targums, in line with Deut 9:4–6, certainly do not hold the view that Israel's election flowed from her own merits. When the Targums speak of the merit (or merits) of the Fathers, matters are more complex. Usually such merits are spoken of in the phrase בזכות (or plural בזכוות). Sometimes this must be translated "because of" or "for the sake of" – and in that case this may be no more than a reference to God remembering his covenant with the patriarchs (compare the prayer of Moses, Exod 32:12–13). But in some instances the expression might mean "by/for/through the merit(s) of." Even in this case, however (and the translation is disputable), McNamara argues that it is not entirely clear that the Targums are going much beyond motifs already present in the Hebrew Bible, into a doctrine of inherited merit that saves Israel.

The frequent Targumic expressions "good works" and "bad works," found neither in the Hebrew Bible nor in the Greek Old Testament, probably find their closest parallels in the Gospel of Matthew, and in certain letters of the Pauline corpus. Both Matthew and the Targums speak comfortably of reward, of course, but the glory is to be given to God. Nevertheless, McNamara records numerous expressions that find no ready parallelism in either the Hebrew Bible or in New Testament writings. For instance, in the Palestinian Targum on Deut 28:31 (on the curses for violating the covenant), the MT's "there shall be no one to help you" is paraphrased "and you shall have no good works before the Lord your God which might deliver you from the hands of your enemies." Similarly, the MT of Isa 26:20 ("Go, my people, enter your chambers, and shut your doors behind you") becomes in Tg. Isa. "Go, my people, make for yourself good deeds which will protect you in time of distress." Such variations can be multiplied many times.

As for passages that treat covenants or offer visions of the future, the Palestinian Targums "expand considerably, and relate the text to later Jewish history and the rewards and punishments in the otherworld, retribution in keeping with observance or neglect of the precepts of the Law."[100] Similarly, the Targums often go beyond the biblical texts in stressing kingdom of God themes (though "kingdom" is notoriously difficult to define) and encouraging messianic expectation. As might be expected, repentance is an accentuated theme in the Targums, "together with the doctrine of God's mercy and forgiveness to those who repent."[101] They "constantly insert mention of obedience to the Law, but as well as this can expand on God's mercy, and

---

[99] Ibid., 319.
[100] Ibid., 337.
[101] Ibid., 348.

insert mention of it in places not required by the translation."[102] Often the insertions and expansions are in line with themes in Deuteronomy.

Although most of his space is devoted to close readings of the Targums, McNamara brings his essay to a close by raising questions about the extent to which the Targums shed light on Sanders's claims regarding covenantal nomism. McNamara argues that the evidence from the Targums of the Pentateuch and of the Prophets does not warrant associating the Aramaic paraphrases with any one particular section of Judaism of the Second Temple period. (The presence of the doctrine of resurrection shows they did not originate in Sadducean circles, however.) The Targums "remain faithful to the biblical teaching that election is of God's grace and free will, not because of Israel's righteousness."[103] By and large, McNamara affirms, their references to good works, evil works, and punishments and rewards are in keeping with the language of the Gospels. And although the Targums deploy surrogates to refer to God (Memra, Shekinah, fear of the Lord), these surrogates, though frequent, are not universally used, and the God of Israel remains a living God, seen most clearly in the language of prayer.

Sanders does not treat the Targums separately, largely because he is not persuaded that their dating is early enough to make these translations relevant. Here, of course, McNamara demurs. But McNamara's objection to Sanders has more to do with the categories deployed than with the specific evidence of the Targums. "Covenant" calls to mind a relation with a living God, and looks backward and forward in time to what God has done and will do; "nomism" denotes a static position, conformity to certain rules. Covenant cannot be defined by law – whether law as it is understood at Qumran or in later rabbinic tradition. McNamara writes, "To me . . . it is questionable whether 'covenantal nomism' is an apt description of any form of Jewish religion."[104] The proper response to covenant is obedience, as Sanders rightly insists, and at given times in history that voice finds expression in law. But that voice could speak again: that is the nature of the vitality of covenant and of covenant obedience.

David M. Hay begins his treatment of Philo[105] by outlining what we know of Philo's eight non-exegetical treatises, what they contain, including their distinctive emphases. Whatever the debates among contemporary students of Philo, Philo himself certainly did not think he was betraying Scripture: doubtless he simply did not discern any insuperable difficulty between Scripture and the best of the pagan world. Philo's treatments embrace a mix of literal and allegorical explanations, though he leans more heavily on the

---

[102] Ibid.

[103] Ibid., 352.

[104] Ibid., 355.

[105] "Philo," 357–79.

latter. Although most of his focus is on the individual, one treatise deals with metaphysical and cosmological issues (viz. *On the Creation of the World*).

"At the heart of Philo's religious philosophy is a concern to portray the pilgrimage of the soul to God."[106] Thus his "insiders" are those who share this outlook; his "outsiders" are "all those who refuse to make their relationship to God their chief business in life."[107] Moreover, this stance is commonly allied with a metaphysical dualism: drawing near to God means turning away from the body and the senses. Although Philo can speak of sins and of forgiveness, he prefers to talk in terms of human weakness and the acquisition of virtue, about inspired reason standing over against the passions. The serpent in Gen 3 does not symbolize evil or Satan, but pleasure. In his exposition of Gen 3:24–4:1, mind (Adam) unites with the senses (Eve) and in consequence comprehends external phenomena and is deluded into thinking that this is its own doing. What human beings ought to strive for is mystical union with God.

Within this outlook, then, "Israel" connotes the community of all who "see God." The term is not coincident with all who are Israelites by natural descent. Its applicability depends on closeness to and devotion to the Mosaic revelation (interpreted, of course, through the Philonic grid). Philo uses the word "covenant" only rarely. He understands that the Jews have a unique relationship to God, established through Moses at Sinai. Moreover, they serve as priestly intercessors on behalf of humanity. Nevertheless, Hay insists, this does not really square with Sanders's covenantal nomism. As far as covenantal nomism is concerned, "getting in" focuses on the community as the recipient of God's grace and promises, whereas Philo is interested in the individual's search for God. Moreover, the notion of "staying in" and preserving oneself by works presupposes an eschatological orientation, but Philo has no clear idea on such subjects. Not only does Philo say little about covenants, but the framework of his thought is not soteriological. So it seems a bit forced to squeeze Philo into the covenantal nomism rubric. Philo does not exclude Gentiles, but clearly hopes that many will become Jewish proselytes. With but rare exceptions, Philo shows little interest in apocalyptic or nationalistic eschatology. Nowhere does he speak of Jews or Gentiles being "saved" after death.

Philo considers the Law of Moses to be the Law of Nature, and the patriarchs were "living laws." In consequence, the Law of Moses is for all of humanity, and those who live by it are "citizens of the world" – indeed, only they are! As for such laws as those dealing with circumcision, Sabbath, and the like, allegory can disclose their inner substance, but this is not a substitute for literal observance. A child is like pure wax, inexperienced in both good

---

[106] Ibid., 364.
[107] Ibid., 365.

and evil: both good and evil can be inscribed. Because of defects in education, however, a child is attracted to evil before he or she is old enough for reason to kick in. Only God can forgive sin, which is a violation of the Law of Nature, which is God's law. Our part is to repent, and to make public confession (to deter others). Repentance occupies the second place after perfection; it is symbolized by Enoch. Moses prescribes certain sacrifices for sin, and these are the most complete and appropriate means. "Pentateuchal references to the wrath of God and dire consequences of disobedience are designed to awaken the claims of conscience and prompt repentance. . . . The true 'cure' for sin lies in divine forgiveness on the one hand, and, on the other, a sinner's conversion to a better life through the elimination of vice and acquisition of virtue."[108] Conscience itself is God's word or reason (λόγος) within each individual. Repentance is itself grounded in God's grace. Philo does not think that human beings simply earn God's forgiveness and mercy. "He certainly often stresses that human beings have free will and that they must cooperate with God in acquiring the virtues. . . . Yet Philo does not think of human will as absolute and his concept of grace is not synergistic."[109]

Markus Bockmuehl begins his essay[110] by asserting that questions about the "pattern of religion" in the Qumran community have become far more difficult in recent years than they were a quarter of a century ago, owing to the plethora of new sources and the exponential increase of secondary studies. The challenge does not lie in the numbers alone, but in the diversity of the sources.

Although a meaningful discussion of Qumran's soteriology must certainly take into account the contributions of E. P. Sanders and other early contributors, something is to be said for the view that their agenda is often driven by some form of Christian concerns rather than by the texts at hand. Still, many Jewish texts *do* raise questions about human salvation, so an examination of the sources is important. Bockmuehl avers that he cannot examine all the new material that treats temple, calendar, ritual, and much more. Instead, he focuses on the *Community Rule* (1QS), including some of the newly published fragments from Cave 4, and from time to time makes additional reference to other Qumran sources, especially CD, 1QH, and 4QMMT.

After a brief survey of the contents of 1QS, Bockmuehl elucidates the "elements of a doctrine of salvation"[111] found in this document. (1) How does election link up with the people of God, corporately considered? The crucial question is whether the community sees itself as the elect, over against Israel,

---

[108] Ibid., 377.
[109] Ibid., 378.
[110] "1QS and Salvation at Qumran," 381–414.
[111] Ibid., 388.

and if so on what ground – and in particular whether that ground is in some way their superior righteousness. Bockmuehl argues that the evidence is ambiguous. At the very least, a case can be made for the view that the community sees itself to be eschatologically representative rather than substitutive for the nation as a whole. "Remnant" language is common in CD and 1QM, and this is of course a biblical *topos*. Certainly the community can refer to itself as "Israel"; joining the community means joining the definitive "covenant of God." Yet elsewhere the texts can speak of those "in Israel" or those "of Israel" who repent – which demonstrates that "Israel" is not restricted in its use to referring exclusively to the community. True, the Qumran community embraces a narrower vision of God's faithful community in the present hour than was held by many other Jews. But the community may see itself as the vanguard of the nation and the land, which is of course a typically sectarian response. (2) As for the individual, there is a complex tension between voluntarism and predestination. On the one hand, especially in 1QS and 1QH a personal commitment to Jewish faith and practice is of decisive importance; moreover, individuals may become apostate. On the other hand, the destiny of both the just and the wicked is foreordained by God. "Salvation, on this view, could never be a matter of human merit."[112] (3) The words for "righteousness" or "justification" can certainly be used forensically (Bockmuehl thinks 1QS 10–11 is especially significant). Nevertheless it is through God's righteous character and acts that sins can be forgiven. Nevertheless, such forgiveness is not available for those who are unrepentant or for those outside the community. "Thus, atonement for sins is an act of God *for believers*: God does *not* atone for the sins of Belial's lot (2:8)."[113] It is not too surprising, then, that 1QS "should come to view priestly atonement for sin as located exclusively within the remit of the sect."[114] Moreover, alienation from the Jerusalem temple invariably leads to diverse forms of atonement outside the sacrificial cult. In the "Words of the Luminaries," just as Moses atoned for rebellious Israel in the desert, so now "we atone for our sin and the sin of our fathers" (4Q504 1–2.ii.9–10, vi.5–6; 4:5–7). Even if the community understood such atonement to function in deliberate analogy to the atonement available in the temple cult, a shift in categories and focus is unavoidable. Further, in 1QS 3:3–9 a significant connection is drawn between ritual purity and atonement for sins, though to be sure the ritual is effective only through the Holy Spirit.

"For the Qumran Community, therefore, atonement for sin remains the prerogative of God himself. Its appropriation, however, is possible only to

---

[112] Ibid., 397.
[113] Ibid., 400.
[114] Ibid.

repentant members of the sect, since its sacrificial locus comes to be situated very specifically in the worship and praxis of the *yahad*."[115]

In the most innovative section of his paper, Bockmuehl examines the additional fragments that make possible a redactional history of *Serekh Ha-Yahad*. Granted the cogency of his reconstruction, the redactional direction is certainly toward more rules, more emphasis on priestly functions, more severe rules relating to expulsion, a more narrowly sectarian stance.

Bockmuehl holds that although his findings "are not fundamentally incompatible" with those of Sanders,[116] the availability of more sources, the sheer diversity of perspectives in the documents, the arrival of more discriminating analytical methods, and the possibilities of tracing redactional development, conspire to confirm the "intrinsically unsystematic soteriology"[117] of a central document like 1QS. "If the direction of my redactional analysis is correct," Bockmuehl writes, "we might have in Qumran a developing example of the sort of exclusivistic preoccupation with 'works of the law' against which Paul of Tarsus subsequently reacts in his letters to Gentile Christians. If, by contrast, it could be shown after all that 4QS^b and 4QS^d represent the later recension of the *Serekh*, the conclusion would have to be that Paul was not alone in his reaction against narrow religious exclusivism. Either way, the soteriology of the scrolls is clearly not a monolithic theological construct be remained subject to flux and development over an extended period of time."[118]

The contribution of *Mark Seifrid* to this volume does not treat yet another literary corpus of Second Temple Judaism, but offers a study of "righteousness" language, especially צדק and cognates, in the Hebrew Bible and in early Judaism.[119] He begins by surveying several tensions arising from earlier studies. Gerhard von Rad championed the view that "righteousness" in the Hebrew Bible is consistently salvific. But this view does not account for "a small but conspicuous group of texts in which a punitive form of divine righteousness appears."[120] On the other hand, those who want to link divine righteousness and retribution must account for the fact that "saving righteousness" occurs about four times more frequently than punitive divine justice. A second tension arises between those who think that the righteousness vocabulary bears the sense of "accordance with a norm" and those who prefer "fidelity to a relationship." Clearly, the former might usefully be tied to notions of punitive righteousness; if the latter is adopted, at very least the way

---

[115] Ibid., 402.
[116] Ibid., 412.
[117] Ibid., 113.
[118] Ibid., 413–4.
[119] "Righteousness Language in the Hebrew Scriptures and Early Judaism," 415–42.
[120] Ibid., 415.

is clear to think of righteousness in salvific terms: "God's righteousness consists in his fidelity to his people in saving them."[121]

It may help to put some of this into historical perspective. Albrecht Ritschl argued that the notion of retributive justice, with its connections with the courtroom, is a product of the pagan world. God's righteousness is simply the consistency of God's actions in line with his aim to bring salvation to the world. God is not interested in some sort of mechanical relation between worthiness and reward or punishment, but in the organic relation between beginning and result. In response, Hermann Cremer argued that in the Hebrew Bible God's righteousness does not have to do with some future goal of salvation, but with his present activity in establishing justice and protecting it. For Cremer, then, the punishment of the wicked was an essential element in the salvation of the righteous. For God, ruling and judging belong together; the Bible speaks of concrete acts of God's judgment. On these points, Cremer is demonstrably and entirely correct. At this juncture, however, he introduces a more questionable conclusion. Although God's judging activity is, for Cremer, always two-sided (i.e. it includes both the punishment of the oppressors and the salvation of the oppressed), nevertheless the actual "righteousness" terminology is connected only with the latter, i.e. with the saving dimension of God's action. (Clearly, this view influenced von Rad.)

Further, Cremer argued that the biblical usage does not embrace the concept of a norm. Rather, it has to do with the relationship between a person and an idea, between thought and language. But here, of course, he opens himself to the sort of trenchant linguistic criticism ably put forward by James Barr half a century later. Indeed, there are "at least two fundamental errors in Cremer's treatment of the vocabulary of righteousness from which scholarship in large measure has yet to free itself."[122] (1) Cremer is engaged in an obvious quest for a *Grundbegriff* that can be applied to every occurrence of צדק. There is nothing *intrinsically* mischievous about such a quest, but it is wrong-headed when it overrides the actual empirical evidence. It is the same sort of error made by von Rad in his sweeping generalization (above). (2) In line with his attempt at defining a univocal *Grundbegriff*, Cremer says the word-usage is always "social and forensic."[123] In other words, it has to do with a relationship between persons. But the usage is too diverse to accommodate this reductionism: the word group can be applied to various objects of commerce and cult, and can be used in impersonal metaphors (e.g. "paths of righteousness," Ps 23:3).

Often appeal is made to Gen 38:26 to argue that "justice" or "righteousness" is primarily relational, such that whatever norms may be appealed to are

---

[121] Ibid. 416.

[122] Ibid., 418.

[123] Cited in Seifrid, "Righteousness Language," 418.

contained within the relationship. Seifrid shows that this is not the case: there is an external norm, a community norm, that excuses Tamar for her actions. This is entirely in line with the work of Hans Heinrich Schmid, who has shown that notions of legitimacy and normativity are associated with the צדק-group throughout Northwest Semitic. Franz Reiterer has extended these findings by engaging in a componential analysis of צדק-terms, grouping the texts into three categories: juridical, ethical-social, and conflictual-military. Failure to absorb these lessons has led to serious mistakes in highly influential studies, such as that of John Ziesler, whose categories of forensic/status versus activity/behavior mirror Protestant/Catholic debates, but do not deal responsibly with the linguistic data on their own terms.

Perhaps a still more common claim is that "God's righteousness" means something like "covenant-faithfulness." This "presupposes that the idea of a promissory covenant is both fundamental and pervasive within the Hebrew Scriptures, a matter which is highly debated."[124] More importantly, Seifrid shows that ברית and צדק-terms only very rarely occur in proximity to each other, despite their high frequencies. Moreover, in the Hebrew Bible "one generally does not 'act righteously or unrighteously' with respect to a covenant. Rather, one 'keeps,' 'remembers,' 'establishes' a covenant, or the like. Or, conversely, one 'breaks,' 'transgresses,' 'forsakes,' 'despises,' 'forgets,' or 'profanes' it."[125] Righteousness language is more commonly found in parallel with terms for rectitude over against evil. By contrast, expressions such as חסד and אמונה (with their "associations of enduring friendship"[126]) are prominent when covenantal relations are in view. "All 'covenant-keeping' is righteous behavior, but not all righteous behavior is 'covenant-keeping.' It is misleading, therefore, to speak of 'God's righteousness' as his 'covenant-faithfulness.'"[127] Worse, once this mistake has been linked to the reductionistic categorization of "covenant" as promissory covenant, then (it is argued) God is righteous because he has promised to save. This is very close to Ritschl's idealistic interpretation, and ignores advances from Cremer on.

Further, if Schmid is right in his insistence that righteousness language in the Hebrew Bible "has to do in the first instance with God's ordering of creation, its relative distance from covenantal contexts is entirely explicable."[128] It is not an accident that righteousness terminology, only rarely linked with covenant, is very frequently associated with the vocabulary of ruling and judging. This is what might be called a creational context for

---

[124] Ibid., 423.
[125] Ibid., 424.
[126] Ibid.
[127] Ibid.
[128] Ibid., 425.

righteousness, as opposed to a covenantal context. And this in turn "both illumines and delimits Cremer's claims regarding the concreteness and salvific character of righteousness language."[129]

Within this framework, Seifrid seeks to ground his work on many passages, while drawing out finer distinctions: masculine צדק usually signifies the abstract concept of "right order" or what is morally right, while the feminine צדקה tends to refer to a concrete thing, a righteous act or a vindicating judgment. These distinctions Seifrid links to the approximately fifteen instances in the Hebrew Bible where God's righteousness is conceived in punitive or retributive terms, all of them in juridical contexts.

Turning to the literature of Second Temple Judaism, Seifrid observes how little detailed semantic work has been done, despite the sweeping claims often made. Nevertheless, Sanders's linking of being "righteous" with "being in the covenant" or with "(Israel's) covenant status" does not stand up well either in Qumran or in the rabbinic materials. And similarly, to understand "the righteousness of God" and "justification" in Paul as God's "covenant-faithfulness" to Israel is badly to misunderstand antecedent usage and Pauline texts alike. When Paul speaks of the "revelation of God's righteousness" (Rom 1:17), the associations with the Psalms and Isaiah show that the expression belongs to creational categories:

> God appears in such texts as creator, lord, and king, who "rules and judges" the entire earth. Naturally, he acts in faithfulness toward his people, contends with their enemies, and executes judgment on their behalf. Yet his acts of "justification" do not represent mere "salvation" for Israel, or even merely "salvation." They constitute the establishment of justice in the world which Yahweh made and governs. Indeed, they may be seen to entail his own justification as the true God over against the idols. The nations are to anticipate that Yahweh will bring about justice for them, even as he has brought it about for Israel. This perspective is apparent, for example, in Psalm 98:1–3, which speaks of Yahweh revealing his "righteousness" to the eyes of the nations. The psalm continues by calling on creation (the sea, the inhabitants of the earth, the rivers and mountains) to rejoice before Yahweh, the king, and to await joyfully his judgment of the earth "in righteousness and equity" (Ps 98:4–9).[130]

The final substantive essay in this volume, prepared by *Roland Deines*, is a fresh, major study of the Pharisees,[131] and aims to overturn some commonly received positions. The subject, Deines points out, is important for several reasons. The second volume of this set on *Justification and Variegated Nomism* is on Paul, and Paul characterizes himself as κατὰ νόμον Φαρισαῖος (Phil 3:5), which raises the question as to what "Pharisee" means. Moreover, this question forms a link between Paul and Jesus, since his most important interlocutors and opponents were Pharisees. But for our purposes, identifying

---

[129] Ibid., 426.
[130] Ibid., 441.
[131] "The Pharisees Between 'Judaisms' and 'Common Judaism'," 443–503.

the beliefs, practices, and influence of the Pharisees is of paramount importance, because a great deal of contemporary scholarly conviction so emphasizes many conflicting "Judaisms" that one can scarcely posit the dominant influence of the Pharisees without an immediate and vociferous challenge. Such debates inevitably influence how we "read" Paul. Although Sanders can speak of a "Common Judaism," he does not think it is significantly shaped by Pharisaism.

The problem of assigning the right place to the Pharisees is aggravated by two additional things: (1) There is systematic "rejection of all attempts to attribute individual texts from the area of apocryphal and pseudepigraphic literature to the Pharisees or other known groups."[132] Obviously one ought to begin by treating each text on its own. But if that methodological scrupulousness becomes a doctrinaire restriction, on the ground that each text contains its own form of "Judaism," the conclusions are being tied up with the presuppositions. (2) The tendency in recent scholarship to refer to Pharisees and other groups as "sects," with that word's overtone of separation, of being on the outside of the culture and the culture's religion and reacting against them, begs a number of fundamental issues, even while it "strengthens this tendency to speak of individual Judaisms."[133]

Obviously these developments must be reinforced by casting doubt on the three- or four-fold division of Judaism that Josephus presupposes. This is done by depreciating the Pharisees, exaggerating the influence of Sadducees both politically and religiously, and insisting that Josephus' divisions are misleading simplifications. The result is "a far-reaching denial of Pharisaic influence on the world it shared with other Jews."[134] The modification advanced by Sanders – that there was a "Common Judaism" that held sway during the period Sanders defines, viz. 63 B.C. to A.D. 66 – was a religion of priesthood and temple. What Sanders has shown, Deines argues, is that Judaism "is to be understood as *one* religion, and was perceived as such by outsiders."[135] But then the question immediately arises: What were the roots of this "Common Judaism"?

Deines tracks these roots from the main themes of Deuteronomistic thought, especially cultivated by the Pharisees. Though demonstrably it contributed to the portrait of "Common Judaism," the priestly-levitical literature of the chronicler tended toward an exclusive-elite outlook. "To this strongly priestly-oriented tradition, however, the Qumran writings and the Essenes in their description by Josephus may be ascribed, and with qualifica-

---

[132] Ibid., 448.
[133] Ibid., 449.
[134] Ibid., 451–2.
[135] Ibid., 453.

tion also the Sadducees."[136] What precipitated the next stage was the pressure brought to bear by Antiochus IV Epiphanes. The diverse parties were forced to take common action, and in this framework adherence to Torah became of paramount importance. Even the slaughter of sixty Hasideans by Alcimus could not initially break up the coalition. But with their first successes behind them, the coalition quickly dissolved and the three principal parties described by Josephus found their voices competing. At issue was the way forward for the nation as a whole.

At this juncture Deines unpacks the heart of his argument. Within Palestinian Judaism, he argues, 4QMMT proves to be a document that reflects party formation. Its concern to preserve the newly acquired purity of the temple, its focus on Torah observances, and not least the seriousness of its tone reflect the "determination with which struggles about these questions were carried out."[137] By careful analysis of the identity of the "we"-group, the "you"-group (singular and plural), and the "they"-group, Deines argues that 4QMMT "remains an important, early and decisive piece of evidence for the popularity of that position which generally is identified as Pharisaic. Furthermore, the impression we glean from 4QMMT supports the reliability of Josephus' tripartite characterization of Judaism prior to A.D. 70."[138] This in turn leads to careful evaluation of the evidence from Josephus, followed by probes into, inter alia, *Jubilees, Psalms of Solomon, Assumption of Moses, 1 Enoch, Lives of the Prophets, Scroll of Fasting, Liber antiquitatum biblicarum*, and *4 Ezra*. These texts Deines assigns to three groups, according to their date. The oldest group, written in the context of the Maccabean uprising, "do not yet contain clear controversies between parties, even though the authors take divergent positions."[139] The middle group is "characterized by vehement internal Jewish conflict in which questions of correct purity and holiness in cult and personal life play a central role."[140] The last group, written after A.D. 70, largely leave behind these controversies, in the attempt "to convince the nation of the necessity to turn back to the law."[141] Deines's purpose is to demonstrate that, while there is a demonstrable trajectory, the diversity of Judaism thus unpacked, the so-called "Judaisms," does not in fact go beyond Josephus' description of the religious movements of his people.

At this juncture, Deines offers his own definition and summary of Pharisaism. The flexibility of the term in the sources is part of its strength.

---

[136] Ibid., 455.
[137] Ibid., 462.
[138] Ibid., 474.
[139] Ibid., 490.
[140] Ibid.
[141] Ibid.

Above all, it designates primarily "a *particular relationship to the Law*."[142] It embraces a non-exclusive understanding of tradition, such that diverse opinions can be tolerated and evaluated provided they can be shown to stand in continuity with Torah tradition. Precisely because Jesus placed his own authority *above* that of Torah tradition, he constituted an unacceptable threat. Much of Sanders's "Common Judaism" is simply pharisaic influenced Judaism. This leads to careful delineation of the various parties identified by Josephus, culminating with a critical suggestion: Pharisaism was

> a separate movement *within* the nation *for* the nation, whose legitimacy was indeed *accepted* by large parts of the people, even though its requirements were not *observed* to an equal extent. This provides us in my opinion also with justification to consider Pharisaism as normative Judaism, not because all *lived* according to Pharisaic halakah, but because Pharisaism was by the majority acknowledged as legitimate and authentic interpretation of the divine will for the chosen nation.[143]

In short, Deines concludes that Pharisaism was "*the fundamental and most influential religious movement within Palestinian Judaism between 150 B.C. and A.D. 70.*"[144]

2. Further Studies

Apart from the preceding two chapters, which respectively have studied "righteousness" words and Pharisaism, this volume has proceeded by evaluating various corpora linked with Second Temple Judaism. One can easily see, however, that it might be useful to examine certain related topics across the literature. In this brief section I shall summarize two or three such studies, all of which appeared late enough that their findings were not incorporated into the foregoing discussions.

First to be considered is the published form of a doctoral dissertation written at Aberdeen University by Mark Adam Elliott, *The Survivors of Israel: A Reconsideration of the Theology of Pre-Christian Judaism.*[145] Elliott's argument is subtle and complex. In brief, he argues that during this period many Jewish groups thought of *themselves* as the elect, in a doctrine that might almost be called special election. This was linked up in their own minds with the tradition of remnant theology that arose within the Hebrew canon itself. These "remnant groups" constituted a kind of "movement of dissent"; indeed, "it would appear that the idea of a remnant (even where the term is not used specifically) granted *theological legitimation* for the

---

[142] Ibid., 493 (emphasis his).
[143] Ibid., 501 (emphasis his).
[144] Ibid., 503 (emphasis his).
[145] Grand Rapids: Eerdmans, 2000.

emergence of this movement."[146] Necessarily the groups connected with this movement of dissent were minority groups, even if they sometimes wielded substantive influence, for remnant theology is minority theology. More importantly, their voices were largely nonnationalistic. They constitute "too *important* a voice in Judaism for contemporary scholars to go on referring to nationalistic voices as if *they* were the only significant ones, particularly, one might add, in the context of prolegomena to the study of the New Testament."[147]

Worried not only about future apocalyptic terrors, but about the judgments apparently *already* taking place, these groups espoused not only a remnant theology, but what Elliott calls a "destruction-preservation soteriology"[148] – i.e. a pervasive pattern of salvation in which hope in the future turns on passing through severe judgment first. The problem they faced was this: Granted the wickedness of Israel, and, to some extent, even of the righteous, where in the biblical history is there a paradigm of salvation that could again become effective when the covenant, including their provisions for atonement, become ineffective in maintaining Israel in her righteous status? Elliott identifies two: a second deluge motif, and a new exodus motif. The conclusion is that "*salvation is experienced by means of, as well as in the midst of, danger and judgment.*"[149] And in such paradigms, there is salvation only for the remnant, with a kind of vindication of the sectarian group by the rest of Israel.

Elliott concludes that a nationalistic view of election theology does not accurately reflect at least some important pre-Christian Jewish groups, and that some sort of "special election" existed long before the New Testament period. Elliott then teases out some of the theological and historical implications of his findings, most of which do not directly concern us here. Although he does not spell it out in these terms, Elliott's work, to the extent that it is right, does not bear directly on questions of "works righteousness" or the like, but it does directly contradict the pattern of covenantal nomism that Sanders deploys as an over-arching category to explain all (or at least most) of this literature.

In addition to Elliott's published monograph, two other recent dissertations have shed light on the complexities of Second Temple Judaism and the questions we are addressing, while dealing with topics slightly adjacent to our own. The first, by Steven M. Bryan, treats "Jesus and Israel's Traditions of Judgment and Restoration."[150] Much of this work we need not consider here,

---

[146] Ibid., 242–3.
[147] Ibid., 243.
[148] Ibid., 575, passim.
[149] Ibid., 595 (emphasis his).
[150] Ph.D. dissertation submitted to the University of Cambridge in August, 1999.

since its concern is to place Jesus in the appropriate matrix of Israel's traditions of judgment and restoration. But it is precisely in the delineation of that matrix that Bryan offers a number of shrewd observations. For many Jews, election, purity, temple, and land were "all interrelated aspects of a vision of the eschaton and of a program for achieving that vision. For all the differences within first-century Judaism concerning how purity should be pursued, there remained broad agreement that the present persistence of impurity was a hindrance to the full realization of God's presence in Israel."[151] Jesus' emphasis on national judgment was fully in line with prophetic denunciations in the Hebrew canon (though it went beyond them in several respects), but this did not mean Jesus was abandoning the ideal of purity.

> Rather, it appears that Jesus drew on alternative sacred traditions according to which God's people would only be constituted as a pure society through the sanctification of the whole earth by an eschatological action of God. Perhaps the actions of the priest and the Levite in the parable of the good Samaritan are caricatured. But the reality behind the caricature is a society whose patterns of relation are structured in part by grades of purity.[152]

Much of the work is a defense of this conclusion.

The second dissertation, written by Simon James Gathercole, is titled "After the New Perspective: Works, Justification and Boasting in Early Judaism and Romans 1–5."[153] Once again, the focus on Paul does not immediately concern us (as it will concern us in the second volume of this set), but the first two chapters set about the task of exploring the extent to which Jewish texts prior to A.D. 70 reflect the theme of final vindication taking place on the basis of obedience to the Law. "Sanders' approach to the Jewish literature in general and the DSS in particular . . . loads the theological freight on the past ('getting in') and the present ('staying in'). The taxonomy of 'getting in' and 'staying in' itself considerably downplays eschatological judgment (and by extension the role of works in that judgment) in the pattern of Jewish soteriology. The mystery of existence, 'the secret of what *will* be' includes the 'birthtimes of salvation' and 'who is to inherit glory and trouble',[154] implying a considerable future dimension in the theology of the group."[155] Gathercole argues strenuously that neither an over-emphasis on realized eschatology nor a constant focus on the corporate dimensions of salvation can finally obscure the evidence: "Final judgment on the basis of works permeates Jewish theology, Qumran included."[156]

---

[151] Ibid., 150.
[152] Ibid.
[153] Ph.D. dissertation submitted to the University of Durham in March, 2001.
[154] The reference is to 4Q417 1.i.11.
[155] Gathercole, "Works, Justification and Boasting," 97.
[156] Ibid., 97.

3. Concluding Reflections

It is time to bring these threads together. If in the preceding summaries I have tried to represent the authors of the essays or dissertations as accurately as possible, the following conclusions are to be blamed on no-one but me.

(1) Transparently, these scholars are not all in perfect agreement. Seifrid and Bockmuehl hold slightly different interpretations of key passages from the Dead Sea Scrolls; Spilsbury is very cautious about how much can be inferred about religious movements in Second Temple Judaism from the writings of Josephus, while Deines judges that much more can be said. Elliott is convinced that each group thinks of itself as the object of special election; Bockmuehl argues that the community at Qumran thought of itself as the eschatological representative of Israel rather than its substitute. Similarly, Deines would dissent from Elliott because the former sees Pharisaism as a separatist movement *within* the nation *for* the nation.

(2) Several of the scholars found that at least parts of their respective corpora could be usefully described as reflecting covenantal nomism. One conclusion to be drawn, then, is not that Sanders is wrong everywhere, but he is wrong when he tries to establish that his category is right everywhere.

(3) There is strong agreement that covenantal nomism is at best a reductionistic category. Sometimes it is the balance of things that drives us toward this judgment. A book may be shown to have its inspiration in biblical ideas, but if all its inspiration is found in *one kind* of biblical ideas, while complementary biblical ideas are completely ignored, the resulting synthesis may be far removed from the result of reading the entire Hebrew canon. The extremely strong focus on personal worth and meritorious righteousness in Judith or Tobit cannot be overlooked; Sirach stands somewhat apart from other wisdom books. The Additions to Esther, doubtless written when the people of God were hard-pressed, certainly enjoin personal faithfulness, but the focus of the Additions as a whole never really calls into question whether or not the people will persevere to the end. In Bauckham's assessment, *2 Enoch* is even more attached to works righteousness than *4 Ezra*, while *2 Baruch* mentions God's mercy, but that mercy is poured out on those who deserve it. Recall his conclusion, even regarding *4 Ezra*: that book, he writes, "does rather importantly illustrate how the basic and very flexible pattern of covenantal nomism could take forms in which the emphasis is overwhelmingly on meriting salvation by works of obedience to the Law, with the result that human achievement takes center-stage and God's grace, while presupposed, is effectively marginalized."[157] The entire focus of 4 Maccabees is on reason/Law: all the attention is devoted to "staying in," with nothing left for

---

[157] Bauckham, "Apocalypses," 174.

"getting in." In the *Testament of Moses*, the people "get in" by grace, but they "stay in" by God's determined grace as well. Temporal judgments may have to be faced by God's people, but God's grace ensures their final victory, since the world was made for them. The "staying in" of the people as a whole is as certain as God's grace in electing them in the first place – and that means that one of the pegs of Sanders's covenantal nomism does not seem to fit. The Tannaitic literature boasts competing theologies, but part of this heritage is certainly replete with merit theology. *L.A.B.* is highly selective in its re-telling of the Old Testament story, precisely so that its emphases (drawn from the period of the Judges) underline the importance of faithfulness and persever-ance while assuring them that God won't finally abandon his people.

(4) But covenantal nomism is not only reductionistic, it is misleading, and this for two reasons.

First, deploying this one neat formula across literature so diverse engenders an assumption that there is more uniformity in the literature than there is. In Philo, for instance, there is no real notion of being "saved" in any of the traditional senses. In Sanders's usage, the "getting in" of covenantal nomism is bound up with how the community becomes the people of God. Philo is really not interested in this (though he does hold that Israel has a special relationship with God): his focus is on the individual's pilgrimage toward God. Compare the "getting in" and "staying in" here, with whatever they mean in the Tannaitic literature, in Josephus, in the apocalypses: Sanders's formula is rather difficult to falsify, precisely because it is so plastic that it hides more than it reveals, and engenders false assumptions that lose the flavor, emphases, priorities, and frames of reference, of these diverse literary corpora.

Second, and more importantly, Sanders has erected the structure of covenantal nomism as his alternative to merit theology. At one level, of course, he has a point. Earlier analyses of the literature of Second Temple Judaism often found merit theology everywhere, and Sanders, as we have seen, is right to warn against a simple arithmetical tit-for-tat notion of payback. Even where some of the apocalypses use the language of weighing deeds in the balance and the like, it is possible to understand the relevant passages as reflecting a holistic assessment of an entire life and its direction. Nevertheless, covenantal nomism as a category is not really an alternative to merit theology, and therefore it is no real response to it. Over against merit theology stands grace (whether the word itself is used or not). By putting over against merit theology not grace but covenant theology, Sanders has managed to have a structure that preserves grace in the "getting in" while preserving works (and frequently some form or other of merit theology) in the "staying in." In other words, it is as if Sanders is saying, "See, we don't have merit theology here; we have covenantal nomism" – but the covenantal nomism he constructs is so flexible that it includes and baptizes a great deal of merit theology.

In fact, both poles – "getting in" and "staying in" – need nuancing. We have seen that the first pole is more stable in this literature than the second: the assumption is that Israel is God's people by grace. Well and good. But does this refer to the entire people at the moment of their initial calling? What about the entry of the individual, especially when what the individual is entering is a special community, as at Qumran? And what happens when the election-category of "getting in" becomes more commonly a source of boasting than a source of gratitude and obligation (a problem that already surfaces in the Hebrew prophets)? But the "staying in" pole is even more problematic. If Gathercole is right, the emphasis on "getting in" and "staying in" may unwittingly downplay the importance of eschatological judgment, and avoid questions about the role of works in that judgment in the various Jewish soteriologies. But even what "staying in" means is almost infinitely flexible. Is all of this obedience or law-keeping cast as a matter of faithful conformity to God's gracious revelation, such conformity enabled and empowered by God's help? Or is it sometimes cast as the human contribution to the entire scheme, such that it is entirely appropriate to conclude that a Judith, for instance, earns her reward, or that the Tannaitic literature includes a large stream of works-righteousness (even while it includes other and competing streams), or that *2 Enoch* and *4 Ezra* and *2 Baruch*, on almost any calcula- tion, portray kinds of merit theology that are difficult to escape, or that the martyrs in 4 Maccabees exercise at least some atoning function by their death, and not merely an exemplary function? In other words, does it not appear that covenantal nomism has become a rubric so embracing that it includes within its capacious soul huge tracts of works-righteousness or merit theology? True, the literature is so diverse that what expressions such as "works- righteousness" and "merit theology" might mean needs teasing out in each case, just as covenantal nomism needs teasing out. But it appears that the category of covenantal nomism cannot itself accomplish what Sanders wants it to accomplish, viz. serve as an explanatory bulwark against all suggestions that some of this literature embraces works-righteousness and merit theology, precisely because covenantal nomism embraces the same phenomena. Sanders has to some extent constructed a "heads I win, tails you lose" argument: it is rhetorically effective, but not a fair reflection of the diverse literature.

(5) But the problem is deeper. In some of this literature the very categories of covenantal nomism seem mistaken. Josephus' approach to the relationship between God and his people is arguably more indebted to the ancient systems of benefaction and patronage (hence Spilsbury's "patronal nomism") than to notions of grace and obedience. But that inevitably introduces a "tit-for-tat" reciprocity in the relationship that is finally a long way removed from the

biblical heritage. In *Jubilees*, election is certainly by grace. But that is mere initiation; final salvation finally depends on obedience. More importantly, for the Jews for whom *Jubilees* is written, the "getting in" is by birth; it is something inherited. All the focus of their own experience is on staying in. It appears that Enns is right: in the configuration of *Jubilees* the "getting in" is not really into salvation, but into a kind of preliminary election, with the salvation being accomplished by the "staying in." It is difficult not to conclude that the categories of covenantal nomism are sometimes mistaken. In several of these sources (e.g. Philo, *Sibylline Oracles*), God's Law is either for Gentiles as well as Jews, or it is for all because it is nothing more than the finest articulation of the law of nature. Philo is primarily interested in portraying the pilgrimage of the individual soul to God, not least by the acquisition of virtue. It is extremely difficult to see how covenantal nomism is a suitable category here at all.[158]

---

[158] There are other elements in the "new perspective" that make a similarly reductionistic and sometimes misleading appeal to documents of Second Temple Judaism. One thinks in particular of the sweeping exegetical conclusions drawn by N. T. Wright and others, based on the thesis that Jews of the period were convinced they were still living in the exile, and were anticipating relief from this suffering. Recent studies on this aspect of the debate on the "new perspective" are beyond the scope of this volume, but one might usefully consult James M. Scott, ed., *Exile: Old Testament, Jewish, and Christian Conceptions* (JSJSup 56; Leiden: Brill, 1997); Carey C. Newman, ed., *Jesus and the Restoration of Israel: A Critical Assessment of N. T. Wright's Jesus and the Victory of God* (Downers Grove: IVP, 1999). The problems with the view that within Second Temple Judaism the exile was ongoing may be summarized as follows (I here follow Bryan, "Jesus and Israel's Traditions," 9–12, whose summary is excellent): (1) Although the examples Wright cites (notably Tobit 14:5–7) show that at very least the exile could serve as a powerful motif through which people could talk about what was wrong with the nation, it is not clear that they took the exile to be literally ongoing. There was in Israel a persistent way of thinking about history and eschatology, an ongoing tradition by which crucial events in the past pointed the way to the future. Thus Ps 95 looks back at the rebellion of Israel at Meribah; Isaiah takes up the exodus motif (and Mark picks it up from Isaiah: see Rikki Watts, *Isaiah's New Exodus and Mark* [WUNT 88; Tübingen: Mohr (Siebeck), 1997]). Thus to pick up the exile theme was not necessarily the same thing as saying that the exile was ongoing, and that this formed part of the nation's existential self-awareness. After all, Tobit 14:5 itself acknowledges the first return from exile, which is then kept separate from the "times of fulfillment." (2) Some of the passages Wright cites in support of his view point in a rather different direction. True, in Neh 9:36 Ezra laments that the people remain slaves in their own land. But recent scholarship has shown how much Ezra-Nehemiah look at things through the lens of a partially realized eschatology. "In other words, the problem of Ezra-Nehemiah is not so much one of continuing exile but of incomplete restoration; for the author(s) of Ezra-Nehemiah, to equate the two, as Wright does, would have been to deny a key moment in the out-working of God's eschatological purposes" (Bryan, "Jesus and Israel's Traditions," 10). (3) Several scholars appeal to texts in *Jubilees* to argue that there was widespread perception that the exile was ongoing. But the texts in *Jubilees* (e.g. ch. 23) call to mind Deuteronomic curses (e.g. Deut 32) in which exile is merely one curse of many. *Jub.* 23 insists that this "evil generation" is experiencing all of the curses, not just exile; indeed, the emphasis on exile is

(6) The unsuitability of the terminology becomes more acute in the light of Seifrid's essay. If "covenant" and "righteousness" are not customarily linked in Scripture, and if there are very good reasons for thinking that God's righteousness must be understood first and foremost in a creational context (with the result that God's righteousness simply cannot be identified with God's covenantal faithfulness), the fundamental assumptions behind covenantal nomism begin to crumble.

(7) One can scarcely fail to note the frequency with which several scholars in these pages comment that their corpora largely fit the category of covenantal nomism, only to go on to show that the fit isn't very good, especially with some part of their respective corpora. Thus Falk, for instance, is fairly generous toward Sanders, but then draws attention to sources that raise the prospect of sinlessness, which means there is no need for grace. More importantly, entrance into the covenantal community that sang the *Hodayot* was *not* by the racial and covenantal election of Deut 7 and 10, but by personal choice: one could not become a member of the community any other way. But since the community saw itself as faithful adherents to the covenant (i.e. the covenant of the community!), the notion of "getting in" by grace seems rather far removed. Similarly, the *Lives of Adam and Eve* reports the elaborate penance necessary to return to God – but this is the Adamic equivalent of *entering* the covenant, of "getting in." On the face of it, the entrance in this case is not particularly marked by grace.

(8) Several authors track a trajectory of developments within the corpus of literature for which they are responsible. Thus Bockmuehl reconstructs the textual development of 1QS over a couple of centuries, and argues that its direction is precisely toward the sort of "works of the law" that the apostle Paul would have opposed. Deines groups much of the literature into three periods, and it is the second period (leading up to the fall of Jerusalem and its temple) that presupposes not only heated competition among the groups that made up Judaism in the first century, but the rising influence of Pharisaism.

(9) One hesitates to raise this last point, because in the nature of the case it is hard to prove. The so-called *Annales* school of historiography in France attempts to understand the ordinary bloke, the common person, of a particular place and time, rather than the literary deposit. The fact that one of the foundation documents of the Church of England is the Thirty-Nine Articles

---

reduced. "This downgrading of the exile may have been the author's way of dealing with the fact that the expected restoration had not accompanied the sixth century return" (Ibid., 11). (4) In at least some of the relevant texts, the fact that restoration promises have not been completed is evidence not that the original exile is ongoing, but that the nation is sunk in a *further* cycle of sin/exile/restoration (e.g. *T. Naph.* 4; *2 Bar.* 53–74). (5) "It is difficult to imagine that in the heady days of Hasmonean success, people still widely perceived themselves to be in exile" (Bryan, "Jesus and Israel's Traditions," 12).

does not mean that ordinary Anglicans do not ever cross an imaginary line away from the Articles, into a fairly crass merit theology. How many first-century Jews on the street might well have felt more comfortable with laws and merit theology than with the complexities of the more literary preserves of Second Temple Judaism?

Examination of Sanders's covenantal nomism leads one to the conclusion that the New Testament documents, not least Paul, must not be read against this reconstructed background – or, at least, must not be read *exclusively* against this background. It is too doctrinaire, too unsupported by the sources themselves, too reductionistic, too monopolistic. The danger is that of the "parallelomania" about which Sandmel warned us,[159] by which texts are domesticated as they are held hostage to the ostensible background called forth by appealing to certain other antecedent texts. One of the hopes of the editors of this pair of volumes is that the breaking up of fallow ground attempted in this first volume will lead to fresh exegesis of crucial Pauline texts in the next.

---

[159] Samuel Sandmel, "Parallelomania," *JBL* 81 (1962): 2–13.

Index of Ancient Names

Index of Modern Names

Scripture Index

Scripture references follow the order of the Hebrew Bible

Index to Apocrypha

Index to Pseudepigrapha

Index to Qumran Texts

Index to Philo

Index to Josephus

Index to Mishnah and Other Rabbinic Sources

Index to Targums

Index to Miscellaneous Texts

Subject Index